Late Quaternary Chronology and Paleoclimates of the Eastern Mediterranean

Ofer Bar-Yosef   Renee S. Kra
Editors

LATE QUATERNARY CHRONOLOGY AND PALEOCLIMATES OF THE EASTERN MEDITERRANEAN

RADIOCARBON
Department of Geosciences
The University of Arizona
4717 E. Ft. Lowell Road
Tucson, Arizona 85712 USA

American School of Prehistoric Research
Peabody Museum
Harvard University
11 Divinity Avenue
Cambridge, Massachusetts 02138 USA

Library of Congress Cataloging-in-Publication Data

Late Quaternary chronology and paleoclimates of the eastern Mediterranean / Ofer Bar-Yosef, Renee S. Kra, editors.
    p.   cm.
    Includes bibliographical references.
    ISBN 0-9638314-1-0 (acid-free) : $45.00
     1. Paleolithic period—Middle East. 2. Neolithic period—Middle East. 3. Paleoclimatology—Middle East—
Quaternary. 4. Paleoecology—Middle East—Quaternary. 5. Radiocarbon dating—Middle East. 6. Middle East—
Antiquities.
   I. Bar-Yosef, Ofer. II. Kra, R. S. (Renee S.)
   GN772.32.M628L38 1994
   939′.4—dc20   94-6891
                                                                 CIP

© 1994 *RADIOCARBON*, Department of Geosciences, The University of Arizona, Tucson, Arizona.
All rights reserved. This work may not be translated or copied in whole or in part without the written permission of the publisher (*RADIOCARBON*, Department of Geosciences, The University of Arizona, 4717 E. Ft. Lowell Road, Tucson, Arizona, 85712 USA), except for brief excerpts in connection with reviews or scholarly analysis. Use in connection with any form of information storage and retrieval, electronic adaptation, computer software, or by similar or dissimilar methodology now known or hereafter developed is forbidden. The contents of the papers herein are the responsibility of the authors.

Printed and bound by Braun-Brumfield, Inc., Ann Arbor, Michigan in the United States of America.

ISBN 0-9638314-1-0 *RADIOCARBON*, The University of Arizona, Tucson, Arizona, USA

CONTENTS

v

IV. BIOZONES OF THE LEVANT

V. SUMMARY

DATING EASTERN MEDITERRANEAN SEQUENCES: INTRODUCTORY REMARKS

OFER BAR-YOSEF and RENEE S. KRA

INTRODUCTION

The original goal for a pre-conference workshop in May 1991[1] organized by the editors of this volume was aimed at reporting and discussing the most up-to-date radiometric age determinations, in relation to changing paleoclimates, for the Upper Pleistocene and Holocene of the eastern Mediterranean. Major issues of current debate on the emergence of anatomically modern humans and the origins of agriculture were discussed at the symposium by active researchers in this area. The workshop served as an introduction to, rather than as a means to, a solution of myriad research problems. In addition to participants of the workshop, we invited those who could not attend to send written contributions for publication. We would like to thank all the participants and contributors for their patience and trust in this long-evolving process.

The present volume represents major achievements in the field of Upper Pleistocene and Early Holocene chronology in a region that covers the area from the foothills of the Taurus-Zagros Mountains through the Levant to northeast Africa. The paleoclimatic record in the last 20,000 yr is the most pertinent for understanding the origins of cultivation, domestication and settlement of pastoral communities. This is not to say that climate change was primarily responsible for such important social/economic innovations. However, we believe that, in order to have a meaningful discussion involving the role of climate as a trigger for change, we should examine the available scientific records. The chronological resolution of climate shifts is, as yet, unsatisfactory for those who study the fine-grained pattern of social and economic developments that are becoming clear in archaeological records (*e.g.*, Bar-Yosef 1990; Bar-Yosef and Belfer-Cohen 1992; Bar-Yosef and Meadow, in press; Miller 1992; Moore 1989; Moore and Hillman 1992).

In addition to a synthesis of interdisciplinary, interpretive data and discussions, we provide our readers with date lists and tables of the currently available results of varied radiometric measurements, such as thermoluminescence (TL), electron spin resonance (ESR), uranium/thorium (U/Th), and radiocarbon (^{14}C). We do not offer dendrochronologically calibrated ^{14}C dates for the last 10,000 yr, but refer the reader to the new, extended and refined calibration data and software, in *CALIBRATION 1993* (Stuiver, Long and Kra 1993; Stuiver and Reimer 1993). We use the original, uncalibrated BP dates, which we prefer to bp, commonly cited by British schools, with laboratory code designations and numbers, wherever possible, for easy reference. Rapid advancements in the field of dendrochronology may improve even the most recent curves, making current data obsolete. Thus, the reader can recalculate the original date according to the latest, state-of-the-art calibrations to obtain the most accurate values.

In this chapter, we present our views on some of the "burning" dating issues. We begin with the Middle Paleolithic, a period associated with the emergence of modern humans and a subject of continuing controversy. Several interpretations have been offered, for example, for cave sequences, designation of human fossils and cultural affiliation of the archaeological remains. In this volume, we focus mainly on issues relating to several dating techniques, and address the question of sample provenience. The issue of context becomes more complex when ^{14}C determinations, crucial to the construction of a Neolithic regional sequence, are considered. We illustrate such difficulties with

---

[1] The 14th International Radiocarbon Conference, Tucson, Arizona, 20-24 May 1991

Late Quaternary Chronology and Paleoclimates of the Eastern Mediterranean
Edited by O. Bar-Yosef and R. S. Kra. RADIOCARBON 1994, pp. 1–12

examples from the well-known site of Jericho. We have also asked Dr. H. T. Waterbolk to comment on the ^{14}C dates of this area (Waterbolk 1987, this volume), and we thank him for his thoughtful essay. Finally, we turn to some aspects of dating paleoclimatic sequences. Although much research has been undertaken, especially in the palynology of the area (*e.g.*, van Zeist and Bottema 1991), little information can be contributed to the understanding of long-term climate change.

THE IMPACT OF TL, ESR, U/Th DATES

Human fossils uncovered in Near Eastern caves, especially those from the Galilee/Mt. Carmel region, have been at the center of a heated debate about the origin of modern humans. For quite some time, scholars generally accepted that the area accommodated at least two groups of fossils. One group, uncovered in Skhul and Qafzeh Caves, demonstrated morphological features resembling those of Upper Paleolithic Cro-Magnons. At one time, these Mousterian human remains were named "Proto-Cro-Magnons", presumably indicating their ancestry of the Upper Paleolithic populations of Eurasia. In the absence of other criteria, these skeletal remains were placed chronologically at 50,000–40,000 yr ago (*e.g.*, Trinkaus 1984). The second group included the "Western Asia Neanderthals", *i.e.*, the woman from Tabun, the adult burial from Amud, the baby from Kebara and the human remains uncovered in Shanidar Cave in Iraqi Kurdistan.

Following the first report on microfauna from excavations at Qafzeh Cave (Vandermeersch 1969) and at Tabun Cave, Layer C (Jelinek *et al.* 1973; Jelinek 1982a,b; Farrand 1979), Haas (in Jelinek *et al.* 1973) noticed the discrepancies between the relative chronologies of these two sites. It was only with the completion of Tchernov's (1981, 1984, 1988, 1992, this volume) major study and revisions that the relative antiquity of the Qafzeh assemblages within the Middle Paleolithic sequence of the Levant was established. On the basis of this information, together with an alternative geomorphological and paleoclimatic interpretation of the hominid-bearing levels in Qafzeh (XXIV–XVII), Bar-Yosef and Vandermeersch (1981) (see also Bar-Yosef 1989a,b) suggested a date of 80,000– 100,000 yr for the lowermost levels in the cave.

Although amino acid racemization (AAR) dates measured by Masters (1982) indicated that the lower levels at Qafzeh were older than 50,000 BP (Farrand, this volume), the series of thermoluminescence (TL) dates (Valladas *et al.* 1988), followed by electron spin resonance (ESR) dates (Schwarcz *et al.* 1988), established the general age for the fossils. Figure 1 presents the set of available dates. The chapters by Mercier and Valladas and by Schwarcz provide a summary of ages determined by these three methods; Farrand reappraises the determinations.

Even if the current TL results from the lower levels at Tabun Cave, Mercier and Valladas (this volume) establish an important conclusion that the Middle Paleolithic sequence in the Near East is as old as that of South Africa or western Europe (Clark 1992). It is also clear that hominids that are viewed as possible ancestors of the modern *Homo sapiens sapiens* are as old, in the Near East, as those in Klasies River Mouth, Border Cave and Kibish Omo.

An important issue rarely raised regarding the TL and ESR dates is the nature of context within the site. In most cases, when dates of Acheulean or Mousterian levels become available, discussion focuses on the human fossils, and not on their provenience. Most of us are aware that the dating of the fossils is indirect, based on datable substances, such as animal teeth, bones, burned flints, grains of sand and interbedded speleothems (Geyh, this volume). Often, the radiometric readings from the site or the level in question are averaged. For example, the Qafzeh dates are cited as 92,000 ± 5000 yr, whereas the real range from layers that are *ca.* 1.5 m thick is between 82,000 and 109,000 yr. ESR dates from the same layers yielded averages of 96,000 ± 13,000 yr for early

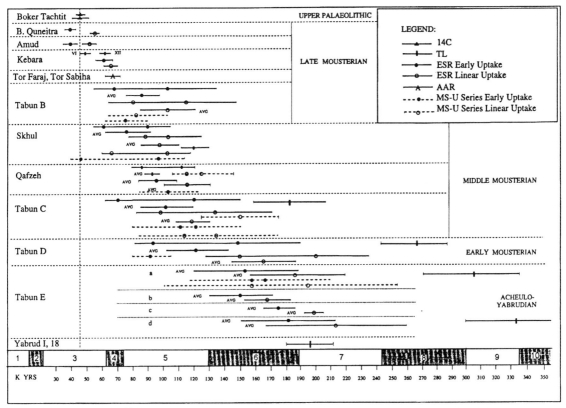

Fig. 1. A distribution of ^{14}C, TL, ESR, AAR and mass spectrometric U-series dates, based on Valladas *et al.* (1987, 1988), Mercier and Valladas (this volume), Grün and Stringer (1991), Grün, Stringer and Schwarcz (1991), Schwarcz *et al.* (1988), Stringer *et al.* (1989), Mercier *et al.* (1993) and Marks (1983). The vertical line at the left indicates the beginning of the Upper Paleolithic at *ca.* 46,000 yr, based on the ^{14}C dates from Boker Tachtit and the TL dates from Kebara.

uptake (EU), and 115,000 ± 15,000 for linear uptake (LU). The dated samples derived from only the lower part of the Mousterian sequence in Qafzeh, essentially Layers XVII–XXIV, where hominids were uncovered. It should be remembered that the upper part of the Mousterian accumulation is, as yet, undated. Unfortunately, composite geological/archaeological profiles from the dated sites, indicating the position of the dated samples, have not yet been published. The result is that most of us cannot re-examine the relation between dated fossils and the context of the site. Even more problematic is the dating of isolated teeth and burned flints from sites excavated in the past when systematic recording was not a standard field technique. In such cases, however, scholars are fully aware of these pitfalls (*e.g.*, Grün, Stringer and Schwarcz 1991; Grün and Stringer 1991; Stringer *et al.* 1989; Mercier *et al.* 1993).

The advantage of the published TL and ESR dates of burned flints or animal teeth is that they raise questions concerning site-formation processes. Since Schiffer's (1976, 1987) pioneering essays and the drive to implement contextual archaeology (Butzer 1982), there has been considerable progress in understanding site-formation, or sedimentary processes. Although many archaeologists recognize such effects of macroprocesses as alluviation, colluviation, fluvial morphology and loess deposition, attention to microprocesses such as human intervention, disturbances caused by activity of earthworms and other burrowing animals and insects (bees, ants), and minor diagenesis, is far from adequate. In the last decade, micromorphology has contributed a great deal to enabling archaeologists to understand the importance of microscopic examination for recognizing invisible (to the naked eye) formative mechanisms (Goldberg 1980; Courty, Goldberg and MacPhail 1989; Gé *et al.* 1993 (see papers in Goldberg *et al.* 1993)). There is a growing awareness that these phenomena, if not identified, can mask significant natural and induced effects. Intermittent occupations by hyenas and humans are more easily discernible by examining microscopic slides than profiles of excavated squares. Only when sterile levels are reached (a phenomenon common in rockshelters in northern latitudes or high altitudes, but hardly known from the Levant) can the remains of hyena dens be isolated by the excavators.

The TL dates from Qafzeh Cave are consistent (Aitken and Valladas 1992), and although the dated flints were found in assigned levels, they still could have migrated from their original, *in-situ* positions. Perhaps it is more realistic to consider that the range of Qafzeh dates (82,000–109,000 TL yr) indicates the slow accumulation of the hominid-bearing levels, which took some 20,000 to 25,000 yr.

Similarly, we may infer, from the TL dates of Kebara Cave (Valladas *et al.* 1987), some conclusions about the formation processes at this site. As a reminder, the dates are as follows:

Unit VI	48,300 ± 3500
Unit VII	51,900 ± 3500
Unit VIII	57,300 ± 4000
Unit IX	58,400 ± 4000
Unit X	61,600 ± 3600
Unit XI	60,000 ± 3500
Unit XII	59,900 ± 3500

Laville and Goldberg (1989) and Goldberg and Laville (1991) interpret these dates as a rather rapid accumulation of 3.5 m of anthropogenic-biogenic deposits. The burial of KNH-2 was found at the base of Unit XI and in Unit XII. This should lead us to the cautious conclusion that we simply have no idea what kind of hominid produced the lithic assemblages uncovered in the upper section of the Mousterian sequence. The study of the artifacts clearly indicates minor trends of change in production of blanks, or core reduction techniques. While the lithic industry of Units XII–IX is essentially the same, and is based on what is known as Levallois convergent preparation, Meignen and Bar-Yosef (1991) and Bar-Yosef and Meignen (1992) recorded a slight shift to more radial blanks in Units VIII–VII.

A more general conclusion regarding the Mousterian chronology can be reached when we combine the available TL dates from Kebara Cave with preliminary ESR readings that cluster around 55,000–48,000/47,000 BP from Amud Cave (Grün and Stringer 1991). Amud Cave contained a burial of an adult Neanderthal that was uncovered in the 1960s (Suzuki and Takai 1970). Thus, if we can demonstrate that the similarities between the lithic assemblages and the hominids are valid, then it is highly probable that the so-called Mediterranean Neanderthals prevailed in the Levant during the entire sequence of the Late Mousterian.

In sum, the acknowledgment that Near Eastern caves are not stable depositional traps would soon lead to trials in reconstruction of assemblages. Experimental studies on the movement of artifacts have demonstrated that displacements of 10–20 cm can be expected over time (*e.g.*, Villa and Courtin 1983). One of us (O. B.-Y.) briefly conducted such an experiment in Kebara, and found that Mousterian pieces could have been moved as much as 15–20 cm. From this, we can deduce that dated teeth and burned flints, even when exact provenience is well known, could have originated in older or younger levels. Thus, we must evaluate available TL and ESR dates with caution and encourage more systematic studies.

Finally, the paleoanthropological questions concerning modern humans coming "Out of Africa" are directly related to dated industries and sites in Ethiopia, Sudan and Egypt. The work of Wendorf, Schild, Close and their associates (this volume) in the eastern Sahara is a crucial contribution to this problem. These authors describe and evaluate the nature and dating of the various levels by different techniques. The TL, ESR and other uranium (U)-series dating techniques enable us to date sites that are beyond the current reach of ^{14}C. However, one crucial cultural change occurred more or less at the range of overlap between oldest ^{14}C dates and a few of the newly published U-series dates, namely the transition from the Middle to Upper Paleolithic. This cultural shift is the second problem tied to the origin of modern humans. As mentioned above, it was believed for a long time that the Near Eastern so-called "Proto-Cro-Magnons" could have been the ancestors of European Upper Paleolithic Cro-Magnons, to whom the term, *Homo sapiens sapiens*, was applied originally. Establishing the antiquity of the Skhul-Qafzeh fossils only helps to focus the debate. While some of us view the need for an additional mutation to reach the cultural level of the Upper Paleolithic technological and cultural achievements, others simply regard the shift as gradual or even rapid, but occurring within the same world populations. The claim for revolutionary transformation suggests tracing its origin in the Middle/Upper Paleolithic of a certain region. Therefore, dating sites, assemblages and cultures plays an important role in supporting one hypothesis or another.

The earliest ^{14}C dates for the beginning of the Upper Paleolithic technological change in lithics are *ca.* 48,000–40,500 BP from the site of Boker Tachtit (Marks 1983; Phillips, this volume). Other dates from a somewhat later context in Kebara cave, where the Transitional industry or Emiran (Gilead 1989) is missing ages in the range of 43,000–46/47,000 BP, support the dates from the Negev. Although the TL dates for Kebara (see above) are not available for Unit V, the latest Mousterian layer, the date of Unit VI, 48,300 ± 3500 BP, indicates that the transition from the Middle to Upper Paleolithic took place *ca.* 47,000–45,000 BP. Additional dates are needed, but from Temnata cave in Bulgaria, similar TL dates for the earliest Upper Paleolithic were recently obtained (S. Kozłowski, personal communication). However, the degree of potential discrepancy between TL and ^{14}C dates for this period is, as yet, unknown, especially when calibrated ^{14}C dates tend to gain a few hundred to 1000 yr every 10 millennia. Under such circumstances, ESR dates for Skhul cave, including those calculated as EU and tested by mass spectrometry (McDermott *et al.* 1993), and samples that provide readings in the range of 45,000–40,000 yr for Mousterian teeth, are too young and should be considered intrusive or mixed. These dates should receive the same cautious attention given to ^{14}C dates that are inconsistent with other dates from neighboring sites.

RADIOCARBON DATE AND SITE-FORMATION PROCESSES

Archaeologists often use ^{14}C dates to propose or advocate a hypothesis or a preferred chronology (see Phillips; Byrd; Garrard, Baird and Byrd; Cauvin and Stordeur; Simmons and Wigand; Kozłowski, all this volume). Rarely does a discussion concerning the contextual relation between the supposedly dated layer and the date (or dates) precede the final conclusions. Neglected also is the identification of the charcoal sample to a wood species that may indicate the source of discrepancies between the expected date and the actual result. The same holds true when the effects of site-formation processes are not taken into account. On the occasions when context is treated as a significant factor in formulating a meaningful interpretation, the accuracy of the available dates may be questioned. We choose to demonstrate these difficulties by examining the site of Jericho.

Jericho is a well-known mound in which the lower part of the sequence contains Late Natufian and Early Neolithic remains, subdivided into Pre-Pottery Neolithic A and B (subsequently, PPNA and PPNB) (Kenyon 1957; Kenyon and Holland 1981, 1983). (The Late Natufian dates to 11,000–10,300 ± 100 BP, the PPNA to 10,300 ± 100–9300 ± 200 BP and the PPNB to 9300 ± 200–7800

± 500 BP.) Although most archaeologists acknowledge the gap between the PPNA and the PPNB, little attention has been paid to the hiatus between the Late Natufian and the PPNA. The most attractive architectural remains are the PPNA tower and the wall that protects the tower and the settlement (Bar-Yosef 1986). While searching for the northern continuation of the alleged "town wall" that was first uncovered in the Western Trench, Kenyon (1957; Kenyon and Holland 1981) excavated another sector (M) just 20 m away. Instead of the Neolithic wall or brickmud houses, she exposed PPNA deposits, and suggested that these levels were the core of the settlement, which she named "Proto-Neolithic". Close examination of the lithics persuaded Crowfoot-Payne (1983) that the material from area M was the same as that from the PPNA, and should be included in what she termed the Sultanian industry. There is also no evidence that the PPNA deposits in this location are earlier than the structures in the Western Trench.

Dating the PPNA in Jericho was important, especially during the 1950s, when Robert Braidwood and his associates tried to uncover early farming communities in the foothills of the Zagros Mountains (Braidwood and Howe 1960). The first ^{14}C dates from Jericho, the GL series (see Kuijt and Bar-Yosef, this volume) turned out to be too young (Burleigh 1983). Both the Pennsylvania and British Museum Laboratories provided another series of ^{14}C dates (Stuckenrath 1963; Barker and Mackey 1963; Burleigh 1983; Kuijt and Bar-Yosef, this volume). Since the dates became available in the literature before the publication of the archaeological profiles, they are organized, in most lists, from the oldest to the youngest (*e.g.*, Weinstein 1984). However, when the various dates are placed on the published profile (Kenyon and Holland 1981; Fig. 2), the emerging picture is slightly different. Only one date near 10,000 BP comes from the lower part of the Neolithic sequence. The earliest levels (*ca.* 1 m above bedrock) were not dated. As Figure 2 demonstrates, a few dates are not in stratigraphic order. Beyond controversies concerning interlaboratory correlations, such disagreements derive from the fact that intrusive charcoal cannot be identified. Thus, the archaeologist should consider the building, leveling and digging activities carried out by Neolithic villagers, as well as the use of old wood, before rejecting or accepting ^{14}C determinations. Finally, for those concerned with the Neolithic chronology of the Levant, we note that the end of the Jericho PPNA deposits is marked by dates in the range of 7300 to 7200 BP. When compared to the northern Levant (*ca.* 10,000–9500 in Mureybet Phase II (Kuijt and Bar-Yosef, this volume)), these ^{14}C results indicate that the PPNA lasted longer in the south (Rollefson 1989).

Undoubtedly, many ambiguities in the interpretation of charcoal dates will be resolved when seeds or other organic substances, such as rope made of grass and twined objects made of linen, can be dated directly from the original context. The accelerator mass spectrometric (AMS) dates measured by the Oxford Accelerator Laboratory (Housley, this volume) demonstrate their value for archaeological interpretations. In recent years, AMS dates have enabled paleoethnobotanists and other researchers to determine earlier phases of plant cultivation (*e.g.*, Moore 1991; Moore *et al.* 1986; Moore and Hillman 1992; Bar-Yosef *et al.* 1991; Miller 1992). AMS dating also enables researchers to identify mixed assemblages, for example, when seeds found in the Natufian deposits of Hayonim Terrace, Ain Mallaha or Nahal Oren, were determined to be clearly intrusive (*e.g.*, Housley, this volume; Valla 1991; Legge 1986).

[14]C dating can also remove uncertainties involved in the investigation of monocultural and often monolevel sites. Such an approach was developed in the arid areas of the Near East, and the chapters by Cauvin and Stordeur; Garrard, Baird and Byrd; and Avner, Carmi and Segal (all this volume) are among the best examples.

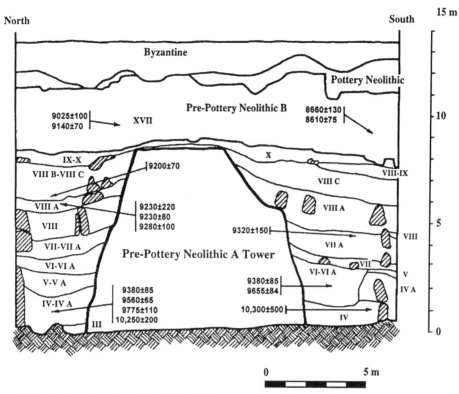

Fig. 2. A schematic section of the Jericho PPNA tower redrawn from the original section (Kenyon and Holland 1981, plate 238). The tower is represented by the heavy black line, and on each side, the PPNA stratigraphic units are given (Stages IV–X). The hatched blocks mark the position of the house walls. The distribution of the available radiometric dates demonstrates problems in interpreting the rate of deposition, the use of dead wood, the re-use of wooden posts and the redeposition of charcoal flecks.

PALEOCLIMATE CHANGE AND THE ARCHAEOLOGICAL RECORD

The third section of this volume focuses on paleoclimate changes in the eastern Mediterranean during the past 20,000 yr. The chapters by Fontugne *et al.*; Goldberg; Frumkin *et al.*; El-Moslimany; and Baruch present marine, terrestrial and palynological data and interpretations of climate change. Comparisons among their results enable the reader to assess the different approaches and techniques, the limitations of the studies and the level of current knowledge. On reading these chapters, it becomes clear that marine records are the most complete, followed by the palynological sequences from lakes, and finally, the geomorphological observations. The reader will also observe that, on a regional scale, the information is not spread evenly. Although additional marine sequences can be obtained, it will be difficult to find lakes where they do not exist today, such as in the southern Levant. It is unfortunate that the Dead Sea area still does not have a complete palynological record for the past 20,000 yr. Comprehensive documentation for this area would, undoubtedly, answer questions on the impact of the Younger Dryas on the vegetational history of this particular drainage basin.

It is superfluous to stress the importance of ^{14}C dating of marine and pollen records. For measuring marine samples, AMS technology requires only milligram-sized samples; however, pollen-core samples are still measured by conventional techniques (*e.g.*, liquid scintillation or gas-proportional counting). The need to have as many measurements as possible is clearly demonstrated by the absence of correlation among dates for the final millennia of the Pleistocene between the Ghab in northern Syria and the Hula Valley in Israel (Baruch, this volume). Difficulties in matching events in ocean and pollen records to a well-founded ^{14}C time scale inhibit better understanding of complex relations between temperature change, precipitation and vegetational response intervals of abrupt climate change. Our inability to reach a sound chronological framework for the eastern Mediterranean impacts on the interpretation of archaeological studies and historical documents of the Holocene. Ample evidence implies that environmental deterioration and resource depletion began with the establishment of farming communities. However, this was not a linear trend. Paleo-climatic evidence and modeling for the Holocene (*e.g.*, COHMAP 1988) show that certain fluctuations are well recorded in areas where agriculture and pastoralism were introduced much later than in the Levant or the Near East, in general. Bruins (this volume) discusses the most obvious effects of humans on their immediate environments of the semi-arid region of the Negev. Avner, Carmi and Segal (this volume) describe human occupations that precede the last three millennia. They also demonstrate that ^{14}C dating is the most important tool in identifying the human presence in the desert when there are no characteristic stone tools or sherds.

The last section of this volume contains a summary by Tchernov that demonstrates the use of faunal assemblages for reconstructing the past biogeography of the region as well as for establishing the relative chronology. It was, for example, the presence of archaic species of rodents in the hominid-bearing layers at Qafzeh that hinted at the antiquity of the site when compared to the caves in Mt. Carmel (Tchernov 1981). In addition, discussions concerning terrestrial climate reconstruction must take into account the known behavior and foraging strategies of small mammals such as rodents or reptiles (*e.g.*, lizards). The presence of "self-domesticated" species, such as the house mouse (*Mus musculus*) has important implications for archaeological interpretations. When well preserved (Weiner and Bar-Yosef 1990) and found *in situ*, animal bones provide datable substance. An example of their excellent application for archaeological interpretation is in the Abu Hureyra sequence (Moore 1992).

CONCLUDING REMARKS

We hope that this volume will evoke a cautious, or even skeptical, spirit of investigation. We encourage more radiometric analyses, but only when they include broad interdisciplinary data on stratigraphic, hydrologic, marine, palynologic and sedimentary processes. All this, with a view toward weighing the implications of and evaluating the dates for interpretations of evolutionary thresholds. The lists and tables of dates provided here will enable the energetic reader to test his or her new hypotheses on one or more of the evolutionary issues that currently circulate in the literature. We hope that, by providing the reader with such a compendium, in spite of the gaps of information on the regions not fully documented here, such as the Zagros Mountains of Iran or of Anatolia, our audience will come to appreciate the major progress in research of Late Quaternary Chronology and Paleoclimates of the Eastern Mediterranean.

ACKNOWLEDGMENTS

We thank all the authors of this volume for their contributions, cooperation and perseverance. Thanks are also due the reviewers of the original manuscripts for offering constructive comments and improving the quality of the end-product. We are grateful to David Pilbeam and C. C. Lamberg-Karlovsky for their constant support. The American School of Prehistoric Research, Harvard University, is gratefully acknowledged for their trust and support, and Peabody Museum Publications, for their role in the promotion of this book. We are indebted to John W. Martin,

Tucson, for designing the cover. We thank Austin Long, Editor of *RADIOCARBON*, for quietly overseeing the publication; we cannot give enough praise to Assistant Editors, David R. Sewell and Kimberley L. Tanner, for their professional commitment, diligence and expertise in producing this book.

REFERENCES CITED

Aitken, M. J. and H. Valladas
   1992   Luminescence dating relevant to human origins. *Philosophical Transactions of the Royal Society of London* B 337:139–144.
Avner, U., I. Carmi and D. Segal
   1994   Neolithic to Bronze Age settlement of the Negev and Sinai in light of radiocarbon dating: A view from the southern Negev. This volume.
Bar-Yosef, O.
   1986   The walls of Jericho: An alternative interpretation. *Current Anthropology* 27:157–162.
   1989a   Geochronology of the Levantine Middle Palaeolithic. In *The Human Revolution: Behavioural and Biological Perspectives on the Origins of Modern Humans*, pp. 589–610. Edinburgh University Press, Edinburgh.
   1989b   Upper Pleistocene cultural stratigraphy in southwest Asia. In *Patterns and Processes in Later Pleistocene Human Emergence*, pp. 154–179. Cambridge University Press, Cambridge.
   1990   The Last Glacial Maximum in the Mediterranean Levant. In *The World at 18,000 BP*. Vol. 2, *Low Latitudes*, pp. 58–72. Unwin Hyman, London.
Bar-Yosef, O. and A. Belfer-Cohen
   1992   From foraging to farming in the Mediterranean Levant. In *Transitions to Agriculture in Prehistory*, pp. 21–48. Prehistory Press, Madison, Wisconsin.
Bar-Yosef, O., A. Gopher, E. Tchernov and M. E. Kislev
   1991   Netiv Hagdud – An Early Neolithic village site in the Jordan Valley. *Journal of Field Archaeology* 18(4): 405–424.
Bar-Yosef, O. and R. H. Meadow
   The Origins of Agriculture in the Near East. School of American Research, Santa Fe. In press.
Bar-Yosef, O. and L. Meignen
   1992   Insights into Levantine Middle Paleolithic cultural variability. In *The Middle Paleolithic: Adaptation, Behavior, and Variability*, pp. 163–182. University of Pennsylvania, The University Museum, Philadelphia.
Bar-Yosef, O. and B. Vandermeersch
   1981   Notes concerning the possible age of the Mousterian Layers at Qafzeh Cave. In *Préhistoire du Levant*, edited by J. Cauvin and P. Sanlaville, pp. 555–569. Maison de l'Orient, CNRS, Lyon.
Barker, H. and Mackey, J.
   1963   British Museum natural radiocarbon measurements IV: *Radiocarbon* 5:104–108.
Baruch, U.
   1994   The late Quaternary pollen record of the Near East. This volume.
Braidwood, R. and B. Howe (editors)
   1960   *Prehistoric Investigations in Iraqi Kurdistan*. Studies in Ancient Oriental Civilization 31. Oriental Institute, Chicago.
Bruins, H.
   1994   Comparative chronology of climate and human history in the southern Levant from the Late Chalcolithic to the Early Arab period. This volume.
Burleigh, R.
   1983   Appendix C: Radiocarbon dates. In *The Excavations at Jericho*, edited by K. M. Kenyon, pp. 501–504. London, British School of Archaeology, Jerusalem.
Butzer, K. W.
   1982   *Archaeology as Human Ecology: Method and Theory for Contextual Approach*. Cambridge University Press, Cambridge.
Byrd, B.
   1994   Late Quaternary hunter-gatherer complexes in the Levant between 20,000 and 10,000 BP. This volume.
Cauvin, J. and D. Stordeur
   1994   Radiocarbon dating El-Kowm: Upper Paleolithic through Chalcolithic. This volume.

Clark, J. D.
    1992   African and Asian perspectives on the origins of modern humans. *Philosophical Transactions of the Royal Society* 337:201–215.
COHMAP
    1988   Climatic changes of the last 18,000 years: Observations and model simulations. *Science* 241:1043–1052.
Courty, M. A., P. Goldberg and R. MacPhail
    1989   *Soils and Micromorphology in Archaeology*. Cambridge University Press, Cambridge.
Crowfoot-Payne, J.
    1983   The flint industries of Jericho. In *Excavations at Jericho*, pp. 622–759. The British School of Archaeology in Jerusalem, London.
El-Moslimany, A.
    1994   Evidence of Early Holocene summer precipitation in the continental Middle East. This volume.
Farrand, W. R.
    1979   Chronology and paleoenvironment of Levantine prehistoric sites as seen from sediment studies. *Journal of Archaeological Science* 6:369–392.
    1994   Confrontation of geological stratigraphy and radiometric dates from Upper Pleistocene sites in the Levant. This volume.
Fontugne, M., M. Arnold, L. Labeyrie, M. Paterne, S. E. Calvert and J.-C. Duplessy
    1994   Paleoenvironment, sapropel chronology and Nile River discharge during the last 20,000 years as indicated by deep-sea sediment records in the eastern Mediterranean. This volume.
Frumkin, A., I. Carmi, I. Zak and M. Magaritz
    1994   Middle Holocene environmental change determined from the salt caves of Mount Sedom, Israel. This volume.
Garrard, A., D. Baird and B. Byrd
    1994   The chronological basis and significance of the Late Paleolithic and Neolithic sequence in the Azraq Basin, Jordan. This volume.
Gé, T., M. Courty, W. Matthews and J. Wattez
    1993   Sedimentary formation processes of occupation surfaces. In *Formation Processes in Archaeological Contexts*, edited by P. Goldberg, D. Nash and M. D. Petraglia, pp. 149–163. Prehistory Press, Madison.
Geyh, M. A.
    1994   The paleohydrology of the eastern Mediterranean. This volume.
Gilead, I.
    1989   The Upper Paleolithic in the southern Levant: Periodization and terminology. In *Investigations in Southern Levantine Prehistory*, edited by O. Bar-Yosef and B. Vandermeersch, pp. 231–254. BAR International Series 497, British Archaeological Reports, Oxford.
Goldberg, P.
    1980   Micromorphology in archaeology and prehistory. *Paléorient* 6:159–164.
    1994   Interpreting late Quaternary continental sequences in Israel. This volume.
Goldberg, P. and H. Laville
    1991   Etude geologique des depots de la grotte de Kebara (Mont Carmel): Campagne 1982–1984. In *Le Squelette Mousterien de Kebara 2, Mt. Carmel, Israël*, edited by O. Bar-Yosef and B. Vandermeersch, pp. 29–42. Maison de l'Orient, CNRS, Lyon.
Goldberg, P., D. Nash and M. D. Petraglia (editors)
    1993   *Formation Processes in Archaeological Contexts*. Prehistory Press, Madison.
Grün, R. and C. B. Stringer
    1991   Electron spin resonance dating and the evolution of modern humans. *Archaeometry* 33(2):153–199.
Grün, R., C. B. Stringer and H. P. Schwarcz
    1991   ESR dating of teeth from Garrod's Tabun Cave collection. *Journal of Human Evolution* 20(3):231–248.
Housley, R.
    1994   Eastern Mediterranean chronologies: The Oxford AMS contribution. This volume.
Jelinek, A. J.
    1982a   The Middle Palaeolithic in the southern Levant with comments on the appearance of modern *Homo sapiens*, pp. 57–104. BAR International Series 151, British Archaeological Reports, Oxford.
    1982b   The Tabun Cave and Paleolithic Man in the Levant. *Science* 216:1369–1375.
Jelinek, A. J., W. R. Farrand, G. Haas, H. A. and P. Goldberg
    1973   New excavations at the Tabun Cave, Mount Carmel, Israel, 1967–1972; A preliminary report. *Paléorient* 12:151–183.
Kenyon, K.
    1957   *Digging Up Jericho*. Benn, London.

Kenyon, K. and T. Holland
1981   *Excavations at Jericho, Vol. 3: The Architecture and Stratigraphy of the Tell.* British School of Archaeology in Jerusalem, London.
1983   *Excavations at Jericho.* British School of Archaeology, London.
Kozłowski, S.
1994   Radiocarbon dates from Aceramic Iraq. This volume.
Kuijt, I. and O. Bar-Yosef
1994   Radiocarbon chronology for the Levantine Neolithic: Observations and data. This volume.
Laville, H. and P. Goldberg
1989   The collapse of the Mousterian sedimentary regime and the beginning of the Upper Palaeolithic at Kebara. In *Investigations in South Levantine Prehistory*, edited by O. Bar-Yosef and B. Vandermeersch, pp. 75–95. BAR International Series 497, British Archaeological Reports, Oxford.
Legge, A. J.
1986   Seeds of discontent: Accelerator dates on some charred plant remains from the Kebaran and Natufian cultures. In *Archaeological Results from Accelerator Dating*, edited by J. Gowlett and R. E. M. Hedges, pp. 23–35. Alden Press, Oxford.
Marks, A. E.
1983   The sites of Boker Tachtit and Boker: A brief introduction. In *Prehistory and Paleoenvironments in the Central Negev*, Vol. 3, edited by A. E. Marks, pp. 15–37. Southern Methodist University Press, Dallas.
Masters, P. M.
1982   An amino acid racemization chronology for Tabun. In *The Transition from Lower to Middle Palaeolithic and the Origin of Modern Man*, pp. 43–56, edited by A. Ronen. BAR International Series 151, British Archaeological Reports, Oxford.
Meignen, L. and O. Bar-Yosef
1991   Les industries Mousterienne de Kebara. In *Le Squelette Mousterien de Kebara 2, Mt. Carmel, Israël*, edited by O. Bar-Yosef and B. Vandermeersch, pp. 49–76. Maison de l'Orient, CNRS, Lyon.
Mercier, N. and H. Valladas
1994   Thermoluminescence dates for the Paleolithic Levant. This volume.
Mercier, N., H. Valladas, O. Bar-Yosef, C. Stringer and J. L. Joron
1993   Thermoluminescence date for the Mousterian burial site of Es-Skhul, Mt. Carmel. *Journal of Archaeological Science* 20:169–174.
Miller, N. F.
1992   The origins of plant cultivation in the Near East. In *The Origins of Agriculture*, edited by C. W. Cowan and P. J. Watson, pp. 39–58. Smithsonian Institution Press, Washington, DC.
Moore, A. M. T.
1989   The transition from foraging to farming in southwest Asia. In *Foraging and Farming: The Evolution of Plant Exploitation*, edited by D. R. Harris and G. C. Hillman, pp. 620–631. Unwin Hyman, London.
1991   Abu Hureyra 1 and the antecedents of agriculture on the Middle Euphrates. In *The Natufian Culture in the Levant*, edited by O. Bar-Yosef and F. R. Valla, pp. 277–294. International Monographs in Prehistory, Ann Arbor.
Moore, A. M. T., J. A. J. Gowlett, R. E. M. Hedges, G. C. Hillman, A. J. Legge and P. A. Rowley-Conwy
1986   Radiocarbon accelerator (AMS) dates for the Epipaleolithic settlement at Abu Hureyra, Syria. *Radiocarbon* 28(3):1068–1076.
Moore, A. M. T. and G. C. Hillman
1992   The Pleistocene to Holocene transition and human economy in southwest Asia: The impact of the Younger Dryas. *American Antiquity* 57:482–494.
Phillips, J.
1994   The Upper Paleolithic chronology of the Levant and the Nile Valley. This volume.
Rollefson, G. O.
1989   The Late Aceramic Neolithic of the Levant: A synthesis. *Paléorient* 151:168–173.
Schiffer, M. B.
1976   *Behavioral Archaeology.* Academic Press, London.
1987   *Formation Processes of the Archaeological Record.* University of New Mexico Press, Albuquerque.
Schwarcz, H. P.
1994   Chronology of modern humans in the Levant. This volume.
Schwarcz, H. P., R. Grün, B. Vandermeersch, O. Bar-Yosef, H. Valladas and E. Tchernov
1988   ESR dates for the hominid burial site of Qafzeh in Israel. *Journal of Human Evolution* 17:733–737.

Simmons, A. and P. Wigand
  1994   Assessing the radiocarbon determinations from Akrotiri *Aetokremnos*, Cyprus. This volume.
Stringer, C. B., R. Grün, H. P. Schwarcz and P. Goldberg
  1989   ESR dates for the hominid burial site of Es Skhul in Israel. *Nature* 338:756–758.
Stuckenrath, R. Jr.
  1963   University of Pennsylvania radiocarbon dates VI. *Radiocarbon* 5:82–103.
Stuiver, M., A. Long and R. S. Kra (editors)
  1993   Calibration 1993. *Radiocarbon* 35(1):1–244.
Stuiver, M. and P. J. Reimer
  1993   Extended ^{14}C data base and revised CALIB 3.0 ^{14}C age calibration program. *Radiocarbon* 35(1):215–230.
Suzuki, H. and F. Takai (editors)
  1970   *The Amud Man and His Cave Site.* Academic Press of Japan, Tokyo.
Tchernov, E.
  1981   The biostratigraphy of the Middle East. In *Préhistorie du Levant. Chronologie et Organisation de l'Espace Depuis les Origines Jusqu'au VIe Millenaire,* edited by J. Cauvin and P. Sanlaville, pp. 67–97. Maison de l'Orient, CNRS, Lyon.
  1984   *Faunal Turnover and Extinction Rate in the Levant.* The University of Arizona Press, Tucson.
  1988   Biochronology of the Middle Paleolithic and dispersal events of hominids in the Levant. In *L'Homme de Néandertal,* Vol. 2, edited by M. Otte, pp. 153–168. Etudes et Recherches Archeologiques de l'Université de Liège 34, Liège.
  1992   Eurasian-African biotic exchanges through the Levantine corridor during the Neogene and Quaternary. *Courier Forschungsinstitut Senckenberg* 153:103–123.
  1994   New comments on the biostratigraphy of the Middle and Upper Pleistocene of the southern Levant. This volume.
Trinkaus, E.
  1984   Western Asia. In *The Origins of Modern Humans: A World Survey of the Fossil Evidence of Modern Humans,* edited by F. H. Smith and F. Spencer, pp. 251–293. Alan R. Liss, Inc., New York.
Valla, F. R.
  1991   Les Natoufiens de Mallaha et l'espace. In *The Natufian Culture in the Levant,* edited by O. Bar-Yosef, pp. 111–122. International Monographs in Prehistory, Ann Arbor, Michigan.
Valladas, H., J. L. Joron, G. Valladas, B. Arensburg, O. Bar-Yosef, A. Belfer-Cohen, P. Goldberg, H. Laville, L. Meignen, Y. Rak, E. Tchernov, A. M. Tillier and B. Vandermeersch
  1987   Thermoluminscence dates for the Neanderthal burial site at Kebara in Israel. *Nature* 330:159–160.
Valladas, H., J. L. Reyss, J. L. Joron, G. Valladas, O. Bar-Yosef and B. Vandermeersch
  1988   Thermoluminescence dating of Mousterian "Proto-Cro-Magnon" remains from Israel and the origin of modern man. *Nature* 331:614–615.
van Zeist, W. and S. Bottema
  1991   *Late Quaternary Vegetation of the Near East.* Dr. Ludwig Reichert Verlag, Weisbaden.
Vandermeersch, B.
  1969   *Paléontologie Humaine: Les Nouveaux Squelettes Mousteriens Découverts à Qafzeh Israël et Leur Signification.* Academie des Sciences, Seance du 23 mai, 1969, Comptes rendus des seances de l'Academie des Sciences.
Villa, P. and J. Courtin
  1983   The interpretation of stratified sites: A view from underground. *Journal of Archaeological Science* 10:267–281.
Waterbolk, H. T.
  1987   *Working with Radiocarbon Dates in Southwestern Asia.* BAR International Series 379, British Archaeological Reports, Oxford.
  1994   Radiocarbon dating Levantine prehistory. This volume.
Weiner, S. and O. Bar-Yosef
  1990   States of preservation of bones from prehistoric sites in the Near East: A survey. *Journal of Archaeological Science* 17:187–196.
Weinstein, J. M.
  1984   Radiocarbon dating the southern Levant. *Radiocarbon* 26(3):297–366.
Wendorf, F. R. Schild, A. Close, H. Schwarcz, G. Miller, R. Grün, A. Bluszcz, S. Stokes, L. Morawska, J. Huxtable, J. Lundberg, C. Hill and C. McKinney
  1994   A chronology for the Middle and Late Pleistocene wet episodes in the eastern Sahara. This volume.

THERMOLUMINESCENCE DATES FOR THE PALEOLITHIC LEVANT

NORBERT MERCIER and HELENE VALLADAS

Centre des Faibles Radioactivités, Avenue de la Terrasse, Laboratoire Mixte CNRS-CEA
F-91198 Gif sur Yvette, Cedex, France

INTRODUCTION

For the last two decades, the thermoluminescence (TL) technique has been used to date many Near Eastern sites for which radiocarbon (^{14}C) dating was impossible or unreliable. Most initial research concentrated on ceramics, either to identify forgeries, as in the case of the famous Haçilar vessels (Aitken, Moorey and Ucko 1971), or to support controversial ^{14}C dates, as in the case of Egyptian prehistoric vessels from Hemamieh and Qurna-Tarif (Whittle 1975). Since the discovery that TL could be used for heated flint (Göksu *et al.* 1974), the technique has been perfected to become a reliable tool (Aitken, Huxtable and Debenham 1986; Valladas 1992) in dating of Middle and Upper Paleolithic sites.

Although the reliability of this dating method has been repeatedly demonstrated (see, *e.g.*, Valladas 1992, a recent study comparing TL and ^{14}C dates for the same sites), several TL dates for Middle Paleolithic sites in the Levant have been received by some with skepticism. We intend to show that, in most instances, skepticism is unjustified, because it arises from apparent misunderstandings of the technique. We will also point out cases where new measurements may be necessary in light of recent data.

THE DATING OF FLINT

General Principles

Thermoluminescence refers to light emitted, in excess of incandescent glow, by certain solids following exposure to ionizing radiation. When archaeological ceramics or flints are buried, they receive alpha, beta and gamma radiation mostly from the ^{238}U, ^{232}Th and ^{40}K ions contained within the artifacts and in the surrounding soil. The effect of cosmic radiation is of lesser importance, and depends on burial depth. In passing through a material, alpha, beta and gamma rays excite numerous electrons, some of which remain trapped for extended periods of time in energy levels created by crystal defects. In certain minerals, electrons can remain in an excited state for over one million years at ambient temperature. The number of electrons trapped is a function of the accumulated radiation dose received by the mineral. Thus, if the annual radiation dose is known, one can calculate the duration of exposure to ionizing radiation.

When a mineral is heated above a certain critical temperature, the trapped electrons are excited into higher energy levels from which they drop, emitting light, or TL, in the process. The intensity, measured with photomultipliers and recorded as a function of the heating temperature, is proportional to the number of released electrons, which, in turn, is proportional to the number trapped, and consequently, to the total radiation dose received since the mineral was last heated above 500°C. Heating most minerals of archaeological interest above this temperature empties the electron traps, and the refilling process will only begin after the mineral cools.

Paleodose is the total accumulated radiation dose calculated from the measured TL intensity. To convert TL intensity to paleodose, the TL sensitivity of the material must be known; this refers to

Late Quaternary Chronology and Paleoclimates of the Eastern Mediterranean
Edited by O. Bar-Yosef and R. S. Kra. RADIOCARBON 1994, pp. 13–20

13

the ratio between the intensity of the measured TL and the total radiation dose. Sensitivity is determined by measuring the TL induced in the same mineral by a known amount of artificial radiation; the two most common radiation sources are ^{90}Sr and ^{137}Cs. The internal annual radiation dose received by a flint is calculated from the concentrations of the relevant radioisotopes, which are usually determined by neutron activation analysis. The external dose, including cosmic and gamma rays, is measured by planting very sensitive dosimeters, such as $CaSO_4$/Dy, as close as possible to the sampling point.

To obtain the date of human use of an archaeological flint by TL, heating must have occurred during, or soon after such use at a temperature >450°C. Underheated flint should be avoided, because the age will be overestimated due to the presence of trapped electrons remaining from the time preceding its use. Such electrons give rise to "geological TL". Consequently, several methods have been developed to determine if flints from the vicinity of ancient hearths were adequately heated (Valladas 1983; Göksu, Weiser and Regulla 1989). Of course, reheating of an object since its last use will yield a TL date of the heating event. Once the paleodose and the annual dose rate have been calculated, a simple equation (Age = paleodose/dose rate) gives the date of human use of the object, or more precisely, the time elapsed since the last heating.

Reliability of Annual and Paleodose Determinations

The three principal sources of the internal dose (^{238}U, ^{232}Th and ^{40}K) have half-lives over one billion years, so their radiation flux can be considered constant within the comparatively short time span since the dated objects were last heated. In contrast with teeth dated by electron spin resonance (ESR), flints do not exchange radioelements with the surrounding soil, so the measured concentrations can be taken as representing the entire period of burial. These two facts ensure that, in flint, the internal dose remains invariant over very long periods of time.

The external (environmental) dose, on the other hand, may fluctuate, as when the water content of the surrounding soil changes, or some radioelements are leached out or are enriched by water-borne minerals. Consequently, current dosimeter readings can under- or overestimate the amount of environmental radiation received in the past.

As noted earlier, the preferred method for determining annual dose involves burying several dosimeters in the sampling environment. Under certain time constraints, the gamma component of the external dose is measured *in situ* with a portable spectrometer. In some instances, as when the strata of interest have been removed, for example, the external dose is measured in the laboratory by gamma-ray spectrometry on saved soil specimens. Although these results are less reliable, because a small soil volume might not represent a flint's original context, such soil samples can be subjected to detailed U/Th disequilibrium analysis. These data can provide useful information about past radioelement mobility, and enable a better estimate of the mean past external dose. The best solution would be to combine both types of annual dose determinations.

Systematic errors can arise in the determination of the paleodose, itself, if an inadequate function is used to represent the growth of the TL signal *vs.* radiation dose received by the flint. For example, recent work has shown that, at doses higher than 250 Gray (1 Gray = 1J kg^{-1}), an exponential function can underestimate the paleodose and, consequently, the calculated age by 15–20% (Mercier 1992; Sanzelle *et al.* 1993). To avoid this pitfall in computing the paleodose, one must take into account the specific supralinearity (initial non-linearity of the TL growth) of each case (Mercier *et al.* 1992; Sanzelle *et al.* 1993).

Problems

Inadequate knowledge of the past water content of the soil poses a problem in determining the external annual dose. In passing through water, the external radiation is attenuated, so the present radiation flux will not represent that of the past if the water content (measured by drying soil samples at 100°C) was radically different. The best approach is to estimate upper and lower soil moisture limits. The potential maximum (saturation) is measured by laboratory simulation of the pressure to which soil had been subjected at the relevant depth; the minimum can be assumed to be no less than 5% by weight, even for burial sites in semi-arid regions. So, in computing the mean external annual dose, one takes the current water content as a first approximation and includes the upper and lower limits as a systematic component in the final uncertainty given with each date.

Radioelement transport within the soil can constitute a lesser but still important problem. Studies of numerous soils have shown that ^{40}K and U and Th families contribute almost equally to the total external gamma-ray flux (the principal component of the external dose). Mineral leaching and reprecipitation affects only soluble salts found in the exposed environment; the most soluble salts are those of K, U and Ra. Radon loss must also be considered.

Even if there were a 50% uncertainty in the dose attributed to these radioelements, the uncertainty in the calculated external annual dose would be <30%, because K and the entire U series usually contribute only about two-thirds of the total dose, and only soluble salts exposed to water are concerned (Levinson, Bland and Lively 1982). Further, if the internal and external doses are comparable, as is frequently the case, the ultimate impact of this large initial uncertainty will be an error of *ca.* 15% in the estimated annual dose.

Determination of $^{232}Th/^{238}U$, a useful indicator of U mobility, aids greatly in mapping the past radioactive history of the soil. In soils consisting of clay and silt, this ratio tends to have values between 3 and 4, but in the vicinity of bone and teeth, a lower ratio is often observed because the putrefaction of animal tissue produces a chemical environment favoring the reduction of U^{4+} salts to less soluble U^{2+} salts, which precipitate on the bone. Consequently, soil adhering to bone or teeth tends to contain abnormally high U levels, which are not representative of the soil at large and should not be used in the computation of the mean external dose. Such enrichment will result in overestimated environmental annual dose and produce an underestimate of the true age.

LEVANTINE SITES DATED BY THERMOLUMINESCENCE

Reliable dates are most likely obtained 1) when the flint comes from recent excavations and dosimeters can be left for a reasonable length of time close to the recovery site, and 2) when control measurements can be performed in the laboratory on soil specimens collected from the vicinity of the flint. We review TL dates that have been published or are being prepared for publication (see Table 1) and for which we have relevant data. The sites that have been studied are the Hummal Well and Yabroud I shelter in Syria, and the Kebara, Qafzeh, Skhul and Tabun caves in Israel.

Hummal Well

Levels 6b and 1b of Hummal Well were dated at the Oxford Laboratory (1988). The former "consisted of abraded and patinated Mousterian-like blades but the level was far above the other Mousterian layers" (Oxford 1988). The reported mean of three dates was 104,000 ± 9000 BP. The external dose was determined by dosimeters *in situ*, and the average water content of the surrounding soil was assumed to be 3 ± 3%, a value that appears to be too low, particularly since several overlying peaty layers suggest past periods of higher humidity. When we performed gamma-

TABLE 1. Mean Flint Thermoluminescence Ages for Six Levantine Sites

Site	Stratigraphic information	No. of flints	Date (kyr)	Reference
Hummal Well	Mousterian-like industry: Level 6b	3	104 ± 9	Oxford (1988)
	Yabroudian: Level 1b	3	160 ± 22	Oxford (1990)
Yabroud Shelter I	Acheuleo-Yabroudian industry: −4.5 m	6	195 ± 15	Oxford (1990)
Kebara	Mousterian sequence:			Valladas *et al.*
	Unit VI	5	48.3 ± 3.5	(1987)
	Unit VII	5	51.9 ± 3.5	
	Unit VIII	5	57.3 ± 4.0	
	Unit IX	4	58.4 ± 4.0	
	Unit X	7	61.6 ± 3.6	
	Unit XI	5	60.0 ± 3.5	
	Unit XII	7	59.9 ± 3.5	
Qafzeh	Mousterian Levels XVII, XVIII, XIX, XXI, XXII, XXIII	20	92 ± 5	Valladas *et al.* (1988)
Skhul	Mousterian industry: Level B	6	119 ± 18	Mercier *et al.* (1993)
Tabun	Mousterian sequence:			Mercier (1992)
	Unit I	13	134–184	
	Unit II	3	195–263	
	Unit V	4	226–307	
	Unit IX	4	249–297	
	Pre-Mousterian sequence:			Mercier (1992)
	Unit X	2	202–270	
	Unit XI	5	229–296	
	Unit XII	4	273–350	
	Unit XIII	4	331 ± 30*	

*This level consisted of breccia and was unlikely to require a correction for loss of radioelements.

spectrometric analysis on a soil sample from Level 6b, we found a strong ^{226}Ra enrichment, the activity of which was four times greater than that of ^{234}Th. These results suggest a recent enrichment caused by changes in the water table (Levinson, Bland and Lively 1982).

Level 1b contained Yabroudian material buried in travertine. The three flints from this level were dated to 160,000 ± 22,000 BP, and the dosimetric data were radically different from that of Level 6b. Here the external dose (*ca.* 2 mGy) accounted for 95% of total, making the age determination extremely sensitive to measurement errors. Dosimeter values are considerably different from those calculated from U and Th concentrations measured in soil samples (Hennig and Hours 1982). Enrichment in ^{226}Ra similar to that observed in Level 6b would account for this discrepancy. A thorough re-examination of the radioelements and their relative concentrations in this soil is required, because it would appear that the environmental gamma dose measured at present grossly exceeds what must have prevailed in the past. If that were so, the reported ages are underestimated.

Yabroud Shelter I

The Oxford Laboratory (1990) also dated six flints from a level containing Acheuleo-Yabroudian industries in Yabroud Shelter I, giving a highly coherent set of dates, averaging 195,000 ± 15,000 BP. The external dose, determined by gamma spectrometry on soil samples, represented

20–50% of the total annual dose, making the date less sensitive to uncertainties in the external dose measurements. The mean water content was taken to be 9 ± 9%. Because no supralinearity corrections were made, this date and the Hummal Well results may be underestimated by 15–20%.

Kebara

At our laboratory (Valladas *et al.* 1987), we dated 38 flints from the 4-m-deep Mousterian Units VI to XII in Kebara Cave. The results fell into 7 groups of 4 or more flints each. Table 1 shows that the respective group averages rise from 48,300 ± 3500 to 59,900 ± 3500 BP for the layer that yielded a Neanderthal skeleton. We measured the annual external dose with dosimeters planted for one year. Specimens analyzed by gamma spectrometry showed no evidence of significant radio-element migration or loss of radon. After accounting for all uncertainties, a systematic error of ± 7.5% was attributed to the external dose.

Qafzeh

Dates for 20 flints from Mousterian Levels XVII–XIX and XXI–XXIII clustered near 92,000 ± 5000 BP (Valladas *et al.* 1988), making the Proto-Cro-Magnon remains recovered from these strata older than the Kebara Neanderthal. The fortunate high radioelement content of these flints reduced the contribution of external gamma rays to 20–37% of the total annual dose. Consequently, the dates are virtually independent of past variations in the environmental dose. Nevertheless, we made dosimetric and laboratory spectrometric measurements, as in the case of Kebara flints. They revealed no evidence of significant disequilibrium. In view of the apparently rapid sedimentation rate, indicated by the geology of the Mousterian Levels and the measured dates, an isochron test was performed (Aitken and Valladas 1993) to provide an independent estimate of the external dose. Test results confirmed the validity of our calculated ages.

Skhul

Six flints from Mousterian Level B, which contained Proto-Cro-Magnon skeletons, yielded an average age of 119,000 ± 18,000 BP (Mercier *et al.* 1993). Normal dosimetry was not possible since most strata had been removed. Thus, we estimated the external annual dose from clumps of breccia adhering to the limestone walls of the shelter. Although we were concerned with the possible non-representative nature of the measured external dose, the high internal dose in the dated flints reduced the impact of this uncertainty. For example, if an uneven distribution of radio-elements in the surrounding soil introduced a 50% error into the measured external dose, the calculated average age would be off by only 17%. The Skhul average date, even with less reliable dosimetric data, provides extra evidence for the antiquity of modern humans in the Levant.

Tabun

The 39 flints dated by TL (Mercier *et al.*, in press) were collected during the 1967–1972 excavation from units numbered by Jelinek (1981) as I, II, V, IX, X, XI, XII and XIII in the intermediate section of the cave. The external dose, measured by 46 dosimeters distributed among the units, ranged from 840 to 450 μGy yr^{-1}. The relative contribution of the environmental dose to the total dose varied not only among the flints themselves, but from unit to unit, due to differences in radio-element contents. Numerous soil samples collected throughout the year revealed that the water content did not vary significantly from season to season, but remained at a relatively high level of 20–30% by weight. ^{232}Th/^{238}U ratios measured in eight soil samples ranged from 2 to 4.5 (5 samples had normal 3–4 values), from which one can infer that no more than 20% of the total U migrated in any instance.

At the initial stages of our work, the great antiquity of the Tabun dates made it advisable to consider two extreme scenarios for the past radioactive environment, thus the range, instead of a unique date, in Table 1. The upper age limit assumes that the environmental dose did not change significantly in the recent past. Although we have no evidence that the radioelement content of the soil changed dramatically in recent times, we thought it wise to estimate the age one would obtain if U and K leached out to the maximum extent compatible with the radiochemical analysis of the soil. Under the circumstances, gamma doses recorded by the dosimeters would be lower than those received by the flints in the past, and would result in an underestimated age. Because the lower limit represents the worst possible scenario, the true age is somewhere between the two extremes (Mercier 1992).

A THERMOLUMINESCENCE-BASED CHRONOLOGY

Preliminary Comments

In the past, when the Levant Mousterian period was believed to be contemporaneous with the European Late Glacial period, attempts were made to ^{14}C-date the upper levels of various sites. For over ten years, the chronology of the Paleolithic sites in the Levant was woven around the few ^{14}C dates, frequently at the limits of ^{14}C validity (*ca.* 40,000 BP), and around a few U/Th dates, often obtained on single specimens of travertine. It is important to note that these two methods suffer from a common handicap: very small quantities of modern contaminants, if not removed during sample preparation, can have a major impact on the calculated date. Admittedly, great progress has been made in the last two decades in purifying datable samples, particularly in the removal of detritus from travertine dated by the U/Th method (Ku and Liang 1984), yet little can be done about potential recrystallization of secondary carbonates in the interstices of such highly porous material. Although the TL dates also have certain flaws, as shown above, errors are attenuated by the fact that they stem from problems affecting only a fraction of the total annual dose.

Chronology of Middle Paleolithic Sites

On the basis of TL dates for the six sites examined above, we propose a coherent chronology for the pertinent lithic industries and fossil remains of the Levant.

Lithic Industries. In all the Levantine sites that have yielded both the Mugharan and Mousterian industries, the latter are superimposed on the former. The Tabun dates suggest that the replacement of the Mugharan by the Mousterian occurred *ca.* 250,000 BP, during marine isotope stages 8–7. If, as we strongly suspect, the Yabroud I and Hummal Level 1b ages are underestimated, the Mugharan industries did not persist much longer at the two Syrian sites. The first Mousterian industries, Tabun D type (Garrod 1962), were replaced sometime before 150,000 BP by the Tabun C types, which remained dominant until at least *ca.* 90,000 BP, as the Qafzeh excavations have shown (Meignen and Bar-Yosef 1988). The broad scheme outlined here will be refined after longer stratigraphic sequences have been dated.

Human Fossil Remains. The considerable overlap of dates rules out a clear succession of *Homo sapiens neanderthalensis* by *Homo sapiens sapiens.* Among the remains from the six sites, the oldest is a female Neanderthal skeleton from Garrod's Unit C (Unit I in Table 1), dated to pre-170,000 BP. Those succeeding it are early modern humans from strata at Skhul and Qafzeh, dated to 120,000 and 90,000 BP, respectively. The youngest is a Neanderthal from Kebara, dated to *ca.* 60,000 BP. Until more sites and skeletal remains are dated, it is difficult to tell if the two populations coexisted or came in successive waves, and whether the occupations were continuous or intermittent.

CONCLUSIONS

For reasons amply discussed above, not all flint TL dates can be accepted with the same confidence, and some published dates may require remeasurement. The major source of uncertainty lies in the calculations of past environmental doses. The most reliable dates are obtained when *in situ* dosimetry is accompanied by thorough soil analysis. We hope to have shown that, if suitable precautions are taken and all possible sources of errors properly estimated, TL dates are highly credible, within the time limits indicated. Their reliability becomes even more convincing when dates of numerous flints from long stratigraphic sequences are compared.

ACKNOWLEDGMENT

This is Contribution CFR:1552.

REFERENCES CITED

Aitken, M. J., J. Huxtable and N. C. Debenham
    1986   Thermoluminescence dating in the Palaeolithic: Burnt flint, stalagmitic calcite, and sediment. *Association Française pour l'Etude du Quaternaire Bulletin* 26:7–14.
Aitken, M. J., P. R. S. Moorey and P. J. Ucko
    1971   The authenticity of vessels in the Haçilar style. *Archaeometry* 13:89–141.
Aitken, M. J. and H. Valladas
    1993   Luminescence dating relevant to human origins. *Philosophical Transactions of the Royal Society, London* B337:139–144.
Garrod, D. A.
    1962   The Middle Paleolithic of the Near East and the problem of the Mount Carmel man. *Journal of the Royal Anthropological Institute* 92:232–259.
Göksu, H. Y., J. H. Fremlin, H. T. Irwin and R. Fryxell
    1974   Age determination of burnt flint by TL method. *Science* 183:651–654.
Göksu, H. Y., A. Weiser and D. Regulla
    1989   110°C TL peak records the ancient heat treatment of flint. *Ancient TL* 7:15–17.
Hennig, G. J. and F. Hours
    1982   Dates pour le passage entre l'Acheuléen et le Paléolithique moyen à El Kowm (Syrie). *Paléorient* 8(1): 81–83.
Jelinek, A.
    1981   The Middle Palaeolithic in the Southern Levant from the perspective of the Tabun Cave. In *Préhistoire du Levant*, edited by J. Cauvin and P. Sanlaville, pp. 265–280. Maison de l'Orient, CNRS, Lyon.
Ku, T. L. and Z. C. Liang
    1984   The dating of impure carbonates with decay-series isotopes. *Nuclear Instruments and Methods in Physical Research* 223:563–571.
Levinson, A. A., C. J. Bland and R. S. Lively
    1982   Exploration for U ore deposits. In *Uranium Series Disequilibrium: Application to Environmental Problems*, edited by M. Ivanovitch and R. S. Harmon, pp. 351–383. Clarendon Press, Oxford.
Meignen, L. and O. Bar-Yosef
    1988   Kébara et le Paléolithique moyen du Mont Carmel (Israel). *Paléorient* 14(2):123–129.
Mercier, N.
    1991   Flint paleodose determination at the onset of saturation. *Nuclear Tracks* 18:77–79.
    1992   Apport des méthodes radionucléaires de datation à l'étude du peuplement de l'Europe et du Proche-Orient au cours du Pléistocène moyen et supérieur. Ph.D. Dissertation, Université de Bordeaux I, Bordeaux.
Mercier, N., H. Valladas and G. Valladas
    1992   Some observations on paleodose determination in burnt flint. *Ancient TL* 10:28–32.
Mercier, N., H. Valladas, O. Bar-Yosef, B. Vandermeersch, C. Stringer and J. L. Joron
    1993   Thermoluminescence date for the Mousterian burial site of es-Skhul, Mt. Carmel. *Journal of Archaeological Sciences* 20(2):169–174.
Mercier, N., G. Valladas, H. Valladas, A. Jelinek, L. Meignen, J. L. Reyss and J. L. Joron
           TL dates of burnt flints from Jelinek excavations: New Tabun cave chronology and its implications. *Journal of Archaeological Science*, in press.

Oxford Research Laboratory for Archaeology
  1988   *Ancient TL*. Supplement 2:22.
  1990   Date List 4. *Ancient TL* 8(3):43.
Sanzelle, S., J. Faïn, D. Maillier, M. Montret and T. Pilleyre
  1993   Exponential regresssions for TL/ESR using regenerated dose response curves. *Ancient TL* 11:16–14.
Valladas, H.
  1983   Estimation de la température de chauffe des silex préhistoriques par leur thermoluminescence. *Comptes Rendus de l'Academie des Sciences* 296:993–996.
  1992   Thermoluminescence dating of flint. *Quaternary Science Reviews* 11:1–5.
Valladas, H., J. L. Joron, G. Valladas, B. Arensburg, O. Bar-Yosef, A. Belfer-Cohen, P. Goldberg, H. Laville, L. Meignen, Y. Rak, E. Tchernov, A. M. Tillier and B. Vandermeersch
  1987   Thermoluminescence dates for the Neanderthal burial site at Kebara in Israel. *Nature* 330:159–160.
Valladas, H., J. L. Reyss, J. L. Joron, G. Valladas, O. Bar-Yosef and B. Vandermeersch
  1988   Thermoluminescence dating of Mousterian "Proto-Cro-Magnon" remains from Israel and the origin of modern man. *Nature* 331:614–616.
Whittle, E. H.
  1975   Thermoluminescence dating of Egyptian Prehistoric pottery from Hemamieh and Qurna-Tarif. *Archaeometry* 17:119–122.

CHRONOLOGY OF MODERN HUMANS IN THE LEVANT

HENRY P. SCHWARCZ

Department of Geology, McMaster University, Hamilton, Ontario L8S 4M1 Canada

INTRODUCTION

Over the past five years, a major revolution has occurred in our understanding of the chronology of hominid evolution. The geographic focus of much of this revision has been in Israel, to some extent at sites that have been known for a long time. These sites, largely in the Galilee and on Mount Carmel, contain hominid remains that represent two important stages of the evolutionary process: 1) Neanderthals found at Kebara and Tabun in Mount Carmel, and at Amud Cave in the Galilee; 2) anatomically modern hominids ("Modern man") found at Qafzeh Cave in the Galilee, and Skhul on Mt. Carmel. Also, a single, well-preserved cranium found at the Galilean cave of Zuttiyeh appears to be related to the Neanderthal population, yet there are some striking differences.

These sites are all too old to be dated by ^{14}C (whose dating limit is *ca.* 50,000 BP). The sites are in the time range amenable to uranium (U)-series dating, but datable materials (*e.g.*, stalagmites) have not been found in the correct spatial association, although they exist in each cave, and, in some cases, have been dated (Schwarcz, Goldberg and Blackwell 1980). Likewise, there are no volcanic materials suitable for potassium-argon (K/Ar) or argon-argon (^{40}Ar/^{39}Ar) dating. The development of thermoluminescence (TL) dating of burned flint and electron spin resonance (ESR) dating of tooth enamel has made it possible to date these sites.

I review here results obtained from sites at which hominid remains have been found. I shall also review some absolute determinations obtained from purely archaeological sites dating from the same period, roughly the last 200,000 yr. The archaeological record, which these dates represent, forms an important background to hominid evolution. See Schwarcz, Goldberg and Blackwell (1980) for further details on the U-series dating of these sites.

DATING METHODS

Both TL and ESR dating are based on the same physical principle, *i.e.,* trapping electronic charges at defects in crystal lattices. In both cases, the "clock" consists of a buildup of trapped charges at a known rate as a result of radioactive bombardment. The radioactivity occurs in the dated materials themselves (flint or enamel) and in the surrounding sedimentary matrix.

Aitken (1985) described the TL method in detail. In principle, it is applicable to any geological material whose natural TL signal has been set to zero by some physical process at the time of deposition. Currently, two types of materials are widely studied—detrital sediment and siliceous rock (*e.g.,* flint and chert). Detrital sediment, especially loess or dune sands, can be dated if the natural TL signal has been bleached out by sunlight. A related dating method, optically stimulated luminescence (OSL) (Huntley, Godfrey-Smith and Thewalt 1985), makes use of electronic traps that are more easily bleached. Neither of these methods has yet been applied to detrital sediments in Israel, although an attempt was made by Bowman (1984) to date sediment in Tabun.

TL dating can also be applied to siliceous rock, in which the TL signal has been zeroed through heating. Prehistoric lithic artifacts are commonly made of such material: quartzite or quartz-cemented sandstones. Both siliceous clastic sediment and siliceous rock emit light when heated,

Late Quaternary Chronology and Paleoclimates of the Eastern Mediterranean
Edited by O. Bar-Yosef and R. S. Kra. RADIOCARBON *1994, pp. 21–31*

21

as a result of recombination of trapped electronic charges at specific luminescence centers. The traps and centers occur principally in the minerals, quartz and feldspar. The buildup of the trapped charges is approximately proportional to the amount of radiation to which the sample has been exposed.

The age of the sample is calculated from the relation

$$t = D_E / d \qquad (1)$$

where D_E = the equivalent dose, a radiation dose measured in the laboratory that is equivalent to the dose that the sample has received since it was buried, measured in appropriate units (grays, Gy); d is the total dose rate measured in Gy/yr; it is the sum of two components: the external dose rate, d_{ex}, produced by the radioactivity of the surrounding sediment and cosmic rays; and the internal dose rate, d_{in}, produced by radioactivity within the sample. The paleodose is determined from the intensity of light emitted by the sample when it is heated in a TL apparatus (Aitken 1985). This signal is converted to dose by giving the sample an additional artificial dose of gamma radiation and noting the rate at which the intensity increases as a function of added dose. D_E is then determined by back-extrapolation. d_{ex} is either measured by direct dosimetry at the site, or is calculated from the content of U, thorium (Th) and K in the sediment. The internal dose rate, d_{in}, is determined from the composition of the flint. The precision of the method is limited by the uncertainty in the external dose rate, and by the errors in determination of D_E. Typically, errors of 5 to 20% are reported for TL dates on burned flint. These are estimates of precision only, but concordance with other dating methods (U-series and ESR) has been checked in a few instances. The upper age limit for TL dating of burned flint is at least 500,000 yr, whereas the limit of TL (and OSL dating) of sediments is <200,000 yr.

The ESR method is generally applied to material that was formed at the time of deposition and, therefore, does not have to be zeroed. Freshly deposited tooth enamel, in particular, is known to have a zero ESR intensity. D_E is determined from the height of a characteristic signal in the ESR spectrum (at g = 2.0018), found in all tooth enamel and bone. However, bone cannot be dated for reasons explained by Grün and Schwarcz (1987). As with TL, the conversion of the signal height to an equivalent radiation dose is made by giving the sample additional doses of gamma radiation and noting the increase in signal intensity. D_E is then determined by back extrapolation, using an exponential fit to take into account saturation of the signal with added dose. The external dose rate, d_{ex}, is determined as for TL. The internal dose rate, d_{in}, is generated almost entirely by U that has been taken up by the enamel and attached den-tine/cementum since burial. The time-dependence of this uptake process influences the deter-mination of the age. In particular, if we assume that U was taken up early in the burial history (early uptake or EU), calculation of the age from a particular set of ESR data gives the youngest possible age for the sample; later U uptake gives progressively older ages. We find that the best agreement between ESR ages and other independent age estimates is obtained when we assume that U has been taken up by both enamel and dentine at a constant rate throughout the burial history (linear uptake or LU). It is possible to determine the true uptake model by isotopic analysis of U and Th in teeth (Grün, Chadam and Schwarcz 1988). This method has now been employed at some of the Israeli sites by McDermott *et al.* (1993). For further details on ESR dating of tooth enamel, see Grün, Schwarcz and Zymela (1987); for a general description of ESR dating, see Grün (1989).

Some archaeological sites in Israel and elsewhere in this region have also been dated by the U-series methods, specifically, $^{230}Th/^{234}U$ and $^{234}U/^{238}U$ in stalagmitic and spring-deposited calcites.

Schwarcz (1989) described the theory behind this method. Samples of calcite suitable for analysis should be non-porous and free of any detrital particles (sand, windblown dust). Such "clean" deposits of stalagmites or travertines are rarely found in Israel, and most of the dates reported so far have been obtained on partially contaminated samples.

I first review the dating of sites at which anatomically modern hominids, often defined as "Proto-Cro-Magnons" have been recovered, and then turn to the sites that have yielded the so-called "Western Asia Neanderthals". The dates are summarized in Table 1.

Qafzeh

This cave lies in a small wadi (dry river valley) south of the town of Nazareth. The interior of the cave contains Middle Paleolithic artifacts but no hominid remains. Burials of at least 20 modern hominids were found in the terrace in front of the cave (Vandermeersch 1981). The modern aspect of these remains and the lack of other chronometric information led many researchers to argue that they must date to *ca.* 40,000 yr ago (*e.g.*, Trinkaus 1984). Bar-Yosef and Vandermeersch (1981) were first to suggest their greater antiquity. Tchernov (1988) showed that the microfauna from the terrace sediments was most closely allied to an interglacial assemblage known at other sites in Israel. These hominids were found associated with a Middle Paleolithic lithic industry (Boutié 1989), also suggesting that they were older than originally assumed.

The first absolute dates on the site were obtained by H. Valladas and her co-workers (1988), using the TL method on burned flint. They analyzed flints from Layers XVII–XXIII, which yielded ages between 90,000 and 110,000 yr, averaging 92,000 ± 5000 yr. There was no trend of increasing age with depth in the sequence, which suggested that the entire deposit had accumulated rather quickly. The dose received by the flints was dominated by the internal dose, mainly due to U and K in the flint. Therefore, uncertainties in the external dose rate did not contribute significantly to the error in the age. This dose rate was determined using TL dosimeters buried in the site for one year.

Schwarcz *et al.* (1988) reported an ESR study of the same site. We analyzed macrofaunal samples from Layers XV–XXI. The external dose rates were obtained from analyses of dentine/cementum of teeth, from sediment adhering to the teeth and from the dosimetry reported by Valladas *et al.* (1988). The average ages were 96,000 ± 13,000 yr (EU) and 115,000 ± 15,000 (LU) yr. Subsequently, Grün and Stringer (1991) used improved determinations of D_E to obtain ages of 100,000 ± 10,000 (EU) and 120,000 ± 8000 (LU) yr. Both these estimates depend more strongly on the external dose rates than do the TL dates. Aitken and Valladas (1992) re-evaluated the external dose rate at this site by using an isochron plot. They found a dose rate *ca.* 20% higher than that estimated by Valladas *et al.* (1988). Therefore, the true ESR dates would be somewhat lower and would come into closer agreement with the TL dates. The isochron analysis of Aitken also yields a collective age for the entire population of burned flints of 88,000 ± 9000 yr, not significantly different from that reported by Valladas *et al.* (1988). Recently, McDermott *et al.* (1993) obtained U-series ages of 89,000 and 106,000 yr for dentine of two teeth from Layer XIX. Concordance between these ages and EU model ages suggests that EU of U occurred at this site, and the EU ages are more likely to be correct, further strengthening the agreement with the TL ages.

Although there is still some uncertainty (*ca.* ± 5%) in the age of this site, it is generally clear that Proto-Cro-Magnon hominids were present in Israel sometime during the last interglacial (isotope stage 5), *ca.* 90,000–100,000 yr ago. The publication of these radiometric dates initiated a radical revision of the chronology of modern hominids, and inspired researchers to apply these methods to other sites in southwest Asia and Africa where modern hominid fossils were known.

TABLE 1. Age Data for Levantine Sites*

Site	Level	ESR (tooth enamel) EU	ESR (tooth enamel) LU	TL (flint)	U-series	Refs.**
A. Modern hominids						
Qafzeh	XVII-XXI	--	--	92 ± 5	--	V1
Qafzeh	XV-XXII	100 ± 10	120 ± 8	--	--	G&S;
Qafzeh	XIX	103 ± 19	125 ± 22	--	89 ± 3	Mc
Qafzeh	XIX	105 ± 2	115 ± 8	--	106 ± 2	Mc
Qafzeh	XVII-XXI			88 ± 9	--	A&V
Skhul	B	81 ± 15	101 ± 12	--	--	St
Skhul	B	--	--	--	79 ± 4†	Sc2
Skhul	B	--	--	119 ± 18	--	M1
Skhul	B	88 ± 13	102 ± 18	--	80.3 ± 0.6‡	Mc
Skhul	B	56 ± 9	76 ± 19	--	42.8 ± 1.8‡	Mc§
B. Neanderthal						
Amud	B	42 ± 3	49 ± 4	--	--	G&S
Tabun	B	86 ± 11	103 ± 16		--	Gˡ
Tabun	B	76 ± 14	85 ± 18		50.7 ± 0.2‡	Mc
Tabun	C	102 ± 17	119 ± 11	--	--	G⌀
Tabun	C	118 ± 5	127 ± 10	134–184	101.5 ± 2.9‡	Mc, M2
Tabun	D	122 ± 20	166 ± 20	--	--	G⌀
Tabun	D	93 ± 12	152 ± 24	--	110.7 ± 0.9‡	Mc
Tabun	D	--	--	195–297	--	M2
Tabun	Ea	154 ± 34	188 ± 31	--	--	G‡‡
Tabun	Ea	158 ± 41	158 ± 56	--	159 ± 1‡	Mc
Tabun	Ea	167 ± 42	196 ± 57	--	168 ± 2‡	Mc
Tabun	Ea	167 ± 42	196 ± 57	229–296	--	M2,Mc
Tabun	Eb	151 ± 21	168 ± 15	--	--	Gˡ
Tabun	Eb	--	--	273–350	--	M2
Tabun	Ec	176 ± 10	199 ± 7	--	--	G*
Tabun	Ed	186 ± 61	213 ± 46	--	--	G§
Tabun	Ed	--	--	331 ± 30	--	M2
Kebara	VI	--	--	48 ± 3	--	V2
Kebara	VII	--	--	52 ± 4	--	V2
Kebara	VIII	--	--	57 ± 4	--	V2
Kebara	IX	--	--	58 ± 4	--	V2
Kebara	X	60 ± 6	64 ± 6	62 ± 4	--	V2; Sc3
Kebara	XI	--	--	60 ± 4	--	V2
Kebara	XII	--	--	60 ± 4	--	V2
Zuttiyeh	Yabrudian	--	--	--	148 ± 6†	Sc2
Zuttiyeh	Chimney	--	--	--	164 ± 21†	Sc2
C. Archaeological sites						
Biq'at Quneitra		39 ± 6	54 ± 6	--	--	Z
Hayonim	Mousterian	--	--	--	163+60, −40†	Sc2
Nahal Zin: Ein Mor	--	--	--	--	46 ± 3†	Sc2
Nahal Zin: Ein Aqev	--	--	--	--	211 ± 19†	Sc2
Nahal Zin: Ein Aqev	--	--	--	--	80 ± 5†	Sc2
Yabrud	-4.6 m	177 ± 20	231 ± 19	--	--	P&S
Yabrud	-4.6 m	--	--	195 ± 15	--	H

*Ages in thousands of years

**V=Valladas *et al.* (1988); G&S=Grün and Stringer (1991); Sc1=Schwarcz *et al.* (1988); Mc=McDermott *et al.* (1993); A&V=Aitken and Valladas (1992); St=Stringer *et al.* (1989); Sc2=Schwarcz *et al.* (1980); M1=Mercier *et al.* (1993); G=Grün *et al.* (1991); V2=Valladas *et al.* (1987); Sc3=Schwarcz *et al.* (1989); Z=Ziaei *et al.* (1990); P&S=Porat and Schwarcz (ms.); H=Huxtable (ms.); M2=Mercier and Valladas (1994)

†Calcite sample (stalagmite); ‡Tooth, either dentine or enamel; *Avg. of 4 analyses; §Avg. of 5 analyses; ˡAvg. of 7 analyses; ⌀Avg. of 8 analyses; ‡‡Avg. of 10 analyses

Skhul

Skeletal remains representing at least 10 individuals of modern-looking hominids were excavated from this rockshelter, one of a series of sites in Nahal HaMearot (Wadi Mughara) at the foot of Mt. Carmel, studied by Garrod and co-workers in the 1930s (Garrod and Bate 1937; McKown and Keith 1939). The site was essentially destroyed by these campaigns, but a small amount of breccia and some stalagmitic deposits remain. Schwarcz, Goldberg and Blackwell (1980) obtained U-series dates on some of these. A layer of calcite believed to be coeval with the archaeological fill yielded a date of 79,000 ± 4000 yr, but other layers, seemingly of the same generation of calcite, gave ages of >350,000 yr (the limit of the U-series method).

Mammalian teeth from the excavation, curated at the Natural History Museum (London), were used for ESR dating. Samples of the matrix were also recovered from the collection, which could be used to determine the external dose rate, d_{ex}. Seven subsamples from two bovid teeth were dated (Stringer *et al.* 1989). The mean ages were 81,000 ± 15,000 yr (EU) and 101,000 ± 12,000 yr (LU). McDermott *et al.* (1993) dated dentine and enamel from this site by mass-spectrometric U-series methods. One of the two teeth previously discussed by Stringer *et al.* (1989) gave a U-series age of 80,270 ± 550 yr, which concurred with the EU age of the tooth, suggesting an EU of U. The other tooth gave a U-series age of 40,430 ± 210 yr that was distinctly younger than the EU age and suggested post-depositional U uptake. Two other teeth from the same archaeological layer gave analogous U-series and EU ESR ages, but with dates ranging from 43,000 to 45,000 and 46,000 to 55,000 yr, respectively. McDermott *et al.* (1993) suggest a greater complexity in the stratigraphy of this site than was previously assumed. Mercier *et al.* (1993) obtained TL dates on burned flint from this site, which yielded ages ranging from 99,000 to 167,000 yr, with a mean of 119,000 ± 18,000 yr. This result is consistent with the older ESR dates, but none of the samples gave dates as young as the 43,000 to 55,000-yr range seen in some of the U-series and ESR dates on teeth.

Considering the total range of the ESR and TL dates, we have further evidence from this site of the great antiquity of modern hominids in southwest Asia, at a time when Europe was populated by Neanderthals. Therefore, it is interesting to contrast these results with dates obtained on skeletal remains traditionally classified as west Asian Neanderthals from Israel.

NEANDERTHAL SITES FROM ISRAEL

Kebara

Kebara cave also lies on the western slope of Mt. Carmel, and contains a long sequence of archaeological deposits (Arensburg *et al.* 1985; Bar-Yosef *et al.* 1992). The skeleton of a robust Neanderthal male (Rak 1990) was found within the lowest Mousterian levels. The skeleton was buried in a grave that penetrated Layer XII. Valladas *et al.* (1987) obtained TL dates on burned flint from Units VI–XII (increasing in stratigraphic age). The ages increase from 48,300 ± 3500 yr in Unit VI to *ca.* 60,000 yr for Units X–XII. The average age of Units XI and XII is 60,000 ± 6000 yr. As at Qafzeh, d_{ex} is a comparatively small fraction of the total dose rate (20–37%). Schwarcz *et al.* (1989) subsequently dated this site by ESR using tooth enamel from Unit X, above the burial of the Neanderthal but one of the richest units, where a series of "living floors" were found. The external dose (gamma + cosmic ray) was taken from TL dosimetry done by Valladas; this is the dominant component of the total dose. As a result, little difference exists between the EU and LU ages: 60,000 ± 6000 and 64,000 ± 6000 yr, respectively. Porat *et al.* (ms.) have also ESR-dated burned flint from this site. Using the Al center in the ESR spectrum of flint, they obtained an average age of 65,000 ± 14,000 yr, which agrees with the existing TL and ESR dates for the Neanderthal-bearing unit. These ages are comparable to dates obtained for Neanderthal-bearing layers from western Europe (Grün and Stringer 1991), which range from 35,000 to 60,000 yr or greater. With only one exception (St. Cesaire), European Neanderthals are older than the early modern hominids ("Cro-Magnons"), whereas, in Israel, some modern-looking hominids are much older than typical Neanderthals. This situation is further complicated by results from Tabun.

Tabun

Tabun cave is a few hundred meters away from the site of Skhul. The cave contains one of the longest continuous archaeological sequences in southwest Asia. It was originally studied by Garrod and Bate (1937), who found various hominid remains including a fairly complete robust skeleton of a female sometimes classified as Neanderthal, recovered from either the base of Layer B or the top of Layer C. Further excavations at the cave in Layers C–E are discussed in Jelinek *et al.* (1973) and Jelinek (1982).

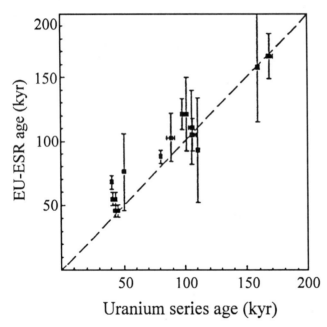

Grün, Stringer and Schwarcz (1991) made ESR age determinations on teeth from the faunal material collected by Garrod and Bate (1937). Sediment attached to other specimens in the museum was used to estimate the gamma dose rate; this estimate is a little higher than the rate measured by direct gamma-ray spectrometry at the site. The ages would be a little older if the latter data were used instead. Teeth with extremely low U concentrations, for which the internal dose was negligible, gave dates consistent with LU (rather than EU) ages for high-U teeth, suggesting that some teeth may have experienced continuous U uptake. The LU ages are typically 17–20% older than the EU ages. McDermott *et al.* (1993) found that mass-spectrometric U-series analyses of some of the teeth agreed with the EU ESR ages, as would be expected if U had been taken up soon after deposition (Fig. 1). The EU ages range from 86,000 ± 11,000 yr for Layer B (the stratigraphically youngest layer studied) to 182,000 ± 61,000 yr for Layer Ed.

Fig. 1. Comparison between U-series and EU-ESR ages on teeth from sites in Israel; from McDermott *et al.* (1993). Reprinted with permission from the authors and *Nature* ©1993 Macmillan Magazines Ltd.

The total set of ages (Fig. 2), although showing great scatter in each layer, indicates that Layers B and C must date to the last interglacial. Thus, at Tabun, we may have evidence for a robust hominid approximately coeval with, or a little earlier than modern-looking hominids at the nearby site of Skhul. If the burial were in Layer B, then the ages of the two taxa are indistinguishable.

This does not require that they were strictly contemporaneous, because the errors in dates at both sites would allow them to have differed in age by several thousand years.

Mercier *et al.* (in press; see also Mercier and Valladas 1994) determined TL ages on burned flint from Jelinek's excavations at Tabun. External dose rates were determined using TL dosimeters emplaced in the section where the flints had been removed. The stratigraphic position of Mercier and Valladas' samples are defined in relation to the stratigraphic units defined by Jelinek, but these can be correlated approximately with those of Garrod and Bate. In general, the ages obtained by Mercier and Valladas are older than those by Grün *et al.* (1991) or McDermott *et al.* (1993) for equivalent strata (Table 1).

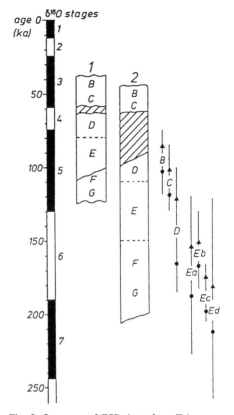

Fig. 2. Summary of ESR dates from Tabun, compared with two other estimates of the age: 1. Jelinek (1982); 2. Bar-Yosef (1989); from Grün, Stringer and Schwarcz (1991). Reprinted by permission of Academic Press.

Amud Cave

A partial Neanderthal skeleton was recovered from Amud Cave in Wadi Amud, northwest of Tiberias (Suzuki and Takai 1970). The skeleton (Amud I) was almost complete, although in poor condition. Other hominid remains were also found in the same stratigraphic unit, Formation B, as well as an extensive faunal assemblage, which has not yet been made available for ESR dating. Excavations were recently renewed at the site and ESR measurements were undertaken by Grün and Stringer (1991), who report preliminary dates on artiodactyl teeth from Formation B: 42,000 ± 3000; 41,000 ± 3000 yr (EU); and 49,000 ± 4000 and 50,000 ± 4000 yr (LU). These dates are younger than those discussed above, but are consistent with the more "progressive" evolutionary features of Amud I (Grün and Stringer 1991:180).

Zuttiyeh

Zuttiyeh is another cave in Wadi Amud, from which a well-preserved hominid cranium was recovered by Turville-Petre (1927). Unfortunately, the stratigraphic position of the skull was not recorded, except that it was found below the lowest archaeological horizon. The residual deposits in the cave consist mainly of calcite-cemented breccias and stalagmitic mounds, some of which have been dated by U-series (Schwarcz, Goldberg and Blackwell 1980). The main stalagmitic mound at the front of the cave contained Acheulo-Yabroudian artifacts, with dates ranging from 148,000 ± 6000 to 97,000 ± 13,000 yr. However, we suggest that travertines inside the cave are more likely to have been associated with the skull; they give dates of 95,000 ± 10,000 and 164,000 ± 21,000 yr, but the samples both were contaminated and the dates suspect. We hope that an ESR date will be obtained on fauna associated with the skull.

PALEOLITHIC SITES IN ISRAEL AND THE SOUTHERN LEVANT

In addition to dates on hominid sites themselves, U-series dates have been obtained on archaeological sites coeval with the hominid sites, which were presumably occupied by either Asian Neanderthals or modern hominids. Schwarcz, Goldberg and Blackwell (1980) discuss some of these dates. The site of Ein Avdat, in the Negev Desert, is particularly interesting in the present context. It is near the site of Boker Tachtit, where Marks (1977) found a lithic industry transitional between Middle Paleolithic (MP) and Upper Paleolithic (UP). At Ein Avdat, a travertine was found to contain artifacts of similar typology. The travertine, which was quite pure, gave a well-defined U-series date of 47,000 ± 3000 yr. Similar dates were obtained by ^{14}C analysis of ostrich eggshells at Boker Tachtit: >43,500, >33,000; and 43,000 ± 2000 yr. These dates show that the MP/UP transition occurred in Israel, at most, a few thousand years earlier than in Europe, where the transition from Mousterian to Aurignacian was ^{14}C dated to *ca.* 40,000 yr (Bischoff *et al.* 1989). This is especially interesting in light of: 1) the early presence of modern hominids in this region (*ca.* 100,000 yr); and 2) a popular assumption that, in western Europe, the MP/UP transition was associated with the replacement of Neanderthals by modern hominids.

At Nahal Aqev, a travertine spring-mound contains sediments correlative with those from a neighboring Mousterian site. The travertine layer underlying these sediments dates to 85,000 ± 10,000 and 74,000 ± 5000 yr; the oldest layers in this mound date to 211,000 ± 19,000 yr. The site of Biq'at Quneitra, on the Golan Heights, has yielded a Mousterian industry. Five bovid teeth from the site yielded ESR dates of 39,000 ± 6000 (EU) and 54,000 ± 6000 (LU) (Ziaei *et al.* 1990). In Syria, the spring mound of El-Kowm consists of a series of travertines in which are embedded Yabroudian and Mousterian artifacts. These have yielded U-series dates: Yabroudian layers range from 156,000 ± 16,000 to 99,000 ± 16,000 yr; a Mousterian layer dated to 76,000 ± 16,000 (Hennig and Hours 1982). These ages agree with TL dates on burned flint from this site (Yabroudian average = 160,000 ± 22,000; Mousterian = 104,000 ± 9,000 (Huxtable, unpublished data). Also in Syria, new studies of Yabroud have begun to yield chronological data of the Yabroudian industry in a layer at 4.6-m depth from Solecki's excavation (Solecki and Solecki 1993). Porat and Schwarcz (1992) obtained ESR dates of 231,000 ± 19,000 (LU), 177,000 ± 20,000 on tooth enamel from 4.6 m below datum, probably Kulturschicht 18 of Rust (1950). This agrees with TL dates of 195,000 ± 15,000 on burned flint obtained by J. Huxtable (Farrand, personal communication 1992).

In summary, a number of sites in this region have yielded dates supportive of the existence of MP industries at *ca.* 100,000 yr, while a Lower Paleolithic, Yabroudian industry is typically dated to 160,000 to 140,000 yr, except at its type locality, Yabroud, where preliminary TL dates on burned flint and ESR dates on tooth enamel suggest ages of *ca.* 200,000 yr.

DISCUSSION AND CONCLUSION

I have summarized the results of TL, ESR and U-series dating at sites in Israel at which the remains of modern and Neanderthal hominids have been uncovered. These data have led to a major revision in the chronology of the emergence of modern man. The new dates have stimulated a great deal of renewed research and discussion on this topic. Bar-Yosef and Meignen (1992:176) suggest a parallel between the industries of Kebara, Units IX and X and that of Layer B in Tabun. This is approximately consistent with estimates of their respective dates: 60,000 and *ca.* 80,000 yr. Similarly, the Qafzeh industry appears to resemble that of Tabun's Layer C, which is also roughly consistent with absolute dating estimates. Microfaunal evidence has also been used to estimate ages of Levantine sites. At Qafzeh, Bar-Yosef and Vandermeersch (1981) used these data to infer an age of *ca.* 100,000 yr, essentially agreeing with both TL and ESR dates. However, at Tabun, faunal evidence (Bar-Yosef 1989) suggests that the boundary between Layers C and D represents a time gap between 100,000 and 60,000 yr, which is much younger than the dates summarized here.

Over the next decade, additional dates will be obtained to strengthen these arguments, and to clarify the chronological placement of the various taxa and their relations to archaeological data. In Israel, particularly, the need for better and more complete data is apparent:

1. The newly developed OSL method (Huntley, Godfrey-Smith and Thewalt 1985) is ideally suited to dating coastal sites, where the silt-sized quartz is wind-blown. OSL signals of this material should have been zeroed by sunlight, and, thus can be dated by measuring the amount of signal that has regrown. Tabun, Kebara and other sites in the Valley of Caves (Nahal Me'arot) could be dated in this way, as long as reliable estimates of the dose rate can be obtained. The time limit for this method is *ca.* 150,000 yr.
2. U-series dating of calcite concretions and encrustations on artifacts at some of the sites discussed above may be feasible, using thermal ionization mass spectrometry. However, the level of contamination may be too high to allow the dating of even carefully selected samples. In the cave of Tabun, in particular, numerous spring deposits formed at various times in the history of the cave should be studied.
3. The ESR isochron method (Blackwell and Schwarcz 1992) may allow us to date tooth enamel more precisely. Subsamples of a single tooth are assumed to have experienced the same external gamma-ray dose, but had internal doses that depended on their uranium content. If a graph of D_E *vs.* d_{in} gives a straight line, then the slope of this line is the age of the sample, and the intercept is a measure of d_{ex}, the external component of d. This method will be especially useful for dating samples from sites whose sedimentary fill was completely removed during excavation, so that no samples of sediment can be obtained for determination of d_{ex}, and can also correct for variation in the external dose rate through time, which occurs when the water content of the sediment changes as a result of climate shift.

ACKNOWLEDGMENTS

This research was partly funded by grants from the National Science Foundation, USA to the University of California (BNS 8801699, to F. C. Howell), and the Social Sciences and Humanities Research Council, Canada. I am grateful to Rainer Grün for his continued assistance and collaboration in much of the work described here. I appreciate the help and encouragement of Ofer Bar-Yosef and Renee Kra in the preparation of this paper.

REFERENCES CITED

Aitken, M.
　　1985　*Thermoluminescence Dating.* Academic Press, London.
Aitken, M. and H. Valladas
　　1992　Luminescence dating and the origin of modern man. In *The Origin of Modern Humans and the Impact of Chronometric Dating*, edited by M. J. Aitken, C. B. Stringer and P. A. Mellars, pp. 27–39. Royal Society, London.
Arensburg, B., O. Bar-Yosef, M. Chech, P. Goldberg, H. Laville, L. Meignen, Y. Rak, E. Tchernov, A.-M. Tillier and B. Vandermeersch
　　1985　Une sépulture néandertalienne dans la grotte de Kebara (Israël). *Comptes Rendus Hebdomadaires des Séances de l'Académie des Sciences* 300:227–230.
Bar-Yosef, O.
　　1989　Upper Pleistocene cultural stratigraphy in southwest Asia. In *Emergence of Modern Humans*, edited by E. Trinkaus, pp. 154–180. Cambridge University Press, Cambridge.

Bar-Yosef, O. and B. Vandermeersch
  1981   Notes concerning the possible age of the Mousterian layers at Qafzeh Cave. In *Préhistoire du Levant*, edited by J. Cauvin and P. Sanlaville, pp. 555–569. Maison de l'Orient, CNRS, Lyon.

Bar-Yosef, O., B. Vandermeersch, B. Arensburg, A. Belfer-Cohen, P. Goldberg, H. Laville, L. Meignen, Y. Rak, J. D. Speth, E. Tchernov, A.-M. Tillier and S. Weiner
  1992   The excavations in Kebara Cave, Mt. Carmel. *Current Anthropology* 33:497–550.

Bischoff, J., N. Soler, N. Maroto and R. Julia
  1989   Abrupt Mousterian/Aurignacian boundary at c. 40 ka BP: Accelerator ^{14}C dates from L'Arbreda Cave, (Catalunya, Spain). *Journal of Archaeological Science* 16:553–576.

Blackwell, B. and H. P. Schwarcz
  1992   Electron spin resonance (ESR) isochron dating: Solving the external gamma problem. *Applied Radiation and Isotopes* 44:243–252.

Boutié, P.
  1989   Etude technologique de l'industrie mousterienne de la Grotte de Qafzeh (près de Nazareth, Israel). In *Investigations in South Levantine Prehistory*. Edited by O. Bar-Yosef and B. Vandermeersch, pp. 213–230. BAR International Series 497, British Archaeological Reports, Oxford.

Bowman, S.
  1984   Thermoluminescence characteristics of sediments from the Tabun cave, Israel. *Nuclear Tracks and Radiation Measurement* 10:731–736.

Garrod, D. and D. Bate
  1937   *The Stone Age of Mount Carmel*, Vol. 1, *Excavations at the Wady el-Mughara*. Oxford University Press, Oxford.

Grün, R.
  1989   Electron spin resonance (ESR) dating. *Quaternary International* 1:65–109.

Grün, R., J. Chadam and H. P. Schwarcz
  1988   ESR dating of tooth enamel: Coupled correction for U-uptake and U-series disequilibrium. *Nuclear Tracks and Radiation Measurement* 14:237–241.

Grün, R. and H. P. Schwarcz
  1987   Some remarks on "ESR dating of bones". *Ancient TL* 5:l–9.

Grün, R., H. P. Schwarcz and S. Zymela
  1987   ESR dating of tooth enamel. *Canadian Journal of Earth Science* 24:1022–1037.

Grün, R. and C. B. Stringer
  1991   Electron spin resonance dating and the evolution of modern humans. *Archaeometry* 33(2):153–199.

Grün, R., C. B. Stringer and H. P. Schwarcz
  1991   ESR dating of teeth from Garrod's Tabun Cave collection. *Journal of Human Evolution* 20:231–248.

Hennig, G. J. and F. Hours
  1982   Dates pour le passage entre l'Achuléen et le Paléolithique moyen à El Kowm (Syrie). *Paléorient* 8:81–84.

Huntley, D. J., D. I. Godfrey-Smith and M. L. Thewalt
  1985   Optical dating of sediments. *Nature* 313:105–107.

Klein, R. G.
  1989   *The Human Career*. University of Chicago Press, Chicago.

Jelinek, A.
  1982   The Middle Paleolithic in the Southern Levant with comments on the appearance of modern *Homo sapiens*. In *The Transition from Lower to Middle Paleolithic and the Origin of Modern Man*, edited by A. Ronen, pp. 57–104. BAR International Series 151, British Archaeological Reports, Oxford.

Jelinek, A., W. R. Farrand, G. Haas, A. Horowitz, and P. Goldberg
  1973   New excavations at the Tabun Cave, Mount Carmel, Israel: A preliminary report. *Paléorient* 1:151–183.

Marks, A.
  1977   *Prehistory and Paleoenvironments in the Central Negev, Israel*, Vol. II, *The Avdat/Aqev Area*, Part 2. Southern Methodist University Press, Dallas.

McDermott, F., R. Grün, C. B. Stringer and C. J. Hawkesworth
  1993   Mass spectrometric U-series dates for Israeli Neanderthal/early modern hominid sites. *Nature* 363:252–255.

McKown, T. D. and A. Keith
  1939   *The Stone Age of Mount Carmel*, Vol. 2, *The Fossil Human Remains from the Levalloiso-Mousterian*. Clarendon Press, Oxford.

Mercier, N., G. Valladas, H. Valladas, A. Jelinek, L. Meignen, J. L. Reyss and J. L. Joron
          TL dates of burnt flints from Jelinek excavations: New Tabun cave chronology and its implications. *Journal of Archaeological Science*, in press.

Mercier, N. and H. Valladas
   1994   Thermoluminescence dates for the Paleolithic Levant. This volume.
Mercier, N., H. Valladas, O. Bar-Yosef, B. Vandermeersch, C. B. Stringer and J. L. Joron
   1993   Thermoluminescence date for the Mousterian burial site of Es-Skhul, Mt. Carmel. *Journal of Archaeological Science* 20(2):169–174.
Porat, N. and H. P. Schwarcz
   1991   Use of signal subtraction methods in ESR dating of burned flint. *Nuclear Tracks and Radiation Measurement* 18:203–212.
Porat, N., H. P. Schwarcz, H. Valladas, O. Bar-Yosef and B. Vandermeersch
   1994   Electron spin resonance dating of burned flint from Kebara Cave, Israel. Ms. submitted to *Geoarchaeology*.
Rak, Y.
   1990   On the differences between two pelvises of Mousterian context from the Qafzeh and Kebara caves, Israel. *American Journal of Physical Anthropology* 81:323–332.
Rust, A.
   1950   *Die Höhlenfunde von Jabrud (Syrien)*. K. Wachholtz, Neumunster.
Schwarcz, H. P.
   1985   ESR studies of tooth enamel. In Proceedings of Fourth Specialist Seminar on TL and ESR Dating, Worms, 1984. *Nuclear Tracks and Radiation Measurement* 10:865–867.
   1989   Uranium series dating of Quaternary deposits. *Quaternary International* 1:7–17
Schwarcz, H. P., W. M. Buhay, R. Grün, H. Valladas, E. Tchernov, O. Bar-Yosef and B. Vandermeersch
   1989   ESR dates for the Neanderthal site of Kebara, Israel. *Journal of Archaelogical Science* 16:653–661.
Schwarcz, H. P., P. Goldberg and B. Blackwell
   1980   Uranium series dating of archaeological sites in Israel. *Israel Journal of Earth Sciences* 29:157–165.
Schwarcz, H. P., R. Grün, B. Vandermeersch, O. Bar-Yosef, H. Valladas and E. Tchernov
   1988   ESR dates for the hominid burial site of Qafzeh in Israel. *Journal of Human Evolution* 17:733–737.
Solecki, R. S. and R. L. Solecki
   1993   The pointed tools from the Mousterian occupations of Shanidar Cave, northern Iraq. In *The Paleolithic Prehistory of the Zagros-Taurus*, edited by D. I. Olszewski and H. L. Dibble, pp. 119–146. The University Museum, University of Pennsylvania, Philadelphia.
Stringer, C. B., R. Grün, H. P. Schwarcz and P. Goldberg
   1989   ESR dates for the hominid burial site of Es Skhul in Israel. *Nature* 338:756–758 .
Suzuki, H. and F. Takai
   1970   *The Amud Man and His Cave Site*. University of Tokyo Press, Tokyo.
Tchernov, E.
   1988   Biochronology of the Middle Paleolithic and dispersal events of hominids in the Levant. In *L'Homme de Néanderthal*, Vol. 2, *L'Environnement*, edited by M. Otte, pp. 153–168. Etudes et Récherches Archéologiques de l'Université de Liège, Liège.
Trinkaus, E.
   1984   Western Asia. In *The Origins of Modern Humans*, edited by F. H. Smith and F. Spencer, pp. 251–293. A. R. Liss, New York.
Turville-Petre, F.
   1927   Researches in prehistoric Galilee (1925–26) and a report on the Galilee skull. *British School of Archaeology in Jerusalem, Bulletin* 14.
Valladas, H., J. L. Joron, G. Valladas, B. Arensburg, O. Bar-Yosef, A. Belfer-Cohen, P. Goldberg, H. Laville, L. Meignen, Y. Rak, E. Tchernov, A. M. Tillier and B. Vandermeersch
   1987   Thermoluminescence dates for the Neanderthal burial site at Kebara cave in Israel. *Nature* 330:159–160.
Valladas, H., J. L. Reyss, G. Valladas, O. Bar-Yosef and B. Vandermeersch
   1988   Thermoluminescence dates of Mousterian "Proto-Cro-Magnon" remains from Israel and the origin of modern man. *Nature* 331:614–616.
Vandermeersch, B.
   1981   *Les Hommes Fossiles de Qafzeh (Israël)*. Maison de l'Orient, CNRS, Lyon.
Ziaei, M., H. P. Schwarcz, C. M. Hall and R. Grün
   1990   Radiometric dating of the Mousterian site at Quneitra. In *Quneitra: A Mousterian Site on the Golan Heights*, edited by N. Goren-Inbar, pp. 232–235. Qedem 31, Hebrew University of Jerusalem, Jerusalem.

CONFRONTATION OF GEOLOGICAL STRATIGRAPHY AND RADIOMETRIC DATES FROM UPPER PLEISTOCENE SITES IN THE LEVANT

WILLIAM R. FARRAND

Exhibit Museum, The University of Michigan, Ann Arbor, Michigan 48109-1079 USA

INTRODUCTION

Recent radiometric ages determined by the thermoluminescence (TL) and electron spin resonance (ESR) methods have raised serious questions about existing interpretations of the late Pleistocene chronology of several important prehistoric sites in the Levant. Such sites as Tabun, Skhul, and Kebara caves on Mount Carmel, Israel, the Cave of Jebel Qafzeh in Nazareth, Israel and Yabrud Rockshelter I, Syria contain records of Middle Paleolithic cultures (Levantine Mousterian, Mugharan and variants) and skeletal remains of both *Homo sapiens neanderthalensis* and anatomically modern *H. sapiens sapiens*. Both physical types are found with essentially the same technological materials (Mousterian artifacts) and appear to have exploited the same kinds of fauna and flora. The chronological relations (and thus, the inferred evolutionary position) of the Neanderthals and anatomically modern populations have been a subject of intense debate since their discovery in the 1930s. The application of radiocarbon (^{14}C) dating, beginning in the 1960s, did little to resolve chronological questions. This was so because the pertinent strata lay at or near the maximum practical limits of the method, or even beyond those limits, where very small amounts of modern contaminants can have very large effects on the apparent dates.

Other dating methods have been tried, such as uranium (U)-series dating (particularly of travertines) and amino-acid racemization (AAR) (of bones and marine shells). U-series is limited by the scarcity of suitable travertines in the pertinent stratigraphic positions, and AAR depends critically on appropriate calibration controls and temperature histories. However, these methods have led to the conclusion that many Middle Paleolithic strata are much older than the limits of ^{14}C dating, that is, well beyond 50,000 or 60,000 yr ago.

This interesting debate has taken on a new dimension with the advent of TL and ESR dating, which have been applied to burned flint artifacts and fossil teeth. Not only are the apparent ages of the critical strata significantly older than previously thought, in some cases, 2 or even 3 times as old as ^{14}C dating had suggested, but also the chronological association of Neanderthals and anatomically modern humans reverses long-standing hypotheses. If the new dates are accepted, anatomically modern humans preceded the Neanderthal populations in the Near East, and the two human groups coexisted for some time. This situation has naturally kindled heated discussions about the evolution of the human species, namely concerning the relations of human physical types to their material culture, the evolution of modern *H. sapiens sapiens* from *H. sapiens neanderthalensis*, and the "Out of Africa" hypothesis of the mitochondrial DNA practitioners. I do not review this debate because it has been discussed elsewhere (Mellars 1990; Otte 1988; Trinkaus 1989).

I review here the credibility of all the radiometric dates. Internal inconsistencies exist within the series of dates from a single method, and there are very large statistical uncertainties around single dates (as much as 20 to 30%), as well as conflicts with dates determined by other methods. In TL and ESR dating, the uncertainties stem from the assumptions of the methods, mainly in environmental radiation dose, in moisture history of the sample since burial and in models of radiation uptake (early, linear or recent). (See also the discussion of these methods by Jelinek (1990a,b) and

Late Quaternary Chronology and Paleoclimates of the Eastern Mediterranean
Edited by O. Bar-Yosef and R. S. Kra. RADIOCARBON 1994, pp. 33–53

33

by Grün *et al.* (1987).) If most of the recently determined TL and ESR dates are accepted, we then must reject essentially all the ^{14}C dates (except infinite ones) on Middle Paleolithic sites in the Near East, as well as some normally acceptable U-series dates. In some cases, the alternative would be to acknowledge striking temporal disjunctions in cultural history and inferred paleoclimates across very short geographical distances.

In this paper, I evaluate the available radiometric dates against the background of geology, sedimentology and stratigraphy of pertinent sites and of related phenomena, such as relict shorelines and littoral dune accumulations along the shores of the Levant. To begin, I examine the cave of Tabun, because its 25-m-thick, stratified sequence has long been the basis of Middle Paleolithic cultural history in the Levant. I will then review the nearby sites of Kebara, Skhul and Qafzeh, all within a 35-km radius, before discussing sites in neighboring Syria and Lebanon. I will not repeat detailed descriptions of these sites, which can be found in the references cited below.

TABUN CAVE, MOUNT CARMEL, ISRAEL[1]

Tabun Cave is located on the face of the Mount Carmel limestone block, a former sea cliff that dominates the Israeli coastal plain for 30 km south of the Carmel promontory in Haifa. The bedrock sill of the cave opening is *ca.* 53 m asl and *ca.* 15 m above the adjacent coastal plain. The Mediterranean coastline is only 2.5 km from the cave, and the present coast is paralleled by 2 or 3, more-or-less continuous eolianite (*kurkar*) ridges constructed of dune sand that accumulated along former shorelines, normally attributed to the last interglacial, or deep-sea isotope stage 5. The eolianite sand is identical to the sandy fill in the lower half of Tabun, which is believed to be also related to former high sea-level stands (Farrand 1979; Jelinek *et al.* 1973).

The sedimentary fill in Tabun was studied in detail by Goldberg (1973) and summarized in Jelinek *et al.* (1973) and Farrand (1979). The sequence is still referred to by the older terminology of Garrod and Bate (1937), as given in Table 1, although the 1967–1971 excavations by Jelinek (1982b) have resulted in a much more detailed stratigraphy.

Garrod's stratigraphy comprised broad subdivisions based variously on lithology or artifacts, and did not relate to the natural stratigraphy of the cave. However, one is forced to rely on Garrod's subdivisions in dealing with materials that she retrieved because she completely removed all the sedimentary fill from the outer chamber of the cave. Thus, there is no way of relating Garrod's finds to Jelinek's stratigraphy in detail. This problem is pertinent here because the teeth dated by Grün, Stringer and Schwarcz (1991) came from Garrod's museum collections in London, and they cannot be related to the site stratigraphy except in the most general terms.

The question of provenience is all the more troublesome because there are lateral (facies) variations within a single Garrod layer across the site. For example, Jelinek found no preserved bones below Layer C in the middle and inner chambers of the cave, and Garrod (1937) noted that bone preservation was quite irregular below Layer C. Bones were preferentially preserved in reddish earth and breccias close to the cave walls, where early cementation of sediments protected the bones from weathering, but they were usually absent in the greenish, whitish or brown sediments in the middle of the cave. This situation is likely to have affected the radiation dose history of the teeth dated by ESR, as well as presenting problems in evaluating the dose by implanting dosimeters at the present time.

---

[1]References: Jelinek *et al.* (1973); Jelinek (1982 a,b)

Table 1. Tabun Cave Stratigraphy

Garrod and Bate (1937)	Jelinek (1982a,b)		
	Major units	Beds	Archaeological facies
Chimney I & II	Not excavated		Late Mousterian
Layer B	Not excavated		
Layer C	I	1 – 26	Later Mousterian
	II	27 – 32	
	III	33 – 36	
	IV	37 – 40	
Layer D	V	41 – 42	Early Mousterian
	VI	43 – 49	
	VII	50 – 58	
	VIII	59 – 61	
	IX	62 – 69	
	X	70 – 72	Transitional
Layer Ea	XI	73 – 77	{ Acheulean / Yabrudian / Amudian / Acheulean
Layer Eb	XII	78 – 80	Acheulean
Layer Ec	?		
Layer Ed	XIII	81 – 85	{ Yabrudian / Acheulean / Yabrudian
Layer F	Not excavated	Not excavated	Acheulean
Layer G	XIV	90A – 90J	Acheulean

The sedimentary sequence begins at the base with a rather thin stratum of strongly deformed loamy sediments (Layer G) that plunge steeply into a karstic bedrock "swallow hole". This is followed by thick sandy sediments (Layer F and Layer Ed), very similar to the coastal eolianites mentioned above, that also subsided into the karstic swallow hole. Above this layer, the sediments gradually become less sandy and more silty (Layers Ec–D), resembling loess, and are variably cemented by secondary phosphate (collophane), presumably originating from the decay of bones formerly present. Garrod's sublayers, Ea, Eb, Ec and Ed, were subdivided typologically (Garrod and Bate 1937), but Goldberg's sedimentological analysis (Fig. 1), which was based on Garrod's drawings, places the sand/silt transition within the lower part of Garrod's Layer E.

These layers are marked by some small offsets and truncations, indicating erosional episodes, and settling and compaction of the sediments. Overlying Layer D is a disturbed zone where original deposits have been eroded or slumped into another karstic swallow hole, inferred to be underlying the sediments in the inner chamber of the cave. This disturbance, not recognized by Garrod, is labeled "C–D" by Jelinek *et al.* (1973), and comprises Units II–VI of the revised stratigraphy (Jelinek 1982a). It is overlain conformably by Garrod's Layer C, a sequence of repeated layers of white ash, black carbon-rich, and brick-red baked sediments. Garrod stated that these "narrow banded hearths of alternating colors, dipping towards the middle [of the cave]" appeared "[a]t the entrance to the inner chamber", but Layer C in the outer chamber of the cave was "made up of hardened earth", black in the east and redder to the west and approximately horizontal (Garrod and Bate 1937).

Layer C passes upward by transition into Layer B, a relatively homogeneous sediment composed of a matrix of reddish brown clay with disseminated head-size limestone boulders derived from the walls of the inner chamber. The red clay is terra rossa soil that washed into the top of the cave through a large "chimney" shaft, open to the surface. The opening of the chimney apparently began during the deposition of Layer C, as shown by its central facies, which is composed of the same kind of sediment as in Layer B (Jelinek 1982a). Above Layer B, more of the red clayey, rocky sediment filled the chimney shaft to within 7 m of the overlying plateau surface. These sediments, Chimney I and II, were entirely removed during Garrod's excavations.

Beds 1–17 of Jelinek's Major Unit I are, in fact, part of Garrod's Layer C, not Layer B, as Jelinek (1982a, b) stated. I made this correlation from depth measurements on Garrod's sections (1937). The banded burned strata of Layer C occur next to the cave walls, but they pass gradually into a reddish brown clayey sediment in the center of the section. A few black, carbonaceous layers could be traced right across the section from wall to wall, through the reddish-brown sediment, demonstrating that the two kinds of sediments accumulated simultaneously side by side. Thus, Layer C, as a lithostratigraphic construct, encompasses these contrasting facies. However, Jelinek notes that the artifacts found in Beds 1–17 (the upper part of his Major Unit I) had closer affinities to those in overlying Layer B than to artifacts in the lower portions of Layer C.

The Tabun sediments comprise a complex sequence of events largely dominated by eolian infilling, first sandy, then silty, ending with the opening of the chimney and inwashing of red soil simultaneous with detachment of blocks of the bedrock wall. Two, or perhaps three, important discontinuities occur in this sequence. The youngest lies between Layers C and D, and is related to the collapse of sediments into the inner-chamber swallow hole. The older discontinuity results from subsidence into the visible swallow hole at the bottom of the outer chamber, the timing of which is not clear. I have postulated (Jelinek et al. 1973; Farrand 1979) that the subsidence of sediments into these swallow holes resulted from a lowered water table consequent to falling levels of the Mediterranean Sea, which, in turn, is related to global glacial-interglacial cycles.

During the Jelinek excavations, we discovered a prominent discontinuity, a high-angle offset, between what seems to be Garrod's Layer E and our Bed 80 (Jelinek et al. 1973). Bed 80 has been renamed Bed 90, or Major Unit XIV, in Jelinek's (1982a) revised stratigraphy. Major Unit XIV has been equated with Garrod's Layer G (Jelinek 1982a), on the basis of the industry, which is more like that of Layer G than like E or F.

Relations are different, however, in the eastern part of the section where Goldberg obtained samples assigned to Layers Ed and F (Fig. 1). In this area, Layer F appears to progress continuously into Layer E. Garrod also noted that it is toward the west side of the outer chamber of the cave that the lower part of Layer E, as well as Layer F, begins to plunge sharply "towards a point lying below the unexcavated western part of the trench" (Garrod and Bate 1937:66). Garrod also noted a fault in Layer E in the buttress (témoin of Jelinek et al. 1973) of sediment that she left on the west side of the outer chamber of the cave. That fault lines up quite well with the slumped interface between our Units XIII and XIV in Square 42. Garrod did not see the continuation of the fault across the area south of the buttress, but she presumed that it was there (Garrod and Bate 1937). Thus, in this western area, Layer E (on the east side of Garrod's fault) slumped down against older sediments equivalent to our Unit XIV (on the west side of that fault), but a continuous section from Layer G up through F into E remains intact on the east side of Garrod's excavated area.

However, there is no strong evidence of *major* interruptions in the sediment sequence between the base of Layer E (*i.e.*, Unit XIII) and the top of Layer D (Unit VII). This inference is reinforced by Jelinek's (1982b) observation of continuity in the artifact assemblages from Layers Ea into D, showing a transition from the latest Mugharan into the earliest Mousterian technology, as well as the lack of abrupt shifts in the percentages of artifact types in Layer E (Jelinek 1982a). Thus, it is misleading when Grün, Stringer and Schwarcz (1991:233) write that "the numerous unconformities in units XIV to II represent several fluctuations of sea level, of unknown magnitude." To the contrary, a general continuity seems to have prevailed from Unit XIII–VII, although this does not preclude episodes of non-deposition and minor truncations documented in our excavations (Jelinek 1982b; ms. in preparation). Thus, it seems that sediments from Units XIII–VII (and the displaced sediments in Units VI–II) accumulated within a single glacial-interglacial cycle.

Corroboration of continuity lies in the pollen record from Tabun, recently restudied by Fish (summarized by Jelinek (1992)). In short, the Tabun pollen record is "remarkable for its complacency and general lack of evidence of marked change in arboreal types" (Jelinek 1992). It reflects dominantly steppic conditions throughout.

With this background, I will discuss radiometric dates from Tabun, which include ^{14}C, AAR, ESR and TL, shown in relation to stratigraphy in Table 2.

TABLE 2. Radiometric Dates (kyr) for Tabun Cave (See text for date sources)

Strata	^{14}C	ESR (EU)	ESR (LU)	Other
B	39.7 ± 0.8	86 ± 11	103 ± 16	
C–Bed 4	51.0 $^{+\ 4.8}_{-\ 3.0}$			51–53 (AAR)
C–Bed 16	45.8 $^{+\ 2.1}_{-\ 1.6}$			
C–Bed 19				60–90 (TL)
C–Bed 22				68–71 (AAR)
C–Undetermined		107 ± 17	119 ± 11	
D	35.4 ± 0.9	122 ± 20	166 ± 20	
Ea		154 ± 34	188 ± 31	83–87 (AAR)
Eb		151 ± 21	168 ± 15	
Ec		176 ± 10	199 ± 7	
Ed		182 ± 61	213 ± 46	

There is much scatter among the 16 ^{14}C dates, presumably owing to contamination by younger organic matter. I have listed only those dates older than 40,000 yr for Tabun C, assuming that it is older than the one result for Tabun B, at 39,000 yr. Ten dates from Tabun C (Bien and Gandolfi 1972), ranging from 23,000 to 38,800 yr are scrambled stratigraphically, and are considered spurious (Jelinek *et al.* 1973). Inadequate pretreatment is presumably to blame, and the samples were also attributed mistakenly to a non-existent "Upper Paleolithic Carmel culture"! (Bien and Gandolfi 1972).

Only three of these ^{14}C dates are credible, at 51,000 and 45,800 BP (GrN-7409 and GrN-7410, respectively), which are indistinguishable statistically, and at 39,700 BP (GrN-2534) (Table 2). Of this group, the oldest ages approximate most closely the true ages. Only with caution do we accept 51,000 BP as a limiting age. Thus, the upper part of Tabun C (or Bed 4 of Major Unit I of Jelinek) is at least 51,000 yr old.

The single date, 39,700 BP, for Tabun B is most likely only a limiting age as well. Unfortunately, the provenience is unknown, except that it was collected "1 meter below the surface" (Vogel and Waterbolk 1963:172). At the time of collection in 1959, the surface of the cave was truncated, eroded and sloping, so that it is difficult to visualize the exact stratigraphic position of the sample. Given the clear evidence for a gradual sedimentological transition from Tabun C to Tabun B, an age difference of some 12,000 yr from the top of Tabun C to some point in Tabun B seems excessive, which throws doubt on 39,700 BP, if 51,000 BP for Tabun C is valid.

Table 2 also shows three AAR ages. The problem here is one of calibration based on an assumed temperature history of the enclosing sediments. A first attempt was made by Bada and Helfman (1976), but later refinements in the calibration were made by Masters (1982), based on the 39,700 BP ^{14}C date from Tabun B and actual ground temperatures measured in the site. Of the resulting ages, the 51,000 or 53,000 BP estimate for Tabun C (exact provenance unknown) is in reasonable agreement with the 51,000 BP ^{14}C age for the top of Tabun C. Thus, the 68,000 or 71,000 BP age for lower Tabun C (Bed 22) is not unreasonable, although a span of some 20,000 yr for the accumulation of 2 m of sediments in Layer C seems too long. If these AAR determinations are correct, relative to the ^{14}C age, then an estimate of 83,000–87,000 yr for Major Unit XI, Bed 75 or 76 (*i.e.*, "Bed 49" of Jelinek's original terminology (Masters 1982) or Tabun Ea of Garrod) is not out of line.

Table 2 summarizes ESR ages determined recently by Grün, Stringer and Schwarcz (1991). These do not agree well with any dates discussed above. If the ESR dates are even approximately correct, then all the other dates listed in Table 2 are in error by a factor of 2 or 3. In fairness, Grün *et al.* recognize that their results are first approximations, given the uncertainties of their sample provenances and environmental dose rates (H. P. Schwarcz, personal communication).

Recent TL dates on burned flints from the Jelinek excavations at Tabun complicate the picture even more (Mercier 1992; Mercier and Valladas 1994). These dates are consistently older than the ESR dates from the same strata (see Table 4). The maximum TL dates, assuming no change in environmental dose with time, are 65,000–137,000 yr older than ESR(LU) dates. Even the youngest TL estimates, considered the "worst possible scenario" by Mercier and Valladas (1994), are 15,000–100,000 yr older than the ESR(LU) ages. The discrepancies are too great to be attributed to the uncertainties in provenance of the ESR samples, discussed above, and thus raise the question of assumptions in both methods.

For an alternate evaluation, I plot the ESR dates against depth (Fig. 1), and include the gross granulometry (sand, silt and clay percentages) of the Tabun section. At the outset, there is much uncertainty about each of the data points, as indicated by the boxes enclosing the ESR dates. Even if the ESR ages are correct, they are likely to fall anywhere within a given box. On the one hand, the vertical positions of the samples dated by Grün, Stringer and Schwarcz (1991) are not known more precisely than the broad designation of Garrod's "layers", as explained above, thus, somewhere between the top and bottom of the box. The depth in Figure 1 is taken from Jelinek (1982a), and may differ somewhat from that of Garrod. On the other hand, the experimental errors associated with the ESR dates are very large, from 10 to >20%, in almost all cases.

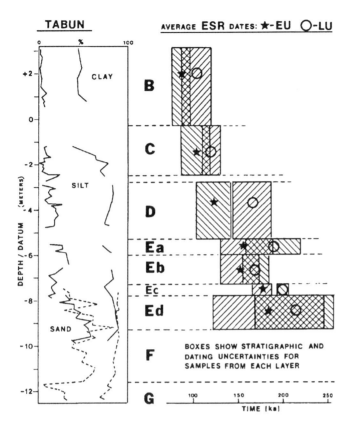

Fig. 1. Plot of ESR dates *vs.* stratigraphic depth and grain size in Tabun. Each average date is based on repeated runs on 2–4 different samples from a given layer (Grün *et al.* 1991). Boxes enclosing the ESR dates indicate the uncertainties in the age estimate and in vertical stratigraphic position (see text). The column on the left portrays the grain-size evolution in the Tabun sedimentary fill plotted *vs.* absolute depth relative to datum, which was the same for Garrod's and Jelinek's excavations. Separate segments on this plot are each derived from separate sampling columns, and the solid and dashed curves (below −8 m) show overlapping sampling columns (replotted from Jelinek *et al.* 1973).

Based on Figure 1, and assuming that the dates are valid, one can estimate the rate of sedimentation in Tabun. A straight-line curve can be drawn through the average ESR dates for Layers Ed–D section and another for C–B, which would indicate sedimentation rates of *ca.* 10 cm/1000 yr and 21 cm/1000 yr, respectively. Because both vertical and horizontal controls on the data points are very loose, we cannot justify drawing more detailed curves than simple, straight lines. I have not included such curves in Figure 1 for fear that uninformed readers will assume that they have more veracity than intended.

The data in Figure 1 imply an essentially uniform sedimentation rate from the base of Tabun E to the top of Tabun D, and a doubling of the rate after the C/D hiatus. As a first approximation, that conclusion is reasonable, but several aspects of the rates are suspect. As discussed above and as shown by the granulometry in Figure 1, Tabun Ed is a very sandy deposit resembling the dune sands of the coastal plain. From Tabun Ec upward through Tabun D, there is an increasing proportion of silt over sand, presumably reflecting a cutoff of the local sand source and prevalence of long-distance silt (loess) input. (See the sedimentation model in Farrand (1979).) This change in input carries with it the implication of a changing sedimentation rate, from relatively fast accumulation of local dune sand (Ed) to slower input of loess (Ec through D), which came from a more distant source. However, no such change is reflected in the data in Figure 1 or by the inferred sedimentation rates suggested above, although some variability could be hidden in the uncertainties underlying that plot, as discussed in the previous paragraph. A doubling (at least) of the apparent sedimentation rate in Tabun C and B relative to the lower section is also reasonable, even if numerical values are suspect, because the reworked terra rossa that washed into the chimney probably accumulated faster than the windblown sediments. This conclusion is partially supported by the abundance of animal bones in the Tabun B and Chimney deposits, implying rapid burial.

However, these apparent sedimentation rates, only 10–20 cm/1000 yr, are quite slow. For comparison, a sedimentation rate based on the Mousterian section at Kebara Cave (see below), as dated by TL ages on burned flint (Valladas *et al.* 1987; Mercier and Valladas 1994), is *ca.* 400 cm in 11,600 yr, or 33 cm/1000 yr. These Kebara sediments are reasonably similar to those of Tabun C. The same rate of *ca.* 33 cm/1000 yr is also derived from the sediments in Franchthi Cave in southern Greece (Jacobsen and Farrand 1987), where it is the average sedimentation rate from Upper Paleolithic through the end of Neolithic time, specifically from 23,000–5000 yr. The Franchthi sediments range from clay loams, with minimal human influence, to Mesolithic and Neolithic accumulations, with considerable anthropogenic input. Similarly, the Tabun sediments, especially Layers E and D, also included a strong anthropogenic influence. Jelinek (1982b) reports >44,000 artifacts recovered from only 90 m^3 of sediment, or nearly 500 artifacts/m^3, on average, for the recent excavations, although they were by no means uniformly distributed. Further, the Franchthi section is interrupted by several unconformities (hiatuses), so that the overall average rate of 33 cm/1000 yr belies the true rates of sediment accumulation that range from at least 50 cm to as much as 3000 cm/1000 yr (Farrand 1993).

Thus, the sedimentation rates implied by the Tabun ESR dates appear much too slow by comparison with comparable sediments observed elsewhere in the region. The TL dates would yield even slower rates. Moreover, the lithological sequence in Tabun implies a single interglacial-glacial cycle from Tabun F through D, then an important interglacial break, followed by the onset in Layer C of the next glacial cycle. ESR(LU) and TL dates span 2 or even 3 interglacials. I conclude, thus, from sedimentation rate arguments, that the ESR(LU) and TL dates for Tabun must be incorrect or that some important hiatuses (intervals of non-deposition) in the Tabun E and D section have not been detected, or some of both.

KEBARA CAVE, MOUNT CARMEL, ISRAEL[2]

The Kebara site is situated only 13 km south of Tabun in a similar geomorphic setting. The known thickness of the sedimentary fill in Kebara is considerably less than that in Tabun, and no cultural deposits older than Middle Paleolithic are known. Yet, similarities exist between the two sites.

Like Tabun, several ^{14}C dates have yielded mixed results, suggesting contamination. The oldest and most trustworthy of the Kebara dates is 41,000 ± 1000 BP (GrN-2561) on "charred wood or bone" at a depth of 2.5 m in the Mousterian section (Vogel and Waterbolk 1963), which is considered culturally equivalent to Tabun B (Meignen and Bar-Yosef 1988). However, this ^{14}C date may be several thousand calendar yr too young. Bard *et al.* (1990) demonstrated that ^{14}C dates are *ca.* 3000 yr too young at 20,000 BP, and in the range of 1000 to 5000 yr too young at 30,000 BP. It will be important to keep this in mind when comparing ^{14}C dates with U-series, TL and ESR dates.

A series of TL dates on burned flint at Kebara (Valladas *et al.* 1987; Mercier and Valladas 1994) ranging from 48,300 to 61,600 for Units VI–XII, are in stratigraphic order within the limits of their standard deviations. ESR dates were determined on cervid and gazelle teeth from Unit X (Schwarcz *et al.* 1989), and these dates average 60,000 ± 6000 (EU model) or 64,000 ± 6000 (LU model), in close agreement with the TL date of 61,600 ± 3600 for the same unit.

---

[2]References: Vandermeersch and Bar-Yosef (1988); Goldberg and Laville (1988)

Thus, all the radiometric dates for Kebara are in reasonable agreement. First, the youngest TL date (48,300 ± 3500) is close to the 41,000 ± 1000 ^{14}C age, especially in view of the realization that the ^{14}C date is too young in sidereal years (see above). Second, the ESR date for Unit X agrees within statistical limits with the TL date for the same unit. Third, the TL ages increase progressively with stratigraphic depth from Unit VI–X, leading to an acceptable rate of sedimentation, as discussed above. These dates imply that the ^{14}C and amino-acid dates for Layer C in Tabun (51,000–*ca.* 70,000) might be approximately correct, and that the Tabun ESR dates are out of line.

CAVE OF JEBEL QAFZEH, NAZARETH, ISRAEL[3]

This site has two parts: a cave with a cultural succession of Bronze, Upper Paleolithic and Middle Paleolithic ages, and a terrace (*le vestibule* of Vandermeersch (1981)) at the entrance to the cave where exclusively Middle Paleolithic remains are preserved. The connection between the cave sediments and the terrace deposits was almost completely removed during excavations in the 1930s. A major unconformity of unknown duration separates the Upper Paleolithic and the underlying, heavily weathered Mousterian beds in the cave.

The terrace deposits enclose abundant remains of human activity: Mousterian artifacts, fauna, ash layers and burials of early, anatomically modern *Homo sapiens sapiens*. These were deposited mostly in the open air and derived from rock debris (*éboulis*) from the adjacent bedrock slopes. Similar deposits were not found inside the cave. The upper terrace layers are more or less firmly cemented with secondary calcium carbonate because they accumulated outside the drip line of the cave entrance and were exposed directly to rainfall and weathering in a semi-arid climate. At a depth of 1–2 m below the present surface, the lower terrace deposits, where most of the human burials were found, are loose, friable and noticeably weathered. The bedrock clasts are rounded, porous and chalky (Vandermeersch 1981; Goldberg 1980).

Burned flint and animal teeth in the Qafzeh terrace deposits were TL- and ESR-dated, respectively. Twenty TL dates on Layers XVII–XXIII were virtually identical, averaging 92,000 ± 5000 (Valladas *et al.* 1988), implying very rapid sedimentation of the 4.5-m-thick terrace sequence, if the dates are correct. Sixteen ESR dates, from Layers XV–XXI (Schwarcz *et al.* 1988), likewise are also strongly clustered, showing no age gradient with stratigraphic depth, tending to reinforce the conclusion of rapid sedimentation. The ESR dates average 96,000 ± 13,000 (EU model) or 115,000 ± 15,000 (LU model), the range of the EU dates being statistically identical with the TL range, and are supported by new work by McDermott and Grün (H. P. Schwarcz, personal communication). The inference of rapid sedimentation is consistent with the sedimentological evidence of coarse, stony sediments, as well as with the observation that the lower terrace sediments are not cemented, which implies that the entire terrace succession must have accumulated too rapidly for cementation to have occurred until after deposition of all the terrace sediments had ceased.

Although the TL and the ESR dates, at least the EU dates, are in agreement both in numerical age and in the implication of very rapid sedimentation, questions remain about their validity. First, Schwarcz *et al.* (1988) express a preference for the LU model. If they are correct, there is some disagreement (greater than the statistical differences) between the TL and ESR dates, *i.e.*, 92,000 *vs.* 115,000 yr. Close agreement of TL with ESR results is usually independent verification of the age estimates (*e.g.*, Schwarcz *et al.* 1988), but, in fact, much of the age calculation depends on the environmental (or external) radiation dose, from enclosing sediments and cosmic radiation, which

[3]References: Vandermeersch (1981); Bar-Yosef and Vandermeersch (1981); Farrand (1979)

is the same for both the TL and the ESR methods. The environmental radiation dose is modulated by moisture conditions in the enclosing sediments, which may vary over the time since burial. These conditions may represent the greatest source of uncertainty in TL and ESR dating, which, then, are not totally independent checks on each other, as has been stated (Jelinek 1992).

In contrast to the TL and ESR dates, AAR of ostrich eggshell from Qafzeh suggests that sedimentation was not as rapid as inferred above. Alloisoleucine/isoleucine (D/L) ratios for shells from Layers XVII–XXI increase progressively with depth from *ca.* 0.6 to 0.9 (Brooks, Kokis and Hare 1992). No calibration is yet available by which to assign absolute ages to these ratios, which imply a time span of 20,000–40,000 yr (depending on the absolute age) for the 0.75-m-thick sediments in this part of Qafzeh (Brooks, Kokis and Hare 1992). This amounts to an average sedimentation rate of *ca.* 2–4 cm/1000 yr for Layers XVII–XXI, which seems rather slow. (See above for sedimentation rates in Tabun and Kebara.) Perhaps the real (average) sedimentation rate lies somewhere between the extremes suggested by ostrich eggshell AAR, ESR and TL dates. In any case, the racemization ratios suggest something unusual in the radiation dose history of the bones and flints measured by ESR and TL, respectively, at Qafzeh. A fluctuating moisture history, complicated by early cementation of the terrace deposits, may be involved (see below).

Masters (1982) reported other AAR dates for Qafzeh, which also disagree with the ESR and TL dates, although some compare favorably with Tabun and Kebara ^{14}C dates. Masters refined earlier estimates of racemization rate constants by using Pallmann temperature vials emplaced in the site sediments. Inconsistencies remain among the various materials dated at Qafzeh, *e.g.*, Upper Paleolithic animal bone from inside the cave is older than underlying hominid fossils of lower strata in the terrace deposits, and animal bones from the terrace are distinctly older than hominids in the same levels. Masters suspects that the Upper Paleolithic bone may have been cooked or at least heated near a hearth, making it appear too old. She mentions the effect of preservatives (and attempts at their removal) on D/L ratios, which may account for the spuriously young ages of the human fossils. She suspects that much less preservative may have been used on the animal bones (Layers XXI–XXII), which appear to be some 20,000 yr older than the contemporary(?) human bones (Layer XVII). However, in light of the ostrich eggshell results, a 20,000-yr difference between Layers XXI and XVII might not be out of line. Taken at face value, the AAR dates for the Mousterian animal bones from the terrace, *ca.* 60,000–80,000 yr, agree with the Mousterian dates from Tabun and Kebara, and with the ESR(EU) dates for Skhul (see below).

SKHUL CAVE, MOUNT CARMEL, ISRAEL[4]

Within 100 m of Tabun is the small Skhul Cave that also has yielded some radiometric dates. Skhul is well known for its group of human remains, presumably burials, of a physical type close to that of the Qafzeh skeletons, that is, anatomically modern *Homo sapiens sapiens*. Like Qafzeh, the Skhul remains are found with a Mousterian industry of the Tabun C variety (Jelinek 1982a, b). ESR dates were determined on two bovid teeth from museum collections (Stringer *et al.* 1989) because the site was completely emptied during the 1930s excavations (Garrod and Bate 1937). The provenience of the specimens is not known exactly, but the stratigraphy of Skhul is much simpler, and the deposits much thinner than those of Tabun. Three runs on one tooth averaged 65,200 yr, and four runs on the other tooth averaged 92,500 by the EU model, or 91,800 and 108,000 yr, respectively, by the LU model. The averages for both teeth are 81,000 ± 15,000 and 101,000 ± 12,000 for the EU and LU models, respectively. Thus, 1 of the 2 teeth agrees with the

---

[4]Reference: Stringer *et al.* (1989)

Qafzeh TL and ESR dates reasonably well, but the other is definitely younger. More recently, Mercier and Valladas (1994) dated Skhul burned flints by ESR, with a weighted average date of 119,000 ± 18,000 yr. Here, as at Tabun, the TL dates are distinctly older than ESR dates.

An independent check on the Skhul ESR dates comes from U-series dating of travertines deposited by carbonate-rich water issuing from the interior of Skhul cave and interfingering with the archaeological sediments. Three of four samples dated (Schwarcz *et al.* 1980) were older than 350,000 yr, presumably as the result of the incorporation of detrital ("dead") limestone dust (Schwarcz *et al.* 1980), but one sample gave a finite age of 79,000 ± 4000. At the time that these results were obtained, Schwarcz *et al.* (1980) thought that the spring activity responsible for the travertine must have ceased prior to the Skhul burials, which were presumed younger than the known ^{14}C ages from neighboring Tabun. At present, the 79,000-yr U-series date appears to agree quite well with the EU model average ESR date of 81,000 yr. However, Stringer *et al.* now argue that the travertine "may have continued to be deposited in this site *after* the burial was emplaced" (my emphasis, Stringer *et al.* 1989:757), because they prefer the LU-model age of 101,000 yr. Unfortunately, no field evidence remains for the interrelations of the travertine and the cave sediments.

EARLY UPTAKE *VS.* LINEAR UPTAKE MODELS

The question of early, linear or even recent radiation uptake in a given site is crucial to understanding TL and ESR age estimates, especially for teeth. Stringer *et al.* (1989:757) claim that "for a given site, LU ages are generally closer to independently determined ages than the minimum possible age defined by EU." This, however, would not seem to be the case for Qafzeh and Skhul, or even for Kebara (Table 3), for the following reason. The environmental radiation dose may have varied, even though "continuous U uptake has occurred until recent times", as postulated by Schwarcz *et al.* (1988). In Qafzeh and Skhul, the uppermost sediments are indurated by secondary carbonates, so that they are like concrete in places. Such cementation, like saturation by groundwater, would damp the external radiation dose (B. Blackwell personal communication), thus imposing a changing radiation dose as a function of site development through time. Moreover, at Qafzeh, some bones and teeth are in cemented sediment, but some are not, which might explain the lack of a gradient in the ESR dates. One might also argue hypothetically that a strictly linear model of environmental radiation uptake is unlikely for any site that has experienced climate change (see also Jelinek 1992). Alternations from glacial to interglacial or pluvial to interpluvial, for example, would have influenced rainfall and groundwater levels, especially in the semi-arid and arid Levant.

TABLE 3. Comparison of ESR (EU) and ESR (LU) Dates of Teeth with Other Methods

Site	Method, material	Age	ESR (EU)	ESR (LU)
Skhul	U-series travertine	79,000 ± 4000	81,000 ± 15,000	101,000 ± 12,000
Qafzeh	TL flint	92,000 ± 5000	96,000 ± 13,000	115,000 ± 15,000
Kebara Bed X	TL flint	61,600 ± 3600	60,400 ± 5900	64,300 ± 5500
Yabrud, 4.6 m	TL flint	195,000 ± 1500	177,000 ± 20,000	231,000 ± 19,000

URANIUM-SERIES DATING OF MOUSTERIAN SITES

Other Mousterian sites have been dated in the 80,000–90,000-yr range by the application of U-series disequilibrium dating of carbonates. For example, Tabun D-type Mousterian industry occurs *ca.* 80,000 yr at open-air sites in the Negev, persisting there until *ca.* 47,000 yr, as dated by U-series data on spring travertines (Schwarcz, Goldberg and Blackwell 1980).

At Naamé on the Lebanese coast, a Middle Paleolithic open-air site with Levallois technology (Tabun C-type) occurs in terrestrial sediments sandwiched between two high stands of sea level, both dated by the U-series method. The underlying marine bed was dated at 93,000 ± 5000 yr, and the overlying marine fossils at 90,000 ± 10,000. See below for more discussion of this site.

These 90,000-yr Mousterian dates are compatible with the TL and ESR(EU) dates for the Mousterian in Qafzeh Cave and with the ESR dates from Skhul. They also agree with some preliminary ESR ages on burned flint from the cave site of Nahr Ibrahim in coastal Lebanon, which contains a Tabun C-type industry, at *ca.* 80,000–92,000 yr (Porat and Schwarcz 1991), reinforcing the dates from Naamé. The dated flints are from basal levels in the Central Gallery at Nahr Ibrahim, and are overlain by Tabun B-type artifacts (L. Copeland, personal communication; Solecki 1975).

The Lebanese U-series dates are also compatible with the ^{14}C and AAR dates on the Tabun D horizon at Tabun. Tabun D-type industries (also called "phase 1 Mousterian" by Jelinek) seem to occur mainly in interior and more arid settings, such as the Negev and Syrian deserts; Yabroud shelter I is an example (Jelinek 1982a; Bar-Yosef 1989). Exceptions are found in Tabun and possibly Hayonim (Jelinek, personal communication), Bezez (Copeland 1983), and perhaps Nahr Ibrahim (north gallery, R. S. Solecki, personal communication). Thus, it is difficult to generalize the relative-age relations of Tabun B-, C- and D-type industries. Their mutual stratigraphic relations are well documented only at the type site of Tabun. Thus, one cannot discount the possibility that Tabun C-type industries were contemporaneous with Tabun D-type assemblages elsewhere.

RELATIONS WITH SEA LEVELS OF ISOTOPE STAGE 5

Israel

The last period of worldwide sea levels as high as, or higher than, those of postglacial (Holocene) time was isotope stage 5, between *ca.* 130,000 and 88,000 yr (Edwards *et al.* 1987; Shackleton 1987). These high sea levels left their mark on the coastal plain of Israel as coast-parallel eolianite *kurkar* ridges, the highest of which follows the modern coastal highway and exposes a complex stratigraphy of reddish brown paleosols (*hamra*) intercalated between eolianite strata (Farrand and Ronen 1974). Of the two more-or-less continuous paleosols, the lower one has yielded a good number of Mousterian artifacts, and the upper one has an Epipaleolithic association (Ronen 1977). Apparently, this prominent *kurkar* ridge is a product of the last interglacial (isotope stage 5) and subsequent sea-level fluctuations. Some shelly material, presumably deposited by wave action, is exposed in the core of this ridge. This should be a beach of isotope stage 5, based on its sharp geomorphic preservation, internal stratigraphy and overlying artifacts. Its age has been estimated both by a U-series date on the beachrock (80,000 yr; Brunnacker, Ronen and Tillmans 1982) and an AAR result on the shells (130,000 ± 10,000 yr; Masters, discussion in Farrand 1982).

The beachrock core of this large *kurkar* ridge was previously correlated with isotope substage 5e (Farrand and Ronen 1974; Farrand 1979), but the absolute ages are not definitive. Perhaps it should be placed in substage 5c, *ca.* 112,000 yr, which is also within the 2 σ range of the AAR date. The overlying *hamra* paleosol with Mousterian artifacts is separated from the beach core by some 5–10 m of dune sand. Thus, the Mousterian (Tabun C-type) industry in the paleosol is younger than 120,000 yr, and probably younger than 110,000 yr, by an indeterminate amount. It is not known from the sporadic occurrence of the artifacts whether they were dropped on the top of the dune sand before, during, or after the red soil formed (but before the soil was buried by the next layer of dune sand). Nevertheless, given the thickness of intervening dune sand, the Mousterian in the *hamra* should be somewhat younger than the ESR dates of 107,000–119,000 yr for Layer C in Tabun (Table 2), but it could be compatible with the ESR(EU) date for Layer B (86,000 yr).

Naamé, Lebanon

The Mousterian of the *hamra* paleosol in Israel could be contemporaneous with the Mousterian of Naamé on the Lebanese coast. The lower sea level at Naamé is marked by deposits with *Strombus bubonius* shells, dated by the U-series method at 90,000 ± 20,000 and 93,000 ± 5000 yr, and the overlying vermetid platform is dated at 90,000 ± 10,000 yr (Leroi-Gourhan 1980). The *Strombus* shoreline is presumably Sanlaville's (1981) Enfean II level, and the vermetid shoreline would be Sanlaville's Naamean, normally correlated with isotope stages 5c and 5a, respectively.

The age and correlation of the Naamé deposits are problematic for several reasons. First, U-series dates on mollusks are questionable, and likely to be "significantly younger" than independently determined ages, on corals, for example, Stearns (1984). Second, *Strombus*-bearing shoreline deposits appear to be restricted to stage 5e around the (western) Mediterranean (Hearty 1986), whereas the Naamé *Strombus* level is correlated with stage 5c. *Strombus* occurs only as "apparently reworked 'beach pebbles'" in deposits younger than those of stage 5e, according to Hearty (1986), but the Naamé *Strombus* level is very rich in warm-water species (Sanlaville 1981). However, Hearty's data are restricted to Mediterranean localities west of the "heel" of Italy, except for one sample from an undated site on the west end of Crete. The possibility that the warm *Strombus* fauna persisted until stage 5c in a refuge in eastern Mediterranean waters cannot be precluded without additional data from Levantine shores, especially because Mediterranean waters east of Crete are *ca.* 3–4°C warmer than those of the western Mediterranean (Farrand 1981). Finally, the two shoreline deposits at Naamé are possibly two minor oscillations of sea level within a single isotope substage, such as 5e or 5c. It seems unlikely, however, that the Naamé *Strombus* could be as young as substage 5a, in view of Hearty's (1986) distributional data from the western Mediterranean.

These sea-level stands have been dated elsewhere in the world at *ca.* 112,000 yr (isotope stage 5c) and 88,000 yr (isotope stage 5a), respectively, by recently refined U-series methods (Edwards *et al.* 1987). Thus, the enclosed Middle Paleolithic beds at Naamé appear to lie in the 90,000 to 115,000-yr range. They are intercalated in marine deposits that must date to some part of isotope stage 5 (130,000–88,000 yr). The Naamé Mousterian is probably situated in isotope substage 5b or 5c. Another site that suggests an association of Levantine Mousterian with interglacial high sea levels is the cave of Ras el Kelb, north of Beirut in Lebanon. A type-C Mousterian industry is interstratified with beach deposits *ca.* 6 m above sea level and is ^{14}C dated to >52,000 yr (Garrod and Henri-Martin 1961).

Bezez Cave and Abri Zumoffen, Lebanon

A modest-sized cave, la Grotte de Bezez, is situated on a former coastal headland, just 800 m from the present Mediterranean coast. The stratigraphy and setting of Bezez Cave is rather similar to that of Tabun, except that Bezez was actually flooded by the sea, which deposited the earliest sediments there. The top of the beach deposit inside the cave is *ca.* 15 m above sea level. The overlying cave sediments enclose an Acheuleo-Yabroudian facies of the Mugharan tradition, in turn, overlain by sterile sediments, then a Tabun type-D Levantine Mousterian industry (Kirkbride 1983).

Less than 100 m north of the cave is a small cave and rockshelter, Abri Zumoffen, which may have been a work station or specialized functional area contemporary with the primary occupation in the cave. On the terrace of the rockshelter, excavations exposed sand and cobble beach deposits and intervening terrestrial sediments and weathered horizons (Copeland 1983). These intercalated sediments lie 12–13 m asl; thus, they are lower and presumably younger than the beach in Bezez Cave. There is some question whether the upper and lower beach deposits in front of Abri Zumoffen represent two separate high stands of sea level or two pulses of a single high stand. Sanlaville (personal communication to Copeland 1983) favors the latter interpretation. Current opinion is that the 12–13 m beach(es) developed during the Enfean stage, and that the 15-m beach (Bezez Cave) dates to a pre-Enfean stage, thus dating to isotope stages 5c and 5e, respectively (Copeland, personal communication). The younger Naamean stage shoreline (isotope stage 5a) is not recognized locally, but it occurs at 10.5 m asl at Naamé, just 30 km to the north.

There appears to be good evidence of human occupation of the Zumoffen terrace and abri contemporary with the 12–13 m shoreline. Unabraded artifacts occur throughout and above the beach sediments, as well as in the intercalated terrestrial sediments. All the artifacts here are classified as either Amudian or "Beach Industry", a variant of the Amudian tradition that was found consistently among the beach deposits during the excavations (Copeland 1983). Copeland believes that this Amudian industry is very similar to the Amudian facies in Tabun and to the "pre-Aurignacian" of Beds 13 and 15 in Yabroud Rockshelter I. The Amudian at Adlun lies in a similar stratigraphic position to that of the Amudian at Tabun and Yabroud in that it is underlain and overlain by artifacts of the Yabroudian facies (Jelinek 1990a).

At Adlun, the Amudian occurs after the +15 m (stage 7) shoreline, and is contemporary with the +12–13 m (stage 5e or 5c) sea level. At nearby Naamé, the Mousterian appears on or above the stage 5e or 5c beach and below the +10 m (stage 5a) sea level. Thus, the Amudian can be dated roughly between 160,000 and 120,000 yr along the coast of Lebanon. At Yabroud, the Amudian occurs 1.0–1.5 m above a horizon loosely dated between 177,000 and 195,000 yr (see next section), so that an age *ca.* 140,000 to 150,000 yr is not unreasonable. Thus, the ESR(EU) date of 154,000 ± 34,000 yr reported for the Amudian facies in Tabun, in Garrod's Layer Ea (or the lower part of Jelinek's Unit XI) agrees with the Lebanese and Syrian sites.

Comparisons with Other Pre-Mousterian ("Mugharan") Sites

Another way of analyzing the ESR dates for the Tabun succession is to look at other sites where the pre-Mousterian assemblages of Tabun have been dated. These assemblages, considered still to be Middle Paleolithic in their general level of technology, have been known variously as Yabroudian, Amudian (or "Pre-Aurignacian") and Acheuleo-Yabroudian. At Tabun and other sites, they appear to be interstratified in various arrangements and are likely to represent local variants or functional specializations within a broader Middle Paleolithic technology. Thus, Jelinek (1982a,b) has grouped them together in the Mugharan tradition that comprises Yabroudian, Amudian and Acheulean facies. The Mugharan tradition appears to span a long time, on the basis of both thickness of sedimentary sequences and absolute age assessments. At Tabun, it comprises all of Layer E, some 4 m thick and spanning 30,000 to 40,000 yr, if the ESR dates are correct.

At Yabroud Rockshelter I, the Yabroudian type site 70 km north of Damascus, Syria, the Mugharan industries span a vertical thickness of 8 m, overlain by another 2 m of assorted Mousterian assemblages (Rust 1950; Farrand 1970). Some preliminary ESR and TL dates on burned flint and horse teeth are now available for a single level, 4.6 m below datum, probably Kulturschicht 18 of Rust (1950), as follows:

Flint ESR	103,000–152,000 ± 15,000–20,000	Average of 2 flints
Flint TL	195,000 ± 15,000	Average of 6 flints
Teeth ESR(EU)	177,000 ± 20,000	9 runs on 3 horse teeth
Teeth ESR(LU)	231,000 ± 19,000	9 runs on 3 horse teeth

The TL-flint determinations were made by J. Huxtable, Oxford University, and all the others by N. Porat, in H. P. Schwarcz's laboratory at McMaster University (Porat and Schwarcz 1991 and unpublished). There is a great deal of scatter. Porat (personal communication) is not satisfied with her flint results, which are much younger than the others. Thus, if the youngest and oldest dates are excluded, the age range for the middle of the Mugharan sequence at Yabroud is somewhere *ca.* 177,000–195,000 yr. Because all these dates are on the same horizon, we cannot yet calculate a rate of sediment accumulation for Yabroud.

In Zuttiyeh Cave, eastern Galilee, Israel, the Yabroudian sequence, dated by U-series analyses of travertines (Schwarcz, Goldberg and Blackwell 1980), begins *ca.* 148,000 (or 164,000) yr and lasts until *ca.* 95,000 yr, some 50,000 or 70,000 yr, after which time it is succeeded by a Mousterian assemblage.

At El-Kowm in northeastern Syria, a number of spring-mound travertines enclosing Mugharan-tradition assemblages have been dated by the U-series and ESR methods (Hennig and Hours 1982). The U-series dates place the Mousterian/Yabroudian transition at *ca.* 80,000 yr, and the Yabroudian extends to >156,000 yr, perhaps to 247,000 yr. Three of the same samples were dated by ESR with mixed results. Two of the three agree with the U-series dates within the broad statistical limits (± 20–25%), but the other is completely disparate. However, these ESR ages are tentative because both the external dose rate and the α-efficiencies were assumed, not actually measured.

CONCLUSIONS

In Table 4, I have correlated the stratigraphic columns for sites discussed in the text by means of radiometric dates and geological arguments, including five alternate positions for Tabun. Previous chronological placement of Tabun, 4th column from left, is essentially that of Farrand (1982) modified by Copeland (1981), antedating the availability of ESR and TL dates. It is based largely on sedimentological and geomorphological arguments, especially sea-level history.

Correlation of certain strata in the sites with sea-level history has been accomplished, in part, by means of the archaeological industries in the sites. It is, of course, dangerous (or at best circular reasoning) to correlate geological stratigraphy on the basis of the archaeological contents. However, it can be helpful as a first approximation, that is, as an "order of magnitude" correlation. For example, the position of the transition from the Mugharan Tradition (of Jelinek 1982a,b) to the Mousterian can be examined. If the ESR(LU) dates for Tabun are accepted at face value, the Mugharan/Mousterian transition differs in age by *ca.* 70,000 yr across the region, that is from *ca.* 180,000 yr at Tabun to *ca.* 110,000 yr at El-Kowm and Zuttiyeh (see also Jelinek 1992). This apparent time span is greater than the total documented durations of the Mugharan and Mousterian traditions, and seems excessive in the general scheme of culture history. I will assume, as a conservative working hypothesis, that such a transition probably differs in age by at most 10,000–20,000 yr (and probably much less), roughly the limit of resolution of the ESR and TL methods, across such a small region as the Levant.

It is clear that the ESR and TL dates for Tabun do not agree well with my previous chronology, but also they disagree seriously with each other. Generally, the ESR(EU) dates agree better with the chronologies proposed here for other sites than the ESR(LU) or TL dates do. This contradicts

TABLE 4. Correlation of Middle Paleolithic Prehistoric Sites

TIME (kyr)	ISOTOPE STAGE (Martinson et al. 1987)	SEA LEVEL & kurkar	TABUN G&B*	AJJ*	TABUN ESR(EU) (Grün et al. 1991)	TABUN ESR(LU) (Grün et al. 1991)	TABUN TL min (Mercier 1992)	TABUN TL max (Mercier 1992)	SKHUL	KEBARA	QAFZEH	NAAME	ADLUN	ZUTTIYEH	YABRUD SHELTER I	EL KOWM
40s	3		B MOUST [≥39c]†							V [>47 c] VI – MOUST [>48 c]	////// **					
50s			C [≥51c]	I						VII [48t] MOUST	IX					
60s			MOUST							X [61t–64eu] MOUST	V MOUST					
70s	4		////// C/D	II–VI					travertine [79u]	XII [60t] MOUST	VI–X MOUST ?? ////// ??					MOUST
80s	5a		D MOUST	VII–IX	B MOUST [86]				B [81eu] MOUST "C"	//////	XI–XIV MOUST	Vermetids [90u]		MOUST		[80u–?]
90s	5b	Naamean	Ea[86aar] MUGHAR AMUD	X					B [101 lu] MOUST "C"	XIV sterile	MOUST XV–XXIV [92u–96eu]			travertine [95–97uJ]		
100s	5c	Hamra w/ MOUST "C"	Eb MUGHAR	XI	C MOUST [102±17] C/D	B MOUST [103±16]					bedrock	MOUST "C"				MOUST "D" [104]
110s	5d		Ec ??		C/D				B [119t] MOUST "C"				Bezez MOUST "D"			
120s	5e	Enfean II Carmel beachrock [aar]	Ed MUGHAR F ACH ??	XIII ??	D MOUST [122±20]	C MOUST [119±11]						Strombus [93u–?]	YABRUD 12 m beach	YABRUD	1–10 MOUST "D"	YABRUD
130s	6		//////			C/D ??	C MOUST [134]	I								
140s			//////		C/D ??									[148uJ]		
150s			//////		Ea [154±34] MUGHAR AMUD									YABRUD		[156u–160u] YABRUD
160s			//////		Eb [151±21] MUGHAR	D MOUST [166±20]							AMUD	[164uJ]	13 & 15 (?) AMUD	
170s			//////		Ec [176±10]										18 YABRUD [177eu]	HUMMAL
180s			//////		Ed [182±61] MUGHAR	Ea [188±31] MUGHAR AMUD		C MOUST [184]							↑ or ↓	
190s		Enfean 1	G ACH	XIV	F ACH?	Eb [168?] MUGHAR Ec [199±7]	D MOUST [195]	II					ACH-YAB		18 YAB [195J]	YABRUD
200–219	7					Ed [213±46] MUGHAR	Ea [202] MUGHAR	X					15 m beach			
220–239							Ea [229] AMUD	XI								
260–279	8						Eb [273] MUGHAR	D [263] MOUST II								
280–299							D [297] MOUST Ea [296]	IX								
>300	9						Ed [331] MUGHAR	Eb [350] Ed [331] XII XIII								

*Stratigraphic units in Tabun: G&B = Garrod and Bate (1937); AJJ = Jelinek (1982a,b)

**Major hiatuses

†Radiometric ages [...] in kyr: c = ^{14}C, t = TL, eu = ESR(EU), lu = ESR(LU), aar = AAR, u = uranium series

Prehistoric industries in caps: MOUSTerian, MUGHARan, AMUDian, YABRUDian, ACHeulean, HUMMALian the preferences of the dating experts for the ESR(LU) model. I have offered an explanation for this based on diagenetic cementation of the enclosing sediments early in burial history that strongly reduces the radiation dose later on. This appears to be the case at Qafzeh and Yabroud, where the ESR(EU) dates agree well with the TL dates for the same strata, and at Skhul where the agreement is good with a uranium-series date on travertine. In Kebara cave, the ESR(EU) date also agrees slightly better with TL dates, although no cementation is involved in this case, and for this reason, it is perhaps significant that the EU and LU estimates are not statistically different.

For Tabun, I have suggested that the average sedimentation rates are unusually low in comparison with rates calculated for similar sites in the region (Fig. 1), although suspected periods of non-deposition within the Tabun sequence obviate the calculation of a meaningful sedimentation rate. These comparisons also point to uncertainties in the ESR and TL dates, although more closely spaced dates from better-controlled stratigraphic positions are needed to confirm this conclusion.

Returning to the correlation with sea-level events, Mousterian artifacts have been found close to Tabun in an interdunal paleosol that must date to isotope stage 5d or 5b, probably the latter (*i.e.*, 90,000–100,000 yr). In this revision, the prominent hiatus between Tabun C and D is correlated with a low sea-level episode within stage 5, either 5d or 5b. At Naamé, a Mousterian site is intercalated between shoreline deposits of isotope stages 5c and 5a, dated *ca.* 90,000 yr, and at Ras el Kelb the Mousterian is associated with isotope stage 5 beach deposits of unknown substage. Therefore, an ESR(LU) date for the Tabun Layer D Mousterian of 166,000 yr seems too old by some 70,000 yr, and the TL dates for Tabun D are even older.

A Mugharan (Amudian facies) industry appears to be coeval with the beach at Abri Zumoffen, and Acheuleo-Yabroudian artifacts overlie the beach deposits in Bezez Cave nearby. These beach deposits are now suggested to be of isotope stage 7. Although far from the sea, Yabroud Rockshelter I provides some support for these correlations, since the Amudian horizons there fall into isotope stage 6 (*cf.* the Tabun ESR(EU) date), or even late stage 7, if the Yabroud TL date of 195,000 yr proves correct.

These correlations place the latter phases of the Mugharan tradition in the range, 120,000–150,000 yr, whereas the earliest Mousterian artifacts are commonly found in association with shorelines of isotope stage 5, suggesting that the Mugharan-Mousterian transition in the Levant took place toward the end of isotope stage 6.

Another approach to the evaluation of the radiometric dates involves paleoclimatic arguments, which are complex because the faunal and pollen records are not complete or unambiguous. There is no established paleoclimatic sequence for the Near East into which one can fit evidence found in these prehistoric sites, nor are the climatic implications of deep-sea isotope curves clear for this area. Humidity fluctuations were probably much more important than changes of temperature here (Farrand 1981). For these reasons, I have decided not to present paleoclimatic interpretations in this paper; see Tchernov (1988, 1993) and Jelinek (1992) for such discussions.

As for the dating of anatomically modern *Homo sapiens sapiens* relative to Neanderthal populations in the area, it appears that the modern humans at Qafzeh date *ca.* 90,000–95,000 yr, and Skhul might be just a bit younger, 81,000 ± 15,000 yr, although statistically, Skhul could be the same age as Qafzeh. The large discrepancy between the two samples dated from Skhul complicates the comparison, however, and AAR dates from Qafzeh argue for a younger age. The TL and ESR dated Neanderthal burial in Unit XII at Kebara postdates the Qafzeh and Skhul humans by 20,000–40,000 yr, but the Neanderthal "woman" in Tabun Layer C appears the same age as, or slightly older than, Qafzeh and Skhul, if one accepts the ESR(EU) dates. However, the stratigraphic position of the Tabun Neanderthal is questionable, given the nature of Garrod's excavations, and it has been suggested (*e.g.,* Copeland 1992) that it should be assigned to Layer B, which, by ESR(EU) dating, is *ca.* 86,000 yr old.

Therefore, the chronological scheme proposed here suggests a reversal of the traditional interpretation that *H. sapiens sapiens* succeeded Neanderthals in the Levant. However, the first appearance of modern humans is not as precocious as inferred from the ESR(LU) dates of 100,000–120,000 yr preferred by Stringer, Schwarcz and colleagues (Stringer *et al.* 1989; Schwarcz *et al.* 1988; Grün, Stringer and Schwarcz 1991) or the TL dates of 134,000–184,000 yr of Mercier (1992).

The age of the earliest Neanderthals in this region is still an open question, however, because most Mousterian sites have not yielded human remains, and one can no longer equate Mousterian artifacts with Neanderthal physical types. The earliest dated occurrence of Neanderthals is only *ca.* 60,000 yr (in Kebara) or perhaps 100,000 yr, depending on the stratigraphic position one accepts for the Tabun specimen. Judging from these dates, the first Neanderthals did not show up in the Levant until after the local appearance of anatomically modern humans. This scenario cannot be validated until human remains are recovered in Mousterian contexts in other sites, such as Naamé, Yabroud, Adlun and el Kowm, which, as proposed here, may date to *ca.* 100,000–120,000 yr.

Finally, it appears that only the ESR(EU) dates for Tabun provide a chronology that is reasonable and coherent with geological placement and radiometric dates for other Levantine sites; likewise, ESR(EU) dates give the most logical chronologies for Skhul, Qafzeh and Yabroud. ESR(LU) dates tend to be some 20,000–30,000 yr too old, whereas TL dates on burned flint commonly are much older, especially at Tabun, Skhul and Yabroud. Other TL flint dates agree very well with ESR(EU) dates, for example at Qafzeh and Kebara. I suspect that depositional and weathering histories, as well as fluctuating moisture, play important roles, not yet understood, in controlling radiation doses at different sites.

ACKNOWLEDGMENTS

I am particularly grateful to Arthur Jelinek, my colleague and director of excavations at Tabun Cave, who has extensively reviewed previous drafts of this paper. His insight has been very helpful in clarifying certain facts and interpretations presented herein. Jelinek agrees in general, if not in every detail, with the views expressed in this paper and has presented a related critique of the recent TL and ESR dates, stressing archaeological and paleoclimatic issues (Jelinek 1992). Thanks also to H. P. Schwarcz, B. Blackwell, L. Copeland and H. Valladas for helpful reviews.

REFERENCES CITED

Bada, J. L. and P. M. Helfman
   1976   Application of amino acid racemization in paleoanthropology and archaeology. *Union Internationale des Sciences Préhistoriques et Protohistoriques,* IXe Congrès, Nice, Colloque I:39–62.
Bard, E., B. Hamelin, R. G. Fairbanks, A. Zindler, G. Mathieu and M. Arnold
   1990   U/Th and ^{14}C ages of corals from Barbados and their use for calibrating the ^{14}C time scale beyond 9000 years BP. *Nuclear Instruments and Methods in Physics Research* B52:461–468.
Bar-Yosef, O.
   1989   Upper Pleistocene cultural stratigraphy in southwest Asia. In *Patterns and Processes in Later Pleistocene Human Emergence,* edited by E. Trinkaus, pp. 154–179. Cambridge University Press, Cambridge.
Bar-Yosef, O. and B. Vandermeersch
   1981   Notes concerning the possible age of the Mousterian layers in Qafzeh Cave. In *Préhistoire du Levant,* edited by J. Cauvin and P. Sanlaville, pp. 281–286. Maison de l'Orient, CNRS, Lyon.
Bien, G. S. and L. J. Gandolfi
   1972   La Jolla natural ^{14}C measurements VI. *Radiocarbon* 14(2):368–379.

Brooks, A. S., J. E. Kokis and P. E. Hare
1992   Dating the origin of modern humans. Paper presented at First Paleoanthropology Society meeting, Pittsburgh.
Brunnacker, K., A. Ronen and W. Tillmans
1982   Die jungpleistozänen Äolianite in der südlichen Küstenzone von Israel. *Eiszeitalter und Gegenwart* 32:23–48.
Copeland, L.
1981   Chronology and distribution of the Middle Paleolithic, as known in 1980, in Lebanon and Syria. In *Préhistoire du Levant*, pp. 239–263. Colloque Internationaux du Centre National de la Recherche Scientifique 598, Paris.
1983   The Levalloiso-Mousterian of Bezez Cave. In *Adlun in the Stone Age,* edited by D. A. Roe, pp. 261–327. BAR International Series 159, British Archaeological Reports, Oxford.
1992   Report on the Royal Society discussion meeting, February 1992: The origin of modern humans and the impact of science-based dating. *Paléorient* 18:142–145.
Edwards, R. L., J. H. Chen, T-L. Ku and G. J. Wasserburg
1987   Precise timing of the last interglacial period from the mass spectrometric determination of thorium-230 in corals. *Science* 236:1547–1553.
Farrand, W. R.
1970   Geology, climate and chronology of Yabrud rockshelter I. *Fundamenta. Monographien zur Urgeschichte*, Reihe A. 2:212–233.
1979   Chronology and palaeoenvironment of Levantine prehistoric sites as seen from sediment studies. *Journal of Archaeological Science* 6:369–392.
1981   Pluvial climates and frost action during the last glacial cycle in the eastern Mediterranean: evidence from archaeological sites. In *Quaternary Paleoclimate*, edited by W. C. Mahaney, pp. 393–410. GeoAbstracts Ltd., Norwich, England.
1982   Environmental conditions during the Lower/Middle Paleolithic transition in the Near East and the Balkans. In *The Transition from Lower to Middle Paleolithic and the Origin of Modern Man*, edited by A. Ronen, pp. 105–112. BAR International Series 151, British Archaeological Reports, Oxford.
1993   Discontinuity in the stratigraphic record: Snapshots from Franchthi Cave. In *Formation Processes and the Archaeological Record*, edited by P. Goldberg, D. Nash and M. D. Petraglia, pp. 85–96. Prehistory Press, Madison.
Farrand, W. R. and A. Ronen
1974   Observations on the kurkar-hamra succession on the Carmel coastal plain. *Tel Aviv* 1:45–54.
Garrod, D. A. E. and D. M. A. Bate
1937   *The Stone Age of Mount Carmel.* Clarendon Press, Oxford, 240 pp.
Garrod, D. A. E. and G. Henri-Martin
1961   Rapport préliminaire sur la fouille d'une grotte à Ras el Kelb, Liban, 1959. *Bulletin du Musée de Beyrouth* 16:61–67.
Goldberg, P.
1980   Micromorphology in archaeology and prehistory. *Paléorient* 6:159–164.
Goldberg, P. S.
1973   Sedimentology, Stratigraphy and Paleoclimatology of Tabun, Mt. Carmel, Israel. Ph.D. Dissertation, Department of Geological Sciences, University of Michigan, Ann Arbor.
Goldberg, P. and H. Laville
1988   Le contexte stratigraphique des occupations paléolithiques de la grotte de Kebara (Israël). *Paléorient* 14:117–122.
Grün, R., C. B. Stringer and H. P. Schwarcz
1991   ESR dating of teeth from Garrod's Tabun cave collection. *Journal of Human Evolution* 20:231–248.
Grün, R., H. P. Schwarcz, and S. Zymela
1987   Electron spin resonance dating of tooth enamel. *Canadian Journal of Earth Sciences* 24:1022–1037.
Hearty, P. J.
1986   An inventory of Last Interglacial (*sensu lato*) age deposits from the Mediterranean basin. *Zeitschrift für Geomorphologie, N. F., Supplement-Band* 62:51–69.
Hennig, G. J. and F. Hours
1982   Dates pour le passage entre l'Acheuléen et le paléolithique moyen à el Kowm (Syrie). *Páleorient* 8:81–83.
Jacobsen, T. W. and W. R. Farrand
1987   *Franchthi Cave and Paralia. Maps, Plans, and Sections.* Indiana University Press, Bloomington.
Jelinek, A. J.
1982a   The Middle Paleolithic in the southern Levant, with comments on the appearance of modern *Homo sapiens*. In *The Transition from Lower to Middle Paleolithic and the Origin of Modern Man*, edited by A. Ronen, pp. 57–104. BAR International Series 151, British Archaeological Reports, Oxford.

Jelinek, A. J.
    1982b   The Tabun Cave and Paleolithic man in the Levant. *Science* 216:1369–1375.
    1990   The Amudian in the context of the Mugharan tradition at the Tabun Cave (Mount Carmel), Israel. In *The Emergence of Modern Humans*, edited by P. Mellars, pp. 81–90. Edinburgh University Press, Edinburgh.
    1992   Problems in the chronology of the Middle Paleolithic and the first appearance of early modern *Homo sapiens* in southwest Asia. In *The Evolution and Dispersal of Modern Humans in Asia*, edited by T. Akazawa, K. Aoki and T. Kimura, pp. 253–276. Tokyo University Press, Tokyo.
Jelinek, A. J., W. R. Farrand, G. Haas, A. Horowitz and P. Goldberg
    1973   New excavations at the Tabun Cave, Mount Carmel, Israel, 1967–1972: A preliminary report. *Paléorient* 1:151–183.
Kirkbride, D.
    1983   The soundings at the Mugharet el-Bezez. In *Adlun in the Stone Age,* edited by D. Roe, pp. 23–61. BAR International Series 159, British Archaeological Reports, Oxford.
Leroi-Gourhan, A.
    1980   Les analyses polliniques au Moyen-Orient. *Paléorient* 6:79–91.
Martinson, D. G., N. G. Pisias, J. D. Hays, J. Imbrie, T. C. Moore, Jr. and N. J. Shackleton
    1987   Age dating and the orbital theory of the Ice Ages: Development of a high-resolution 0 to 300,000-year chronostratigraphy. *Quaternary Research* 27:1–29.
Masters, P. M.
    1982   An amino acid racemization chronology for Tabun. In *The Transition from Lower to Middle Paleolithic and the Origin of Modern Man,* edited by A. Ronen, pp. 43–56. BAR International Series 151, British Archaeological Reports, Oxford.
Meignen, L. and O. Bar-Yosef
    1988   Kebara et le paléolithique moyen du Mont Carmel (Israël). *Paléorient* 14:123–130.
Mellars, P. (editor)
    1990   *The Emergence of Modern Humans: An Archaeological Perspective.* Edinburgh University Press, Edinburgh.
Mercier, N.
    1992   Apport des Méthodes Radionucléaires de Datation à l'Etude du Peuplement de l'Europe et du Proche-Orient au Cours du Pléistocène Moyen et Supérieur. Ph.D. Dissertation, Université de Bordeaux I, France.
Mercier, N. and H. Valladas
    1994   Thermoluminescence dates for the Paleolithic Levant. This volume.
Otte, M. (editor)
    1988   *L'Homme de Néandertal,* Vol. 2, *L'Environnement.* Université de Liège, Liège.
Porat, N. and H. P. Schwarcz
    1991   Use of signal subtraction methods in ESR dating of burned flint. *Nuclear Tracks and Radiation Measurements* 18:203–212.
Ronen, A.
    1977   Mousterian sites in red loam in the coastal plain of Mount Carmel. *Eretz Israel* 13:183–190.
Rust, A.
    1950   *Die Höhlenfunde von Jabrud (Syrien).* K. Wachholtz, Neumunster.
Sanlaville, P.
    1981   Stratigraphie et chronologie du Quaternaire marin du Levant. In *Préhistoire du Levant,* pp. 21–31. Colloques Internationaux du Centre National de la Recherche Scientifique 598, Paris.
Schwarcz, H. P., W. M. Buhay, R. Grün, H. Valladas, E. Tchernov, O. Bar-Yosef and B. Vandermeersch
    1989   ESR dating of the Neanderthal site, Kebara Cave, Israel. *Journal of Archaeological Science* 16:653–659.
Schwarcz, H. P., P. Goldberg and B. Blackwell
    1980   U-series dating of archaeological sites in Israel. *Israel Journal of Earth Sciences* 29:157–165.
Schwarcz, H. P., R. Grün, B. Vandermeersch, O. Bar-Yosef, H. Valladas and E. Tchernov
    1988   ESR dates for the hominid burial site of Qafzeh in Israel. *Journal of Human Evolution* 17:733–737.
Shackleton, N. J.
    1987   Oxygen isotopes, ice volume and sea level. *Quaternary Science Reviews* 6:183–190.
Solecki, R. S.
    1975   The Middle Paleolithic site of Nahr Ibrahim (Asfourieh Cave) in Lebanon. In *Problems in Prehistory,* edited by F. Wendorf and A. E. Marks, pp. 283–295.
Stearns, C. E.
    1984   U-series dating and the history of sea level. In *Quaternary Dating Methods,* edited by W. C. Mahaney, pp. 53–66. Elsevier Science Publications, Amsterdam.

Stringer, C. B., R. Grün, H. P. Schwarcz and P. Goldberg
    1989   ESR dates for the hominid burial site of Es Skhul in Israel. *Nature* 338:756–758.
Tchernov, E.
    1988   Biochronology of the Middle Paleolithic and dispersal events of hominids in the Levant. In *L'Homme de Néanderthal*, Vol. 2, *L'Environnement*, edited by M. Otte, pp. 153–168. Université de Liège, Liège.
Trinkaus, E. (editor)
    1989   *The Emergence of Modern Humans: Biocultural Adaptations in the Later Pleistocene.* Cambridge University Press, Cambridge.
Valladas, H., J. L. Joron, G. Valladas, B. Arensburg, O. Bar-Yosef, A. Belfer-Cohen, P. Goldberg, H. Laville, L. Meignen, Y. Rak, E. Tchernov, A. M. Tillier and B. Vandermeersch
    1987   Thermoluminescence dates for the Neanderthal burial site in Israel. *Nature* 330:159–160.
Valladas, H., J. L. Reyss, J. L. Joron, G. Valladas, O. Bar-Yosef and B. Vandermeersch
    1988   Thermoluminescence dating of Mousterian "Proto-Cro-Magnon" remains from Israel and the origin of modern man. *Nature* 331:614–616.
Vandermeersch, B.
    1981   *Les Hommes Fossiles de Qafzeh (Israël).* Centre National de la Recherche Scientifique, Paris.
Vandermeersch, B. and O. Bar-Yosef
    1988   Evolution biologique et culturelle des populations du Levant au paléolithique moyen—les données récentes de Kebara et Qafzeh (Israël). *Paléorient* 14:115–117.
Vogel, J. C. and H. T. Waterbolk
    1963   Groningen ^{14}C dates IV. *Radiocarbon* 5:163–202.

EASTERN MEDITERRANEAN CHRONOLOGIES: THE OXFORD AMS CONTRIBUTION

RUPERT A. HOUSLEY

Radiocarbon Accelerator Unit, Research Laboratory for Archaeology and the History of Art
Oxford University, 6 Keble Road, Oxford OX1 3QJ, England

INTRODUCTION

From its inception in the early 1980s, the Oxford Radiocarbon Accelerator Unit has had a strong interest in chronological problems in the Near East, and has dated *ca.* 275 samples from the region. Many results have been published in site reports, articles or reviews, and *Archaeometry* date lists; a previous compendium was made by Gowlett and Hedges (1987). For this volume, I have compiled a compendium of many of the Oxford AMS dates to make available a single source of results measured between 1983 and 1993. Comments that accompany the dates mostly represent the thoughts of either the excavator or the submitter of the samples at the time of first publication; unattributed comments were written by the Laboratory, and when further results have altered opinions, these have been included. I have tried to keep sites from a particular area and period together, reporting in chronologically descending order, generally from west to east.

All determinations are in radiocarbon years BP (Before Present, present being AD 1950) using the radiocarbon half-life of 5568 years. We account for isotopic fractionation by either measuring the $\delta^{13}C$ value and normalizing to $-25\%o$, or by using an assumed value (for charcoal $-25\%o$; for bone $-21\%o$ relative to PDB) when no measured value was available. Chemical pretreatment methods depend mostly on when the sample was analyzed and the material of the sample. In the early years of the Laboratory, we generally followed the methods of Gillespie *et al.* (1986); later methods are summarized in Hedges *et al.* (1989, and references therein). Samples with numbers less than OxA-2096 were measured on the iron-graphite system, whereas -2096 and above were analyzed using the CO_2 gas ion source (Bronk and Hedges 1989; Hedges *et al.* 1992). Errors are quoted to one standard deviation and are based on an assessment of all the contributions to the error in the laboratory isotope ratio measurement. $\delta^{13}C$ values are not reported here; they may be found in *Archaeometry* date lists where ^{14}C dates are reported. Descriptions of sample retrieval and preparation, context and comments have been greatly abbreviated by the editors to fit space constraints. Readers are referred to *Archaeometry* date lists and references herein for further details.

Of increasing concern to ^{14}C dates is the problem of dating uncharred bone samples with low collagen content. Most dated samples are charcoal, charred seeds or burned bone, where low protein is not problematic. However, the low collagen content of uncharred bone has prevented dating of these samples, and, even when small amounts survive, diagenetic changes can cause problems through the introduction of carbon of a different age (Hedges and Law 1989). Several dates listed here are on uncharred bone; thus, some may be contaminated. Caution should be used in accepting such measurements, unless either the collagen content was high (in which case, the dates are almost invariably recent or subrecent), or there are corroborating data. For a concise overview of sample treatment, see Hedges (1992) and Hedges and van Klinken (1992).

Late Quaternary Chronology and Paleoclimates of the Eastern Mediterranean
Edited by O. Bar-Yosef and R. S. Kra. RADIOCARBON 1994, pp. 55–73

EGYPT: MIDDLE PALEOLITHIC

Charcoal from Nazlet Safaha-1 and Taramsa-1, from eolian sands filling Late Middle Paleolithic chert extraction pit with cobbles from Middle Pleistocene Nile terrace, 7m above Nile floodplain. NS-1 is near village Nazlet Safaha Garb on W bank of Nile, *ca.* 8km downstream of Dandara temple, near Qena, Upper Egypt (26°7′N, 32°29′E). T-1 is S of Dandara temple (26°5′N, 32°41′E) (Vermeersch *et al.* 1986).

OxA-1901. NS-1 ME88/35/51   6680 ± 80
OxA-2601. NS-1 ME88/33/93   37,200 ± 1300
OxA-2602. T-1 ME89/40/7   38,100 ± 1400
Comment (P.M.V.): OxA-1901 is aberrant. Vegetation and/or soil fauna of Early and Middle Holocene was probably responsible for introducing organic matter into sands surrounding Late Middle Paleolithic artifacts. Date indicates that at 6680 BP plants grew on higher ground than floodplain, and "charcoal" must have been natural wood from Holocene wet period. This concurs with other data (Paulissen and Vermeersch 1987). Dates for OxA-2601, -2602 and chert-knapping technology indicate that mine could have been operating over a long period. These dates are among oldest for chert extraction during Paleolithic. Infinite age was expected, especially for Taramsa date, but, as other dates do not exist for area, we refer to other such sites in Egyptian Sahara, where Wendorf *et al.* (1994) obtained OSL dates of *ca.* 100,000 yr. These dates appear older, but OSL dates on adjacent sand from same context confirm AMS measurements.

EGYPT: LATE PALEOLITHIC

A common problem on sites where early domestication is suspected is that plant or animal remains may be intrusive. Wadi Kubbaniya, S Egypt, provides good example.

OxA-101. Acid, alkali-insoluble matter   350 ± 200
OxA-102. Humic acids   101.5 ± 2.5 pMC
OxA-103. Charcoal   17,150 ± 300
Comment (Lab): OxA-101 and -102 are based on single datestone from 1983 excavations; charcoal date agrees with other conventional dates from site.

Charred plant remains from Early Neolithic (EN) site E-75-6, Nabta Playa, near Egypt-Sudan border (22° 32′N, 30°42′E), 100km W of Abu Simbel. Earlier horizon dated to 8800–8500 BP, and later to 8100–8000, based on conventional ¹⁴C dates on charcoal. Subm. 1991 by F. Wendorf and A. E. Close.

OxA-3214. Cruciferae, feature 1/90   8080 ± 110
OxA-3215. Leguminosae, feature 1/90   8095 ± 120
OxA-3216. *Sorghum*, feature 1/91   7960 ± 100
OxA-3217. *Sorghum*, feature 1/90   8020 ± 160
OxA-3218. *Zizyphus*, feature 1/90   8050 ± 130
OxA-3219. *Sorghum*, feature 3/90   7950 ± 160
OxA-3220. *Zizyphus*, pit 1/90   8025 ± 120
OxA-3221. *Sorghum*, feature 1/90   7980 ± 110
OxA-3222. *Sorghum*, feature 2/90   8060 ± 120
OxA-3484. *Panicum*-type, feature 2/90   7950 ± 90
OxA-3485. *Zizyphus*, pit BB/10   7980 ± 95
Comment (Lab): 1990–1991 excavations uncovered 4 houses and 12 pits in area 10×15m. Sealed by playa clays, 2 houses were circular and 2 were oval. They contained traces of hearths and cooking holes with burnt, ashy deposit rich in plant remains of wide range of taxa (Wendorf *et al.* 1992) representing natural subdesert or sahelian flora. Sorghum and millet correspond to modern wild varieties indicating economy based on gathering wild edible plants, although initial infra-red spectroscopy of lipids in grains (Wasylikowa *et al.*) suggests cultivation. Dates are consistent, indicating features are contemporary with 2nd period of EN occupation of site. Importance lies in scarcity of direct archaeological evidence for domestication of African plants and assumption that it was late secondary development beginning well after wheat and barley were established in Egypt. Evidence for intensive use of sorgum and millets *ca.* 7000 cal BC suggests process started earlier than previously believed.

EGYPT: PREDYNASTIC AND DYNASTIC

Wood charcoal from Predynastic sites, Halfiah Gibli (HG) and Semanineh H (SH), Hiw, Upper Egypt (26°00′N, 32°22′E).

OxA-2182. HG 1   4590 ± 80
OxA-2183. HG 2   4810 ± 80
OxA-2184. SH 3   4860 ± 80
OxA-2185. SH 4   4020 ± 80
Comment (Lab): 1σ age ranges for HG dates are *ca.* 3500–3110 (OxA-2182) and 3700–3370 cal BC (OxA-2183). For SH, age ranges are *ca.* 3780–3530 (OxA-2184) and 2860–2460 cal BC.
Comment (K. Bard): Cal dates for HG and OxA-2184 from SH are as expected for Nagada II sites. OxA-2185 suggests charcoal came from Old Kingdom decayed mudbrick feature. OxA-2184 from SH is earlier than expected for Nagada III site, and unless one accepts earlier chronology of Haas *et al.* (1987), site should be Nagada II–III, based on potsherds from site.

Dried emmer wheat (*Triticum dicoccum*), subm. 1982 by G. C. Hillman, from burial chamber of King Zoser's pyramid, Saqqara (29°51′N, 31°14′ E).

OxA-147. Non-charred emmer grain   4120 ± 150
Comment (G.C.H.): Control sample subm. to study problems of dating organic remains preserved by desiccation.
Comment (Lab): Mean value, 4120 BP, straddles ma-

jor wiggle in 3rd millennium BC on Belfast curve, *ca.* 2600–2860 to 2450–2900 BC at 1σ. Historically derived date is *ca.* 2900 BC.

Straw from mud brick in temple of Tuthmosis IV (XVIII Dynasty), Thebes (25°43′N, 32°36′E). Sample taken directly from standing wall.

OxA-917. E46   **3150 ± 80**

Comment (R. L. Wilson): Calendric estimate for Tuthmosis IV is 1400–1390 BC. Generally, New Kingdom historically derived dates are accurate within *ca.* 10 yr. Date was run as "blind test"; expected age: *ca.* 3100 BP.

Mudbrick straw from Pylon: Temple of Pbes(?) (XXVI Dynasty), Thebes (25°24′N, 32°24′E).

OxA-1185. E52   **2500 ± 80**

Comment (K. G. Games): Sample dated to explain discrepancy between expected historical age (650–610 BC) and measured strength of ancient magnetic field. Cal age range (2σ = *ca.* 800–400 BC) does not resolve problem. Magnetic results favor date at lower end of range.

Neckcord of Bishop Timotheaus from Qasr Ibrim, given to him in Cairo in AD 1372. He died shortly afterwards. Expected age: *ca.* 600 BP.

OxA-613.   **570 ± 200**

Samples from 1986 excavations at Qasr Ibrim, E bank of Lake Nasser, 40km NE of Abu Simbel, Nubia (Rowley-Conwy 1988).

OxA-1060. *Camelus* mandible   **2470 ± 160**

Comment (P.A. Rowley-Conwy): Dates fragment of camel mandible from Napatan (XXV Dynasty) context, but close to area of later disturbance. Cal range, 920–190 cal BC, (2σ) is wide, but date supports presence of camel in region in 1st millennium BC.

OxA-1061. Dessicated camel dung   **2690 ± 90**

Comment (P.A.R.-C.): Pellets of dung from Napatan levels. Cal range, 1040–770 BC (2σ), places this evidence for camel in early 1st millennium BC, consistent with Napatan context.

General Comment: OxA-1060, -1061 are earliest evidence for camel in Nile Valley otherwise put in Ptolemaic period (last 3 centuries BC); thus, introduction was earlier.

OxA-1062. Barley straw (*Hordeum* sp.)   **2800 ± 80**

Comment (P.A.R.-C.): Straw used as temper in mudbrick for constructing S Girdle Wall. Date agrees with early Napatan, and indicates that Qasr Ibrim may not have been occupied before this period.

OxA-1023. Grains of Sorghum bicolor   **1520 ± 50**

Comment (P.A.R.-C.): These grains are morphologically between primitive bicolor-type (present at Qasr Ibrim from *ca.* AD 100) and advanced durra-type (from later contexts). Sample came from "bouquet" of *ca.* 200 heads of sorghum in pit dated archaeo-

logically to either X horizon (*ca.* AD 300–500) or Classic Christian II (*ca.* AD 1000–1200). Date is compatible with X horizon and suggests that some elements of durra developed in or were brought into Nubia during this period. Date of origin and spread of durra is not known.

Comment (Lab): Because Sorghum metabolizes CO_2 by C_4 pathway, isotopic fractionation must be considered. Thus, measured date, 1440 ± 50 BP, was corrected to 1520 ± 50 BP to allow for assumed $\delta^{13}C$ value of −12.5‰ (van der Merwe 1982).

THE LEVANT: UPPER PALEOLITHIC AND EPIPALEOLITHIC

Charcoal subm. 1987 and 1992 by O. Bar-Yosef from Paleolithic Kebara Cave, Mount Carmel (Bar-Yosef *et al.* 1986; Laville and Goldberg 1989). Lithics from units VII–XII are exclusively Mousterian. Units IV–VI have both Middle and Upper Paleolithic (UP) elements. Top of unit V is disturbed, but shows increased Upper Paleolithic material. TL dates of burnt flints from layer VI (Valladas *et al.* 1987) suggest age of 48,000 ± 4000 for this unit.

OxA-1230. IIF Q16d "Hearth"	**36,000 ± 1600**
OxA-1567. IIIBf Q16d "Hearth"	**35,600 ± 1600**
OxA-1568. V Q16a/b	**38,000 ± 2100**
OxA-2800. Charred bone W23c	**33,550 ± 930**
OxA-2799. Bone V23d	**14,500 ± 250**
OxA-3974. Charcoal R15CI	**34,510 ± 740**
OxA-3975. Charcoal Q16dII top	**33,920 ± 690**
OxA-3976. Charcoal Q18b IIIB	**43,500 ± 2200**
OxA-3977. Charcoal Q15 IIIBf	**>43,800**
OxA-3978. Charcoal Q16d IVB	**28,890 ± 400**
OxA-3979. Charcoal Q14d V	**>44,000**
OxA-3980. Charcoal Q15d V	**>44,800**
OxA-3981. Charcoal Q19a VIII	**>44,800**

Comment: Unpublished dates from other labs suggest that OxA-1230 is accurate estimate for age of unit IIF since 36,100 ± 1100 from IIIB supports it. OxA-1567 and -1568 are probably underestimated because unpublished dates, 42,100 ± 2100 from IIIBf and 42,500 ± 1800, are from top of unit V. Disturbance at end of Mousterian (unit VI), caused by slower sedimentation and biological reworking (Laville and Goldberg 1989), along with sedimentary collapse toward sinkhole(s) (shown in tilting UP units) may have led to intrusion of younger charcoal. OxA-2800 falls within range of expected dates for Unit II. OxA-2799 may have been severely contaminated or is unidentified intrusion from previously removed Kebaran layer.

Charcoal excavated by J. Tixier (1969–1975) from Ksar 'Akil rockshelter, Lebanon (32°58′N, 34°48′E).

OxA-1791. KA 1 layer 3 upper	**23,170 ± 400**
OxA-1792. KA 2 layer 3b major	**22,850 ± 400**

OxA-1793. KA 3B layer 3b lower	22,050 ± 360
OxA-1794. KA 4C layer 3bb	22,480 ± 380
OxA-1795. KA 5 layer 3c	22,850 ± 380
OxA-1796. KA 7A,B,C layer 7bb	21,100 ± 500
OxA-1797. KA 8A layer 8a	26,900 ± 600
OxA-1798. KA 10 layer 8ac	29,300 ± 800
OxA-1803. KA 11 layer 9a	30,250 ± 850
OxA-1804. KA 12A,B layer 10 lower	31,200 ± 1300
OxA-1805. KA 13 layer 11bm	32,400 ± 1100

Comment (P. A. Mellars): As discussed by Mellars and Tixier (1989), series of 11 dates on charcoal from Ksar 'Akil provides internally consistent sequence and agrees well with 2 existing dates, 26,500 ± 900 (MC-1191) and 32,000 ± 1500 (MC-1192) from levels 8a and 12 (Tixier and Inizan 1981). Results confirm that entire UP sequence dates before 20,000 BP, and that top "Aurignacian" levels date from *ca.* 30,000–32,000 BP. Thus, earlier "Aurignacian" and "Transitional" industries recovered from underlying levels (*ca.* 10m deep) must be substantially older. Anomalously young date of OxA-1796 strongly suggests contamination by intrusive material (Mellars and Tixier 1989).

Charred bone from Hayonim Cave, stratum D, W Galilee, Israel (29°55′N, 35°13′E), subm. 1990 by O. Bar-Yosef.

OxA-2801. D/J21a/220–230	27,200 ± 600
OxA-2802. D3/G22a/220–240	28,900 ± 650
OxA-2803. D2/J19cd/190–199	15,700 ± 230
OxA-2804. D/H20b/225–230	21,650 ± 340
OxA-2805. D/J20/180–220	29,980 ± 720
OxA-2806. D3/IJ20/200–205	20,810 ± 320

Comment (O. B.-Y.): Layer D was found only in inner part of cave (15–18 m², *ca.* 0.35–0.40m thick); it contained typical late Levantine Aurignacian industry and accumulated in eroded shallow basin created by solution and dripping in Mousterian deposits. Lower sublayer (D4) yielded 1 hearth and 3 white ash pits; middle (D3) contained small, partially built-up hearth and many animal bones; top unit preserved remains of 2 mixed beds (D1 and 2). Several Natufian burials penetrated into this layer. Lithic industry dominated by flake production, re-use of older pieces and many carinated and nosed scrapers and burins. Of special interest are 2 slabs with fine engravings; 1 seems to depict a horse (Belfer-Cohen and Bar-Yosef 1981; Bar-Yosef and Belfer-Cohen 1988). Some UP elements were recovered under Kebaran horizon, but they may not be related to interior lithic assemblage. Dates reflect problems of dating charred bones and site formation processes. OxA-2803, with Hv-2675 (16,240 ± 640 BP), suggest use of cave by Kebarans *ca.* 15,000-16,000 BP. OxA-2804, -2806 suggest earlier use of this part of cave by producers of indeterminate UP industry observed below Kebaran. OxA-2801,

-2802 and -2805 support idea that Levantine Aurignacian at Hayonim Cave is same age as layers VII–III in Ksar 'Akil (Belfer-Cohen and Bar-Yosef 1981; Bar-Yosef and Belfer-Cohen 1988).

Charcoal from several Terminal Pleistocene sites in W Negev, Israel excavated 1980–1982 and 1988 by A. N. Goring-Morris, who subm. samples 1988, 1989. Sites include: Saflulim (30°31′N, 34°33′E); Nahal Sekher 23 (31°6′N, 34°50′E); Shunera XVII, XXI (30°56′N, 34°31′E); Shluhat Qeren II (30°57′N, 34°24′E); Azariq XIII, XVI (30°57′N, 34°25′E); and Hamifgash IV (31°11′N; 34°35′E).

OxA-2136. Saflulim SF J21c	10,930 ± 130
OxA-2137. N. Sekher 23 hearth	12,200 ± 150
OxA-2138. Shunera XXI/1	12,100 ± 140
OxA-2139. Shunera XVII/1	1320 ± 80
OxA-2140. Shluhat Qeren II/1	6740 ± 100
OxA-2141. Azariq XVI/1	160 ± 80
OxA-2142. Azariq XIII/1	15,160 ± 190
OxA-2143. Hamifgash IV/1	16,230 ± 200
OxA-2869. Saflulim SF/4 k20b	11,150 ± 100

Comment (A.N.G-M.): Azariq XVI (OxA-2141), Shluhat Qeren II (OxA-2140) and Shunera XVII (OxA-2139) are intrusive; parts of these sites were exposed and parts were *in situ* in sand. Hearth/ash dumps from which OxA-2139 and -2141 derived were associated with flint assemblages (Goring-Morris 1987). Association also seems secure at Shluhat Qeren II. Saflulim (OxA-2136), based on other Natufian dates (*e.g.*, SMU-10: 10,880 ± 280 from Rosh Horesha), and Hamifgash IV (OxA-2143), whose lithic industry is similar to upper level at Jilat 6, from Azraq 17 Tr. 1 and perhaps Kharaneh IV phase A, seem acceptable. OxA-2143 is more acceptable than previous date, RT-1056: 5820 ± 120. OxA-2869 agrees well with OxA-2136. Both results are consistent with dates from Late Natufian in Mediterranean and confirm that only 1 of 3 dates from adjacent Rosh Horesha, SMU-10: 10,880 ± 280, is reliable for dating Late Natufian. These dates are important contribution to chronology of Late Natufian in Negev and its relation to Harifian, which appears to begin *ca.* 10,750 BP. OxA-2137 seems more reliable than calcium carbonate date, RT-1073: 8700 ± 200, which may relate to deposition of soil carbonates during more humid PPNB period following abandonment of site. Lithic assemblage at N. Sekher resembles Early Natufian, yet retains features of preceding Ramonian. OxA-2138 is problematic. Based on techno-typology, it should fall into early phase of Ramonian, and predate N. Sekher 23. OxA-2142 is also problematic in that it is just feasible, although earlier date was expected. Previous dates from Azariq include RT-1081: 10,700 ± 230 on charcoal and RT-1105: 22,200 ± 400 on soil carbonate from underlying adjacent paleosol. Lithic assemblage is similar to Azraq 17, Tr. 2, which pre-dates assemblage from Tr. 1: 13,260 ± 200 (OxA-869).

Charcoal from two late UP sites in Lower Jordan Valley: Fazaël IX, with flake assemblage (numerous burins) similar to Ksar 'Akil 6, phase IV; Fazaël X has bladelet assemblage with many finely retouched microliths. Subm. 1990 by A. N. Goring-Morris.

OxA-2870. Fz X/1   **15,450 ± 130**
OxA-2871. Fz IX/1   **17,660 ± 160**

Comment (A.N.G.-M.): Dates are problematic; they agree with indications that flake-based Fazaël IX predates bladelet assemblage of Fazaël X. Yet, both dates are late when compared to analogous late UP assemblages elsewhere in Levant, falling within range usually ascribed to early Epipaleolithic Kebaran complex. Comparison of Fazaël IX sample and AMS dates from similar assemblage at Ksar 'Akil reveals discrepancy of *ca*. 7000–8000 yr. Similarly, Fazaël X can be compared to Ohalo II, where ^{14}C dates (see below) cluster *ca*. 19,000 BP, and discrepancy is *ca*. 3500 yr. Worthy of note are dates from early Kebaran site, Urkan e-Rub IIa (see below), which are also late. If these dates are accepted at face value, it would be difficult to place Late Kebaran before relatively well-dated and stratigraphically secure Geometric Kebaran, usually dated from *ca*. 14,500 BP. Thus, there is a question of regional anomaly in lower Jordan Valley resulting in younger dates for samples from Fazaël area.

Charred wild barley seeds, identified by M. E. Kislev, from Early Kebaran site, Ohalo II, lake-edge settlement by Sea of Galilee, Israel (32°45'N, 35°35'E).

OxA-2564. AB87a   **18,680 ± 180**
OxA-2565. C87d   **19,310 ± 190**
OxA-2566. C87d   **19,110 ± 390**

Comment (D. Nadel): Finds from this waterlogged site include a complete human skeleton and *in-situ* pits. Three samples were *Hordeum spontaneum*. OxA-2564 came from circular arrangement of unworked stones, *ca*. 45cm diameter; OxA-2565, -2566 came from largest excavated pit of site. For details, see Kislev, Nadel and Carmi (1992).

Charcoal from Early Kebaran site, Urkan e-Rub IIa, Lower Jordan Valley (32°05'N, 35°25'E) excavated 1985–1988 by E. Hovers; subm. 1989, 1990.

OxA-1503. URIIa-1   **14,440 ± 150**
OxA-2838. URIIa-5 Area A horizon 1   **15,050 ± 160**
OxA-2837. URIIa-4 Area B horizon 1   **14,650 ± 120**
OxA-2841. URIIa-8 Area B horizon 1   **15,730 ± 130**
OxA-2840. URIIa-7 Tr. I horizon 2   **14,880 ± 120**
OxA-2842. URIIa-9 Tr. I horizon 2   **14,980 ± 200**
OxA-2835. URIIa-2 Tr. I horizon 2   **15,190 ± 130**
OxA-2839. URIIa-6 Tr. I horizon 2   **14,800 ± 130**
OxA-2836. URIIa-3 Area C horizon 2   **14,860 ± 130**

Comment (E.H.): Dates are from 2 archaeological horizons separated by *ca*. 30cm of sterile sediments. Lithic assemblages from both horizons were typologically dated to Early Kebaran (Hovers *et al*. 1988; Hovers and Marder 1991). Yet, all dates suggest Late Kebaran/early Geometric Kebaran. OxA-1503 was rejected at first (Hedges *et al*. 1990) for being too young, but current dates concur. With typological data and ^{14}C dates from other sites in S Levant, these dates suggest that division of Kebaran into distinct early and late phases is untenable (Hovers and Marder 1991). Great lithic variability characterizes entire Kebaran in Levant (19,000–14,500 BP).

Samples from Nahal Oren (32°43'N, 34°59'E), 10km S of Haifa in Wadi Fellah, Israel. For discussion of site, see Noy, Legge and Higgs (1973), and for dates, see Legge (1986). Dates are on single grains; OxA-396 on humic acids (Batten *et al*. 1986).

OxA-395. Charred *Triticum*   **3100 ± 130**
OxA-396. Humics of above   **6650 ± 190**
OxA-390. Charred *Triticum*   **>33,000**
OxA-389. Charred *Triticum*   **2940 ± 120**

Comment (Lab): Dates are both older and younger than Kebaran context. OxA-396 is example of grain yielding older humic fraction because it is in older sediments.

Charred bone from Geometric Kebaran site, Neve David (32°49'N, 34°57'E), at foot of W slope of Mt. Carmel, on N bank of Nahal Siah (alt. 60m asl).

OxA-892. Sq. K21 Spit 13   **12,610 ± 130**
OxA-859.   **13,400 ± 180**

Comment (Lab): We cannot determine which date is more relevant to burial.

Charred human bone from Paleolithic cave site of Kebara, Mt. Carmel, Israel.

OxA-2798. D19R   **12,470 ± 180**

Comment (O. Bar-Yosef): Date is clearly Natufian, which is more appropriate than previous estimates given to these burials by Turville-Petre: Ein Gev I (Kebaran), Neve David (Geometric Kebaran), Nahal Ein Gev I (Late "Aurignacian") and Ohalo II (Late UP or Epipaleolithic, pre-Natufian sequence).

Charred seeds from Wadi Hammeh 27, in foothills of Ajlun Highlands, overlooking Jordan Valley, *ca*. 2km NE of ancient site of Pella (modern village of Tabaqat Fahl) (35°38'N, 32°27'E). Coll. by P. C. Edwards and S. Colledge; id. by S. Colledge and G. C. Hillman.

OxA-393. XX/D+/3/4 (unit b)   **11,920 ± 150**
OxA-394. XX/D/4/1   **12,200 ± 160**
OxA-507. XX/D+/5/1   **11,950 ± 160**

Comment (S.C.): OxA-393 consisted of several spp. of small round seeds (*ca.* 290 in collection), including small legumes (*e.g.*, *Trifolium/Ononis* spp.), small cruciferae and ranunculaceae types; OxA-507 from similar collection (*ca.* 160 seeds). OxA-394 was on charred masses of *Chenopodium* seeds. Samples were from deposits in Natufian "house". OxA-394 directly overlay floor level; -507 is closely correlated; -393 was slightly higher in sequence. All layers represent occupation debris, which contained many worked Natufian flint and stone tools. OxA-393 and -507 were dated from humic component, -394 from carbonaceous residue; dates demonstrate early Natufian occupation at *ca.* 12,000 BP (Edwards 1984; Edwards and Colledge 1985).

Lupinus seeds from Hayonim Cave, W Galilee, Israel (29°55′N, 35°13′E), excavated 1965–1979.

OxA-742. H77 4(9.7)	12,360 ± 160
OxA-743. H76 4(5)	12,010 ± 180

Comment (O. Bar-Yosef and M. Hopf): Samples are from early Natufian dwelling (Loc. 4) (Bar-Yosef and Goren 1973; Sillen 1984). Dates were intended to confirm whether Natufians collected pulses; positive results are among few dates for early Natufian sites (Hopf and Bar-Yosef 1987).

Charred wild barley seeds (OxA-1899 and -1900) and charred bone from late Natufian contexts on terrace in front of Hayonim Cave, W Galilee, Israel (29°55′N, 35°13′E), coll. 1987–1990 by R. Buxo i Capdevila and F. R. Valla (Valla *et al.* 1989; Valla, Le Mort and Plisson 1991).

OxA-1899. N 28-2168	10,000 ± 100
OxA-1900. N 35-1894	6970 ± 80
OxA-2568. Fl. K-L-M/33.34	17,420 ± 170
OxA-2569. Fl. K-L-M/33.34	11,220 ± 110
OxA-2570. House 4	11,820 ± 120
OxA-2571. Fireplace 8	9640 ± 100
OxA-2572. Early layer II	11,460 ± 110
OxA-2573. House 9	10,100 ± 160
OxA-2974. Fire pit 8	16,810 ± 210
OxA-2975. Fill behind house 4	11,790 ± 120
OxA-2976. House 4	14,050 ± 140
OxA-2977. House 4	11,720 ± 120

Comment: (F.R.V.): None of dates are exactly in accepted range for late Natufian, *i.e.*, 11,000–10,250 BP. This may be due to post-depositional disturbance, which is most probable explanation for OxA-1900. OxA-1899, from pit high in Natufian sequence, may be correct and indicate Natufian culture persisted for longer duration in Galilee than in other locations in Near East where climate was drier. All dates from Natufian layers at Hayonim Terrace are problematic. OxA-2569, -2570, -2572, 2975, and -2977, ranging from 11,820 to 11,220 BP, may be approximate for layer, but they are not in correct stratigraphic order.

Also, they do not seem to agree with current views of relative chronology as indicated elsewhere by flint industries, stratigraphies and other ^{14}C dates. Mixtures from cave could explain oldest dates. Associated flint industries do not look mixed. OxA-2976 could fit Geometric Kebaran, but this culture does not exist in cave. Where it does exist on terrace, it is not associated with bones (which probably disintegrated in severe weather before Natufian settlement). Most recent dates may be due to intrusions, as some Late Neolithic remains cap Natufian layer in area.

Bitter vetch from Rakefet Cave, Israel (32°39′N, 35°6′E) (Vita-Finzi and Higgs 1970).

OxA-541. *Vicia ervilia* seed	2760 ± 200

Comment (G. C. Hillman): Kebaran-Natufian association is doubtful, as later pits are in vicinity.

Grain from Natufian site, 'Ain Mallaha (Eynan), Israel (33°10′N, 35°33′E) subm. by A. J. Legge from excavations of J. Perrot (1960). For accounts of lithics and burials on site, see Valla (1985), Perrot and Ladiray (1985) and Solivères-Massei (1985).

OxA-543. *Triticum aestivum*	330 ± 100

Comment: Grain is recent bread wheat (Legge 1986).

JORDAN: UPPER PALEOLITHIC AND EPIPALEOLITHIC

Samples from Azraq Basin (Wadi el Jilat (31°30′N, 36°23′E), Wadi el Uwaynid (31°47′N, 36°43′E) and Azraq esh Shishan (31°49′N, 36°50′E), subm. 1986 by A. N. Garrard (Garrard *et al.* 1985; Garrard, Byrd and Betts 1986). Charcoal and burnt bone from sites in Wadi el Jilat thought to belong to UP and Epipaleolithic periods.

OxA-519. Jilat 9 Sq. 1 Burnt bone	21,150 ± 400

Comment: Sample from UP occupation in weathered paleosol. Since no soil forms here under present arid conditions, date indicates more humid climate with continuous, probably steppic vegetation.

OxA-520. Jilat 10 Sq. 7 Charcoal	14,790 ± 200

Comment: This single-phase Epipaleolithic occupation probably represents short-term camp, as many artifacts were conjoinable and tool kit was restricted; it contained few microliths that bore little resemblance to other Epipaleolithic sites in region. Site was in eolian silts indicating dry conditions.

OxA-521. Jilat 8 Sq. 3 Charcoal	13,310 ± 120
OxA-636. Jilat 8 Sq. 3 Burnt bone	10,540 ± 160

Comment: Site was very deflated and, like site 10 and upper phase of site 6, was in eolian silt accumulation. Industry contains elements of all three phases at Jilat 6; mixing probably occurred with earlier periods of deflation and/or rodent burrowing.

OxA-522. Jilat 6 Sq. 4 Charcoal	11,740 ± 80
OxA-523. Jilat 6 Sq. 2 Burnt bone	11,450 ± 200
OxA-524. Jilat 6 Sq. 4 Charcoal	15,520 ± 200
OxA-525. Jilat 6 Sq. 1 Charcoal	16,010 ± 200

OxA-539. Jilat 6 Sq. 1 Charcoal   7980 ± 150

Comment: Samples came from 2m² sounding cut through peak of 18,000m² Epipaleolithic "tell". Trench was 1.5m deep, but only top 1m yielded occupation deposits, divisible into 3 phases separated by semi-sterile deposits. OxA-524, -525 are from top phase of very dense occupation in eolian deposits indicating dry conditions; 3 floor levels, upper 1 consisting of crushed lime and lower 2 of compacted red pigmented surfaces, with many rodent burrows. Lithic assemblage was distinctive; geometric backed-bladelet assemblage dominated by triangles, some lunates and micro-gravettes. Only close parallel was at Ein Gev IV in Palestine, thought to date from 11,000 to 13,000 BP. *Ca.* 20–30 cm of semi-sterile sediments separate underlying short-term middle phase, indicating wetter climate. Industry was distinctive, characterized by large non-geometric microliths; La Mouillah points prominent. Such material was ¹⁴C-dated in Sinai to 12,500–14,000 BP. OxA-522, -523 are from this phase. Lowest phase is short-term occupation with more humid conditions, separated from overlying horizon by 8–12cm of semi-sterile sediments. Industry was dominated by thin, finely made, curved pointed, arched-backed bladelets. Kebara level C, thought to date ≤14,500 BP, shows close parallel. OxA-539, very small piece of charcoal retrieved by flotation, was only datable sample.

Comment (Lab): A.N.G. believes that late date of OxA-539 may be result of contamination during flotation. Inversion in other dates is unexplained.

OxA-526. Jilat 7 Sq. 6 Charcoal   8810 ± 110
OxA-527. Jilat 7 Sq. 8 Charcoal   8520 ± 110

Comment: Industry of this site is similar to early-to-mid-PPNB of Levant; dates are well within expected range. Three clusters of stone structures and stone circle with internal subdivisions were found at site. Preserved plant remains include wild einkorn, emmer, barley, various small-seeded grasses, legumes, cheno-pods, liliaceae, grains of cultivated hulled barley and cultivated einkorn. Faunal remains were almost identical to those on earlier Jilat sites (mainly gazelle, with ass, hare, fox, wolf and tortoise).

Samples subm. 1986 from same survey as above in Wadi el Uwaynid and Azraq esh Shishan areas of Jordan (Garrard 1992; Garrard *et al.* 1985, 1987; Garrard, Byrd and Betts 1986). Three dates obtained from charcoal excavated from early Epipaleolithic (possible UP) site found eroding from alluvial terrace in Wadi el Uwaynid, Site 18, 10km SW of Azraq. Occupational deposits, 70cm thick, were in eolian silts, overlain by unaltered eolian silts and calcreted fluvial deposits. Soils indicate wetter conditions than at present.

OxA-864. Uwaynid 18 Sq. 5 Dep. 15B   19,800 ± 350

OxA-867. Uwaynid 18 Sq. 9 Dep. 19A   23,200 ± 400
OxA-868. Uwaynid 18 Sq. 1 Dep. 3K   19,500 ± 250

Comment (A.N.G.): OxA-864 is from occupational fill at 10cm depth; early Epipaleolithic flint industry resembled middle phase at Uwaynid 14 (OxA-866) and lower phase at Jilat 6 (OxA-539). OxA-867 is from hearth at 55cm depth in occupational fill. Associated flint industry was sparse and undiagnostic. OxA-868 is from hearth in 2nd trench; industry was similar to that of OxA-864.

Charcoal from Wadi el Uwaynid, Site 14, 120m downstream from Uwaynid 18 in similar context.

OxA-865. Uwaynid 14 Sq. 10 Dep. 15   18,900 ± 250
OxA-866. Uwaynid 14 Sq. 5 Dep. 18   18,400 ± 250

Comment (A.N.G.): Three short periods of early-to-mid-Epipaleolithic were evident here. Flint industry from upper phase of occupation (OxA-865) resembled middle phase of Jilat 6 (OxA-522, -523); industry from middle phase resembled lower phase at Jilat 6 (OxA-539) and upper phase at Uwaynid 18 (OxA-864, -868). Microlithic component from upper phase is characterized by La Mouillah points and double-truncated backed bladelets; that from lower phase is dominated by small arched-backed curved-pointed pieces. Date from upper phase is slightly older than that from lower phase; given well-defined stratigraphy, this probably is due to movement of small charcoal flecks by burrowing organisms.

Charcoal from Azraq esh Shishan, Site 17, in eolian silts overlying calcrete in marsh.

OxA-869. Azraq 17 Sq. 11 Dep. 11   13,260 ± 200

Charred bone from Wadi el Jilat, Site 10.

OxA-918. Jilat 10 Sq. 8 Dep. 11   12,700 ± 300
OxA-1000. Jilat 10 Sq. 8 Dep. 11 (repeat) 13,120 ± 180

Comment: Dates are significantly younger than OxA-520, charcoal from same level. Archaeological evidence indicates short-term occupation.

Charcoal from Wadi el Jilat Site 22.

OxA-1770. Jilat 22, 1 6b 13   11,920 ± 180
OxA-1771. Jilat 22, 3 15b 37   13,040 ± 180
OxA-1772. Jilat 22, 3 15b 36   12,840 ± 140

Comment (A.N.G.): 1 of 9 UP and Epipaleolithic sites sounded. Jilat 22 has 3 phases of occupation. Lower 2 are in calcreted marsh deposits, separated by sterile tufa/travertine, which must have formed during intense spring activity. Industry from upper phase (OxA-1770) was Geometric Kebaran, but that from middle phase (OxA-1771, -1772) (obliquely truncated tanged points on blades similar to forms from European UP) has no parallels in Near East. Site was rich in bone and carbonized plant remains.

OxA-2409. Jilat 22, 1 4 17a   13,490 ± 110
OxA-2410. Jilat 22, 1 4 17a   13,540 ± 120

Comment (A.N.G.): Dates relate to lower phase and document blade-dominated assemblages in Levantine "Geometric Kebaran".

THE LEVANT: LATE EPIPALEOLITHIC AND ACERAMIC NEOLITHIC

Charred grain (*Triticum boeoticum*) from Late Epipaleolithic levels at Tell Abu Hureyra (35°52'N, 38° 24'E), Euphrates Valley, Syria. Dates are on carbonized grain fragments of wild einkorn from Tr. E.

OxA-170. Level 261	10,600 ± 200
OxA-171. Level 313	10,600 ± 200
OxA-172. Level 326	10,900 ± 200
OxA-386. Level 276	10,800 ± 160
OxA-397. Level 286	10,420 ± 150
OxA-882. Level 324 basal pit	6100 ± 120
OxA-883. Level 326 basal pit	11,450 ± 300

Comment (G. C. Hillman): *Cf.* BM-1121:10,792 ± 82, on combined charcoal from layer E. Dates show grains are contemporary with Mesolithic levels in which they were found, except for OxA-882 (Harris 1986; Hillman 1975; Hillman, Colledge and Harris 1986).

Comment (A. M. T. Moore): OxA-883 confirms date of establishment of Epipaleolithic settlement at Abu Hureyra (*cf.* OxA-172, -387, -430, -468: Moore *et al.* 1986; Moore 1992). Date is even older than other dates from basal deposits; it may indicate settlement began 100 or 200 yr earlier than estimated 11,100 BP. OxA-882 is later than any known prehistoric occupation at Abu Hureyra.

Charred bone from Tr. E (Legge and Rowley-Conwy 1986). See Batten *et al.* (1986) for discussion of separate humic and fulvic fractions; other dates are on carbonaceous residue of bone, which appear to be most reliable.

OxA-387. Charred phalange of *Bos*		11,070 ± 160
Level 326		
OxA-468. Repeat		11,090 ± 150
OxA-469. Humic acids from OxA-468		10,920 ± 140
OxA-470. Humic acids from OxA-468		10,820 ± 160
OxA-407. Wild sheep Level 275		10,050 ± 180
OxA-408. Humic acids from OxA-407		10,250 ± 160
OxA-471. Repeat, OxA-407		10,620 ± 150
OxA-472. Wild sheep Level 281		10,750 ± 170
OxA-473. Wild sheep Level 281		10,000 ± 170
OxA-430. Gazelle Level 316		11,020 ± 150
OxA-431. Humic acids from OxA-430		10,680 ± 150
OxA-434. Gazelle Level 286		10,490 ± 150
OxA-435. Humic acids from OxA-434		10,450 ± 180
OxA-476. Fulvic acids from OxA-434		9600 ± 200
OxA-474. Wild sheep Level 285		10,930 ± 150
OxA-475. Gazelle Level 252		9060 ± 140

Charred bones from Tr. D, Neolithic levels, near base of W slope, Abu Hureyra (*cf.* Burleigh, Matthews and Ambers 1982).

OxA-876. Wild ass Level 73 Phase 1	8500 ± 90
OxA-877. Sheep/goat Level 70 Phase 1	8300 ± 150
OxA-878. Wild ass Level 68 Phase 4	8490 ± 110
OxA-879. Wild ass Level 41 Phase 4	8570 ± 130
OxA-880. Wild ass Level 10 Phase 4	14,920 ± 180
OxA-881. Sheep/goat Level 32 Phase 7	8870 ± 100

Comment (A.M.T.M.): AMS dates confirm expectations that deposits in Tr. D belong to initial expansion and subsequent floruit of Neolithic settlement, but not final phase of occupation. Samples span entire occupation, from Phase 1 at base to Phase 7 at top. Except for OxA-880, dates are close, and OxA-876, -877, -878 and -879 overlap each other at 1σ, suggesting deposits accumulated rapidly. Dates agree closely with conventional ^{14}C date on charcoal for Phase 3, Tr. D, BM-1721:8410 ± 60 (Burleigh, Ambers and Matthews 1982). Bone of OxA-880 came from Phase 4 level; it may derive from older deposit nearby or be aberrant. OxA-881 is maximum age for pit.

Bone, charred seeds and charcoal from Abu Hureyra 2 (Moore 1975).

OxA-2044. Human bone Tr. A		390 ± 60
OxA-2045. Human bone Tr. B Phase 11		170 ± 60
OxA-1232. Charred bone Tr. B Phase 9		7310 ± 120
OxA-1190. Charred wheat seeds Tr. B,		
Phase 2		8500 ± 120
OxA-2169. Charred seeds Tr. B,		
Phase 2		8640 ± 110
OxA-2168. Twig charcoal Tr. E,		
Phase 5		8330 ± 100
OxA-2167. Charred seeds Tr. E,		
Phase 4		8270 ± 100
OxA-1931. Charred domestic wheat seeds,		
Tr. G Phase 2		7890 ± 90
OxA-1930. Charred *Secale montanum/S.*		
vavilovii **and** *Triticum boeo-*		
ticum **seeds Tr. G Phase 2**		8180 ± 100
OxA-1227. Charcoal Tr. G Phase 3		8320 ± 80
OxA-1228. Charcoal Tr. G subsoil		9680 ± 90

Comment (A.M.T.M.): Tr. B provides most complete sequence of Abu Hureyra 2 occupation. OxA-1190 and -2169 agree well with BM-1722R: 8640 ± 100 (Bowman, Ambers and Leese 1990) from phase 4, slightly later in Tr. B sequence. BM-1122: 9374 ± 72 (Burleigh, Matthews and Ambers 1982) from phase 3 is much earlier. These dates suggest occupation began shortly after 9000 BP. OxA-1232 is latest date for Abu Hureyra 2, suggesting Neolithic settlement continued until end of 8th millennium BP. OxA-2167 and -2168 indicate occupation did not begin in N sector of mound until *ca.* 8300 BP; faunal remains show this coincided with switch from gazelle hunting to large-scale sheep and goat herding (Legge and Rowley-Conwy 1987). OxA-1228 was earliest date for Neolithic settlement and suggests Neolithic village was first inhabited early in 10th millennium BP, although stratigraphic records from site indicate occupation was intermittent until *ca.* 9000 BP. OxA-1930, -1931 and -1227 are much later, suggesting area around Tr. G was not permanently inhabited until 2nd period of expansion of Abu Hureyra 2, from *ca.* 8300 BP. Dominance of sheep and goat in Tr. G indicates these animals replaced gazelle. OxA-1930 and -1931 came from level with mixed wild-type and domesticated cereals. Dates suggest wild cereals were exploited until 9th millennium BP. OxA-2044 and -2045 are from recent burials unrelated to site.

THE LEVANT: ACERAMIC AND POTTERY NEOLITHIC

Charcoal from Early Pre-Pottery Neolithic (PPNA) cave, 'Iraq ed-Dubb (32°20'N, 35°40'E) in forested uplands of NW Jordan (Kuijt, Mabry and Palumbo, in press; Palumbo, Mabry and Kuijt 1991). Sample was from slightly below mud floor of oval stone structure *ca.* 30cm above bedrock.

OxA-2567. Unit D10/12   9950 ± 100

Comment (I.K.): date compares well with PPNA lithics from site (Kenyon 1981). Cave appears to have been occupied at same time as earliest dated Early Neolithic remains from Jericho and slightly earlier than Nativ Hagdud, Gezer, Salibiya IX and Hatoula (Bar-Yosef 1991). Early agricultural villages of Jordan Valley were probably only one aspect of economic system that included small groups living in seasonal camps in forested uplands, who constructed semi-subterranean stone dwellings.

Barley from Netiv Hagdud, "Sultanian" mound in lower Jordan Valley, Israel (31°59'N, 35°26'E) (Bar-Yosef, Gopher and Goring-Morris 1980). Sultanian is heavy-duty tool-oriented facies of PPNA (Crowfoot-Payne 1976). Sample was in rubbish zone, 2.6m below surface, overlain by *ca.* 4 building phases.

OxA-744. *Hordeum spontaneum/distichon* 9700 ± 150

Comment (O. B.-Y.): 1 of earliest well-stratified findings of domesticated 2-rowed barley in Near East.

Organic remains from PPN cave at Nahal Hemar (31°10'N, 35°10'E), Judean Desert, Israel; subm. 1986 by O. Bar-Yosef (1985).

OxA-1013. Plain woven cloth	660 ± 200
OxA-1014. Knots from net	8600 ± 120
OxA-1015. Twined "napkin"	8500 ± 220
OxA-1016. Knotted square	8810 ± 120
OxA-1569. Textile	410 ± 60
OxA-1570. Textile	5980 ± 80

Comment: Dates confirm PPN age of 3 samples; also that OxA-1013 was intrusive. OxA-1569 and -1570

were coll. after plundering of cave and before systematic excavation in June 1983. OxA-1569 does not belong to PPNB, but may originate from layer 1, which contained Chalcolithic to Arabic remains. OxA-1570 indicates brief use of cave during PN/Early Chalcolithic.

Charcoal from statues cache in 'Ain Ghazel (31°54' N, 35°53'E).

OxA-1472.	8660 ± 80
OxA-1473.	8700 ± 80

Comment (K. W. Tubb): Samples were between superimposed figures. Only comparable material was from Jericho. Although Kenyon recorded ^{14}C dates for Neolithic levels (Burleigh 1981b), none was associated with highly stylized paddle-shaped busts found in them, which were thought to represent later development of head discovered by Garstang in 1935, attributed by him to Chalcolithic, but later to PPNB. Garstang head is considered contemporary with 'Ain Ghazel statues, which date to PPNB, based on context and lithics. These results are exciting, as they are earliest large-scale, three-dimensional representations of human form. Sophistication of technology used in their production is impressive when they are placed firmly in middle PPNB (*ca.* 7250–6000 BC).

Azraq esh Shishan, Site 31 is aceramic/ceramic Neolithic transitional site (cut by early Islamic burials, OxA-871), in silt dunes overlying calcretes next to Qa el-Azraq, major playa at center of Azraq Basin.

OxA-870. Charcoal Sq. 1 Dep. 10	8350 ± 120
OxA-871. Bone Sq. 14 Dep. 107	1280 ± 90

Comment (A.N.G.): Site provides earliest dates for ovicaprid pastoralism from E Jordan. Ovicaprid bones are almost entirely absent from UP and Epipaleolithic sites in region as well as from aceramic Neolithic Jilat 7, dated to *ca.* 8500–8800 BP (OxA-526, -527). At Azraq 31, sheep/goat bones are 20–30% of faunal assemblage. Possible sheep bones from *ca.* 7400 BP were found at "Burin Neolithic" Jebel Naja (OxA-375), 50km E of Azraq (see below). Besides ovicaprids, gazelle, cattle and ass bones, Azraq 31 produced cultivated hulled barley (*Hordeum sativum*) and wheat (*Triticum* sp.) seeds, which were also found at Jilat 7.

Charcoal from sites in Wadi Jilat.

OxA-1799. Jilat 7 A 34b	5840 ± 100
OxA-1800. Jilat 13 A 21a 19	7920 ± 100
OxA-1801. Jilat 13 A 15a 9	7870 ± 100
OxA-1802. Jilat 26 Cb 7a 1	8690 ± 110

Comment (A.N.G.): These 3 villages are close to present transition zone between dry steppe and desert, receiving less rainfall than required for dry farming. Sites span period in which cultivation and pastoralism became established in more fertile regions of Near East. Differences of material culture and architecture between Jilat and W Jordan, Palestine and Syria may derive from arid land adaptation. Cultivated barley and einkorn seeds were in earliest PPNB levels at Jilat 7; domestic sheep and goat first appear in early PN at Jilat 13. ^{14}C dates from these sites are critical for determining introduction of cultivars and domestic livestock in drier lands bordering SW arm of "Fertile Crescent". OxA-1799 appears to be intrusive from later occupation.

OxA-1812. Jilat 27 E 41a 7   **5270 ± 90**
Comment (A.N.G.): Flint industry was only broadly comparable with those from better known areas of Levant.

OxA-2969. Jilat 26 Ed 18a   **8740 ± 110**
OxA-2407. Jilat 26 C 12a   **8720 ± 100**
Comment (A.N.G.): Typical "Burin Neolithic" assemblage was associated with classic PPNB tool kit. Dates show Burin site phenomenon developed by middle PPNB. No faunal remains were found at Jilat 26; contemporary levels at other sites in Wadi Jilat lacked evidence for sheep/goat pastoralism.

OxA-2413. Jilat 7 A 34a   **8390 ± 80**
Comment (A.N.G.): Two dates from previous sounding derive from middle PPNB levels (8810 ± 110: OxA-526; and 8520 ± 110: OxA-527); OxA-2413 and OxA-1799 dated previously (5840 ± 100) came from lower phase containing early PPNB assemblage. Both dates are late and may derive from intrusive charcoal. Cultivated wheat and barley were found in all levels, but no domesticated livestock were recognized in preliminary analysis of bones.

OxA-2408. Jilat 25 Aa 19a   **8020 ± 80**
Comment (A.N.G.): Chipped stone assemblage seems to be transitional between PPNB and early Late Neolithic; parallels early levels of Jilat 13. Both sites contain evidence of sheep/goat pastoralism.

OxA-2411. Jilat 13 C 24   **7900 ± 80**
Comment (A.N.G.): Date is close to OxA-1800 and -1801 from earlier phase on same site. Sample came from hearth in later phase of occupation.

OxA-2412. Azraq 31 C 19b   **8275 ± 80**
Comment (A.N.G.): Azraq 31 had at least 2 occupation phases: PPNB and LN. Date from earlier phase is 8350 ± 120: OxA-870; sample was from later occupation. Date is earlier than expected, suggesting charcoal could be residual.

Charcoal from Jebel Naja 2321, aceramic Neolithic site in Black Desert, E Jordan (31°50′N, 37°25′E) (Betts 1983, 1984, 1985). Tr. 400 revealed fill of small hut; trench along outside of hut wall contained 3 firepits, ash, fire-cracked flint and traces of bead-making workshop. 2321 is single-period site.

OxA-375. Level 408 pit   **7430 ± 100**

Comment: 2321 belongs to unique group of sites that contains flint tools unlike any other Near Eastern sequence. Almost 100 of these sites exist and only 1 other was previously excavated in 1930s.

Charcoal from Dhuweila, E Jordan (32°05′N, 37°15′E).
OxA-1636. 2202/4217   **7030 ± 90**
OxA-1637. 2202/2133   **8350 ± 100**
OxA-1728. 4225   **7140 ± 90**
OxA-1729. 4118   **7450 ± 90**
Comment (A. Betts): Dates for LN fit well into time range of lithic typology and stratigraphic sequence of site. Early date (OxA-1637) also fits with previous BM date (8190 ± 60). EN sample confirms late 7th millennium date and is important for comparison with other dated sites of Wadi Jilat. LN dates are important because little is known about post-7th millennium sites in Syrian desert. Many sites fit into 6th/5th to early 4th millennium, but few have enough organic remains for dating. Dhuweila dates enable us to place many sites into broad time scale, and help chart progress of changing subsistence strategies.

Charcoal from EN to LN settlements at Burqu'/Ruweishid (32°40′N, 37°50′E) and Tell el-Hibr, Jordan (32°00′ N, 38°10′E).
OxA-2807. Burqu' 02 203   **144.2 ± 1.0% pMC**
OxA-2808. Burqu' 03 158   **6900 ± 100**
Comment (A.B.): Site 03 has 2 phases. OxA-2808 is from pit cut down from upper, later phase. Typologically, early phase compares with early phases of LN Dhuweila 2 (above). Artifacts from later phase are few and undiagnostic, but date ca. 6/5th millennium is reasonable. This phase could compare with later levels at Dhuweila 2.

OxA-2765. Burqu' 27 141   **7350 ± 80**
OxA-2766. Burqu' 27 142   **7930 ± 80**
Comment (A.B.): Dates are from 1st phase at Site 27. Artifacts from these levels relate to early phases of Dhuweila 2 and Site 03. This phase may represent intermittent use of site from beginning of LN.

OxA-2764. Burqu' 27 132   **7270 ± 80**
Comment (A.B.): Sample is from phase 2 after stone-walled hut was built on deposits of phase 1. Artifacts from phase 2 show development and continuity of phase 1.

OxA-2767. Tell el-Hibr 108   **3950 ± 80**
Comment (A.B.): Date does not appear to fit with stratigraphic evidence and other finds from site.

OxA-2768. Burqu' 35 207   **8140 ± 90**
OxA-2769. Burqu' 35 208   **8180 ± 80**
OxA-2770. Burqu' 37 112   **8270 ± 80**
Comment (A.B.): Typologically, Site 35 is different from Dhuweila 1. Artifacts may represent transitional EN/LN, or early stage of LN. They broadly compare with PPNC at 'Ain Ghazel (Rollefson, Kafafi and

Simmons 1991) dated to end of 7th and early 6th millennium BC.

General Comment: This period saw radical change in settlement patterns and economy. By end of EN, most large mixed-farming villages in fertile areas were abandoned. LN occupation was more ephemeral, with little hunting, more pastoralism and wide-range herding extending to steppic areas. Diversity of sites in steppe reflect these changes: Dhuweila 1 was EN hunting camp, contemporary with final stages of village life in verdant areas. Burqu' sites reflect sequence from E/LN transition through much of LN. Faunal analysis suggests most or all Burqu' sites are seasonal hunter/herder camps, representing earliest pastoral nomadic groups in steppe. Yet cultural assemblages differ, which may reflect seasonality, diverse social groups, task-specific sites, change, or a combination of these.

THE LEVANT: LATE NEOLITHIC, HALAF-UBAID PERIOD

Samples from LN (Halaf-Ubaid) site, Arjoune, Syria (34°33'N, 36°31'E), from fills of habitation pits in 3 parts of site (Tr. V, VI, VII).

OxA-571. Tr. V burnt bone fragment	6510 ± 100
OxA-617. Tr. V pig atlas	6670 ± 140
OxA-650. Tr. V burnt bone fragment	6700 ± 110
OxA-572. Tr. VI burnt bone fragment	4730 ± 100
OxA-573. Tr. VI burnt bone fragment	5650 ± 100
OxA-816. Tr. VI carbonized grain	5810 ± 80
OxA-817. Tr. VI carbonized grain	5850 ± 80
OxA-818. Tr. VI pig ulna	5450 ± 110
OxA-574. Tr. VII burnt bone fragment	6440 ± 90
OxA-575. Tr. VII pig tibia	6600 ± 100
OxA-576. Tr. VII pig tibia	6760 ± 100
OxA-577. Tr. VII human bone	6480 ± 130

Comment: For preliminary account, see Marfoe, Copeland and Parr (1981). Arjoune V and VII are probably contemporary short-term occupations, *ca.* 6600 BP. Arjoune VI is younger.

THE LEVANT: CHALCOLITHIC AND EARLY BRONZE

Samples from Chalcolithic large open-air and subterranean site, Shiqmim, located along Nahal Beersheva, S Israel (31°11'N, 34°38'E).

OxA-2520. Charcoal	5060 ± 140
OxA-2521. Charcoal	5530 ± 130
OxA-2522. Charcoal	5600 ± 130
OxA-2523. Charred seeds	5710 ± 140
OxA-2524. Charcoal	5650 ± 140
OxA-2525. Charred twigs	5385 ± 130
OxA-2526. Charred grain	5540 ± 150

Comment (T. E. Levy): Shiqmim has longest time scale for Chalcolithic in Israel (Levy *et al.* 1991). Only Chalcolithic type site, Tuleilat Ghassul, Jordan, has longer sequence, spanning LN/Chalcolithic transition (Gilead 1988). Unique feature of Beersheva Valley Chalcolithic (*ca.* 4500–3500 BC) is subter-

ranean room and tunnel complexes dug into native loessic soil bordering drainage system (wadi). Dates help establish earliest occupation at Shiqmim and represent 4 archaeological contexts:

1. OxA-2523, -2526 from St. IV are earliest pits at site; 1σ calibration range (Stuiver and Reimer 1986): 4659–4360 cal BC.
2. OxA-2524 was from pioneer phase (St. III) subterranean rooms; 1σ: 4714–4350 cal BC. Date represents initial settlement phase; from floor of underground room 7. OxA-2520 was from small hearth representing last use of underground room 3; 1σ: 4000–3701 cal BC.
3. OxA-2522 dates earliest rectilinear building in lower village; 1σ: 4657–4340 cal BC.
4. OxA-2521, -2525 date large open-air altar; average: 4365–4236 cal BC.

There is some discrepancy between OxA-2522 and dates for open-air altar. Geomorphologically, gravels and other sediment under this building cover altar, and should be later, rather than earlier, than altar. Overlap in standard deviations may indicate rapid in-filling of site just before construction of building, which preceded establishment of planned settlement in St. II. Generally, earliest phases at Shiqmim are contemporary with beginning of Badarian, and end of Fayum EN and Merimda cultures in Egypt.

Two basketry samples found in dry cave, Lower Wadi Makukh, near Jericho, Jordan Valley, Israel (31°50'N, 35°25'E) following intensive plundering. Most material in cave was fragmentary Chalcolithic baskets and mats. One object showed unusual twining technique thought to be Roman.

OxA-1928. Mak. 3 reeds/rushes	5310 ± 80
OxA-1929. Mak. 6 palm leaves	1900 ± 60

Comment (O. Bar-Yosef and T. Schick): dates confirm suspicions of mixed Chalcolithic and Roman material.

Charred grape seed (*Vitis vinifera*) from EB I context and charred olive stone (*Olea europea*) from Chalcolithic context, obtained by wet flotation (non-chemical) at Sataf, W of Jerusalem (31°45'N, 35°15'E).

OxA-3434. Area B/16 *V. vinifera*	4590 ± 70
OxA-3435. Area A/26/B.891 *O. europa*	5270 ± 75

Comment (S. Gibson): OxA-3434 is from debris on floor of EB I house shortly after abandonment (Gibson, Ibbs and Kloner 1991). Other finds include EB I pots, animal bones and mud brick. Date agrees with other ^{14}C dates for EB I from Palestine (*cf.* Gilead 1988). OxA-3435 is from lower 60cm of soil in cave entrance. Other finds from this locus include Chalcolithic/Ghassulian pottery and 1 bone point. Date concurs with known ^{14}C range from other Chalcolithic sites in Palestine, notably Negev Desert and Golan. OxA-3435 is 1st date for Chalcolithic site in central highlands of Palestine.

Wood charcoal from EB site, Tell Yaqush, central Jordan Valley, Israel, excavated 1989 (32°36′N, 35°34′E).

OxA-2809. 6 Q14 L111	4400 ± 70
OxA-2810. 7 Q14 L111	4140 ± 70
OxA-2811. 8 Q14 L111	4420 ± 70
OxA-2812. 9 Q14 L118	4410 ± 70
OxA-2813. 10 Q14 L121	4580 ± 70
OxA-2814. 11 Q14 L120	4480 ± 70

Comment (D. L. Esse): Consistent series of dates for house dated by ceramic assemblage to EB II. OxA-2809, -2810 and -2812 are from courtyard just N of house, from burnt debris overlying packed earth floor, sealed by collapsed mudbrick. OxA-2810 is somewhat later than others, but still within normal limits for EB II. Because samples are wood charcoal, OxA-2810 may be most realistic date for terminal phase of building. OxA-2811 and -2814 came from floor of house; OxA-2812 came from area just NW of house. Range of calibrated dates, *ca.* 3400–2900 cal BC, is consistent for EB II of Palestine, and also agrees with currently accepted Egyptian chronology of First Dynasty, upon which Palestinian relative chronology is based.

Samples from EB settlement, Tell Kerma North, on W(?) bank of Khabur River, Jazirah region of NE Syria (36°27′N, 40°51′E); excavated 1987.

OxA-2082. Charred barley grain	4130 ± 70
OxA-2083. Wood charcoal	4100 ± 70

Comment (Lab): OxA-2082 was from mudbrick building, probably granary, destroyed by fire in early to mid-3rd millennium BC. OxA-2083 was from occupation layer thought to date to same period. 2σ ranges (OxA-2082: *ca.* 2895–2505 cal BC; OxA-2083: *ca.* 2890–2500 cal BC) confirm suggested dates.

Wood from handle of bronze spearhead from MB IIa cemetery, Gesher, central Jordan Valley, Israel (32°36′N, 35°33′E); excavated 1987.

OxA-1955. Grave 13, object 42   **3640 ± 70**

Comment (Y. Garfinkel): When calibrated, (*ca.* 2100–1900 cal BC), date fits well with typology of pottery, and with metal artifacts from cemetery (Garfinkel and Bonfil 1990). Finds agree with date of early MB IIa layers at Tel Afek and Tell el Hayyat. OxA-1955 compares to dates from latter site (Falconer and Magness-Gardiner 1989), *i.e.*, 3460 ± 100 (AA-1236) from phase 5 lower and 3600 ± 60 (AA-1239) from phase 5 upper.

ANATOLIA

Emmer wheat (*T. dicoccum*) from lowest levels of Aceramic Neolithic, Tr. 49 L at Can Hasan, Turkey (37°30′N, 33°30′E); subm. 1982 by G. C. Hillman.

OxA-388. Charred grain   **7910 ± 160**

Comment: Conventional ^{14}C date BM-1667: 8360 ± 60 was from larger collection of wood charcoal. Differences between dates may be explained by:

1. Intrusion of grain: this is excluded because of thick accumulation of decomposed mudbrick overlying and sealing occupation deposit.
2. Higher ^{14}C levels in grain, as single year's growth effect. This seems unlikely in view of tree-ring studies (Stuiver 1982), which do not show significant single-yr departures from 10-yr means.
3. Wood charcoals, probably including species brought in as heavy timber, may have been from wood that grew for several centuries before grain was introduced.

OxA-392. Charred rachis   **250 ± 90**

Comment: Charred rachis (*T. durum*) from small sealed hearth underlying surface, built against top of Neolithic wall in Tr. 48 K. Dates compare with BM-817 (<100 BP) based on large assemblage of wheat grain. Unexpected date prompted AMS date on identifiable remains. Hearth's connection to Neolithic wall looked secure, and cereals included large quantity of grains and spikelet forks of emmer wheat, which seemed unlikely to have been cultivated here in recent times.

Charred wheat grain from Phrygian Gordion, Polatli Province, Turkey, identified as *T. aestivum* (bread wheat) and subm. 1982 by G. C. Hillman.

OxA-145. BPB, SE Room   **2650 ± 150**

Comment (G.C.H): Sample came from inside unbroken vessel securely sealed beneath burnt timbers, associated with destruction of Gordion *ca.* 680 BC.

Comment (Lab): On Belfast curve (Pearson, Pilcher and Baillie 1983), mean value of 2650 BP: *ca.* 800 cal BC, but 1σ extends range down to 540 cal BC.

Human calvaria from Alanya Cave, Kadipinari, Antalya, Turkey, subm. by C. B. Stringer and E. Guleç.

OxA-2233. Calotte 155-2-73   **4910 ± 70**

Comment (C.B.S.): 3 partial hominid crania were embedded in travertine deposits on floor of Alanya Cave, but no directly assoc. materials could provide independent date. One skull (155-1-73) had very robust facial and frontal morphology; calotte (155-2-73) and calvaria (155-3-73) were more gracile. Only 1 of 3 samples contained sufficient collagen for dating, but age obtained suggests calotte may derive from Late Chalcolithic, and travertine formation in cave was recent.

CYPRUS: CHALCOLITHIC AND BRONZE AGE

Charcoal and seeds from Lemba Lakkous (34°50′N, 32°20′E).

OxA-1083. Charred seeds   **4370 ± 90**

OxA-1084. Charred seeds   4280 ± 110
OxA-1085. Charcoal Bldg. 9.1 F1   4820 ± 90
OxA-1086. Charcoal Bldg. 15.1 F34   4770 ± 90
OxA-1087. Charred seeds   4310 ± 80
Comment: OxA-1085, -1086 from buildings of Area I, Period 1 compare well with BM-1543 and overlap with dates from nearby Kissonerga Mylouthkia, which yields different material culture (Burleigh 1981a). Also from Area I, OxA-1083 suggests intrusion or later date for Bldg. 18 (Peltenburg 1985). Seeds from Area II Period 1, OxA-1084, -1087, are later than expected, which may mean primary inland settlement was established well after Area I, or seeds had washed down from higher levels.

Charcoal and seeds from Neolithic–Early Bronze Age site, Kissonerga-Mosphilia (34°50′N, 32°25′E).
OxA-2161. Charcoal, pit 1015   4290 ± 80
OxA-2162. Charcoal, pit 1015   4300 ± 80
Comment (E.P.): Dates assign unique Period 3 hoard to Middle Chalcolithic of Cyprus; they help date earliest Cypriot coroplastic art including birthing figurines and painted building model for contemporary "ridge" houses. Dates agree with most other Period 3 dates (Peltenburg 1991).
OxA-2960. Gramineae Bldg. 834   4220 ± 70
Comment (E.P.): Gap exists between Late Chalcolithic and Middle Chalcolithic. This Period 4 building is stratigraphically earlier than most; date helps to close gap; *cf.* BM-2527, -2529, -2530.
OxA-2961. Charred seeds Bldg. 4   4310 ± 75
OxA-2962. Lens/gramineae Bldg. 1161   4370 ± 70
OxA-2963. Cereals Bldg. 994   4520 ± 80
Comment (E.P.): Rectilinear Bldg. 1161 is stratigraphically earlier than immense circular structures nearby, but OxA-2961, -2962 and BM-2568 suggest either rapid evolution or only recorded Middle Chalcolithic settlement plan in Cyprus.
OxA-2964. Charcoal Pit 1132   4860 ± 80
OxA-2965. Gramineae Pit 1149   5100 ± 80
Comment (E.P.): Earliest Neolithic occupation at Kissonerga is derived from pottery and pits. These samples from Neolithic/Early Chalcolithic confirm stratigraphic sequence for site, but may provide dates for 2nd phase rather than foundation.

Charcoal from Sotira *Kaminoudhia*, 20km W of Limmassol, S Cyprus. Samples came from 2 stratigraphic phases (Swiny 1985).
Phase 1
OxA-3308. Area A Rm. 1 Context 51   3890 ± 90
OxA-3309. Area A Rm. 7 Context 51   3780 ± 90
Comment (S.W.M.): Samples from earlier phase were from Area A. Calibrated 1σ ranges are:
1. van der Plicht (1993) bidecadal curve:
    OxA-3308 (2466–2272; 2256–2202 BC)
    OxA-3309 (2332–2108; 2090–2038 BC)

2. Manning (1993) bidecadal curve:
    OxA-3308 (2476–2212 BC)
    OxA-3309 (2330–2052 BC)
3. Weninger (1993) decadal curve:
    OxA-3308 (2339 ± 122 BC)
    OxA-3309 (2175 ± 141 BC)
Phase 2
OxA-3310. Area A Rm. 7 Context 51   3780 ± 90
OxA-3311. Area A Rm. 7 Context 50   3890 ± 100
OxA-3312. Area A Rm. 4 Context 6   3690 ± 100
OxA-3544. Area C Rm. 2 Context 7a   3840 ± 75
OxA-3545. Area C Rm. 2 Context 18   3860 ± 75
OxA-3546. Area C Rm. 8 Context 8   3760 ± 75
OxA-3547. Area C Rm. 8 Context 7   3860 ± 80
OxA-3548. Area C Rm. 17 Context 8   3800 ± 75
Comment (S.W.M.): Samples were from 2nd, main phase of site. Calibrated 1σ ranges are:
1. van der Plicht (1993) bidecadal curve
    OxA-3310 (2332–2108; 2090–2038 BC)
    OxA-3311 (2480–2200 BC)
    OxA-3312 (2200–1910 BC)
    OxA-3544 (2450–2432; 2402–2370; 2358–2194; 2160–2146 BC)
    OxA-3545 (2454–2424; 2406–2272; 2258–2202 BC)
    OxA-3546 (2282–2106; 2092–2036 BC)
    OxA-3547 (2454–2424; 2408–2270; 2262–2200 BC)
    OxA-3548 (2392–2386; 2336–2132; 2076–2050 BC)
2. Manning (1993) bidecadal curve
    OxA-3310 (2330–2052 BC)
    OxA-3311 (2480–2196 BC)
    OxA-3312 (2197–1920 BC)
    OxA-3544 (2419–2157 BC)
    OxA-3545 (2450–2186 BC)
    OxA-3546 (2278–2046 BC)
    OxA-3547 (2454–2178 BC)
    OxA-3548 (2340–2093 BC)
3. Weninger (1993) decadal curve
    OxA-3310 (2175 ± 141 BC)
    OxA-3311 (2334 ± 136 BC)
    OxA-3312 (2051 ± 142 BC)
    OxA-3544 (2302 ± 118 BC)
    OxA-3545 (2321 ± 111 BC)
    OxA-3546 (2148 ± 119 BC)
    OxA-3547 (2323 ± 116 BC)
    OxA-3548 (2190 ± 129 BC)
General Comment (S.W.M.): Sotira *Kaminoudhia* assemblage belongs to Early Cypriot Red Polished tradition (Swiny 1991), as expected. These are first Early Cypriot dates for Cyprus. Combined dates offer best probability for each phase. Phase 1 average: 2150–2360 BC; Phase 2: 2110–2320 BC (Weninger 1993). Similar ranges suggest short interval between phases. Samples probably derive from firewood or other cultural activity. As long-lived samples (except OxA-3544) they offer *termini post quos* ranges for some points during Phases 1 and 2. Generally, this assem-

blage dates beginning to mature Early Cypriot at *ca.* 2350–2100 BC.

Finely woven wool, dyed with true purple, from box marked "said to be from Enkomi", Bronze Age site.

OxA-544. Textile 1   2025 ± 120
OxA-545. Textile 2   1980 ± 100

Comment (I. D. Jenkins): Cloth may be from tombs near Enkomi. Although orginally thought to be Bronze Age, later date could mean several tombs were in use up to Hellenistic times.

IRAN: NEOLITHIC

Charred goat bones from Bus Mordeh phase at Ali Kosh, early farming village on Deh Luran Plain of Khuzistan, W Iran; subm. 1988 by F. Hole.

OxA-1773. Metapodial 97570   7830 ± 90
OxA-1774. Astragalus 97680   7950 ± 110
OxA-1775. Petrous 100   7480 ± 90

Comment (F.H.): OxA-1773 and -1774 seem to settle age of Bus Mordeh phase at *ca.* 7000 cal BC; they are in correct stratigraphic order since OxA-1773 is *ca.* 1m above OxA-1774. Anomalous date, OxA-1775 probably came from upper layer, perhaps Ali Kosh phase, and was mistakenly placed with bones from Bus Mordeh phase during subsequent analysis.

Charred *Hordeum* (barley) seeds from levels E, D, C-D and B at Tepe Ganj Dareh, early farming site in Zagros Mts. near modern town of Kermanshah, W Iran. Subm. 1989 by P. E. L. Smith.

OxA-2099. GD.F1.70 level B   8840 ± 110
OxA-2100. GD.F1.110 level C-D   9010 ± 110
OxA-2101. GD.F1.129 level D   8850 ± 100
OxA-2102. GD.F1.136 level E   8690 ± 110

Comment (Lab): age range: *ca.* 7000–8000 cal BC.

Comment (P.E.L.S.): Dates are Neolithic, consistent with other 20 dates from site. Seven dates from level E yielded both oldest and youngest ages from site. Whole sequence may be more compressed than expected. We still do not know how much time elapsed between level E (non-architectural, no sign of goat control) to level D (elaborate solid architecture, controlled exploitation of wild goats.

TURKMENIA: NEOLITHIC

Charred grain and chaff fragments from Neolithic settlement of Jeitun, *ca.* 20km N of Ashkhabad, Turkmenia (38°00′N, 58°24′E).

OxA-2912. *T. monococcum* 8 ph. I   7100 ± 90
OxA-2913. *Aegilops* sp. 23 ph. II/III   7180 ± 90
OxA-2914. *Aegilops* sp. 34 ph. III/IV   7270 ± 100
OxA-2915. *T. monococcum* 52 ph. IV   7200 ± 90
**OxA-2916. *T. monococcum*, cereal
              frags. 54 below ph. IV**   7190 ± 90

Comment (S. Limbrey): Dates firmly establish farming in central Asian desert by later 6th millennium BC, and suggest short occupation of site. Dates also confirm use of cultivated einkorn, which, together with naked and hulled barley, dominates cereal assemblage.

ACKNOWLEDGMENTS

I would particularly like to thank the following people who, over the years, have helped produce the dates listed here: C. Anglias, A. D. Bowles, A. R. T. Brian, J. F. Foremen, R. Gillespie, J. A. J. Gowlett, R. E. M. Hedges, E. Hendy, M. J. Humm, I. A. Law, P. Leach, C. Parry, C. B. Ramsay, G. Tyrrell and G. J. van Klinken. Further, I thank the editors of *Archaeometry* for their kind permission to reproduce all the original sections from the date lists. Finally, I express my appreciation to all the archaeologists who supplied the samples and their subsequent comments that appear here in abbreviated form.

REFERENCES CITED

Bar-Yosef, O.
    1985   A cave in the desert: Nahal Hemar. Jerusalem, *Israel Museum* 258.
    1991   The Early Neolithic of the Levant: Recent advances. *Quarternary Review of Archaeology* 12:1–18.
Bar-Yosef, O. and A. Belfer-Cohen
    1988   The Early Upper Palaeolithic in Levantine caves. In *The Early Upper Paleolithic: Evidence from Europe and the Near East,* edited by J. A. Hoffecker and C. A. Wolf, pp. 23–42. BAR International Series 437, British Archaeological Reports, Oxford.
Bar-Yosef, O., A. Gopher and A. N. Goring-Morris
    1980   Netiv Hagdud: A "Sultanian" mound in the lower Jordan Valley. *Paléorient* 6:201–206.
Bar-Yosef, O. and N. Goren
    1973   Natufian remains in Hayonim Cave. *Paléorient* 1:49–68.

Bar-Yosef, O., B. Vandermeersch, B. Arensburg, P. Goldberg, H. Laville, L. Meignen, Y. Rak, E. Tchernov and A.-M. Tillier
   1986   New data on the origin of modern man in the Levant. *Current Anthropology* 27(1):63–64.
Batten, R., R. Gillespie, J. A. J. Gowlett and R. E. M. Hedges
   1986   The AMS dating of separate fractions in archaeology. *Radiocarbon* 28(2A):698–701.
Belfer-Cohen, A. and O. Bar-Yosef
   1981   The Aurignacian at Hayonim Cave. *Paléorient* 7(2), 19–42.
Betts, A.
   1983   Black Desert Survey, Jordan: First preliminary report. *Levant* 15:1–10.
   1984   Black Desert Survey, Jordan: Second preliminary report. *Levant* 16:25–34.
   1985   Black Desert Survey, Jordan: Third preliminary report. *Levant* 17:29–52.
Bowman, S. G. E., J. C. Ambers and M. N. Leese
   1990   Re-evaluation of British Museum radiocarbon dates issued between 1980 and 1984. *Radiocarbon* 32(1):59–79.
Bronk, C. R. and R. E. M. Hedges
   1989   Use of the CO_2 source in radiocarbon dating by AMS. *Radiocarbon* 31(3):298–304.
Burleigh, R.
   1981a   Radiocarbon dates for Lemba. In *Chalcolithic Cyprus and Western Asia*, edited by J. Reade, p. 21. British Museum Occasional Paper 26.
   1981b   Appendix C: Radiocarbon dates. In *Excavations at Jericho III*, edited by K. M. Kenyon, pp. 501–504. British School of Archaeology in Jerusalem, London.
Burleigh, R., J. Ambers and K. Matthews
   1982   British Museum natural radiocarbon measurements XV. *Radiocarbon* 24(3):262–290.
Burleigh, R., K. Matthews and J. Ambers
   1982   British Museum natural radiocarbon measurements XIV. *Radiocarbon* 24(3):229–261.
Crowfoot-Payne, J.
   1976   The terminology of the Aceramic Neolithic period in the Levant. In *Deuxième Colloque sur la Terminologie de la Préhistoire du Proche Orient*, edited by F. Wendorf, pp. 131–137. Nice, UISPP Congress.
Edwards, P. C.
   1984   Two Epipalaeolithic sites in the Wadi Hammeh (Area XX). In *Preliminary Report of the University of Sydney's Fifth Season of Excavation (1982–83) at Pella in Jordan*, edited by A. McNicoll, W. Ball, S. Bassett, P. Edwards, P. Macumber, D. Petocz, T. Potts, L. Randle, L. Villiers and P. Watson, pp. 55–86. Annual Department of Antiquities of Jordan 28.
Edwards, P. C. and S. M. Colledge
   1985   The Natufian settlement in the Wadi Hammeh (Area XX). In *Preliminary Report on a Sixth Season of Excavation by the University of Sydney at Pella in Jordan (1983–84)*, edited by T. F. Potts, S. M. Colledge and P. C. Edwards, pp. 182–196. Annual Department of Antiquities of Jordan 29.
Falconer, S. E., and B. Magness-Gardiner
   1989   Hayyat (Tell el). In *Archaeology of Jordan II 1. Field Reports. Survey and Sites A–K*, edited by D. Homes-Fredericq and J. B. Hennessy, pp. 254–261. Akkadica Supplementum VII. Leuven, Peeters.
Garfinkel, Y., and R. Bonfil
   1990   Graves and burial customs of the Middle Bronze IIa period at Gesher. *Eretz-Israel* 21:132–147.
Garrard, A. N., A. Betts, B. Byrd and C. Hunt
   1987   Prehistoric environment and settlement in the Azraq Basin: An interim report on the 1985 excavation season. *Levant* 19:5–25.
Garrard, A. N., B. Byrd and A. Betts
   1986   Prehistoric environment and settlement in the Azraq Basin: An interim report on the 1984 excavation season. *Levant* 18:5–24.
Garrard, A. N., B. Byrd, P. Harvey and F. Hivernel
   1985   Prehistoric environment and settlement in the Azraq Basin: A report on the 1982 survey season. *Levant* 17:1–28.
Gibson, S., B. Ibbs and A. Kloner
   1991   The Sataf Project of Landscape Archaeology in the Judaean Hills: A preliminary report on four seasons of survey and excavation (1987–89). *Levant* 23:29–54.
Gilead, I.
   1988   The Chalcolithic period in the Levant. *Journal of World Prehistory* 2:397–443.
Gillespie, R., J. A. J. Gowlett, E. T. Hall and R. E. M. Hedges
   1984   Radiocarbon measurement by accelerator mass spectrometry: An early selection of dates. *Archaeometry* 26(1):15–20.
Gillespie, R., J. A. J. Gowlett, E. T. Hall, R. E. M. Hedges and C. Perry
   1985   Radiocarbon dates from the Oxford AMS system: Archaeometry datelist 2. *Archaeometry* 27(2):237–246.

Gillespie, R., R. E. M. Hedges and M. J. Humm
  1986   Routine AMS dating of bone and shell proteins. *Radiocarbon* 28(2A):451-456.
Goring-Morris, A. N.
  1987   *At the Edge: Terminal Pleistocene Hunter-Gatherers in the Negev and Sinai.* BAR International Series 361, British Archaeological Reports, Oxford.
Gowlett, J. A. J., E. T. Hall, R. E. M. Hedges and C. Perry
  1986   Radiocarbon dates from the Oxford AMS system: Archaeometry datelist 3. *Archaeometry* 28(1):116-125.
Gowlett, J. A. J. and Hedges, R. E. M.
  1987   Radiocarbon dating by Accelerator Mass Spectrometry: applications to archaeology in the Near East. In *Chronologies du Proche Orient*, edited by O. Aurenche, J. Evin and F. Hours, pp. 121-144. BAR International Series 379, British Archaeological Reports, Oxford.
Gowlett, J. A. J., R. E. M. Hedges, I. A. Law and C. Perry
  1986   Radiocarbon dates from the Oxford AMS system: Archaeometry datelist 4. *Archaeometry* 28(2):206-221.
  1987a   Radiocarbon dates from the Oxford AMS system: Archaeometry datelist 5. *Archaeometry* 29(1):125-155.
Haas, H., J. Devine, R. Wenke, M. Lehner, W. Wolfli and G. Bonani
  1987   Radiocarbon chronology and the historical calendar in Egypt. In *Chronologies du Proche Orient*, edited by O. Aurenche, J. Evin and F. Hours, pp. 585-606. BAR International Series 379, British Archaeological Reports, Oxford.
Harris, D. R.
  1986   Plant and animal domestication and the origins of agriculture. In *Archaeological Results from Accelerator Dating*, edited by J. A. J. Gowlett and R. E. M. Hedges, pp. 5-12. *Oxford Committee for Archaeology Monograph* 11.
Hedges, R. E. M.
  1992   Sample treatment strategies in radiocarbon dating. In *Radiocarbon After Four Decades: An Archaeological Perspective*, edited by R. E. Taylor, A. Long and R. S. Kra, pp. 165-183. Springer-Verlag, New York.
Hedges, R. E. M., R. A. Housley, C. R. Bronk and G. J. van Klinken
  1990   Radiocarbon dates from the Oxford AMS system: Archaeometry datelist 11. *Archaeometry* 32(2):211-237.
  1991a   Radiocarbon dates from the Oxford AMS system: Archaeometry datelist 12. *Archaeometry* 33(1):121-134.
  1991b   Radiocarbon dates from the Oxford AMS system: Archaeometry datelist 13. *Archaeometry* 33(2):279-296.
  1992a   Radiocarbon dates from the Oxford AMS system: Archaeometry datelist 14. *Archaeometry* 34(1):141-159.
  1992b   Radiocarbon dates from the Oxford AMS system: Archaeometry datelist 15. *Archaeometry* 34(2):337-357.
Hedges, R. E. M., R. A. Housley, I. A. Law and C. R. Bronk
  1989   Radiocarbon dates from the Oxford AMS system: Archaeometry datelist 9. *Archaeometry* 31(2):207-234.
  1990   Radiocarbon dates from the Oxford AMS system: Archaeometry datelist 10. *Archaeometry* 32(1):101-108.
Hedges, R. E. M., R. A. Housley, I. A. Law and C. Perry
  1988a   Radiocarbon dates from the Oxford AMS system: Archaeometry datelist 7. *Archaeometry* 30(1):155-164.
Hedges, R. E. M., R. A. Housley, I. A. Law, C. Perry and J. A. J. Gowlett
  1987b   Radiocarbon dates from the Oxford AMS system: Archaeometry datelist 6. *Archaeometry* 29(2):289-306.
Hedges, R. E. M., R. A. Housley, I. A. Law, C. Perry and E. Hendy
  1988b   Radiocarbon dates from the Oxford AMS system: Archaeometry datelist 8. *Archaeometry* 30(2):291-305.
Hedges, R. E. M., R. A. Housley, C. Bronk Ramsay and G. J. van Klinken
  1993a   Radiocarbon dates from the Oxford AMS system: Archaeometry datelist 16. *Archaeometry* 35(1):147-167.
  1993b   Radiocarbon dates from the Oxford AMS system: Archaeometry datelist 17. *Archaeometry* 35(2):305-326.
Hedges, R. E. M., M. J. Humm, J. Foreman, G. J. van Klinken and C. R. Bronk
  1992   Developments in sample combustion to carbon dioxide, and the Oxford AMS carbon dioxide ion source system. *Radiocarbon* 34(3):306-311.
Hedges, R. E. M. and I. A. Law
  1989   The radiocarbon dating of bone. *Applied Geochemistry* 4:249-253.
Hedges, R. E. M., I. A. Law, C. R. Bronk and R. A. Housley
  1989   The Oxford accelerator mass spectrometry facility: Technical developments in routine dating. *Archaeometry* 31(2):99-114.
Hedges, R. E. M. and G. J. van Klinken
  1992   A review of current approaches in the pretreatment of bone for radiocarbon dating by AMS. *Radiocarbon* 34(3):279-291.
Hillman, G. C.
  1975   Plant food economy at Tell Abu Hureyra: A preliminary report. In *Excavation at Tell Abu Hureyra in Syria: A Preliminary Report*, edited by A. M. T. Moore, pp. 50-77. Proceedings of the Prehistoric Society 41.
Hillman, G. C., S. M. Colledge and D. R. Harris
  1986   Plant food economy during the Epi-palaeolithic period at Tell Abu Hureyra, Syria: Dietary diversity, seasonality and

modes of exploitation. Paper precirculated and presented at the Symposium on Recent Advances in the Understanding of Plant Domestication and Early Agriculture, World Archaeology Congress, Southampton.

Hopf, M. and O. Bar-Yosef
1987   Plant remains from Hayonim cave, western Galilee. *Paléorient* 13:117–120.

Hovers, E., L. K. Horwitz, O. Bar-Yosef and C. Cope-Miyashro
1988   The site of Urkan e-Rub IIa: A case study of subsistence and mobility patterns in the Kebaran period in the Lower Jordan Valley. *Mitekufat Haeven* 21:20–48.

Hovers, E. and O. Marder
1991   Typo-chronology and absolute dating of the Kebaran complex: Implications from the second season of excavation at Urkan e-Rub IIa. *Mitekufat Haeven* 24:34–58.

Kenyon, K. M. (editor)
1981   *Excavations at Jericho III*. British School of Archaeology in Jerusalem, London.

Kislev, M. E., D. Nadel and I. Carmi
1992   Epi-paleolithic (19,000 BP) cereal and fruit diet at Ohalo II, Sea of Galilee, Israel. *Review of Palaeobotany and Palynology* 71:161–166.

Kuijt, I., J. Mabry and G. Palumbo
1991   Early Neolithic use of upland areas of Wadi El-Yabis: Preliminary evidence from the excavations of 'Iraq ed-Dubb, Jordan. *Paléorient* 17:99–108.

Laville, H. and P. Goldberg
1989   The collapse of the Mousterian sedimentary regime and the beginning of the Upper Palaeolithic at Kebara Cave, Mount Carmel. In *Investigations in South Levantine Prehistory*, edited by O. Bar-Yosef and B. Vandermeersch, pp. 75–95. BAR International Series 497, British Archaeological Reports, Oxford.

Legge, A. J.
1986   Seeds of discontent: Accelerator dates on some charred plant remains from the Kebaran and Natufian cultures. In *Archaeological Results from Accelerator Dating*, edited by J. A. J. Gowlett and R. E. M. Hedges, pp. 13–21. Oxford Committee for Archaeology Monograph 11.

Legge, A. J. and P. Rowley-Conwy
1986   New radiocarbon dates for early sheep at Tell Abu Hureyra, Syria. In *Archaeological Results from Accelerator Dating*, edited by J. A. J. Gowlett and R. E. M. Hedges, pp. 23–35. Oxford Committee for Archaeology Monograph 11.
1987   Gazelle killing in Stone Age Syria. *Scientific American* 255(8):88–95.

Levy, T. E., D. Alon, D., C. Grigson, A. Holl, P. Goldberg, Y. Rowan and P. Smith
1991   Subterranean settlement in the Negev Desert, *ca.* 4500–3700 BC. *Research and Exploration* 7:394–413.

Manning, S. W.
1993   *CALMAKER*. A centralising probabilistic computer calibration programme.

Marfoe, L., L. Copeland and P. J. Parr
1981   Arjoune 1978: Preliminary investigation of a prehistoric site in the Homs Basin, Syria. *Levant* 13:1–27.

Mellars, P. A. and J. Tixier
1989   Radiocarbon accelerator dating of Ksar 'Aqil (Lebanon) and the chronology of the Upper Palaeolithic sequence in the Middle East. *Antiquity* 63:761–768.

Moore, A. M. T.
1975   The excavation of Tell Abu Hureyra in Syria. *Proceedings of the Prehistoric Society* 41:50–77.

Moore, A. M. T., J. A. J. Gowlett, R. E. M. Hedges, G. C. Hillman, A. J. Legge and P. A. Rowley-Conwy
1986   Radiocarbon accelerator (AMS) dates for the Epipalaeolithic settlement at Abu Hureyra, Syria. *Radiocarbon* 28(3):1068–1076.
1992   The impact of accelerator dating at the early village of Abu Hureyra on the Euphrates. *Radiocarbon* 34 (3): 850–858.

Noy, T., A. J. Legge and E. S. Higgs
1973   Recent excavations at Nahal Oren, Israel. *Proceedings of the Prehistoric Society* 39:75–99.

Palumbo, G., J. Mabry, J. and I. Kuijt
1990   The 1989 Wadi el-Yabis survey excavation project. *Annual of the Department of Antiquities of Jordan* 34:95–118.

Paulissen, E. and P. M. Vermeersch
1987   Earth, man and climate in the Egyptian Nile Valley during the Pleistocene. In *Prehistory of Arid North Africa*, edited by A. Close, pp. 29–67. Southern Methodist University Press, Dallas.

Pearson, G.W., J. R. Pilcher and M. G. L. Baillie
1983   High precision ^{14}C measurement of Irish oaks to show the natural ^{14}C variations from 200 BC to 4000 BC. *Radiocarbon* 25(2):179–186.

Peltenburg, E. J.
　1985　Lemba Archaeological Project I: Excavations at Lemba Lakkous 1976–1983. *Studies in Mediterranean Archaeology* 70(1).
　1991　Lemba Archaeological Project II: A ceremonial area at Kissonerga. *Studies in Mediterranean Archaeology* 70(3).
Perrot, J.
　1960　Le gisement natoufien de Mallaha (Eynan), Israel. *L'Anthropologie* 70:437–483.
　1984　Structures d'habitat, mode de vie et environnement. Les village souterrains des pasteurs de Béersheva dans le sud d'Israël, au IVe millénaire avant le l'ère chrétienne. *Paléorient* 10:75–96.
Perrot, J. and D. Ladiray
　1985　Le sepultures natoufiennes de Mallaha (Eynan). *Mémoires et Travaux du Centre de Recherche Français de Jérusalem* 4(1).
Rollefson, G., Z. Kafafi and A. Simmons
　1991　The Neolithic village of 'Ain Ghazal, Jordan. *BASOR Supplement* 27:95–116.
Rowley-Conwy, P. A.
　1988　The camel in the Nile Valley: New radiocarbon accelerator (AMS) dates from Qasr Ibrim. *Journal of Egyptian Archaeology* 74:245–248.
Sillen, A.
　1984　Dietary change in the Epi-Palaeolithic and Neolithic of the Levant: The Sr/Ca evidence. *Paléorient* 10(1):149–155.
Solivères-Massei, O.
　1985　Les hommes de Mallaha. *Mémoires et Travaux du Centre de Recherche Français de Jérusalem* 3.
Stuiver, M.
　1982　A high-precision calibration of the AD radiocarbon time scale. *Radiocarbon* 24(1):1–26.
Stuiver, M. and P. J. Reimer
　1986　A computer program for radiocarbon age calibration. *Radiocarbon* 28(2B):1022–1030.
Swiny, S.
　1985　Sotira-*Kaminoudhia* and the Chalcolithic/Early Bronze Age transition in Cyprus. In *Archaeology in Cyprus 1960–1985*, edited by V. Karageorghis, pp. 115–124. Nicosia, A. F. Leventis Foundation.
　1991　Reading the prehistoric record: A view from the south in the late third millennium BC. In *Cypriot Ceramics: Reading the Prehistoric Record*, edited by J. A. Barlow, D. L. Bolger and B. Kling, pp. 37–44. Philadelphia, A. G. Leventis Foundation and the University Museum of Archaeology and Anthropology.
Tixier, J. and M. L. Inizan
　1981　Ksar' Aqil: Stratigraphie et ensembles lithiques dans le Paléolithique supérieur: Fouilles 1971–1975. In *Préhistoire du Levant*, edited by J. Cauvin and P. Sanlaville, pp. 353–367. Maison de l'Orient, CNRS, Lyon.
Valla, F. R., F. Le Mort and H. Plisson
　1991　Les fouilles en cours sur la Terrasse d'Hayonim. In *The Natufian Culture in the Levant*, edited by O. Bar-Yosef and F. R. Valla, pp. 93–110. International Monographs in Prehistory, Archaeology Series 1, Ann Arbor.
Valla, F. R., H. Plisson and R. Buxo i Capdevila
　1989　Notes préliminaires sur les fouilles en cours sur la Terrasse d'Hayonim. *Paléorient* 15(1):245–257.
Valladas, H., J. L. Joron, G. Valladas, B. Arensburg, O. Bar-Yosef, A. Belfer-Cohen, P. Goldberg, H. Laville, L. Meignen, Y. Rak, E. Tchernov, A. M. Tillier and B. Vandermeersch
　1987　Thermoluminescence dates for the Neanderthal site at Kebara in Israel. *Nature* 330:159–160.
Vallat, F.
　1985　Les industries de silex de Mallaha (Eynan) et du Natoufien dans le Levant. *Mémoires et Travaux du Centre de Recherche Français de Jérusalem* 3.
van der Merwe, N. J.
　1982　Carbon isotopes, photosynthesis and archaeology. *American Scientist* 70:596–606.
van der Plicht, J.
　1993　The Groningen radiocarbon calibration program. *Radiocarbon* 35(1):231–237.
Vermeersch, P. M., E. Paulissen, G. Gijselings and J. Janssen
　1986　Middle Palaeolithic chert exploitation pits near Qena (Upper Egypt). *Paléorient* 12:61–65.
Vita-Finzi, C. and E. S. Higgs
　1970　Prehistoric economy in the Mount Carmel area of Palestine: Site catchment analysis. *Proceedings of the Prehistoric Society* 36:1–37.
Wasylikowa, K., J. R. Harlan, J. Evans, F. Wendorf, R. Schild, A. E. Close, H. Królik and R. A. Housley
　1993　Examination of botanical remains from Early Neolithic houses at Nabta Playa, Western Desert, Egypt, with special reference to sorghum grains. In *The Archaeology of Africa: Food, Metals and Towns*, edited by T. Shaw, P. Sinclair, B. Andah and A. Okpoku, pp. 154–164. Routledge, London.

Wendorf, F., A. E. Close, R. Schild, K. Wasylikowa, R. A. Housley, J. R. Harlan and H. Królik
   1992   Saharan exploitation of plants 8,000 years BP. *Nature* 359:721–724.
Wendorf, F., R. Schild and A. E. Close
   1993   *Egypt During the Last Interglacial: The Middle Paleolithic of Bir Tarfawi and Bir Sahara East.* Plenum Press, New
         York.
Wendorf, F., R. Schild, A. E. Close, H. P. Schwarcz, G. H. Miller, R. Grün, A. Bluszcz, S. Stokes, L. Morawska, J. Huxtable,
J. Lundberg, C. L. Hill and C. McKinney
   1994   A chronology for the Middle and Late Pleistocene wet episodes in the eastern Sahara. This volume.
Weninger, B.
   1993   CALKN.EXE. Kalibration bis ca. 18000 cal BC.

PALEOENVIRONMENT, SAPROPEL CHRONOLOGY AND NILE RIVER DISCHARGE DURING THE LAST 20,000 YEARS AS INDICATED BY DEEP-SEA SEDIMENT RECORDS IN THE EASTERN MEDITERRANEAN

MICHEL FONTUGNE, MAURICE ARNOLD, LAURENT LABEYRIE, MARTINE PATERNE
STEPHEN E. CALVERT[1] *and JEAN-CLAUDE DUPLESSY*

Centre des Faibles Radioactivités, Laboratoire mixte CNRS/CEA, Domaine du CNRS
F-91198 Gif sur Yvette, Cedex, France

INTRODUCTION

The Mediterranean Sea lies in a zone separating a region of hot, dry climate to the south from a region of warm, humid climate to the north. At present, the hydrological balance of the basin is dominated by net evaporative loss of water in addition to that supplied from precipitation and runoff. Thus, its circulation is that of a classical "negative estuary" (Miller 1983). The surface-water loss is compensated by a flow of water from the surface Atlantic through the Straits of Gibraltar (Béthoux 1984), and a return flow of deep water exports highly saline water from the Mediterranean to intermediate depths of the Atlantic (Wüst 1935).

Various lines of evidence show that the climate and hydrological balance in the eastern basin of the Mediterranean changed drastically during the last glacial maximum (LGM) and during the LGM-Holocene transition. Such evidence comes from the records of sedimentation, pollen and faunal analyses, and stable isotope variations in foraminifera preserved in deep-sea cores. The sedimentary changes include the accumulation of a distinctive organic-rich horizon, or sapropel (Kullenberg 1952), during the late stages of glacial retreat; this accumulation may have been caused by complete stagnation of the eastern basin (Bradley 1938), thereby inducing preferential preservation of organic matter. Accumulation also may have been a consequence of increased primary production as a result of a different mode of circulation (Berger 1976; Calvert 1983). The pollen evidence traces the changes in vegetation around the margins of the basin, which reflect changes in terrestrial climates (Cheddadi and Rossignol-Strick 1994), whereas the record of variations in the oxygen isotopic composition of foraminifera in the eastern Mediterranean can be interpreted in terms of temperature and salinity changes of the near-surface waters (Williams, Thunell and Kennett 1978). The latter are likely to have changed markedly due to the semi-isolated location of the eastern Mediterranean, and to the different precipitation regimes that existed over the basin and the adjacent land areas during the LGM and the transition to Holocene conditions.

Although palynological studies of high-resolution sediment records from continental sequences in Greece, Turkey and the Near East (Wijmstra 1969; Bottema 1974; van Zeist and Bottema 1977; Bottema and van Zeist 1981) have provided valuable information on climatic changes in this region, such studies are relevant only to local vegetation. Information is also available from paleo-lake levels or river terraces (Street and Grove 1979; Adamson *et al.* 1980; Paulissen and Vermeersch 1989) or terrestrial faunal analysis (Goodfriend 1988; Goodfriend and Magaritz 1988). However, such studies are frequently hampered by the lack of a reliable chronology due to the occurrence of frequent hiatuses in continental sequences, especially during arid or hyperarid phases. In addition, the ^{14}C dating method, which is used commonly to provide accurate chronologies in

---

[1]Department of Oceanography, University of British Columbia, Vancouver, British Columbia, Canada V6T 1Z4

Late Quaternary Chronology and Paleoclimates of the Eastern Mediterranean
Edited by Ofer Bar-Yosef and R. S. Kra. RADIOCARBON 1994, pp. 75–88

75

such studies, is often not applicable in arid or semi-desert environments, such as those surrounding the eastern Mediterranean. This is because, in general, only shells or carbonate deposits are available for dating, and the hard-water effect, recrystallization, or ingestion of fossil carbonates by terrestrial mollusks often lead to dating errors (Evin *et al.* 1980; Goodfriend 1987; Evin 1991).

In contrast to problems encountered with continental records, climatic information recorded in deep-sea cores is applicable over a large spatial scale, but generally at lower temporal resolution. The value of such marine records lies in our ability to link them directly to the record of global climatic fluctuations. Further, tephrochronology (Ninkovitch and Heezen 1965; Keller 1971; Vinci 1985; Paterne *et al.* 1986; Paterne, Guichard and Labeyrie 1988) and progress in ^{14}C dating techniques, such as accelerator mass spectrometry (AMS) using foraminifera (Arnold *et al.* 1987) are now capable of furnishing very accurate time scales.

We review here the evidence that has been obtained on sediment cores, concentrating on paleoceanographic changes that occurred during the last glacial-interglacial transition. Some palynological and faunal studies of deep-sea cores have already been published; new information on sapropel chronology and the influence of Nile discharge on sapropel formation in the eastern Mediterranean are presented.

POLLEN AND FAUNAL ANALYSIS

Analysis of marine cores has produced a correlation of continental paleoclimatic records with the oxygen isotopic record of global ice volume and regional climate. In the eastern Mediterranean, pollen records are available from three areas, namely the eastern part of the Tyrrhenian Sea (Rossignol-Strick and Planchais 1989), the Adriatic Sea (Rossignol-Strick, Planchais and Paterne 1992), and the Ionian Sea (Cheddadi, Rossignol-Strick and Fontugne 1991) and Levantine Basin (Cheddadi 1988; Cheddadi and Rossignol-Strick 1994) (see Table 1). Two main types of vegetation presently characterize the eastern Mediterranean borderlands. Trees are dominant in the north and east, whereas the south is a rather treeless semi-desert or desert. Strictly Saharan vegetation is poorly represented in the pollen assemblages in these records, which consequently contain little information on paleoenvironments of northern Africa. The principal taxa present include the tree genera, *Pinus, Quercus, Cedrus* and *Olea*, and the herbaceous plants, *Artemisia, Ephedra*, Chenopodiaceae, Gramineae and Cyperaceae. These forms are present in all the records, and their variations in abundance form the basis of climatic interpretation.

On the basis of this information, the vegetation and climate developed in a similar manner in southern Europe and the Near East. During the last glacial maximum (*ca.* 18,000–20,000 BP), a sagebrush semi-desert, dominated by *Artemisia* with interspersed *Pinus*, was present at all elevations. The closest present analogues for the Ionian Sea borderlands are found on the southern slopes of the Altai Mountains in central Asia (Cheddadi, Rossignol-Strick and Fontugne 1991) or in the Ukrainian-type grass steppe for southern Italy (Rossignol-Strick and Planchais 1989). Such vegetation characterizes regions with low minimum precipitation (100–350 mm/yr) and very cold winters with numerous freezing days (<–15°C). The harshness of the winter diminished toward the southeast. Summer mean temperatures are estimated to have been between 21° and 24°C for southern Italy, and between 27° and 35°C in the Near East. However, isolated refuges of deciduous temperate forest were present at mid-altitude, where precipitation was higher, due to orographic effects, and temperatures were not too low (Rossignol-Strick and Planchais 1989; Rossignol-Strick, Planchais and Paterne 1992). During the slow onset of deglaciation between 18,000 and 13,000 BP, semi-desert vegetation was progressively replaced in the central Mediterranean by a more severe desert, sparsely occupied by Chenopodiaceae. Around 14,000 BP, the lowland grass steppe was

TABLE 1. Core Locations, Water Depths and the Minimum $\delta^{18}O$ Values of *Globigerinoides Ruber* During the Beginning of Sapropel Deposition

Core	Lat N	Long E	Depth (m)	$\delta^{18}O$	Corrected $\delta^{18}O$	Reference
BAN 8409 GC	34.32	20.02	3405	-0.7	-0.7	C,R-S&F*
V10-67	34.70	20.72	2890	-1.2	-1.2	V-G*
DED87-06	36.04	21.24	3620	-0.25	-0.25	This work
MD 84-657	34.05	21.52	2373	-0.67	-0.67	This work
RC 9-183	34.50	23.42	2684	-0.7	-0.7	This work
80 KB 11	36.50	24.33	795	-0.86	-1.01	This work
82 KS 04	34.43	24.55	1446	-1.2	-1.2	This work
MD 84-656	33.38	24.77	2100	-1.57	-1.57	This work
67MO 3	34.42	24.83		-0.6	-0.6	V-G,D&Z*
RC9-181	33.42	25.02	2286	-1.17	-1.17	V-G,R&C*
RC 9-180	34.08	25.67	2653	-0.53	-0.53	This work
81 MC 30	34.10	25.95	2774	-1.21	-1.21	This work
TR 171-27	33.83	25.98	2680	-1.1	-1.1	W&T*
CHN119-6PG	33.26	26.00	2372	0.11	0.11	J&W*
81 MC 28	34.60	26.07	2938	-0.99	-0.99	This work
81 MC 09	35.65	26.25	2287	-0.4	-0.55	This work
75-KS52	34.00	26.32	3118	-0.75	-0.75	V-G,D&Z*
81 MC 08	35.78	26.60	718	-0.12	-0.27	This work
V 10-49	36.08	26.83	1170	-0.91	-1.06	This work
75 KS50	34.68	27.00	2290	-0.75	-0.75	V-G,D&Z*
V10-58	35.96	27.08	2547	-0.6	-0.6	S*
82 KS 01	34.37	27.15	2150	-0.75	-0.75	V-G,D&Z*
80 KB 28	34.85	27.25	2150	-0.35	-0.35	V-G*
75 KS 26	36.08	27.30	1517	-0.1	-0.35	V-G,D&Z*
V 10-51	35.92	27.30	791	-1.02	-1.16	This work
RC 9-178	33.73	27.92	2628	-1.25	-1.25	This work
TR 172-22	35.32	29.02	3150	-0.5	-0.5	T,W&K*
CHN119-12PG	32.38	29.23	2289	-0.18	+0.07	J&W*
MD84-655	32.32	30.02	1465	-0.18	+0.07	This work
CHN119-16PG	33.25	30.33	2523	-0.23	+0.02	J&W*
P6508-36	32.73	30.52	2000	-0.88	-0.63	J&W*
CHN119-18PG	34.35	30.93	2484	0.08	+0.02	J&W*
MD84-650	33.67	31.45	2360	-0.66	-0.41	This work
RC 9-176	36.02	31.47	2465	0.22	+0.47	This work
CHN119-22PG	32.77	31.89	1581	-0.59	-0.34	J&W*
C6157	33.17	32.17	1900	−1.00	-0.75	L&P-G*
RC 9-174	32.97	32.42	1397	-0.76	-0.51	This work
MD84-642	32.68	32.58	1260	-1.15	-0.90	This work
MD84-641	33.03	32.63	1375	-1.37	-1.12	F&C*
MD 90-964	33.05	32.64	1375	-1.16	-0.91	This work
MD84-639	33.66	32.70	870	-0.6	-0.35	This work
CORE 17	35.50	33.33	850	-0.6	-0.35	B*
CORE 190	36.00	33.38	832	-0.4	-0.05	B*
MD84-627	32.23	33.75	1185	-1.39	-1.14	T*
GA32	31.95	34.35	590	-1.93	-1.68	L*
MD84-629	32.07	34.35	745	-1.69	-1.44	This work
MD84-632	32.85	34.38	1425	-1.57	−1.32	This work

*C,R-S&F = Cheddadi, Rossignol-Strick and Fontugne (1991); V-G = Vergnaud-Grazzini (1975); V-G,D&Z = Vergnaud-Grazzini, Devaux and Znaidi (1986) V-G,R&C = Vergnaud-Grazzini, Ryan and Cita (1977); W&T = Williams and Thunell (1979); J&W = Jenkins and Williams (1984); S = Shackleton, unpublished; T,W&K = Thunell, Williams and Kennett (1978) L&P-G = Luz and Perelis-Grossowicz (1980); F&C = Fontugne and Calvert (1992); B = Buckley *et al.* (1982); T = Tucholka *et al.* (1987); L = Luz (1979) progressively replaced by a continental semi-desert in southern Italy. At around 12,000 BP, the trend of increasing aridity was interrupted by a more humid period, characterized by the reintroduction of sagebrush in lowland areas around the Ionian Sea, and oak and grass forest-steppe at mid-elevation (Cheddadi, Rossignol-Strick and Fontugne 1991).

The beginning of the Holocene period *ca.* 10,000 BP is marked by the expansion of deciduous oak and the masking of herbaceous vegetation in the pollen record. This reforestation occurred along with an increase in humidity, which followed the second pulse of meltwater discharge into the global ocean (Bard *et al.* 1987). It also coincides with the beginning of a period of high freshwater discharge into the eastern Mediterranean from the Nile and perhaps other rivers (see below). The maximum in summer precipitation occurred around 8000 BP, followed by a continuous trend to aridification since this time (Cheddadi, Rossignol-Strick and Fontugne 1991). Such palynological studies provide semi-quantitative information only on changes in humidity, whereas information on temperature variations must be derived using other methods (Guiot 1990; Guiot *et al.* 1989).

The qualitative reconstruction of the surface-water temperature of the LGM in the eastern Mediterranean is based on the distribution of planktonic microfossils; the early work has been reviewed by Thunell (1979). Thiede (1978) and Thunell (1979) used transfer functions (Imbrie and Kipp 1971) to link planktonic foraminiferal assemblages in surface sediments to overlying surface-water characteristics (mainly temperature and salinity), which allowed quantitative reconstruction, such as those obtained by CLIMAP (1976). The first reconstructions for the Mediterranean Sea used transfer functions based on Atlantic surface sediment data (CLIMAP Project Members, 1976; Luz and Bernstein 1976), but these are not reliable for the Mediterranean. New transfer functions derived by Thiede (1978) and Thunell (1979) were used to reconstruct the last glacial maximum. However, certain fossil assemblages found in Mediterranean glacial sediments have no modern equivalents, thereby limiting the reliability of the results. Nevertheless, the results of Thiede (1978) and Thunell (1979) are similar. Thiede (1978) obtained winter and summer sea-surface temperatures of 13° and 19°C, respectively, in the Alboran Sea, and 18° and 26°C, respectively, in the Levantine Basin. Thunell (1979) found winter temperatures slightly lower for the central Mediterranean. Both authors found a large temperature anomaly in the Aegean Sea and south of Crete, where the mean winter temperature was 6°C cooler than at present, and the mean summer temperature was 4°C cooler. They explained this anomaly by an influx of cold glacial runoff through the Aegean Sea originating from the summer melting of glaciers in eastern Europe and western Siberia. These temperature estimates are consistent with the information provided by palynological studies, which show that cooler conditions prevailed in the central eastern Mediterranean (Ionian) Sea borderlands compared to southern Italy or the Levantine Basin (Cheddadi, Rossignol-Strick and Fontugne 1991). No reconstructions are available for other areas for this period.

FRESHWATER INPUT TO THE EASTERN MEDITERRANEAN

Palynological data reviewed above show that the borderlands of the eastern Mediterranean received very low precipitation during the LGM. However, the input of large amounts of freshwater into the eastern Mediterranean during glacial retreat was used by Olausson (1961) to explain the formation of sapropels, organic-rich horizons intercalated in the normal calcareous sediments of this basin. The source of this input was ascribed to the Black Sea, and foraminiferal analysis of sediment cores (Thunell and Lohmann 1979) appeared to support this suggestion. Subsequently, the oxygen isotopic composition of planktonic foraminifera present in the sapropels was shown to reflect the presence of a low-salinity surface layer in the eastern basin at this time (Williams, Thunell and Kennett 1978). Rossignol-Strick (1983, 1985) suggested that the source of this fresh water was the Nile River, whose runoff is modulated by variations in the intensity of the Arabian Sea monsoon.

Further insight into this phenomenon is available from detailed chronologies of sapropel formation and the gradient in the isotopic composition of foraminifera throughout the eastern Mediterranean. The beginning of sapropel deposition and its duration are not well constrained, in spite of the availability of many radiocarbon dates of deep sea cores (Olsson 1959; Olsson and Broecker 1959; Östlund and Engstrand 1960; Pastouret 1970; Buckley and Willis 1969; Buckley *et al.* 1982; Delibrias, Guillier and Labeyrie 1974, 1986; Gillot and Capron 1973; Stanley and Maldonado 1977; Rossignol-Strick *et al.* 1982; Znaidi 1982; Sutherland, Calvert and Morris 1984; Murat 1984; Troelstra *et al.* 1991). These results are reported in Figure 1. Taken at face value, they show that the latest sapropel event occurred between 15,000 and 4000 BP, the modal value being between 7000 and 9000 BP. The long period of increased freshwater input suggested by these data is not consistent with pollen data or with information on continental paleoenvironments. Moreover, the duration of the event appears to be substantially different in cores collected in close proximity. Such a wide variability in ages is mainly due to the low resolution that results from conventional radiocarbon dating of thick sediment sections and to the different types of material dated (carbonate or organic matter that may contain a non-negligible amount of old terrestrial carbon). Therefore, these data cannot provide reliable information on the synchroneity or duration of the sapropel event over the eastern Mediterranean as a whole, and consequently, do not allow a reliable reconstruction of the paleoenvironment at this time.

To address these questions, we discuss seven cores collected during the cruises, ETNA 82 of the *R/V Suroit*, and NOE and DEDALE of the *M/S Marion Dufresne*. The locations and depths of cores are shown in Table 1. Cores KET 8216, KET 8222 and DED 8706 are considered to represent the Adriatic, and the western and the eastern Ionian Seas, respectively. Cores MD 84627, 84639, 84641 and 84650 cover the Levantine Basin. Murat (1984) and Murat and Got (1987) described the lithology of the cores and identified the sapropel. Paterne *et al.* (1986) Paterne, Guichard and Labeyrie (1988), Tucholka *et al.* (1987) and Fontugne *et al.* (1989) checked the stratigraphy using oxygen isotope measurements and tephrochronology. AMS *14C* measurements were made on *Globigerinoides ruber,* or mixed planktonic foraminifera (KET 8216) when *G. ruber* was not sufficiently abundant. To check the presence of hiatuses in the cores, we sampled the first centimeter at the top and the base of the sapropel, and the first centimeter immediately below and above the sapropel. The results have been corrected for a reservoir age of 400 yr (Broecker and Peng 1982; Bard *et al.* 1987), a value consistent with direct measurements of Mediterranean shells from museums by Delibrias (1989). The data are summarized in Table 2.

The ages of the levels below the sapropel fall in a fairly narrow range (9040 ± 140 to 9580 ± 120 BP), and have a mean value of 9300 BP. The adjacent level at the base of sapropel also has a narrow range of ages (8150 ± 140 to 8960 ± 130 BP), with a mean and modal value of 8570 BP. The similar ages of these two levels and their consistent age differences underline the synchroneity of the beginning of sapropel formation over a large area of the eastern Mediterranean. Such a result is in good agreement with the age assigned to this event by Troelstra *et al.* (1991).

In contrast to the close agreement between the ages at the base of the sapropel shown in Table 2, the upper part of the sapropel and the oxidized level immediately above have a much larger age range (5970 ± 170 to 7630 ± 130 BP and 5650 ± 140 to 7660 ± 110 BP, respectively). These results are interpreted as a reflection of oxidation of organic matter in the upper part of the sapropel by downward diffusion of dissolved oxygen after the cessation of sapropel formation when the sediment-pore waters change from anoxic to oxic conditions (Pruysers, DeLange and Middleburg

1991). Thus, the age of the top unit identified by the color and organic content is not the true age, since an unidetermined part of the sapropel has been secondarily reoxidized. However, an oxide-rich layer above the sapropel in the Adriatic Sea is considerably younger (Fontugne *et al.* 1989).

These results show clearly that the conditions that led to the formation of sapropel S1 are not directly associated with glacial freshwater discharge from the Black Sea (Olausson 1961), because the maximum runoff from south-central Europe and western Siberia occurred during the first step of the deglaciation at *ca.* 13,000 BP (Denton 1981), significantly before the beginning of sapropel formation. The chronology is consistent with the sapropel being a direct response to the large discharge of the Nile, which, in turn, reflects the insolation-driven variations of the African Monsoon (Rossignol-Strick 1985). However, the time-transgressive termination of sapropel formation does not permit an estimation of the length of the Mediterranean pluvial period; only the beginning of sapropel formation can be considered as a chronological reference.

To determine the impact of freshwater input to the eastern Mediterranean during the Holocene, we used the variations of the $^{18}O/^{16}O$ ratio of planktonic foraminifera as a tracer of the variations of near-surface salinities, as originally described by Williams, Thunell and Kennett (1978). As fresh water is depleted in the heavy oxygen isotope, compared with sea water, the $\delta^{18}O$ value of calcite tests of planktonic foraminifera, such as *Globigerinoides ruber* (which depends on the isotopic composition of sea water), will record the occurrence of freshwater input and the variation of the salinity gradient (Duplessy 1982). However, the $\delta^{18}O$ of foraminifera also depends on the temperature of sea water in which the foraminifera lived, with a decrease of *ca.* 0.25‰ for every 1°C temperature increase. Fortunately, the surface-temperature gradient in the Levantine Basin is small (<1°C), and we have assumed that it was constant over the entire Holocene period.

Data from 47 cores, including some already published (see references in Table 1), were used to reconstruct the paleosalinity gradient at the start of the sapropel deposition period. The $\delta^{18}O$ values were determined on the same morphological form of *G. ruber* to avoid the variability in isotopic fractionation caused by biological effects (Emiliani 1969). Because of the variability of the $\delta^{18}O$ records within sapropel S1 in the cores referenced in Table 1, we took the most negative values of *G. ruber* from the sapropel in each core to examine the regional salinity gradient in the eastern Mediterranean during this event (Figure 2). The lowest $\delta^{18}O$ values (−1.5 to −2.0‰) occur along the Sinai and Israeli coasts and increase steadily to the west. Such a pattern follows the present sea-surface circulation, where the Nile River discharge is driven toward the east (Lacombe and Tchernia 1972). The trend of increasing $\delta^{18}O$ values to the west continues to roughly 30°E longitude, where positive values are found. The values decrease again south of Crete, and are as negative as those found off Sinai toward the African coast. Aegean Sea values are slightly higher than those intermediately south of Crete.

These $\delta^{18}O$ changes cannot be the result of sea-surface temperature variations because of the marked east-west isotopic gradient in the eastern part of the basin and the large changes in $\delta^{18}O$ over relatively small distances in the area around Crete. The distribution of $\delta^{18}O$ values shown in Figure 2 appears to indicate that there were two freshwater sources for the eastern Mediterranean at the beginning of the sapropel event. Clearly, one was the Nile River, whose influence was limited to the area east of 30°E. The other appears to have been south of Crete, and may have originated in North Africa (Cyrenaica and/or Libya). High lake levels throughout this region between 7000 and 9000 BP (Street and Grove 1979; Nicholson and Flohn 1980) probably indicate significant freshwater drainage to the central Mediterranean during sapropel S1 formation.

TABLE 2. AMS ¹⁴C ages of the Base and the Top of Sapropel S1

Core*	KET 8216	KET 8222	DED 8706	MD 84639	MD 84650	MD 84641	MD 84627
Depth (m)	1166	1691	3620	870	2360	1375	1185
Below	9380 ± 140		9040 ± 140	9580 ± 120	9130 ± 150	9360 ± 130	8440 ± 160
Base	8610 ± 110	8600 ± 140	8150 ± 140	8960 ± 100	8720 ± 130	8300 ± 110	8630 ± 130
Top	6270 ± 110		6960 ± 150	7630 ± 130	7650 ± 140	6670 ± 100	5970 ± 170
Above	6270 ± 110		6410 ± 140	7660 ± 110	6790 ± 120	6310 ± 100	5650 ± 140

*Core locations: KET 8216: 41.51°N 17.93°E. KET 8222: 37.63°N 16.88°E. The locations of the other cores are given in Table 1.

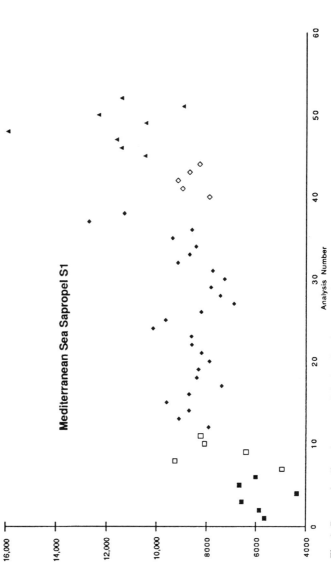

Fig. 1. Reported radiocarbon ages of the basal and upper horizons of sapropel S1 in eastern Mediterranean cores. ▲ – below the sapropel; ♦ – sapropel; ◇ – base of sapropel; □ – top of sapropel; ■ – above sapropel.

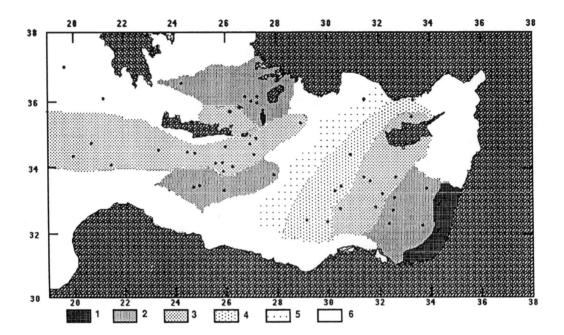

Fig. 2. Distribution of the lowest $\delta^{18}O$ values of *Globigerinoides ruber* in Sapropel S1 in cores from the eastern Mediterranean. The $\delta^{18}O$ value at each location has been normalized to a temperature of 25°C. For the cores from the Levantine Basin, the summer temperature was, on average, 1°C higher, whereas in the area south of Crete, it was roughly 0.5°C lower (Thiede 1978). Legend: 1: <−1.3; 2: −1.3 to −0.90; 3: −0.9 to −0.3; 4: −0.3 to +0.1; 5: >+0.1; 6: no data.

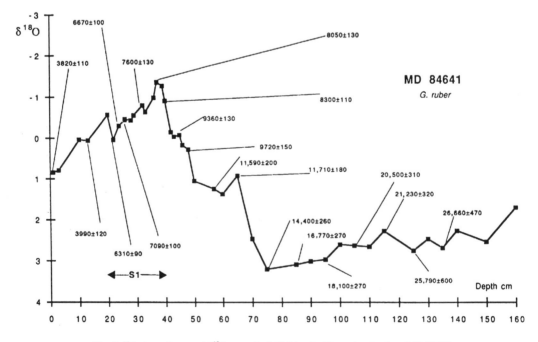

Fig. 3. ^{14}C chronology and $\delta^{18}O$ record of *Globigerinoides ruber* in Core MD 84641

Further data are needed to determine more precisely the source of these waters. The rather high $\delta^{18}O$ values encountered in the area south of Crete and the sharp NWSE $\delta^{18}O$ gradient between the Aegean Sea and the Levantine basin suggest that the contribution of fresh water from the Black Sea to the eastern Mediterranean was minor. The distribution of $\delta^{18}O$ values shown in Figure 2, which closely reflects the salinity pattern, indicates that sea-surface circulation does not appear to have been very different from the present, and that the Nile was not the only freshwater source for the eastern Mediterranean during the formation of sapropel S1. Whether these freshwater sources were responsible for bottomwater anoxia as a result of water column stratification (Kullenberg 1952; Olausson 1961), or for a circulation reversal leading to increased primary production in this basin (Berger 1976; Calvert 1983) is unknown.

Unfortunately, the duration of the period of increased runoff from North Africa cannot be determined from the chronology of sapropel formation, because of the wide variation in the ^{14}C ages at the top of this unit (Table 2). On the other hand, the dating of the oxygen isotope record in an undisturbed sediment core, which is mainly a record of salinity and/or freshwater input during the Holocene period, provides the best estimate of the duration of this major pluvial period. Core MD 84641 was chosen for this study because of its proximity to the Nile River mouth, because of the presence of a relatively thick and unbioturbated sapropel S1 and because of the relatively high sedimentation rate (10 cm/1000 yr) in the core that provides a high-resolution record. Standard methods were used to separate and clean *G. ruber* samples (Duplessy 1978), which were dated by the ^{14}C AMS technique (Arnold *et al.* 1987). The results are presented in Figure 3.

The $\delta^{18}O$ record is similar to that believed to represent the World Ocean. The inflection point at 75 cm (14,400 ± 260 BP), marking the beginning of the $\delta^{18}O$ decrease, indicates the beginning of deglaciation in the northern hemisphere, and its age agrees with that recorded in the North Atlantic Ocean (Bard *et al.* 1987). Between 75 and 48 cm (14,400–9750 BP), the $\delta^{18}O$ values decrease, recording the temperature increase during the first step of deglaciation; between 11,700 and 10,000 BP, a marked plateau in $\delta^{18}O$ values, with a small increase at around 60 cm, may signify a pause in the deglaciation (Duplessy *et al.* 1981). Between 48 and 37 cm (9300–8050 BP), $\delta^{18}O$ values indicate maximum freshwater input; marine faunal or pollen analyses for this period (Luz and Berstein 1976; Cheddadi 1988) show that such low $\delta^{18}O$ values are not affected by temperature variations. After an abrupt increase after 8000 BP, $\delta^{18}O$ values increase progressively to reach present values at 4000 BP.

This record shows that major freshwater flooding occurred over a period of less than 1300 yr, that is, between 9300 and 8000 BP, (the sharp peak in $\delta^{18}O$ values). However, the influence of freshwater input extended over a much longer interval, namely from 9300 to 4000 BP, considerably longer than that represented by the duration of the sapropel. Evidently, freshwater flooding had to be above a critical threshold to induce sapropel formation. The reversal of the climatic trend toward drier conditions at 8000 BP agrees well with the marine palynological record (Cheddadi, Rossignol-Strick and Fontugne 1991) and observations from continental records (Street and Grove 1979; Nicholson and Flohn 1980).

CONCLUSION

Although marine records do not necessarily offer the best resolution, they do, with the support of accurate isotopic records and absolute chronologies, allow reliable climatic reconstructions at regional scales, permitting correlation with continental sequences. Palynological records have provided information on the vegetational pattern around eastern Mediterranean borderlands, and point to the drier and cooler climatic conditions during the last glacial maximum. Marine faunal and pollen analyses show that, during this period, the harsher conditions were focused in the central eastern Mediterranean. The oxygen isotopic record from marine cores has clearly demonstrated significant freshwater inputs to the eastern Mediterranean during the period of formation of the last sapropel, and has shown that this supply was not from a single source, such as the Nile River. Additional sources in North Africa or a precipitation increase over the entire basin are possible. This pluvial period started *ca.* 9300 BP and ended after *ca.* 4000 BP.

ACKNOWLEDGMENTS

We thank the following: C. Vergnaud-Grazzini, who provided us with an unpublished oxygen isotopic stratigraphy of Core KS 8204; A. Murat for samples from Aegean Sea cores; H. Leclaire and C. Neuman for micropaleontological studies; B. Lecoat, J. Antignac and A. Vigot for technical assistance in mass spectrometry; and E. Kaltenacker and P. Maurice for ^{14}C AMS dating. This study was supported by the Commissariat à l'Energie Atomique (CEA) and Centre National de la Recherche Scientifique (CNRS). Cruise ETNA 82, of the French *R/V Le Suroit*, was supported by Centre National pour l'Exploitation de l'Océan (CNEXO). Cruises DEDALE 86, 87, NOE-MARM-ED 84 of the *R/V Marion Dufresne* were supported by Terres Australes et Antarctiques Françaises (TAAF). The participation of SEC in this study was supported by the Natural Sciences and Engineering Research Council of Canada (NSERC), the Canada Council and CEA/CNRS.

REFERENCES CITED

Adamson, D. A., F. Gasse, F. A. Street and M. A. J. Williams
    1980   Late Quaternary history of the Nile. *Nature* 288:50–55.
Arnold, M., E. Bard, P. Maurice and J. C. Duplessy
    1987   [14]C dating with the Gif-sur-Yvette tandetron accelerator: Status report. *Nuclear Instruments and Methods in Physical Research* B29:120–123.
Bard E., M. Arnold, P. Maurice, J. Duprat, J. Moyes and J. C. Duplessy
    1987   Retreat velocity of the North Atlantic polar front during the last deglaciation determined by ^{14}C accelerator mass spectrometry. *Nature* 328:791–794.
Berger, W. H.
    1976   Biogenous deep-sea sediments: Production, preservation and interpretation. In *Chemical Oceanography*, edited by J. P. Riley and R. Chester, pp. 265–388. Academic Press, London.
Béthoux, J. P.
    1984   Paléo-hydrologie de la Mediterranée au cours des derniers 20,000 ans. *Oceanologica Acta* 6:225–267.
Bottema, S.
    1974   Late Quaternary vegetation history of NW Greece. Unpublished Ph.D. Dissertation, University of Groningen, The Netherlands.
Bottema, S. and W. van Zeist
    1981   Palynological evidence for the climatic history of the Near East, 50,000–60,000 BP. Colloque International du CNRS 598:111–132.
Bradley, W. H.
    1938   Mediterranean sediments and Pleistocene sea levels. *Science* 88:376–379.
Broecker, W. S. and T.-H. Peng
    1982   *Tracers in the Sea*. Eldigio Press, New York.
Buckley, H. A., L. R. Johnson, N. J. Shackleton and R. A. Blow
    1982   Late glacial to recent cores from the eastern Mediterranean. *Deep Sea Research* 35:739–766.
Buckley, J. D. and E. H. Willis
    1969   Isotope radiocarbon measurements VII. *Radiocarbon* 11:53–105.
    1970   Isotope radiocarbon measurements VIII. *Radiocarbon* 12(1):87–129.
Calvert, S. E.
    1983   Geochemistry of Pleistocene sapropels and associated sediments from the eastern Mediterranean. *Oceanologica Acta* 6:255–267.
Cheddadi, R.
    1988   Paléoclimats au nord de la Méditerranée orientale depuis 250,000 ans. Analyse pollinique et stratigraphie isotopique de quatre carottes marines. Unpublished Ph.D. Dissertation, University of Montpellier, France.

Cheddadi, R. and M. Rossignol-Strick
  1994   Palaeovegetation and palaeoclimate of the eastern Mediterranean borderlands during the last 250 kyr. *Paleoceanography,* in press.
Cheddadi R., M. Rossignol-Strick and M. Fontugne
  1991   Eastern Mediterranean palaeoclimate from 26 to 5 ka B.P. documented by pollen and isotopic analysis of a core in the anoxic Bannock Basin. *Marine Geology* 100:53–66.
Cita, M. B. and D. Grignani
  1982   Nature and origin of Late Neogene Mediterranean sapropels. In *The Nature and Origin of Cretaceous Carbon-Rich Facies,* edited by S. O. Schlanger and M. B. Cita, pp. 165–196. Academic Press, London.
Cita, M. B., C. Vergnaud-Grazzini, C. Robert, H. Chamley, N. Ciaranfi and S. d'Onofrio
  1977   Paleoclimatic record of a long deep-sea core from the eastern Mediterranean. *Quaternary Research* 8:205–235.
CLIMAP Project Members
  1976   The surface of the ice age earth. *Science* 191:1131–1137.
Delibrias, G.
  1989   Carbon 14. In *Nuclear Methods of Dating,* edited by E. Roth and Poty. CEA, Paris.
Delibrias, G., M. T. Guillier and J. Labeyrie
  1974   Gif natural radiocarbon measurements VIII. *Radiocarbon* 16(1):15–94.
  1986   Gif natural radiocarbon measurements X. *Radiocarbon* 28(1):9–68.
Denton, G. H. and T. J. Hughes (editors)
  1981   *The Last Great Ice Sheets.* John Wiley & Sons, New York.
Duplessy, J. C.
  1978   Isotope studies. In *Climatic Change,* edited by J. Gribbins, pp. 46–67. Cambridge University Press, Cambridge.
  1982   Glacial to interglacial contrast in the northern Indian Ocean. *Nature* 295:494–498.
Duplessy, J. C., G. Delibrias, J. L. Turon, C. Pujol and J. Duprat
  1981   Deglacial warming of the northeast Atlantic Ocean: Correlation with the palaeoclimatic evolution of the European continent. *Palaeogeography, Palaeoclimatology, Palaeoecology* 35:121–144.
Emiliani, C.
  1969   A new micropaleontology. *Micropaleontology* 15:265–300.
Evin, J.
  1991   Fiabilité des matériaux utilisés en datation par le radiocarbone. Master's Thesis, University of Lyon I, France.
Evin, J., J. Marechal, C. Pachiaudi and J. J. Puissegur
  1980   Conditions involved in dating terrestrial shells. *Radiocarbon* 22(2):545–555.
Fontugne, M. R., M. Arnold, L. D. Labeyrie and J.-C. Duplessy
  1989   Initiation de la stratification de la Méditerranée orientale et débit du Nil à l'Holocène. In *Past and Future Evolution of Deserts, Actes Colloque PICG* 252, Jerba, Tunisia.
Fontugne, M. R. and S. E. Calvert
  1992   Late Pleistocene variability of the carbon isotopic composition of organic matter in the eastern Mediterranean: Monitor of changes in carbon sources and atmospheric CO_2 concentrations. *Paleoceanography* 7:1–20.
Fontugne, M. R., M. Paterne, S. E. Calvert, A. Murat, F. Guichard and M. Arnold
  1989   Adriatic deep water formation during the Holocene: Implication for the reoxygenation of the deep eastern Mediterranean Sea. *Paleoceanography* 4:199–206.
Gilot, E. and P. C. Capron
  1973   Louvain natural radiocarbon measurements XII. *Radiocarbon* 15(1):127–133.
Goodfriend, G. A.
  1987   Radiocarbon age anomalies in shell carbonate of land snails from semi-arid areas. *Radiocarbon* 29(2):159–167.
  1988   Mid Holocene rainfall in the Negev Desert from ¹³C of land snail shell organic matter. *Nature* 333:757–760.
Goodfriend, G. and M. Magaritz
  1988   Paleosol and late Pleistocene rainfall fluctuation in the Negev Desert. *Nature* 332:144–146.
Guiot, J.
  1990   Methodology of the last climatic cycle reconstruction from pollen data. *Palaeogeography, Palaeoclimatology, Palaeoecology* 80:49–69.
Guiot, J., A. Pons, J. L. de Beaulieu and M. Reille
  1989   A 140,000 year climatic reconstruction from two European pollen records. *Nature* 338:309–313.
Imbrie, J. and N. G. Kipp
  1971   A new micropaleontological method for quantitative paleoclimatology: Application to a late Pleistocene Caribbean core. In *The Late Cenozoic Glacial Ages,* edited by K. K. Turekian, pp. 71–181. Yale University Press, New Haven.

Jenkins, J. A. and D. F. Williams
    1984   Nile water as a cause of eastern Mediterranean sapropel formation: Evidence for and against. *Marine Micropaleontology* 9:521–534.
Keller, J.
    1971   The major volcanic events in recent eastern Mediterranean volcanism and their bearing on the problem of Santorini ash layers. In *Acta of the 1st International Scientific Congress on the Volcano of Thera*, pp. 152–169. Archaeological Services of Greece, Athens
Kullenberg, B.
    1952   On the salinity of the water contained in marine sediments. *Goteborgs Kunliga Vetenskapsoch Vitterhets-Samhalle. Handlingar* 6B:3–37.
Lacombe, H. and P. Tchernia
    1972   Caractères hydrologiques et circulation des eaux en Méditerranée. In *The Mediterranean Sea*, edited by D. J. Stanley, pp. 25-36. Dowden, Hutchinson and Ross, Stoudsburg, Pennsylvania.
Luz, B.
    1979   Paleo-oceanograghy of the post glacial eastern Mediterranean. *Nature* 278:847–848.
Luz, B. and M. Bernstein
    1976   Planktonic foraminifera and quantitative paleoclimatology of the eastern Mediterranean. *Marine Micropaleontology* 1:307–323.
Luz, B. and L. Perelis-Grossowicz
    1980   Oxygen isotopes, biostratigraphy and recent sedimentation rates in the eastern Mediterranean off Israel. *Israeli Journal of Earth Science* 29:140–146.
Miller, A. R.
    1983   The Mediterranean Sea, A. Physical aspects. In *Ecosystems of the World*, vol. 26, edited by B. H. Ketchum, pp. 219–251. Elsevier, Amsterdam, The Netherlands.
Murat A.
    1984   Séquences et paléoenvironnements marins quaternaires: Une marge active: L'arc hellénique oriental. Master's Thesis, University of Perpignan, France.
Murat, A. and H. Got
    1987   Middle and late Quaternary depositional sequences and cycles in the eastern Mediterranean. *Sedimentology* 34:885–899.
Nicholson, S. E. and H. Flohn
    1980   African environmental and climatic changes and the general atmospheric circulation in the Late Pleistocene and Holocene. *Climatic Change* 2:313–348.
Ninkovitch, D. and B. C. Heezen
    1965   Santorini tephra. *Submarine Geology and Geophysics*. Colston Papers 17:413–452.
Olausson, E.
    1961   Studies of deep-sea cores. *Report of the Swedish Deep Sea Expedition* 8:335–391.
Olson, E. A. and Broecker, W. S.
    1959   Lamont natural radiocarbon measurements V. *American Journal of Science Radiocarbon Supplement* 1:1–28.
Olsson, I.
    1959   Uppsala natural radiocarbon measurements I. *American Journal of Science Radiocarbon Supplement* 1:87–102.
Östlund, H. G. and L. G. Engstrand
    1960   Stockholm natural radiocarbon measurements III. *American Journal of Science Radiocarbon Supplement* 2:186–197.
Pastouret, L.
    1970   Etude sédimentologique et paléoclimatique de carottes prélevées en Méditerranée orientale. *Thethys* 2: 227–266.
Paterne, M., F. Guichard and J. Labeyrie
    1988   Explosive activity of the south Italian volcanoes during the past 80,000 years as determined by marine tephrochronology. *Journal of Volcanology and Geothermal Research* 34:153–172.
Paterne, M., F. Guichard, J. Labeyrie, P. Y. Gillot and J. C. Duplessy
    1986   Tyrrhenian Sea tephrochronology of the oxygen isotope record for the past 60,000 years. *Marine Geology* 72:259–285.
Paulissen, E. and P. Vermeersch
    1989   Le comportement des grands fleuves allogènes: L'exemple du Nil saharien au Quaternaire supérieur. *Bulletin de la Société Géologique de France* 8:73–83.

Pruysers, P. A., G. J. DeLange and J. J. Middleburg
1991   Geochemistry of eastern Mediterranean sediments: Primary sediment composition and diagenetic reactions. *Marine Geology* 100:137–154.
Rossignol-Strick, M.
1983   African monsoons, an immediate climate response to orbital insolation. *Nature* 304:46–49.
1985   Mediterranean Quaternary sapropels, an immediate response of the African Monsoon to variation of insolation. *Palaeogeography, Palaeoclimatology, Palaeoecology* 49:237–263.
Rossignol-Strick, M., W. Nesteroff, P. Olive and C. Vergnaud-Grazzini
1982   After the deluge: Mediterranean stagnation and sapropel formation. *Nature* 295:105–110.
Rossignol-Strick, M. and N. Planchais
1989   Climate patterns revealed by pollen and isotope records of a Tyrrhenian sea core. *Nature* 342:413–416.
Rossignol-Strick, M., N. Planchais and M. Paterne
1992   Vegetation dynamics and climate during the deglaciation in an Adriatic record. *Quaternary Science Reviews* 11:415–423.
Stanley, D. J. and A. Maldonado
1977   Nile Cone: Late Quaternary stratigraphy and sediment dispersal. *Nature* 266:129–135.
Street, F. A. and A. T. Grove
1979   Global maps of lake-level fluctuations since 30,000 yr B.P. *Quaternary Research* 12:83–118.
Sutherland, H., S. E. Calvert and R. J. Morris
1984   Geochemical studies of the recent sapropel and associated sediment from the Hellenic Outer Ridge, eastern Mediterranean Sea. I. Mineralogy and chemical composition. *Marine Geology* 56:79–92.
Thiede, J.
1978   A glacial Mediterranean. *Nature* 276:680–683.
Thunell, R. C.
1979   Eastern Mediterranean Sea during the last Glacial Maximum: An 18,000 year B.P. reconstruction. *Quaternary Research* 11: 353–372.
Thunell, R. C. and G. P. Lohmann
1979   Planktonic foraminiferal fauna associated with eastern Mediterranean Quaternary stagnations. *Nature* 281:211–213.
Thunell, R. C., D. F. Williams and J. P. Kennett
1977   Late Quaternary paleoclimatology, stratigraphy and sapropel history in the eastern Mediterranean. *Marine Micropaleontology* 2:371–388.
Troelstra, S. R., G. M. Ganssen, K. van der Borg, and A. F. M. de Jong
1991   A late quaternary stratigraphic framework for the eastern Mediterranean sapropel S1 based on AMS *14C* dates and stable oxygen isotopes. *Radiocarbon* 33(1):15–21.
Tucholka, P., M. R. Fontugne, F. Guichard and M. Paterne
1987   The Blake magnetic polarity episode in cores from the Mediterranean Sea. *Earth and Planetary Science Letters* 86:320–326.
van Zeist, W. and S. Bottema
1977   Palynological investigation in western Iran. *Paleohistoria* 19:19–85.
Vergnaud-Grazzini, C.
1975   δ18O changes in foraminifera carbonates during the last 105 years in the Mediterranean Sea. *Science* 190: 272–274.
Vergnaud-Grazzini, C., M. Devaux and J. Znaidi
1986   Stable isotope "anomalies" in the Mediterranean Pleistocene records. *Marine Micropaleontology* 10:35–69.
Vergnaud-Grazzini, C., W. B. F. Ryan and M. B. Cita
1977   Stable isotope fractionation, climate change and episodic stagnation in the eastern Mediterranean during the Late Quaternary. *Marine Micropaleontology* 2:353–370.
Vinci, A.
1985   Distribution and chemical composition of tephra layers from eastern Mediterranean abyssal sediments. *Marine Geology* 64:143–155.
Williams, D. F. and R. C. Thunell
1979   Faunal and oxygen isotopic evidence for surface water salinity changes during sapropel formation in the eastern Mediterranean. *Sedimentary Geology* 23:81–93.
Williams, D. F., R. C. Thunell and J. P. Kennett
1978   Periodic freshwater flooding and stagnation of the eastern Mediterranean Sea during the Late Quaternary. *Science* 201:252–254.

Wijmstra, T. A.
   1969   Palynology of the first 30 meters of a 120 m deep section in northern Greece. *Acta Botanica Neerlandica* 18:511–527.
Wüst, T. A.
   1935   Die Stratosphäre. *Wissenschaftliche Ergebnisse der Deutschen Atlantischen Expedition auf dem Forschungs- und Vermessungsschiff "Meteor"* 6:109–288.
Znaidi, J.
   1982   Les grands évènements climatiques du Quaternaire récent en Méditerranée orientale: La réponse sédimentaire, microfaunique et isotopique. Master's Thesis, Université Pierre et Marie Curie, Paris.

INTERPRETING LATE QUATERNARY CONTINENTAL SEQUENCES IN ISRAEL

PAUL GOLDBERG[1]

Institute of Archaeology, Hebrew University, Jerusalem 91905 Israel

INTRODUCTION

For decades, Israel and the Near East have been the focus of paleoenvironmental research involving archaeology, botany, zoology and earth science. Israel's particular position at the corners of three continents is significant because a strong ecological gradient exists here, and past changes in climate and environments should be registered in geological sequences. This is equally true for biological sequences, which are discussed elsewhere in this volume (*e.g.*, Fontugne *et al.* 1994).

Geological studies have been undertaken in a wide range of sediments and environments that include lacustrine, alluvial and colluvial, eolian (dunes and loess), coastal and cave sites (Goldberg and Bar-Yosef, in press). Resolution of these environmental changes increases after *ca.* 25,000–30,000 BP with the emergence of reliable chronologies provided by radiocarbon dates and the appearance of *in-situ* archaeological sites.

Although stratigraphic and geomorphologic sequences from Israel have been documented in detail, the methods used to translate these sequences into paleoenvironmental reconstructions commonly are diverse. Here, I attempt to summarize and discuss the geological evidence and strategies that have been employed to make these reconstructions. I emphasize sediments, soils, and geomorphologic criteria, and additional corroborative data from other disciplines will be mentioned where appropriate. Because this paper focuses on the geographic area of present-day Israel, I have deliberately confined myself to works performed within these boundaries. Thus, information from neighboring Egypt, Jordan, Lebanon and Syria will be mentioned only in passing.

THE REGION

Israel is situated at the transition between the subhumid Mediterranean zone in the north and the arid region of the Negev Desert in the south (Fig. 1). The climate is characterized by relatively short cool, rainy winters and long, hot summers. Precipitation, falling in the winter months (mostly between mid-November and mid-March), varies from a maximum of *ca.* 1000 mm in the Galilee in the north to less than 50 mm in the southern Negev. Temperatures show greater local variation, with the coolest mean annual temperatures in the mountains of the north (Galilee and Mt. Hermon) and central area (Judean Mountains, central and southern Transjordanian plateau) and the central Negev Plateau; the warmest temperatures are in the Jordan Valley and Arabah, which are parts of the Syrian-African Rift (Atlas of Israel 1970).

The most informative and complete continental sequences in Israel are found in fluvial, eolian and lacustrine deposits—commonly associated with paleosols—in the Negev/Sinai and Jordan Valley regions. Here, periods of erosion and deposition are well expressed and associated with archaeological/prehistoric sites.

[1]Present address: Texas Archaeological Research Laboratory, University of Texas, Austin, Texas 78712-1100 USA

Late Quaternary Chronology and Paleoclimates of the Eastern Mediterranean
Edited by O. Bar-Yosef and R. S. Kra. RADIOCARBON 1994, pp. 89–102

Lacustrine Sediments

Exposures of lacustrine sediments are essentially confined to the central and lower Jordan Valley areas. In the Hula Depression of the northern Jordan Valley, stratigraphic paleoenvironmental information derives from boreholes that have yielded data from pollen (Horowitz 1979; Weinstein-Evron 1990; Baruch and Bottema 1991) and diatoms (Ehrlich 1973). The most prominent, extensive and stratigraphically complete lacustrine sediments are those of the Lisan Formation. These were deposited in a Late Pleistocene saline lake that extended from the Sea of Galilee in the north to Hazeva, south of the modern Dead Sea. Considerable research has been done on these sediments, including studies of lithology, mineralogy and diagenesis, geochemistry and diatoms (*e.g.*, Begin, Ehrlich and Nathan 1974, 1980; Katz, Kolodny and Nissenbaum 1977; Gardosh 1987). There are various interpretations regarding the salinity of the water body, documentation of the shrinkage of the lake, itself, and its paleoclimatic history.

The Lisan Formation is generally characterized by alternating laminae of aragonite with local appearances of gypsum and diatomite and detritus-rich layers. Such layers interfinger with wadi gravels at the margins of the lake. Neev and Emery (1967) interpreted the sediments of the Lisan Formation to represent a more humid climate with a greater runoff/evaporation ratio than occurs at present. Both ^{14}C dates obtained from tufa, driftwood and aragonite at various stratigraphic locations near the top of the Lisan deposits (Vogel and Waterbolk 1972), and uranium-series (U-series) determinations (Kaufman 1971), have yielded roughly comparable results, which show that the lake existed from at least 60,000 to *ca.* 15,000 or 17,000 yr ago; the highest level attained by the lake was at *ca.* −180 m (Neev and Emery 1967).

In the original report by Neev and Emery (1967), the Dead Sea stage began *ca.* 15,000 yr ago, during a period with low runoff/evaporation ratio, which indicated a dry climate. Shortly after this, pluvial conditions caused the lake to rise, reaching its maximum between 12,000 and 10,000 BP, and continuing to *ca.* 6500 BP, when desiccation ensued. Contemporary archaeological studies at that time (*i.e.,* 1967) report a cultural gap between the Neolithic and Chalcolithic periods, which is supported by the proposal of the latest dry period. Thus, it appears that no clear climatic change occurred during the transition from the Pleistocene to Holocene. A decade later, Neev published a revised version of the Late Quaternary history of the Lisan/Dead Sea epic (Neev and Hall 1977). They cautioned against a "pseudo-paradoxical trap", *viz.,*

> that within troughs of the intermediate lakes (i.e., lakes between the present Dead Sea basin and basins to the north, such as the Kinneret) evaporitic sediments represent pluvial periods, while the fresh water sediments consisting of coarse detritus and thick alluvial clay beds (cf. Unnamed Clastic Unit of Begin et al., 1974 – see below) represent the interpluvial (interglacial) periods (Neev and Hall 1977:2).

Basing their conclusions on these principles, new uranium/thorium and ^{14}C dates (Kaufman 1971) and new stratigraphic information, Neev and Hall (1977:2) stated: "(a) The Lisan pluvial period appears to have ended some 13,000 to 11,000 years ago. (b) An interpluvial (interglacial) stage occurred some 17,000 to 15,000 years ago between two pluvial stages of the Lisan period". Between 13,000 and 11,000 BP and at *ca.* 10,000 BP, Lake Lisan rapidly and completely dried up. The lake subsequently refilled, which lasted until *ca.* 7000 BP, and which seems to reflect a "pluvial" period.

Begin, Erlich and Nathan (1974, 1980), who studied the lateral and temporal changes in the mineralogy and diatoms from several columnar sections along the entire length of the Lisan basin, suggest a slightly different sequence of events. Their results show an increase in the ratio of chemical to detrital sediments from the lower Laminated Member to the upper White Cliff Member, which contains some thick beds of gypsum and aragonite in the south and diatomite in the north. Overlying these lacustrine sediments, and best exposed in the area north of the present Dead Sea, are predominantly reddish sands, silts and clays—the "Unnamed Clastic Unit"—that represent colluvially and alluvially derived *terra-rossa*-like soils that were stripped from the Samarian hills to the west. Begin, Erlich and Nathan (1974:24) explain these trends as resulting from "a decrease in the supply of detrital sediments and an increase in salt concentration of Lake Lisan with time". They interpreted this to represent a general trend toward climatic aridity throughout the Late Pleistocene, with greater precipitation/evaporation ratios at the base of the Lisan Formation, some 60,000 yr ago, culminating in maximum aridity *ca.* 19,000 yr ago. The deposition of the "Unnamed Clastic Unit" coincides with a return to "pluvial" conditions, when upland soils were eroded. Their interpretation disagrees with that of Neev and Hall (1977), who claimed such detrital masses correspond to "interpluvial" periods.

In a geochemical study of the sediments, Katz, Kolodny and Nissenbaum (1977) documented the geochemical history of Lake Lisan by measuring strontium, sodium and calcium, as well as carbon and oxygen isotopes. The Ca and Sr results show an overall decrease in Sr/Ca ratios in aragonite, and initial values similar to those of the present-day Dead Sea. This indicates "good long term mixing of the lake" (Katz, Kolodny and Nissenbaum 1977:1626), characterized by initial hypersaline water body with contributions of freshwater. They calculated a depth of Lake Lisan between 400 and 600 m. The $\delta^{18}O$ values in the aragonites are high, which they interpreted to represent higher rates of evaporation possibly related to the higher level of the water body (−180 m). Although it is not clear exactly when this occurred, it would appear to correspond to the Upper Member, which would be *ca.* 40,000 to 18,000 yr old (see also Gardosh, Kaufman and Yechieli 1991). The authors did not discuss finer temporal detail.

In another geochemical endeavor, Gardosh (1987) studied the concentrations of water-soluble salts from the Samra (precursor to Lake Lisan) and Lisan Formations. He found that the Na/Cl ratio declines upward within the Lisan Formation. Concomitantly, Mg/Cl, Ca/Cl and Sr/Cl ratios increase at the top of the Formation. These trends increasingly reflect the composition of spring brines. "This change can be created by a constant discharge of spring brines and a decrease in discharge of fresh water, its water composition gradually changed under the influence of the spring brines" (Gardosh 1987:88). This model is more consistent with the conclusions reached by Begin, Erlich and Nathan (1974) than with those of Katz, Kolodny and Nissenbaum (1977). Gardosh (1987) offers no explanation for these diametrically opposing interpretations of the same body of sediment.

Studies of the shoreline facies of the Lisan Formation show similar trends. Druckman, Magaritz and Sneh (1987) studied ooids interfingered with sands and gravels, which were deposited along the margins of Lake Lisan. Aragonitic ooids from an outer zone, close to the shoreline, were partially or completely dissolved. Plant remains apparently associated with an upper oolite layer yielded a ^{14}C date of 14,600 ± 240 BP; aragonitic ooids from below this were 20,400 ± 400 BP.

...oolitic shoals found at an elevation of 180m below sea level and dated at about 14,000 years B.P. indicate that Lake Lisan of that time was a saline lake from which aragonite ooids could precipitate. Since ooids are a deposit of shallow water, this also marks the approximate lake level at that time.

From the areal distribution of the oomoldic diagenetic facies, which surround the lake shoreline..., it is reasonable to assume that fresh water (discharged into the lake by streams) saturated the porous aquifers surrounding the lake and caused the leaching of the aragonite ooids and precipitation of the calcitic cements (Druckman, Magaritz and Sneh 1987:106).

Thus, ooid dissolution is tied to a higher water table associated with a humid climate from *ca.* 14,000 to 13,000 BP. This water table was lowered with a rapid retreat of the lake after this time, which the authors ascribe to climatic change, rather than tectonic subsidence.

Geomorphologic studies of the distribution and stratigraphic position of prehistoric sites in the lower Jordan Valley also contribute to our understanding of the final stages of lacustrine deposition and retreat of Lake Lisan. In the area of the Salibiya Basin in the lower Jordan Valley (Fig. 1), several prehistoric sites occur within or on sedimentary units that are contemporary with the Lisan Formation (Bar Yosef, Goldberg and Leveson 1974; Schuldenrein and Goldberg 1981). Here, the retreat of Lake Lisan (Hovers and Bar-Yosef 1987; Bar-Yosef 1987) was accompanied by pre-historic occupations whose ages decrease with elevation; Epipaleolithic sites containing Kebaran and Geometric Kebaran industries (*ca.* 17,000–13,500 BP) are generally found between −180 m, and −193 m and −203 m (Hovers 1989). The spatial patterning of these sites suggests that Lake Lisan was essentially at its maximum elevation until the end of the Geometric Kebaran (*ca.* 13,000 BP).

Natufian sites are located in gullies and eroded pockets that developed on the Lisan marls as the lake retreated; the lowermost sites are at −215 and −230 m. Erosion ceased with the deposition of

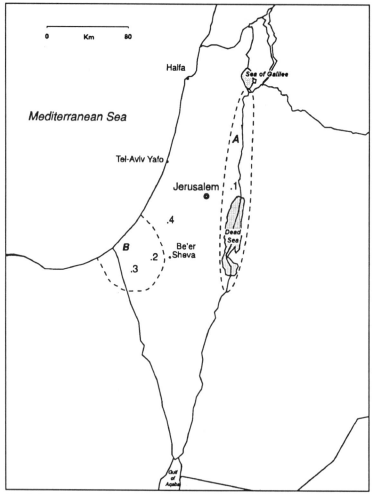

Fig. 1. Location map of sites discussed in the text. A. Jordan Valley; B. Western and northern Negev; 1. Fazael/Salibiya; 2. Shiqmim (Chalcolithic site); 3. Nahals Nizzana and Shunera; 4. Nahal Lachish.

pinkish brown silts that are partially contemporaneous with and slightly postdate the early Pre-Pottery Neolithic (PPNA site of Salibiya IX; Bar-Yosef 1980). *In-situ* salami-shaped masses of algal tufa were found locally within the lowermost centimeters of these silts, and clearly rest upon Late Natufian sites; their formation is associated with freshwater seeps emanating from small, localized depressions. Presumably, these acted as loci for the abundant waterfowl as well as the water mole, *Arvicola*, that was recovered from the contemporaneous PPNA site of Gilgal, dated to 10,100–9400 BP (Noy, Schuldenrein and Tchernov 1980; Bar-Yosef *et al.* 1991).

Deposition continued during the Early Holocene, when the neighboring PPNA settlement of Netiv Hagdud was covered with bouldery gravel. This deposition ended with basin-wide erosion, which is estimated to have begun in mid-Holocene times, possibly after the Chalcolithic period (*ca.* 6500 BP; Goldberg and Bar-Yosef 1990). The geomorphologic and palynologic evidence in the Salibiya depression suggests that climatic conditions were wetter during the Geometric Kebaran and Early Natufian, and became increasingly arid during the late Natufian (Schuldenrein and Goldberg 1981; Leroi-Gourhan and Darmon 1987; Engstrom, Hansen and Wright 1990; Baruch and Bottema 1991). This drier period is tentatively correlated with the Younger Dryas (YD), recently recognized as a worldwide phenomenon (Fairbanks 1989). These observations and the emplacement of Natufian and Neolithic sites in time demonstrate that the reconstruction of the so-called Lake Beisan of Koucky and Smith (1986) clearly is untenable.

A similar trend comes from Wadi Fazael, *ca.* 7 km north of the Salibiya Basin (Bar-Yosef, Goldberg and Leveson 1974; Schuldenrein and Goldberg 1981). Here, several *in-situ* prehistoric sites in alluvial and colluvial contexts provide additional paleoenvironmental data (Table 1). Bar-Yosef, Goldberg and Leveson (1974) believed that changes in climate better explained the geomorphologic evidence than did recent tectonic movements or changes in base level of the final Lisan/proto-Dead Sea lake. Thus, alluviation during the Kebaran and Geometric Kebaran, and deposition of colluvium during the early Natufian, were interpreted to represent a distinctly wetter interval, although the late Natufian seemed to mark an increase in aridity. These interpretations are borne out by the pollen results of Leroi-Gourhan and Darmon (1987) cited above.

TABLE 1. The Sequence of Geomorphologic Events in the Wadi Fazael Basin*

Period	Event
Natufian	4b Erosion continues at least to present wadi bed
Natufian	4a Colluviation of dark stony clay
Natufian	3b Erosion at least to present wadi bed and deposition of gravels
Geometric Kebaran	3a Colluviation of yellowish red stony clay
Geometric Kebaran	2 Minor channeling phase and filling
Kebaran 1	Alluviation of gravels and clays 3–5 m thick with Site Fz VIII

*Based on Bar-Yosef, Goldberg and Leveson (1974); events in descending order

Additional stratigraphic evidence of several ^{14}C dates of tufa and oolites associated with former levels of Lake Lisan (Begin *et al.* 1985) supports the sequences described above. In spite of contamination problems involved with dating these types of materials, the results also indicate that Lake Lisan fluctuated notably during the last 30,000 yr. The dates from Begin *et al.* (1985), for example, suggest that the lake retreated from −180 to −370 m between 21,000 and 17,000 BP, followed by a rise to *ca.* −180 m *ca.* 14,000 BP, and a retreat shortly thereafter. Such assessments are tempered by archaeological field data from this area (Hovers 1989; see above), which show that the fluctuations illustrated by Begin *et al.* (1985) are roughly in the proper temporal position but their amplitude should be reduced.

In summary, the data from Lake Lisan show more agreement between Neev and Hall's (1977) and Begin, Erlich and Nathan's (1974, 1980) revised profiles, than with Neev and Emery's (1967) first profile. Both Neev and Begin appear to agree that Lake Lisan was high until *ca.* 18,000 BP, representing conditions effectively wetter than today's. The two versions diverge after this, wherein Neev calls for a drier period between 18,000 and 15,000 BP, followed by a pluvial period and subsequent rise of the lake until *ca.* 12,000 BP. Begin, Ehrlich and Nathan (1974) envisage a generally pluvial period from 18,000–12,000 BP, as represented by the "Unnamed Clastic Unit"; for Neev and Hall (1977), such a clastic unit signifies dry interpluvial conditions.

The geoarchaeological sequence at Wadis Fazael and Salibiya and associated pollen data support the chronological correlation and climatic interpretation of Begin, Erlich and Nathan (1974, 1980) of a wetter climate between 18,000 and 12,000 BP. Post-Lisan history from Natufian and PPN sites indicates moist conditions, but drying for the Early Natufian (*ca.* 12,000–11,000 BP), until the end of the Late Natufian (*ca.* 11,000–10,600 BP). The PPN (*ca.* 10,000–8500 BP) was characterized by a water table rise, alluviation and presumably wetter conditions; the second half of the Holocene was marked by increasing aridity (*cf.* Goldberg and Rosen 1987).

Fluvial and Slope Sediments in Southern Israel

Fluvial sediments were discussed briefly in the section on the Jordan Valley lacustrine deposits. However, they are more widespread in much of the central and western Negev regions, extending into Sinai (Goldberg 1986; Goldberg and Bar-Yosef, in press). Although early Late Pleistocene sediments and terraces can be found, I confine my discussion to those in the latter part of the profile, where Upper Paleolithic, Epipaleolithic and Historic period sites are found.

In the central and western Negev and Sinai, the past 35,000 yr are characterized by alternate periods of aggradation and degradation, in which numerous prehistoric sites are associated with the aggradational episodes: Upper Paleolithic sites occur over an area that stretches from Wadi El-Arish in Sinai, even to the Wadi Feiran system in Southern Sinai (Phillips 1988), to Nahal Besor (Fig. 1), one of the principal drainages of the western and central Negev. In these larger drainages, including Nahal Nizzana and Wadi Qudeirat, Upper Paleolithic sites can be found in massive fluvial sands, clays and loessial silts that often show signs of standing water. Individual beds of these fine-grained materials can be traced over tens of meters, indicating deposition by low-energy, possibly perennial streams associated with local ponding under wetter climatic conditions. These inferences are based on the ubiquity of the deposits over the region, their fine-grained nature and the lateral extent of the bedding.

Bands of pedogenic carbonate nodules are widespread in these alluvial silts in the Negev. In an isotopic study of three of the stratigraphically highest set of nodules, Goodfriend and Magaritz (1988) obtained ^{14}C dates of *ca.* 13,000, 28,000 and 37,000 BP (also, see below). They believed that these nodules formed during a much wetter period than the present, because, under dry conditions, similar to those of today, there could be little pedogenesis. After the deposition of the fluvial silts associated with Upper Paleolithic sites, widespread erosion and downcutting occurred over much of this region, beginning *ca.* 23,000–25,000 BP, and continuing for *ca.* 10,000 yr. It is worth mentioning that relatively few prehistoric sites were found for this period, despite recent extensive surveys conducted in the area (Goldberg 1986). Aggradation recurred for a brief time between *ca.* 15,000 and 13,000 BP. In Qadesh Barnea, for example, this was characterized by the accumulation of distinctly gleyed sands and silts associated with Epipaleolithic occupations that were ^{14}C dated to *ca.* 14,500–12,500 BP. As before, this alluvial phase was ascribed to a pulse of wetter conditions, on the basis of its regional extent, associated high groundwater table and the relative ubiquity of numerous Epipaleolithic sites over much of the area, including northern and southern Sinai (Goldberg 1984; 1986).

Holocene fluvial sequences also occur over this broad region, and extend northward into the lower Shefela region, near the ancient city of Lachish (Fig. 1). In the Be'er Sheva Valley, for example, architectural and cultural remains at the Chalcolithic site of Shiqmim (Fig. 1) (*ca.* 6200–5600 BP; Levy *et al.* 1991) interfinger with *ca.* 2–3 m of alluvial sands and silts that overlie more than 3 m of well-rounded gravel containing Chalcolithic pottery (Goldberg 1987; Goldberg and Bar-Yosef, in press). At this same location, deposition during Chalcolithic times was later terminated by erosion, which lasted until the Byzantine period, when more than 2 m of massive alluvial silts began to be deposited, continuing until the Crusader period. This late Historic interval of silt deposition was not a local event; deposits of similar age and style can be found over most of the western and northern Negev (Goldberg and Bar-Yosef, in press). In the Shefela, Byzantine sites appear partially buried by clayey alluvial and colluvial soils (personal observations in the Tel Yarmuth area; Goldberg 1988).

Later Holocene deposits are more typical in the northern Negev and southern Shefela regions (Fig. 1). They are distinct coarse- and fine-grained depositional units containing pottery that encompass Early Bronze (EB) through Byzantine periods (Rosen 1986a,b). Rosen recognized channel gravels and finer-grained deposits for the EB, and interpreted them to depict floodplain environments, with ponding and weak pedogenesis of a somewhat moister climate than that of the present. The overlying sediments are associated with the Middle Bronze Age I (MB I), and consist of laminated fine-grained sediments, pointing to rapid floodplain aggradation. This was ascribed to fluctuating rainfall conditions, resulting in landscape instability and stripped hillslopes (Rosen 1986b). Erosion, associated with drier conditions, occurred during the MB II through Late Bronze Age (LB). During the Iron Age, deposition of angular, poorly sorted gravel and sandy silt were attributed to short-distance transport, similar to colluviation of materials from nearby Tell Lachish. This is related to the destruction and subsequent abandonment of the site. Rosen (1986b) believes that this event can be linked to neglect of agricultural fields, which brought about soil erosion.

Coastal Sediments

Pleistocene coastal sediments abound in Israel, and are characterized by cemented and friable calcarenites (*kurkar*) and reddish sandy loams (*hamra*) (Horowitz 1979; Neev, Bakler and Emery 1987). The sediments have been studied from numerous exposures in the western third of the country, as well as from hundreds of boreholes (*e.g.*, Issar 1968; Gvirtzman *et al.* 1983/1984). Although numerical dates are inconclusive, the stratigraphic evidence indicates that the earliest *hamra/kurkar* sequences are Middle Pleistocene, and tend to occur in the easternmost extents of the coastal region. In the northern coastal plain, for example, undated Mousterian implements occur in a >1-m-thick *hamra* that overlies at least two separate *kurkar* units. Higher in the profile is a thinner *hamra*, associated with Epipaleolithic sites (Ronen 1977; Farrand and Ronen 1974; Ronen *et al.* 1975; Ronen and Kaufman 1976). Westward, *hamra/kurkar* sequences become successively younger, with the latest Pleistocene and Holocene profiles occurring along semicontinuous coastal cliff sections (Gvirtzman *et al.* 1983/84).

In the Netanya area, for example, Gvirtzman *et al.* (1983/84) describe a coastal cliff section that consists of two interbedded eolianites beds (*kurkar*) and two *hamras*, capped by unconsolidated yellow and light-brown sandy units. The upper *hamra* contains Epipaleolithic implements, whereas the loose sands encompass archaeological remains ranging from EB to Byzantine Ages.

Unfortunately, in spite of their ubiquity and abundant study, the *kurkar* and *hamra* units provide little unequivocal paleoclimatic information. This is primarily a result of the lack of chronological control, because most of these sediments and soils are beyond the range of ^{14}C dating, although Epipaleolithic tools are found consistently in the uppermost *hamra*. The depositional context of the sandstones and the mode of formation of the loams are also difficult to interpret, despite the quantity of exposures, as well as borehole and analytical data (Issar 1968; Yaalon 1967; Yaalon and Dan 1967; Gvirtzman *et al.* 1983/1984). For example, it is not clear to what extent the sandstones are continental (eolian or beach) or shallow marine, nor whether the sandstones and loams are related to transgressions, regressions or both (see Farrand and Ronen 1974). It is normally difficult to distinguish nearshore eolian sands from marine sands when examining samples from boreholes. Further, although some of the *hamras* are clearly sedimentary in origin (personal observations at Evron Quarry), others are more readily interpretable in terms of pedogenic processes (Yaalon and Dan 1967; Karmeli, Yaalon and Ravina 1968; Dan, Yaalon and Koyum-djisky 1969). The origin of the prominent so-called *café au lait hamra* has been notoriously difficult to determine. Much more work is needed to understand the origin, timing and processes of formation of these deposits and materials.

Eolian Sediments (Dunes and Loess)

In addition to coastal sands described above, other eolian sediments are characterized by both sand (dunes) and silt (loess) deposits, mostly in the western Negev and Sinai, Egypt, where prehistoric sites are plentiful and provide firm chronological control. Most of this information is based on recently published surveys and detailed excavations of prehistoric sites, in association with good geological exposures in the Nahals Nizzana, Shunera, Sekher and Be'er Sheva (Goring-Morris 1987; Goring-Morris and Goldberg 1990). Data from these surveys and excavations show that most of the dunes rest unconformably on vast silty alluvial deposits that contain Late Mousterian through Upper Paleolithic sites (see above). These sediments are usually in the form of terraces which, depending upon locality, were developed between *ca.* 25,000 and 15,000 BP (Goring-Morris and Goldberg 1990; Goldberg 1986).

The first occurrences of sandy deposits resting upon this Upper Paleolithic "undercoating" are found in northern and eastern Sinai, and are dated to *ca.* 25,000 BP. However, as one moves eastward toward the Nahal Be'er Sheva drainage, initial indications of dune incursion from the west become successively younger, such that, in Nahal Nizzana, the 20,000(?)-yr-old site of Azariq XIII is situated at the base of the dune complex. *Ca.* 15 km to the east, in the Shunera area, the earliest sites at the base of the dunes, resting upon eroded fluvial silts, and associated with Upper Paleolithic sites, date to *ca.* 16,000–20,000(?) BP; in Nahal Sekher, again, *ca.* 50 km east of this, eolian dunes occur in association with Epipaleolithic sites that are *ca.* 14,500 yr old (*e.g.*, site Nahal Sekher 22) (Goring-Morris 1987; Goring-Morris and Goldberg 1990). It appears that, overall, the period of *ca.* 25,000–18,000 BP could be characterized by increasing aridity, based on the timing of the movement of the dune sand, prior to its stabilization. On a much more local scale, dune mobilization can be documented during the Neolithic, Chalcolithic and Byzantine periods (Goring-Morris and Goldberg 1990), generally tied to overall aridity for the western Negev/eastern Sinai. However, as discussed elsewhere (Goldberg 1986; Goldberg and Bar-Yosef 1990), geomor-phologic changes associated with Byzantine settlements cannot be discussed in paleoclimatic terms alone. Intensive settlement and human activity in the Negev at this time may have been partly responsible for these changes.

Isotope Studies

We have gained much valuable information from isotope studies of soil carbonates and snails (Magaritz, Kaufman and Yaalon 1981; Magaritz 1986; Goodfriend 1988, 1989, 1990, 1991). As mentioned above, Goodfriend and Magaritz (1988) used ^{14}C to date carbonate nodules from fluvial sequences in the Negev. Magaritz, Kaufman and Yaalon (1981) also studied oxygen and carbon isotopes of soft and hard carbonate nodules from soils in the western part of the country, from the northern Negev to an area near Haifa in the north (Fig. 1). δ^{13}C values were too variable to permit reconstruction of former climates. On the other hand, δ^{18}O values were much more uniform, particularly for hard nodules, which were collected from different Late Pleistocene parent materials. ^{14}C dates of these nodules ranged between 12,600 and 14,870 BP, then appeared to be acceptable, because they formed in carbonate-free material, and were consistent with other stratigraphic evidence, including mean residence time of organic matter and the occurrence of Epipaleolithic artifacts in certain locations. Magaritz, Kaufman and Yaalon (1981:170) concluded that

> about 15,000 to 10,000 years ago two different types of climate-related processes occurred in the Israeli coastal plain. First, nodule formation occurred in three widely spaced soils of significantly different ages.... And secondly, the red Mediterranean Hamra loam...formed in an area of over 100 km² in the near-coastal environment.... Both processes were promoted by increased moisture availability. This can be due to a change in the precipitation/evaporation (P/E) ratio, i.e., different rainfall distribution.

In a similar study, Magaritz (1986) examined carbonate nodules from eolian loess in the Netivot section, northern Negev (Bruins and Yaalon 1979) and a fluvial/lacustrine sequence from Ramat Hovav, western Negev (Yair and Enzel 1987). In the upper part of the Netivot section, which is of concern here, the upper two horizons dated to 7240 BP and 13,630 BP. These and underlying nodules exhibited isotopic compositions that resembled those from nodules to the north, from areas with predominant Mediterranean climates. This suggests, "...that for this short period [14,000-11,000 BP] the desert boundary moved southward and pedogenesis occurred in the whole region studied" (Magaritz 1986:226). This interpretation can also be applied to the uppermost, Holocene horizon, which is roughly coeval with the beginning of the Chalcolithic period (see Shiqmim, above).

The upper part of the Ramat Hovav section consists of late Pleistocene alluvial and eolian sandy silts, overlain by gypsiferous sabkha deposits and loose eolian sand, respectively. ^{14}C ages range from *ca.* 25,900–21,890 BP for the lower unit, to 11,680–10,300 BP for the upper sabkha deposits; unconformities separate these units, as well as the sabkha and dune deposits. Oxygen and carbon isotopes from carbonates show enrichment from the lower to upper horizons, and "may correspond to a change in either the source of the air masses or in the evaporation process" (Magaritz 1986:228). At *ca.* 18,000 BP, prior to the formation of the sabkha and dune deposits, the climate was distinguished by marked aridity.

Goodfriend (1988, 1989, 1990, 1991) studied the carbon isotope ratios of organic matter from Holocene land snails in the Negev in order to monitor changes in the distribution of C_3 and C_4 plants, and to infer climatic shifts in this area, which exhibits a strong precipitation gradient. Snail samples were obtained from archaeological sites, and from both natural and artificial cuts, as well as rodent burrow middens; bulk samples were used for ^{14}C dating. The results show that, during the Middle Holocene (*ca.* 6500–3000 BP), the transition zone between pure C_3 and mixed C_3 and C_4 plants was *ca.* 20 km south of its current location, and "implies significantly greater rainfall in the region at that time" (Goodfriend 1990:196). In a parallel study of oxygen isotope ratios, δ^{18}O values changed systematically within the Holocene; Early Holocene ratios were similar to modern ratios, with a regular decrease that reaches minimum values at *ca.* 6500–6000 BP (Goodfriend 1991) (Fig. 2). After this, $\delta^{18}O$ values increase until 3500 BP, when they reach modern values. These trends are interpreted in terms of changes in atmospheric circulation patterns, with increased frequency of storms arriving from northeastern Africa *ca.* 6500–6000 BP (Goodfriend 1991).

DISCUSSION AND CONCLUSION

Several factors should be considered when analyzing the data presented above. First is the size and distribution of the area under discussion. Although the region is compact, north to south climatic gradients are steep, and annual climatic variability is high, as recent winter (1991/1992) snow-storms clearly illustrate. In addition, Quaternary sequences are both spotty and discontinuous within a given subregion. For example, in the Jordan Valley, deposits of the former Lake Lisan are quite extensive, and they are exposed, albeit with some variability, over a linear distance of almost 200 km. In the area of the western Negev, there is also some geographical and geological congruity, with widespread fluvial deposits containing calcareous soils covered by eolian sands. However, correlation of these two regions, separated only by *ca.* 60 km, and with diverse geological contexts of deposition, is not obvious.

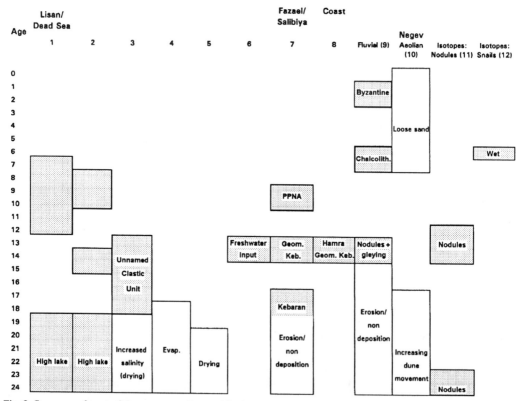

Fig. 2. Summary of most of the sequences discussed in the text. Principal references: 1. Neev and Emery (1967); 2. Neev and Hall (1977); 3. Begin, Ehrlich and Nathan (1974, 1980); 4. Katz, Kolodny and Nissenbaum (1977); 5. Gardosh (1987); 6. Druckman, Magaritz and Sneh (1987); 7. Bar-Yosef, Goldberg and Leveson (1974); Schuldenrein and Goldberg (1981); Begin *et al.* (1985); 8. Issar (1968); Farrand and Ronen (1974); Gvirtzman *et al.* (1983/1984); 9. Goldberg (1986); Goldberg and Bar-Yosef (in press); 10. Goring-Morris (1987); Goring-Morris and Goldberg (1990); 11. Magaritz, Kaufman and Yaalon (1981); Magaritz (1986); Goodfriend and Magaritz (1988); 12. Goodfriend (1988, 1989, 1990, 1991).

For the Jordan Valley, the general level of Lake Lisan seems to have been high throughout the Late Pleistocene, although estimates vary as to when the Lisan stage ended. Models of Begin, Erlich and Nathan (1974) and Neev and Hall (1977) place this stage at *ca.* 18,000 BP, whereas data from Fazael and Salibiya (Schuldenrein and Goldberg 1981) suggest that the lake level was high until Geometric Kebaran times, *ca.* 14,000 BP. The latter interpretation agrees with Begin *et al.*'s (1985) reconstruction, which also shows >150-m fluctuations of the lake levels from *ca.* 30,000–14,000 BP, with higher stages at *ca.* 23,000 and 21,000 BP. However, it should be noted that the chronology of their curve is based heavily on ^{14}C dates of algal stromatolites, which, in thin section, show abundant detrital (dead) carbonates. Despite the drying trends indicated within the Lisan sediments themselves (Begin, Erlich and Nathan 1974), the presence of high lake levels and the stratigraphic data from Fazael (where alluviation is associated with Kebaran sites; Bar-Yosef, Goldberg and Leveson 1974), as well as pollen data (Leroi-Gourhan and Darmon 1987), suggest generally wetter conditions at this time in the Jordan Valley. This is not the case for the western Negev, where, from *ca.* 25,000–14,500 BP, widespread erosion and dune incursion suggests arid, and probably cold, conditions. It would appear then, that, in the central part of the country, a band of wetter climate existed. Butzer (1978) postulated such a configuration, and Goldberg (1986) and Goldberg and Bar-Yosef (1982) commented on it.

This regional disparity in inferred climate is not present during the Geometric Kebaran period (*ca.* 14,500–12,500 BP). Geological, palynological and faunal evidence from this period show that the climate was uniformly and distinctly wetter than at present. In the Jordan Valley, this is illustrated by the pollen data and alluviation associated with high Lisan Lake levels. In the Negev and Sinai, this inference is derived from high water tables, prevalent alluviation and the widespread distribution of Geometric Kebaran and Mushabian sites over the entire area. Strong isotopic evidence from carbonate nodules also exists from the Negev and coastal regions. A distinct calcic horizon can be found in the Fazael area, where it developed within and just below the Geometric Kebaran units, which directly overlie the horizon containing Kebaran artifacts. Such soils do not form under present arid conditions, where leaching is insufficient to mobilize carbonates to this extent. Finally, increased quantities of fresh water were responsible for alteration of the Lisan oolites, as Druckman, Magaritz and Sneh (1987) documented.

The Pleistocene/Holocene transition (*ca.* 12,000–10,000 BP) is particularly well represented in the northern half of the country, and was marked by a shift to drier conditions and increased temperature at *ca.* 11,000 BP. A colder and drier spell was reconstructed for the 11,000–10,000 BP time span, generally correlated with the "Younger Dryas" (Baruch and Bottema 1991; Baruch 1994; Magaritz and Goodfriend 1987). Evidence for a Holocene "Early Neolithic Pluvial" is confined to the Jordan Valley, where the abundant PPN sites with fauna, pollen and plant remains are recorded (Bar-Yosef *et al.* 1991). In the Negev, little stratigraphic information is extant, and most prehistoric sites are found on the surface, without stratigraphic contexts, or in locally mobilized dunes, such as in the Nahal Sekher area. The Jordan Valley contains little stratigraphic information for most of the later Holocene. In contrast, both the carbon isotopic data on snails (Goodfriend 1990) and massive alluviation during the Chalcolithic period in the Western Negev point to wetter conditions *ca.* 6000–7000 BP (Goldberg 1987). Faunal data from this site support this conclusion as well (Grigson, personal communication 1987). Also within the western and northern Negev is the ubiquitous occurrence of fluvial silts dating to the Byzantine through the Crusader periods (Goldberg 1986; Goldberg and Bar-Yosef 1990). The deposition of these silts can be interpreted in both climatic (greater precipitation) and anthropogenic (landscape clearing resulting in surface erosion) terms, and arguments are made for both (Goldberg and Bar-Yosef 1990). The stratigraphic sequences summarized above unquestionably provide important insights for distinguishing paleoenvironmental changes. Yet, the data are still incomplete in terms of temporal and geographic detail, despite the relatively small size of the country. More refined and exacting research is needed to fill these gaps.

REFERENCES CITED

Atlas of Israel
  1970   *Atlas of Israel.* Survey of Israel, Ministry of Labor, Jerusalem. Elsevier, Amsterdam.
Baruch, U.
  1994   The Late Quaternary pollen record of the Near East. This volume.
Baruch, U. and S. Bottema
  1991   Palynological evidence for climatic fluctuations in the southern Levant ca. 17,000 to 9,000 yrs ago. In *The Natufian Culture in the Levant*, edited by O. Bar-Yosef and F. R. Valla. International Monographs in Prehistory, Ann Arbor.
Bar-Yosef, O.
  1980   A figurine from a Khiamian site in the lower Jordan Valley. *Paléorient* 6:193–200.
  1987   Prehistory of the Jordan Rift. *Israel Journal of Earth Sciences* 36:107–119.
Bar-Yosef, O., P. Goldberg and T. Leveson
  1974   Late Quaternary stratigraphy and prehistory of Wadi Fazael, Jordan Valley: A preliminary report. *Paléorient* 2:415-428.
Bar-Yosef, A. Gopher, E. Tchernov and M. E. Kislev
  1991   Netiv Hagdud: An early Neolithic village site in the Jordan Valley. *Journal of Field Archaeology* 18:406–424.
Begin, Z. B., W. Broecker, B. Buchbinder, Y. Druckman, A. Kaufman, M. Magaritz and D. Neev
  1985   Dead Sea and Lake Lisan Levels in the Last 30,000 Years: A Preliminary Report. Internal Report, Geological Survey of Israel.
Begin, Z. B., A. Ehrlich and Y. Nathan
  1974   Lake Lisan: The Pleistocene precursor of the Dead Sea. *Bulletin, Geological Survey of Israel* 63:32.
  1980   Stratigraphy and facies distribution in the Lisan Formation: New evidence from the area south of the Dead Sea, Israel. *Israel Journal of Earth Sciences* 29:182–189.
Bruins, H. and D. H. Yaalon
  1979   Stratigraphy of the Netivot section in the desert loess of the Negev (Israel). *Acta Geologica Academiae Scientiarum Hungarica* 22:161–169.
Butzer, K. W.
  1978   The Late Prehistoric environmental history of the Near East. In *The Environmental History of the Near and Middle East Since the Last Ice Age*, edited by W. C. Brice, pp. 5–12. Academic Press, London.
Dan, J., D. H. Yaalon and H. Koyumdjisky
  1969   Catenary soil relationships in Israel, 1. The Netanya Catena on coastal dunes of the Sharon. *Geoderma* 2:95–120.
Druckman, Y., Magaritz, M. and A. Sneh
  1987   The shrinking of Lake Lisan, as reflected by the diagenesis of its marginal oolitic deposits. *Israel Journal of Earth Sciences* 36:101–106.
Ehrlich, E.
  1973   Quaternary diatoms of the Hula Basin. *Bulletin, Geological Survey Israel* 58:1–40.
Engstrom, D. R., B. C. S. Hansen and H. E. Wright, Jr.
  1990   A possible Younger Dryas record in southeastern Alaska. *Science* 250:1383–1385.
Fairbanks, R. G.
  1989   A 17,000-year glacio-eustatic sea level record: Influence of glacial melting rates on the Younger Dryas event and deep-ocean circulation. *Nature* 342:637–642.
Farrand, W. R. and A. Ronen
  1974   Observations on the kurkar-hamra succession on the Carmel Coastal Plain. *Tel-Aviv* 1:45–54.
Fontugne, M., M. Arnold, L. Labeyrie, S. E. Calvert, M. Paterne and J.-C. Duplessy
  1994   Paleoenvironment, sapropel chronology and Nile River discharge during the last 20,000 years as indicated by deep-sea sediment records in the eastern Mediterranean. This volume.
Gardosh, M.
  1987   Water composition of Late Quaternary lakes in the Dead Sea Rift. *Israel Journal of Earth Sciences* 36:83–89.
Gardosh, M., A. Kaufman and Y. Yechieli
  1991   A reevaluation of the lake sediment chronology in the Dead Sea Basin based on new ^{230}TH/U [sic] dates. *Abstract*, Israel Geological Society Annual Meeting: 42–43.

Goldberg, P.
1984 Late Quaternary history of Qadesh Barnea, northeastern Sinai. *Zeitschrift für Geomorphologie* 28:193–217.
1986 Late Quaternary environmental history of the Southern Levant. *Geoarchaeology* 1:225–244.
1987 Geology and stratigraphy of Shiqmim. In *Shiqmim I, Prehistoric Investigations of Early Farming Societies of the Northern Negev, Israel*, edited by T. E. Levy, pp. 35–43. BAR International Series 356, British Archaeological Reports, Oxford.
1988 Environmental setting of Tel Yarmuth. In *Yarmouth 1*, edited by P. Miroschedji, pp. 105–112. Editions Recherches sur les Civilisations, Paris.

Goldberg, P. and O. Bar-Yosef
1982 Environmental and archaeological evidence for climatic change in the southern Levant and adjacent areas. In *Paleoclimates, Paleoenvironments and Human Communities in the Eastern Mediterranean Region in Later Prehistory*, edited by J. L. Bintliff and W. van Zeist, pp. 399–414. BAR International Series 133, British Archaeological Reports, Oxford.
1990 The effect of man on geomorphological processes based upon evidence from the Levant and adjacent areas. In *Man's Role in the Shaping of the Eastern Mediterranean Landscape*, edited by G. Entjes-Nieborg and W. van Zeist, pp. 71–86. Balkema, Rotterdam.
   Sedimentary environments of prehistoric sites in Israel and the southern Levant. In *Proceedings of the Lubbock Lake Symposium*, edited by E. Johnson. Texas Technology Press, Lubbock, in press.

Goldberg, P. and A. Rosen
1987 Holocene palaeoenvironments in Israel. In *Shiqmim I, Prehistoric Investigations of Early Farming Societies of the Northern Negev, Israel*, edited by T. E. Levy, pp. 23–33. BAR International Series 356, British Archaeological Reports, Oxford.

Goodfriend, G. A.
1988 Mid-Holocene rainfall in the Negev Desert from ^{13}C of land snail shell organic matter. *Nature* 333:757–760.
1989 Complementary use of amino-acid epimerization and radiocarbon analysis for dating of mixed-age fossil assemblages. *Radiocarbon* 31(3):1041–1047.
1990 Rainfall in the Negev Desert during the Middle Holocene, based on ^{13}C of organic matter in land snail shells. *Quaternary Research* 34:186–197.
1991 Holocene trends in ^{18}O in land snail shells from the Negev Desert and their implications for changes in rainfall source areas. *Quaternary Research* 35:417–426.

Goodfriend, G. A. and M. Magaritz
1988 Paleosols and late Pleistocene rainfall fluctuations in the Negev Desert. *Nature* 332:144–146.

Goring-Morris, N. A.
1987 *At the Edge: Terminal Pleistocene Hunter-Gatherers in the Negev and Sinai*. BAR International Series 361, British Archaeological Reports, Oxford.

Goring-Morris, N. A. and P. Goldberg
1990 Late Quaternary dune incursions in the southern Levant: Archaeology, chronology and palaeoenvironments. *Quaternary International* 5:113–137.

Gvirtzman, G., E. Schachnai, N. Bakler and S. Ilani
1983/ The stratigraphy of the Kurkar Group (Quaternary) of the coastal plain of Israel. Geological Survey
1984 of Israel. *Current Reports*: 70–82.

Horowitz, A.
1979 *Quaternary of Israel*. Academic Press, New York.

Hovers, E.
1989 Settlement and subsistence patterns in the Lower Jordan Valley from Epipalaeolithic to Neolithic times. In *People and Culture in Change*, edited by Israel Hershkovitz, pp. 37–51. BAR International Series 508, British Archaeological Reports, Oxford.

Hovers, E. and O. Bar-Yosef
1987 Prehistoric survey of eastern Samaria: A preliminary report. *Israel Exploration Journal* 37:77–87.

Issar, A.
1968 Geology of the central coastal plain of Israel. *Israel Journal of Earth Sciences* 17:16–29.

Karmeli, D., D. H. Yaalon and I. Ravina
1968 Dune sand and soil strata in Quaternary sedimentary cycles of the Sharon coastal plain. *Israel Journal of Earth Sciences* 17:45–53.

Katz, A., Y. Kolodny and Y. Nissenbaum
1977 The geochemical evolution of the Pleistocene Lake Lisan-Dead Sea system. *Geochimica et Cosmochimica Acta* 41:1609–1626.

Kaufman, A.
1971   U-series dating of Dead Sea Basin carbonates. *Geochimica et Cosmochimica Acta* 35:1269–1281.
Koucky, F. L. and R. H. Smith
1986   Lake Beisan and the prehistoric settlement of the Northern Jordan Valley. *Paléorient* 12:27–36.
Leroi-Gourhan, A. and F. Darmon
1987   Analyses palynologiques de sites archéologiques du pléistocène final dans la vallée du Jourdain. *Israel Journal of Earth Sciences* 36:65–72.
Levy, T. E., D. Alon, C. Grigson, A. Holl, P. Goldberg, Y. Rowan and P. Smith
1991   Subterranean Negev settlement. *National Geographic Research and Exploration* 7(4):394–413.
Magaritz, M.
1986   Environmental changes recorded in the Upper Pleistocene along the desert boundary, southern Israel. *Paleogeography, Paleoclimatology, Paleoecology* 53:213–229.
Magaritz, M. and G. A. Goodfriend
1987   Movement of the desert boundary in the Levant from the latest Pleistocene to early Holocene. In *Abrupt Climatic Change: Evidence and Implications*, edited by W. H. Berger and L. D. Labeyrie, pp. 173–183. Reidel, Dordrecht.
Magaritz, M., A. Kaufman and D. H. Yaalon
1981   Calcium carbonate nodules in soils: $^{18}O/^{16}O$ and $^{13}C/^{12}C$ ratios and ^{14}C contents. *Geoderma* 25:157–172.
Neev, D., N. Bakler and K. O. Emery
1987   *Mediterranean Coasts of Israel and Sinai.* Taylor and Francis, New York.
Neev, D. and K. O. Emery
1967   The Dead Sea. *Bulletin, Geological Survey of Israel* 41:1–147.
Neev, D. and J. Hall
1977   Climatic fluctuations during the Holocene as reflected by the Dead Sea levels. Paper presented at the International Conference on Terminal Lakes, Ogden, Utah.
Noy, T., J. Schuldenrein and E. Tchernov
1980   Gilgal, a Pre-Pottery Neolithic A site in the lower Jordan Valley. *Israel Exploration Journal* 30:63–82.
Phillips, J. L.
1988   The Upper Paleolithic of the Wadi Feiran, southern Sinai. *Paléorient* 14(2):183–200.
Ronen, A.
1977   Mousterian sites in red loam in the coastal plain of Mount Carmel. *Eretz Israel* 13:183*–190*.
Ronen, A. and D. Kaufman
1976   Epi-Paleolithic sites near Nahal Hadera, central coastal plain of Israel. *Tel-Aviv* 3:16–30.
Ronen, A., D. Kaufman, R. Gophna, N. Bakler, P. Smith and A. Amiel
1975   The Epi-Paleolithic site of Hefziba, central coastal plain of Israel. *Quartär* 26:53–72.
Rosen, A.
1986a   Alluvial stratigraphy of the Shephela and its paleoclimatic implications. *Geological Survey of Israel, Jerusalem, Report* GSI/25/86.
1986b   Environmental change and settlement at Tel Lachish, Israel. *BASOR* 266:45–58.
Schuldenrein, J. and P. Goldberg
1981   Late Quaternary palaeoenvironments and prehistoric site distribution in the lower Jordan Valley: A preliminary report. *Paléorient* 7:57–72.
Vogel, J. C. and H. T. Waterbolk
1972   Groningen radiocarbon dates X. *Radiocarbon* 14(1):6–11.
Weinstein-Evron, M.
1990   Palynological history of the Last Pleniglacial in the Levant. Les Industries à Pointes Foliacées du Paléolithique Supérieur Européen, Kraków 1989. *Etudes et Recherches Archéologiques de l'Université de Liège* 42:9–25.
Yaalon, D. H.
1967   Factors affecting the lithification of eolianiate and interpretation of its environmental significance in the coastal plain of Israel. *Journal of Sedimentary Petrology* 37:1189–1199.
Yaalon, D. H. and J. Dan
1967   Factors controlling soil formation and distribution in the Mediterranean coastal plain of Israel during the Quaternary. *Proceedings of the VII INQUA Congress* 9, Boulder, Colorado: 321–338.
Yair, A. and Y. Enzel
1987   The relationship between annual rainfall and sediment yield in arid and semi-arid areas. The case of the northern Negev. *Catena Supplement* 10:121–135.

THE LATE QUATERNARY POLLEN RECORD OF THE NEAR EAST

URI BARUCH

Israel Antiquities Authority, P.O. Box 586, Jerusalem 91004 Israel

INTRODUCTION

Palynological evidence gathered in the Near East over the past 35 years indicates that the vegetation of the region was subject to many fluctuations during Late Quaternary times. Due to the relative scarcity of pollen-bearing sediments in this part of the world (as compared, for example, with western Europe) palynological information for the region is unevenly distributed (Fig. 1). The two main centers for research are in Anatolia, where W. van Zeist and S. Bottema, Biologisch Archaeologisch Instituut, State University of Groningen, The Netherlands, conducted intensive studies, and the southern Levant, which has been investigated by several scientists, including the present author. Evidence from farther inland is much scarcer. Vegetational changes of the Late Pleistocene and Early Holocene are viewed as resulting from climatic events, whereas those of the later Holocene are considered mainly the result of anthropogenic interference. As the results of most studies discussed in the following have already been published in detail, this paper focuses mainly on principal trends in the vegetational history of the Near East, and particularly on chronostratigraphic aspects of the pollen record in various parts of the region, rather than on events at specific sites. Radiocarbon (^{14}C) dates are discussed in terms of years before present (BP), and are uncalibrated, unless otherwise indicated.

THE PLENIGLACIAL

Chronologically, this period corresponds to the main phase of the last glacial period, up to ca. 14,000 BP, that is, to isotopic stages 2–3 in terms of deep sea-core stratigraphy (Shackelton and Opdyke 1973). The earlier phase of this time span was marked by moderate (interstadial) climatic conditions in the northern hemisphere, whereas, in the later phase, more severe conditions prevailed, as northern hemisphere glaciers advanced to their maximum southern limit.

Only four pollen sites in the Near East yielded palynological evidence for the period before the past 20,000 yr. As these sites are separated by several hundred kilometers, their respective pollen records provide a rather fragmentary picture of the regional history of vegetation.

The Southern Levant

One of the longest sedimentary sequences in the Near East is in the Hula Valley, which occupies the northernmost of the three main basins located in the southern Levantine segment of the Syro-African Rift system. Lake sediments have accumulated here since early Quaternary times (Horowitz 1979), but as a result of large drainage operations carried out in the 1950s, the lake, which once covered a large portion of the valley, has been reduced to a few small ponds confined to a nature reserve in the south. Precipitation in the valley ranges from 700 to 450 mm (decreasing from north to south), whereas on the adjacent mountains, it fluctuates (with local topography) between 1000 and 500 mm. According to Zohary (1973, 1980), the now almost completely destroyed climax vegetation of the area is dominated by *Quercus ithaburensis,* scattered patches of which may still be encountered in the valley and on the lower reaches of the surrounding slopes. Above 400–500 m, Tabor oak park forest is replaced by typical Mediterranean maquis of *Quercus*

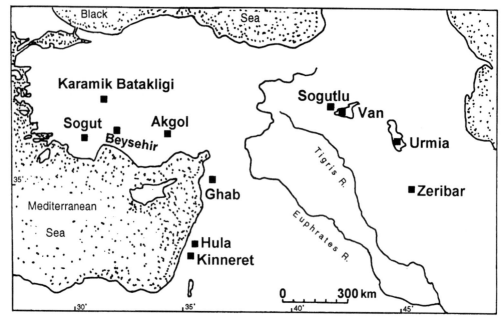

Fig. 1. Location map of pollen diagram site in the Near East

calliprinos and *Pistacia palaestina*, which, above 800 m, are joined by the deciduous Quercus boissieri.

The vegetational history of the Hula Valley in the period under consideration is recorded palyno-logically in the upper part of a 120-m-long core, studied by Weinstein-Evron (1983). Two dates obtained from the top 10 m of the core gave ages on the order of 40,000–42,000 BP. Weinstein-Evron based the chronological framework of her diagram on the correlation of her Zones 13–15 with Zone U3 of the Ghab diagram from the northern Levant (see below), and on her view that the lowest pollen assemblage zones of her diagram (1–5), indicating dry conditions, should be correlated with the last interglacial. Accordingly, Weinstein-Evron's diagram is chronologically bracketed by dates of *ca.* 46,000 BP and 10,000 BP.

Oak and grass pollen dominate the diagram. Grass must have originated mainly from local plants growing on the lake shore, whereas oak undoubtedly derived from forests surrounding the lake, both in the valley and on the adjacent hillsides. The arboreal pollen/non-arboreal pollen (AP/NAP) ratio fluctuates between 20% and 50% along the 15 pollen assemblage zones into which the diagram was divided, pointing to considerable shifts in the extent of the forest around the lake during the period covered by the pollen diagram. Zone 5, which demonstrates the lowest total AP values (20–25%) and the highest chenopod values (*ca.* 40%), seems to represent the driest period. The following period, corresponding to Zone 6, was probably the most humid, as AP values increase to 60%.

As no differentiation has been made, in Weinstein-Evron's diagram, between deciduous and ever-green oak pollen types, the relative proportion of each in the actual vegetation is not known. However, based on results obtained in a study of a younger core from the same area (Baruch and Bottema 1991; see discussion below), we speculate that most oak pollen grains in Weinstein-Evron's core originated in deciduous oaks, and probably mainly Tabor oak. Toward the upper part of the diagram, especially from Zone 12 on, the pollen evidence suggests cooler conditions in the

Hula area, as the relative frequency of *Cedrus* pollen grains increases. However, until more precise chronological control of Weinstein-Evron's diagram becomes available, the exact period during which this and other events recorded in the diagram occurred will remain a matter of sheer speculation.

The later part of the Pleniglacial in the Hula is covered by a pollen diagram prepared by Baruch and Bottema from a 17-m-long core taken *ca.* 5 km south of Weinstein-Evron's core (Fig. 2). The diagram reflects only the events recorded in the lowest 6 m of the core, representing the period from 17,000 to 9000 BP. The chronology of the sequence is anchored by four ^{14}C dates (Fig. 2). As stated above, the AP is dominated by deciduous (presumably Tabor) oak pollen, and the NAP is dominated by grass pollen. As may be inferred from the low AP values in the lowest section of the diagram, before the beginning of the Late Glacial (*ca.* 14,000 BP), climatic conditions in the Hula area must have been drier (and cooler) than at present.

The Northern Levant

A pollen diagram covering the past 45,000 yr was prepared by Niklewski and van Zeist (1970) from a 7-m-long core retrieved from the Ghab valley in northwestern Syria. Annual precipitation

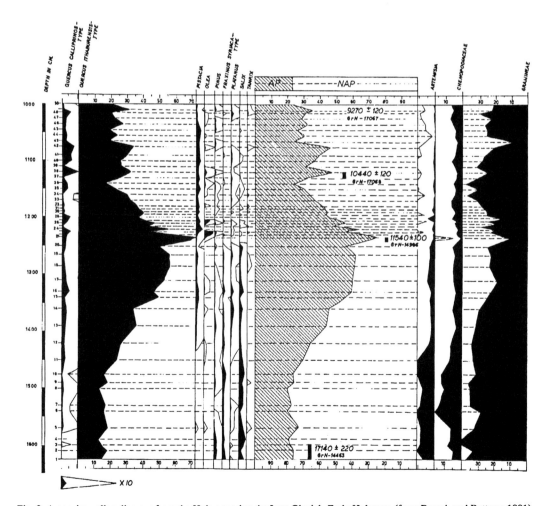

Fig. 2. A concise pollen diagram from the Hula covering the Late Glacial–Early Holocene (from Baruch and Bottema 1991)

fluctuated here with local topography from 1300 mm in the uplands to 600 mm in the lowlands. The main natural vegetational belts on the surrounding hillsides, presently largely degraded, consist of, in ascending altitudinal order, *Ceratonia siliqua* – *Pistacia lentiscus* park forest, *Quercus calliprinos* – *Pistacia palaestina* maquis and *Quercus infectoria* forest.

Three ^{14}C dates place the pollen diagram between *ca.* 45,000 BP and 9000 BP. Deciduous oaks dominate the AP; Artemisia and chenopods dominate the NAP. Marked fluctuations of the AP/NAP ratio characterize the 21 pollen assemblage zones of the diagram, suggesting considerable shifts in forest cover versus steppe during the Pleniglacial. Presumably, these shifts resulted from climatic fluctuations involving both temperature and precipitation. However, as there are too few ^{14}C dates in the diagram, little else can be concluded about these events.

Although it may be possible to demonstrate similarities between the Ghab diagram and Weinstein-Evron's diagram from the Hula, the poor chronological control of both records renders largely speculative any attempt to correlate climatic events of the northern and southern Levant during the Pleniglacial.

Western Iran

Van Zeist and Bottema (1977) undertook pioneering research in Near Eastern palynology in western Iran, subsequently constructing a pollen diagram from a 40-m-long core from Lake Zeribar (Fig. 3), a small lake situated in an intermontane valley, 1300 m above sea level (asl). The vegetation around the lake consists of remnants of deciduous-oak forest dominated by *Quercus brantii*. Annual precipitation is 600–800 mm, and January and July mean temperatures are *ca.* 2°C and 28°C, respectively.

Zones 1–3 of the Zeribar diagram represent the Pleniglacial, ^{14}C-dated between 42,000 and 14,000 BP. The sequence is dominated by NAP, with *Artemisia* and chenopods (especially *Atriplex*-type) forming the bulk of the assemblage, while AP values are no more than 5%. These data point to severe continental conditions in the inner Zagros during the Pleniglacial. The vegetation was dominated by steppe and desert plants, with isolated stands of deciduous oaks, especially in the early part of the period; the climate, which was undoubtedly cooler than at present, must also have been significantly drier. Toward the final stages of this period conditions seem to have become even more harsh, as the corresponding segment of the diagram shows almost total disappearance of arboreal vegetation from the Zeribar area; this is most conspicuous in Subzone 3b, chronologically coinciding with the peak of glaciation in the northern hemisphere. Continuing global temperature decline seems to have been coupled, in the eastern Zagros, with further decline in humidity.

Western Anatolia

The longest pollen record from this part of the Near East comes from Karamik Batakligi (van Zeist, Woldring and Stapert 1975). This former lake, 1000 m asl, is now largely a marsh, with little open water. Annual precipitation, including summer rains, is *ca.* 480 mm; January and July mean temperatures are *ca.* 0°C and 22°C, respectively. Information on extant local vegetation is scarce; however, it is severely disturbed as a result of long-term human intervention. Its composition is essentially steppic, with very few trees.

The base of the 6-m-long core retrieved from Karamik Batakligi was ^{14}C-dated to *ca.* 20,000 BP. Assuming a constant rate of sedimentation between the lowermost (5.75–6.00 m) and an overlying dated level (3.75–4.00 m), Zones 1–2 of the Karamik Batakligi pollen diagram (Fig. 4), with inferred ages of *ca.* 20,000–18,500 and 18,500–14,500 BP, respectively, probably represent the

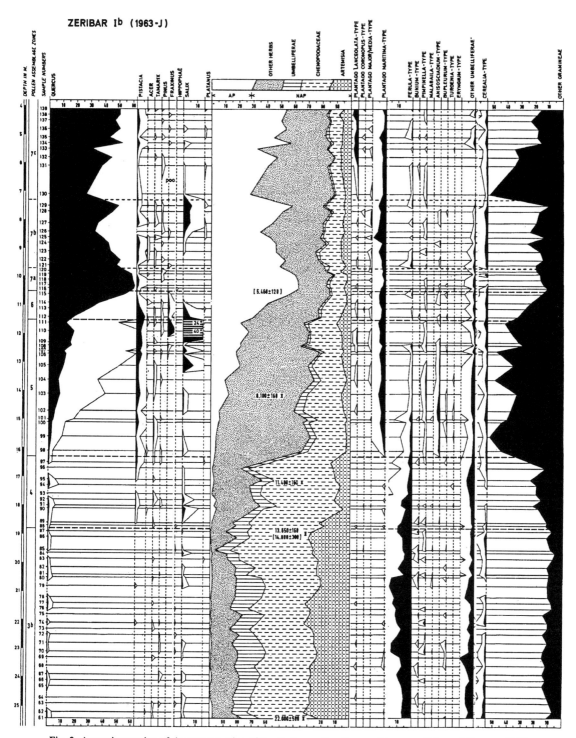

Fig. 3. A concise version of the upper section of the Zeribar pollen diagram (from van Zeist and Bottema 1977)

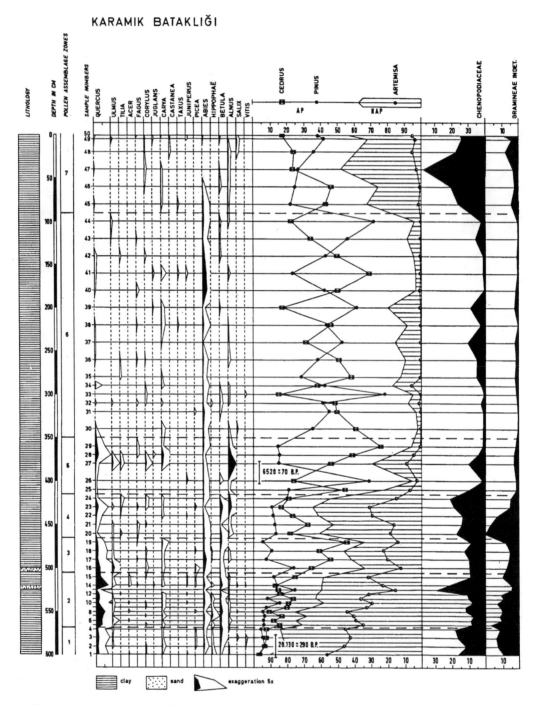

Fig. 4. A concise version of the Karamik Batakligi pollen diagram (after van Zeist, Woldring and Stapert 1975)

Pleniglacial. Zone 1, coinciding with the peak of northern hemisphere glaciation, is characterized by high relative frequency of herbaceous pollen, overwhelmingly dominated by *Artemisia* (up to ca. 60%), accompanied by chenopods, grasses and composites. The vegetation probably was

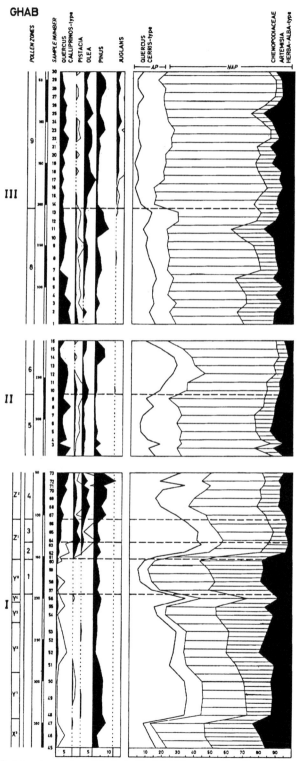

GHAB

steppic, reflecting dry and cool conditions. The diagram also suggests that an open, deciduous-oak forest was present on the surrounding hillsides, replaced at higher elevations by a conifer belt consisting of *Cedrus, Abies* and *Pinus*.

THE LATE GLACIAL – EARLY HOLOCENE

The Late Glacial (*ca.* 14,000 to 10,000 BP) was marked in the northern hemisphere by conspicuous climate changes associated with rapid glacial retreat, eventually bringing about the end of the Ice Age. The glacial regime deteriorated rapidly through a series of fluctuations, the most widely recognized of which are the Allerød warm oscillation (12,000–11,000 BP) and the Younger Dryas cold oscillation (11,000–10,400 BP). Climatic amelioration marked the beginning of the Holocene (*ca.* 10,000 BP), with northern-hemisphere climate reaching an optimum in the so-called Atlantic period (8000–5000 BP). These events are also reflected in the Near Eastern pollen record.

The Levant

Levantine palynological evidence for the Late Glacial and Early Holocene is principally concentrated in two sites, the Ghab in northwest Syria and the Hula Valley. A concise version of the Late Pleistocene–Holocene pollen diagram from the Ghab is shown in Figure 5 (van Zeist and Woldring 1980). The Late Glacial is covered here by Zone 1 of the lower section (I), and the Early Holocene by Zones 2–6. A ^{14}C date of 10,080 ± 55 BP (GrN-5810) was obtained from the 1.29–1.37-m level, corresponding to the boundary between Zones 1 and 2.

Fig. 5. A concise version of the Late Glacial–Holocene pollen diagram from the Ghab (from van Zeist and Woldring 1980)

High AP values, in the range of 45%, have been demonstrated for the period immediately preceding Zone 1 of the present diagram (Zone Y4 of the Late Holocene diagram (Niklwesky and van Zeist 1970)). However, a sharp decline in AP values marked the next period, represented by Zone 1 of the present diagram (corresponding to subzone Y5 of the original diagram), which covers the interval from ca. 14,000–11,000 BP, when AP values decreased to almost 10%, their lowest values for the entire sequence. A complete reversal of this trend occurred in Zones 2 and 3, where the AP values rose again, reaching their apex at the end of Zone 2 and beginning of Zone 3, with values of *ca.* 60%. Thus, it appears that following a period (during the final stages of the Late Pleistocene) when climatic conditions in the Ghab area were favorable for the expansion of arboreal vegetation, during the period corresponding to the European Late Glacial, the forests in the Ghab area contracted to their smallest extent ever. Apparently, the global rise in temperatures that was now taking place, especially conspicuous during the Allerød interstadial (*ca.* 12,000–11,000 BP), was not sufficiently compensated for in the Ghab area by a parallel rise in precipitation, and severe aridity thus resulted. However, conditions altered from *ca.* 11,000 BP onward, as indicated by the beginning of forest re-expansion. No doubt, this was triggered by the global decline in temperatures during the Younger Dryas, which, in the Ghab, seems to have led to a marked change in the runoff/evaporation ratio. However, it is possible that absolute values of precipitation were also increasing. A further increase in precipitation must have occurred at the onset of the Holocene, since forests continued to expand despite the renewed rise in global temperatures.

As one may conclude from the Hula diagram (Fig. 2), events in the southern Levant seem to have followed an opposite course. In Spectrum 11 (Fig. 2), which marks the beginning of the Late Glacial, AP values increase to *ca.* 30%, a 10% rise from the preceding period. AP values continued to rise throughout the first half of the Late Glacial, culminating in Spectrum 21, dated to *ca.* 11,500 BP, at *ca.* 75%. The sharp rise in AP percentages resulted principally from a rise in the relative frequency of deciduous oaks, presumably due to a major expansion of the Tabor oak park-forest in the Hula region. Because the culmination of this process largely coincided with the first half of the Allerød (marked by a global rise in temperatures), this rise in humidity most probably resulted from actual increase in precipitation. The sharp decrease in AP values over the next 1000 yr (*ca.* 11,500–10,500 BP) suggests a marked forest decline in the Hula area, thus reflecting severe deterioration in climate conditions in northern Israel. As temperatures were presumably still high at the beginning of this stage (coinciding with the second half of the Allerød) only a slight drop in annual precipitation was necessary to trigger this process. Precipitation must have dropped significantly after this, because despite global temperature decline during the Younger Dryas, arboreal vegetation in the Hula region continued to contract. Just before the beginning of the Holocene, climatic conditions in the southern Levant seem to have become almost as harsh as in the Pleniglacial maximum, some 7000 yr earlier. However, at the beginning of the Holocene, relative humidity increased again in the Hula area, as the pollen record shows forest re-expansion. Since global temperatures were also rising at this time, the rise in relative humidity could only have resulted from a major increase in precipitation. Nevertheless, conditions were not as favorable for tree growth as during the first half of the Late Glacial; the deciduous oak forest did not regain its former expanse, and evergreen oaks, which are somewhat more drought-resistant, spread slightly.

The opposing trends of the Ghab and the Hula pollen diagrams of this period raise the question whether the Late Glacial – Early Holocene pollen record at these sites truly reflects the climatic histories of the areas, or whether it is an artifact of a dating error. The possibility of a dating error in the Hula diagram is highly unlikely, because 1) the relevant section of the Hula core has four consistent ^{14}C dates, and 2) the diagram is similar to the corresponding, well-dated section of an earlier unpublished diagram (prepared by Tsukada) from another Hula core (Bottema and van Zeist

1981; van Zeist and Bottema 1982). However, a dating error in the Ghab diagram should be seriously considered, as the suggested chronology of the relevant section here is based on a single ^{14}C date (Niklewski and van Zeist 1970; van Zeist and Woldring 1980).

An alternative explanation could be that the climatic regime in the Levant during the final stages of the Pleistocene and the Early Holocene differed from the present, in that the Levant may have been divided into northern and southern provinces, marked by diachronic climatic histories (whereas today it is regarded as a single climatic province). Rognon (1987) attempted to explain the implications of this situation in terms of the atmospheric circulation patterns of the period.

Western Iran and Eastern Anatolia

Western Iran and eastern Anatolia are considered here together because the pollen diagrams of these two adjacent regions are quite similar. In the Zeribar pollen diagram (Fig. 3), the Late Glacial coincides largely with Zone 4. AP values are very low (<5%), although they increase slightly from the preceding period. *Artemisia* and chenopods dominate the pollen spectra, indicating that the vegetation was still steppic in character. AP values in Zone 5 gradually increase (*ca*. 10,500–6000 BP), suggesting gradual expansion of forests in the Zeribar area. As *Quercus* and *Pistacia* formed the main components of this forest, one may infer that a variety of very open oak-pistachio forest ("forest-steppe") had become established around Lake Zeribar. Herbaceous pollen percentages remained high, but declines in the *Artemisia* and chenopod pollen curves and the rise of the Gramineae curve seem to reflect the replacement by a grass steppe of a steppe dominated by the former. The pollen record of Zone 5 clearly points to a significant increase in humidity in the Zeribar area, albeit still far below modern values.

Zone 6 of the Zeribar diagram reflects sharply accelerating forest expansion on the hill-slopes around the lake, corresponding to a rapid replacement of the oak-pistachio steppe-forest by a dense forest vegetation, similar to the Zagros oak woodland presently prevalent in the area. Humidity probably increased greatly in a relatively short time (no more than 1000 yr). *Ca*. 5500 BP, the inferred date of the Zone 6/7 boundary, the oak forest in the Zeribar area reached its maximum expansion, suggesting a further rise in humidity.

Lake Urmia, 150 × 15–50 km, 1280 m asl and *ca*. 350 km north of Lake Zeribar, produced a similar pollen diagram (Bottema 1986). The lake is presently surrounded by *Artemisia* steppe, while remnants of a deciduous *Quercus brantii* steppe-forest dot the adjacent hillsides. Large areas to the east and southeast are covered with halophytic vegetation. A 4.5-m-long core was analyzed and two ^{14}C dates obtained. Zone Y (divided into three subzones) covers the period 13,200–9540 BP, largely corresponding to the Late Glacial. As in Zeribar Zone 4, with which it may be correlated, Urmia Zone Y shows low AP values (<5%), and high NAP values, dominated by *Artemisia* and chenopods. An exclusively *Artemisia* steppe must have surrounded Lake Urmia during Zone Y time, indicating arid conditions. However, a somewhat moister climate is believed to have set in during Subzone Y2 (the Allerød?), causing a slight expansion of Gramineae at the expense of *Artemisia*. Subzone Z1 (9500–*ca*. 8000 BP?) shows slightly increased AP values, mainly accounted for by *Pistacia*. Upland vegetation must have been still largely devoid of arboreal vegetation, but *Pistacia atlantica* may have become more widespread in dry wadi beds. Most striking is the sharp decrease in *Artemisia* and the matching rise in Gramineae, which suggests a replacement of *Artemisia* steppe by grass steppe. This is similar to Zeribar Zone 5, discussed above, where a much more prominent rise in AP values was noted. In Lake Urmia, the corresponding rise in humidity must have been far slower. Subzone Z2 shows higher AP values, indicating continually rising humidity. Oak forest was expanding, but the pollen record implies that various other species, such as junipers and *Acer*, also settled in favorable areas. *Ca.* 6500 BP, the Subzone Z2/Z3 boundary, the forest in Lake Urmia attained its maximum extent, indicating that relative humidity had reached its present-day level.

Similar results were obtained from Lake Van and Sogutlu, 30 km apart from each other, in the Taurus Mountains of eastern Anatolia, 1650 m and 1400 m asl, respectively (van Zeist and Woldring 1978; van Zeist and Bottema 1991). Annual precipitation in the Lake Van area is 300–400 mm; natural vegetation is steppe with oak-woodland at higher elevations. Zones 1–3 of the Lake Van pollen diagram (11,300–8000 BP) are characterized by high NAP values; chenopods dominate, but high percentages of *Artemisia*, Gramineae, other composites and *Umbelifrae* are also present (Fig. 6). Steppe and desert steppe must have prevailed around Lake Van during this period, indicating arid conditions. During Zones 4–5, (*ca.* 7350–4500 BP), AP values gradually increased,

LAKE VAN, EAST TURKEY

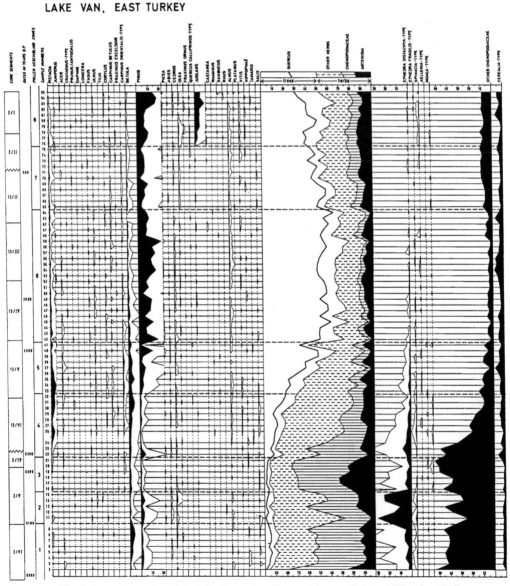

Fig. 6. A concise version of the Lake Van pollen diagram (after van Zeist and Woldring 1978)

signifying a marked expansion of the oak forest. At higher elevations, pine expanded, evidenced by increased *Pinus* percentages. These events clearly indicate a significant rise in humidity. Humidity must have reached its highest (present-day?) level in the Lake Van area during the following period, corresponding to Zone 6 (4500–2600 BP), as one may deduce from the fact that AP values have reached their maxima here. The Sogutlu diagram covers a shorter period than that of the Lake Van diagram, but the picture is similar.

To summarize the evidence from the western Zagros–eastern Taurus belt, the Late Glacial must have been generally dry over the entire region, with steppe to desert-steppe dominating the landscape in the lowlands, and impoverished woodlands scattered on the hillsides. It is questionable to what extent the relatively high global temperatures, especially during the Allerød, contributed to the overall aridity in this mountainous area. Above 1000 m, temperature could still be the limiting factor for the spread of arboreal vegetation, but little precipitation must have been the main factor. Compared with more northerly sites, the climate in the Zeribar area seems to have become slightly more humid during this period, because the first, albeit very faint signs of forest expansion are noted. The vegetal landscape altered significantly in the course of the Early Holocene, with steppe and desert-steppe replaced gradually by forest. However, the onset and pace of the process was not consistent throughout the region. In the south, the Zeribar area, forest expansion began earlier, at the beginning of the Holocene, and lasted longer, culminating only after some 5000 yr. Farther north, in the Urmia region, forest expansion began *ca.* 9500 BP, *i.e.,* 1000 yr later, but culminated *ca.* 6500 BP, 1000 yr earlier than in Zeribar. To the northwest, in the Van/Sogutlu area, forest expansion began even later, *ca.* 7350 BP, and ended only *ca.* 4000 BP. During the first half of the Holocene, forest expansion must have been accompanied by a marked rise in precipitation, and perhaps in temperatures. The diachronic beginnings of forest expansion in the western Zagros–eastern Taurus belt may indicate that climate amelioration started in the south and gradually spread northward; the diachronic culmination of forest expansion may be attributed to different local conditions in, for example, topography and soil composition.

South-Central and Western Anatolia

Palynological evidence for the Late Glacial–Early Holocene of south-central Anatolia is confined to Lake Akgol, the remnant of former Lake Konia, in the eastern Konia plain, 1000 m asl (Bottema and Woldring 1986). Present-day mean annual precipitation is <300 mm. No natural vegetation exists today, due to agricultural activity, but it is believed to have been dominated by *Artemisia* steppe (Bottema and Woldring 1986; van Zeist and Bottema 1991). Conifer forest can be found on north-facing slopes of the mountains to the south of the plain.

The Akgol pollen diagram was drawn from a 6-m-long core taken from a drained marsh by the lakeside. The base of the diagram was ^{14}C-dated to *ca.* 13,000 BP. Zone X (subdivided into four subzones) and Subzone Y1 represent the Late Glacial. The boundary between Subzone X4 and Y1 was ^{14}C-dated to *ca.* 11,000 BP; the Early Holocene is represented by Subzone Y2 and lower Zone Z. The boundary between Zones Y and Z was ^{14}C-dated to *ca.* 8000 BP.

Zone X shows generally low AP values (10% maximum). *Artemisia* and chenopods alternately dominate the sequence, suggesting prevailing desert and steppe vegetation around Lake Konia during most of the Late Glacial. Pine and deciduous oak probably dotted the surrounding hillsides. The climate was probably much drier than today. During the time of Subzone X3, Artemisia values decreased markedly, matched by a parallel rise in Gramineae percentages; a slight rise in deciduous oaks is also noted. Climatic conditions during this period, which largely coincides with the Allerød, must have become somewhat more humid. The spread of forest in the Konya plain started between

11,000 and 10,000 BP (Subzone Y1), which partially corresponds with the European Younger Dryas. Initially, the pollen evidence points to marked expansion of *Betula*. The birch forest apparently developed on the higher reaches of the mountain slopes around the Konya basin. In Subzone Z1, *Betula* decreases while deciduous oaks reach their maximum. Later, at *ca.* 8000 BP or possibly somewhat later, *Pinus* and *Cedrus* values rise sharply, while those of deciduous oaks decline, suggesting the spread of conifer forest at the expense of broad-leaved forest. Birch forest expansion around Lake Konya at the end of the Late Glacial must have been triggered by increased precipitation. Higher global temperatures at the beginning of the Holocene must have caused the replacement of birch by deciduous oaks, whereas higher precipitation levels probably accounted for the subsequent replacement of deciduous broad-leaved forest by conifer forest (Bottema and Woldring 1986).

In the pollen diagram of Karamik Batakligi, *ca.* 300 km to the northwest, the Late Glacial is represented in Zone 3 (Fig. 4). *Cedrus* dominates the arboreal pollen, and increases during this phase, reaching a maximum of *ca.* 60% near the Zone 3/4 boundary (*ca.* 11,600 BP). As this period was characterized by global warming, precipitation probably rose significantly. *Cedrus* declines sharply in the early stage of Zone 4 (corresponding to the Younger Dryas), which suggests a reversed climatic trend toward aridity. Relatively low AP values imply that the climate must have remained comparatively dry during the remainder of Zone 4 (the upper boundary is dated to *ca.* 8200 BP), but during Zone 5, the conifer forest, with *Cedrus* and *Pinus* alternately dominating, began to re-expand. The forest extended to its maximum during the early stages of Zone 6, reaching an apex sometime after 5850 BP, the inferred date of the Zone 5/6 boundary.

For southwestern Anatolia, palynological evidence is available from Sogut Golu and Beyşehir Golu (van Zeist, Woldring and Stapert 1975; Bottema and Woldring, 1986). As both pollen diagrams are similar, only that of Beyşehir Golu (Beysehir II) is considered here. Beyşehir Lake, 1200 m asl, lies in a transitional vegetation zone. To the east and the north is a mixed steppe-forest of broad-leaved trees and conifers, led by *Quercus pubescens, Pinus nigra* and *Juniper* species; to the west and south, a conifer forest of *Pinus nigra, Cedrus libani, Abies cilicica* and *Juniper excelsa* constitutes the natural plant cover. Annual precipitation is *ca.* 500 mm; mean January and August temperatures are *ca.* 0°C and 22°C, respectively. The base of the Beyşehir II diagram was ^{14}C-dated to *ca.* 15,400 BP (Fig. 7). However, this is the only ^{14}C date for this diagram. Pollen Zone 1 (*ca.* 15,000–12,300 BP), which covers the end of the Pleniglacial and the early stages of the Late Glacial, is characterized by low AP values (10–20% maximum), suggesting aridity. Zone 2 (12,300–10,900 BP), largely corresponding to the Allerød of northwest Europe, shows considerably higher AP values, dominated by *Pinus*. Global temperature rise was probably accompanied, locally, by a marked increase in average annual precipitation. A drastic decline of pine (and total AP values) mark the beginning of Zone 3, probably reflecting a decrease in global temperatures during the Younger Dryas. However, the trend subsequently reversed again, presumably marking the beginning of the Holocene. AP values rise, this time including those of both pine and cedar, as well as of oak. The conifer forest must have expanded on the hillsides south and west of the lake, while the mixed broad-leaved, needle-leaved woodland expanded to the north and east. The renewed rise of global temperatures during the Early Holocene must have been accompanied by a significant rise in humidity. Local forests attained their largest extent at *ca.* 6000 BP, but humidity must have continued to increase for a few thousand years, as oak almost disappeared, and pine expanded at the expense of cedar during the interval of Zone 4.

THE LATE HOLOCENE

The Late Holocene is marked in the Near East by a growing human impact on vegetation. I discuss this subject only briefly, as it has already been reviewed extensively (*e.g.,* Baruch 1990; Bottema

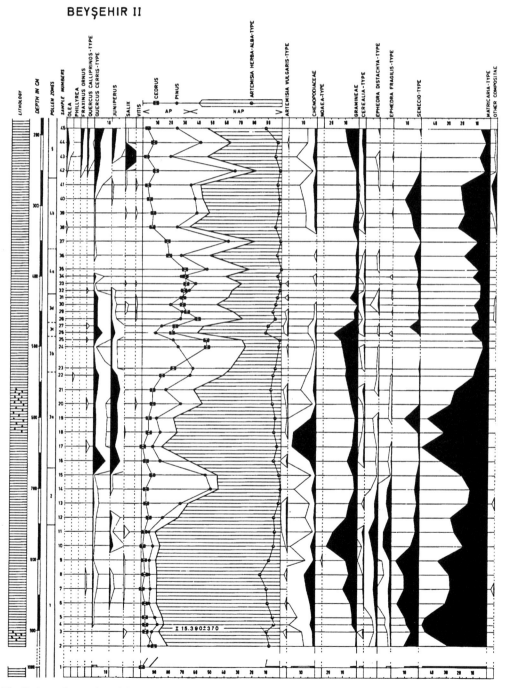

Fig. 7. A concise version of the Beyşehir II pollen diagram, covering the Late Glacial–Early Holocene (from Bottema and Woldring 1986)

and Woldring 1990; van Zeist and Bottema 1991). Anthropogenic disturbance of natural vegetation becomes evident in pollen diagrams from the eastern Mediterranean during the second half of the 2nd millennium BC. The Beyşehir I diagram (van Zeist, Woldring and Stapert 1975) (Fig. 8) is viewed as the type-section for the Late Holocene in the eastern Mediterranean. The anthropogenic phase in this, as well as in other eastern Mediterranean diagrams with similar traits, has been referred to as the Beyşehir Occupation Phase (Bottema and Woldring 1990). It is marked by a rapid decline of natural forest components (conifer and deciduous oak in western Anatolia, evergreen oak in the Levant), the rise of cultivated trees (*e.g., Fraxinus ornus* in western Anatolia, *Olea, Juglans* and *Vitis,* in western Anatolia and the Levant, *Ceratonia* in the southern Levant), and the rise of "anthropogenic indicators" (*i.e.,* plant taxa characteristic of disturbed habitats).

BEYŞEHIR I

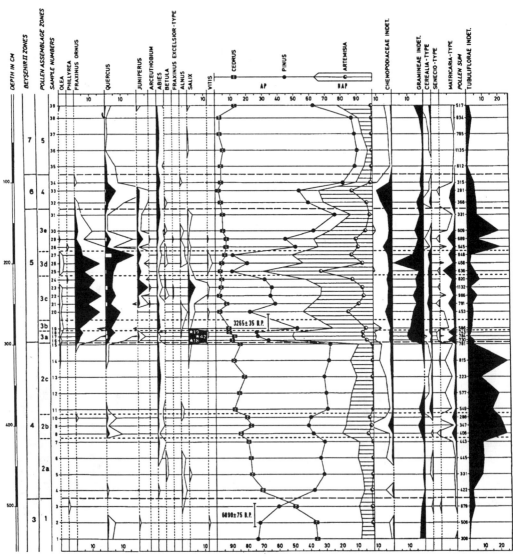

Fig. 8. A concise version of the Beyşehir I pollen diagram covering the later Holocene (from van Zeist, Woldring and Stapert 1975)

These events are attributed to large-scale forest clearing, similar to that apparent in western European pollen diagrams from the same period; deliberate cultivation along with its corollary, the spread of weeds, is evident. Due to subsequent weakening of human intervention, the anthropogenic phase is followed by forest regeneration. The Beyşehir Occupation Phase should be dated to *ca.* 3200–2000 BP, on the basis of uncalibrated ^{14}C dates (Bottema and Woldring 1990). Calibration would add *ca.* 200 yr to these dates. In the southern Levant, similar events (Fig. 9) were dated, on the basis of calibrated ^{14}C dates, to *ca.* 2250 BP–800 AD, that is, nearly 1000 yr later (Baruch 1986, 1990, 1993). The discrepancy between the radiometric dates of the southern Levantine diagrams and those of southwestern Anatolia, however, may be due to the fact that the latter were not corrected for hardwater effect (Baruch 1993).

CONCLUDING REMARKS

Reconstruction of Near Eastern vegetational history on the basis of palynology is still largely fragmentary, mainly because site-to-site correlation of the pollen record is difficult. Distances between coring sites, particularly in eastern regions, are very large; most diagrams do not stretch beyond

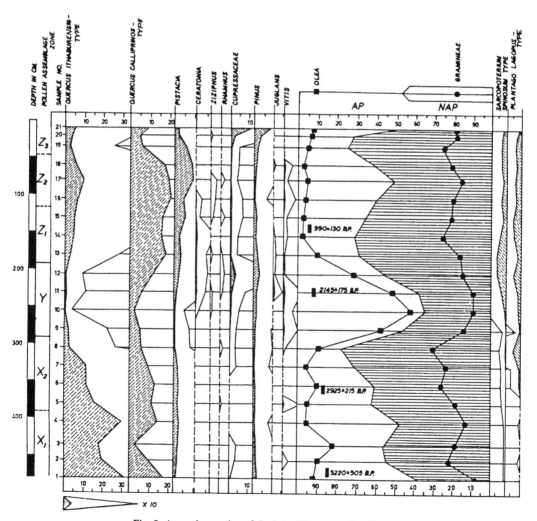

Fig. 9. A concise version of the Lake Kinneret pollen diagram

the past 15,000–20,000 yr, at most; and perhaps most important is the fact that there are too few ^{14}C dates. Despite these drawbacks, some generalizations can be made (Fig. 10).

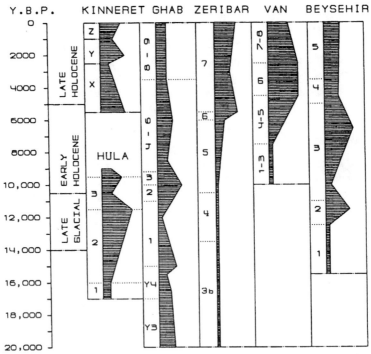

Fig. 10. Schematic pollen diagrams showing major trends in vegetational history of the areas discussed here

It appears that the Pleniglacial was generally dry in all regions of the Near East. However, in isolated niches in the Levant (as shown, *e.g.*, in Weinstein-Evron's diagram from the Hula, and in Niklewsky and van Zeist's diagram from the Ghab) and in southwestern Anatolia (as shown in the Sogut Golu diagram), conditions must have been favorable for tree growth, at least periodically. Aridity also characterized the Late Glacial, but in places such as the Ghab, conditions seem to have become particularly harsh during the Allerød. Southwest Anatolia and the southern Levant depart from the general trend (as seen in Bottema and Woldring's diagrams from Beyşehir, and Baruch and Bottema's diagram from the Hula), as remarkable forest expansion occurred here during this period. Increased local precipitation must have compensated for the global temperature rise, thus encouraging general forest expansion in the Near East at the beginning of the Holocene. However, this process was not synchronic over the entire area, as the forest contracted in the southern Levant. Simultaneous expansion of the forest in the northern Levant may indicate that the climatic amelioration that characterized the southern Levant during the Late Glacial slowly shifted northward during the ensuing millennia.

This possibility becomes even more plausible when one studies the succeeding pollen zones in these as well as other Near Eastern diagrams. Figure 8 shows the general trend of events. In the southern Levant, the forest attained its largest expansion in the Allerød, 12,000–11,000 BP; in the northern Levant, the apex was only *ca.* 2000 yr later, or 10,000–8000 BP, and in south-central and southwestern Anatolia, at 8000–7000 BP. In the eastern Taurus–western Zagros belt, forests expanded at a much slower rate, culminating only some 6500–5500 yr ago in southern localities

(Lakes Zeribar and Urmia), and only 4500 yr ago in northern areas (Lake Van and Sogutlu). By the end of the Atlantic period, or soon afterward, modern climatic conditions appear to have set in over the entire region, and forest expansion halted. Subsequent anthropogenic influences then masked all natural expressions of climatic fluctuations in the pollen record.

REFERENCES CITED

Baruch, U.
1986   The late Holocene vegetational history of Lake Kinneret (Sea of Galilee), Israel. *Paléorient* 12(2):37–48.
1990   Palynological evidence of human impact on the vegetation as recorded in Late Holocene lake sediments in Israel. In *Man's Role in the Shaping of the Eastern Mediterranean Landscape,* edited by S. Bottema, G. Entjes-Neiborg, and W. van Zeist, pp. 283–293. A. A. Balkema, Rotterdam.
1993   The Palynology of Late Holocene Cores from the Dead Sea. Ph.D. Dissertation, The Hebrew University of Jerusalem.
Baruch, U. and S. Bottema
1991   Palynological evidence for climatic changes in the Levant *ca.* 17000–9000 B.P. In *The Natufian Culture in the Levant,* edited by O. Bar-Yosef and F. R. Valla. International Monographs in Prehistory, Ann Arbor.
Bottema, S.
1986   A late Quaternary pollen diagram from Lake Urmia (northwestern Iran). *Review of Palaeobotany and Palynology* 47:241–261.
Bottema, S. and W. van Zeist
1981   Palynological evidence for the climatic history of the Near East 50000–6000 B.P. In *Préhistoire du Levant,* edited by J. Cauvin and P. Sanlaville, pp. 115–132. Maison de l'Orient, CNRS, Lyon.
Bottema, S. and H. Woldring
1986   Late Quaternary vegetation and climate of southwestern Turkey, Part II. *Paleohistoria* 26:123–149.
1990   Anthropogenic indicators in the pollen record of the Eastern Mediterranean. In *Man's Role in the Shaping of the Eastern Mediterranean,* edited by S. Bottema, G. Entjes-Neiborg, and W. van Zeist, pp. 231–264. A. A. Balkema, Rotterdam.
Horowitz, A
1979   *The Quaternary of Israel.* Academic Press, New York.
Niklweski, J. and W. van Zeist
1970   A late Quaternary pollen diagram from northwestern Syria. *Acta Botanica Neerlandica* 19:737–754.
Rognon, P.
1987   Relations entre phases climatiques et chronologiques au Moyen Orient de 16,000-4,000 B.P. In *Chronologies du Proche Orient,* edited by O. Aurenche, J. Evin and F. Hours, pp. 189–206. BAR International Series 379, British Archaeological Reports, Oxford.
Shackelton, N. J. and N. D. Opdyke
1973   Oxygen isotope and palaeomagnetic stratigraphy of Equatorial Pacific core V28-238: Oxygen isotope temperatures and ice volumes on a 10^5 year and 10^6 year scale. *Quaternary Research* 3:39–55.
van Zeist, W. and S. Bottema
1977   Palynological investigations in western Iran. *Palaeohistoria* 19:19–87.
1982   Vegetation history of the Eastern Mediterranean and the Near East during the last 20000 years. In *Palaeoclimates, Palaeoenvironments and Human Communities in the Eastern Mediterranean Region in Later Prehistory,* edited by J. L. Bintliff and W. van Zeist, pp. 277-321. BAR International Series 133, British Archaeological Reports, Oxford.
1991   *Late Quaternary Vegetation of the Near East.* Ludwig Reichert, Weisbaden.
van Zeist, W. and H. Woldring
1978   A postglacial pollen diagram from Lake Van in east Anatolia. *Review of Palaeobotany and Palynology* 26:249–276.
1980   Holocene vegetation and climate of northwestern Syria. *Palaeohistoria* 22:111–125.
van Zeist, W., H. Woldring and D. Stapert
1975   Late Quaternary vegetation and climate of southwestern Turkey. *Palaeohistoria* 17:53–143.
Weinstein-Evron, M.
1983   The palaeoecology of the Early Würm in the Hula basin, Israel. *Paléorient* 9(1):5–19.
Zohary, M.
1973   *Geobotanical Foundations of the Near East* (2 vols.). Gustav Fischer, Stuttgart.
1980   *The Vegetal Landscape of Israel.* Am-Oved, Tel-Aviv (in Hebrew).

EVIDENCE OF EARLY HOLOCENE SUMMER PRECIPITATION IN THE CONTINENTAL MIDDLE EAST

ANN P. EL-MOSLIMANY

Palynological Consultants, P.O.B. 367, Seahurst, Washington 98062 USA

INTRODUCTION

The present climate of the Middle East is characterized by a prolonged period of summer drought and highly variable winter precipitation. This climate is transitional between the zone dominated by the Indian monsoon to the south and that of evenly distributed precipitation to the north. Climatic boundaries have shifted in the past, but the extent and timing of those shifts are largely undocumented. I summarize here the botanical evidence for Early Holocene summer precipitation in the Middle East in the presently dry-summer region, from the Arabian desert to northern Syria. In regions where some summer precipitation occurs today, rainfall was probably more common in summer during the Early Holocene.

DESERT REGIONS

Many remnants of desert lakes date to this period. Playas commonly form during the winter even today. However, with the onset of summer drought, lakes evaporate, sediments dry and are blown away. In the Early Holocene, summer precipitation apparently prevented deflation and allowed year-to-year accumulation. The fossil lakes of the Rub' Al-Khali (Empty Quarter) and the Mundafan Basin of Saudi Arabia have been the basis of an exhaustive study by McClure (1976, 1978, 1984). The radiocarbon dates for the Holocene series range from 10,000 to 5000 yr BP, and primarily cluster *ca.* 8250–7000 BP. Additional Holocene playa or lake remnants have been dated to *ca.* 8400 BP at Wadi Al-Luhy in Saudi Arabia (Hotzl, Krämer and Maurin 1978), to *ca.* 7800 BP on the island of Bahrain in the Arabo-Persian Gulf (Doornkamp, Brunsden and Jones 1980), and from *ca.* 8500–7800 BP in the northern Arabo-Persian Gulf (El-Moslimany 1983, 1990). Whitney, Faulkender and Rubin (1983) report a series of lakes that were extant *ca.* 8500–5300 BP in the northern desert of Saudi Arabia.

The most consistent characteristic of Early Holocene pollen assemblages in the Middle East is the high percentage of Poaceae (grass) pollen relative to that in modern pollen samples. This phenomenon is seen in the Early Holocene sediments from the Rub' Al-Khali and from the northern Arabo-Persian Gulf (El-Moslimany 1983, 1990), as well as in the long pollen diagrams from the present summer-dry region (Fig. 1). At present, the Rub' Al-Khali is the largest sand desert in the world. It is surrounded by high terraces that contributed alluvial sediments to the basin prior to the onset of Pleistocene aridity. The low erratic precipitation is generally confined to the winter months. Pollen accumulating at present represents existing dune vegetation, primarily *Cyperus conglomeratus* and *Calligonum*. In Holocene lake sediments, Chenopodiaceae and *Plantago* are the most important pollen types, with Poaceae pollen averaging *ca.* 14%, as compared to 1% in modern surface samples (El-Moslimany 1990).

Rainfall in Kuwait and southern Iraq averages <100 mm/yr. In the low-lying deserts, vegetation is dominated primarily by desert scrub and annuals, registered in modern pollen assemblages by high values for Chenopodiaceae, *Plantago*, Compositae and other herbaceous pollen types. Freshwater sediments exposed by tidal scour on the floor of the northern Arabo-Persian Gulf date to the

Late Quaternary Chronology and Paleoclimates of the Eastern Mediterranean
Edited by O. Bar-Yosef and R. S. Kra. RADIOCARBON 1994, pp. 121–130

121

Early Holocene (*ca.* 7800–8500 BP). Freshwater peat, as well as lacustrine and estuary sediments, were analyzed from grab samples and short Pfleger cores. Pollen assemblages in these sediments were compared with those in 25 modern pollen samples obtained from various environments in Kuwait and southern Iraq. Poaceae pollen, which averages only *ca.* 2% in modern samples, ranges from 28% to 80% and averages 52% of the total pollen present in these Early Holocene samples (El-Moslimany 1990).

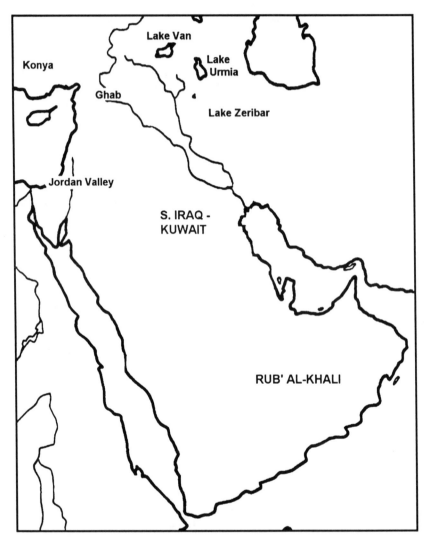

Fig. 1. Map of the Middle East, showing sites with pollen indicators of summer precipitation in the Early Holocene

The relatively high representation of the Poaceae family in the Early Holocene suggests the occurrence of summer precipitation. Representatives of the grass family are adapted to almost every environment that supports vegetation, but grasses generally play a dominant role in vegetation only where there is adequate moisture during the growing season. In addition, grasses adapted to summer aridity produce less pollen than those growing in regions of summer precipitation (El-

Moslimany 1987). The degraded state of the vegetation caused by overgrazing is probably not an important factor in the contrast between the high percentages of Poaceae pollen in Early Holocene environments and the very low percentages of Poaceae pollen today. In Kuwait, a large tract of land has been protected from overgrazing for the past 15 yr, yet grass pollen in surface samples from this reserve is no higher than elsewhere in Kuwait (El-Moslimany, unpublished data).

KURDISTAN

Pollen diagrams from permanent lakes in less arid parts of the region provide more complete records than do the geographically and temporally discrete pollen assemblages in remnants of desert lakes and ponds. Only in these long pollen diagrams are there records of the dry-summer climates and climatic transitions preceding and following periods of Early Holocene summer rainfall. Figure 2 shows curves that were constructed for two pollen indicators of summer precipitation, based on pollen diagrams of three lakes: Lake Zeribar (van Zeist and Bottema 1977); Lake Urmia and Lake Van (Bottema 1986). The first indicator is the ratio between Poaceae (grass), an indicator of rainy summers, and Chenopodiaceae plus *Artemisia*, non-arboreal pollen indicators of dry summers; this ratio is expressed as P/A+C. The second indicator is the pollen of *Quercus* (oak), which is the most important pollen-producing deciduous tree. Increasing values indicate summer rainfall. This interpretation, based on modern ecology (El-Moslimany 1986, 1987) and studies of present-day pollen accumulation (El-Moslimany 1990), differs from that of the authors of the pollen diagrams, who do not consider the factor of seasonality. The scrubby vegetation is attributed to aridity, not specifically to summer drought. They relate the gradual increase in *Quercus* pollen over a period of 5000 yr to a corresponding gradual increase in overall precipitation.

The lakes mentioned above lie within the arc formed by the Zagros-Taurus Mountains of Kurdistan, coinciding roughly with border regions separating modern Iraq from Iran and Turkey. The diagram from a fourth lake, Lake Mirabad, is not considered here, because the earliest sediments examined were apparently deposited after summer precipitation was already well established. Also, the grass curve is highly erratic and probably under the control of local conditions, such as the intermittent spread of grasses across a dried lake-bottom (van Zeist and Bottema 1977). No ^{14}C dates are available for Lake Van, which was originally dated from varves, and which has an uncertain chronology. I assume here that its vegetational history is in accord with that of other lakes of Kurdistan. The justification for this is discussed by Bottema (1986). Figure 2 suggests a similar chronology for changes in seasonality. It focuses on indicators of one specific climatic factor, summer precipitation. The data are based on pollen diagrams from lakes that differ in climate and vegetation. This difference may explain why the indicators of summer precipitation appear 1000 yr earlier in the Lake Zeribar diagram than in the diagram of Lake Urmia. Both lakes are at 1300-m elevations. Lake Zeribar has an annual rainfall estimated at 800 mm; no rain falls in summer. Summer drought is less severe at Lake Urmia, but it lies in the rain shadow of the Zagros Mountains, where total annual rainfall is only 200–300 mm.

Artemisia herba-alba, a species totally resistant to summer drought, is present in the Lake Zeribar region. *Artemisia fragrans*, which depends on some summer precipitation, is found at Lake Urmia. Assuming that climate and vegetation were similar to present conditions, the earliest effect at Lake Urmia, prior to the onset of increasing summer precipitation, may have been for *A. fragrans* to have replaced *A. herba-alba*, thus delaying the increase in Poaceae pollen. Pollen of the two *Artemisia* species has not been distinguished in the Urmia pollen diagram, so that such a change is not evident. Non-arboreal vegetation responds quickly to climatic variations; thus, the ratio between the two rainfall indicators, P/A+C, is a sensitive marker of seasonality. Because of the inherently slower response time of trees, the *Quercus* curve is expected to increase more slowly.

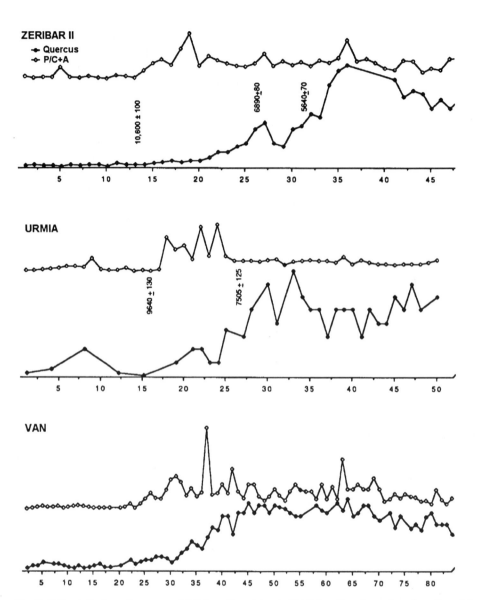

Fig. 2. Pollen indicators of summer rainfall from three lakes in Kurdistan. Sample numbers from the original pollen diagrams are shown on the horizontal axis. Values for *Quercus* pollen and the ratio of Poaceae to Chenopodiaceae plus *Artemisia* are based on percentages of total pollen counts from the published pollen diagrams.

At both Lake Urmia and Lake Zeribar, *Quercus* pollen reached its maximum after the P/A+C curve; at Lake Zeribar, this *Quercus* peak occurred almost 5000 yr later! When conditions became favorable for *Quercus*, the trees probably were quite far away. The amount or the regularity of summer precipitation may also have affected the rate of *Quercus* immigration.

NORTHWESTERN SYRIA

A pollen diagram based on a series of samples from the archaeological site of Tell Mureybet (Leroi-Gourhan 1974) indicates summer precipitation during the Early Holocene. The samples are ^{14}C-dated from *ca.* 10,400 BP to 7600 BP. After *ca.* 10,000 BP, cereal and other Poaceae pollen increased at the expense of Chenopodiaceae. This was attributed to an increase in moisture, but Chenopodiaceae are notoriously influenced by human activity, and there is an uncertain link between their abundance in archaeological deposits and climatic factors. However, Poaceae pollen is high throughout the deposits, reaching 60–70% of the total pollen between 8000 and 7600 BP. Poaceae pollen comprises only 3.8% of modern samples taken in the vicinity (Bottema and Barkoudah 1979).

The Ghab valley of the Orontes River lies *ca.* 175 km southwest of Tell Mureybet, at an elevation of 190 m, between the Alaoite and Zawiye Mountains of northwestern Syria. Data from three separate cores (van Zeist and Woldring 1980) are combined to include the entire Holocene period. Figure 3 is from Ghab I, dated to the Early Holocene (van Zeist and Bottema 1982). *Quercus* pollen is present throughout the original long Ghab diagram (Niklewski and van Zeist 1970). Perhaps this less continental region was more susceptible to incursions of summer rainfall. The period preceding 10,000 BP was apparently dry during the summer, although it followed another phase of high values of both deciduous oak pollen and high P/C+A ratios. This earlier period seems to coincide with a very minor increase in summer rainfall indicators that can be seen *ca.* 12,000 BP at the Kurdistan lakes (Fig. 2). The rise in oak pollen and P/A+C at this time is minimal at Lake Zeribar and Lake Van, but a little stronger at Lake Urmia. It is doubtful that summer precipitation was occurring in the Taurus-Zagros arc. The minor indications at these sites were more likely due to pollen that was carried into the lakes from distant sources.

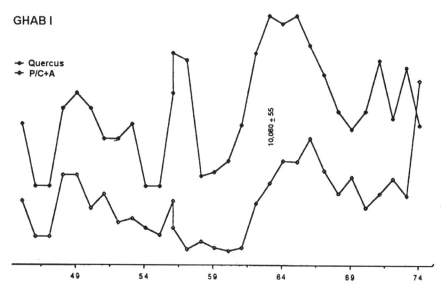

Fig. 3. (See Fig. 2.) Pollen indicators of summer rainfall from the Ghab I pollen diagram, Ghab valley, northwestern Syria

SOUTHWESTERN TURKEY

A pollen diagram from Akgöl Adabag on the Konya plain in southwestern Turkey (Bottema and Woldring 1987) is useful for comparison, because it lies within a zone that has less summer drought than any of the other sites. Modern vegetation in the mountains surrounding Konya reflects more evenly distributed precipitation, but pollen assemblages from the Late Glacial and Early Holocene were similar to those in Kurdistan. One difference was the early appearance of *Betula* (beech) pollen. Because *Betula* is a deciduous tree that was probably also responding to summer precipitation, it was added to the pollen of *Quercus* in Figure 4. *Betula* and other deciduous pollen types are included in the other pollen diagrams, but are relatively minor components, and are disregarded here.

Based on the very low summer precipitation indicators prior to *ca*. 12,500 BP, I infer that summer aridity in Konya was comparable to the more continental sites (Fig. 4). The vigorous response of these indicators after *ca*. 12,500 BP leaves little doubt that summer precipitation was occurring in this region just as it was in northwestern Syria. Because the Akgöl Adabag core extends back only to *ca*. 13,000 BP, it is not possible to state with certainty that deciduous *Quercus* was present in this core during the Pleistocene, as it was near Ghab.

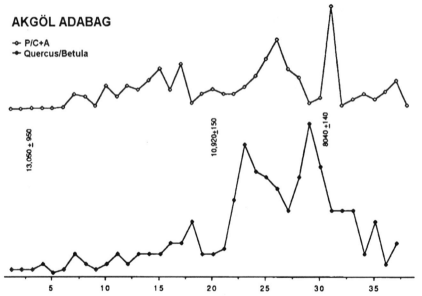

Fig. 4. (See Fig. 2.) Pollen indicators of summer rainfall from the Akgöl Adabag pollen diagram, Konya, southwestern Turkey

The Younger Dryas began *ca*. 11,000 BP, and apparently affected summer moisture conditions. At sites where pollen indicators of summer moisture had increased, they now fell. This can be seen at Ghab (Fig. 3) and Akgöl Adabag (Fig. 4), and to a lesser extent at Urmia (Fig. 2). This effect probably resulted from the lowering of the Mediterranean's sea-surface temperature that occurred during the Younger Dryas (Rossignol-Strick *et al.* 1982). Because the Mediterranean Sea is the primary moisture and energy source for the regional climate, a change in surface temperature would have had a considerable impact. Conversely, the warming sea-surface at 12,000 BP and 10,000 BP may have been a factor in the initiation of summer precipitation at some sites *ca*. 12,000 BP and, more regionally, at 10,000 BP.

JORDAN VALLEY

Horowitz and Gat (1984) compared Late Pleistocene, Middle Holocene and Recent pollen percentages of deciduous oak and evergreen oak in pollen diagrams from the Hula Valley, Lake Kinneret and the Dead Sea. They observed that oak pollen in recent sediments is primarily from evergreen trees, but the Middle Holocene and Pleistocene samples are dominated by deciduous oak, and they attribute this to summer precipitation during the Pleistocene and Middle Holocene. My interpretation differs slightly. A deciduous forest can maintain itself on favorable sites in the summer-dry climate, if it is not disturbed. Evidence for this is provided by the extensive deciduous forests that thrived in this region until the last few centuries. Thus, the presence of deciduous oak in the Middle Holocene and the Pleistocene may be due to surviving forests that had come into existence much earlier. Lack of deciduous oak pollen in modern samples may reflect the inability of destroyed forests to recover under the present inhospitable climate (El-Moslimany 1986).

EXPANDED RANGE OF WHEAT SPECIES

Remains of wheat species that prefer summer rainfall are found in Early Holocene archaeological sites far to the east and south of present regions of summer precipitation. The wild progenitors of domesticated wheat include diploid einkorn (*Triticum boeoticum*) and tetraploid emmer (*T. dicoccoides*). Two races or subspecies of *T. boeticum* occur. A smaller, one-seeded ecotype (*T. boeticum* ssp. *aegilopoides*) grows in the southern Balkans and western Anatolia. A larger, two-seeded ecotype (*T. boeticum* ssp. *thaudar*) shares the habitat of *T. boeticum* ssp. *aegilopoides*, but also extends into the summer-dry regions of the Euphrates basin. *T. dicoccoides* is much more restricted, and apparently, is well adapted to conditions of summer drought (Zohary 1969).

The unusually high percentages of cereal pollen (up to 8%) at the Late Paleolithic site of Tell Mureybet (10,500–9500 BP) suggested to Leroi-Gourhan (1974) that cereals were being tended at the site. This is supported by the presence of morphologically wild-type seeds of *T. boeticum* ssp. *thaudar* (van Zeist and Casparie 1968). Though able to grow in summer-dry regions, *T. boeticum* does not occur naturally near Tell Mureybet today.

Renfrew (1969) observed that the one-grained variety of einkorn, *T. boeticum* ssp. *aegilopoides*, and its domesticated counterpart occur much earlier than the two-grained types, and at sites far to the east of the modern range of distribution, Jarmo (*ca.* 8750 BP) and Ali Kosh (*ca.* 9500–6750 BP). It has since also been reported from Abu Hureyra (11,500–10,500 BP) (Hillman 1975). This is of particular significance, because the one-grained *T. boeticum* ssp. *aegilopoides* is characteristic of the cooler Balkans and western Anatolia, and is less adapted to summer drought. It is difficult to explain such great distances between the natural stands and these early archaeological sites, except by an extension of their ranges during that time, which could best be explained by some summer precipitation.

Helbaek (1960) noted that club wheat (*T. compactum*) does not thrive on irrigated land, and prefers summer rainfall, along with other species of the hexaploid bread-wheat group. Thus, the presence of club wheat at Tell Ramad (9000–7000 BP) and bread wheat (*T. aestivum*) at Tepe Sabz (*ca.* 7500–7000 BP) (Renfrew 1969) may indicate summer precipitation. Figure 5 shows the Early Holocene sites that are presently outside the range of summer precipitation, and where one-grained *T. boeticum* and hexaploid wheats grew.

Hexaploid wheats are thought to have originated from hybrids between an ancestor of *Aegilops squarrosa* and domesticated *T. dicoccoides*. Because the two modern species do not have a common distribution, it has been assumed that emmer wheat must have been carried by early farmers to natural stands of *A. squarrosa* in the south Caspian region for this cross to have taken place (Zohary 1969). Jarman (1972) points out the incongruity of "the supposed most likely place of origin" and its earliest recorded occurrences at Knossos, Crete and Tell Ramad, Syria. The evidence of Early Holocene summer precipitation suggests a response to this objection. *T. dicoccoides* was not necessarily transported to the moist-summer region where *A. squarrosa* thrived. Instead, the opportunity for hybridization could have occurred when the extension of summer precipitation allowed *A. squarrosa* to spread into the range of *T. dicoccoides*.

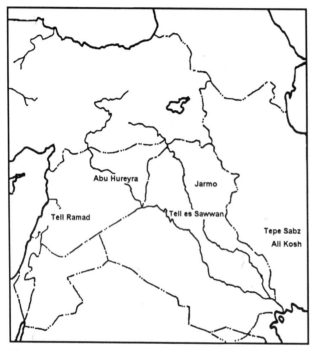

Fig. 5. Early Holocene sites of one-seeded einkorn and hexaploid wheat

SUMMARY AND CONCLUSION

The consistency within individual pollen diagrams between the two curves that indicate summer precipitation supports the idea of a period of Early Holocene summer precipitation. That similar patterns occur regionally further strengthens the hypothesis. A phase of Early Holocene summer precipitation also explains some of the anomalies in the patterns of wheat distribution now and in the Early Holocene. The botanical evidence is supported by Horowitz and Gat (1984), whose isotopic composition data indicate that paleowaters in the Nubian sandstone aquifers of the Sinai and southern Israel resulted from a precipitation regime that differed from the present winter-rainfall climate. In addition, the formation of a sapropel layer in the Mediterranean 9000–6000 BP is attributed to stagnation caused by freshwater flooding. The input probably originated from North Africa and was due to increased monsoonal precipitation (Fontugne *et al.* 1994).

For the lower latitudes of Asia and Africa, evidence of increased summer precipitation during the Early Holocene has culminated in a model of strengthened monsoons due to stronger summer insolation (Kutzbach and Guetter 1986). This increase in summer precipitation has been deduced primarily through the study of changing lake levels (Street and Grove 1979). Based on the observation that lake levels did not rise during that period, it has been concluded that summer precipitation did not extend into the mid-latitudes of the Middle East (Street-Perrott and Roberts 1983). However, lake level is not a valid indicator of summer rainfall in the Middle East, where winter precipitation dominates. Even at its maximum, summer rainfall was probably only a small percentage of the total annual precipitation. Obviously, a combination of low winter precipitation and moderate summer rainfall would tend to result in less water in lakes and elsewhere. Indeed, other pollen data suggest that winter precipitation was relatively low in the Early Holocene (El-Moslimany 1986). A relatively small amount of summer precipitation can modify the vegetation considerably, but would not result in increased erosion or a higher water table. Only where winter precipitation is extremely low can summer precipitation make a positive physical impact, as it has in the formation of lakes in desert regions.

The end of the summer-rainfall climate is not recognized in the pollen diagrams as clearly as is the onset, although the lack of lake sediments in the desert region after *ca.* 7000 BP may be significant. Because all of the available pollen diagrams are percentage diagrams, each curve relates to the abundance of the others, and cannot be considered independently. Although deciduous forests required summer rainfall to expand their ranges from glacial refuges, in most areas, they were able to persist after summer drought was re-established. Thus, decreases in deciduous tree pollen generally are as likely to reflect forest cutting than a return to summer drought (El-Moslimany 1986). Once deciduous trees were established, their pollen largely masked the pollen of the non-arboreal groups that had provided evidence of seasonal variation in precipitation. Also, the effect that arboreal vegetation has on the relative abundance of pollen of Poaceae, *Artemisia* and Chenopodiaceae is not known.

Regional summer precipitation was probably variable enough to result in chronologies that differed from place to place. Summer precipitation may have been affected by an enhanced monsoon in the south, and by a southern shift in summer rainfall in eastern Europe. Winter precipitation began to increase throughout the eastern Mediterranean *ca.* 6000 BP. Some areas may have been affected by interacting climate systems, thus extending the period favorable for the growth and expansion of deciduous trees. This may have been the case at Lake Zeribar, where *Quercus* pollen continued to increase until *ca.* 5500 BP.

REFERENCES CITED

Bottema, S.
  1986   A late Quaternary pollen diagram from Lake Urmia, northwestern Iran. *Review of Palaeobotany and Palynology* 47:241–261.
Bottema, S. and Y. Barkoudah
  1979   Modern pollen precipitation in Syria and Lebanon and its relation to vegetation. *Pollen et Spores* 11:427–480.
Bottema, S. and H. Woldring
  1987   Late Quaternary vegetation and climate of southwestern Turkey, Part II. *Palaeohistoria* 26:124–149.
Doornkamp, J., D. Brunsden and D. Jones
  1980   *Geology, Geomorphology and Pedology of Bahrain.* GeoAbstracts, Norwich, England.
El-Moslimany, A.
  1983   History of Climate and Vegetation in the Eastern and Middle East from the Pleniglacial to the Mid-Holocene. Ph.D. Dissertation, University of Washington, Seattle.
  1986   Ecology and late Quaternary history of the Kurdo-Zagrosian oak forest near Lake Zeribar, Kurdistan, western Iran. *Vegetatio* 68:55–63.
  1987   The late Pleistocene climates of the Lake Zeribar region, Kurdistan, western Iran, deduced from the ecology and pollen production of nonarboreal pollen. *Vegetatio* 72:131–139.
  1990   Ecological significance of common nonarboreal pollen: Examples from drylands of the Middle East. *Review of Palaeobotany and Palynology* 64:343–350.
Fontugne, M., M. Arnold, L. Labeyrie, M. Paterne, S. E. Calvert and J.-C. Duplessy
  1994   Paleoenvironment, sapropel chronology and Nile River discharge during the last 20,000 years as indicated by deep-sea sediment records in the eastern Mediterranean. This volume.
Helbaek, H.
  1960   The paleoethnobotany of the Near East and Europe. In *Prehistoric Investigations in Iraqi Kurdistan*, edited by R. Braidwood and B. Howe, pp. 99–117. Studies in Ancient Oriental Civilization 31. University of Chicago Press, Chicago.
Hillman, G.
  1975   The plant remains from Tell Abu Hureyra: A preliminary report. *Proceedings of the Prehistoric Society* 41: 50–77.

Horowitz, A. and J. R. Gat
   1984   Floral and isotopic indications for possible summer rains in Israel during wetter climates. *Pollen et Spores* 26:61–68.
Hötzl, H., F. Krämer and V. Maurin
   1978   Quaternary sediments. In *The Quaternary Period in Saudi Arabia*, edited by S. Al-Sayari and J. Zötl, pp. 202–209. Springer-Verlag, New York.
Jarman, H. N.
   1972   The origins of wheat and barley cultivation. In *Papers in Economic Prehistory* 15, edited by E. S. Higgs, pp. 15–26. Cambridge University Press, Cambridge.
Kutzbach, J. and P. Guetter
   1986   The influence of changing orbital parameters and surface boundary conditions on climate simulations for the past 18 000 years. *Journal of Atmospheric Science* 43:1726–1759.
Leroi-Gourhan, A.
   1974   Etudes palynologiques des derniers 11,000 ans en Syrie semi-désertique. *Paléorient* 2:443–451.
McClure, H.
   1976   Radiocarbon chronology of late-Quaternary lakes in the Arabian Desert. *Nature* 26:755–756.
   1978   Ar Rub' Al Khali. In *The Quaternary Period in Saudi Arabia*, edited by S. Al-Sayari and J. Zötl, pp. 252–263. Springer-Verlag, New York.
   1984   Late Quaternary Geology of the Rub' Al-Khali. Ph.D. Dissertation, University of London.
Niklewski, J. and W. van Zeist
   1970   A late Quaternary pollen diagram from northwest Syria. *Acta Botanica Neerlandica* 19:737–754.
Renfrew, J.
   1969   The archeological evidence for the domestication of plants. In *The Domestication and Exploitation of Plants and Animals*, edited by P. J. Ucko and G. W. Dimbleby, pp. 149–172. Aldine, Chicago.
   1973   *Paleoethnobotany. The Prehistoric Food Plants of the Near East and Europe.* Columbia University Press, New York.
Rossignol-Strick, M., W. Nesteroff, P. Olive and C. Vergnaud-Grazzini
   1982   After the deluge: Mediterranean stagnation and sapropel formation. *Nature* 295:105–110.
Street, F. and A. Grove
   1979   Global maps of lake-level fluctuations since 30,000 years BP. *Quaternary Research* 12:83–118.
Street-Perrott, A. and N. Roberts
   1983   Fluctuations in closed lakes as an indicator of past atmospheric circulation patterns. In *Variations in the Global Water Budget*, edited by F. A. Street-Perrott, M. A. Beran and R. Ratcliffe, pp. 331–345. Reidel, Dordrecht, The Netherlands.
van Zeist, W. and S. Bottema
   1977   Palynological investigations in western Iran. *Palaeohistoria* 19:19–85.
   1982   Vegetational history of the eastern Mediterranean and the Near East during the last 20000 years. In *Palaeoclimates, Palaeoenvironments and Human Communities in the Eastern Mediterranean Region in Later Prehistory*, edited by J. Bintliff and W. van Zeist, pp. 277–321. BAR International Series 133, British Archaeological Reports, Oxford.
van Zeist, W. and W. A. Casparie
   1968   Wild einkorn wheat and barley from Tell Mureybit in northern Syria. *Acta Botanica Neerlandica* 17:44–53.
van Zeist, W. and H. Woldring
   1978   A postglacial pollen diagram from Lake Van in east Anatolia. *Review of Palaeobotany and Palynology* 26:249–276.
   1980   Holocene vegetation and climate of northwestern Syria. *Palaeohistoria* 22:112–125.
Whitney, J., D. Faulkender, and M. Rubin
   1983   The environmental history and present condition of the northern sand seas of Saudi Arabia. Saudi Deputy Ministry of Mineral Resources. *USGS Open File Report* OF-O3-95.
Zohary, D.
   1969   The progenitors of wheat and barley in relation to domestication and agricultural dispersal in the Old World. In *The Domestication and Exploitation of Plants and Animals*, edited by P. J. Ucko and G. W. Dimbleby, pp. 47–66. Aldine, Chicago.

THE PALEOHYDROLOGY OF THE EASTERN MEDITERRANEAN

MEBUS A. GEYH

Niedersächsisches Landesamt für Bodenforschung, Postfach 510153, D-30631 Hannover, Germany

INTRODUCTION

The eastern Mediterranean is a narrow transition zone from humid to arid climate. Precipitation amounts up to 2000 mm in the Anti-Lebanon Mountains. Along the coast, the mean annual rainfall is 800 mm. Farther south and east, the climate becomes semi-arid to arid, with a mean annual precipitation of <200 mm. Most rainfall occurs during the short winter; summer is long and hot.

In Lebanon and Galilee, the humid climate is mainly controlled by precipitation from the Westerlies, which bring marine storms during the cold season. The summer climate is determined by the location of the Inter-Tropical Convergence Zone (ITCZ) over the deserts of the Sahara and Arabia. In autumn and spring, dust storms with hot, dry winds govern the weather, sometimes interrupted by sporadic heavy rain (Khamsin) storms. Arid climatic conditions prevail in Syria, Iraq, Jordan and northern Saudi Arabia. Sporadic rainfall in the southeast is often brought on by monsoons.

As a climate transition zone, the eastern Mediterranean is ideal for studying climate changes of the past. Paleohydrologic, paleoclimatic, geomorphologic, archaeologic and environmental-isotope proxy data are available. Hydrologic reconstructions of prehistoric times are based mainly on multidisciplinary studies involving proxy data from natural archives that yield dates with different precisions. In the eastern Mediterranean, such archives include ancient sea levels of both Lake Lisan and the Dead Sea (Begin *et al.* 1985; Klein 1986; Frumkin *et al.* 1991), soil and sediment profiles and, most important, pollen assemblages of peat and lake deposits (Horowitz 1979).

For historical times, written reports, diaries, religious legends from the Bible and archaeologic findings often contain previously undeciphered proxy data with valuable paleoclimatic and paleo-hydrologic information (Issar 1990). Such proxy data include crop yields, prices and quality of foodstuffs, flood records, unusual and catastrophic weather conditions and dates of floral cycles, as well as migration schedules of birds.

Environmental Isotope Dates and Paleohydrologic Information

Environmental isotopes provide the most accurate and precise chronometers of paleohydrologic and paleoclimatic events (Geyh and Schleicher 1990). Among these isotopic dating methods, ^{14}C is the most reliable for a great variety of materials. Abundant climatologically relevant ^{14}C data from the eastern Mediterranean are available for the last 30,000 yr. Fewer absolute uranium/thorium (U/Th) dates, mainly from calcareous samples, have been determined. Much ^{14}C data can be obtained from studying speleothems and groundwater.

Speleothems are deposited and groundwater is recharged only during humid or pluvial periods. For speleothems to form, dripwater from the roof of a cave must contain a high concentration of CO_2 and HCO_3, both formed in the topsoil. These dissolved inorganic carbon (DIC) compounds in groundwater contain ^{14}C-free carbon from dissolved fossil lime and ^{14}C-rich carbon of the contemporaneous biogenic CO_2 from the time of recharge.

Late Quaternary Chronology and Paleoclimates of the Eastern Mediterranean
Edited by O. Bar-Yosef and R. S. Kra. RADIOCARBON 1994, pp. 131–145

As a result, the initial ^{14}C value of newly formed secondary limestone is less than that of contemporaneous atmospheric CO_2, which explains why conventional ^{14}C ages of speleothems are greater than those of coeval organic matter (Franke 1951). A "reservoir correction" must be made to convert the ^{14}C time scale of a speleothem into a conventional ^{14}C time scale. Unfortunately, because of the prevailing kinetic isotope fractionation during limestone precipitation, no geochemical or physical procedure exists for estimating this correction, for example, by $\delta^{13}C$ values (Fanditis and Ehhalt 1970; Hendy 1971). Empirically deduced values for the reservoir correction are based on ^{14}C dating of both charcoal or other organic material and the coeval secondary limestone. Stalagmites that grew until sampling yield estimates of this correction by extrapolation of the ^{14}C ages from the base to the top (Talma and Vogel 1992). The correction biases generally range from several centuries to three millennia and are always smaller than those for DIC in groundwater, as isotope exchange occurs between the bicarbonate in the drip water and the atmospheric CO_2. In central Europe, the speleothem correction is *ca.* −900 yr (Geyh 1970).

As no suitable coeval organic and calcareous samples in Israeli caves were suitable for estimating the reservoir correction, I use the European value, at least for the Holocene. This seems justifiable, as the correction bias for groundwater dates is very close to −1300 yr for both the Upper Galilee and southern Germany, where the most speleothem samples were collected. The precision of the correction bias for speleothem is better than ± 500 yr.

Groundwater dating is beset by the same hydrochemical problem. Correction models to estimate the initial ^{14}C activity based on the alkalinity of the groundwater and/or on $\delta^{13}C$ values of DIC have been proposed (*e.g.*, Gonfiantini 1972; Fontes 1985), but the results are often misleading (Geyh 1992). Empirically obtained estimates may be suitable alternatives. Both the lime content and its contribution to the topsoil of the catchment area are important parameters (Geyh 1972). More reliable and precise values are obtained by comparing the results of extensive isotope hydrology studies with the paleoclimates of the study area (Geyh 1992).

As both groundwater and speleothems develop only during pluvial periods, the frequency distribution (histogram) of the corresponding ^{14}C dates may reflect the paleohydrology of the area. Geyh and Streif (1970) first applied this method while studying eustatic sea-level changes. Careful study showed that the wiggles in the ^{14}C calibration curve (Stuiver and Kra 1986; Stuiver and Reimer 1993) used for converting conventional ^{14}C years into solar years affect the shape of the ^{14}C histogram (Geyh 1980). The most critical periods of the calibration curve are characterized by pronounced wiggles, *e.g.*, the 3rd and 9th millennia BP (Becker, Kromer and Trimborn 1991). Both the steadily increasing difference between the U/Th and ^{14}C ages of coeval coral samples (Bard *et al.* 1990; Stuiver and Reimer 1993) and the small variations in the CO_2 content of continental ice (Barnola, Korotkevich and Lorius 1987), for the period 30,000–13,000 BP, support the assumption that the frequency distribution of ^{14}C dates for the Upper Pleistocene are only slightly truncated due to the wiggles of the ^{14}C calibration curve.

Stable isotope compositions of carbon and oxygen are also valuable paleohydrologic proxy data, obtained from marine and limnologic mollusk shells (Goodfriend 1986, 1988), marine and limnologic sediment cores (Luz 1982; Stiller *et al.* 1984), speleothems (Issar 1990; Issar *et al.* 1992) and groundwater (Geyh *et al.* 1985; Geyh 1992). The prerequisite for a paleohydrologic evaluation of isotope proxy data is careful examination of possible diagenetic processes that may have masked or truncated primary paleohydrologic information. Variations of $\delta^{13}C$ values from mollusk shells may relate mainly to changes in precipitation and the source of CO_2. $\delta^{18}O$ values are governed by temperature, precipitation source and evaporation effects. The more continental the origin of the rain and the lower the temperatures, the larger the depletion in heavy oxygen isotopes.

THE PALEOHYDROLOGIC SETTING

Results of Conventional Paleohydrologic Methods

The ancient terminal Lake Lisan, and its much smaller successor, the Dead Sea, belong to the Jordan River system, which provides most valuable hydrological information for the eastern Mediterranean for the Upper Pleistocene and Holocene. Neev and Emery (1967) evaluated the levels of Lake Lisan for the Upper Pleistocene; Klein (1986) and Frumkin *et al.* (1991) investigated the Holocene. They interpreted large fluctuations in the lake levels as results of changes in precipitation and evaporation, thus as transitions between humid and arid climates. Begin *et al.* (1985) described the Upper Pleistocene history of Lake Lisan levels most precisely. They evaluated maximum lake levels by dating algal stromatolites and ooliths, as well as by studying ancient human settlements along the coast (Fig. 1). High lake levels existed at *ca.* 24,000, 20,500 and 15,000–14,000 BP, low levels at 30,000, 23,000 and 17,000 BP (Yechieli *et al.* 1993). Uncertainties of up to 2000 yr are possible due to the reservoir effect and contamination.

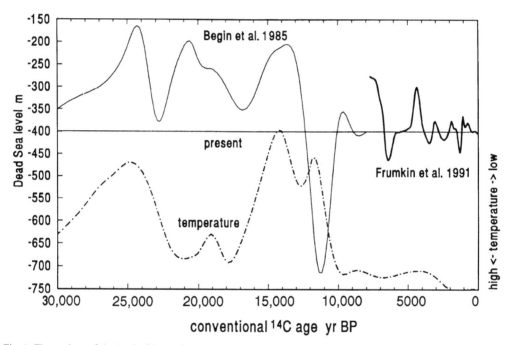

Fig. 1. Fluctuations of the level of Lake Lisan based on the occurrence of stromatolites, the formation and modulation of salt caves in Mount Sedom and archaeological studies of the upper Pleistocene (Begin *et al.* 1985) and the Holocene (Frumkin *et al.* 1991). A relative temperature curve derives from pollen analysis of samples from the northern catchment area of Lake Lisan (Weinstein 1976)

The level of Lake Lisan was never higher than *ca.* 13,000 BP (Bølling/Allerød), the pre-Holocene wet period, which ended abruptly at 10,500 BP, as documented in Dead Sea sediments (Magaritz *et al.* 1991; Yechieli *et al.* 1993). The absolute minimum lake level at −700 m msl, 300 m below the present Holocene level, was reached *ca.* 11,000 BP, as derived from a ^{14}C date of organic matter and an existing underground drainage system (Neev and Emery 1967). At this time, the desert extended to the north (Magaritz and Goodfriend 1987). This event is probably coincident with the cold Younger Dryas period (Yechieli *et al.* 1993). There is a remarkable resemblance between the fluctuations of the Lake Lahontan in Nevada (Broecker and Orr 1958; Benson 1981) and Lake Lisan, which is interpreted as a reflection of global climate change at the mid-northern latitudes (Begin *et al.* 1985).

These lake-level fluctuations are also well correlated with palynologically derived temperature variations determined from core material taken in the northern part of the Lake Lisan catchment area (Weinstein 1976). High lake levels at 24,000 and 14,000 BP corresponded to low temperatures. In contrast, the palynological evidence of a small drop in temperature *ca.* 20,500 BP correlates with a high lake level (Fig. 1).

The sharp rise in global temperature by *ca.* 7°C (Talma and Vogel 1992; Stute *et al.* 1992) and the inferred 30% increase in atmospheric CO_2 at 10,000 BP (Barnola, Korotkevich and Lorius 1987) coincide with a rise of temperature and precipitation in the eastern Mediterranean and northern Africa. The Neolithic revolution in the Near East may be the human response to this dramatic climate change. The culture of the pre-pottery Neolithic people flourished in Jericho and settlements and forests existed in the Negev and Sinai (Issar 1992). Rainfall was twice as high as at present in the northern Negev (Goodfriend 1987; Magaritz and Goodfriend 1987) but not as high as that of the Late Pleistocene. A high Dead Sea level until *ca.* 7500 BP follows from the absence of salt caves of Mount Sedom (Frumkin *et al.* 1991).

Based on archaeological studies from Lake Huleh, Moore (1973) observed that the climate became dry between 7500 and 7000 BP. A drop in Dead Sea level by >100 m and the widely distributed deposition of a salt crust (Frumkin *et al.* 1991) confirmed this finding. However, Goodfriend, Magaritz and Carmi (1986) and Goodfriend (1988) detected humid conditions in the Negev between 7000 and 6500 BP (if the dates are precise). Vegetation from 7000–6000 BP reflects a warm climate (Horowitz 1979). Marshes and swamps slowly disappeared. The Chalcolithic culture (6550–5500 BP) developed during this period of gradual desiccation.

After *ca.* 5500 BP, precipitation increased and temperatures decreased. The Dead Sea level rose by 100 m. Magaritz *et al.* (1991) found evidence for a moist period at *ca.* 5000 BP, which lasted a maximum of 500 yr. During this time, the ancient town of Arad flourished, with 2000–3000 inhabitants who practiced irrigation agriculture (Amiran 1991). Oaks were deposited in the salt caves at Mount Sedom. Neev and Emery (1967) found a high Dead Sea level at 4400 BP. Arad and the Negev were abandoned *ca.* 4600 BP, when a polar climate invaded the North American Boreal forest, and Saharan oases began to shrink. The climate of the early Bronze Age (5400–4400 BP) in the eastern Mediterranean was dry compared to that of the early Holocene.

Neev and Emery (1967) found evidence for another rapid drop in moisture in Dead Sea sediments between 4600 and 3700 BP. Arid conditions were also inferred for the interval, 4750–3250 BP, on the basis of dates for the northern Negev (Goodfriend 1986). Halite was formed in Dead Sea sediments at 4000 BP. According to Magaritz *et al.* (1991), the driest period of the Holocene began about this time. Issar (1990, 1992) interpreted the movement of peoples from Mesopotamia and Canaan into Egypt as a response to climatic deterioration prompted by the northward movement of the desert belt (Pachur and Braun 1980). *Ca.* 4000 BP, the climate in Ethiopia became more humid and the headwaters of the Nile higher. When the monsoonal belt moved southward 400 years later, the level of the Nile fell, sand storms destroyed crops and famine engulfed Egypt. The Hebrews returned to Palestine (Issar 1990). Data from studies of salt caves by Frumkin *et al.* (1991) and geomorphology by Klein (1982) indicate that the Dead Sea level was *ca.* 20 m higher from 3200–3000 BP. The Iron Age began at the end of this short humid period and settlements reappeared in the Negev, but the Dead Sea basin became drier. At 2900 BP, the Dead Sea level was at least 60 m lower than 600 yr before, indicated by the Mezad Gozal fortress at <−396 m msl

(Klein 1982). Olive trees disappeared and the natural forest started to expand. Desiccation continued until at least 2300 BP. A short humid period followed between 2000 and 1700 BP, indicated by a higher Dead Sea level (Klein 1982, 1986; Frumkin *et al.* 1991). A relatively humid climate also prevailed in the Negev and Levant after 300 BC and AD 600. Terraced irrigation agriculture was practiced locally (Issar 1992). The next dry period was interrupted by slightly more moisture between 1000 and 800 BP (Issar and Tsoar 1987; Issar 1992). *Ca.* AD 500, olive trees disappeared and the natural forest expanded, indicating a warmer and drier climate. Desertification increased, sand dunes in the northern Sinai became active and invaded the Mediterranean coastal plain (Issar 1992). The last increases of the Dead Sea level were from AD 1200–1300 and AD 1550–1650 (Klein and Flohn 1987).

PALEOHYDROLOGIC EVIDENCE FROM ISOTOPE DATA

Radiocarbon Dates

Unpublished ^{14}C dates of 41 stalagmites from 10 caves strongly confirm that the eastern Mediterranean was wetter and colder during the Upper Pleistocene than during the Holocene. Figure 2 is a superposition of bars, each starting and ending with the ^{14}C dates of the top and bottom samples, respectively, from the sampled stalagmites. Continuous and rather constant growth of the stalagmites was confirmed by ^{14}C dating of several samples taken along their axes. Figure 2 reflects intensive speleothem formation during the Upper Pleistocene compared to the Holocene. This agrees with the high level of Lake Lisan (Fig. 1). The apparently discordant data at *ca.* 30,000 BP may be due to contamination of old calcareous samples. The minimum temperature at 23,000 BP coincided with a low lake level. During a short period of optimum growth conditions, between

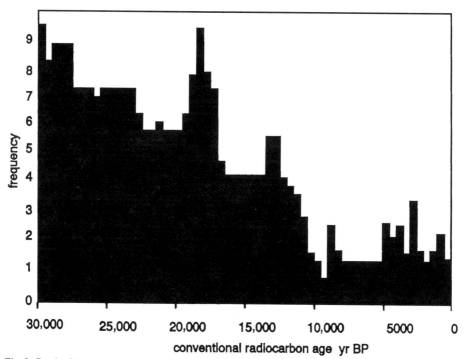

Fig. 2. Graph of the growth periods of stalagmites collected from caves in northern Israel, a superposition of bars, each starting and ending with the ^{14}C dates of the top and bottom samples, respectively, taken from the sampled stalagmites. Intensified speleothem formation reflects a more humid period during the Upper Pleistocene than during the Holocene.

20,500 and 19,000 BP, tall and long stalagmites formed. Never before or afterwards has such an intensive stalagmatic growth been reflected. Three specimens from two caves, each a maximum of 1000 yr old, grew *ca.* 18,500 BP (uncorrected ^{14}C age). The reservoir correction for speleothem dates could have been –3000 yr instead of –900 yr at this time, if the caves were overlain by soil. With the large correction, the maximum level of Lake Lisan and the peak growth of speleothems (Neev and Emery 1967) would correlate with extreme humidity. Stalagmites grew at a slower rate when the climate became drier and warmer during the Holocene. The small wiggles of the graph (Fig. 2) may be caused by statistical artifacts.

Figure 3 represents 72 ^{14}C dates for DIC in deep groundwater collected in the arid Dawwa basin in Syria, the arid Hamad area in southern Syria, Jordan, eastern Iraq and northern Saudi Arabia (Geyh *et al.* 1985), and provides independent paleohydrologic information. The samples were collected from wells with fresh groundwater (electrical conductivity values below 3500 μS cm^{-1} and absence of tritium). An estimate of the initial ^{14}C content yielded a reservoir correction of –1300 ± 500 yr (Geyh 1992) derived from the model by Gonfiantini (1972).

A humid period at *ca.* 30,000 BP is similar to the speleothem data. The times of the top levels of Lake Lisan and temperature peaks at 24,000, 20,500 and 14,000 BP (Fig. 1) concur with the peaks of the groundwater graph at 23,500, 20,500 and 18,500, are less pronounced at 15,000 and 12,500 BP, and confirm the general temperature history given in Figure 1. Groundwater recharge and speleothem growth peaked *ca.* 18,000 BP, when global temperature was at a minimum. Groundwater recharge culminated during the Neolithic pluvial between 9500 and 6500 BP. The period between 6500 and 4500 BP was drier and groundwater recharge decreased to a minimum after 4000 BP.

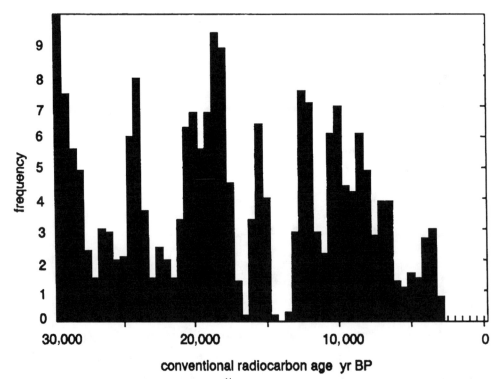

Fig. 3. Seventy-two conventional and uncorrected ^{14}C dates from the DIC of fresh groundwater samples collected in the Dawwa basin and the Hamad region (Geyh *et al.* 1985). Maxima and minima represent humid and dry periods, respectively.

$\delta^{13}C$ and $\delta^{18}O$ Data

Flohn (1991) developed a feedback model for abrupt global climate change resulting from modification of atmospheric CO_2 concentration due to oceanic upwelling and downwelling. Changes in precipitation in semi-arid and arid regions affect the distribution of C_4 and C_3 plants (Magaritz *et al.* 1991; Talma and Vogel 1992). Leavitt and Long (1989) noted drought-related changes in the $\delta^{13}C$ value of wood resulting from stomatal closure and CO_2 fixation during photosynthesis. In turn, $\delta^{13}C$ and $\delta^{18}O$ values for fossil biological and calcareous material, at least from climate-sensitive regions, may be complex proxy data of environmental paleohydrologic parameters such as temperature, relative humidity and soil moisture (Leavitt and Danzer 1992). $\delta^{18}O$ values of calcareous material are governed mainly by the oxygen isotope composition of water in the local environment. $\delta^{13}C$ and $\delta^{18}O$ proxy data from biogenic carbonates, mollusk shells and corals also provide paleoclimatic and paleohydrologic information (*e.g.*, Goodfriend and Magaritz 1987; Issar *et al.* 1992).

The case for non-biogenic carbonates such as speleothems is more complex. Both the $\delta^{18}O$ values of secondary carbonates and the δ^2H values of pore water contain temperature information if carbonate forms under isotopic equilibrium (Fanditis and Ehhalt 1970; Hendy 1971; Schwarcz *et al.* 1976; Harmon *et al.* 1978; Rozanski and Dulinski 1988). Kinetic isotopic fractionation usually governs speleothem formation and obscures, at least theoretically, inherent paleoclimatic information (Fornaca-Rinaldi, Panichi and Tongiorgi 1968; Hendy 1971). Fanditis and Ehhalt (1970) found that the kinetic isotopic fractionation of secondarily precipitated carbonate depends upon the hardness of the drip water, which is influenced by CO_2 formation in topsoil and, thus, from the climate. Therefore, it is not surprising that even $\delta^{18}O$ and ^{13}C records of speleothem formed under kinetic isotopic fractionation may reflect climate changes. The cumulative, splined $\delta^{18}O$ and $\delta^{13}C$ records of speleothem from the eastern Mediterranean (Fig. 4) using 245 stable isotope dates from 19 stalagmites collected in six caves is one example (Issar 1990; Issar *et al.* 1992). Similar $\delta^{13}C$ and $\delta^{18}O$ curves indicate that kinetic isotopic fractionation occurred during stalagmite formation and that simple translation of $\delta^{18}O$ values in temperatures is not possible (Hendy 1971).

Contrary to the theoretical expectations described above, the cold and probably humid periods at 30,000, 25,500, 20,500 and 18,000 BP in the eastern Mediterranean are clearly visible in the $\delta^{18}O$ and $\delta^{13}C$ records. Except for the coldest period of the last Pleniglacial the hydrologic fluctuations are not evident in the $\delta^{18}O$ record. The humid period at the beginning of the Holocene is reflected in a pronounced $\delta^{18}O$ minimum. Low $\delta^{18}O$ values were also found in marine sediments from the eastern Mediterranean and the Red Sea, and were interpreted as an indicator of increased precipitation and stronger admixture of fresh water (Luz 1982).

The period following 5500 BP needs special attention. Stable isotope records obtained from sediments of Lake Kinneret (Stiller *et al.* 1984), from mollusk shells of the eastern Mediterranean (Kaufman and Magaritz 1980; Fig. 5) and from the speleothems discussed here correlate well, taking into account a correction bias of −500 yr of the speleothem time scale *vs.* that of Mediterranean mollusks. The latter may have an additional correction bias of −400 yr for the reservoir effect. Kaufman and Magaritz (1980) interpreted negative $\delta^{18}O$ values in mollusks as an indication of intensified rainfall that resulted in a decline of salt content in the Mediterranean Sea along the coast. Issar (1990) and Issar *et al.* (1992) constructed $\delta^{13}C$ and $\delta^{18}O$ master curves, which are used as a paleohydrologic reference. The trends as well as the peaks and lows of the smoothed $\delta^{18}O$ and $\delta^{13}C$ speleothem curves correlate well with those of limnic sediments from the Sea of Galilee.

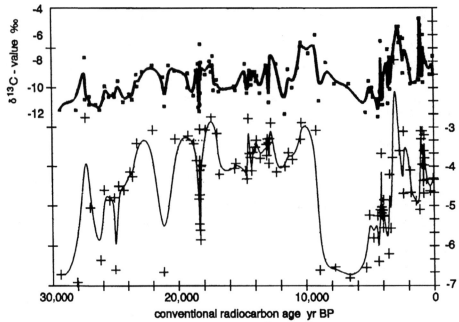

Fig. 4. The similarity of the cubic spline of both cumulative $\delta^{18}O$ and $\delta^{13}C$ records of 19 stalagmites from 6 caves in northern Israel reflects kinetic isotope fractionation, but also paleoclimate changes.

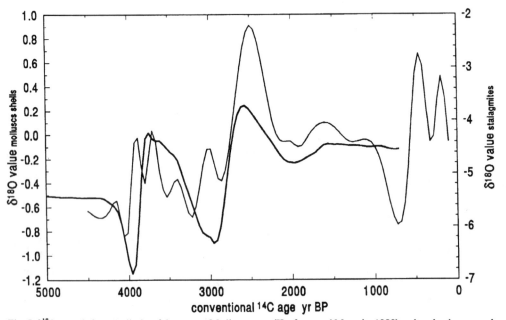

Fig. 5. $\delta^{18}O$ records from mollusks of the eastern Mediterranean (Kaufman and Magaritz 1980) and speleothem samples from caves in Israel. The reservoir corrections for ^{14}C dates of speleothem and mollusks are assumed to differ by 400 yr. Relatively humid periods are shown by lows of the $\delta^{18}O$ curves.

REGIONAL AND GLOBAL PALEOHYDROLOGY

Whether the paleohydrology of the eastern Mediterranean is specific to that region or is a reflection of global paleoclimate still is a debated issue. Paleohydrologic data from arid North Africa (the Sahara) in the west and western India in the east may contribute to the solution of this problem. Field observations show that the climate before 30,000 to *ca.* 25,000 BP was moist and relatively dry in Africa and the eastern Mediterranean until *ca.* 20,000 BP (Butzer 1979). The climate then became humid in the eastern Mediterranean, but remained hyperarid in the Sahara (*Hyperaride postatérien*) until *ca.* 12,500 BP (Butzer 1979; Muzzolini 1985; Pachur and Hoelzmann 1991). Later, many African closed lakes rose. Global hyperaridity characterized the period at *ca.* 11,000 BP; the level of Lake Lisan was at a minimum and lakes regressed in northwestern India (Singh, Joshi and Singh 1972) and Africa (Butzer 1979; Street-Perrott and Grove 1976). Yechieli *et al.* (1993) correlate these observations with the Younger Dryas, the end of the Pleistocene. The succeeding *Grand Humide* in the Sahara (12,000–7500 BP; Geyh and Jäkel 1974; Rognon 1976; Muzzolini 1985) coincided with the wet climate in the eastern Mediterranean. Evidence came from high levels of many African closed lakes, extensive Nile floods, the high level of Lake Lisan and intensified speleothem growth in the eastern Mediterranean.

Global aridity characterized the millennium from 7500–6500 BP (*Grand Aride mi-holocène*). Sediment studies of two ancient lakes in the Thar desert (Singh, Joshi and Singh 1972; Wasson, Smith and Agrawal 1984) provide evidence for this paleohydrologic deterioration extending to the Indian subcontinent (Fig. 6). The *Humide néolithique* followed from 6000–4500 BP. African animals were painted on rocks in the Sahara. Nicholson (1980) reported considerably moister climate in the northern and southern fringes of the Sahara between 6000 and 5000 BP than at present. High Nile floods were also reported. The climate in the eastern Mediterranean became wetter at the beginning and drier at the end of this period. Nicholson and Flohn (1980) assumed a northward shift in the mean ITCZ. From a Greenland ice core, Hammer, Clausen and Dansgaard (1980) found that global climates were wetter than now for this period.

The *Aride post-néolithique* (Muzzolini 1985) in the Sahara commenced *ca.* 4500–4000 BP, accompanied by the disappearance of traditional grazing areas, decreasing Nile floods and severe droughts. Similar climatic development is known for Iraq, Iran (Amiran 1991) and the Punjab. Issar (1992) reports increasing soil salination in Mesopotamia *ca.* 4000 BP. In the Punjab, the Old-Hakra River system began to disappear, the Harappa culture ended, groundwater recharge ceased (Geyh 1992) and lakes disappeared in northwestern India (Singh, Joshi and Singh 1972). Issar (1992) explains the cultural and political development in this area as a response to climate change in Egypt and the eastern Mediterranean. According to his interpretation, each latitudinal shift of the monsoonal belt forced the historically known population movements in this region.

Comparison of climatic development in the eastern Mediterranean with the global hemispheric mean temperature curve (Wigley 1988) reveals that temperature and precipitation do not correlate well throughout the Holocene. Low temperatures at 4500, 3200, 2100 and 1000 BP apparently occurred with relatively humid periods. In contrast, the change of moderate to low temperature during the Early Holocene related to a transition from a lengthy pluvial period to a short, dry period.

Paleoclimatic modeling can explain this long-term trend. Kutzbach and Street-Perrott (1985) simulated long-term climate in northern hemisphere tropics. They found strengthened monsoonal circulation and increased precipitation over Africa and Arabia, probably accompanied by a northward shift of the mean ITCZ, from 15,000 BP onward, culminating between 9000 and 6000 BP.

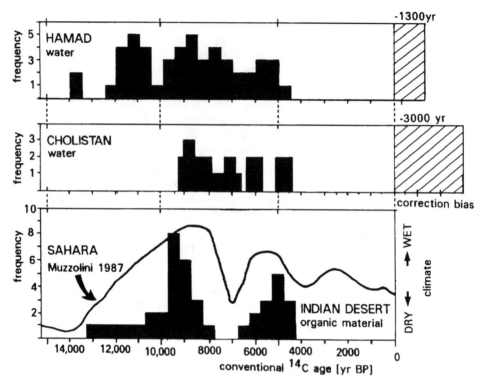

Fig. 6. Periods of existence of two ancient lakes in the Thar Desert in India and Pakistan (Singh, Joshi and Singh 1972; Wasson, Smith and Agrawal 1984), groundwater recharge in the Thar Desert and the Hamad region as well as the generalized climatic development in the Sahara (Muzzolini 1985)

However, the time resolution of 3000 yr is not sufficient to explain the dry millennium between 7500 and 6500 BP.

Nicholson and Flohn (1980) developed a hypothesis for the Late Pleistocene to Middle Holocene climate based on climatic asymmetry between northern and southern Atlantic Oceans caused by the release of meltwater and icebergs into the northern Atlantic. Ocean cooling diminished evaporation, thus, continental precipitation by *ca.* 20 % at *ca.* 10,000 BP. After climate amelioration during the next 2000 yr, at *ca.* 7500 BP, 3 M km^3 of ice and meltwater were evacuated from Hudson's Bay. At the same time, the eastern Mediterranean and Africa became dry again. Climatic asymmetry between both sides of the Atlantic remained until 4000 BP, when the Laurentian ice shield completely disintegrated. This coincided with the onset of global desiccation. The mean ITCZ moved southward.

Short-term climate variations of a millennium or even a century can be observed through a feedback mechanism arising from ocean upwelling and downwelling. Decreased CO$_2$ and water vapor can be forced by intensified equatorial ocean upwelling resulting in a less effective natural greenhouse effect. Intensified downwelling of warm water will increase CO$_2$ content and water vapor; a release of volcanic CO$_2$ may trigger this mechanism (Flohn 1983, 1991).

As stated above, $\delta^{13}C$ and $\delta^{18}O$ records of calcareous matter may be a rather complex reflection of paleoclimate and paleohydrology. Despite this, the maxima and minima of the running mean curve of $\delta^{13}C$ values from wood samples (Leavitt and Danzer 1992) and our composite $\delta^{13}C$ curve from Israeli stalagmites (Fig. 7) agree rather well, at least since 16,000 BP, although the trends of the absolute values differ. These $\delta^{13}C$ trend differences may stem from bias fluctuations and erroneous dates in the older part of the time scale as the stable isotope curve is a superposition of segments obtained from 19 stalagmites collected in six caves.

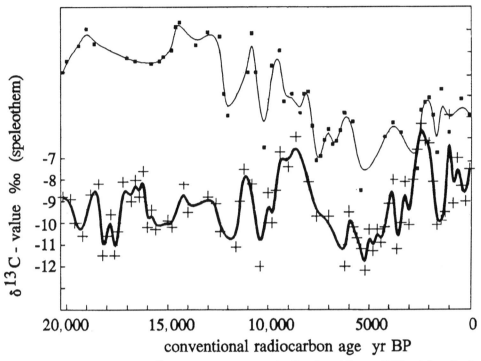

Fig. 7. Running mean of published $\delta^{13}C$ values from wood samples (Leavitt and Danzer 1992) and the splined $\delta^{13}C$ curve for Israeli stalagmites plotted above the ^{14}C time scale

As the Pleistocene portion of the $\delta^{13}C$ curve for wood cannot be interpreted as a reflection only of global climate (Krishnamurthy and Epstein 1990), the similarity to isotopic records from Israel (Luz 1982; Stiller *et al.* 1984; Kaufman and Magaritz 1980) obtained from both biogenic and non-biogenic calcareous matter raises the question whether global paleoclimatic and paleohydrologic change influences the stable isotopic composition of atmospheric CO_2. Before this question is answered and the effects are understood, reliable paleoclimatic and paleohydrologic conclusions cannot be drawn from carbon isotopic composition records.

SUMMARY

The paleohydrologic evolution of the eastern Mediterranean region shows some distinct peculiarities to that of the Sahara and the globe. The most pronounced climate variations at the transition from the Late Pleistocene to the Holocene are explained by the movement of the ITCZ. This movement changed the monsoonal influence on the eastern Mediterranean and the African climate. Small differences in the climatic records of both regions may be explained by inaccurate estimates of the reservoir correction of the ^{14}C ages or unreliable results of ^{14}C dating. Changes are generally synchronous with the global paleohydrologic regime, although the climatic development in different parts of the world may show different trends. Global warming may have contributed to the desiccation of the regions with weather governed by the Westerlies, whereas those whose weather is governed by the monsoons became more humid.

142   *M. A. Geyh*

Acknowledgments

The paleohydrologic interpretation of our isotope data, most of which have not been published, was highly encouraged by Dr. Arie Issar of the Jacob Blaustein Institute for Desert Research in Sede Boqer, Israel. The groundwater samples were collected by Drs. W. Wagner and D. Plöthner of the Federal Institute of Geosciences and Natural Resources in Hannover, Germany, and by Dr. R. Rajab of ACSAD in Damascus, Syria. Stalagmites were sampled by Drs. H. W. Franke of Munich, Germany, and E. Wakshal of the Hebrew University, Rehovot, Israel, in caves in the Upper Galilee, with financial support from the German Research Foundation (DFG).

References Cited

Amiran, H. K.
  1991   The climate of the ancient Near East. The early third millennium BC in the northern Negev of Israel. *Erdkunde* 45(3):153–162.
Bard, E., B. Hamelin, R. B. Fairbanks and A. Zindler
  1990   Calibration of the radiocarbon time scale over the past 30,000 years using mass-spectrometric U-Th ages from Barbados corals. *Nature* 345:405–410.
Barnola, J.-M., Y. S. Korotkevich and C. Lorius
  1987   Vostok ice core provides 160,000 year record of atmospheric CO_2. *Nature* 329:408–414.
Becker, B., B. Kromer and P. Trimborn
  1991   A stable-isotope tree-ring time scale of the Late Glacial/Holocene boundary. *Nature* 353:647–649.
Begin, Z. W., W. Broecker, B. Buchbinder, Y. Druckman, A. Kaufman, M. Magaritz and D. Neev
  1985   Dead Sea and Lake Lisan levels in the last 30,000 years: A preliminary report. *Israel Geological Report* 29/85:1–18.
Benson, L. V.
  1981   Palaeoclimatic significance of lake level fluctuations in the Lahontan Basin. *Quaternary Research* 16:390–403.
Broecker, W. S and P. L. Orr
  1958   Radiocarbon chronology of Lake Lahontan and Lake Bonneville. *Bulletin of the Geological Society of America* 69:1009–1032.
Butzer, K.W.
  1979   Climatic patterns in an un-glaciated continent. *Geographical Magazine* 51:201–208.
Fanditis, J. and D. H. Ehhalt
  1970   Variations of the carbon and oxygen isotope composition in stalagmites and stalactites: evidence of non-equilibrium isotopic fractionation. *Earth and Planetary Science Letters* 10:1336–144.
Flohn, H.
  1983   A climatic feedback mechanism involving oceanic upwelling, atmospheric CO_2 and water vapor. In *Variations in the Global Water Budget,* edited by A. Street-Perrott, M. Beran and R. Ratcliffe, pp. 403–418. Reidel Publishing Company, Dordrecht.
  1991   Recent climatic evolution as scenario for abrupt paleoclimatic events? In *Paläoklimaforschung,* Vol. 1, *Klima-geschichtliche Probleme der letzten 130,000 Jahre,* edited by B. Frenzel, pp. 165–176. Akademie der Wissen-schaften und der Literatur, Mainz.
Fontes, J. C.
  1985   Some considerations on groundwater dating using environmental isotopes. In *Hydrogeology in the Service of Man,* pp. 118–154. International Association of Hydrogeologists, Cambridge.
Fornaca-Rinaldi, G., C. Panichi, and E. Tongiorgi
  1968   Some causes of the variation of the isotopic composition of carbon and oxygen in cave concretions. *Earth and Planetary Science Letters* 4:321–324.
Franke, H. W.
  1951   Altersbestimmungen an Kalzit-Konkretionen mit radioaktivem Kohlenstoff. *Naturwissenschaften* 38:527.
Frumkin, A., M. Magaritz, I. Carmi and I. Zak
  1991   The Holocene climatic record of the salt caves of Mount Sedom, Israel. *The Holocene* 1(3):191–200.
Geyh, M. A.
  1970   Zeitliche Abgrenzung von Klimaänderungen mit ^{14}C- Daten von Kalksinter und organischen Substanzen. *Beihefte zum Geologische Jahrbuch* 98:15-22.
  1972   Basic studies in hydrology and ^{14}C and ^3H measurements. In *Proceedings of the 24th International Geological Congress, Montreal* 11:227–234.

Geyh, M. A.
1980   Holocene sea-level history: Case study of the statistical evaluation of ^{14}C dates. *Radiocarbon* 22 (3):695–704.
1992   The ^{14}C time-scale of groundwater: Correction and linearity. In *Isotope Techniques in Water Resources Development*, pp. 167–177. International Atomic Energy Agency, Vienna.

Geyh, M. A. and D. Jäckel
1974   Late Glacial and Holocene climatic history of the Sahara desert derived from a statistical assay of ^{14}C dates. *Palaeogeography, Palaeoclimatology, Palaeoecology* 15:205-208.

Geyh, M. A., J. Khouri, R. Rajab and W. Wagner
1985   Environmental isotope study in the Hamad region. *Geologisches Jahrbuch*, Series C, 38:3-15.

Geyh, M. A. and H. Schleicher
1990   *Absolute Age Determination*. Springer Verlag, Heidelberg.

Geyh, M. A. and J. Streif
1970   Studies on coastal movements and sea-level changes by means of the statistical evaluation of ^{14}C data. In *Report on the Symposium on Coastal Geodesy*, edited by Rudolf Sigl, pp. 599–611. International Union of Geodesy and Geophysics, Munich.

Gonfiantini, R.
1972   Notes on isotope hydrology. Internal IAEA report, International Atomic Energy Agency, Vienna.

Goodfriend, G. A.
1986   Holocene shifts in rainfall in the Negev desert as inferred from isotopic, morphological and faunal analysis of fossil land snails. In *Book of Abstracts and Reports from the Conference of Abrupt Climatic Change*, edited by W. H. Berger and L. D. Labeyrie, pp. 122–124. Ref.-Series 86-8. Scripps Institute of Oceanography, La Jolla.
1987   Chronostratigraphic studies of sediments in the Negev desert, using amino acid epimerization analysis of land snail shells. *Quaternary Research* 28:374–392.
1988   Mid-Holocene rainfall in the Negev desert from ^{13}C of land snail shell organic matter. *Nature* 333:757–760.

Goodfriend, G. A. and M. Magaritz
1987   Carbon and oxygen isotope composition of shell carbonate of desert land snails. *Earth and Planetary Science Letters* 86:377–388.

Goodfriend, G. A., M. Magaritz and I. Carmi
1986   A high stand of the Dead Sea at the end of the Neolithic period: Paleoclimatic and archaeological implications. *Climatic Change* 9:349–356.

Hammer, C. U., H. B. Clausen and W. Dansgaard
1980   Greenland ice sheet evidence of post-glacial volcanism and its climate impact. *Nature* 288:230–235.

Harmon, R. S., P. Thompson, H. P. Schwarcz and D. C. Ford
1978   Late pleistocene paleoclimate of North America as inferred from stable isotope studies of speleothems. *Quaternary Research* 9:54–70.

Hendy, C. W.
1971   The isotope chemistry of speleothems I. *Geochimica et Cosmochimica Acta* 35:801–824.

Horowitz, A.
1979   *The Quaternary of Israel*. Academic Press, New York.

Issar, A. S.
1990   *Water Shall Flow from the Rock*. Springer-Verlag, Heidelberg.
1992   The Impact of Climate Variations on Water Management Systems and Related Socioeconomic Systems. *UNESCO/IHP Project* IIc, in press.

Issar, A. S. and H. Tsoar
1987   Who is to blame for the desertification of the Negev? In *The Influence of Climate Change and Climatic Variability on the Hydrologic Regime and Water Resources*, edited by S. I. Solomon, M. Beran and W. Hogg, pp. 587–583. IAHS Publication 168. International Association of Hydrological Sciences, Wallingford.

Issar, A. S., Y. Govrin, M. A. Geyh, E. Wakshal and M. Wolf
1992   Climate changes during the Upper Holocene in Israel. *Israel Journal of Earth Sciences* 40:219-223.

Kaufman, A. and M. Magaritz
1980   The climatic history of the eastern Mediterranean as recorded in mollusk shells. *Radiocarbon* 22 (3):778–781.

Klein, C.
1982   Morphologic evidence of lake level changes, western shore of the Dead Sea. *Israel Journal of Earth Sciences* 31:67–94.
1986   *Fluctuations of the Level of the Dead Sea and Climatic Fluctuations in Israel During Historical Times*. Ph.D. Dissertation, Hebrew University of Jerusalem.

Klein, C. and H. Flohn
   1987   Contributions to the knowledge of the fluctuations of the Dead Sea Level. *Theoretical and Applied Climatology* 38:151–156.
Krishnamurthy, R. V. and S. Epstein
   1990   Glacial-interglacial excursion in the concentration of atmospheric CO_2: Effect in the $\delta^{13}C/^{12}C$ ratio in wood cellulose. *Tellus* 42B:423–434.
Kutzbach, J. E. and F. A. Street-Perrott
   1985   Milankovitch forcing of fluctuations in the level of tropical lakes from 18 to 0 kyr BP. *Nature* 317:130–134.
Leavitt, S. W. and A. Long
   1989   Drought indicated in carbon-13/carbon-12 ratios of southwestern tree rings. *Water Resources Bulletin* 25(2): 341–347.
Leavitt, S. W. and S. R. Danzer
   1992 $\delta^{13}C$ variations in C_3 plants over the past 50,000 years. *Radiocarbon* 34(3):783–791.
Luz, B.
   1982   Palaeoclimatic interpretation of the last 20,000 yr record of deep-sea cores around the Middle East. In *Palaeoclimates, Palaeoenvironments and Human Communities in the Eastern Mediterranean Region in Later Prehistory*, edited by J. L. Bintliff and W. van Zeist, pp. 41–61. BAR International Series 133, British Archaeological Reports, Oxford.
Magaritz, M. and G. A. Goodfriend
   1987   Movement of the desert boundary in the Levant from latest Pleistocene to early Holocene. In *Abrupt Climatic Change: Evidence and Implications*, edited by W. H. Berger and L. D. Labeyrie, pp. 173–183. Reidel, Dordrecht.
Magaritz, M., S. Rahner, Y. Yechieli and R. V. Krishnamurthy
   1991 $^{13}C/^{12}C$ Ratio in organic matter from the Dead Sea area: Paleoclimatic interpretation. *Naturwissenschaften* 78:453–455.
Moore, A. M. T
   1973   The Late Neolithic in Palestine. *Levant* 5:36–68.
Muzzolini, A.
   1985   Les climats au Sahara et sur ses bordures, du Pléistocène final à l'aride actual. *Empúries* 47:8–27.
Neev, D. and K. O. Emery
   1967   The Dead Sea: Depositional processes and environments of evaporites. *Bulletin of the Geological Survey of Israel* 41:1–147.
Nicholson, S. E.
   1980   Saharan climate in historical times. In *The Sahara and the Nile: Quaternary Environments and Archaeological Occupation in Northern Africa*, edited by M. A. J. Williams and H. Faure, pp. 173–200. Balkema, Rotterdam.
Nicholson, S. E. and H. Flohn
   1980   African environmental and climatic changes and the general atmospheric circulation in Late Pleistocene and Holocene. *Climatic Change* 2:313–348.
Pachur, H.-J. and G. Braun
   1980   Theh paleoclimate of the Central Sahara, Libya and the Libyan desert. *Paleoecology of Africa* 12:352–363.
Pachur, H.-J. and P. Hoelzmann
   1991   Paleoclimatic implications of Late Quaternary lacustrine sediments in western Nubia, Sudan. *Quaternary Research* 36:257–276.
Rozanski, K. and M. Dulinski
   1988   Deuterium and oxygen-18 content of fluid inclusions trapped in carbonate cave deposits. *Freiberger Forschungshefte*, Series C, 420:92–105.
Rognon, P.
   1976   Essai d'interprétation des variations climatiques au Sahara depuis 40.000 ans. *Revue de Géographie Physique et de Géologie Dynamique*, 2nd ser., 18:251–282.
Schwarcz, H. P., R. S. Harmon, P. Thompson and D. C. Ford
   1976   Stable isotope studies of fluid inclusions in speleothems and their palaeoclimatic significance. *Geochimica et Cosmochimica Acta* 40:657–665.
Singh, G., R. L. Joshi and A. P. Singh
   1972   Stratigraphic and radiocarbon evidence for the age and the development of three salt lake deposits in Rajasthan, India. *Quaternary Research* 2:496–505.
Stiller, M., A. Ehrlich, U. Pollingher, U. Baruch and A. Kaufman
   1984   The Late Holocene sediments of Lake Kinneret (Israel): Multidisciplinary study of a 5 m core. *Geological Survey of Israel Current Research* 1983/84:83–88.

Street-Perrott, F. A. and A. T. Grove
    1976   Environmental and climatic implication of late Quaternary lake level fluctuation in Africa. *Nature* 261: 385–390.
Street-Perrott, F. A. and N. Roberts
    1983   Fluctuations in closed-basin lakes as an indicator of past atmospheric circulation patterns. In *Variations in the Global Water Budget*, edited by A. Street-Perrott, M. Beran and R. Ratcliffe, pp. 331–345. Reidel, Dordrecht.
Stuiver, M. and R. S. Kra (editors)
    1986   Calibration Issue. *Radiocarbon* 28(2B):805–1030.
Stuiver, M. and P. J. Reimer
    1993   Extended ^{14}C data base and revised Calib 3.0 ^{14}C age calibration program. *Radiocarbon* 35(1):215–230.
Stute, M., P. Schlosser, J. F. Clark and W. S. Broecker
    1992   Paleotemperatures in the southwestern United States derived from noble gases in groundwater. *Science* 256: 1000–1003.
Talma, A. S. and J. C. Vogel
    1992   Late Quaternary paleotemperature derived from a speleothem from Cango Caves, Cape Province, South Africa. *Quaternary Research* 37:203–213.
Wasson, R. J., G. I. Smith and D. P. Agrawal
    1984   Late Quaternary sediments, minerals, and inferred geochemical history of Didwana lake, Thar desert, India. *Palaeogeography, Palaeoclimatology, Palaeoecology* 46:345–372.
Weinstein, M.
    1976   The Late Quaternary vegetation of the northern Golan. *Pollen and Spores* 18:553–562.
Wigley, T. M. L.
    1988   The climate of the past 10,000 years and the role of the sun. In *Secular Solar and Geomagnetic Variations in the Last 10,000 Years*, edited by F. R. Stephenson and A. W. Wolfendale, pp. 209–224. Kluwer, Dordrecht.
Yechieli, Y., M. Magaritz, Y. Levy, U. Weber, U. Kafri, W. Woelfli, and G. Bonani
    1993   Late Quaternary geological history of the Dead Sea area, Israel. *Quaternary Research* 39:59–67.

A CHRONOLOGY FOR THE MIDDLE AND LATE PLEISTOCENE WET EPISODES IN THE EASTERN SAHARA

FRED WENDORF[1], ROMUALD SCHILD[2], ANGELA E. CLOSE[1], HENRY P. SCHWARCZ[3] GIFFORD H. MILLER[4], RAINER GRÜN[5], ANDRZEJ BLUSZCZ[6], STEPHEN STOKES[7] LIDIA MORAWSKA[8], JOAN HUXTABLE[7], JOYCE LUNDBERG[9] CHRISTOPHER L. HILL[1] and CURTIS McKINNEY[10]

INTRODUCTION

The Eastern Sahara, particularly the southwestern part of Egypt, is today one of the driest places on Earth. The mean annual rainfall is <1 mm per annum and, except in the few places where water can be found close to the surface, there are almost no signs of life nor vegetation. Nevertheless, it has long been known that even this driest part of the Sahara was once much wetter, that, at times, it had large permanent lakes, and that artifacts have been found in the sediments of these lakes. Acheulean handaxes are associated with some of the fossil lakes, indicating that they probably existed in the Middle Pleistocene, during the period of the Lower Paleolithic. Other lakes have yielded Middle Paleolithic artifacts, some of which are similar to the Late Pleistocene Mousterian of southwestern Asia and Europe (Tixier 1967), whereas others have been assigned to a Middle Paleolithic entity named the Aterian, which is known only from North Africa (Caton-Thompson 1946). There seem to be no Upper or Late Paleolithic sites in the Sahara, suggesting that the most recent Late Pleistocene lacustrine event occurred during the Middle Paleolithic.

Until recently, attempts to establish an absolute chronology for the lacustrine events in the Sahara were unsuccessful. Numerous radiocarbon dates were obtained on carbonates from these lakes. Absolute ages tended to cluster between 20,000 and 40,000 BP, which many believed represented the period of the Saharan Middle Paleolithic lakes (Chavaillon 1973; Conrad 1972; Ferring 1975; Pachur *et al.* 1990; Rognon and Williams 1977; Tillet 1983), even though there were more advanced, Upper Paleolithic complexes in the Nile Valley (Vermeersch *et al.* 1984) and Cyrenaica (McBurney 1967), with radiocarbon dates on charcoal yielding ages of at least 35,000 yr. It is not likely that the Middle Paleolithic would have survived in the Sahara for several thousand years after the Upper Paleolithic had appeared nearby (see Wendorf and Schild [1980:228–234]).

Uncertainties in the ages of Middle Paleolithic lakes are now being resolved through the use of new dating techniques. Together with careful stratigraphic studies, these techniques reveal that the Middle Paleolithic sequence consists of several lacustrine episodes in the Eastern Sahara, that the most recent of these was probably >60,000 yr ago and possibly >70,000 yr ago, and that the

[1]Department of Anthropology, Southern Methodist University, Dallas, Texas 75275 USA
[2]Institute of Archaeology and Ethnology, Polish Academy of Sciences, Solidarnosci 105, PL-00-140 Warsaw, Poland
[3]Department of Geology, McMaster University, Hamilton, Ontario, L8S 4M1 Canada
[4]Center for Geochronological Research, INSTAAR and Department of Geological Sciences, University of Colorado, Boulder, Colorado 80309-0450 USA
[5]Research School of Earth Sciences, The Australian National University, GPO Box 4, Canberra 2601 Australia
[6]Radiocarbon Laboratory, Silesian Technical University, PL-44-100 Gliwice, Poland
[7]Research Laboratory for Archaeology and the History of Art, Oxford University, 6 Keble Road, Oxford, OX1 3QJ, UK
[8]Department of Chemical Engineering, University of Toronto, Toronto, Ontario, M5S 1A1 Canada
[9]Department of Geography, Carleton University, Ottawa, Ontario, K1S 5B6 Canada
[10]Center for American Archeology, Box 366, Kampsville, Illinois 62053 USA

Late Quaternary Chronology and Paleoclimates of the Eastern Mediterranean
Edited by O. Bar-Yosef and R. S. Kra. RADIOCARBON 1994, pp. 147–168

earliest Middle Paleolithic lacustrine event could be >200,000 yr old. These new data come from two adjacent depressions in the Egyptian Sahara known as Bir Tarfawi and Bir Sahara East.

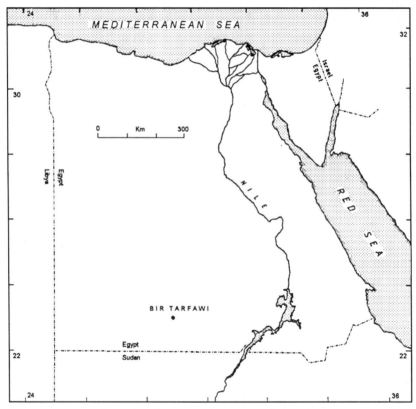

Fig. 1. Map of Egypt showing location of Bir Tarfawi

The depression of Bir Tarfawi is 400 km west of Aswan in southwestern Egypt (Fig. 1); Bir Sahara East lies *ca.* 10 km to the west. Both depressions are deflated into a deep bed of sandstone and conglomerate laid down during the Paleozoic and Tertiary. Inset within each depression are several smaller sub-basins, the oldest and highest of which contain lake sediments associated with Late Acheulean artifacts. Each depression also contains clear evidence for five separate Middle Paleolithic lacustrine events, and in Bir Tarfawi, there is an additional Middle Paleolithic playa-basin, which, we believe, precedes the earliest permanent Middle Paleolithic lake. In 1973–1974, some excavations were carried out in both depressions at the localities with Acheulean and Middle Paleolithic artifacts (Wendorf and Schild 1980); more extensive excavations were carried out in 1986–1988 (Wendorf *et al.* 1987; 1990).

The Bir Tarfawi depression is a long, narrow, north-south trough with three separate sub-basins. The most extensive work has been in the northernmost sub-basin (Section BT-A), where we have stratigraphic evidence of the sequence of lacustrine events. The sequence at Bir Sahara East was equally complex, but more of the sediments have been eroded, and they are now within a single sub-basin.

Several techniques have been used to determine the ages of the major geological events at Bir Tarfawi and Bir Sahara East: uranium (U) series (McKinney 1993; Schwarcz and Morawska 1993), electron spin resonance (ESR) (Robins 1993; Schwarcz and Grün 1993), two varieties of thermoluminescence (TL) (fine quartz and burned sediment) (Bluszcz 1993; Huxtable 1993), optical, or optically stimulated luminescence (OSL) (Stokes 1993), and amino acid racemization of ostrich eggshell (Miller 1993). A few radiocarbon measurements were also obtained (Haas and Haynes 1980). A total of 160 age determinations were made.

Wherever possible, we have attempted to apply several techniques to the same beds, to determine whether the techniques are applicable only to particular sedimentary conditions, whether they yield similar age estimates, and whether they provide internally consistent and precise dates. We expected grossly similar results to emerge, and, to some extent, that expectation has been fulfilled. However, there are discrepancies among age estimates obtained by different methods, and none of them appears to yield completely reliable or consistent results, although some are better than others.

THE STRATIGRAPHIC SEQUENCE AT BIR TARFAWI

Late and Final Acheulean

The Acheulean localities have received only limited study. Highly cemented marls that accumulated in deep-water sediments provide evidence for the existence of permanent, Late Acheulean lakes at each end of the Tarfawi depression (Sections BT-A and BT-C). The bases of the lakes are at about the same elevation (*ca.* 247 m msl), but the lake in Section BT-A was much larger and the accumulated sediments thicker. The lake at the southern end of the depression (Section BT-C) seems to have been a series of interdunal ponds; occasional handaxes were found embedded in the marls that accumulated in the centers of the ponds, suggesting that the ponds were occasionally dry or almost dry. One of the dated samples (Table 1) comes from a spring vent adjacent to the margin of the northern Late Acheulean lake. The top of the spring vent is at the same elevation as the base of the lake, and blocks of silica-cemented sand appear around the rim and on its deflated slope. Final Acheulean handaxes can also be seen on the slope and in the eye of the vent.

TABLE 1. Age Estimates for the Late Acheulean Lakes

Sample no.	Material	Location	Age (kyr)
Thermoluminescence (Quartz)			
GdTL-168	Sand	Below limestone, Sec. BT-C	165 ± 22
Uranium Series			
87BTF-17	Limestone	Late Acheul. basin, Sec. BT-A	448 ± 47
87BTF-19	Cemented sand	Final Acheul. spring, Sec. BT-A	542 ± 389
87BTF-51.01	Limestone	Acheul. basin, Sec. BT-C	>350 (*ca.* 600)

The Sand Pan and Tarfawi White Lake

During the major period of aridity after the Late Acheulean lacustrine interval, shore- and shallow-water deposits disappeared from the Acheulean basin, leaving only deep-water marls as an isolated remnant. To the west of this remnant, aeolian deflation cut another depression, the floor of which is at 244.4 m, or 2.6 m below the deepest part of the Acheulean lake. Later, when moist conditions returned, this hollow was filled by the first lake in the northern sub-basin (BT-A) to be associated with Middle Paleolithic artifacts (the Tarfawi White Lake; Table 2). The artifacts were found *in situ* below the deep-water sediments of the lake (Site E-88-14), suggesting that they probably represent occupations of an early phase of the wet interval. There is no eolian sand in the marls of this lake (or in the subsequent Grey Phases of the East Lake), indicating that the surrounding landscape was covered by vegetation and, hence, that there was considerable local rainfall. However, the very high concentrations of uranium and calcium in their sediments show that the lakes were spring-fed (the local sediment is all quartz sand).

TABLE 2. Age Estimates for the Tarfawi White Lake

Sample no.	Material	Location	Age (kyr)
Uranium series			
87BTF-33	Marl	Tr. 14/86, Bed 9	152 ± 39
40M1	Marl	Tr. 14/86, Bed 9	160 $^{+5}_{-2.5}$
87BTF-32	Marl/mollusks	Tr. 10/86, Bed 6	242 ± 22
87BTF-21	Marl	Tr. 14/86, Bed 3	265 ± 89
Electron Spin Resonance			
	Mollusks	Tr. 10/86, Bed 6	28.2

Along and slightly above the western edge of the central sub-basin at Tarfawi (Section BT-B) is a small depression containing sediments of an ephemeral lake (the Sand Pan); three associated Middle Paleolithic sites have been excavated (E-86-1, E-87-1, E-87-4) (Table 3). The Sand Pan may be older than the Tarfawi White Lake, but there is no direct stratigraphic relation between them. The eastern edge of the Sand Pan is cut by the large hollow in the central sub-basin, which contains sediments of lakes believed to be the equivalents of the Grey and Green phases of the East Lake in the northern sub-basin. Also at the same elevation as the Tarfawi White Lake is a nearby remnant of marl, which is probably of the same age. Again, however, we could not establish the precise stratigraphic association between the Sand Pan and the remnant.

TABLE 3. Age Estimates for Sand Pan, Section BT-B

Sample no.	Material	Location	Age (kyr)
Thermoluminescence (Quartz)			
GdTL-177	Sand	E-86-1, Cultural layer	≤280
GdTL-177a	Sand	E-86-1, Cultural layer	110 ± 25
Amino Acid Racemization			
AAL-4809 AAL-4983	Eggshell	E-86-1, Cultural layer	
AAL-5206 AAL-5207	Eggshell	E-87-1, Cultural layer	175 $^{+70}_{-35}$
AAL-5221	Eggshell	E-87-4, Cultural layer	
AAL-4810 AAL-5205	Eggshell	E-86-1, Cultural layer E-87-1, Cultural layer	200–225 $^{+90}_{-45}$

The floor of the Sand Pan is at 246 m, or 1.6 m higher than the floor of the Tarfawi White Lake. The deposits in the two basins clearly represent different sedimentological conditions. The Sand Pan held local runoff water only seasonally, whereas the Tarfawi White Lake was a large, deep, permanent and partially spring-fed lake. It is possible that the Sand Pan was formed during a minor moist episode during the dry period that followed the Tarfawi White Lake. However, in light of their relative elevations, it seems more likely that the Sand Pan occurred before the Tarfawi White Lake, and marks a brief humid phase during the arid period after the Acheulean lake.

The East Lake

A prolonged interval of hyperaridity separates the Tarfawi White Lake from the next lacustrine episode. During this period, the water table fell to a level only slightly higher than that of today, the landscape surrounding the former White Lake was eroded, and the wind excavated a large hollow down to an elevation of 242 m, or 2.4 m below the bottom of the White Lake, leaving two large remnants of firmly cemented, deep-water carbonates to the north and west of the hollow.

In the succeeding wet interval, a lake developed in the hollow adjacent to the remnants of the Tarfawi White Lake. Four lacustrine events in the East Lake sequence were separated from each other by periods of aridity. All four phases occupied the same depression, so that each wet episode is regarded as only a phase in the complicated history of that lake. In the northern sub-basin at Bir Tarfawi, the first three wet phases of the East Lake are named Grey Phases 1, 2 and 3 (Tables 4–6); a significant change in the color of the sediments caused the fourth wet episode to be named the Green Phase (Table 7). The sediments of this last phase contain more sand and silt than those of the three Grey phases, and there are only occasional thin patches of carbonates, suggesting that the lake during the Green Phase was not as deep as the earlier lakes, and was more playa-like.

The beginning of Grey Phase 1 is signaled by a rise in the water table, which produced a shallow marsh, and then a small lake (*ca.* 60 m in diameter) in the bottom of the hollow. Slope-wash sediments, marking the appearance of local rainfall, immediately overlie the marsh deposits, followed by the sands and silts of a somewhat larger, but seasonally fluctuating lake. The four lakes of the East Lake sequence varied in size, but all were highly unstable, with strong seasonal variation. There were periods when the deepest parts of the lakes were dry, and cracks developed in their beds; some of these dry periods may have been seasonal; they were certainly minor when compared to the major arid periods that separated the four lacustrine phases. The major arid periods were of sufficient duration and intensity for the lakes to dry, for their bases to be eroded and deepened, for most of their beaches to disappear, and for the outlines of the basin to reshape. For example, in the dry interval between Grey Phase 1 and 2, the wind excavated a hole to approximately the same level as the bottom of the Grey Phase 1 lake (242 m). The erosion between Grey Phase 2 and 3 was less severe; it cut only to 243 m, but it removed almost all of the non-calcareous, shallow-water sediments of the Grey Phase 2 lake. The base of the Green Phase was at 244 m, and the highest preserved silts of that event are at 245 m.

In the central sub-basin at Tarfawi (BT-B), the base of the lacustrine sediments was not exposed, but we observed deposits of two superimposed lacustrine episodes (Tables 8 and 9). The upper unit (Table 9) has the same color and elevation as the deposits of the Green Phase in the northern sub-basin, and the two lakes are regarded as contemporary and possibly interconnected at their maximal stand. A period of lower water table and deflation separates these green silts from the underlying unit of lacustrine sediments. It is most economical to correlate this lower lacustrine unit in the central sub-basin with Grey Phase 3 in the northern sub-basin (Table 8).

After the Green Phase, there is no evidence of lacustrine sedimentation in any of the Tarfawi sub-basins, although occasional patches of salt crust can be seen in small depressions deflated into the top of the green silt. These salt crusts are attributed to ephemeral pools that probably formed during the early Holocene. Neolithic artifacts are often found near them.

TABLE 4. Age Estimates for Grey Phase 1 at Section BT-A

Sample no.	Material	Location	Age (kyr)
Uranium Series			
170E1	Tooth enamel	BT-14, Bed 1i	Infinite
169D1	Dentine	BT-14, Bed 1d	85 ± 2
169E1	Tooth enamel	BT-14, Bed 1d	Infinite
166E1	Tooth enamel	BT-14, Bed 1a	260^{+40}_{-20}
166D1	Tooth enamel	BT-14, Bed 1a	Infinite
200s1	Eggshell	BT-14, Bed 1a	140^{+20}_{-10}
87BTF-2	Carbonate	BT-14, Bed 1d	70 ± 36
87BTF-3	Carbonate	BT-14, Bed 1d	93 ± 40
87BTF-1	Carbonate	BT-14, Bed 1d	96 ± 18
87BTF-44	Eggshell	BT-14, Bed 1d	136 ± 3
87BTF-42	Eggshell	BT-14, Bed 1d	137 ± 3
87BTF-43	Eggshell	BT-14, Bed 1d	122 ± 3
87BTF-40	Eggshell	BT-14, Bed 1a	179 ± 19
87BTF-41	Eggshell	BT-14, Bed 1a	126 ± 8
*Electron Spin Resonance**			
87-8	Tooth enamel	BT-14, Bed 1i	121 ± 6
BT-7	Tooth enamel	BT-14, Bed 1i	171 ± 6
87-3	Tooth enamel	BT-14, Bed 1d	138 ± 5 / 144 ± 9
87-4	Tooth enamel	BT-14, Bed 1d	147 ± 6 / 149 ± 7
87-2	Tooth enamel	BT-14, Bed 1d	114 ± 7 / 110 ± 7
87-5	Tooth enamel	BT-14, Bed 1a	139 ± 6 / 154 ± 7
87-1	Tooth enamel	BT-14, Bed 1a	140 ± 7 / 162 ± 7
87-6	Tooth enamel	BT-14, Bed 1	130 ± 6 / 115 ± 6 / 146 ± 9
BT-4	Tooth enamel	BT-14, Bed 1	121 ± 10 / 121 ± 6
BT-10	Tooth enamel	BT-14, Bed 1	151 ± 11
--	Tooth enamel	BT-14, Bed 1d	175.4
Optical			
OX$_{OD}$748(T)-1	Sand	BT-14, Bed 1d	129 ± 7.7
Thermoluminescence (Burned Quartzitic Sandstone)			
OXTL506x	Burned rock	BT-14, Bed 1d	96 ± 14
Amino Acid Racemization			
AAL-4804			
AAL-4807			
AAL-4808			
AAL-4981			
AAL-4982	Eggshell	BT-14, Bed 1d	130
AAL-5215			
AAL-5216			
AAL-5217			
AAL-5223			
Radiocarbon			
SMU-214	Organic residue	BT-14, Bed 1h	21.95 ± 0.49

*All the ESR dates in these tables are based on the linear uptake model.

TABLE 5. Age Estimates for Grey Phase 2 at Section BT-A

Sample no.	Material	Location	Age (kyr)
Uranium Series			
87BTF-12B	Marl	Tr. 6/74, Bed 2j	113 ± 23
88BTN-T6/74-2	Marl	Tr. 6/74, Bed 2m	139 ± 32
88BTN-T6/74-1	Marl	Tr. 6/74, Bed 2m	102 ± 30
87BTF-11B	Marl	Tr. 7/74, Bed 2l	131 ± 27
88BTN-T7/74-2	Marl	Tr. 7/74, Bed 2m	188 ± 27
88BTN-T7/74-1	Marl	Tr. 7/74, Bed 2m	339 ± 72
87BTF-8	Carbonate	BT-14, Bed 2c	156 ± 43
171E1	Tooth enamel	BT-14, Bed 2c	Infinite
87BTF-22B	Marl	Pool, Tr. 3/86, Bed 5	101 ± 12
87BTF-22A	Carbonate	Pool, Tr. 3/86, Bed 4	82 ± 10
Electron Spin Resonance			
--	Tooth enamel	BT-14, Bed 2c	211.2
--	Snail shells	Pool, Tr. 3/86, Bed 5a	43.2
87-9	Tooth enamel	BT-14, Bed 2	167 ± 9 / 262 ± 13
87-7	Tooth enamel	BT-14, Bed 2	178 ± 9 / 199 ± 10
Optical			
$OX_{OD}748(T)$-3	Sand	BT-14, Bed 2c	119.3 ± 22.9
Amino Acid Racemization			
AAL-4806 / AAL-5218	Eggshell	BT-14, Bed 2c	125
Radiocarbon			
SMU-205	Carbonaceous rock	Pool, Bed 4	26.53 ± 0.47
SMU-2146	Soil	Pool, bed 2, base	47.14 ± 4.36 / 50.32 ± 7.13
SMU-177	*Melanoides*	BT-14, Tr. 6/74, Bed 2m	44.19 ± 1.38

Middle Paleolithic archaeological materials have been found with sediments of all the wet episodes in the northern and central sub-basins at Bir Tarfawi. The associated faunal remains, which are particularly abundant in the Grey and Green Phase sediments in the northern sub-basin, include white rhinoceros (*Ceratotherium simum*), giraffe (*Giraffa camelopardalis*), buffalo (*Pelorovis antiquus*), wild camel (*Camelus thomasi*), wild ass (*Equus africanus*), large antelopes (including greater kudu [*Tragelaphus strepsiceros*] and others), reduncine antelopes (probably kob [*Kobus kob*] and waterbuck [*K. ellipsiprymnus*]), large gazelle (*Gazella dama*), small gazelle (*G. dorcas*?) and perhaps red-fronted gazelle (*G. rufifrons*), warthog (*Phacochoerus aethiopicus*), spotted hyena (*Crocuta crocuta*) and probably striped hyena (*Hyaena hyaena*), jackal (*Canis aureus* or *C. adustus*), small cat (probably the common wild cat, *Felis silvestris*), porcupine (*Hystrix cristata*), hare (*Lepus capensis* or *L. whytei*), and both the bones and eggshells of ostrich (*Struthio camelus*) (Gautier 1993).

TABLE 6. Age Estimates for Grey Phase 3 at Section BT-A

Sample no.	Material	Location	Age (kyr)
Uranium Series			
87BTF-12A	Marl	Tr. 6/74, Bed 3h	132 ± 18
88BTN-T6/74-4	Marl	Tr. 6/74, Bed 3h	156 ± 20
88BTN-T6/74-3	Marl	Tr. 6/74, Bed 3g	146 ± 24
88BTN-T7/74-4	Marl	Tr. 7/74, Bed 3g	146 ± 31
88BTN-T7/74-3	Marl	Tr. 7/74, Bed 3g	153 ± 27
88BTN-T7/74-5	Marl	Tr. 7/74, Bed 3i	127 ± 30
87BTF-11A	Marl	Tr. 7/74, Bed 3i	112 ± 26
167D1	Dentine	BT-14, Bed 3a	Infinite
87BTF-9	Marl	BT-14, Bed 3a(?)	289 ± 28
Electron Spin Resonance			
BT-6	Tooth enamel	BT-14, Bed 3	234 ± 23
Optical			
$OX_{OD}748(T)-6$	Sand	BT-14, Bed $3e_3$	$96.4^{+7.2}_{-10.9}$
Amino Acid Epimerization			
AAL-4805⎫ AAL-5219⎭	Eggshell	BT-14, Bed 3	125

TABLE 7. Age Estimates for the Green Phase at Section BT-A

Sample no.	Material	Location	Age (kyr)
Uranium Series			
87BTF-10	Carbonate	BT-14, Bed 4a	115 ± 22
Electron Spin Resonance			
--	Eggshell	BT-14, Bed 4d	12
--	Eggshell	BT-14, Bed 4d	12.8
--	Tooth enamel	BT-14, Bed 4d	145.2
BT-3	Tooth enamel	BT-14, Bed 4	106 ± 7
Thermoluminescence (Quartz)			
GdTL-171	Sand	BT-14, Bed 4a	70 ± 10
Optical			
$OX_{OD}748(T)-7$	Sand	BT-14, Bed 4a	$71.4^{+8.2}_{-7.1}$
Amino Acid Racemization			
AAL-4515⎫ AAL-4802⎪ AAL-4803⎬ AAL-4980⎭	Eggshell	BT-14, Bed 4d	100^{+10}_{-20}

TABLE 8. Age Estimates for Grey Phase 3, East Lake, at Section BT-B

Sample no.	Material	Location	Age (kyr)
Uranium Series			
87BTF-39	Limestone	E-87-3, Bed 1	118 ± 39
87BTF-36	Limestone	Tr. 13/86, Bed 11	289 ± 87
87BTF-37	Marl	Tr. 17/87, Bed 11, top	440 ± 751
87BTF-39A	Limestone	Tr. 1, Bed 1	172 ± 43

TABLE 9. Age Estimates for the Green Phase, East Lake, at Section BT-B

Sample no.	Material	Location	Age (kyr)
Uranium Series			
87BTF-38	Limestone	E-87-2, Tr. 17, Bed 13	490 ± 209
87BTF-26	Carbonate	E-87-2, Bed 6	220 ± 28
87BTF-14:01	Carbonate	E-87-2, Bed 6d	302 ± 265
87BTF-14:02	Carbonate	E-87-2, Bed 6d	195 ± 123
87BT-28	Carbonate	E-86-2, Bed 8(?)	154 ± 169
Electron Spin Resonance			
--	Tooth enamel	E-87-2	208
--	Tooth enamel	E-87-2	190
Thermoluminescence (Quartz)			
GdTL-178	Sand	E-86-2, Bed 7f	≤285
GdTL-178a	Sand	E-86-2, Bed 7	60 ± 15
Amino Acid Racemization			
AAL-5220 ⎱ AAL-5306 ⎰	Eggshell	E-87-3, Bed 2b	125
AAL-5222	Eggshell	E-86-2, Bed 6	125

A marginal peaty pool associated with an early part of Grey Phase 2 in the northern sub-basin yielded several thousand bones, which include 51 identified taxa of amphibians, reptiles, birds and small mammals, and 8 identified taxa of freshwater fish (Kowalski *et al.* 1989; Van Neer 1989); all of these are extant species (there are extinct forms among the large mammals). The remains of crocodiles, water turtles and fish provide evidence for a large lake, which, at times, must have been connected to the river net of sub-Saharan Africa. Among the fish are Nile perch (*Lates niloticus* and *Bagrus*), both of which require deep, well-oxygenated water. The fish taxa are typical of the present-day Nile, Chad and Niger basins, and suggest a water connection with one of those systems, possibly the Nile, by way of the Wadi Howar in northwestern Sudan, and one of the buried channels discovered by ground-penetrating radar (McCauley *et al.* 1982).

Remains of the small mammals and birds suggest that the lake was large, shallow and entropic, with reed beds over much of its surface. The surrounding landscape was probably a savanna with clumps of trees close to the water. Some rodent species live today no closer than 1200 km to the south, which corresponds approximately to the 500 mm isohyet, which means that the rainfall during this period was at least 500 mm per year. The birds are more varied in their distributions, but several species, all of which breed in Africa, exist today only in central and southern Africa. Both small mammals and birds strongly suggest that the increased rainfall of this lake episode occurred as a result of a northward shift of the tropical monsoon.

THE STRATIGRAPHIC SEQUENCE AT BIR SAHARA EAST

Final Acheulean Springs

At Bir Sahara East, Final Acheulean handaxes were dropped by deflation onto the surface around several fossil spring vents near the southern margin of the depression, but none of the sites at which they were found have been dated. Site BS-14 is surrounded by sediments of a carbonate-rich groundwater-fed pool, the base of which is at about the same elevation as the bases of the Late Acheulean lakes at Bir Tarfawi (247 m).

The Sahara White Lake and the Sand Sheet

A major period of aridity followed the Final Acheulean, when a large eolian depression formed at the southern end of the present Bir Sahara East depression and north of the Final Acheulean spring vents. The base of this hollow was at *ca.* 243 m asl, or *ca.* 4 m below the bottom of the spring pool at BS-14. The bottom of the hollow is now occupied by a small remnant of carbonate-cemented sands and marls, evidence of a fairly large, and probably deep, freshwater Sahara White Lake. Middle Paleolithic artifacts occur on the deflated surface around this remnant, but it was not studied in detail, and the provenience of the artifacts was not established. There are no dates for this event.

The stratigraphic relation between the Sahara White Lake and other events in the Bir Sahara East depression has not been established, but it is likely that the Sahara White Lake was followed by an arid period, when the present morphology of the depression was created. North of the Sahara White Lake remnant, the wind excavated a large, deep hollow to a depth of 236.5 m asl, *ca.* 6.5 m below the base of the lowest remaining portion of the Sahara White Lake. During this arid interval, a sand sheet entered the hollow from the north. No cultural remains can be regarded as contemporary with the Sand Sheet, but Middle Paleolithic artifacts were found in the top few centimeters of it at one site (E-88-1). The artifacts are not abraded, and therefore, are probably later than the Sand Sheet, itself. We believe that they were worked into the Sand Sheet by pedogenic processes (Table 10).

TABLE 10. Age Estimates for Site E-88-1 (in the top of the sand sheet)

Sample no.	Material	Location	Age (kyr)
Amino Acid Racemization			
AAL-5413	Eggshell	E-88-1	$175 \, ^{+70}_{-35}$
AAL-5414	Eggshell	E-88-1	>250

The West Lake

After the encroachment of the Sand Sheet, there still remained a large hollow in the central portion of the basin, the bottom of which was below 240 m asl. This was partially filled by the sediments of four lacustrine intervals separated by arid episodes. This series has been named Phases 1–4 of the West Lake.

Phase 1, the earliest lake in the sequence, covered an area of several hundred square meters, and had sufficient depth and permanence for carbonate precipitation to develop. The deepest sediments of Phase 1 were not exposed, but they are below 240 m asl, and their eroded surface is at 242 m asl. There are no dates for this interval. The base of West Lake 2 was also not exposed, but again it was below 240 m. At its maximum, West Lake Phase 2 left sediments as high as 247 m; it was the deepest and largest lake in this sequence (Table 11). The base of Phase 3 of the West Lake is at 242 m (Table 12); the base of Phase 4 is at 244 m (Table 13).

TABLE 11. Age estimates for Phase 2, West Lake, at Bir Sahara East

Sample no.	Material	Location	Age (kyr)
Uranium Series			
87BSH-10:1	Marl	E-88-11, Bed 8a	148 ± 60
87BSH-10:2	Marl	E-88-11, Bed 8a	257 ± 171
87BSH-13	Carbonate	E-88-11, Bed 6	203 ± 71
87BSH-12	Carbonate	BS-11, Bed 5	339 ± 156
87BSH-11	Carbonate	BS-11, Bed 5	381 ± 96
87BSH- 7	Limestone	E-88-11, Bed 9	307 ± 110
Thermoluminescence (Quartz)			
GdTL-202	Sand	Tr. 3, Bed 6, Sec.BS-A	>125
GdTL-164	Sand	BS-12, Tr. 5/73, Bed 4	84 ± 10
GdTL-166	Sand	BS-1, Tr. 7/73, Bed 16	105 ± 15
Thermoluminescence (Burned Sediment)			
OXTL506a	Burned silt	BS-1, Bed 7	105.4 ± 10.5
OXTL506b	Burned silt	BS-1, Bed 9	108.6 ± 10.6
Optical			
$OX_{OD}748(S)-2$	Sand	E-88-11, Bed 5 (base)	$103.9\ ^{+9.5}_{-13.2}$
Radiocarbon			
SMU-81	Large shells	BS-16, Bed 4	>41.45
SMU-82	Small shells	BS-16, Bed 4	40.71 ± 3.27
SMU-218	Peat	BS-16, Bed 3	33.08 ± 1.12
SMU-95	Peat humates	BS-16, Bed 3 (top)	37.74 ± 1.98
SMU-108	Peat humates (?)	BS-16, Bed 3 (top)	28 ± 1.25
SMU-215	Carbonate	BS-16, Bed 3	34.6 ± 0.97
SMU-80	*Melanoides*	BS-13 (=Bed 7, E-88-2)	32.78 ± 0.9

There is evidence of carbonate precipitation at all phases of the West Lake, except Phase 4, suggesting that the first three lakes were permanent and relatively deep. The sediments of Phase 4, like those of the Green Phase at Bir Tarfawi, are mostly silts with occasional carbonate lenses, which may record the presence of an ephemeral lake during that period.

Concentrations of Middle Paleolithic artifacts have been found in the deposits of each phase of the West Lake sequence, except Phase 4. Site E-88-2 is probably contemporary with Phase 4, but its precise stratigraphic position could not be determined. The artifacts were buried in a foredune

TABLE 12. Age Estimates for Phase 3, West Lake, at Bir Sahara East

Sample no.	Material	Location	Age (kyr)
Thermoluminescence (Quartz)			
GdTL-200	Sand	Tr. 14/88, Bed 10	291 ± 65
Optical			
OX$_{OD}$748(S)-3a	Sand	Tr. 14/88, Bed 10	71.1 $^{+2.8}_{-6.0}$*

*This sample may actually refer to Phase 4 of the West Lake

TABLE 13. Age Estimates for Phase 4, West Lake, at Bir Sahara East

Sample no.	Material	Location	Age (kyr)
Thermoluminescence (Quartz)			
GdTL-167	Sand	BS-15, Bed 18	65 ± 9
GdTL-201	Sand	Tr. 14/88, Bed 17	84 ± 91*
Optical			
OX$_{OD}$748(S)-1	Sand	E-88-2, Bed 8	42.8 $^{+2.7}_{-4.32}$**
OX$_{OD}$748(S)-4	Sand	Tr. 15/88, Bed 22, base	55.9 $^{+17.3}_{-14.1}$**
OX$_{OD}$748(S)-3	Sand	Tr. 14/88, Bed 17	114 $^{+9.8}_{-11.2}$†
Amino Acid Racemization			
AAL-5415⎫ AAL-5416⎬ AAL-5418⎭	Eggshell	E-88-2, Bed 8	125
AAL-5417	Eggshell	E-88-2, Bed 8	100
Radiocarbon			
SMU-75	*Corbicula*	BS-15, Bed 9	30.87 ± 1
SMU-79	*Melanoides*	BS-15, Bed 9	>44.7

*This sample refers to an arid episode between Phases 3 and 4 of the West Lake.
**These two samples refer to an arid episode after West Lake Phase 4.
†This sample may actually refer to West Lake 3.

deposited along the shore of the Phase 4 lake, but the dune cannot be directly tied to the lacustrine sediments.

Faunal remains are not as abundant in Bir Sahara East as they were in the northern sub-basin at Bir Tarfawi. However, the range of megafauna is similar, and includes the extinct camel (*Camelus thomasi*), white rhinoceros (*Ceratotherium simum*), buffalo (*Pelorovis antiquus?*), warthog (*Phacochoerus aethiopicus?*) and wild ass (*Equus asinus*) (Gautier 1980:319; Gautier 1993).

Phase 4 of the West Lake is the last lacustrine event in the Bir Sahara East depression. Although there is no evidence of a Holocene lake or playa, there is a shallow channel cut into a remnant of the West Lake sediments in one area near the center of the depression. This channel is filled with silt and contains Neolithic artifacts.

DISCUSSION OF THE DATES

We developed a model for the chronology of the Lower and Middle Paleolithic wet phases in the Eastern Sahara, which, with the stratigraphic sequence of lacustrine sediments, provides the basis for evaluating age determinations obtained from Bir Tarfawi and Bir Sahara East. Our model is based on the following data.

First, in both the Nile Valley and Cyrenaica, the earliest Upper Paleolithic is firmly ^{14}C-dated between 40,000 and 30,000 BP (McBurney 1967; Paulissen and Vermeersch 1987). It is unlikely that Middle Paleolithic technology and typology would continue virtually unchanged in the Sahara if there were Upper Paleolithic populations in adjacent areas. Thus, the Middle Paleolithic in the Sahara must be older than 40,000 BP.

Second, the stratigraphy in the Nile Valley shows two major episodes of wadi aggradation in the Late Pleistocene and Holocene. The more recent is early Holocene, and the older one, containing reworked Middle Paleolithic artifacts, precedes two Late Pleistocene Nilotic alluviations, one of which is associated with late Middle Paleolithic, and the other, with Late Paleolithic (Schild and Wendorf 1989). There is no evidence for wadi activity, slopewash or other indication of local rainfall during the entire period of the two Late Pleistocene Nilotic alluviations, which suggests a long interval of hyperaridity that coincided with the later part of the Middle Paleolithic and all of the Late Paleolithic in the Nile Valley of Egypt. There could not have been sufficient rainfall during this period of hyperaridity to create the large permanent Middle Paleolithic lakes in the Eastern Sahara, some of which enjoyed *ca.* 500 mm of rainfall per annum, as indicated by the fauna (Kowalski *et al.* 1989). Thus, we conclude that the Middle Paleolithic lakes must have occurred during wet periods, antedating the Late Pleistocene Nilotic alluviations.

Numerous ^{14}C dates confirm that the Late Paleolithic Nilotic alluviation began before 20,000 BP and ended *ca.* 12,500 BP. Several TL and infinite ^{14}C dates for the Late Middle Paleolithic alluviation show that the period began *ca.* 60,000 BP and ended before 40,000 BP (Wendorf and Schild 1989). If the TL dates are correct, then the latest, pre-Holocene wet episode in Egypt occurred >60,000 yr ago.

Our model correlates the wadi deposits stratigraphically below those of the Late Pleistocene alluviations (containing older Middle Paleolithic artifacts) with the Middle Paleolithic wet phases in the Sahara. Thus, the Middle Paleolithic wadi deposits along the Nile and the Middle Paleolithic lacustrine events in the Eastern Sahara are older than 60,000 BP. Thus, we reject all the finite ^{14}C dates from our previous work at Bir Tarfawi and Bir Sahara East (Haas and Haynes 1980), a position that is supported by the infinite ^{14}C dates obtained from sediments overlying those with the finite dates (Wendorf and Schild 1980:228–234, 247–257).

This interpretation has not been widely accepted, because several researchers believe that there was a wet period in the Sahara between 40,000 and 20,000 yr ago (Conrad 1972; Petit-Maire 1991; Pachur *et al.* 1990; Rognon and Williams 1977; Servant and Servant-Vildary 1972). However, all the ^{14}C dates indicating such a late wet phase are on carbonates, which are notoriously susceptible to exchanges of both older and younger carbon.

The lower age limit in our model is based on the chronology of the Late and Final Acheulean in Africa. At Lake Ziway in Ethiopia, the latest Acheulean appears just below an early Middle Paleolithic stratum, for which there is a potassium/argon (K/Ar) date of 235,000 ± 5000 BP (Wendorf *et al.* 1975; Wendorf, Close and Schild, in press). Another Late Acheulean at Kapthurin, in the Baringo Basin of northern Kenya, has a K/Ar date of 230,000 BP (Leakey *et al.* 1969). These dates suggest that the beginning of the Middle Paleolithic, or Middle Stone Age, in Africa should not be older than *ca.* 230,000 yr. From a survey of the Middle Stone Age of East Africa, Clark (1988:291) has concluded that the Middle Stone Age began at least 200,000 yr ago.

We can also evaluate the dates on the basis of the stratigraphy in the basins. The sequence in the northern sub-basin (BT-A) at Bir Tarfawi provides the best stratigraphic control. Here, the older lake sediments, those of the Acheulean and Tarfawi White Lakes, occur as two sets of remnants perched above the basin that held the deposits of the East Lake; the four phases of the East Lake are superimposed in a single basin. Most of the stratigraphic sequence in the central sub-basin (BT-B) is also well established. The basin of the Sand Pan is cut by the hollow containing the lakes of the Green and Grey Phases. We believe that Green and Grey Phases in this sub-basin were contemporary with the last two phases of the East Lake in the northern sub-basin, and that the lakes in the two sub-basins were probably interconnected. We are not certain of the age of the Sand Pan, except that it is older than the Grey Phase in the central sub-basin. We think it is likely that the Sand Pan is older than the Tarfawi White Lake of the northern sub-basin.

The stratigraphic sequence is also straightforward at Bir Sahara East, although some of the details are not established by direct superposition. The only part of the sequence for which there is much doubt is the position of the Sahara White Lake. However, the elevation of its base and the firm cementation of the marl capping the remnant argue that it precedes all of the West Lake. Within the West Lake sequence, the four phases are superimposed in the same basin.

The water tables in Bir Tarfawi and Bir Sahara East are presently at the same level. The simplest correlation of the sequences in the two depressions assumes that the Acheulean and Middle Paleo-lithic lakes in the two depressions were simultaneous responses to changes in the local environ-ment. This hypothesis is supported by the similarities in the number of lacustrine events and by the pattern of those events. The second Middle Paleolithic lake in each depression (East Lake Grey Phase 1 and West Lake Phase 1) was much smaller than the later lakes. The third and fourth Middle Paleolithic lakes in each depression (East Lake Grey Phases 2 and 3, and West Lake Phases 2 and 3) were the most extensive and deepest lakes. The fifth Middle Paleolithic wet event in each depression produced a shallow, playa-like lake.

Unfortunately, there are some disturbing differences. The Acheulean lakes and spring pools are at the same elevations, and thus, fit the model that they were simultaneous responses to changes in the local environment. However, the lowest sediments of the Sahara White lake are *ca.* 1.4 m lower than the base of the Tarfawi White Lake, and, even more disconcerting, the lower deposits of the West Lake Phases 1 and 2 are more than 2 m below the lowest parts of East Lake Grey Phase 1 and 2 in Bir Tarfawi. Phase 1 of the West Lake was several times larger than its supposed equivalent at Bir Tarfawi. Finally, the sediments of Grey Phase 2 of the East Lake and Phase 2 of the West Lake have very different $^{234}U/^{238}U$ ratios (Schwarcz and Morawska 1993), which indicates that they were not created by the same water source, although it might not necessarily mean that they were not contemporary.

We had anticipated that the absolute age determinations would resolve the question of correlation between the two depressions, but the available measurements are not sufficiently consistent to do this. In fact, many of the dates are so widely dispersed that some support can be found for almost any correlation (Figs. 2 and 3). The U-series results on sediments seem to be the least consistent, and some effort has been made to develop an explanation for these results. For example, marls of the Grey and Green Phases in the northern sub-basin at Bir Tarfawi (Section BT-A) yield many U-series dates that are out of stratigraphic order (Fig. 2). Schwarcz and Morawska (1993) propose to resolve this problem by using the isochron approach (Schwarcz and Latham 1989). The method is based on the assumption that these sediments are composed of two components: 1) chemically precipitated calcite, whose $^{230}Th/^{234}U$ age is equal to the age of deposition; 2) detritus from which some uranium and thorium are leached during analytical procedures. The analytical data represent mixtures of these two components. On a graph of $^{230}Th/^{232}Th$ *vs.* $^{234}U/^{232}U$, if the data yield a straight line, then the slope of the line gives the value of the $^{230}Th/^{234}U$ of component (1). Also, a straight line on a plot of $^{234}U/^{232}Th$ *vs.* $^{238}U/^{232}Th$ has a slope equal to the $^{234}U/^{238}U$ ratio of (1). The age of the deposits can then be obtained by substituting these new values of $^{230}Th/^{234}U$ and $^{234}U/^{238}U$ into the age equation. The graphs for the Grey and Green Phases in the northern sub-basin at Bir Tarfawi show good correlation between the isotope ratios, and the slopes are well defined. The ages for the Grey and Green Phases as determined by these slopes are as follows:

Unit	Age
Grey Phase 1 + 2	105,000 ± 15,000
Grey Phase 2	105,000 ± 23,000
Grey Phase 3	141,000 ± 3000
Green Phase	114,000 ± 10,000

These results, however, are not in stratigraphic order, possibly because the isochron method was intended for samples with $^{230}Th/^{232}Th$ values of <20, whereas these samples have values that far exceed that amount. The age calculations for Grey Phases 1 and 2 are also much younger than the average of the U-series age determinations by mass spectrometry on four (of five) ostrich eggshells from Grey Phase 1 (131,000 ± 7000). (The fifth eggshell [87BTF40] had a much larger error, and fell outside error ranges of the other four.) The uranium isochron for the samples from Grey Phase 3 shows little scatter, which suggests that the isochron date for this unit may be correct, and that Phase 3 was *ca.* 141,000 BP yr ago. We may then assume that Grey Phases 1 and 2 are only slightly older, and that when the water table fell after Grey Phase 3, it remained above the marls of Grey Phases 1 and 2, so that some portions of these beds were isotopically altered, causing the primary age of *ca.* 141,000 BP to be reset to the younger age indicated by the isochron slope.

An age estimate of 141,000 BP for Grey Phase 1 also agrees with the ESR measurements for that unit, which gave an average linear uptake age of 151,000 ± 39,000. If all sub-samples with ages more than one standard deviation away from the mean are excluded, the average is 138,000 ± 19,000. On the other hand, the 141,000 date does not agree with the OSL or TL measurements, which places Grey Phase 1 at 129,000 ± 7700 (OSL) and 96,000 ± 14,000 (TL). The OSL result is very close to the mass-spectrometric U-series dates on eggshell. There are no TL dates for Grey Phases 2 and 3, but the OSL measurements for those units are 119,300 ± 22,900 for Grey Phase 2, and 96,400 +7200/-10,900 for Grey Phase 3. The latter is five standard deviations younger than the U-series isochron date calculated for that event.

The optical technique provides the most internally consistent suite of dates for the Bir Tarfawi and Bir Sahara East sequences. The only results that do not agree with the known stratigraphy are those for Phases 3 and 4 of the West Lake. It is possible that these samples may have been switched during handling. The OSL dates also tend to agree with most of the TL dates.

The ostrich-eggshell racemization ratios for the eggshell from Grey Phase 1 provided the calibration point for that chronology, and the 130,000 age indicated by the mass-spectrometric U-series measurements was the selected date for the calibration. The Grey Phase 1 samples were deeply buried (1.5–2.5 m below the surface), well below the level where surface heat would effect the ratios. Eggshells from the sediments of Grey Phases 2 and 3 show almost the same ratios as those of Phase 1. This may mean that all three Grey Phases occurred in a brief period of time, but it is

162

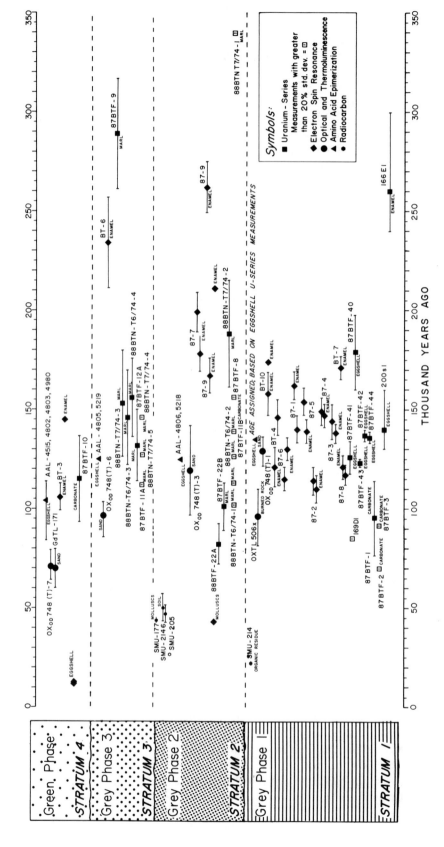

Fig. 2. Distribution of available age estimates for the four phases of the East Lake at Bir Tarfawi

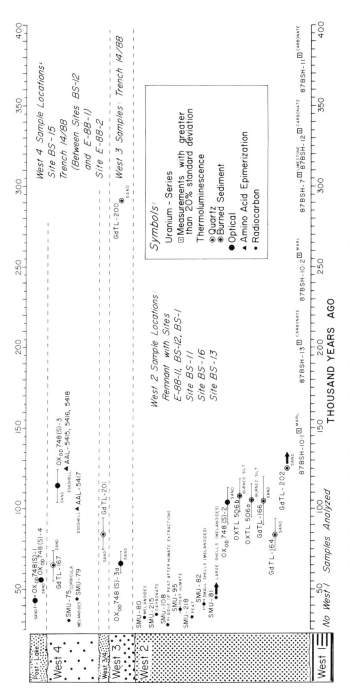

Fig. 3. Distribution of available age estimates for the four phases of the West Lake at Bir Sahara East

also possible that the ratios of the samples from Grey Phases 2 and 3 may have been altered by surface heat. If this were the case, the lakes would be somewhat younger than the ratios show. The OSL dates for the same deposits are significantly younger (119,000 and 96,000 BP, although one of these has a large standard error).

The problem of heat alteration must also be considered in evaluating the dates for the eggshell samples from the Sand Pan and from Site E-88-1 in the Sand Sheet, both of which may be younger than the ratios indicate. None of the samples was deeply buried, so that where there are two sets of ratios, as at these two sites, the younger dates are more likely to be correct, and even these should be seen as maximal. Thus, the sites in the Sand Pan and Site E-88-1 are probably no older than 175,000 yr, and perhaps younger. Heat alteration may also explain the racemization dates of *ca.* 125,000 for Sites E-86-2, E-87-3 and E-88-2. These three sites should be approximately contemporary with the Green Phase in the northern sub-basin at Bir Tarfawi, which had a racemization ratio equivalent to an age of *ca.* 100,000 yr (which should, again, be seen as maximal because of possible heat alteration). OSL and TL measurements from several sites place the Green Phase at <114,000 yr ago.

Although the various dates obtained do not help us in the details of correlating the Bir Tarfawi and Sahara East sequences, the overall suite is encouragingly close to our general model (outlined above) for the chronology of the Middle Paleolithic in this region. Except for a very few measurements that fall outside the expected limits (all of which are also beyond the error ranges of other measurements from the same unit), the dates are within the predicted age range for the Middle Paleolithic wet periods in the eastern Sahara: between 230,000 and 60,000 yr ago. The only technique that consistently yields results of a younger age is ^{14}C, and this is not unexpected.

It is also reassuring that the dates generally agree with the known stratigraphic sequences in the two depressions. The oldest dates tend to be with the oldest lakes, and the youngest with the most recent, although there are exceptions. However, the scatter of dates for each event is so wide, particularly for those events that have the greatest frequency of dated samples, that no precise age can be established for any of them (Figs. 2 and 3). We had also hoped to use this series of dates to relate the terrestrial climatic sequence in the eastern Sahara to the oxygen-isotope record in deep-sea sediments. Again, a precise correlation is not possible, although several relevant observations may be made.

There are two competing chronological models for dating global climatic change. One draws on external influences, particularly changes in solar radiation (Imbrie and Imbrie 1980; Berger and Loutre 1991). Rossignol-Strick (1983) suggests a correlation between insolation maxima and monsoon intensification. The ages of the insolation maxima are determined through the astronomical theory of global climatic change, which forms the basis for the SPECMAP marine-isotope chronology, placing the onset of the Last Interglacial at *ca.* 127,000 yr (Martinson *et al.* 1987).

The second model is based on internal boundary conditions, or a combination of these with solar radiation (Prell and Kutzbach 1987), and infers that Saharan climates are related to such factors as global ice volume, sea-surface temperatures and the value of atmospheric carbon dioxide (for discussion, see Hill *et al.* [ms.]). Of three independent chronologies for these internal boundary phenomena, the first is based on oxygen-isotope ratios and a time scale derived from the rate of Antarctic snow accumulation in the Vostok ice core. This indicates a period of 24,000 yr of maximum warmth and high levels of carbon dioxide, reaching a peak at 135,000 BP (Barnola *et al.* 1987:410). The second chronology is from a calcite vein in the Great Basin of North America, dated by U-series. This chronology has isotopic signals of higher temperatures for a period of

20,000 yr, beginning at 140,000 ± 1000 BP (Winograd *et al.* 1988, 1990). The third chronology is based on the dates of high sea levels, represented by beach features and corals. These dates vary considerably, and there is no consensus on the precise age of the last major high sea stand. Moore (1982) places it at 135,000 yr, but high sea levels are dated by Chen *et al.* (1991:95) between 133,000 and 110,000 yr, and by Edwards *et al.* (1987) between 130,000 and 122,000 yr. However, Muhs and Szabo (1991:239) report a high sea stand beginning as early as 141,000 BP and lasting for *ca.* 20,000 yr.

The independent chronologies are similar to the U-series isochron and ESR ages for the three Grey Phases at Bir Tarfawi. This would suggest that monsoonal rainfall in the Tarfawi region began slightly before or at the onset of the Last Interglacial, around 140,000–135,000 yr. However, in the Great Basin calcite sequence, the Last Interglacial is documented as a single period of higher temperatures, rather than a series of pulsations, as indicated by the Egyptian lake sequences. The previous major episode of increased temperatures (and, presumably, monsoonal intensification) is >250,000 BP. According to our model, this is too early for the Tarfawi White Lake and its associated Middle Paleolithic archaeology.

In contrast, astronomical theory places the insolation maxima, theoretically correlated with monsoonal intensification, at 197,000, 173,000, 126,000, 104,000, 82,000 and 10,000 yr (Berger and Loutre 1991:312). (There are other minor maxima, but of lower intensity than the 10,000-yr maximum that produced only ephemeral lakes in southern Egypt; we assume that these also would have been too minor to result in permanent lakes in the area.) The insolation peak at 126,000 yr has the strongest signal, and it is tempting to relate it to the three Grey Phases, all of which are believed to fall within a period of a few millennia. Such a correlation is possible if Grey Phase 1 was *ca.* 133,000–130,000 yr, and coincided with the beginning of deglaciation and with the onset of that period of solar intensity. The Green Phase might then relate to, or slightly precede, the 104,000-yr or the 82,000-yr maximum. All of these correlations are in general agreement (within 2 standard deviations) with most of the mass-spectrometric U-series, OSL and TL dates.

Neither of these models conflicts with the hypothesis that increased monsoonal activity in East Africa correlates with deglaciation, rather than with maximum insolation (Hillaire-Marcel *et al.* 1986:Table 1; Lézine and Casanova 1991:310).

Unfortunately, the Tarfawi and Bir Sahara East age measurements do not provide us with sufficient evidence to choose between the competing chronological schemes. The U-series isochron dates and ESR measurements generally support the independent chronology that dates the Stage 6/5 boundary between 135,000 and 145,000 yr. The mass-spectrometric U-series eggshell, OSL and TL dates generally support the SPECMAP chronology based on astronomical theory. At this point, we cannot choose between them. The dating evidence firmly indicates only that major wet episodes occurred between 140,000 and 100,000 yr. The dates are not sufficiently precise to permit us to determine on which side of the Stage 6/5 boundary these episodes occurred, or whether they straddle it. Given the difficulties inherent in the various techniques, this problem is not likely to be resolved soon. The mass-spectrometric dates on ostrich eggshells seem to hold the most promise, but the difficulty lies in locating appropriate samples.

The wide dispersal of the dates for Bir Tarfawi and Bir Sahara East (Figs. 2 and 3) suggests that results obtained by the techniques used here should be approached with caution. U-series, ESR and TL dates have sometimes been used to support complicated climatic sequences, occasionally with limited or no stratigraphic control for the dated samples (Fontes and Gasse 1991; Petit-Maire 1991; Szabo *et al.* 1989). Such approaches place much more confidence in the indicated ages than would seem justified by the results from Bir Tarfawi and Bir Sahara East. As yet, these techniques cannot provide the level of precision or replication available with ^{14}C dating in later periods. It is a cliché of ^{14}C dating that it is reliable only when multiple measurements provide a tight or patterned cluster. With the techniques used for dating the Middle Paleolithic, it seems that the only way to obtain a tight cluster is to avoid multiple dates.

ACKNOWLEDGMENTS

The fieldwork on which this paper is based was carried out by the Combined Prehistoric Expedition, jointly sponsored by Southern Methodist University, the Polish Academy of Sciences and the Geological Survey of Egypt. We wish to thank the Egyptian General Petroleum Company and the Egyptian Antiquities Organisation for their cooperation and assistance. Financial support was provided by U. S. National Science Foundation Grants BNS-8518574 (to F.W.), BNS-8805555 and BNS-9010622 (to G.H.M.), and grants from the Canadian Natural Sciences and Engineering Research Council and Social Sciences and Humanities Research Council (to H.P.S.).

REFERENCES CITED

Barnola, J. M., D. Raynaud, Y. S. Korotkevich and C. Lorius
　　1987　Vostok ice core provides 160,000-year record of atmospheric CO_2. *Nature* 329:408–414.
Berger, A. and M. K. Loutre
　　1991　Insolation values of the climate of the last 10 million years. *Quaternary Science Reviews* 10(4):297–317.
Bluszcz, A.
　　1993　Thermoluminescence dating of deposits from the area of Bir Sahara East and Bir Tarfawi. In *Egypt During the Last Interglacial*, edited by F. Wendorf, R. Schild, A. E. Close and associates, pp. 224–226. Plenum Press, New York.
Caton-Thompson, G.
　　1946　*The Aterian Industry: Its Place and Significance in the Palaeolithic World.* Royal Anthropological Institute of Great Britain and Ireland, London.
Chavaillon, N.
　　1973　L'Atérien de Hassi-Ouchtat dans le mons d'Ougarta (Sahara nord-occidental). *Libyca* 21:91–138.
Chen, J. H., H. A. Curran, B. White and G. J. Wasserburg
　　1991　Precise chronology of the Last Interglacial period: ^{234}U-^{230}Th data from fossil coral reefs in the Bahamas. *Geological Society of America Bulletin* 103:82–97.
Clark, J. D.
　　1988　The Middle Stone Age of East Africa and the beginnings of regional identity. *Journal of World Prehistory* 2:235–305.
Conrad, G.
　　1972　Les fluctuations climatiques récentes dans l'est du Sahara occidental algérien. In *Actes du Congrès Panafricain de Préhistoire, VI Session*, pp. 343–349. Dakar, Senegal.
Edwards, R. L., J. H. Chen, T. L. Ku and G. J. Wasserburg
　　1987　Precise timing of the Last Interglacial period from mass spectrometric determination of Thorium-230 in corals. *Science* 236:1547–1553.
Ferring, C. R.
　　1975　The Aterian in North African prehistory. In *Problems in Prehistory: North Africa and the Levant*, edited by F. Wendorf and A. E. Marks, pp. 113–126. Southern Methodist University Press, Dallas.
Fontes, J. and F. Gasse
　　1991　Palhydaf (palaeohydrology in Africa) program: Objectives, methods, major results. *Palaeogeography, Palaeoclimatology, Palaeoecology* 84:191–215.
Gautier, A.
　　1980　Contributions to the archaeozoology of Egypt. In *Prehistory of the Eastern Sahara*, by F. Wendorf and R. Schild, pp. 317–344. Academic Press, New York.
　　1993　The Middle Paleolithic archaeofaunas from Bir Tarfawi (Western Desert, Egypt). In *Egypt During the Last Interglacial*, edited by F. Wendorf, R. Schild, A. E. Close and associates, pp. 121–141. Plenum Press, New York.
Haas, H. and C. V. Haynes
　　1980　Discussion of radiocarbon dates from the Western Desert. In *Prehistory of the Eastern Sahara*, by F. Wendorf and R. Schild, pp. 373–378. Academic Press, New York.

Hill, C. L., F. Wendorf and Angela E. Close
Global climatic change and Pleistocene pluvials in Saharan North Africa. Submitted to *Quaternary Research.*
Hillaire-Marcel, C., O. Carro and J. Casanova
1986 ^{14}C and Th/U dating of Pleistocene and Holocene stromatolites from East African paleolakes. *Quaternary Research* 25:213–239.
Huxtable, J.
1993   Thermoluminescence dates for burnt earth sample from Bir Sahara East and a burnt core from Bir Tarfawi. In *Egypt During the Last Interglacial,* edited by F. Wendorf, R. Schild, A. E. Close and associates, pp. 227–228. Plenum Press, New York.
Imbrie, J. and J. Z. Imbrie
1980   Modelling the climatic response to orbital variations. *Science* 207:942–953.
Kowalski, K., W. Van Neer, Z. Bochenski, M. Mlynarski, B. Rzebik-Kowalska, Z. Szyndlar, A. Gautier, R. Schild, A. E. Close and F. Wendorf
1989   A Last Interglacial fauna from the eastern Sahara. *Quaternary Research* 32:335–341.
Leakey, M., P. V. Tobias, J. E. Martyn and R. E. F. Leakey
1969   An Acheulean industry with prepared core technique and the discovery of a contemporary hominid mandible at Lake Baringo, Kenya. *Proceedings of the Prehistoric Society* 35:48–76.
Lézine, A.-M. and J. Casanova
1991   Correlated oceanic and continental records demonstrate past climate and hydrology of North Africa (0–140 ka). *Geology* 19:307–310.
McBurney, C. B. M.
1967   *The Haua Fteah (Cyrenaica) and the Stone Age of the Southeast Mediterranean.* Cambridge University Press, Cambridge.
McCauley, J. F., G. G. Schaber, C. S. Breed, M. J. Grolier, C. V. Haynes, B. Issawi, C. Elachi and R. Blom
1982   Subsurface valleys and geoarchaeology of the eastern Sahara revealed by shuttle radar. *Science* 218:1004–1020.
McKinney, C.
1993   Bir Tarfawi: A stratigraphic test of uranium-series dating. In *Egypt During the Last Interglacial,* edited by F. Wendorf, R. Schild, A. E. Close and associates, pp. 218–223. Plenum Press, New York.
Martinson, D. G., N. G. Pisias, J. D. Hays, J. Imbrie, T. C. Moore and N. J. Shackleton
1987   Age dating and the orbital theory of the ice ages: Development of a high-resolution 0 to 300,000-year chrono-stratigraphy. *Quaternary Research* 27:1–27.
Miller, G. H.
1993   Chronology of hominid occupation at Bir Tarfawi and Bir Sahara East, based on the epimerization of isoleucine in ostrich eggshells. In *Egypt During the Last Interglacial,* edited by F. Wendorf, R. Schild, A. E. Close and associates, pp. 241–254. Plenum Press, New York.
Moore, W. S.
1982   Late Pleistocene sea level history. In *Uranium-Series Disequilibrium: Applications to Environmental Problems,* edited by M. Ivanovich and R. S. Harmon, pp. 481–495. Clarendon Press, Oxford.
Muhs, D. R. and B. Szabo
1991   New uranium-series ages of the Waimanalo Limestone, Oahu, Hawaii and paleoclimatic implications for the Last Interglacial period. *Geological Society of America Abstracts with Program* 23(5):239.
Pachur, H., S. Kröpelin, P. Hoelzmann, M. Goschin and N. Altmann
1990   Late Quaternary fluvio-lacustrine environments of Western Nubia. *Berliner Geowissenschaftlichen Abhandlungen* (A) 120:203–260.
Paulissen, E. and P. M. Vermeersch
1987   Earth, man and climate in the Egyptian Nile Valley during the Pleistocene. In *Prehistory of Arid North Africa: Essays in Honor of Fred Wendorf,* edited by A. E. Close, pp. 19–67. Southern Methodist University Press, Dallas.
Petit-Maire, N.
1991   Recent Quaternary climatic change and man in the Sahara. *Journal of African Earth Sciences* 12 (1/2):125–132.
Prell, W. L. and J. E. Kutzbach
1987   Monsoon variability over the past 150,000 years. *Journal of Geophysical Research* 92(D-7):8411–8425.
Robins, D.
1993   ESR study of materials from the excavation of Middle Paleolithic sites at Bir Tarfawi. In *Egypt During the Last Interglacial,* edited by F. Wendorf, R. Schild, A. E. Close and associates, pp. 238–240. Plenum Press, New York.
Rognon, P. and M. A. J. Williams
1977   Late Quaternary climatic changes in Australia and North Africa: A preliminary interpretation. *Palaeogeography, Palaeoclimatology, Palaeoecology* 21:235–327.

Rossignol-Strick, M.
    1983   African monsoons, an immediate climatic response to orbital insolation. *Nature* 304:46–49.
Schild, R. and F. Wendorf
    1989   The Late Pleistocene Nile in Wadi Kubbaniya. In *Stratigraphy, Paleoeconomy and Environment, Prehistory of Wadi Kubbaniya*, Vol. 2, assembled by F. Wendorf and R. Schild, edited by A. E. Close, pp. 15–100. Southern Methodist University Press, Dallas.
Schwarcz, H. P. and R. Grün
    1993   Electron spin resonance dating of tooth enamel from Bir Tarfawi. In *Egypt During the Last Interglacial*, edited by F. Wendorf, R. Schild, A. E. Close and associates, pp. 234-237. Plenum Press, New York.
Schwarcz, H. P. and A. G. Latham
    1989   Dirty calcite, I. Uranium-series dating of contaminated calcites using leachate alone. *Isotope Geoscience* 80: 35–43.
Schwarcz, H. P. and L. Morawska
    1993   Uranium-series dating of carbonates from Bir Tarfawi and Bir Sahara East. In *Egypt During the Last Interglacial*, edited by F. Wendorf, R. Schild, A. E. Close and associates, pp. 205–217. Plenum Press, New York.
Servant, M., and S. Servant-Vildary
    1972   Nouvelles données pour une interprétation paléoclimatique de séries continentales du Bassin Tchadien (Pléistocène récent, Holocène). In *Palaeoecology of Africa*, Vol. 6, edited by E. M. Van Zinderen Bakker, pp. 87–92. Balkema, Rotterdam.
Stokes, S.
    1993   Optical dating of sediment samples from Bir Tarfawi and Bir Sahara East: an initial report. In *Egypt During the Last Interglacial*, edited by F. Wendorf, R. Schild, A. E. Close and associates. Plenum Press, New York.
Szabo, B. J., C. V. Haynes, Jr. and T. A. Maxwell
    1989   Uranium-series dated authigenic carbonates and Acheulian sites in southern Egypt. *Science* 243:1053–1056.
Tillet, T.
    1983   *Le Paléolithique du Bassin Tchadien Septentrional (Niger-Tchad)*. CNRS, Paris.
Tixier, J.
    1967   Procédés d'analyse et questions de terminologie concernant l'étude des ensembles industriels du Paléolithique récent et de l'Epipaléolithique dans l'Afrique du Nord-Ouest. In *Background to Evolution in Africa*, edited by W. W. Bishop and J. D. Clark, pp. 771–820. University of Chicago Press, Chicago.
Van Neer, W.
    1989   Recent and fossil fish from the Sahara and their palaeohydrological meaning. In *Palaeoecology of Africa*, Vol. 20, edited by J. A. Coetzee, pp. 1–18. Balkema, Rotterdam.
Vermeersch, P. M., E. Paulissen, G. Gijselings, M. Otte, A. Thomas, P. Van Peer, and R. Lauwers
    1984   33,000 year old chert mining site and related *Homo* in the Egyptian Nile Valley. *Nature* 309:342–344.
Wendorf, F., A. E. Close and R. Schild
    1987   Recent work on the Middle Palaeolithic of the Eastern Sahara. *The African Archaeological Review* 5:49–63. Africa during the period of *Homo sapiens neanderthalensis* and his contemporaries. In *Scientific and Cultural History of Mankind*, edited by S. J. De Laet. UNESCO, Paris, in press.
Wendorf, F., A. E. Close, R. Schild, A. Gautier, H. P. Schwarcz, G. H. Miller, K. Kowalski H. Królik, A. Bluszcz, D. Robins and R. Grün
    1990   Le dernier interglaciaire dans le Sahara oriental. *L'Anthropologie* 94:361–391.
Wendorf, F., R. L. Laury, C. C. Albritton, R. Schild, C. V. Haynes, P. E. Damon, M. Shafiqullah and R. Scarborough
    1975   Dates for the Middle Stone Age of East Africa. *Science* 187:740–742.
Wendorf, F. and R. Schild (editors)
    1980   *Prehistory of the Eastern Sahara*. Academic Press, New York.
    1989   Summary and synthesis. In *Late Paleolithic Archaeology*, Vol 3. *Prehistory of Wadi Kubbaniya*, assembled by F. Wendorf and R. Schild, edited by A. E. Close, pp. 768–824. Southern Methodist University Press, Dallas.
Wendorf, F., R. Schild (assemblers) and A. E. Close (editor)
    1984   *Cattle-Keepers of the Eastern Sahara: The Neolithic of Bir Kiseiba*. Institute for the Study of Earth and Man, Southern Methodist University, Dallas.
Winograd, I. J., T. B. Coplen, K. R. Ludwig, B. J. Szabo, A. C. Riggs, and K. M. Revesz
    1990   Continuous 500,000-year climatic record from Great Basin vein calcite: 1. The ^{18}O time series. *Geological Society of America Abstracts with Program* 22(7):209.
Winograd, I. J., B. J. Szabo, T. B. Coplen and A. C. Riggs
    1988   A 250,000-year climatic record from Great Basin vein calcite: Implications for the Milankovitch theory. *Science* 242:1276–1280.

THE UPPER PALEOLITHIC CHRONOLOGY OF THE LEVANT AND THE NILE VALLEY

JAMES L. PHILLIPS

Department of Anthropology, University of Illinois at Chicago, Chicago, Illinois 60680 USA

INTRODUCTION

Over the past 15 years, the chronology of the Upper Paleolithic of the Levant and the Nile Valley has been vastly complemented by the accumulation of new radiometric dates from three main dating methods: 1) standard radiocarbon (^{14}C) methodology with new and improved counters; 2) accelerator mass spectrometry (AMS) dates from, notably, Oxford, Arizona and Groningen; and 3) thermoluminescence (TL) dates. The Upper Paleolithic period, generally acknowledged as *ca.* 40,000–20,000 BP in the Levant and the Nile Valley, has been enriched with dates from previously excavated rockshelter sites, such as Ksar 'Akil (Mellars and Tixier 1989), Kebara and Hayonim (Bar-Yosef 1991) and from newly exposed sites in Jordan (Garrard and Gebel 1988), Sinai (Phillips 1988) and Egypt (Close 1980, 1984, 1988). Table 1 lists ^{14}C and TL dates for the Upper Paleolithic of the Levant and the Nile Valley.

The Upper Paleolithic period follows quite different paths in the Levant and in the Nile Valley. Assemblages that lack Levallois technology occur quite early in the Levant (by *ca.* 40,000 BP in the Negev and Sinai), whereas the Levallois technique was used in the Nile Valley until virtually the end of the Pleistocene (*e.g.*, the Sebilian). Several archaeological cultures in the Nile Valley used the Levallois technique to varying degrees, but with decreasing frequency over time. For example, during the early Halfan, Levallois technology was used extensively, whereas during the late Halfan it was barely used at all (Marks 1968).

Further, the ecological situations of the two archaeological cultures in the Levant (Ahmarian and Levantine Aurignacian) are quite different from those in the Nile Valley. As northeastern Africa became increasingly hyperarid, a riverine environment was clearly an attraction, and sites concentrated near permanent water (springs, lakes, small rivers or marshes). Despite many surveys, no archaeological sites belonging to the Upper Paleolithic were recovered in either the eastern or western deserts of Egypt or the Sudan.

The topography of the two areas was also quite different. In the Levant, several microenvironments occupied a varied landscape of mountains, hills, valleys (such as the Jordan Valley with Lake Lisan) and coastal areas in the north; open steppe usually existed in the more marginal southern Levant, with the exception of the mountainous area of south-central Sinai. The landscape of the Nile Valley was quite uniform.

THE LEVANT

The earliest Upper Paleolithic assemblages in the Levant were found in the south, in the Negev and Sinai, namely at Boker A and Abu Noshra II in the south, and at Qafzeh in the north. These sites belong to the Ahmarian complex, and appeared *ca.* 8000 yr earlier than the Levantine Aurignacian at Ksar 'Akil, Lebanon. These early Ahmarian sites contained fully developed Upper Paleolithic blade/bladelet assemblages. Backed blades and bladelets, perforators, truncations, burins and end-scrapers comprised the tool assemblages, which also included single-platform blade cores and cresting and core tablets. The punch technique of indirect percussion was used extensively. The

Late Quaternary Chronology and Paleoclimates of the Eastern Mediterranean
Edited by O. Bar-Yosef and R. S. Kra. RADIOCARBON 1994, pp. 169–176

development of this process can be traced to the site of Boker Tachtit in the Negev (Marks 1983), where the transition from late Mousterian to the early Upper Paleolithic occurred from *ca.* 48,000–40,000 BP (Table 1). Thus, the earliest Upper Paleolithic assemblages in the Levant are found in the southern Levant. The fauna recovered from the early Ahmarian sites represent locally available species: deer, pig and cattle in the north; ostrich eggshells were the only evidence of fauna recovered from the early Negev and Sinai sites, except at Abu Noshra, where cattle, pig, gazelle, ibex, wolf, fox, cat, fish and bird remains were recovered.

The Levantine Aurignacian, on the other hand, first appeared in the north, at Ksar 'Akil, Lebanon, at *ca.* 32,000 BP, and it was not until *ca.* 26,000 BP that it replaced the Ahmarian in the southern Levant, near Ein Avdat in the Negev. The Levantine Aurignacian is characterized by rockshelter habitations in the northern Levant, with retouched, generally thick and irregular blades, and a variety of burins and steep end scrapers making up the majority of the lithic tool assemblages. Bone tools were abundant, and split-based points were found at Kebara and Hayonim. The technology was dominated by flakes over blades; it appears that direct percussion was used in most reduction sequences. The fauna consists of a variety of deer; pig and cattle were also found frequently in the assemblages.

It is clear from Table 1 that some late dates, such as those from Ein Aqev: Level 5, Uwaynid 18, Fazael IX and X, all with Levantine Aurignacian assemblages, overlap dated Epipaleolithic Kebaran sites, such as Ohalo II on the shore of the Sea of Galilee. Whether the Levantine Aurignacian continued in the southern Levant while the Kebaran developed in the north is a question that needs to be addressed, especially in relation to new pollen data from the Dead Sea and Lake Hula (Baruch and Bottema 1991). Also important to know is how long the Ahmarian lasted as a separate techno-complex. A case can be made that the Ahmarian existed for only *ca.* 12,000 yr, from *ca.* 40,000–28,000 BP, and that the sites of Ein Aqev East in the Negev and WH618H1 and WH784x in Jordan, dated between *ca.* 20,000 and 16,000 BP, are not actually Ahmarian, but represent evolved groups with different adaptation patterns from those typically Ahmarian.

THE NILE VALLEY

Until recently, material comparable in age, lithic typology and technology to Upper Paleolithic sites in the Levant were unknown in the Nile Valley. Excavation near Armant has produced evidence of sites that date from *ca.* 35,000–30,000 BP (Vermeersch *et al.* 1982). Nazlet Khater-4 was a flint mine that yielded a restricted tool kit, consisting of retouched blades, denticulates and bifacial adzes, the latter being used for quarrying. It is unclear whether evidence of the Levallois technique exists at this site. A bit upstream from Nazlet Khater-4, on the east bank of the river near Qena, the site of Shuwikhat-1 (Paulissen and Vermeersch 1987) provides a TL date on burned clay of 24,700 ± 2500 BP. A second site, E71K9, located farther upstream near Isna, dates to 21,640 ± 1520 BP (Table 1). Together, these sites represent the Shuwikhat industry, characterized by denticulated blades, a variety of burins, end scrapers on blades, perforators and truncations. These assemblages are the closest to the Ahmarian during the Upper Paleolithic of the Nile Valley, and, with Nazlet Khater-4, are the only sites in the Nile Valley dated between 40,000 and 20,000 BP.

Although the unnamed tradition from Nazlet Khater-4 and Nazlet Khater-1 and the Shuwikhat tradition are the only true Upper Paleolithic industries in the Nile Valley, several others that retain some Upper Paleolithic traits date from *ca.* 20,000–17,000 BP, contemporary with the Epipaleolithic Kebaran of the Levant. Following the Shuwikhat tradition, the Egyptian Fakhurian, Kubbaniyan, Idfuan, and the lower Nubian Halfan are the earliest dated traditions, although Wendorf and Schild (1989), basing their conclusions on stratigraphy, believe that the Gemaian of the Second

Cataract is earlier, probably dating between 25,000 and 20,000 BP. These complexes are nearly contemporaneous and share a number of features, including settlement patterns and food resources.

The Fakhurian is known from sites near Isna, on the west bank of the river, and from three sites in Wadi Kubbaniya. Fish remains were abundant at several sites. Mammalian fauna include harte-beest, cattle and hippo. The Fakhurian, as well as most of the other Late Paleolithic sites on the Nile, is characterized by bladelet or microblade assemblages, depending on the raw material, some with Levallois technique, which is absent, however, from the Fakhurian assemblages. These are characterized by *mèche de forêt* and backed bladelets, with occasional end-scrapers and burins. Fakhurian assemblages date between 20,600 and 17,370 BP (Table 1).

The Kubbaniyan is the most studied of the Late Paleolithic traditions in the Nile Valley. Sites cluster in the Wadi Kubbaniya near Aswan, and downriver some 150 km near Isna. Fifty-eight ^{14}C determinations were obtained from seven sites, indicating occupation from *ca*. 18,500–17,000 BP. Using plant and animal remains, researchers have interpreted the settlement system as a series of seasonal movements of Kubbaniyan populations among sites located "in the main dune field, in the fronting plain, and in the relatively flat but high area near the wadi mouth" (Wendorf and Schild 1989:801). The Kubbaniyan lithic tradition contains some Levallois blank production, especially for burins and retouched flakes (Wendorf and Schild 1989). Ouchtata retouched bladelets are the dominant tool type in the earlier periods, and scaled pieces dominate in the later Kubbani-yan (Wendorf and Schild 1989). Multiple platform flat cores, made on Egyptian flint, were found in the sites near Isna; the sites in Wadi Kubbaniya contained mostly Nile pebbles used as raw material.

The Halfan tradition is known only from sites in Lower Nubia, near the Second Cataract. Fauna consists of hartebeest and cattle at the Khor Musa wadi sites; fish remains were abundant at sites located slightly downriver, in Egyptian Nubia. The Halfan industry is microlithic, produced on small Nile pebbles. The Halfan flake characterizes the tradition; it is a variant of the Levallois flake. Backed bladelets are the dominant tool type, many being blunted with Ouchtata retouch. The Halfan dates to *ca*. 19,500–17,500 (Wendorf and Schild 1989).

The Idfuan tradition was found at sites between Kom Ombo and an area slightly north of Isna, on the west bank of the river. These sites date between 18,000 and 17,000 BP; thus, they are approxi-mately contemporary with the Late Kubbaniyan (Wendorf and Schild 1989). Debitage consisted of Levallois and Halfan flakes and numerous blades produced from opposed platform cores. Formal tools were rare, and were mainly retouched and denticulated blades. Fish, hartebeest and wild cattle remains were recovered in abundance.

CONCLUSION

The most recent chronological evidence gathered from the Levant and the Nile Valley indicates that the Upper Paleolithic began in the southern Levant as a direct descendent of the late Middle Paleolithic Mousterian; the transition is found at the site of Boker Tachtit in the Negev. The Upper Paleolithic occurred later in the Nile Valley; remains are quite sparse, and there are no direct ante-cedents. Inhabitants of the southern Levant settled in open-air sites, which were organized toward locales near recurring natural resources, especially springs, lakes and ponds. Animal remains tend to represent the diverse environmental setting, for example, the mountainous region of southern Sinai and the northern Negev/Sinai border. Settlement in the northern Levant, on the other hand, was oriented toward forested areas and related fauna (*e.g.* deer); sites were generally found in rockshelters.

In the Nile Valley, Upper Paleolithic sites are found in riverine environments; their inhabitants exploited fish and shellfish; fauna included hartebeest, cattle and gazelle. The retention of the Levallois technique in many of the lithic traditions after 30,000 BP is unique to the Nile Valley; it was retained neither in the Levant nor Europe during the Upper Paleolithic. Thus, Upper Paleolithic populations of the Levant and the Nile Valley do not appear to share "cultural identities", attesting to a lack of population movement between Africa and southwestern Asia. It was not until the Mushabian tradition in the southern Levant that a North African presence can be found in Asia.

TABLE 1. ^{14}C Dates of the Upper Paleolithic in the Levant and Nile Valley

Site, context	Date (yr BP)	Lab no.*	Material	Tradition	Reference
ISRAEL					
Kebara					
IIf	36,000 ± 1600	OxA-1230	Charcoal	Ahmarian	Hedges *et al.* 1990:113
IIBf	35,600 ± 1600	OxA-1567	Charcoal	Ahmarian	Hedges *et al.* 1990:113
V	38,000 ± 2100	OxA-1568	Charcoal	Ahmarian	Hedges *et al.* 1990:113
W23c 400-405	33,550 ± 930	OxA-2800	Bone	Lev Aurignacian	Hedges *et al.* 1992:151
26	20,450 ± 300	RT-227	Ash	Lev Aurignacian	Henry and Servello 1974:33
Hayonim D	16,240 ± 640	Hv-2675	Bone	Lev Aurignacian	Gilead 1991:120
Hayonim D	20,810 ± 320	OxA-2806	Bone	Lev Aurignacian	Bar-Yosef 1991:85
Hayonim D	21,650 ± 340	OxA-2804	Bone	Lev Aurignacian	Bar-Yosef 1991:85
Hayonim D	27,200 ± 600	OxA-2801	Bone	Lev Aurignacian	Bar-Yosef 1991:85
Hayonim D	28,900 ± 650	OxA-2802	Bone	Lev Aurignacian	Bar-Yosef 1991:85
Hayonim D	29,980 ± 720	OxA-2805	Bone	Lev Aurignacian	Bar-Yosef 1991:85
Fazael IX	17,760 ± 160	OxA-2871	Charcoal	Lev Aurignacian	Hedges *et al.* 1992:342
Fazael X	15,450 ± 130	OxA-2870	Charcoal	L. Aurignacian(?)	Hedges *et al.* 1992:342
NEGEV					
Boker Tachtit/1	47,280 ± 9050	SMU-580	Charcoal	Trans Ahmarian	Marks 1983:37
Boker Tachtit/1	46,930 ± 2420	SMU-259	Charcoal	Trans Ahmarian	Marks 1983:37
Boker Tachtit/1	>45,620	SMU-184	Charcoal	Trans Ahmarian	Marks 1983:37
Boker Tachtit/4	35,055 ± 4100	SMU-579	Charcoal	Ahmarian	Marks 1983:37
Boker A	>33,600	SMU-181	Charcoal	Ahmarian	Marks 1977:9
Boker A	>33,420	SMU-260	Charcoal	Ahmarian	Marks 1977:9
Boker A	37,920 ± 2810	SMU-578	Charcoal	Ahmarian	Marks 1983:37
Boker BE					
III	27,450 ± 1130	SMU-188	Charcoal	Ahmarian	Marks 1977:9
III	26,600 ± 500	SMU-229	Charcoal	Ahmarian	Marks 1977:9
III	26,030 ± 600	SMU-288	Charcoal	Ahmarian	Marks 1977:9
II	26,950 ± 520	SMU-227	Charcoal	Ahmarian	Marks 1977:9
II	24,630 ± 390	SMU-565	Charcoal	Ahmarian	Marks 1983:37
I	25,610 ± 640	SMU-186	Charcoal	Lev Aurignacian	Marks 1983:37
Ein Aqev					
12	19,980 ± 1200	SMU-5	Charcoal	Lev Aurignacian	Marks 1976:230
11	17,390 ± 560	SMU-8	Charcoal	Lev Aurignacian	Marks 1976:230
9	17,890 ± 600	SMU-6	Charcoal	Lev Aurignacian	Marks 1976:230
7	17,510 ± 560	I-5495	Charcoal	Lev Aurignacian	Marks 1976:230
5	16,900 ± 250	I-5494	Charcoal	Lev Aurignacian	Marks 1976:230
Shunera XVI	16,100 ± 150	Pta-3403	Eggshell	Lev Aurignacian	Goring-Morris 1987:63
Shunera XVI	15,800 ± 160	Pta-3702	Eggshell	Lev Aurignacian	Goring-Morris 1987:63
Shunera XVI	16,200 ± 170	RT-227	Ash	Lev Aurignacian	Goring-Morris 1987:63
JORDAN					
Jilat 9	21,150 ± 400	OxA-519	Bone	Lev Aurignacian	Garrard and Gebel 1988:319
Uwaynid 18	23,200 ± 400	OxA-867	Charcoal	Lev Aurignacian	Garrard and Gebel 1988:326
Uwaynid 18	19,800 ± 350	OxA-864	Charcoal	Lev Aurignacian	Garrard and Gebel 1988:326
Uwaynid 18	19,500 ± 250	OxA-868	Charcoal	Lev Aurignacian	Garrard and Gebel 1988:326

TABLE 1. (Continued)

Site, context	Date (yr BP)	Lab no.*	Material	Tradition	Reference
Uwaynid 14	18,900 ± 250	OxA-865	Charcoal	Proto-Kebaran?	Garrard and Gebel 1988:325
Uwaynid 14	18,400 ± 250	OxA-866	Charcoal	Proto-Kebaran?	Garrard and Gebel 1988:325
WH 618 HI	20,300 ± 300	Ua-4395	Charcoal	Ahmarian?	Coinman 1990:324
WH 784x	19,000 ± 1300	Ua-4396	Charcoal	Ahmarian?	Coinman 1990:324
LEBANON					
Ksar 'Akil					
I	23,170 ± 400	OxA-1791	Charcoal	Proto-Kebaran?	Mellars and Tixier 1989:764
I	22,850 ± 400	OxA-1792	Charcoal	Proto-Kebaran?	Mellars and Tixier 1989:764
I	22,050 ± 360	OxA-1793	Charcoal	Proto-Kebaran?	Mellars and Tixier 1989:764
I	22,480 ± 380	OxA-1794	Charcoal	Proto-Kebaran?	Mellars and Tixier 1989:764
I	22,850 ± 380	OxA-1795	Charcoal	Proto-Kebaran?	Mellars and Tixier 1989:764
III	21,100 ± 500	OxA-1796	Charcoal	Lev Aurignacian	Mellars and Tixier 1989:764
III	26,900 ± 600	OxA-1797	Charcoal	Lev Aurignacian	Mellars and Tixier 1989:764
III	29,300 ± 800	OxA-1798	Charcoal	Lev Aurignacian	Mellars and Tixier 1989:764
III	26,500 ± 900	MC-1191	Charcoal	Lev Aurignacian	Mellars and Tixier 1989:764
IV	30,250 ± 850	OxA-1803	Charcoal	Lev Aurignacian	Mellars and Tixier 1989:764
VI	31,200 ± 1300	OxA-1804	Charcoal	Lev Aurignacian	Mellars and Tixier 1989:764
VI	32,400 ± 1100	OxA-1805	Charcoal	Lev Aurignacian	Mellars and Tixier 1989:764
VI	32,000 ± 1500	MC-1192	Charcoal	Lev Aurignacian	Mellars and Tixier 1989:764
6–7m	28,840 ± 380	GrN-2195	Shell	Lev Aurignacian	Henry and Servello 1974:32
SINAI					
Lagama VII	>19,000	RT-413A	Charcoal	Lagaman	Bar-Yosef and Phillips 1977:264
Lagama VII	31,210 ± 278	SMU-185	Charcoal	Lagaman	Bar-Yosef and Phillips 1977:264
Lagama VII	34,170 ± 3670	SMU-172	Charcoal	Lagaman	Bar-Yosef and Phillips 1977:264
Lagama VIII	32,980 ± 2140	SMU-119	Eggshell	Lagaman	Bar-Yosef and Phillips 1977:264
Lagama VIII	30,360 ^{13}C/^{12}C				
Lagama IIID	30,050 ± 1240	SMU-118	Eggshell	Lagaman	Bar-Yosef and Phillips 1977:264
Lagama IIID	30,360 ^{13}C/^{12}C				
QB 501	33,800 ± 940	Pta-2819	Eggshell	Ahmarian	Gilead 1991:119
QB 601	32,470 ± 780	Pta-2964	Eggshell	Ahmarian	Gilead 1991:119
Abu Noshra 1	29,580 $^{+1610}_{-1340}$	B-13198	Charcoal	Ahmarian	Phillips 1987:113
Abu Noshra 1	25,950 ± 360	B-13897	Matrix	Ahmarian	Unpublished
Abu Noshra 1	>30,440	B-12125	Charcoal	Ahmarian	Phillips 1987:113
Abu Noshra 1	31,330 ± 2880	SMU-1824	Charcoal	Ahmarian	Unpublished
Abu Noshra 1	35,824 ± 1090	SMU-2254	Charcoal	Ahmarian	Unpublished
Abu Noshra 1	35,805 ± 1520	SMU-2007	Charcoal	Ahmarian	Phillips 1988:187
Abu Noshra II	31,023 ± 8537	SMU-1772	Charcoal	Ahmarian	Phillips 1988:187
Abu Noshra II	31,585 ± 2275	SMU-1762	Charcoal	Ahmarian	Phillips 1988:187
Abu Noshra II	33,470 ± 680	ETH-3075	Charcoal	Ahmarian	Unpublished
Abu Noshra II	33,940 ± 790	ETH-3076	Charcoal	Ahmarian	Unpublished
Abu Noshra II	38,924 ± 1529	SMU-2122	Charcoal	Ahmarian	Phillips and Gladfelter 1989:119
Abu Noshra II	48,250 ± 2810	SMU-2372	Charcoal	Ahmarian	Unpublished
Abu Noshra VI	31,100 ± 300	SMU-2371	Charcoal	Ahmarian	Unpublished
A 306a	27,100 ± 410	Pta-2950	Eggshell	Ahmarian	Gilead 1984:140
EGYPT					
Tahta Area					
Shuwikhat I	24,700 ± 2500	OxTL-253	Clay	Shuwikhat	Paulissen and Vermeersch 1987:48
Nazlet Khater 1	31,650 $^{+3600}_{-2500}$	GrN-11298	Charcoal	No appellation	Vermeersch *et al.* 1982:627
Nazlet Khater 4	35,100 ± 1100	GrN-11296	Charcoal	No appellation	Vermeersch *et al.* 1982:627
Nazlet Khater 4	32,100 ± 700	GrN-11297	Charcoal	No appellation	Vermeersch *et al.* 1982:627
Nazlet Khater 4	33,100 ± 650	GrN-11299	Charcoal	No appellation	Vermeersch *et al.* 1982:627
Nazlet Khater 4	34,950 ± 600	GrN-11301	Charcoal	No appellation	Vermeersch *et al.* 1982:627
Nazlet Khater 4	30,360 ± 2310	Lv-1129	Charcoal	No appellation	Vermeersch *et al.* 1982:627

TABLE 1. (Continued)

Site, context	Date (yr BP)	Lab no.*	Material	Tradition	Reference
Nazlet Khater 4	33,280 ± 1280	Lv-1140	Charcoal	No appellation	Vermeersch *et al.* 1982:627
Nazlet Khater 4	30,980 ± 2850	Lv-1141D	Charcoal	No appellation	Vermeersch *et al.* 1982:627
Nazlet Khater 4	31,320 ± 2310	Lv-1142	Charcoal	No appellation	Vermeersch *et al.* 1982:627
Isna/Idfu Area					
E71K1	19,720 ± 180	SMU-1816	Shell	Fakhurian	Close 1988:171
E71K1	18,070 ± 330	I-3416	Shell	Fakhurian	Close 1984:20
E71K3	17,640 ± 300	I-3415	Shell	Fakhurian	Close 1984:20
E71K9	21,640 ± 1520	OxTL-161c1	TL	Shuwikhat	Close 1988:171
E71P1, Area A	18,180 ± 190	SMU-1817	Shell	Idfuan	Close 1984:20
E71P1, Area C	18,150 ± 190	SMU-1815	Shell	Kubbaniyan-like	Close 1984:20
E67K12	19,000 ± 365	SMU-365	Shell	Industry "D"	A. Close, pers. commun.
Wadi Kubbaniya					
E-81-3	18,120 ± 670	SMU-1036	Charcoal	Fakhurian	Haas 1989:276
E-81-3	18,360 ± 790	SMU-1129	Charcoal	Fakhurian	Haas 1989:276
E-81-4	20,690 ± 280	SMU-1037	Charcoal	Fakhurian	Haas 1989:276
E-81-4	18,440 ± 690	SMU-1131	Charcoal	Fakhurian	Haas 1989:276
E-82-3	19,810 ± 310	SMU-1136	Charcoal	Fakhurian	Haas 1989:276
E-81-6	18,010 ± 340	SMU-1033	Charcoal	Fakhurian	Haas 1989:276
E-81-6	19,350 ± 370	SMU-1033	Charcoal	Fakhurian	Haas 1989:276
E-81-6	17,370 ± 550	SMU-1033	Charcoal	Fakhurian	Haas 1989:276
E-81-6	19,030 ± 180	SMU-1157	Charcoal	Fakhurian	Haas 1989:276
E-78-3	18,470 ± 200	SMU-997	Charcoal	Kubbaniyan	Haas 1989:276
Layers 3-4	18,080 ± 170	SMU-994	Charcoal	Kubbaniyan	Haas 1989:276
Layers 3-4	17,450 ± 1000	AA-96	Charcoal	Kubbaniyan	Haas 1989:276
Layer 5	18,310 ± 570	SMU-1019	Charcoal	Kubbaniyan	Haas 1989:276
Layer 5	820 ± 500	AA-98	Cereal	Kubbaniyan	Haas 1989:276
Layer 5	1090 ± 50	AA-97	Cereal	Kubbaniyan	Haas 1989:276
Layer 7	18,500 ± 180	SMU-995	Date-stone	Kubbaniyan	Haas 1989:276
Layer 7	350 ± 200	OxA-101	Date-stone	Kubbaniyan	Haas 1989:276
Layer 7	101.5pMC**	OxA-102	Charcoal	Kubbaniyan	Haas 1989:276
Layer 8	17,150 ± 300	OxA-103	Charcoal	Kubbaniyan	Haas 1989:276
Layer 10	18,320 ± 150	SMU-1038	Charcoal	Kubbaniyan	Haas 1989:276
Layer 18	18,660 ± 270	SMU-1137	Charcoal	Kubbaniyan	Haas 1989:276
Layer 18/20	18,590 ± 170	SMU-1150	Charcoal	Kubbaniyan	Haas 1989:276
Layer 20	18,500 ± 220	Gd-1522	Charcoal	Kubbaniyan	Haas 1989:276
Layer 20	18,100 ± 140	AA-2028	*Cyperus*	Kubbaniyan	Haas 1989:276
Layer 20	16,960 ± 210	SMU-599	Charcoal	Kubbaniyan	Haas 1989:276
Layer 20/21	18,110 ± 160	Gd-1520	Charcoal	Kubbaniyan	Haas 1989:276
Layer 22	18,000 ± 200	AA-2029	*Cyperus*	Kubbaniyan	Haas 1989:276
Layer 22?	17,930 ± 380	SMU-596	Charcoal	Kubbaniyan	Haas 1989:276
Layer 23	18,140 ± 400	Gd-2091	Charcoal	Kubbaniyan	Haas 1989:276
Layer 24	18,470 ± 180	Gd-1610	Charcoal	Kubbaniyan	Haas 1989:276
Layer 24	17,870 ± 140	AA-2030	*Cyperus*	Kubbaniyan	Haas 1989:276
Above Layer 24	18,080 ± 350	Gd-2092	Charcoal	Kubbaniyan	Haas 1989:276
E-81-1					
Layer b	18,030 ± 300	SMU-1379	Charcoal	Kubbaniyan	Haas 1989:276
Layer b	17,490 ± 190	AA-2034	*Cyperus*	Kubbaniyan	Haas 1989:276
Layer c	17,530 ± 170	AA-2035	*Cyperus*	Kubbaniyan	Haas 1989:276
Layer c	17,750 ± 180	SMU-1035	Charcoal	Kubbaniyan	Haas 1989:276
Layer d	17,560 ± 220	AA-2036	*Cyperus*	Kubbaniyan	Haas 1989:276
Layer e	17,430 ± 280	AA-2037	*Cyperus*	Kubbaniyan	Haas 1989:276
Layer f	17,990 ± 150	AA-2038	*Scirpus*	Kubbaniyan	Haas 1989:276
Layer f	18,350 ± 290	SMU-1463	Charcoal	Kubbaniyan	Haas 1989:276

Table 1. (Continued)

Site, context	Date (yr BP)	Lab no.*	Material	Tradition	Reference
Layer f	18,130 ± 310	SMU-1380	Charcoal	Kubbaniyan	Haas 1989:276
Layer g	17,210 ± 260	AA-2039	*Cyperus*	Kubbaniyan	Haas 1989:276
E-78-2	19,100 ± 2130	SMU-1401	Charcoal	Kubbaniyan	Haas 1989:276
E-78-2	16,540 ± 1160	SMU-1400	Charcoal	Kubbaniyan	Haas 1989:276
E-78-4					
Level h	17,860 ± 320	SMU-1378	Charcoal	Kubbaniyan	Haas 1989:277
Level f	17,810 ± 150	AA-2033	*Cyperus*	Kubbaniyan	Haas 1989:277
Level f	17,620 ± 340	Gd-2093	Charcoal	Kubbaniyan	Haas 1989:277
Level e	17,640 ± 140	Gd-1612	Charcoal	Kubbaniyan	Haas 1989:277
Level 3	17,710 ± 160	SMU-1016	Charcoal	Kubbaniyan	Haas 1989:277
Level c/d	17,950 ± 225	AA-2032	*Cyperus*	Kubbaniyan	Haas 1989:277
Level c	17,870 ± 180	SMU-1018	Charcoal	Kubbaniyan	Haas 1989:277
Level c	17,800 ± 170	Gd-1611	Charcoal	Kubbaniyan	Haas 1989:277
Level b	17,740 ± 170	SMU-1017	Charcoal	Kubbaniyan	Haas 1989:277
Level b	17,300 ± 160	AA-2031	*Cyperus*	Kubbaniyan	Haas 1989:277
Level a	17,670 ± 250	SMU-616	Charcoal	Kubbaniyan	Haas 1989:277
Level a	17,380 ± 340	SMU-617	Hhumates	Kubbaniyan	Haas 1989:277
Level a	17,100 ± 540	SMU-623	Charcoal	Kubbaniyan	Haas 1989:277
Level a	19,060 ± 1000	AA-224A	Charcoal	Kubbaniyan	Haas 1989:277
Level a	18,020 ± 525	AA-224B	Charcoal	Kubbaniyan	Haas 1989:277
Level a	239 ± 5pMC**	AA-226	Cereal	Kubbaniyan	Haas 1989:277
Level a	133 ± 5pMC**	AA-227	Cereal	Kubbaniyan	Haas 1989:277
Level a	2670 ± 250	AA-225	Cereal	Kubbaniyan	Haas 1989:277
Level a	4850 ± 200	AA-228	Cereal	Kubbaniyan	Haas 1989:277
E-87-7/Tr 7	17,850 ± 200	SMU-592	Charcoal	Kubbaniyan	Haas 1989:277
Tr 8	17,130 ± 200	SMU-595	Charcoal	Kubbaniyan	Haas 1989:277
E-83-2	16,660 ± 370	SMU-1221	Charcoal	Kubbaniyan	Haas 1989:277
E-78-9	18,230 ± 200	SMU-1226	Shell	Kubbaniyan	Haas 1989:277
EGYPTIAN NUBIA					
Ballana 8859	18,650 ± 500	WSU-318	Charcoal	Halfan	Marks 1968:396
SUDANESE NUBIA					
Khor Musa 443	17,670 ± 400	SMU-576	Charcoal	Halfan	Marks 1968:396
Khor Musa 443	17,250 ± 330	SMU-576	Charcoal	Halfan	Marks 1968:396
Khor Musa 443	16,550 ± 500	WSU-201	Charcoal	Halfan	Marks 1968:396
Khor Musa 2014	19,200 ± 375	WSU-332	Charcoal	Halfan	Marks 1968:396

* OxA=Oxford Accelerator; RT=Rehovot; Hv=Hannover; SMU=Southern Methodist University; I=Teledyne Isotopes; Pta= Pretoria; Ua=Uppsala Accelerator; MC=Monaco; GrN=Groningen; B=Bern; ETH=Zürich; OxTL= Oxford; Lv=Louvain; AA=Arizona Accelerator; Gd=Gdansk/Gliwice; WSU=Washington State University
**pMC=percent modern carbon

REFERENCES CITED

Baruch, U. and S. Bottema
    1991   Palynological evidence for climatic changes in the Levant *ca.* 17,000–9000 BP. In *The Natufian Culture in the Levant*, edited by O. Bar-Yosef and F. Valla, pp. 11–20. International Monographs in Prehistory, Ann Arbor.

Bar-Yosef, O.
    1991   The archaeology of the Natufian layer at Hayonim cave. In *The Natufian Culture in the Levant*, edited by O. Bar-Yosef and F. Valla, pp. 81–92. International Monographs in Prehistory, Ann Arbor.

Bar-Yosef, O., and J. L. Phillips (editors)
    1977   *Prehistoric Investigations in Gebel Maghara, Northern Sinai.* Monographs of the Institute of Archaeology, Hebrew University, Jerusalem.

Close, A. E.
    1980   Current research and recent radiocarbon dates from northern Africa. *Journal of African History* 21:145–167.

Close, A. E.
    1984   Current research and radiocarbon dates from northern African, II. *Journal of African History* 25:1–24.
    1988   Current research and radiocarbon dates from northern Africa, III. *Journal of African History* 29:145–176.
Coinman, N.
    1990   Refiguring the Levantine Upper Paleolithic: A Comparative Examination of Lithic Assemblages From the Southern Levant. Ph.D. Dissertation, Arizona State University, Tempe.
Garrard, A. N. and H.-G. Gebel (editors)
    1988   *The Prehistory of Jordan: The State of the Research in 1986.* BAR International Series 396, British Archaeological Reports, Oxford.
Gilead, I.
    1984   Paleolithic sites in northeastern Sinai. *Paléorient* 10:135–142.
    1991   The Upper Paleolithic period in the Levant. *Journal of World Prehistory* 5 (2):105–154.
Goring-Morris, A. N.
    1987   *At the Edge: Terminal Pleistocene Hunter-Gatherers in the Negev and Sinai.* BAR International Series 361, British Archaeological Reports, Oxford.
Haas, H.
    1989   The radiocarbon dates from Wadi Kubbaniya. In *The Prehistory of Wadi Kubbaniya*, Vol. 2, *Stratigraphy, Paleoeconomy, and Environment*, edited by A. E. Close, pp. 274–279. Southern Methodist University Press, Dallas.
Hedges, R. E., R. A. Housley, I. A. Law and C. R. Bronk
    1990   Radiocarbon dates from the Oxford AMS system: Archaeometry date list 10. *Archaeometry* 32:101–108.
Hedges, R. E., R. A. Housley, C. R. Bronk and G. J. van Klinken
    1992   Radiocarbon dates from the Oxford AMS system: Archaeometry date list 14 and 15. *Archaeometry* 34 (parts 1 and 2):141–159, 337–357.
Henry, D. O. and F. Servello
    1974   Compendium of carbon-14 determinations derived from Near Eastern prehistoric sites. *Paléorient* 2:19–44.
Marks, A. E.
    1968   The Halfan industry. In *The Prehistory of Nubia*, edited by F. Wendorf, pp. 393–460. Fort Burgwin Research Center and Southern Methodist University Press, Dallas.
    1976   Ein Aqev: A Late Levantine Upper Paleolithic site in the Nahal Aqev. In *Prehistory and Paleoenvironments in the Central Negev, Israel*, Vol. I, edited by A. E. Marks, pp. 227–291. Southern Methodist University Press, Dallas.
    1977   Introduction: A preliminary overview of the central Negev prehistory. In *Prehistory and Paleoenvironments in the Central Negev, Israel*, Vol. II, edited by A. E. Marks, pp. 3–34. Southern Methodist University Press, Dallas.
    1983   The sites of Boker Tachtit and Boker: A brief introduction. In *Prehistory and Paleoenvironments in the Central Negev, Israel*, Vol. III, edited by A. E. Marks, pp. 15–37. Southern Methodist University Press, Dallas.
Mellars, P. and J. Tixier
    1989   Radiocarbon-accelerator dating of Ksar 'Aqil (Lebanon), and the chronology of the Upper Paleolithic sequence in the Near East. *Antiquity* 63 (241):761–768.
Paulissen, E. and P. M. Vermeersch
    1987   Earth, man, and climate in the Egyptian Nile Valley during the Pleistocene. In *Prehistory of North Africa: Essays in Honor of Fred Wendorf*, edited by A. E. Close, pp. 29–67. Southern Methodist University Press, Dallas.
Phillips, J. L.
    1987   Sinai during the Paleolithic: The early periods. In *Prehistory of North Africa: Essays in Honor of Fred Wendorf*, edited by A. E. Close, pp. 105–121. Southern Methodist University Press, Dallas.
    1988   The Upper Paleolithic of the Wadi Feiran, southern Sinai. *Paléorient* 14 (2):183–200.
Phillips, J. L. and B. G. Gladfelter
    1989   A survey in the upper Wadi Feiran basin, southern Sinai. *Paléorient* 15 (2):113–122.
Vermeersch, E. M., E. Paulissen, G. Gijselings, M. Otte, A. Thoma and C. Charlier
    1984   Une minière de silex et un squelette du paléolithique supérieur ancien à Nazlet Khater, Haute Egypte. *L'Anthropologie* 88:231–244.
Vermeersch, P. M., M. Otte, E. Gilot, E. Paulissen, G. Gijselings and D. Drappier
    1982   Blade technology in the Egyptian Nile Valley: Some new evidence. *Science* 216:626–628.
Wendorf, F. and R. Schild
    1989   Summary and synthesis. In *The Prehistory of Wadi Kubbaniya*, Vol. 3, *Late Paleolithic Archaeology*, edited by A. E. Close, pp. 768–824. Southern Methodist University Press, Dallas.

THE CHRONOLOGICAL BASIS AND SIGNIFICANCE OF THE LATE PALEOLITHIC AND NEOLITHIC SEQUENCE IN THE AZRAQ BASIN, JORDAN

ANDREW GARRARD[1], DOUGLAS BAIRD[2] and BRIAN F. BYRD[3]

INTRODUCTION

Prior to the 1970s, most research on the Late Paleolithic and Neolithic of the Levant was undertaken in a 100-km-wide corridor running adjacent to the eastern Mediterranean seaboard. With isolated exceptions, this was confined to regions presently lying in the moist steppe and woodland belt. More recently, researchers have become increasingly interested in the drier steppe and sub-desert regions to the south and east of the "Levantine corridor." There have been three main attractions: 1) the relatively good preservation of open sites and prehistoric land surfaces, which results from the lack of recent vegetational or agricultural disturbance and urban development; 2) the desire for greater understanding of the diversity of environments and human behavioral systems in the Levant during the Late Pleistocene and Early Holocene; 3) the wish to shed further light on the major economic, demographic and social changes of this time period, particularly, the economic intensification that eventually led to agriculture and pastoralism, the increasing sedentism and population nucleation, and the social and ideological changes reflected in increased exchange of "exotics," mortuary practices and ritual paraphernalia.

We concern ourselves here with the chronological results and significance of field research undertaken in the Azraq Basin of central-northern Jordan (Fig. 1), largely between 1982 and 1989. The present environment of this region has been described previously (Nelson 1973; Garrard *et al.* 1988a). In brief, the Basin covers *ca.* 12,000 km^2 of the Jordanian plateau. Elevations vary from *ca.* 500 m, at its center, to 1800 m in the Jebel Druze region to the north, to 600–900 m along its other boundaries. Surface lithology consists of basalts in the north and flint-rich limestone, chalks and marls to the south. The mean annual rainfall, limited to the winter, ranges from 200 mm in the northwest to less than 50 mm in the southeast (Fig. 1). Considerable variation in annual rainfall has been recorded. Reliable "dry" cultivation can be practiced only where annual rainfall regularly exceeds 200 mm. At present, irrigation cultivation is limited to the Azraq oases at the center of the Basin. Elsewhere in the region, attempts are occasionally made at "opportunistic" cultivation in seasonally moist alluvial areas, but the products are usually for animal grazing rather than human consumption. Presently, most of the area is used only for goat, sheep and camel pastoralism.

Field research for the Azraq Project has focused on three areas: the Azraq oases at the center of the Basin, a section of Wadi el-Uwaynid, which lies 10 km to the west of Azraq, and Wadi el-Jilat, which lies in a steppe-desert transition area (presently receiving *ca.* 100 mm annual precipitation) 55 km to the southwest (Fig. 1). More than 100 prehistoric sites were found during survey, and soundings and excavations of various scales were undertaken at 21 localities, 18 of which are demonstrably late Upper Paleolithic, Epipaleolithic or Neolithic. Because the region is largely virgin territory, we are very reliant on radiocarbon (^{14}C) dates for our basic chronology. Many Late Paleolithic and some Neolithic chipped stone assemblages obtained during survey and excavations differ from those described from better known areas of the Levant. These could not be dated reliably by relative techniques. We obtained 41 ^{14}C dates from 13 Late Paleolithic and Neolithic sites

[1]Institute of Archaeology, University College London, 31–34 Gordon Square, London WC1H 0PY, England
[2]Department of Archaeology, University of Edinburgh, 16–20 George Square, Edinburgh EH8 9JZ, Scotland
[3]Brian F. Mooney Associates, 9903-B Businesspark Avenue, San Diego, California 92131 USA

Late Quaternary Chronology and Paleoclimates of the Eastern Mediterranean
Edited by O. Bar-Yosef and R. S. Kra. RADIOCARBON 1994, pp. 177–199

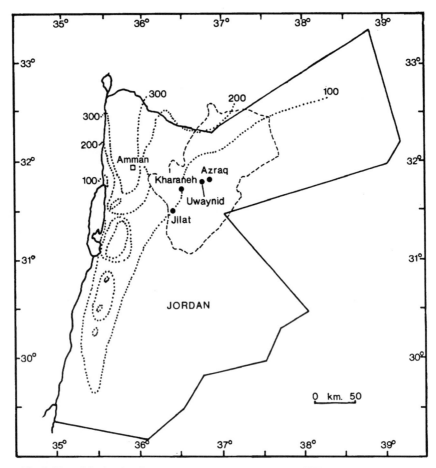

Fig. 1. Map of Jordan showing present rainfall in mm per annum [·····], Azraq drainage basin [⌐˙⌐], and sites and survey areas described in text

in the region (Figs. 2, 3). Given that large charcoal samples were rare at many of the localities, all but one of these samples was dated using accelerator mass spectrometry (AMS). Samples were dated at the NSF-Arizona Radioisotope Accelerator Facility (AA) at The University of Arizona and the Radiocarbon Accelerator Unit (OxA) at Oxford University.

Virtually all the dated samples were collected *in situ,* and, in most cases, their chronological order corresponds to the stratigraphic sequence. However, at Jilat 6, 7 and 8, we observed reversals in which early contexts yielded young dates (for details, see compendium below). There are four possible reasons for this: 1) contamination of the samples by more recent carbon; 2) physical penetration of the sample material downward through the sedimentary column; 3) statistical anomalies; and 4) inaccuracies in the dating procedure. The first, third and fourth reasons are difficult to demonstrate, but the second is a logical possibility for samples <3 mm in diameter. Root systems, worms, burrowing insects, rodents and fissures resulting from soil desiccation can all contribute to an unexpected result. Surprisingly, the anomalous dates obtained from Jilat 6, 7 and 8 were all much younger than the cultural material found during systematic surface survey or excavation. If a physical process was the reason for the anomaly, we assume that the samples derive from small-scale, localized human activities that were not detected during fieldwork, or perhaps from charcoal

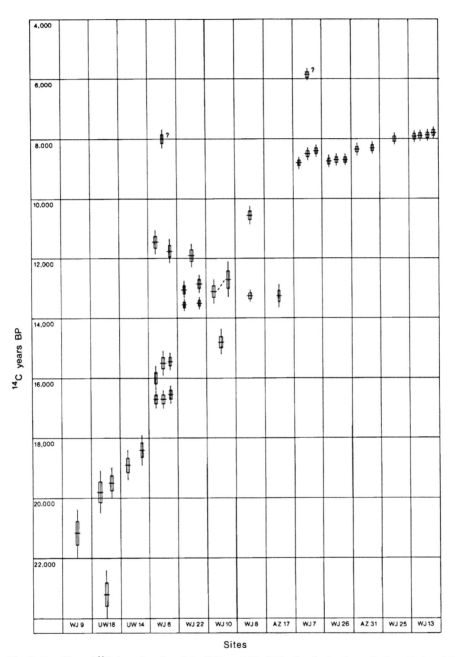

Fig. 2. Uncalibrated ^{14}C dates from late Paleolithic and Neolithic sites in the Azraq Basin, with 1 and 2 σ error bars. WJ = Wadi Jilat; UW = Uwaynid; AZ = Azraq. Neolithic dates are also shown in Fig. 3.

derived from natural "bush" fires. In some instances, we also found older residual charcoal in younger cultural contexts (*e.g.*, Azraq 31).

A general commentary follows on the significance of the dates to our knowledge of Levantine paleoenvironments, settlement patterns, and developments in technology and subsistence strategies. A compendium at the end of this paper begins with notes on each of the Upper Paleolithic, Epi-

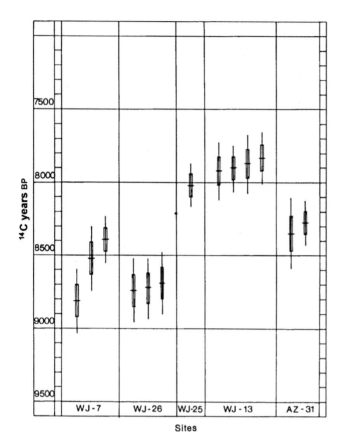

Fig. 3. Uncalibrated ^{14}C dates from Neolithic sites in the Azraq Basin, with 1 and 2 σ error bars. These dates are also shown in Fig. 2.

paleolithic and Neolithic sites that were tested or partially excavated during the Azraq Project. The sites from the three study areas, Wadi el-Jilat, Wadi el-Uwaynid and Azraq, are listed in the compendium in approximately chronological order (see Figs. 2, 3), according to the following format:

Name, previous names, UTM grid reference

1. Cultural period, context or location
2. Surface exposure and surface area
3. Date of surface survey
4. Date and area of soundings and excavations
5. Bibliographic references; in addition to the cited literature, see Wright (1991, 1993) on ground-stone assemblages, Reese (1991) on marine shells and Colledge (1991) on plant remains.

Contents of Sounding

6. Sedimentological context of occupations, nature of structural remains
7. Chipped stone industry
8. Other utilized stone, bone, shell
9. Faunal remains
10. Floral remains
11. Burials
12. Uncalibrated ^{14}C dates (lab no., sample no., material, date) reported in years before present (BP), with comments.

THE PALEOENVIRONMENTAL SEQUENCE

Geomorphological and Sedimentary Contexts of Sites

A study of the geomorphological and sedimentary context of the sites in Wadi el-Jilat, Wadi el-Uwaynid and Azraq is being undertaken by Christopher Hunt (see Garrard *et al.* 1988b for further information).

Wadi el-Jilat

Wadi el-Jilat is a tributary of the Wadi ed-Dabi (Dhobai), which drains through the southwestern sector of the Azraq Basin (Fig. 1) and cuts through a transitional zone between steppe and desert. The area presently receives 100 mm mean annual rainfall. Perennial grasses and other vegetation secure unconsolidated sediments in the western portion of the Jilat drainage, but the eastern end is actively deflating. Geomorphological and archaeological field research was undertaken in a 10-km stretch, cross-cutting that boundary. A series of aggradational units were identified in the valley floor, each consisting of deposits from various sources (fluvial, colluvial and eolian). These had been subjected to post-depositional changes and cycles of erosion. The late Upper Paleolithic site of Jilat 9, which was dated to 21,150 ± 400 BP (the earliest of the Jilat sites under consideration), was found eroding from the upper levels of a low-energy fluvial deposit (aggradation unit B). This may have accumulated during a drying-out phase, when soil erosion was more intense in the valley. Besançon, Geyer and Sanlaville (1989) suggested that wadi aggradation in the Azraq Basin was greatest during "catapluvial" phases.

With one notable exception, the Epipaleolithic occupations (*ca.* 20,000–12,000 BP) in the valley were contained in loessic silts that overlie an earlier lithified aggradation complex (D). The upper settlement horizon at Jilat 6, dated between 16,700 ± 140 and 15,470 ± 130 BP, overlies a 1.7-m-thick deposit of eolian silts. The occupational horizon at Jilat 10, dated between 14,790 ± 200 and 12,700 ± 300 BP, was found eroding from the uppermost levels of a 2.5+ m-thick accumulation, and the occupational horizons at Jilat 8, dated to 13,310 ± 120 BP, were contained within 0.5 m of loess. Eolian silts are not collecting in the valley floor at the present time, for two possible reasons: 1) a large-scale reduction in sediment supply relative to the period following the cold, dry Last Glacial Maximum (for a discussion of general conditions in the southern Levant at this time, see Bar-Yosef (1990) and Baruch and Bottema (1991)); 2) there is very little vegetation to anchor wind-blown silts (*cf.* Yaalon and Dan 1974). Apart from climate changes, 8000 yr of pastoralism has undoubtedly greatly reduced vegetation density in the region. Goldberg (1986) has noted a similar reduction in loess accumulation in the central and northern Negev.

Pedogenic horizons in the loess units show the development of blocky or prismatic soil structures as a result of clay illuviation. This probably occurred during non-depositional periods when vegetation became established over the silt surfaces. Striking evidence of pedogenic activity under what was probably a damper regime than the present extended down from the surface of the basal occupation at Jilat 6, thought to date to *ca.* 19,000–20,000 BP. The lower and middle occupational phases of Jilat 22, dated between 13,540 ± 120 and 12,840 ± 140 BP, are embedded in indurated marsh sediments containing *Phragmites* stems and rhizomes in growth position. Presumably, the site was occupied during the dry season or periods of drought. At present, there are no springs in the valley and the only surface water is that which becomes temporarily trapped in potholes after winter storms. The paleomarsh deposits suggest either local spring activity or damming of the valley. Interestingly, the 14th–13th millennium BP is a period when wet conditions occurred in northern Sinai and the Negev (Goldberg 1986), the Lisan Basin (Begin *et al.* 1985) and the Hulah Valley (Baruch and Bottema 1991). With the exception of Jilat 32, located on a hillside in colluvium, all the Neolithic sites that we studied (Jilat 7, 13, 23, 24, 25, 26) are contained in shallow silts overlying the older lithified aggradation unit D. It is hoped that laboratory analysis of these sediments will provide more information on the environment of deposition.

Wadi el-Uwaynid

Wadi el-Uwaynid is a major section of one of the principal drainage systems discharging through the western sector of the Basin. The study area lies at the margins of a basalt outlier, 10 km west of Azraq and 50 km northeast of Jilat. The two sites that have been sounded lie *ca.* 110 m apart. Occupation at Uwaynid 18 dated between 23,200 ± 400 and 19,500 ± 250 BP; at Uwaynid 14, between *ca.* 20,000 and 18,400 ± 250 BP. The cultural horizons at Uwaynid 18 are contained in eolian silts which have undergone pedogenesis; those at Uwaynid 14 are more clayey, and gleying suggests a relatively high water table. The sites lie close to a spring, which may be of some antiquity. Following occupation, more eolian and fluvial silts and sands covered the sites and calcretes formed in the surface horizons. Calichification is suggestive of a regime of higher rainfall or higher water table than at present, but with strong seasonal drought (Chapman 1974; Sakaguchi 1987).

Azraq

Several areas were surveyed around the Azraq oases, but soundings were restricted to three Epipaleolithic and Neolithic sites lying on the southern side of the marshes at Azraq esh-Shishan. In each case, the archaeological deposits lie in eolian silts, but at Azraq 17 Trench 2, dated to 13,260 ± 200 BP, they extend into indurated marsh deposits containing *Phragmites* in growth position.

Summary

The geomorphological and sedimentary context of the Azraq Basin sites indicates that loess accumulated in the western drainage systems between 20,000 and 13,000 BP, probably continuing on a smaller scale until the Neolithic. Evidence of wetter events or locally higher water tables was found in sediments of *ca.* 20,000–19,000 BP at Jilat 6 and Uwaynid 18, of *ca.* 13,500–12,800 BP at Jilat 22 and of Terminal Pleistocene or Early Holocene date in the Wadi el-Uwaynid. Comparisons are made with the regional evidence.

Faunal Remains

Faunal remains were retrieved from most of the late Upper Paleolithic, Epipaleolithic and Neolithic Azraq Basin sites. Andrew Garrard and Rebecca Montague (Garrard *et al.* 1988b) analyzed material recovered before 1985, and Louise Martin studied more recent material (Baird *et al.* 1992; Garrard *et al.* 1994). The assemblages from Jilat and Uwaynid are characteristic of steppe and subdesert environments, whereas those from the vicinity of the Azraq oases also contain features indicative of nearby springs and tracts of marshland. The most common species represented at the sites antedating 8000 BP are *Gazella* sp., *Equus* sp., *Lepus capensis* and *Testudo* sp. *Bos primigenius* was important locally in the vicinity of Azraq. Post-8000 BP, *Capra* sp. and *Ovis* sp. are common. Because they are exceedingly scarce in collections antedating 8500 BP and rare in the period 8500–8000 BP (see section below on Transitions to Cultivation and Pastoralism), this dramatic change is thought to relate to the introduction of domestic livestock.

The majority of the gazelle bones could not be identified by species, but horn cores from the early Epipaleolithic site of Uwaynid 18 were identified as *Gazella subgutturosa*, which was common until recently throughout the Syrian and Arabian steppe and desert (Harrison 1968). Both *Equus hemionus/asinus* and *Equus hydruntinus* were identified from dental remains (based on criteria in Davis (1980)). The latter was represented by two mandibular tooth rows at the Natufian site of

Azraq 18. This represents the latest recorded occurrence of this species in the Levant (Uerpmann 1987). A single first phalanx of *Camelus dromedarius* was found in a secure context at Uwaynid 18. Apart from a phalanx from the early Epipaleolithic site of Madamagh, in southwestern Jordan, this is the only camel bone known from an Epipaleolithic context in the Levant (Uerpmann 1987). Other species from the sites included *Canis lupus, Vulpes* sp., *Felis* sp, *Sus scrofa* and a range of birds including *Struthio camelus* (ostrich).

The scarcity of caprine (sheep and goat) bones in contexts antedating 8500 BP is surprising. Only three bones were attributable to this group from more than 10,000 identified from this time range (Baird *et al.* 1992). Wild sheep were identified from the Late Pleistocene of the central Negev (Butler *et al.* 1977) and the Ras en-Naqb area of southern Jordan (Henry *et al.* 1985). One might have expected sheep and goat to be at home in the steppelands of the limestone-chalk region of the Azraq Basin. The absence of wild goat or ibex in the study areas is not so surprising, as these animals prefer the sanctuary of cliffs in more craggy terrain (Schaller 1977). Ibex bones were found in the Late Natufian site of Khallat Anaza in craggy basalt in the northernmost part of the Basin (Garrard 1985).

Botanical Remains

Samples were collected from each site for pollen analysis, but pollen grains proved scarce and poorly preserved. Extensive soil flotation has yielded small quantities of carbonized seeds, as well as woody and parenchymatous tissue. Susan Colledge is presently studying this material. The botanical material from the upper phase of Jilat 6, dated from 16,700 ± 140 to 15,470 ± 130 BP, was described briefly (Garrard *et al.* 1988b). Unfortunately, the seed remains can be identified only to family or genus level, which is insufficient for detailed environmental reconstruction. The majority of the seeds derive from chenopods, which are a widespread element in the present steppe and subdesert flora. Plant remains were found at several of the Neolithic sites. Most identifiable seeds came from Early and Middle PPNB occupations at Jilat 7 (*ca.* 9500–8400 BP) and from early Late Neolithic levels at Jilat 13 (7920 ± 100 to 7830 ± 90 BP). The species found include wild and domestic barley and einkorn, domestic emmer, lentil, pistachio and fig (Garrard *et al.* 1994).

At present, wild barley and einkorn do not grow in the Jilat region, and the nearest regular cultivation of domestic cereals is practiced around the Hammam villages *ca.* 35 km northwest of Jilat. "Opportunistic" cultivation of barley is attempted occasionally in seasonally moist valley floors between Jilat and Hammam, but the barley often remains unharvested and is suited only for animal grazing. Currently, there are no springs in the Jilat valley that would allow irrigation cultivation, and the wadi is entrenched in the vicinity of the sites. Both grain and chaff remains (*e.g.*, glumes, rachis fragments) were found in the archaeological samples, which indicates that final processing of Neolithic cereals was done locally. However, their presence does not necessarily mean that they were grown locally; it is possible that they were imported from areas to the west and that the wild-type cereals were weeds of cultivation.

SETTLEMENT PATTERNS

When fewer ^{14}C dates were available, Garrard (1991) speculated that there may have been three peaks in settlement in the Azraq Basin. He suggested that these occurred from 22,000–18,000, 14,000–12,000 and 9500–7000 BP. However, newly acquired dates force a revision of this hypothesis. Examination of the ^{14}C dates, supported by further analysis of survey and excavation data, suggests more continuous use of the western and central Azraq Basin through the Late Pleistocene and Early Holocene (Fig. 2). However, a closer look at these data reveals gaps in our knowledge; for example, no settlement has been found that dates to the mid- to late 11th and early 10th millennia BP, contemporary with the Harifian, Khiamian and PPNA. By contrast, in the Negev and northern Sinai, where far more extensive survey and excavation have been undertaken, settlement seems to peak in the mid-11th millennium or Harifian (Goring-Morris 1989).

Late Upper Paleolithic and Epipaleolithic Settlement

A distinctive feature of survey on the Jordanian plateau has been the finding of extensive, partially deflated sites dating to the mid-Epipaleolithic. The largest of these are Jilat 6 and Kharaneh 4 (Garrard *et al.* 1985; Garrard, Byrd and Betts 1986; Garrard and Byrd 1992; Muheisen 1985, 1988). These sites lie 25 km apart in parallel drainages running through the western sector of the Basin (Fig. 1). Both have dense surface canopies of artifacts of over *ca.* 2 ha. Whereas the upper *in-situ* levels of Jilat 6 were dated between 16,700 ± 140 and 15,470 ± 130 BP, the upper phase (D) at Kharaneh 4 was recently ^{14}C-dated between 15,700 and 15,200 BP (Muheisen, personal communication). Considerable surface spread of artifacts may derive from what were formerly smaller-scale overlapping occupations. However, systematic surface survey of the western half of the main concentration at Jilat 6 shows that the deflated material has much in common technologically with the assemblage in the upper excavated horizon. This suggests that the material derives from groups with a broadly similar lithic tradition. The small sounding at Jilat 6 revealed two ocher-pigmented surfaces, and what is considered an artifical silt floor (Phase A, Loci 6, 8, 10 in Fig. 4), whereas the limited excavations at Kharaneh 4 exposed a semicircle of postholes and two burials (Muheisen 1985, 1988).

Jilat 6 and Kharaneh 4 are remarkable in demonstrating the repeated use of highly specific open-air localities during extended periods of the late glacial. These two sites are also unusual for this period in that they contain structural and mortuary remains (*cf.* Bar-Yosef and Belfer-Cohen 1989). The reason for repeated occupation is unclear. One possibility is that they lie close to active springs in an otherwise arid area. If this is the case, the sites may have served as seasonal aggregation centers. We found sedimentary and fossil evidence for a marsh environment at the nearby site of Jilat 22, in levels from 13,540 ± 120 to 12,840 ± 140 BP, but this is substantially later than the upper excavated phase at Jilat 6. Other explanations for repeated occupation may be that the sites were used for caching supplies or had social or territorial significance (Garrard and Byrd 1992).

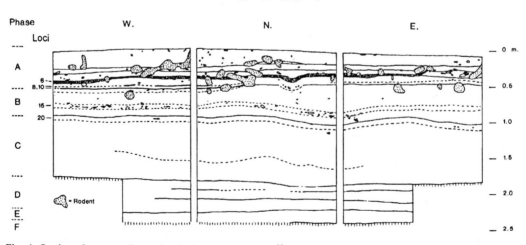

Fig. 4. Sections from sounding at Wadi Jilat 6. Phase A: 6 ^{14}C dates: 16,700–15,470 BP; Phase B.15: 2 ^{14}C dates: 11,740–11,450 BP; Phase C.20: 1 ^{14}C date: 7980 BP

Neolithic Settlement

Pre-Pottery and early Late Neolithic settlements in the Azraq Basin are much smaller than many contemporary sites in the presently moist steppe and Mediterranean woodland habitats. In terms of surface scatter, the largest Neolithic site is Jilat 26, at 0.78 ha². By contrast, contemporaneous occupation at 'Ain Ghazel (*ca.* 8700 BP) is thought to have covered 4.5 ha, and late PPNC 'Ain Ghazel (*ca.* 7700 BP) 12.5 ha (Rollefson and Kohler-Rollefson 1989). Structural remains at Neolithic sites in the Azraq Basin are also flimsier and suggest seasonal use (Garrard *et al.* 1994). PPNB dwellings in Wadi el-Jilat (Jilat 7, 26, 32) are typically curvilinear (rarely rectilinear) and semi-subterranean, and had substructures built from upright slabs of stone. The internal diameter was usually *ca.* 3–3.5m, although some were smaller. The dwellings frequently had internal hearths and partitions constructed from upright slabs or coursed stones. Superstructures are thought to have been made from organic materials that could have been removed for re-use elsewhere. The early Late Neolithic structures (Jilat 13, 25 and Azraq 31) are similar, but larger. The oval structure at Jilat 25 had internal dimensions of 7 × 4.5 m, and that at Jilat 13, 10 × 6 m. As Garrard *et al.* (1994) suggest, this could mean larger co-resident groups (required by the integration of herd husbandry with traditional activities pursued in the steppe), or that the structures housed both humans and domestic animals.

CHIPPED STONE TECHNOLOGY

Late Upper Paleolithic and Epipaleolithic Technology

Chipped stone assemblages from the Late Upper Paleolithic and Epipaleolithic sites in the Azraq Basin were described previously (Garrard, Byrd and Betts 1986; Garrard *et al.* 1987; Byrd 1988; Byrd and Garrard 1990; Garrard and Byrd 1992). Blade and bladelet cores predominate at all the sites. Single-platform forms are most common (38%–78% of total cores); opposed-platform types occur in moderate proportions (13%–42% of total cores). Flake cores occur in low to moderate proportions (0%–21% of total cores), being most prevalent at the latest occupations (the upper phase of Jilat 22—11,920 ± 180 BP—and Natufian Azraq 18). Core sizes from occupation horizons reflect the predominant blanks that were removed. Thus, very small bladelet cores were dominant during the lower phase of Uwaynid 14, whereas both small bladelet and massive blade cores were retrieved from the middle phase of Jilat 10 and Jilat 22.

Blades and bladelets provided blanks for most of the retouched tools. Flake tools did not account for more than 4% of retouched tool assemblages. Bladelets were more commonly used than blades, except at:

1. Late Upper Paleolithic Jilat 9: 21,150 ± 400 BP (5% bladelet tools)
2. Jilat 10: 14,790 ± 200 to 12,700 ± 300 BP (17% bladelet tools)
3. Jilat 22 middle phase: 13,040 ± 180 to 12,840 ± 140 BP (7% bladelet tools).

Jilat 10 and 22 are very unusual for the time period, as they contain many blade tools (Byrd 1988; Garrard and Byrd 1992).

The microburin technique appears to have been in common usage in the Azraq Basin from *ca.* 20,000 BP (Byrd 1988). The adjusted microburin index (Marks and Larson 1977) from the upper phase of Uwaynid 18, dated between 19,800 ± 350 and 19,500 ± 250 BP, was 41.51. The index continued at levels between 20.77 and 61.86, except at:

1. Jilat 10: 14,790 ± 200 to 12,700 ± 300 BP (microburins absent)
2. Azraq 17, Trench 2: 13,260 ± 200 BP (microburins very rare)
3. Azraq 18: Natufian (microburins rare).

The most common forms of retouched blade tools were end scrapers, notches/denticulates, burins and non-standardized retouched pieces. At Jilat 22, middle phase (13,040 ± 180 to 12,840 ± 140), a form known as Jilat knives accounted for 51% of the total retouched tools. This tool has a pronounced tang at one end, and is obliquely truncated into a point at the other end. A use wear study by Mark Becker showed that Jilat knives were hafted and probably used as knives rather than projectile points (Garrard and Byrd 1992). No other sites investigated in the Azraq Basin or, indeed, in the Near East, are known to have produced this tool.

Temporal trends in the retouched bladelet tool category from the Azraq Basin sites:

1. 21,150 ± 400 BP: Jilat 9 contained a small number of backed bladelet fragments.
2. 19,800 ± 350 to ? 18,400 ± 250 BP: Uwaynid 18, upper phase; Uwaynid 14, middle phase; Jilat 6, lower phase: mainly narrow, finely made, curved, pointed, arched-backed pieces.
3. 18,900 ± 250 to ? 18,400 ± 250 BP: Uwaynid 14, upper phase; Jilat 6, middle phase: mainly la Mouillah points and double truncated backed bladelets made on large robust bladelets.
4. 16,700 ± 140 to 15,470 ± 130 BP: Jilat 6, upper phase: mainly small asymmetric and symmetric triangles plus microgravette points.
5. 14,790 ± 200 to 12,700 ± 300 BP: Jilat 10, Azraq 17, Trench 2: thin bladelets with marginal retouch. This form is unusual for the time range; however, 3 ^{14}C dates were obtained from Jilat 10 and 1 from Azraq 17, Trench 2. Byrd (1988) and Byrd and Garrard (1990) argued that the date from the latter may be anomalous, and that the assemblage may date to the late Upper Paleolithic.
6. 13,310 ± 120 to 11,920 ± 180 BP: Jilat 8, Jilat 22, upper phase: mixture of trapezes, rectangles, lunates, triangles.
7. ? 11,500–11,000 BP: Azraq 18: mainly lunates retouched by helwan, bipolar and abrupt techniques, plus retouched bladelets.

Neolithic Technology

The site compendium contains details of the chipped stone assemblages from the Neolithic sites sounded or excavated during the Project: 1) main core reduction strategies; 2) predominant blank and debitage types; 3) use of exotic raw materials; 4) point types; and 5) other characteristic retouched tool types. For further information see Baird *et al.* (1992) and Garrard *et al.* (1994). Generally, production technology shows considerable continuity from Early PPNB until the early Late Neolithic. For example, opposed platform reduction strategies that included the production of naviform cores, and a tabular flint-adapted reduction strategy that also produced naviform cores (Nissen, Muheisen and Gebel 1987) are important from the PPNB to the early Late Neolithic. Associated with this is the relative importance of blades and bladelets in the tool blank and debitage categories.

Several temporal trends should be noted. The Early PPNB is distinguished by the proportion of exotic material used, the importance of bladelet blanks and debitage, and change-of-orientation reduction strategies, as opposed to platform methods. The Jilat 25 assemblage attests to a change in technology in the early Late Neolithic. This involves a shift away from opposed platform techniques and the abandonment of naviform methods, which maximized blade and bladelet production, to single platform and change-of-orientation strategies, maximizing flake production. As evidence from Azraq 31 and Jilat 13 illustrate, this process was not straightforward.

We also observe considerable continuity in the character of some tool assemblages from Middle PPNB to Late Neolithic. Assemblages with relatively high proportions of truncation burins, drill bits on burin spalls and bifacials occur in the Middle PPNB at Jilat 26, and in the later Middle or

Late PPNB phase in Jilat 7. These seem to become particularly frequent assemblage types during the Late Neolithic in the steppe (Betts 1987). There is also continuity in point types between the PPNB and earliest Late Neolithic. The earliest Late Neolithic levels at Jilat 13 contain significant proportions of Amuq as well as some Byblos points. At this site, there is also a very clear sequence in the appearance of Late Neolithic point types. The earliest types are Nizzanim and Herziliya points, the former being particularly common. Low proportions of Haparsah points and Transverse arrowheads appear later in the sequence. The ^{14}C dates demonstrate that these developments occurred relatively rapidly in the first half of the 8th millenium BP. At this stage, the early appearance of Transverse arrowheads must be accepted with caution.

The evidence provided by absolute dating documents the interassemblage variability on coeval sites in the steppe and desert areas during the 9th to 8th millenium BP. Thus, while a "burin site" type assemblage is present at Middle PPNB Jilat 26 and in the latest PPNB phases at Jilat 7, the assemblages at contemporary and/or later Middle PPNB Jilat 7, Middle or Late PPNB Jilat 32 and Late PPNB Azraq 31 are far removed from the "burin site" type. The same phenomenon occurs in relation to the technology in the early Late Neolithic. At early phase Jilat 13 and probably Azraq 31, production strategies are similar to those of the PPNB. At coeval Jilat 25, manufacturing techniques are substantially different. In this case, at least, if one takes into account the possibility of two standard deviations' variance in dates, chronological development may be a significant factor.

TRANSITIONS TO CULTIVATION AND PASTORALISM

One objective of the Azraq Basin has been to determine the involvement of the populations of the oasis and steppe environments of the east Jordanian plateau in early Near Eastern cultivation and pastoralism. In particular, we have attempted to determine: 1) whether domestication occurred locally, or whether the first cultivars and domestic livestock were introduced from elsewhere (see Wright 1971; Hole 1984); and 2) some of the factors behind the first use of domesticates in this region (see Kohler-Rollefson 1988; Rollefson and Kohler-Rollefson 1989).

Cultivation

Susan Colledge is studying the plant remains from the Azraq Basin sites and has identified domestic einkorn and barley from the Early PPNB levels at Jilat 7 (Garrard *et al.* 1994). From the associated lithic assemblage, this seems likely to date to the second half of the 10th millennium BP. Both chaff (rachis and glume fragments) and grain were found, indicating that final processing prior to consumption was done locally. We cannot yet demonstrate that cultivation was practiced locally, but further analysis of associated plant remains should help clarify this possibility. The overlying Middle PPNB levels at Jilat 7 contain domestic einkorn and barley, and also lentil and domestic emmer. All four species have also been found in the early Late Neolithic levels at Jilat 13, dating to the early 8th millennium BP.

Although controversy still exists over the antiquity of the earliest morphologically domestic cereals in the Near East (Kislev 1989), researchers generally agree that cereals were being cultivated in the Damascus Basin and the Jordan Valley by the early to mid-10th millennium BP (Zohary and Hopf 1988; Hillman and Davies 1990). Unfortunately, no sites have been found in the Azraq Basin from this time period; thus, we are unable to determine whether cultivars appeared before the Early PPNB, or whether the progenitors of domestic cereals grew locally. The only earlier seed assemblage from this locality is from the upper phase at Jilat 6, which antedates the early phase at Jilat 7 by at least six millennia. Remains from this phase yielded no progenitors of the later domesticates (Garrard *et al.* 1988b).

Pastoralism

Louise Martin is studying the Neolithic faunal remains from the Azraq Basin sites, and has demonstrated that caprine (sheep and goat) bones are extremely rare in contexts antedating the mid-9th millennium BP (only 3 caprine bones were identified amongst >10,000 bones; see Baird *et al.* 1992). Levels dating to the first half of the 9th millennium BP at Jilat 7 contained no caprine bones. By contrast, abundant sheep and goat bones have been found in early Late Neolithic contexts dating to the terminal 9th or early 8th millennium BP. These bones are abundant at Jilat 25, dating to 8020 ± 80 BP, also in levels dating to 7920 ± 100 and 7900 ± 80 BP at Jilat 13, and in broadly contemporaneous levels at Azraq 31 (Baird *et al.* 1992; Garrard *et al.* 1994).

We are less clear about the exploitation of caprines between the mid- and terminal 9th millennium BP. It is possible that the settlement at Jilat 7 continued into this period, as a date of 8390 ± 80 BP was obtained on a charcoal sample from the site. However, this sample was from an Early PPNB context, where it would have been intrusive. Whether or not this is the case, no caprine bones were found at Jilat 7. At Azraq 31, levels dating to 8350 ± 120 BP contained 2 caprine bones amongst a sample of 56. A similar proportion was found in contemporary levels that may be contaminated (8 bones amongst 260: Baird *et al.* 1992). Therefore, it is possible that herded sheep and goats were present in the steppe during the second half of the 9th millennium BP, but more excavations and larger sample sizes are needed for clarification.

Much controversy still surrounds the beginning of close herding and selective breeding of livestock in the Near East (Horwitz 1989). Helmer (1988, 1989) believes he can demonstrate size changes in goats by the end of the 10th millennium BP and in sheep by the middle of the 9th millennium BP. Kohler-Rollefson, Gillespie and Metzger (1988:424–425) noted increased deformities in foot bones of goats from early 9th millennium BP 'Ain Ghazel, Jordan, which they believe resulted from "unsuitable husbanding conditions as well as human protection from predators". At Tell Abu Hureyra, on the Middle Euphrates in northern Syria, Legge and Rowley-Conwy (1987) record a marked increase in caprines at *ca.* 8300 BP.

The extreme scarcity of caprine bones in mid-9th millennium BP levels in the Azraq Basin sites makes it unlikely that caprines were domesticated locally in the limestone steppe. They were probably introduced from the west. Kohler-Rollefson (1988) and Rollefson and Kohler-Rollefson (1989) suggested that pastoralism in the Jordanian steppe may have developed in response to the deterioration of environments around PPNB farming villages in more fertile habitats to the west. The authors hypothesize that this was caused by overgrazing and/or browsing, cultivation methods and woodland clearance. We are unable to determine, with certainty, whether the Azraq Basin sites were occupied by herders from communities to the west, or whether the groups exploiting this region were indigenous. However, there are many elements of continuity in architectural and lithic traditions between the PPNB and early Late Neolithic in the steppe (Garrard *et al.* 1994).

COMPENDIUM OF UPPER PALEOLITHIC, EPIPALEOLITHIC AND NEOLITHIC SITES OF THE AZRAQ PROJECT, WITH RADIOCARBON DATES

Late Paleolithic Sites

JILAT 9 (2.509 E × 34.863 N)

1. Late Upper Paleolithic site eroding from fluvial terrace of Wadi Jilat.
2. Surface deflated; artifacts spread over 6750 m².
3. Systematic surface survey 1982.
4. Two 4-m² soundings excavated in 1984.
5. Refs: Garrard *et al.* (1985:11–13, 1986:7–9, 1988b:46–47); Byrd (1988).
6. Upper stratigraphy of Trench 1 comprises 55–60 cm of fluvially deposited silts with lenses of fine sand. Subsequently altered by pedogenesis. Artifacts and bones in upper 25 cm.
7. Retouched chipped stone tools: 5% are microliths, mainly fragments of backed bladelets. Only 1 microburin found. Non-microlithic tools (mainly on blades), principally end-scrapers, non-standardized retouched pieces and notches/denticulates.
9. Faunal remains predominantly from *Testudo*. Also some *Equus, Gazella* and *Lepus* bones.
12. One AMS date from base of cultural horizon:
OxA-519. WJ9/1/2a Burned bone **21,150 ± 400**

UWAYNID 18 (2.849 E × 35.188 N)

1. Late Upper Paleolithic and Early Epipaleolithic site with two superimposed phases of occupation. In eolian silts in terrace of Wadi Uwaynid.
2. Eroding from terrace. Thought to have covered *ca.* 875 m².
3. Systematic surface survey 1984.
4. Two soundings (10 m² total) excavated 1985.
5. Refs: Garrard *et al.* (1987:9–15, 1988b:46–47); Byrd (1988).

Upper Occupational Phase

6. 15 cm of dense occupational material in eolian silts. These subsequently underwent pedogenesis, developing a blocky structure, and were later subjected to considerable carbonate induration.
7. Retouched chipped stone tools: 89% are microliths, mainly narrow, finely made, curved, pointed, arched-backed pieces (*cf.* Uwaynid 14 middle occupational phase, Jilat 6 lower occupational phase). Adjusted microburin index is 41.51 (Marks and Larson 1977).
8. Two basalt handstones and two irregular pestle fragments. *Dentalium* beads.
9. Faunal remains, predominantly *Gazella, Equus* and *Testudo*.

12. Two AMS dates:
OxA-864. UW18.5.15b Wood charcoal **19,800 ± 350**
OxA-868. UW18.1.3k Wood charcoal **19,500 ± 250**
Lower Occupational Phase

6. Hearth containing burned basalt pebbles; in eolian silts *ca.* 45 cm below upper occupational phase.
7. Chipped stone assemblage sparse.
12. One AMS date:
OxA-867. UW18.9.19a Wood charcoal **23,200 ± 400**

UWAYNID 14 (2.851 E × 35.187 N)

1. Early Epipaleolithic site with three superimposed phases of occupation. In clayey silts in terrace of Wadi Uwaynid.
2. Eroding from terrace. Original extent uncertain.
3. Systematic surface survey 1984.
4. Two soundings (10 m² total) excavated 1985.
5. Refs: Garrard *et al.* (1985:15, 1987:8–15, 1988b:46–47); Byrd (1988).

Upper Occupational Phase

6. Thin horizon (2 cm) of artifacts and bones with hearth. In clayey silts that have undergone gleying, suggestive of high water table and marshy conditions.
7. Retouched chipped stone tools: 86% are microliths, mainly la Mouillah points and double truncated backed bladelets. Made on larger bladelet blanks than those used in middle phase (*cf.* middle occupational phase Jilat 6). Adjusted microburin index is 39.30.
9. Sparse faunal remains.
12. One AMS date:
OxA-865. UW14.10.15 Wood charcoal **18,900 ± 250**
Middle Occupational Phase

6. Thin scatter (2 cm) of artifacts, bone and charcoal in clayey silts; 15–20 cm below upper occupational phase. For sedimentary context, see above.
7. Retouched chipped stone tools: 95% are microliths, mainly narrow, finely made, arched-backed, curved, pointed pieces (*cf.* upper occupational phase Uwaynid 18, lower occupational phase Jilat 6). Adjusted microburin index is 20.77.
9. Sparse faunal remains.
12. One AMS date:
OxA-866. UW14.5.18 Wood charcoal **18,400 ± 250**
Comment: The mean for this date is 500 yr youn-

ger than that obtained on the sample from the overlying phase. However, if one compares the dates at two standard deviations (2 σ), there is considerable overlap. Note that the lithic assemblage in this middle phase is very similar to that from the upper occupational phase at neighboring Uwaynid 18, which has been dated to between 19,800 ± 350 and 19,500 ± 250. This suggests that the dated sample at Uwaynid 14 may derive from the occupation above.

Lower Occupational Phase

7. Sparse, chipped stone assemblage in clayey silts, 15 cm below middle occupational phase.
12. No ^{14}C date.

JILAT 6 (Wadi Dhobai K) (2.544 E × 34.888 N)

1. Early Epipaleolithic site with three superimposed occupational phases. In eolian silts on terrace of Wadi Jilat.
2. Surface deflated. Artifacts spread over 19,175 m².
3. Systematic surface survey in 1982.
4. Waechter and others excavated sounding in 1937–1938. Garrard and others excavated single 4 m² sounding in 1984.
5. Refs: Waechter *et al.* (1938); Garrard *et al.* (1985:15–17, 1986:12–17, 1988b:44–47); Byrd (1988); Garrard and Byrd (1992).

Upper Occupational Phase (A)

6. 40–60 cm of ashy silts containing high density of artifacts and bones. The lower 30 cm of sediment is characteristic of compressed and trampled occupational surfaces. Distinctive compressed silt layer (Fig. 4, Unit 6) and two horizontal ocher pigmented surfaces (Fig. 4, Units 8, 10), with lipped-up edges running through excavation area, are thought to have formed the floors of a structure.
7. Retouched chipped stone tools: 68% are microliths, mainly asymmetric and symmetric triangles. Also, microgravette points and curved, pointed, arched-backed pieces. Adjusted microburin index is 55.66. Non-microlithic tools, mainly end scrapers, burins, non-standardized retouched pieces.
8. Two fragments from basalt artifacts, 1 incised pebble. Also shell beads and bone tools.
9. Faunal remains: diverse species including birds, but dominated by *Gazella*.
10. Seed remains mainly from chenopods. No cereals.
12. Six tightly clustered AMS dates from both Oxford and Arizona laboratories have mean ranges of 16,700 to 15,470 BP:

AA-5494. WJ6.3.9a Wood charcoal **16,700 ± 140**
AA-5493. WJ6.2.3a Wood charcoal **16,695 ± 120**
AA-5491. WJ6.1.7b Wood charcoal **16,575 ± 120**
OxA-525. WJ6.1.5a Wood charcoal **16,010 ± 200**
OxA-524. WJ6.4.8a Wood charcoal **15,520 ± 200**
AA-5492. WJ6.1.8a Wood charcoal **15,470 ± 130**

Middle Occupational Phase (B)

6. 40–55 cm horizon of eolian silts with fine columnar structure resulting from weak pedogenic activity. Contains a well-defined 5–7-cm-thick occupational horizon (Fig. 4, Unit 15). This is separated from the cultural deposits above and below by sterile eolian silts.
7. Retouched chipped stone tools: 74% are microliths, mainly robust la Mouillah points (*cf.* upper occupational phase, Uwaynid 14). Also, double-truncated, backed bladelets and Qalkhan points. Adjusted microburin index is 24.32. Non-microlithic tools, mainly notches/denticulates and non-standardized retouched pieces.
8. Shell bead, bone points.
9. Faunal remains, mainly *Equus, Gazella, Testudo.*
12. Charcoal scarce, but two AMS dates obtained:

OxA-522. WJ6.4.12a Wood charcoal **11,740 ± 180**
OxA-523. WJ6.2.12a Burned bone **11,450 ± 200**
Comment: The dates are 4–5 millennia younger than those from the phase above! The sedimentary and structural features in the overlying horizon, which include trampled surfaces and artificially laid floors, preclude any major geological inversion of sediments. Thus, the anomalously young dates must result from one of the reasons described in the text above. No material consistent with these dates was found in surface survey. As indicated above, the lithic assemblage from the middle occupational phase at Jilat 6 is similar to that in the upper occupational phase at Uwaynid 14, which has been dated to 18,900 ± 250 BP.

Lower Occupational Phase (C)

6. Massive eolian silt, 85–95 cm thick, with a strong columnar structure resulting from pedogenic activity under a moister regime. Occupational horizon found in upper 5–7 cm of deposit (Fig. 4, Unit 20).
7. Retouched chipped stone tools: 81% are microliths, mainly narrow, finely made, curved, pointed arched-backed pieces (*cf.* upper occupational phase at Uwaynid 18 and the middle

occupational phase at Uwaynid 14). The adjusted microburin index is 54.86. Non-microlithic tools are mainly truncations and non-standardized retouched pieces.

8. Bone pendant.

9. Faunal remains, mainly *Gazella, Equus, Testudo.*

12. No charcoal obtained during excavation, but a small fragment (<3 mm diameter) was obtained by flotation.

OxA-539. WJ6.1.14a Wood charcoal **7980 ± 150**
Comment: This date was 8 millennia younger than the dates obtained for the uppermost phase, and 4 millennia later than those obtained for the middle phase! For possible explanations, see above. No material consistent with this date was found during surface survey. As indicated above, the lithic assemblage in the lower occupational phase at Jilat 6 is very similar to that in the upper occupational phase at Uwaynid 18 and the middle occupational phase at Uwaynid 14. The former has been ¹⁴C dated to between 19,800 ± 350 and 19,500 ± 250 BP.

JILAT 22 (Wadi Dhobai I) (2.559 E × 34.888 N)

1. Middle Epipaleolithic site with three superimposed occupational phases. In eolian silts and indurated marsh deposits in terrace of Wadi Jilat. Adjacent to present gorge.

2. Surface deflated; artifacts spread over 3500 m².

3. Systematic survey in 1982, 1984.

4. Single sounding of 4 m² excavated 1987, 1988.

5. Refs: Garrard *et al.* (1985:17); Garrard and Byrd (1992).

Upper Occupational Phase (B)

6. Very ashy silt (20–35 cm thick) with high densities of artifacts and bones.

7. Retouched chipped stone tools: 42% are microliths, mainly backed bladelet fragments including some with truncations. Complete microlithic assemblage includes trapeze-rectangles, la Mouillah points, triangles and lunates. Adjusted microburin index is 36.1. Non-microlithic tools are mainly end scrapers, burins, notches/denticulates and non-standardized retouched pieces.

8. Five fragments from basalt artifacts, shell beads.

9. Faunal remains dominated by *Gazella, Testudo.*

12. One AMS date:

OxA-1770. WJ22.1.6b Wood charcoal **11,920 ± 180**

Middle Occupational Phase (C)

6. Indurated calcareous silts (10–27 cm thick) with high density of artifacts, bone and charcoal. *Phragmites* stems and rhizomes in growth position, in the lower part (marsh deposit).

7. Retouched chipped stone tools: 7% are microliths, mainly backed bladelet fragments, some with truncations. Non-microlithic tools (mainly on blades): 51% of total retouched tool assemblage are "Jilat knives". This form has a pronounced tang at one end and is obliquely truncated into a point at the other end. Other blade tools include burins, notches/denticulates and non-standardized retouched pieces.

8. Shell beads.

9. Faunal remains dominated by *Gazella, Testudo.* Many bird bones.

12. Two AMS dates:

OxA-1771. WJ22.3.15b Wood charcoal **13,040±180**
OxA-1772. WJ22.3.15b Wood charcoal **12,840±140**

Lower Occupational Phase (E)

6. Occupational horizon, 10–11 cm thick, in strongly indurated calcareous silts containing *Phragmites* stems and rhizomes in growth position (marsh deposit). Separated from middle occupational phase by 38–60 cm of archaeologically sterile marsh deposits.

7. Because of difficulties of excavating the indurated unit, the lithic assemblage available for study was small, resembling that of the middle occupational phase.

9. Identifiable faunal remains sparse.

12. Two AMS dates:

OxA-2410. WJ22.1/4.17a Wood charcoal **13,540±120**
OxA-2409. WJ22.1/4.17a Wood charcoal **13,490±110**

JILAT 10. (2.510 E × 34.869 N)

1. Middle Epipaleolithic site in eolian silts on terrace of Wadi Jilat.

2. Uncertain of original extent, as eroding from side of silt sheet. Probably small scale.

3. Systematic surface survey 1982, 1984.

4. Two 4 m² soundings excavated 1984.

5. Refs: Garrard *et al.* (1985:13–15, 1986:9, 1988b:46–47); Byrd (1988).

6. Trench 2 revealed 10–20 cm thick occupational horizon eroding from a former hollow in eolian silt sheet.

7. Retouched chipped stone tools: 17% are microliths, mainly backed bladelet fragments (some with truncations) and thin bladelets with marginal or thin retouch. No microburins. Non-microlithic tools (mainly on blades) are principally end scrapers, burins, truncations and non-standardized

retouched pieces.
8. Shell beads.
9. Faunal remains mainly *Equus, Testudo.*
12. Three AMS dates:
OxA-520. WJ10.7.11b Wood charcoal **14,790 ± 200**
OxA-1000. WJ10.8.11 Wood charcoal **13,120 ± 180**
OxA-918. WJ10.8.11 Wood charcoal **12,700 ± 300**
Comment: OxA-1000 and -918 were obtained from the same sample.

JILAT 8. (Wadi Dhobai E2) (2.552E × 34.887N)

1. Middle Epipaleolithic site in eolian silts on terrace of Wadi Jilat. Adjacent to present gorge.
2. Surface deflated; artifacts spread over 6300 m².
3. Systematic surface survey 1982.
4. Single 4-m² sounding excavated 1984.
5. Refs: Garrard *et al.* (1985:10–11, 1986:9-12, 1988b:46–47); Byrd (1988).
6. 40–50 cm of eolian silts containing lenses of artifacts and bones.
7. Retouched chipped stone tools: 73% are microliths, mainly backed bladelet fragments, often showing truncations. Complete forms include trapeze/rectangles, la Mouillah points and curved pointed, arched-backed pieces. Adjusted microburin index is 38.17. Non-microlithic tools are mainly end scrapers.
8. Two fragments from basalt artifacts. Shell beads.
9. Faunal remains dominated by *Gazella, Testudo.*
12. Two AMS dates were obtained on samples from the base of the sounding:
OxA-521. WJ8.3.4c Wood charcoal **13,310 ± 120**
OxA-636. WJ8.3.4d Burned bone **10,540 ± 160**
Comment: The date obtained on the fragment of burned bone is very young. No cultural material of this period was identified during surface survey.

AZRAQ 17 (2.939 E × 35.239 N)

1. Two-phase site including Middle Epipaleolithic occupation. In silts and indurated marsh deposits close to perennial springs at South Azraq.
2. Surface deflated; artifacts spread over 3100 m².
3. Systematic surface survey in 1984.
4. Two soundings, 15 m², excavated 1985.
5. Refs: Garrard *et al.* (1987:18–19, 1988b:46–47); Byrd (1988).
Trench 1
6. <15 cm of occupational material in silts covering former channel fill.
7. Retouched chipped stone tools: 83% are microliths, mainly broken backed bladelets, many of

which have truncations. Also some lunates and triangles. Adjusted microburin index is 61.86. Non-microlithic tools are mainly non-standardized retouched pieces.
8. One basalt vessel fragment.
9. Faunal remains dominated by *Gazella.*
12. No ¹⁴C date.

Trench 2
6. <30 cm of occupational material contained in ashy silts covering indurated marsh deposits.
7. Retouched chipped stone tools: 55% are microliths. As in Trench 1, there is a substantial number of broken backed bladelets, some with truncations. The most common microlithic tools are very thin bladelets with marginal or thin retouch. Microburins are rare. Non-microlithic tools are mainly end scrapers, burins and non-standardized retouched pieces.
8. Three fragments from basalt artifacts plus 2 handstones; shell beads.
9. Faunal remains dominated by *Gazella.*
12. One AMS date:
OxA-869. AZ17.11.11 Wood charcoal **13,260 ± 200**

AZRAQ 32 (3.007 E × 35.288 N)

1. Early or Middle Epipaleolithic site eroding from eolian silts close to the former spring of Ain el-Beidha.
2. Surface deflated; artifacts spread over 3600 m².
3. Surface survey 1989.
4. 1 m² sounding excavated 1989.
5. Refs: Garrard *et al.* (ms. in preparation).
6. Upper 20 cm of sounding comprises eolian silts. Occupation limited to top 10 cm.
7. Chipped stone material awaiting analysis. Microlithic component characterized by large asymmetric triangles.
8. Fragment from basalt artifact plus handstone.
12. No ¹⁴C dates.

AZRAQ 18 (2.936 E × 35.227 N)

Late Epipaleolithic (Natufian) site in eolian silts close to spring at South Azraq.
2. Surface deflated; artifacts spread over 1400 m².
3. Systematic surface survey 1984.
4. Single sounding of 6 m² excavated 1985.
5. Refs: Garrard *et al.* (1987:20–21, 1988b:46–47); Byrd (1988); Garrard (1992).
6. 30 cm of dense occupational material contained in carbonate indurated silts of eolian origin.
7. Retouched chipped stone tools: 84% are microliths, mainly lunates retouched by helwan, bipolar

and abrupt techniques. Adjusted microburin index is 5.07. Non-microlithic tools, mainly non-standardized retouched pieces and truncations.

8. Ten fragments from basalt and sandstone artifacts including handstones and perforated stones. Shellbeads and bone tools.

9. Faunal remains dominated by *Bos, Equus, Gazella*.

11. Crushed skulls and disarticulated postcranial bones of up to 11 humans in depressions underlying main occupation.

12. No ^{14}C dates.

Neolithic Sites

JILAT 7 (Wadi Dhobai C) (2.546 E × 34.884 N)

1. Early, Middle and possibly Late PPNB site in silts on terrace of Jilat, adjacent to present gorge.

2. Surface deflated; artifacts spread over 2250 m^2.

3. Systematic surface survey 1982.

4. Two soundings excavated 1984: Trenches 1 and 2 (8 m^2). Three trenches excavated 1987, 1988: Areas A–C (77 m^2).

5. Refs: Garrard *et al.* (1985:17–18, 1986:17–23, 1988b:44–48, 1994).

Early PPNB

6. Early PPNB horizon in basal levels of adjoining areas, A and C. Structures and features cut into bedrock.

7. *Chipped Stone Industry*:

a. Cores (in order of importance): single platform and change of orientation blade/bladelet cores; opposed platform blade/bladelet cores including some naviform types; a specialized opposed platform reduction strategy, adapted to the exploitation of tabular flint material, which produced naviform cores (Nissen, Muheisen and Gebel 1987:98).

b. Blanks and debitage: blade/bladelets more important than flakes. Former category dominated by bladelets.

c. Raw material: exotic (possibly heat treated) material present in relatively high proportions. Very little obsidian.

d. Points: Khiam and Helwan points. Only one Byblos point in a large sample.

e. Other characteristic tool types: Hagdud truncations; piercers with relatively thin bits; inversely, alternately retouched blades and bladelets.

8. Other stone artifacts include basalt grinding slabs, handstones, shaft straighteners, stone vessels. Also, a few stone and shell beads.

9. Faunal remains diverse but dominated by *Gazella* and *Lepus*. No signs of *Capra/Ovis*.

10. Plant remains: *Hordeum spontaneum, H. sativam, Triticum monococcum, Pistacia, Ficus*.

12. Comparative typology of the points suggests the assemblage must date to the second half of the 10th millennium BP. Two AMS dates:

OxA-2413. WJ7.A.34a Wood charcoal **8390 ± 80**

OxA-1799. WJ7.A.34b Wood charcoal **5840 ± 100**

Comment: Both results are later than the chipped stone assemblage with which they occur. This must result from 1) intrusion; 2) contamination; or 3) statistical anomalies or inaccuracies in the dating procedure. The older sample possibly intruded from a late Middle or Late PPNB occupation phase on the site. No archaeological source was found in surface survey or excavation for the youngest date.

Middle PPNB

6. Middle PPNB horizon found in all trenches. Several structures relate to this phase. In Area B, a curvilinear, semi-subterranean structure was excavated; it was built from upright slabs of limestone. Internal diameter 3.6 m. Internal partitions. Probably organic superstructure.

7. *Chipped Stone Industry*:

a. Cores: opposed platform blade/bladelet cores include many classic naviform types. Also, specialized tabular flint adapted opposed platform reduction strategy.

b. Blanks and debitage: blade/bladelets outnumber flakes.

c. Raw material: exotic material rare. Very little obsidian.

d. Points: Byblos and occasional Jericho points.

e. Other characteristic tool types: range of piercer types. Many burins, a range of types.

8. Other stone artifacts include basalt vessels, shaft straighteners, pestles, grinding slabs, handstones and incised, grooved and perforated stones. Also, stone beads, bone tools and shell beads.

9. Animal remains as for Early PPNB.

10. Plant remains: *Hordeum spontaneum, H. sativam, Triticum boeoticum, T. monococcum, T. dicoccum, Lens, Pistacia, Ficus*.

12. Two AMS dates from Trench 2 date this phase to the first 2/3 of the 9th millennium BP:

OxA-526. WJ7.6.28a Wood charcoal **8810 ± 110**

OxA-527. WJ7.8.25a Wood charcoal **8520 ± 110**

Later Middle or Late PPNB

6. Found in upper levels of curvilinear structure in area B.

7. *Chipped Stone Industry*:

a. Cores: opposed platform blade/bladelet cores including classic naviform type. Tabular adapted opposed platform strategy present. Amorphous cores relatively common.

b. Blanks and debitage: blade/bladelets outnumber flakes, including rather numerous, relatively long blades.

c. Raw material: exotic material rare. Very little obsidian.

d. Points: Byblos points.

e. Other characteristic tool types: various piercers including drill bits on spalls. Burins important, with significant numbers of truncation burins. Blades with oblique retouch as backing.

12. No direct dates. A sample dated to second half of 9th millennium BP that appeared intrusive in Early PPNB levels in Area A possibly belongs to this phase.

JILAT 26 (Wadi Dhobai A) (2.542 E × 34.882 N)

1. Middle PPNB site in silts on terrace of Jilat, adjacent to present gorge.

2. Surface deflated; artifacts spread over 7850 m².

3. Systematic surface survey 1985.

4. Five trenches excavated 1987, 1988: Areas A–E (164.50 m²).

5. Refs: Garrard *et al.* (1994).

6. Surface survey revealed semi-circle of *ca.* 18 curvilinear and 2 rectilinear structures. Also external "bins", hearths and bedrock mortars. Excavation undertaken in rectilinear structure (Area A); curvilinear structure (Area C); external activity areas (Areas B, D, E). From excavation, the structures appear to be semi-subterranean and built in the typical Jilat style (see Jilat 7 Middle PPNB).

7. *Chipped Stone Industry*

a. Cores: opposed platform blade/bladelet cores include classic naviform type. Tabular adapted opposed platform strategy dominates.

b. Blanks and debitage: blade/bladelets more important than flakes.

c. Raw material: exotic materials rare, no cores. Obsidian absent.

d. Points: Byblos dominate, but significant numbers of Amuq present.

e. Other characteristic tool types: range of piercers include drill bits on burin spalls. Truncation burins. Bifacials include foliate related pieces. Blades with oblique retouch as backing.

N.B. Although technology is uniform across the site, there is some variation in the proportion of tool types. Points are relatively uncommon, but more frequent in Area A. Truncation burins very common in Areas B and C. Piercers relatively uncommon, but more frequent in Area E. Bifacials occur only in Area B.

8. Ground stone artifacts, stone and shell beads rare. However, there are two concentrations of bedrock mortars.

9/10. Animal and plant remains sparse.

12. Three AMS dates date site to first half of 9th millennium BP. Two were obtained from early fills of curvilinear structure in Area C, which had many concave truncation burins among tool types:

OxA-2407. WJ26.C.12a Wood charcoal **8720 ± 100**
OxA-1802. WJ26.Cb.7a Wood charcoal **8690 ± 110**

A third date was obtained from an external activity area (E), which was also associated with concave truncation burins:

OxA-2969. WJ26.Ed.18a Wood charcoal **8740 ± 110**

JILAT 32 (2.512 E × 34.867 N)

1. Middle or possibly Late PPNB site on hillside in Wadi Jilat.

2. Largely buried by colluvium and eolian sediments.

3. Surveyed in 1988.

4. Single sounding, 5 m², excavated in 1989.

5. Refs: Baird *et al.* (1992).

6. Sounding revealed oval structure cut into hillside, with substructure built from upright slabs. Internal dimensions, 1.5 × 3.6 m, remodeled.

7. *Chipped Stone Industry*

a. Cores: opposed platform blade/bladelet cores include classic naviform type. Tabular adapted opposed platform strategy present.

b. Blanks and debitage: blade/bladelets more important than flakes.

c. Raw material: exotic material rare, no cores. Obsidian absent.

d. Points: only Byblos points from excavation area. Helwan and Byblos points from surface survey.

e. Other characteristic tool types: few burins. Inversely retouched blade/bladelets.

8. Basalt handstones. Mortar and pestle from late level.

9. Faunal remains dominated by *Lepus*.

12. No ¹⁴C dates. Technology and tool types are similar to those in Middle PPNB phase at Jilat 7.

AZRAQ 31 (2.944 E × 35.225 N)

1. Late PPNB, Late Neolithic site in silts between playa and marshes at Azraq.
2. Surface deflated; artifacts spread over 4600 m².
3. Systematic surface survey 1982.
4. Two soundings excavated 1985: Trenches 1 and 2 (9 m²). Three 3 × 3 m trenches excavated 1989: Areas A–C (27 m²).
5. Refs: Garrard *et al.* (1985:17–19, 1987:21–23, 1988b:44–48); Baird *et al.* (1992).

Late PPNB

6. Late PPNB hearths, ashy occupation spread and cobbled platform in Trench 1 and adjacent Area A.
7. *Chipped Stone Industry*
   a. Cores: opposed platform blade/bladelet cores include classic naviform type. Tabular adapted opposed platform strategy present.
   b. Blanks and debitage: blade/bladelets more important than flakes.
   c. Raw material: exotic material absent. Obsidian absent.
   d. Points: Byblos points.
   e. Other characteristic tool types: various piercer types include a distinctive form with long thick bits. Various burin types. Some relatively large blade tools. Sickles with limited retouch. Also present but possibly intrusive: truncation burins, drill bits on burin spalls and bifacials.
8. Stone, shell and bone beads.
9. Faunal remains, mainly *Gazella, Bos, Equus.* Very few *Capra/Ovis* bones (3.5%), *Lepus.*
10. Sparse seeds, mainly Cyperaceae. Some *Hordeum* seeds and rachis fragments from secure PPNB contexts.
12. Phase dated to second half of 9th millennium BP. One AMS date:
OxA-870. AZ31.1.10 Wood charcoal **8350 ± 120**

Late Neolithic

6. Area C contains sequence of structural remains with substructures built from upright slabs (as with Jilat Neolithic structures). The adjacent area B contains pits and "midden" deposits.
7. *Chipped Stone Industry*
   a. Cores: opposed platform blade/bladelet cores include classic naviform type. Tabular adapted opposed platform strategy present.
   b. Blanks and debitage: blade/bladelets more important than flakes.
   c. Raw material: exotic material rare, no cores. Obsidian present.

d. Points (in order of importance): Amuq, Nizzanim, Herziliya, Byblos.
   e. Other characteristic tool types: angle burins including truncation types. Drill bits on burin spalls. Bifacials (tile knives and foliates). Sickles include types with bilateral gloss. A flake adze.
8. Basalt handstone, perforated stones, shaft straightener, pebble mortars. Bone beads and points. Shell beads. Many barrel and disk-shaped stone beads made on site from imported Dabba "marble".
9. Faunal remains dominated by *Gazella,* but substantial numbers of *Capra/Ovis* also.
12. One AMS date obtained from Area C structure:
OxA-2412. AZ31.C.19b Wood charcoal **8275 ± 80**
Comment: The date is early and sample is thought to derive from Late PPNB occupation. Later burials have cut into the Neolithic occupation. The following date derives from one such burial in Trench 2:
OxA-871. AZ31.14.107 Unburned bone **1280 ± 90**

JILAT 25 (Wadi Dhobai D) (2.543 E × 34.884 N)

1. Early Late Neolithic site in silts on terrace of Jilat, adjacent to present gorge.
2. Surface deflated; artifacts spread over 3200 m².
3. Systematic surface survey 1985.
4. Single trench of 21 m² excavated 1988.
5. Refs: Garrard *et al.* (1994).
6. Surface survey revealed single oval structure measuring 7.0 × 4.5 m. Trench excavated across eastern end. Although larger than Jilat PPNB structures, built in same manner (see Jilat 7: Middle PPNB).
7. *Chipped Stone Industry*
   a. Cores: single platform and change of orientation cores. Some opposed platform cores present. Naviform absent.
   b. Blanks and debitage: flakes more important than blades/ bladelets.
   c. Raw material: exotics and obsidian absent.
   d. Points: Nizzanim points.
   e. Other characteristic tool types: angle burins, particularly truncation types. Drill bits on burin spalls. Bifacials (tile knives and foliates).
8. Many Dabba "marble" beads in various stages of production. Range of other stone tools include basalt handstones, shaft straighteners, stone vessel fragments and some that may have been used in bead making. Few shell beads.

9. Faunal remains: sample small, but *Capra/Ovis* dominant.

10. Plant remains sparse.

12. Dated to late 9th/early 8th millennium BP. One AMS date:

OxA-2408. WJ25.Aa.19a Wood charcoal **8020 ± 80**

JILAT 13 (Wadi Dhobai B) (2.542 E × 34.882 N)

1. PPNB and Late Neolithic site in silts on terrace of Jilat, adjacent to present gorge.

2. Surface deflated; artifacts spread over 800 m².

3. Systematic surface survey 1985.

4. Waechter and others excavated sounding in 1937–1938. Garrard and others excavated three adjoining trenches (A–C) with total area of 73.5 m² in 1987, 1988.

5. Refs: Waechter *et al.* (1938); Garrard *et al.* (1994).

6. Surface survey revealed an oval structure, 10 × 6 m; this was almost completely excavated in 1987–1988. Although larger than Jilat PPNB structures, it was built in same tradition (see Jilat 7: Middle PPNB). Several modifications were made to the structure, *e.g.*, a substantial pavement was added in a late phase.

7. *Chipped Stone Industry: Earliest Phases of Structure:*

a. Cores: opposed platform blade/bladelet cores include classic naviform type. Tabular adapted opposed platform strategy present.

b. Blanks and debitage: blade/bladelets more important than flakes.

c. Raw material: exotic material rare, no cores. Obsidian present.

d. Points (in order of importance): Nizzanim, Byblos, Herziliya and Amuq.

e. Other characteristic tool types: angle burins include significant proportion of truncation types. Drill bits on burin spalls. Bifacials (tile knives and foliates). Blades with oblique retouch as backing. Endscrapers.

7. *Chipped Stone Industry: Latest Phases of Structure*

a. Cores: opposed platform blade/bladelet cores may include rare classic naviform type. Single platform and change of orientation cores. Tabular adapted opposed platform strategy present.

b. Blanks and debitage: blade/bladelets more important than flakes.

c. Raw material: exotic material rare, no cores. Obsidian present.

d. Points (in order of importance): Nizzanim,

Byblos, Herziliya, Amuq, Haparsah (and Transverse) arrowheads.

e. Other characteristic tool types: angle burins include significant number of truncation types. Drill bits on burin spalls. Bifacials (tile knives and foliates). Blades with oblique retouch as backing. Large blades with truncations (morphology of blanks suggestive of Canaanean blades).

8. Other stone artifacts: relatively few grinding or pounding tools. Figurines, engraved slabs, perforated stones, dressed pillars present. Numerous Dabba "marble" beads in various stages of manufacture. Also shell beads, mother-of-pearl, and a range of bone beads and tools.

9. Faunal remains: preliminary analysis revealed numerous *Gazella*, *Lepus* and *Capra/Ovis* bones.

10. Plant remains: as for Jilat 7, Middle PPNB phase.

12. The structure and its fills, excavated in 1987–1988, was dated to first half of 8th millennium BP. Two AMS dates from early fills of structure:

OxA-1800. WJ13.A.21a Wood charcoal **7920 ± 100**
OxA-1801. WJ13.A.15a Wood charcoal **7870 ± 100**

Two ¹⁴C dates from hearths, either contemporary with or later than the late phase pavement:

OxA-2411. WJ13.C.24 Wood charcoal **7900 ± 80**
UB-3462. WJ13.C.22 Wood charcoal **7830 ± 90**

Comment: We were surprised that these dates were so similar to the dates from the early fills, because this late phase contains Transverse arrowheads and tools resembling Canaanean blades. OxA-2411 is an AMS date from Oxford, and UB-3462 is a conventional date from a larger sample analyzed in the Belfast laboratory. Both were collected *in situ* from stone-lined hearths.

JILAT 23 (Wadi Dhobai G) (2.553 E × 34.888 N)

1. Late Neolithic site in silts on terrace of Jilat, adjacent to present gorge.

2. Surface deflated; artifacts spread over 4700 m².

3. Systematic surface survey 1985.

4. Three 1 m² soundings excavated 1985.

5. Refs: Garrard *et al.* (1987:7–8).

6. Surface survey revealed two small stone circles of 5-m diameter adjoining large circular enclosure of 18-m diameter. Soundings cut across walls of enclosure, stone circle and within stone circle.

7. *Chipped Stone Industry:*

a. Cores: single platform cores and flake cores.

b. Blanks and debitage: flakes more important than blade/ bladelets.

c. Raw material: exotic material and obsidian absent.

d. Points: one Nizzanim point.

e. Other characteristic tool types: truncation burins. Drill bits on spalls. Bifacials (tile knives and foliates).

12. No ^{14}C date.

JILAT 24 (Wadi Dhobai E1) (2.549E × 34.887 N)

1. Late Neolithic site in silts on terrace of Jilat, adjacent to present gorge.
2. Surface deflated; artifacts spread over 700 m².
3. Systematic surface survey 1985.
4. Excavated 6 m² sounding 1985.
5. Refs: Garrard *et al.* (1987:7–8).

6. Surface survey revealed single stone circle of 3.5-m diameter. Sounding cut across wall.

7. *Chipped Stone Industry*:
   a. Cores: single platform cores, flake cores. Some opposed platform blade/bladelet cores.
   b. Blanks and debitage: flakes more important than blade/bladelets.
   c. Raw material: exotic material and obsidian absent.
   d. Points: absent from excavated sample. One Byblos point from surface.
   e. Other characteristic tool types: truncation burins. Drill bits on spalls. Bifacials (tile knives and foliates). One stone bead.

12. No ^{14}C date.

ACKNOWLEDGMENTS

We are extremely grateful to the Radiocarbon Accelerator Unit, Oxford and the NSF-Arizona Radio-isotope Accelerator Facility, Tucson, Arizona, for providing the ^{14}C dates upon which this article is based. We are also indebted to our research colleagues for their contributions to this article, particularly, Susan Colledge, Christopher Hunt, Louise Martin and Katherine Wright. The Azraq Project was generously sponsored by the following: the British Academy, the British Institute at Amman for Archaeology and History, the British Museum, the Leverhulme Trust, the Renaissance Trust and the Wainwright Fund. Research on the chipped stone assemblages (by B. F. B.) was supported by grants from the American Centre for Oriental Research (Amman), the National Endowment for the Humanities and the Wenner-Gren Foundation for Anthropological Research.

REFERENCES CITED

Baird, D., A. Garrard, M. Martin, and K. Wright
   1992   Prehistoric environment and settlement in the Azraq Basin: An interim report on the 1989 excavation season. *Levant* 24:1–31.

Bar-Yosef, O.
   1990   The Last Glacial Maximum in the Mediterranean Levant. In *The World at 18,000 b.p.*, Vol. 2, *Low Latitudes*, edited by C. Gamble and O. Soffer, pp. 58–77. Unwin Hyman, London.

Bar-Yosef, O. and A. Belfer-Cohen
   1989   The origins of sedentism and farming communities in the Levant. *Journal of World Prehistory* 3:447–498.

Baruch, U. and S. Bottema
   1991   Palynological evidence for climatic changes in the Levant *ca.* 17,000–9000 BP. In *The Natufian Culture in the Levant*, edited by O. Bar-Yosef and F. R. Valla, pp. 11–20. International Monographs in Prehistory, Ann Arbor.

Begin, Z.B., W. Broecker, B. Buchbinder, Y. Druckman, A. Kaufman, M. Magaritz and D. Neev
   1985   Dead Sea and Lake Lisan Levels in the Last 30,000 Years. Unpublished Geological Survey of Israel Report 29/85.

Besançon, J., G. Geyer and P. Sanlaville
   1989   Contribution to the study of the geomorphology of the Azraq Basin, Jordan. In *The Hammer on the Rock. Studies in the Early Palaeolithic of Azraq, Jordan*, edited by L. Copeland and F. Hours, pp. 7–63. BAR International Series 540, British Archaeological Reports, Oxford.

Betts, A. V. G.
   1987   Recent discoveries relating to the Neolithic periods in eastern Jordan. In *Studies in the History and Archaeology of Jordan* 3, edited by A. Hadidi, pp. 225–240. Department of Antiquities, Amman.

Butler, B. H., E. Tchernov, H. Hietala and S. Davis
   1977   Faunal exploitation during the Late Epipalaeolithic in the Har Harif. In *Prehistory and Paleoenvironments in the Central Negev, Israel*, Vol. 2, edited by A. E. Marks, pp. 327–345. Southern Methodist University Press, Dallas.

Byrd, B. F.
    1988   Late Pleistocene settlement diversity in the Azraq Basin. *Paléorient* 14(2):257–264.
Byrd, B. F. and A. N. Garrard
    1990   The Last Glacial Maximum in the Jordanian Desert. In *The World at 18,000 b.p.*, Vol. 2, *Low Latitudes*, edited
           by C. Gamble and O. Soffer, pp. 78–96. Unwin Hyman, London.
Chapman, R. W.
    1974   Calcareous duricrust in Al-Hasa, Saudi-Arabia. *Bulletin of the Geological Survey of America* 85:119–130.
Colledge, S.
    1991   Investigations of plant remains preserved in Epipalaeolithic sites in the Near East. In *The Natufian Culture in
           the Levant*, edited by O. Bar-Yosef and F. R. Valla, pp. 391–398. International Monographs in Prehistory, Ann
           Arbor.
Davis, S.
    1980   Late Pleistocene and Holocene equid remains from Israel. *Zoological Journal of the Linnean Society* 70:289–
           312.
Garrard, A. N.
    1985   Appendix 1. Faunal remains. In Black Desert Survey, Jordan: Third preliminary report, edited by A. Betts.
           Levant 17:39–49.
    1991   Natufian settlement in the Azraq Basin, eastern Jordan. In *The Natufian Culture In the Levant*, edited by O.
           Bar-Yosef and F. R. Valla, pp. 235–244. International Monographs in Prehistory, Ann Arbor.
Garrard, A. N., D. Baird, S. Colledge, L. Martin and K. I. Wright
    1994   Prehistoric environment and settlement in the Azraq Basin: An interim report on the 1987 and 1988 excavation
           seasons. *Levant* 26.
Garrard, A. N., A. Betts, B. Byrd, S. Colledge and C. Hunt
    1988a   Summary of palaeoenvironmental and prehistoric investigations in the Azraq Basin. In *The Prehistory of Jor-
           dan*, edited by A. N. Garrard and H.-G. Gebel, pp. 311–337. BAR International Series 396, British Archaeo-
           logical Reports, Oxford.
Garrard, A. N., A. Betts, B. Byrd and C. Hunt
    1987   Prehistoric environment and settlement in the Azraq Basin. An interim report on the 1985 excavation season.
           Levant 19:5–25.
Garrard, A. N. and B. F. Byrd
    1992   New dimensions to the Epipalaeolithic of the Wadi Jilat in central Jordan. *Paléorient* 18(1):47–62.
Garrard, A. N., B. Byrd and A. Betts
    1986   Prehistoric environment and settlement in the Azraq Basin. An interim report on the 1984 excavation season.
           Levant 18:5–24.
Garrard, A. N., B. Byrd, P. Harvey and F. Hivernel
    1985   Prehistoric environment and settlement in the Azraq Basin. Report on the 1982 survey season. *Levant* 17:1–28.
Garrard, A. N., S. Colledge, C. Hunt and R. Montague
    1988b   Environment and subsistence during the late Pleistocene and early Holocene in the Azraq Basin. *Paléorient*
           14(2):40–49.
Goldberg, P.
    1986   Late Quaternary environmental history of the southern Levant. *Geoarchaeology* 1:225–244.
Goring-Morris, A. N.
    1989   Developments in terminal Pleistocene hunter-gatherer sociocultural systems: A perspective from the Negev and
           Sinai Deserts. In *People and Culture in Change*, edited by I. Hershkovitz, pp. 7–28. BAR International Series
           508, British Archaeological Reports, Oxford.
Harrison, D. L.
    1968   *The Mammals of Arabia*. Vol. 2. Benn, London.
Helmer, D.
    1988   Les animaux de Cafer et des sites précéramiques du sud-est de la Turquie: Essai de synthèse. *Anatolica*
           15(1):37–48.
    1989   Le développement de la domestication au Proche-Orient de 9,500 à 7,500 b.p.: Les nouvelles données d'El
           Kowm et de Ras Shamra. *Paléorient* 15(1):111–121.
Henry, D. O., P. Turnbull, A. Emery-Barbier and A. Leroi-Gourhan
    1985   Archaeological, faunal and pollen evidence from Natufian and Timnian sites in Southern Jordan. *Bulletin of
           the American Schools of Oriental Research* 257:45–64.
Hillman, G. C. and M. S. Davies
    1990   Measured domestication rates in wild wheats and barley under primitive cultivation, and their archaeological
           implications. *Journal of World Prehistory* 4:157–222.

Hole, F.
  1984   A reassessment of the Neolithic Revolution. *Paléorient* 10:49–60.
Horwitz, L. K.
  1989   A reassessment of caprovine domestication in the Levantine Neolithic: Old questions, new answers. In *People and Culture in Change*, edited by I. Hershkovitz, pp. 153–181. BAR International Series 508, British Archaeological Reports, Oxford.
Kislev, M. E.
  1989   Pre-domesticated cereals in the Pre-Pottery Neolithic A period. In *People and Culture in Change*, edited by I. Hershkovitz, pp. 147–151. BAR International Series 508, British Archaeological Reports, Oxford.
Kohler-Rollefson, I.
  1988   The aftermath of the Levantine Neolithic Revolution in the light of ecological and ethnographic evidence. *Paléorient* 14(1):87–93.
Kohler-Rollefson, I., W. Gillespie and M. Metzger
  1988   The fauna from Neolithic 'Ain Ghazal. In *The Prehistory of Jordan*, edited by A. N. Garrard and H.-G. Gebel, pp. 423–430. BAR International Series 396, British Archaeological Reports, Oxford.
Legge, A. J. and P. A. Rowley-Conwy
  1987   Gazelle killing in Stone Age Syria. *Scientific American* 257(2):76–84 (English edition).
Marks, A. E. and P. A. Larson, Jr.
  1977   Test excavations at the Natufian site of Rosh Horesha. In *Prehistory and Paleoenvironments in the Central Negev, Israel*, Vol. 2, edited by A. E. Marks, pp. 191–232. Southern Methodist University Press, Dallas.
Muheisen, M.
  1985   L'épipaléolithique dans le gisement de Kharaneh IV. *Paléorient* 11(2):149–160.
  1988   Le gisement de Kharaneh IV, note sommaire sur la phase D. *Paléorient* 14:265–269.
Nelson, B.
  1973   *Azraq Desert Oasis*. Allen Lane, London.
Nissen, H., M. Muheisen and H.-G. Gebel
  1987   Report on the first two seasons of excavation at Basta (1986–1987). *Annual of the Department of Antiquities of Jordan* 31:79–119.
Reese, D. S.
  1991   Marine shells in the Levant: Upper Palaeolithic, Epipalaeolithic and Neolithic. In *The Natufian Culture in the Levant*, edited by O. Bar-Yosef and F. R. Valla, pp. 613–628. International Monographs in Prehistory, Ann Arbor.
Rollefson, G. and I. Kohler-Rollefson
  1989   The collapse of early Neolithic settlements in the Southern Levant. In *People and Culture in Change*, edited by I. Hershkovitz, pp. 73–89. BAR International Series 508, British Archaeological Reports, Oxford.
Sakaguchi, Y.
  1987   Paleoenvironments in the Palmyra district during the late Quaternary. *Bulletin of the University Museum, University of Tokyo* 29:1–27.
Schaller, G. B.
  1977   *Mountain Monarchs: Wild Sheep and Goat of the Himalaya*. University of Chicago Press, Chicago.
Uerpmann, H.-P.
  1987   *The Ancient Distribution of Ungulate Mammals in the Middle East*. Reichert, Wiesbaden.
Waechter, J., V. Seton-Williams, D. M. Bate and L. Picard
  1938   The excavations at Wadi Dhobai 1937–1938 and the Dhobaian industry. *Journal of the Palestine Oriental Society* 18:172–186, 292–298.
Wright, G. A.
  1971   Origins of food production in Southwestern Asia: A survey of ideas. *Current Anthropology* 12:447–477.
Wright, K. I.
  1991   The origins and development of ground stone assemblages in Late Pleistocene Southwest Asia. *Paléorient* 17(1):19–45.
  1993   Early Holocene ground stone assemblages in the Levant. *Levant* 25:93–111.
Yaalon, D. H. and J. Dan
  1974   Accumulation and distribution of loess-derived deposits in the semi-desert and desert fringe areas of Israel. *Zeitschrift für Geomorphologie Supplement* 20:91–105.
Zohary, D. and M. Hopf
  1988   *Domestication of Plants in the Old World*. Clarendon, Oxford.

RADIOCARBON DATING EL-KOWM: UPPER PALEOLITHIC THROUGH CHALCOLITHIC

JACQUES CAUVIN and DANIELLE STORDEUR

Institut de Préhistoire Orientale, Jalès, F-07460 Berrias, France

INTRODUCTION

The El-Kowm basin (Palmyra Desert, Syria) was first inhabited in the Middle Acheulean. To date, five sites (Nadaouiyeh 1, Umm el Tlel, El-Kowm 1, El-Kowm 2, Qdeir 1) have been excavated, revealing archaeological remains from the Lower, Middle and Upper Paleolithic, as well as the Epipaleolithic (Geometric Kebaran and Early Natufian) and the Neolithic (Cauvin 1983). A gap in the occupation of this oasis is evidenced during the Pre-Pottery Neolithic A (PPNA) and early Pre-Pottery Neolithic B (PPNB). The basin was re-occupied at the end of the PPNB, and habitation continued through the Pottery Neolithic (PN) period and up to Late Uruk. We report here 12 ^{14}C dates from 5 sites in the El-Kowm basin. The results are in years before present (BP) and are un-calibrated. Five uranium (U)-series and electron spin resonance (ESR) dates from the Early to Middle Paleolithic precede the ^{14}C dates.

U-SERIES AND ESR DATES

Early–Middle Paleolithic (Yabrudian)

Five dates (Hennig and Hours 1982) have been obtained by other dating methods (U-series and ESR) by the Institute of Physics, University of Köln (ESR) and the Institute for Physical Chemistry, University of Köln (^{60}Co gamma rays). All samples were obtained from travertine levels near four springs of the El-Kowm Basin. These levels were contemporaneous, or immediately over- or underlying Yabrudian levels. The samples were taken from sections of deep wells dug by contemporary peasants for irrigation:

1. Humm 2 – a travertineous conglomerate containing Yabrudian industry in a well at Hummal. Corrected age = 156,000 yr.
2. Oumm 3 – an analogous deposit in Umm el Tlel well. Early and Middle Paleolithic levels have not been excavated. Corrected age = 139,000 yr.
3. Oumm 4 – travertine from Umm Qubeiba well between Yabrudian and Levalloiso-Mousterian levels. Corrected age = 76,000 yr.
4. Oumm 5 – travertine from the same well, underlying the Yabrudian. Corrected age = 245,000 yr.
5. Tell 6 – travertine contemporaneous with Yabrudian from the well of Tell Aarida. Corrected age = 99,000 yr.

Comment: The Yabrudian fills a transitional period between the Early Paleolithic (Acheulean) and the Middle Paleolithic of Syria. According to Hours (1992), these dates indicate that the Yabrudian culture probably lasted from 150,000 to 100,000 yr. The Levalloiso-Mousterian could have begun *ca.* 80,000 yr ago, directly following the initial Hummalian phase, found also in the wells of Hummal (Hours 1982) and Umm el Tlel. Even though these dates seem early, if one considers other dates from Zuttiyeh and Naame (Lebanon) for the beginning of the Levalloiso-Mousterian (*ca.* 90,000 yr ago), one can accept that the transition from Early to the Middle Paleolithic in Syria occurred not only during the Thyrrhenian interpluvial, but as early as the penultimate pluvial.

Late Quaternary Chronology and Paleoclimates of the Eastern Mediterranean
Edited by O. Bar-Yosef and R. S. Kra. RADIOCARBON 1994, pp. 201–204

RADIOCARBON DATES

Upper Paleolithic

Two charcoal samples from the site of Umm el Tlel were submitted for ^{14}C age determination by accelerator mass spectrometry (AMS) in cooperation with Hélène Valladas, Gif-sur-Yvette. Miquel Molist collected the samples while excavating a test pit (Molist and Cauvin 1990).

Gif A-90034. Layer V   **30,310 ± 670**
Gif A-90004. Layer XI   **30,790 ± 760**
Comment: The industry of Layer V at Umm el Tlel resembles that of Layers 10B through 10H in Tixier's excavations at Ksar 'Akil (Tixier and Inizan 1981; Molist and Cauvin 1990). Thus, the date of Layer V coincides well with the material culture attributed to Aurignacian B of the Levant. However, in view of the character of the lithic industry of Layer XI, in which numerous Levallois elements are present, M.-C. Cauvin considers the date too young.

Epipaleolithic

In the course of excavating the same test pit at Umm el Tlel, a charcoal sample was retrieved from the Geometric Kebaran level.

Gif A-90039.   **20,370 ± 330**
Comment: M.-C. Cauvin considers this date too old, in view of the lithic industry. The second excavation of the Geometric Kebaran levels at this site by Gabriel Alcade will probably yield more samples for dating.

Final Pre-Pottery Neolithic B

Final PPNB (or PPNC) is an aceramic culture of the desert zone of Syria and Jordan, contemporaneous with the earliest coastal cultures with dark-face burnished ware (DFBW) pottery (*cf.* Amuq A). Final PPNB is very well represented in the El-Kowm basin, with numerous surface sites as well as stratified levels in 4 sites, 2 of which are juxtaposed in the village of El-Kowm.

El-Kowm 1

This large tell, 20 m above the plain, consists essentially of final PPNB levels. However, some remains of Early Natufian and Geometric Kebaran were also found at the base of these levels (Cauvin, Coqueugniot and Nierlé 1982). Also visible were some Paleolithic levels in the section of a well adjacent to the tell. Only two charcoal samples from different PPNB layers have been dated, both belonging to the final phases of occupation (Dorneman 1986). The samples were dated in 1973 at Groningen and are, from top to bottom:

GrN-6777. Marche III, Phase D, Level (2) (5)   **7290 ± 45**
GrN-6778. Marche IV, Level (2), Room 1   **7400 ± 45**
Comment: We should note that, if the Marche IV sample correlates to an *in-situ* architectural layer, then that of Marche III correlates to a disturbed layer with depressions or pits that contain ceramics attributed to the PN period. The contours of these depressions have not all been identified. GrN-6778 is probably associated with the later ceramic phase.

El-Kowm 2 – Caracol

The tell of El-Kowm 2 is immediately adjacent to El-Kowm 1. It is much smaller and was excavated by D. Stordeur (1989; Stordeur, Maréchal and Molist 1991; Cauvin 1982) from 1978 to 1986. Five dates were obtained at the Lyon Radiocarbon Laboratory with the help of Jacques Evin.

Ly-2520. Upper Level AIV	**7680 ± 200**
Ly-2521. Upper Level AV	**7760 ± 280**
Ly-4438. Lower Level AI	**7760 ± 510**
Ly-4400. Test pit at boundary of occupation surface	**8030 ± 80**
Ly-4439. Test pit at boundary of occupation surface	**7400 ± 300**

Comment: The dates correlate well with the first half of the eighth millennium BP. These results were expected, despite large statistical errors.

Qdeir 1

Qdeir 1 is a hill composed of aeolian sediment near a spring (*tertre de source; cf.* Besançon and Sanlaville 1991), with interstratified levels of final PPNB. The Qdeir 1 site was first tested by Aurenche and Cauvin (1982) and is currently under excavation by D. Stordeur. This single date derives from the first test pit.

Ly-2578. Sondage 1980   **7560 ± 430 BP**

Comment: Continued efforts to date this site are essential because of the problem of charcoal preservation in highly saline sediments. It is important to determine whether this site, which is a semi-nomadic occupation, is contemporary with the surrounding sedentary settlements in the El-Kowm basin (Cauvin 1987–1988). Further AMS dating is planned by H. Valladas.

Pottery Neolithic

No date exists for the PN of the El-Kowm Basin, perhaps with the exception of El-Kowm 1, GrN-6778 (see above).

Late Uruk

One date was obtained from bones at the site of El-Kowm 2, which represents an occupation without architecture, probably of late or final Uruk (Cauvin and Stordeur 1985).

Ly-2318. Fosse XGG   **5930 ± 300**

Comment: Poor preservation of the collagen caused a large statistical error. The Uruk occupation is approximately contemporaneous with the first urban settlements of the middle Euphrates Valley (Habuba Kabira, Sheikh Hassan, top). It probably represents a nomadic aspect of the same culture.

REFERENCES CITED

Aurenche, O. and M. C. Cauvin
    1982   Qdeir 1, campagne 1980: Une installation néolithique du VIIe millénaire. *Cahiers de l'Euphrate* 3:51–78.
Besançon, J. and P. Sanlaville
    1991   Une oasis dans la steppe aride syrienne: La cuvette d'El Kowm au Quaternaire. *Cahiers de l'Euphrate* 5/6:11–32.
Cauvin, J.
    1982   L'oasis d'El Kowm au néolithique. Bilan après trois campagnes: Méthodes, problèmes et premiers résultats. *Cahiers de l'Euphrate* 3:93–98.
    1983   Cinq années de recherches (1978–1983) dans l'oasis d'El Kowm (Syrie). *Les Annales Archéologiques Arabes Syriennes: Revue d'Archéologie et d'Histoire* 23(1):165–177.

Cauvin, J.
1987–   L'occupation préhistorique du désert Syrien: Nouvelles recherches dans la cuvette d'El Kowm (1984–1989).
1988   *Les Annales Archéologiques Arabes Syriennes: Revue d'Archéologie et d'Histoire* 37–38:51–65.

Cauvin, J. and D. Stordeur
1985   Une occupation d'époque Uruk en Palmyrène: Le niveau supérieur d'El Kowm 2–Caracol. *Cahiers de l'Euphrate* 4:191–205.

Cauvin, M. C., E. Coqueugniot and M.-C. Nierlé
1982   Rapport préliminaire sur la campagne 1980 d'El Kowm 1. *Cahiers de l'Euphrate* 3:27–32.

Dornemann, R. H.
1986   A Neolithic village at Tell el Kowm in the Syrian desert. *Studies in Ancient Oriental Civilization* 93. Oriental Institute of the University of Chicago, Chicago.

Hennig, G. J. and F. Hours
1982   Dates pour le passage entre l'Acheuléen et le Paléolithique moyen à El Kowm (Syrie). *Paléorient* 8(1):81–84.

Hours, F.
1982   Une nouvelle industrie en Syrie entre l'Acheuléen supérieur et le Levalloiso-moustérien. In *Archéologie au Levant*. Collection de la Maison de l'Orient Méditerranéen, Série Archéologique 12, pp. 33–46. Maison de l'Orient, Lyon.

Molist, M. and M.-C. Cauvin
1990   Une nouvelle séquence stratifiée pour la préhistoire en Syrie semi-désertique. *Paléorient* 16(2):55–63.

Stordeur, D.
1989   El Kowm 2–Caracol et le PPNB. *Paléorient* 15(1):102–110.

Stordeur, D., C. Maréchal and M. Molist
1991   Stratigraphie générale du tell néolithique d'El Kowm 2–Caracol (Syrie). *Cahiers de l'Euphrate* 5/6:33–46.

Tixier, J. and M. L. Inizan
1981   Ksar' Aqil: Stratigraphie et ensembles lithiques dans le Paléolithique supérieur: Fouilles 1971–1975. In *Préhistoire du Levant*, edited by J. Cauvin and P. Sanlaville, pp. 353–367. Maison de l'Orient, CNRS, Lyon.

LATE QUATERNARY HUNTER-GATHERER COMPLEXES IN THE LEVANT BETWEEN 20,000 AND 10,000 BP

BRIAN F. BYRD

Brian F. Mooney Associates, 9903-B Businesspark Avenue, San Diego, California 92131-1120 USA and Department of Anthropology, University of California, San Diego, La Jolla, California 92093 USA

CLASSIFICATION, CHIPPED STONE INDUSTRIES AND HUNTER-GATHERERS

The extensive research on late Quaternary hunter-gatherer settlements in the Levant has resulted in an exceedingly rich and comprehensive archaeological database from a relatively restricted geographical area. The period between *ca.* 20,000 and 10,000 BP is generally termed the Epipaleolithic and was, initially, strongly correlated with the appearance, numerical dominance and persistence of backed retouched microliths as elements in composite tools (Perrot 1966). This notion has since been revised, based on the results of subsequent field research.

During more than 50 years of research, many terms have been used to characterize the microlithic archaeological assemblages and groups of assemblages of this era. These include Bergian, Geometric Kebaran, Falitian, Hamran, Harifian, Hureyran, Kebaran, Madamaghan, Mushabian, Natufian, Nebekian, Nizzanan, Qalkhan and Ramonian (Bar-Yosef 1970; Copeland and Waechter 1968; Garrod 1932; Goring-Morris 1987; Henry 1982; Marks and Scott 1976; Olszewski 1984; Phillips and Mintz 1977; Rust 1950; Turville-Petre 1932). Of these, only five designations are widely accepted as representative patterns in the archaeological record: Geometric Kebaran, Harifian, Kebaran, Mushabian and Natufian (Bar-Yosef 1991a; Valla 1988a). In addition, all but the Harifian have been subject to finer temporal (early, late, *etc.*) and spatial (typically termed groups) subdivision. The remaining terms are of only historical interest or are used by those who coined them.

The reasons for all this terminology and associated controversies lie in varying objectives of the classifications and the criteria used to create them. Ambiguities can be seen in the varied use of such terms as industry, complex, culture and entity directly after the name (*e.g.*, the Natufian industry (Garrod 1932) *vs.* culture (Garrod 1958)). Some terms distinguish a single site, some much more. Each of these units of classification was primarily based on the associated chipped stone industries, although other archaeological characteristics, such as bone tools, groundstone, burials, architecture, site size and site thickness, have also been considered occasionally (particularly with respect to the Natufian, *e.g.*, Garrod 1958). The chipped stone criteria focus on variability in form, manufacturing technique and size of retouched and backed microliths (generally, the predominant tool forms that are considered the hallmark of this period). The primary analytical emphasis has been placed on variation in frequency of tools within this group, especially in types of geometric and non-geometric microliths. This research emphasis has developed principally because these tools show the widest range of variation and patterning. The nature and frequency of other lithic tools, along with elements of the reduction sequence (including the predominant blank types selected for retouching, core morphology and technology) have played a more limited role in distinguishing groups of assemblages.

Two new bodies of evidence stemming from radiometric dating have further complicated the classification and understanding of late Quaternary hunter-gatherers in the Levant. Bladelet blanks

Late Quaternary Chronology and Paleoclimates of the Eastern Mediterranean
Edited by O. Bar-Yosef and R. S. Kra RADIOCARBON 1994, pp. 205–226

205

and retouched and backed microlithic tools are now widely documented at Upper Paleolithic sites dating at least as early as 30,000 BP (Bar-Yosef and Belfer-Cohen 1977; Bar-Yosef and Phillips 1977; Gilead 1983, 1988; 1991:121–125; Phillips 1994). Hence, the perception that bladelets and retouched microliths were the distinctive addition to the tool kit of the Epipaleolithic is no longer valid.[1] The second development entailed the discovery of sites with lithic industries dating later than 20,000 BP that contain retouched bladelets very similar to pre-20,000 BP occupation horizons, or very few retouched and backed microliths (Garrard, Baird and Byrd 1994; Garrard and Byrd 1992; Gilead 1991; Goring-Morris 1987). In the western Levant, such sites are called either terminal or late Upper Paleolithic, implying a late persistence of hunter-gatherer groups carrying out an Upper Paleolithic life style.

These two developments have led to a re-evaluation of the utility of the term, *Epipaleolithic*. Gilead (1984, 1991:133) suggests that the term be used only for the Natufian, and Bar-Yosef restricts it to the Geometric Kebaran and later (Bar-Yosef and Vogel 1987:220). Others, including myself, have simply dropped the term (*e.g.*, Goring-Morris 1987; Henry 1989).

The lack of rigorously defined terminology and classification systems is a major impediment to meaningful comparisons among regional assemblages where classificatory objectives must be problem-oriented. Bar-Yosef and Vogel (1987:220–221) noted that classification systems associated with the late Quaternary are either numerical-temporal or cultural-historical (*e.g.*, Aurenche *et al.* 1981; Bar-Yosef 1970). The latter generally aim at identifying hunter-gatherer social units in the Levant to facilitate understanding the causes and mechanisms behind the transition to a settled, food-producing economy (Bar-Yosef 1991a); this subject has received the most interest during the past 20 years.

Henry (1989:79–89) has proposed the most explicitly defined classification to identify socio-economic hunter-gatherer units during the late Quaternary—a three-tiered hierarchy, proceeding from the actual archaeological assemblages to create phases/facies, industries and complexes. The evidence upon which his classification is built is drawn primarily from quantitative analysis of stone tool types (particularly backed microliths), tool blank size and microburin indexes (micro-burins being a specialized technique for truncating bladelets while shaping them into backed microliths). His study reaffirms the equivalence of 4 of the 5 primary late Quaternary units, for which he uses the term, *complex* (Kebaran, Geometric Kebaran, Mushabian and Natufian). The Harifian is subsumed as an industry within the Natufian complex. Here, I use *complex* to refer to each of the five primary late Quaternary units, and the slightly more restrictive *industry* for more selective samples of assemblages in other circumstances.

Recently, researchers have attempted to distinguish late Quaternary social groups and their territorial extent, inferring that expressions of style (*e.g.*, equally viable choices made for manufacturing a microlithic tool) can be identified in the archaeological record (*e.g.*, Bar-Yosef and Vogel 1987; Close 1989; Goring-Morris 1987; Shennan 1989; Sheppard 1987; Wiessner 1989). Such studies in the Levant have focused on use-intensity of the microburin technique, the type of retouch used on the backed bladelets, and their size and shape. However, some changes in microlithic tool form may be functional, related to the method of hafting into wood or bone shafts for hunting (Bar-Yosef 1987; Kukan 1978; Valla 1987). Examination of reduction strategies, particularly the

---

[1]Goring-Morris (1987:88–93) has offered an alternative intriguing hypothesis regarding the sequence of developments in the Upper Paleolithic that may have led to the widespread use of backed microliths as composite tool pieces (but see Marks 1988).

production of the ubiquitous microlithic tools, offers the best opportunity for identifying regional traditions and group boundaries during this era (Bar-Yosef 1991b,c). In this paper, I examine the correlation between current nomenclature for prehistoric hunter-gatherer complexes in the Levant between 20,000 and 10,000 BP, incorporating recent field investigations and radiocarbon dates.

RADIOCARBON DATES

Many ^{14}C dates have been obtained from occupation horizons dating between 20,000 and 10,000 BP. Table 1 is a compilation of the 232 assays currently available from occupation horizons. At times I use the term, *occupation horizon*, instead of *site*, because many sites have multiple occupation horizons. The number of ^{14}C dates has increased rapidly during the past 15 yr because of the increased pace of field research, the advent of accelerator mass spectrometry (AMS) and its ability to date much smaller samples, and recognition of the advantage of obtaining multiple dates from single-occupation horizons.

Results listed in Table 1 derive from 19 ^{14}C laboratories. The Oxford AMS laboratory analyzed the most samples. A variety of materials were assayed, the most prominent being wood charcoal, along with ash, charred seeds, burned bone, unburned bone, humic acids and ostrich shell. Of these assays, *ca.* 20% are considered by most researchers to be unreliable or probably unreliable because the dates fall well outside the established range of the archaeological complexes and/or the other dates obtained from that occupation horizon (Table 1). In addition, the number of questionable dates would be increased if they were critically evaluated. Although the percentage of dubious dates may appear rather high, this should not be viewed as unexpected.

The primary causes for unreliable results appear to be post-depositional disturbance, and outdated or varied laboratory techniques, particularly for some of the first dates measured (Waterbolk 1987). The strength of association between dated items and the overall artifact assemblage from a deposit has long been a major interpretive problem. This is now magnified by the use of very small fragments of wood charcoal and seeds through AMS dating, which are much more amenable to movement than larger materials. More reliance on *in-situ* samples, particularly from such features as hearths or trammeled surfaces, might reduce these difficulties. The problem is further magnified by the dating of *old wood*, wood that is either long-lived and/or has been re-used (Bar-Yosef 1989; Kuijt and Bar-Yosef 1994; Schiffer 1986; Waterbolk 1987:43). Further use of charred seeds will reduce this dating distortion.

The probability of obtaining reliable dates from only 1 or 2 samples is quite small. Several archaeologists working in the Levant now submit a substantial series of samples from a single, restricted occupation horizon, which is an ideal procedure (*e.g.,* Nadel and Hershkovitz 1991; Garrard and Byrd 1992; Hovers and Mardel 1991; Moore 1992). It is generally apparent from *cluster dating* which assays fall outside the main cluster. Cluster dating can be expensive, and may be appropriate only where existing information is weak or contradictory. However, an intensive dating scheme cannot guarantee accurate ages for a cultural assemblage if other factors systematically bias the inferences of association or the dates themselves.

[14]C dates in Table 1 are separated into two geographical units: the eastern and western Levant (the Rift system, extending from the Red Sea northward through the Jordan Valley, is the dividing line), subdivided into chipped stone and/or cultural complexes. This geographical division was used because the southwestern Levant has been well documented; the cultural traditions and industrial sequences are best known and most appropriate for this area. The western Levant is divided into six groups of complexes: *Late/Terminal Upper Paleolithic,* Kebaran, Geometric Kebaran, Mushabian and related industries, Natufian and Harifian. In contrast, the eastern Levant has only recently

witnessed rigorous fieldwork (both survey and excavations), and is not yet well understood. Although the same terms have been applied to newly excavated sites in the east, emerging results suggest some distinctive and widely varying lithic complexes. Thus, I subdivide eastern sites into non-Natufian microlithic, non-microlithic, and Natufian and related northern Syrian industries.

CORRELATION OF HUNTER-GATHERER COMPLEXES AND RADIOCARBON DATES

Western Levant

Forty-eight distinct occupation horizons have been dated in the western Levant. Of the 141 ^{14}C samples currently available (61% of the total sample), 25 are considered unreliable, and 8, probably unreliable. The summary of the chipped stone industries in the western Levant draws extensively from the following publications: Bar-Yosef (1970, 1981, 1989, 1990); Bar-Yosef and Belfer-Cohen (1989, 1992); Bar-Yosef and Phillips (1977); Bar-Yosef and Vogel (1987); Goring-Morris (1987); Henry (1983, 1989); and Valla (1988b).

Late/Terminal Upper Paleolithic (pre-20,000–ca. 16,000 BP). Chipped stone assemblages vary widely in character within this group of sites; they represent a coherent entity only in juxtaposition with the Kebaran complex (Ferring 1977, 1980; Gilead 1991; Goring-Morris 1980, 1987:57–97; Marks 1976). These assemblages are distinguished from the Kebaran by types of microliths, and, to some extent, on core-reduction technologies. *Lamelles dufour*, twisted bladelets typically with interior lateral retouch, are common at some sites, whereas finely retouched microliths are more prevalent at others. The frequency of microliths varies widely, from <10% to >60%.

The six occupation horizons listed in Table 1, with ^{14}C dates younger than 20,000 BP, are labeled Late or Terminal Paleolithic. The 13 ^{14}C assays range primarily from 18,000 to 16,000 BP, and the dated sites of this *complex* are in the Mt. Carmel area, the Negev and the Jordan Valley. Although the dates overlap with Kebaran dates, ^{14}C dates for broadly contemporary Kebaran occupation exist nearby only in the west-central area. These assemblages are considered to represent a continuation of earlier Upper Paleolithic tool traditions in the Negev and Jordan Valley by populations coeval with the Kebaran (Bar-Yosef 1981:391; Goring-Morris 1987:444). Rigorous evaluation of site-specific functional variation may alter these interpretations (Valla 1988c).

Kebaran (19,000–14,500 BP). The definition of the Kebaran complex is based largely on a high frequency of microliths and the prevalence of particular forms of non-geometric microliths (Bar-Yosef 1975, 1981). The microburin technique was not used regularly to truncate microliths prior to backing. Spatial variability has long been noted during the Kebaran, and four regional groups distinguished (*e.g.*, Bar-Yosef 1970). The Kebaran has also been subdivided into early and late, based on relative frequency of non-geometric microliths. The term, *Kebaran ancien*, has also been suggested to precede the early Kebaran, particularly in the northwest Levant (Besançon *et al.* 1975; Valla 1988a). It is characterized by finely or semi-abrupt retouched bladelets, whereas the Kebaran is typified by abrupt retouch. However, no dates are available from these occupation horizons. The early Kebaran is dominated generally by micropoints, curved or arched backed bladelets and microgravettes. Predominant obliquely truncated and backed microliths characterize the late Kebaran, although curved backed bladelets are also present (Bar-Yosef and Vogel 1987:225). Bar-Yosef (1981:392-393, 1990) suggests considerable variability existed during the early Kebaran (accounting for most of the spatial subdivisions), whereas more homogeneity is hypothesized for the late Kebaran.

Two-thirds of the 35 dates from 6 sites are from recently dated sites, Ohalo II and Urkan-e-Rub, west-central Levant. The overall temporal distribution of dates confirms previous estimates for the duration of the Kebaran (Bar-Yosef 1990; Bar-Yosef and Vogel 1987; Valla 1988a). Gilead (1991), has hypothesized that many Kebaran sites on the coastal plain are actually Upper Paleolithic and antedate 20,000 BP. Hovers and Mardel (1991) also suggest that the late Kebaran dates from Urkan-e-Rub, which is dominated by curved micropoints, may indicate that the criteria used to differentiate early and late Kebaran must be revised. These criteria (a gradual shift from predominant curved backed microliths to obliquely truncated microliths), however, are supported by stratigraphic evidence from sites in the environs of Urkan-e-Rub and elsewhere (Bar-Yosef 1990; Goring-Morris 1980). More dates are needed to resolve these issues.

Geometric Kebaran (14,500–13,000 BP). This complex is characterized by bladelets fashioned into backed microliths. The production of more straight-backed non-geometric forms, and the appearance and widespread use of geometric trapeze-rectangle microliths, represent the major distinctions separating this complex from late Kebaran assemblages (Bar-Yosef and Belfer-Cohen 1989: 462–463; Henry 1989:93–94; Valla 1988b). The microburin technique was used only occasionally to truncate microliths during their manufacture.

In contrast to the Kebaran, fewer dates (20) but many more sites (12) characterize the Geometric Kebaran complex. Except for Neve David, all these sites are located in the Sinai and Negev. Their temporal range does not appear to overlap with the Kebaran, which is not surprising, given the dearth of dates from Geometric Kebaran sites in the west-central Levant. Geometric Kebaran assemblages have also been subdivided into two groups, based on widths of backed microliths. The cluster of assemblages with narrow microliths is thought to be older (Bar-Yosef 1981:397–398), but this distinction is not supported by recent dates from Neve David (Kaufman 1988).

Mushabian (14,000–12,800 BP). The Mushabian complex is distinguished by predominant non-geometric backed bladelets, the production of which entailed intensive use of the microburin technique (Phillips and Mintz 1977). The dominant microliths are arched backed bladelets that include typically La Mouillah points. These and other characteristics of the chipped stone industry show similarities with North African industries; thus, an eastern origin has been suggested for the Mushabian. The Mushabian and related industries are restricted to the Negev and Sinai in the western Levant, where 15 dates from 9 occupation horizons were obtained from sites mostly in the Sinai. The range of dates and stratigraphic evidence suggest contemporaneity with the Geometric Kebaran for some time, and that their territories overlapped in parts of the Negev/Sinai (Bar-Yosef and Belfer-Cohen 1989:464; Henry 1989:144). Temporal and regional subdivisions have been proposed for the Mushabian complex, and many have been given discrete names (*e.g.*, Goring-Morris 1987; Henry 1989:97–102; Marks and Simmons 1977), but none has been fully accepted (Goring-Morris 1988; Henry 1988a; Valla 1988c). Bar-Yosef and Belfer-Cohen (1989:465) and Henry (1988a:58) also hypothesized that the late Mushabian may be contemporary with the early Natufian, although the range of dates and their error limits make this difficult to demonstrate.

Natufian (12,800/12,500–10,500 BP). The definition of Natufian is based on a series of site characteristics, many of which lie outside the domain of the chipped stone industries (*e.g.*, Bar-Yosef 1983; Byrd 1989a; Garrod 1958; Henry 1985). Key features of the chipped stone industries include smaller cores, wider and shorter blanks, the use of the microburin technique, predominant geometric lunates, backed and unbacked sickle blades and more massive tools (Bar-Yosef and Valla 1991; Perrot 1966; Valla 1975, 1984). Several attributes distinguish early and late Natufian assemblages, including smaller lunates and a corresponding decline in Helwan (or bifacial) backing (Bar-Yosef and Valla 1979). The Natufian is the most heavily dated late Quaternary complex in the Levant, with 39 dates from 12 sites. However, over 25% of the dates are unreliable.

Harifian (10,700–10,000 BP). The Harifian has many similarities with later Natufian occupation, including small lunates (Goring-Morris 1991; Scott 1977). The Harif point, manufactured using the microburin technique, is the assemblage's unique feature; the point appears to have been hafted in the same manner as subsequent Neolithic projectile points (Bar-Yosef 1987). The Harifian is the most geographically and temporally restricted complex dated to the Late Pleistocene. Its distribution is limited to portions of the Negev and Sinai, and appears to have persisted for less than a millennium. Only four sites have been dated, but 19 assays are now available. The dates are extremely consistent, and confirm suggestions of a relatively short episode. It appears likely that the Harifian is an outgrowth of local late Natufian settlement, although dates for the late Natufian of Rosh Horesha are very close to those of the Harifian sites.

Summary. This 10,000-yr period prior to the Neolithic is relatively well dated in the western Levant, and the longevity of each of the main microlithic complexes is relatively well established. But there are major dating gaps among geographical regions: the Negev/Sinai is well dated, whereas the west-central area has limited evidence for the Kebaran and Geometric Kebaran, and the north-central Levant has no dates at all. More dates are needed to resolve the following issues: 1) whether some *Kebaran* microlithic coastal sites are, in fact, pre-20,000 BP Upper Paleolithic; 2) the geographical and temporal extent of the *Terminal/Late Upper Paleolithic* complex; 3) the timing of the transition from the Geometric Kebaran to the Natufian, and from the Natufian to the Neolithic.

Eastern Levant

Only 91 dates from 32 occupation horizons are available from the eastern Levant (39% of the total); 9 are unreliable and 8 are probably unreliable. Compared to the Western Levant, this smaller suite of dates indicates the shorter period of intensive field research. The following discussion of the chipped stone assemblages and possible correlations with the western Levant primarily draws upon summarized results from recent field projects (*e.g.*, Byrd 1988; Byrd and Garrard 1990; Clark *et al.* 1988; Edwards 1987; Edwards *et al.* 1988; Garrard *et al.* 1986, 1987, 1988; Garrard, Baird and Byrd 1994; Henry 1988b, 1989; Jones 1983; Muheisen 1988a; Olszewski *et al.* 1990).

Non-Natufian Microlithic (20,000 BP–?). For this period, 39 dates from 15 sites, several of which have multiple occupation horizons, have been obtained. Most derive from the Azraq Basin of the east-central Levant with another cluster of dated sites from Wadi Hasa in the southeast. Ten of the sites, with >66% of the ^{14}C assays, have yielded dates between 20,000 and 14,300 BP—coeval with the Kebaran of the western Levant. The literature reveals a consistent developmental sequence characterized initially by production bladelets that have been backed and retouched into narrow microliths. In the Jordan Valley, narrow straight-backed and obliquely truncated non-geometric microliths dominate an early dated assemblage, without microburins, at Wadi Hammeh 26 (Edwards 1987). Ein Gev I, much farther north in the Jordan Valley, is characterized by obliquely truncated and backed bladelets and no microburin technique (Bar-Yosef 1970). In the southeastern Levant, the main chipped stone assemblage from Madamagh is dominated by long, narrow, finely retouched and backed bladelets, including arched-backed and truncated pieces often with visible microburin scars (Kirkbride 1958). My re-analysis of this assemblage and Schyle and Uerpmann's (1988:47–52) narrow section cut in the lower remnants of the old excavation trench revealed *Lamelles dufour* in the oldest levels.

Virtually all sites in the Azraq Basin antedating 15,000 BP demonstrate heavy utilization of the microburin technique. Narrow, finely retouched and backed arch-backed bladelets dominate the earliest dated sites, whereas slightly younger (stratigraphically) occupation horizons in the Azraq

Basin yield larger backed tools, including more La Mouillah points and double-truncated pieces (Byrd 1988). The succeeding occupation phase at Jilat 6 is dominated by both small- and moderate-sized symmetrical and asymmetrical triangles, along with small numbers of microgravette points. This phase, A, is now well dated to between 16,500 and 15,500 BP.

Kharaneh IV has also yielded a long and detailed stratigraphic succession and many ^{14}C dates (Muheisen 1983, 1988a,b). Its sequence of assemblages begins with narrow, finely retouched blade-lets, then narrow backed microliths (either arch-backed or obliquely truncated), and finally, much wider, more geometric, truncated and/or backed microliths. The final phase of occupation also has a considerable number of atypical, wide *trapezes* and an occasional *lunate*. This well-documented sequence is consistent with technological and tool-production patterns dated in the western Levant from pre-20,000 BP to the Geometric Kebaran, whereas the previously published dates from Kharaneh IV are much younger (13,970–9840 BP). Based on two new dates from the final phase (D) of occupation (M. Muheisen, personal communication), the previous bone dates appear in-correct and the timing of the Kharaneh IV microlith developmental sequence probably parallels that documented in other portions of the Azraq Basin.

The five remaining non-Natufian microlithic sites have yielded dates almost exclusively later than 14,000 BP. This suite of dates, including 2 unreliable and 6 probably unreliable dates, is problem-atic. Problems include gross internal inconsistency (Jilat 8, Tabaqat al-Bumma), assemblages that date either during or later than the Natufian time range but lack corresponding characteristics (Jilat 22 and possibly Tor Hamar), and assemblages that share more characteristics with either Kebaran or late Upper Paleolithic complexes, rather than post-Kebaran complexes from the western Levant (Azraq 17 and Tabaqat al-Bumma). Given our current understanding of the development of the chipped stone industry in the Levant, I suggest that only the oldest dates from Jilat 8 and Tabaqat al-Bumma, and possibly the Tor Hamar date, should be considered consistent with that information.

The three problematic sites in the east-central Levant are quite varied. The dated assemblage from Trench 2, Azraq 17 contains extremely long and narrow, finely retouched bladelets and a few backed bladelet fragments, similar to Kharaneh IV Phase A. In contrast, *contemporary* Jilat 8 is dominated by backed non-geometric microliths, including small, curved pointed backed tools, La Mouillah points, and some small narrow, trapeze-rectangles. Phase B of Jilat 22 is similar to Jilat 8, but also includes a few triangle- and lunate-shaped tools. Two problematic assemblages are outside the Azraq Basin. Tor Hamar has a single basal date from a multilevel site. The associated chipped stone assemblage includes arched backed bladelets and La Mouillah points (Henry 1988b). In contrast, Tabaqat al-Bumma has yielded four widely distributed dates. The associated microlithic assemblage includes narrow, obliquely truncated and backed bladelets and some micropoints (Banning *et al.* 1992), and appears to share many similarities with nearby Wadi Hammeh 26. The microburin technique was consistently used at Jilat 8, Jilat 22 and Tor Hamar.

Non-Microlithic (ca. 14,000–13,000 BP). Only 7 dates from 3 occupation horizons (including 2 occupation horizons from 1 site) comprise this category. Although they have been found only in the Jilat drainage of the Azraq Basin, they are noteworthy because they are essentially non-micro-lithic assemblages (>80% of the retouched tools), contemporary with the Geometric Kebaran and Mushabian of the western Levant. The few microliths recovered are diverse, finely retouched bladelets, La Mouillah points and some possible trapeze-rectangles. A novel, tanged knife is the predominant tool type recovered at Jilat 22 Phase C (Garrard and Byrd 1992). Made on a blade, it has no known parallels in the Levant. Non-microlithic horizons may represent both task-specific localities that are part of microlithic tool traditions (Jilat 10), and the first indications of a distinct industry characterized by a dearth of microliths and unique tanged tools (Jilat 22). Much more work is needed to understand fully the implications of these preliminary results.

Natufian and Related Industries (12,800/12,500–10,000 BP). These industries are the best dated in the eastern Levant, although the 45 dates came from only five sites. Three sites are dated to the early Natufian in the south and central areas; their ^{14}C results are the oldest for the Natufian, and demonstrate Natufian occupation during the 13th millennium BP. Henry (1982:438) suggested that the Natufian emerged as a distinct complex on the Jordanian plateau, but we cannot be sure of this, given the large error ranges for the dates in the Hisma area. The technological and typological characteristics, including Helwan retouch and large lunates, of these Natufian sites concurs with dated Natufian sites in the southwestern Levant, and differences appear to be related to variation in subsistence practices between environmental zones (Byrd 1989a,b; Edwards 1987; Henry 1989).

In contrast, the two sites dated to the late Natufian (Abu Hureyra and Mureybet) are in the extreme north, and appear to have some chipped-stone features that set them apart from contemporaneous occupation in the central and southern areas, although these distinctions are not universally accepted (Bar Yosef and Valla 1991; Cauvin 1991; Calley 1986; Olszewski 1991). Abu Hureyra has the most impressive dating sequence, consisting of 26 assays (Moore 1992; Moore *et al.* 1986). This data set has provided a firm chronological foundation for Abu Hureyra, although the proposed 1500-yr pre-Neolithic occupation span may be erroneously exaggerated by the outliers.

Summary. As a whole, the eastern Levant is not well dated; no dates exist north of the Yarmouk River, from sites prior to 11,200 BP, and relatively few dates are available from the highlands and the Jordan Valley. More arid areas, such as Wadi Hasa and Azraq Basin, have yielded more dates. The most, and most consistent, dates fall between 20,000 and 14,500 BP. With the exception of Natufian and related sites, dates younger than 14,500 BP are extremely variable. Further research will probably document the coexistence of discrete hunter-gatherer social units with differing microlithic traditions. This may include occupation in arid areas contemporary with the early Natufian. No firm evidence exists of non-Natufian lithic assemblages contemporary with the Natufian. Many more dates are needed to clarify inconsistencies and differing claims for the affiliation of undated sites.

Several new insights into lithic technology and tool production have resulted from dating eastern Levantine sites. First, extensive use of the microburin technique started at 20,000 BP, which continued for 9000 yr. The hypothesized African origin of the technique in the Mushabian of the Negev and Sinai, >6000 yr later (Henry 1974), now must be re-evaluated. Second, geometric-like microlithic assemblages from the Azraq Basin antedate 15,000 BP (contemporary with the late Kebaran). These include a microlithic assemblage with abundant small and medium triangles from Jilat 6 Phase A and a microlithic assemblage dominated by atypical wide *trapezes* from Kharaneh IV Phase D. Third, sites dominated by non-microlithic assemblages date between 13,600 and 12,700 BP (contemporary with the Geometric Kebaran). These settlements contained totally undocumented tanged knives associated with some backed microliths. Finally, early Natufian sites are firmly dated before 12,000 BP.

DISCUSSION

When both radiometric and relative data derived from the stratigraphic superposition of undated assemblages are integrated, it is apparent that the Levant as a whole, was host to a succession of microlithic chipped-stone manufacturing developments. This is confirmed in several localities in the eastern and western Levant, and there seem to be no stratigraphic exceptions to this pattern.

The sequence runs from thin, finely retouched and backed microliths, to somewhat larger microliths with more obliquely retouched ends, to more geometric forms that include triangles or trapeze-rectangles, and finally, to predominant lunates. This patterning supports previous reconstructions of technological progression preceding the Neolithic.

New dates on a series of assemblages has indicated that this developmental succession is not parallel temporally between subregions, and that particular *stages* in this sequence may not have occurred in certain areas of the Levant. The strongest evidence to for these trends is from Late/Terminal Upper Paleolithic horizons in the western Levant, and *non-microlithic assemblages* in the eastern Levant. Other recent results suggest restricted group boundaries, a mosaic of adaptive strategies and varied interaction spheres of distinct hunter-gather populations during much of the 10,000 yr under consideration (*e.g.*, Gilead 1988). The greatest homogeneity across the Levant occurred only during the Natufian, and intensified social interaction between hunter-gatherer groups probably played a prominent role in this development. A prominent future research objective should be to identify fully these patterns, to reconstruct the social mechanisms behind their origins and determine the effect they had on the subsequent emergence of settled food-producing villages whose establishment and progress were lengthy and regionally varying (Byrd 1991).

Spatial and temporal information derived from intensive survey, site discovery, excavation and dating can be used to distinguish possible hunter-gatherer units and their territorial range, including coexistence of different social groups. Geographic extent and duration of discrete hunter-gatherer social units can only begin to be reconstructed for the Negev and Sinai, where >280 sites have been surveyed (Goring-Morris 1989). Hunter-gatherer complexes elsewhere in the western Levant, particularly the Kebaran, Geometric Kebaran and Natufian, serve only as time-stratigraphic units at present. No firm evidence exists of contemporaneous hunter-gatherer social units or their territorial boundaries, with the possible exception of those assemblages termed Late/Terminal Upper Paleolithic. Evidence from these post-20,000 BP sites is too disparate to reconstruct with any confidence (Valla 1988a,c).

If these terms, with the exception of the Natufian, are now applied to *similar* or *coeval* assemblages in the eastern Levant before field projects, detailed analyses and quantitative comparisons are completed, then extant terms will probably lose the meaning they currently convey, and will be restricted to time-stratigraphic units. There is also the danger that these terms will suffer the same fate as *Epipaleolithic*, particularly as more sites with varied lithic assemblages are ^{14}C dated to the same period. Such labeling may serve to mask differences and discourage research aimed at reconstructing hunter-gatherer social boundaries and territories. The evidence reviewed in this paper has outlined some distinctions between the chipped stone assemblages of the eastern and western Levant. These differences reveal considerable potential for reconstructing discrete hunter-gatherer social units, but this will not be possible without rigorous quantitative comparison and many more dates.

The commonalities between the chipped stone assemblages from the southwestern and southeastern Levant clearly prompted the use of the existing labels. For example, sites with small and narrow trapezes and rectangles, comparable to those found at Geometric Kebaran sites, are documented in the highlands of the eastern Levant, from the Hisma through the Petra area, and farther north into the Palmyra Basin (Henry 1988b; Schyle and Uerpmann 1988; Fujimoto 1979). Henry's regional study of the Hisma region resulted in a detailed succession of industries with a variety of new local terms and broader labels (*e.g.*, Henry 1988b, 1989). Some of the more interesting observations derived from this research are related to the transition between complexes, particularly the

Geometric Kebaran and the Natufian.[2] Unfortunately, very few dates were obtained from these sites. The use of the terms, *Mushabian complex* and *Madamaghan industry* (*e.g.*, Henry 1989), for a restricted number of southeastern Levantine sites appears to be unsubstantiated, because there are so few sites and ^{14}C dates and limited typological and quantitative agreement (Byrd 1988; Valla 1988a,c). The Mushabian is a relatively well-defined, restricted hunter-gatherer complex; I suggest that it be confined to sites in the Negev and Sinai until strong evidence can support its broader geographical distribution. As yet, we have no evidence of analogous assemblages in other parts of the eastern Levant (Byrd 1988).

Emerging regional patterns are distinct to groups of assemblages in the eastern Levant, most notably, those with various-sized triangles. Such sites have been found in the Hisma, the Petra area, the Azraq Basin, the eastern Jordan Valley and the el-Kowm Basin (Bar-Yosef 1970; Cauvin and Coqueniot 1988; P. Edwards, personal communication; Henry 1988b; Schyle and Uerpmann 1988). I also consider the Qalkhan assemblages of the Hisma as a variant of this trend. Based on analogy from the radiometric and stratigraphic evidence from the Azraq Basin, these assemblages probably date prior to 15,000 BP (contemporary with the late Kebaran; see also Valla 1988a). Once they are reported fully and compared rigorously, they will no doubt warrant a separate *complex* label. More restricted evidence of regional patterns are also evident somewhat later in the eastern Levant. This includes the undated Falitien backed-blade assemblage of Yabroud (Rust 1950), and assemblages with broad, double-truncated and sometimes backed microliths in *trapeze* and *lunate* shapes from the Azraq Basin (Muheisen 1988a). These assemblages precede the Natufian, and, the latter antedates 15,000 BP, based on new dates from Kharaneh IV. Finally, a non-microlithic assemblage with tanged points dates to the 14th millennium BP; the full implications of its discovery are still obscure, but this may be the first trace of contemporaneous hunter-gatherers primarily exploiting the more arid regions to the south and east.

The diverse and rugged landscape of the Levant affected interaction among hunter-gatherer bands. East-west interaction in the central Levant during much of this period was inhibited by Lake Lisan, which diminished in size very late in the Pleistocene (Bar-Yosef 1990:332; Macumber and Head 1991). However, contact between the Negev/Sinai and the southeastern Levant would have been much easier at this time. Chipped stone assemblages are not the only line of evidence that can be used for tracing interaction spheres. Trade goods, particularly marine shell, found at virtually all sites of this era, bear much information on this issue.

In addition to variation in chipped stone manufacture between western and eastern Levant, different types of settlement patterns have been encountered. In particular, the extent and duration of occupation in the more arid regions of the eastern Levant appear to parallel trends more closely in the fertile west-central Levant than in the arid Negev and Sinai. Limited survey of the arid steppe and desert of the eastern Levant has revealed occupations between 20,000 and 15,000 BP, which contrasts sharply with the dearth of information from the Negev and Sinai during this period, despite extensive survey and excavation (Goring-Morris 1991). Similarly, early Natufian settlements are now documented in the arid steppe and desert margins of the eastern Levant (*e.g.*, Byrd and Colledge 1991; Garrard 1991). Thus, settlements were not restricted to the Mediterranean forest and wet steppe during the early Natufian, as previously suggested (*e.g.*, Henry 1985; Bar-Yosef and Belfer-Cohen 1989).

---

[2]Goring-Morris (1987) *vs.* Henry (1988a) have also suggested that this transition was a result of post-depositional mixing, rather than an actual transition.

Why should settlement distribution differ between arid areas of the eastern Levant and the Negev and Sinai? Current information about settlement in the eastern Levant is not detailed enough to answer this question, although two possible interpretations can be offered. First, hunter-gatherers may have exploited both the arid areas and more fertile highlands of the eastern Levant on a seasonal basis. If so, territories may have been organized with an east-west orientation. Alternatively, the arid steppe and desert may have witnessed year-round settlement, and in certain locations, settlement organization may have included both macro and micro bands. Exploitation during the harshest times of the year may have centered around periodic springs and oases where unprecedentedly large sites occur, with thick deposits of dwellings and burials (Muheisen 1988a; Garrard and Byrd 1992). Recent evidence suggests that unique, logistically organized settlement patterns were established prior to 15,000 BP along the eastern edge of the Levant.

Semimobile groups appear to have populated the western Levant before 13,000 BP, with foraging group size estimated at 10–20 people (Bar-Yosef and Belfer-Cohen 1989; Perevolotsky and Baharav 1987). Bar-Yosef and Belfer-Cohen (1989:451) also suggest that, in the Levant, "the optimum exploitation territory for a band of hunter-gatherers" would be 300–500 km^2 in the Mediterranean forest and *ca.* 500–2000 km^2 in the steppe and desert. If the latter is used as a rough estimate, then more than six foraging groups, with only minimal territory overlap, could have inhabited just the Azraq Basin. During periods of harsher conditions, group territory may have increased to compensate for the decrease in potential food resources; but even if it increased by a magnitude of five, the arid eastern margins of the Levant could have supported hunter-gatherer bands. However, the density and archaeological visibility of sites may be much more limited if populations were required to move more frequently, in smaller groups, and farther, from camp to camp. The virtual absence of evidence for contemporaneous settlement in the more fertile highlands precludes testing of these hypotheses.

These new results have implications for detailed models proposed for the transition to sedentism and food production, which were primarily based on the robust results from the western Levant (*e.g.*, Bar-Yosef and Belfer-Cohen 1991; Henry 1989). These models suggest a series of expansions and contractions of hunter-gatherer populations that exploited the arid areas when climatic conditions were optimal, and largely abandoned them when the climate worsened. Revision of these models is needed to incorporate the new results from the eastern Levant, where there is little evidence for major periods of abandonment, and, thus, less potential for expansion. More attention must be focused on the role of social dynamics, particularly group cooperation and interaction, in these developments, and less on environmental factors.

CONCLUSION

In this overview of research on hunter-gatherers in the Levant between 20,000 and 10,000 BP, I have examined the correlation between current nomenclature for prehistoric hunter-gatherer complexes and recent ^{14}C dates. The distinction and reconstruction of the extent of hunter-gatherer social units are extremely important for Southwest Asian research, but achieving these objectives is a formidable task. Only in the Negev and Sinai can such research be attempted realistically. In the remainder of the western Levant, the data are more sparse, particularly outside coastal areas. Knowledge of the eastern Levant is still preliminary, although it is apparent that occupation in this region varies considerably. Given that the west-central Levant has been considered the core area of hunter-gatherer occupation, caution must be exercised in creating dichotomies between *center and periphery* (*e.g.*, Champion 1989), because this may bias perceptions about the role of different localities in subsequent developments.

Present needs are obvious: 1) intensive survey projects in restricted regions, followed by the excavation of both stratified and single-episode sites to identify emerging patterns in the archaeological record; 2) *cluster dating* of key assemblages that appear to be relatively undisturbed; 3) more detailed reporting and comparison based on more standardized sets of attributes (*e.g.*, Henry 1989). Only in this manner, with an emphasis on regional studies, can we attempt to reconstruct hunter-gatherer group territories in other areas of the Levant. Tremendous potential exists for gaining further insights into how and why hunter-gatherer adaptations changed during the millennium preceding the shift toward more permanent settlement and food production.

ACKNOWLEDGMENTS

The research contributions of Andrew Garrard and Ofer Bar-Yosef, along with discussions I have had with them, have contributed significantly to this paper. I thank Mujahed Muheisen for providing unpublished dates from Kharaneh IV, Jim Phillips for providing the unpublished date from Arabi I, and E. B. Banning for providing unpublished dates from Tabaqat al-Bumma. My own research on the chipped stone assemblages from the Azraq Basin has been supported by grants from the National Endowment for the Humanities and the Wenner-Gren Foundation for Anthropological Research. This article was written while I held a National Endowment for the Humanities University Teacher's Fellowship; their support is gratefully acknowledged. Finally, I would like to thank my wife, Seetha Reddy, for her support during the writing of this paper.

TABLE 1. ^{14}C Dates from the Levant Between 20,000 and 10,000 BP

Site	Provenience	^{14}C age (BP)	Material	Lab no.*	Reference**
WESTERN LEVANT					
Late/Terminal Upper Paleolithic					
Ein Aqev	12	19,980 ± 1200†	Charcoal	SMU-5	M
(D31)	9	17,890 ± 600	Charcoal	SMU-6	M
	11	17,390 ± 560	Charcoal	SMU-8	M
	7	17,510 ± 290	Charcoal	I-5495	M
	5	16,900 ± 250	Charcoal	I-5494	M
Fazaël IX		17,660 ± 160	Charcoal	OxA-2871	OxA
Fazaël X	M10b-c	15,450 ± 130	Charcoal	OxA-2870	OxA
Hayonim	D	16,240 ± 640	Charred bone	Hv-2675	H&S
Sefunim	8a	12,250 ± 65‡	Charcoal	Hv-4074	R
	8a	10,960 ± 390‡	Collagen	Pta-2827	R
Shunera XVI		16,200 ± 170	Ash	RT-227	G-M
		16,100 ± 150	Ostrich eggshell	Pta-3403	G-M
		15,800 ± 160	Ostrich eggshell	Pta-3702	G-M
Kebaran					
Hamifgash IV	1	16,230 ± 200	Charcoal	OxA-2143	OxA
Nahal Oren	308.0/28	3100 ± 130‡	Wheat seeds	OxA-395	OxA
	308.0/28	6650 ± 190‡	Humic acid from OxA-395	OxA-396	OxA
	307.0/32.33	>33,000	Wheat seeds	OxA-390	OxA
	307.0/33	2940 ± 120‡	Wheat seeds	OxA-389	OxA
	L IX	18,250 ± 320	Bone	UCLA-1776c	N,L&H
	L VIII, Rect. 300-6	16,880 ± 340	Bone	UCLA-1776b	N,L&H
	L VIII, Rect. 300-6	15,800 ± 300	Bone	UCLA-1776a	N,L&H
Ohalo II	AB 87a,212.12	18,680 ± 180	Wild barley	OxA-2564	OxA
	AB 87d,212.20-25	19,310 ± 190	Wild barley	OxA-2565	OxA
	C87d,212.25-30	19,110 ± 390	Wild barley	OxA-2566	OxA

TABLE 1. (Continued)

Site	Provenience	^{14}C age (BP)	Material	Lab no.*	Reference**
Ohalo II	C88b 212.16-18	19,400 ± 220	Charcoal	Pta-5375	N&H
	D89a 212.06-14	19,600 ± 400	Charcoal	Pta-5386	N&H
	C85a 212.15-19	20,100 ± 440	Charcoal	Pta-5387	N&H
	C89a 212.15-20	18,360 ± 230	Charcoal	RT-1244	N&H
	AB87 - surface	15,550 ± 130†	Charcoal	RT-1246	N&H
	B85c 212.15-16	19,800 ± 360	Charcoal	RT-1248	N&H
	B89b 212.15-20	19,250 ± 460	Charcoal	RT-1250	N&H
	B85b 212.12-14	19,000 ± 190	Charcoal	RT-1251	N&H
	B89b 212.13-15	18,900 ± 400	Charcoal	RT-1252	N&H
	E86b 212.38-43	17,500 ± 200†	Charcoal	RT-1297	N&H
	B88d 212.10	19,500 ± 170	Charcoal	RT-1342	N&H
	C85c 212.10	18,600 ± 220	Charcoal	RT-1343	N&H
	AB87c 212.15	18,700 ± 180	Charcoal	RT-1358	N&H
Rakefet	--	18,910 ± 300	Bone	I-6865	N,L&H
Urkan-e-Rubb	IIa-1	14,440 ± 150	Charcoal	OxA-1503	OxA
	IIa-1	15,190 ± 130	Charcoal	OxA-2835	OxA
	IIa-1	14,860 ± 130	Charcoal	OxA-2836	OxA
	IIa-1	14,650 ± 120	Charcoal	OxA-2837	OxA
	IIa-1	15,050 ± 160	Charcoal	OxA-2838	OxA
	IIa-1	14,800 ± 130	Charcoal	OxA-2839	OxA
	IIa-1	14,880 ± 120	Charcoal	OxA-2840	OxA
	IIa-1	15,730 ± 130	Charcoal	OxA-2841	OxA
	IIa-1	14,980 ± 200	Charcoal	OxA-2842	OxA
Shunera XVII	1	1320 ± 80‡	Charcoal	OxA-2139	OxA
Geometric Kebaran					
Arabi I		14,500 ± 190	Charcoal	SMU-2373	P
Azariq XVI	1	160 ± 80‡	Charcoal	OxA-2141	OxA
Lagama North VIII		12,900 ± 500†	Charcoal	Pta-2730	G-M
Mushabi XIV	2	14,330 ± 120	Charcoal	SMU-226	B-Y&P
	2	13,750 ± 285	Charcoal	QC-201	B-Y&P
	2	13,830 ± 490	Charcoal	RT-447D	B-Y&P
	2	13,690 ± 150	Charcoal	MC-991	B-Y&P
	2	14,500 ± 100	Charcoal	RT-473B	B-Y&P
Mushabi XVI	--	13,060 ± 220	Charcoal	RT-447C	B-Y&P
Mushabi XVII	--	14,170 ± 480	Charcoal	SMU-661	G-M
Mushabi XVIII	--	13,930 ± 110	Charcoal	SMU-217	B-Y&P
Nahal Rut XVII	--	4620 ± 180‡	Charcoal	RT-1071	G-M
Nahal Zin D5	8, rodent hole	13,170 ± 230	Charcoal	I-5497	G-M
	8, rodent hole	18,840 ± 680†	Charcoal	SMU-?	G-M
	4&5, firepits	15,820 ± 730†	Charcoal	Tx-1121	G-M
Neve David		13,400 ± 180	Charred bone	OxA-859	OxA
	K21,13	12,610 ± 130	Charred bone	OxA-892	OxA
Qadesh Barnea	8D/E	13,930 ± 120	Charcoal	Pta-2159	B-Y
	G	14,130 ± 160	Charcoal	Pta-2158	B-Y
Shunera III		5210 ± 70‡	Ostrich eggshell	Pta-3696	G-M
Mushabian and Related Industries of the Negev					
Mushabi I	Surface	13,310 ± 100	Ostrich shell	SMU-117	B-Y&P
Mushabi V	Hearth	12,990 ± 110	Charcoal	SMU-171	B-Y&P
	Hearth	12,700 ± 90	Charcoal	Pta-2157	B-Y&P
Mushabi XIV	1	13,800 ± 150	Charcoal	RT-473A	B-Y&P
	1	12,900 ± 235	Charcoal	QC-202	B-Y&P
	1, hearth	13,260 ± 200	Charcoal	MC-992	B-Y&P
	1, hearth	13,900 ± 400	Charcoal	RT-417	B-Y&P

TABLE 1. (Continued)

Site	Provenience	¹⁴C age (BP)	Material	Lab no.*	Reference**
Mushabi XIV	1, hearth	13,800 ± 130	Charcoal	SMU-225	B-Y&P
Nahal Zin	D101B8	13,530 ± 144	Charcoal	SMU-268	G-M
Nahal Sekher	NS 23	12,200 ± 150	Charcoal	OxA-2137	OxA
Shluhat Qeren II	1	6740 ± 100‡	Charcoal	OxA-2140	OxA
Shunera II		6860 ± 250‡	Charcoal	Pta-3002	G-M
Shunera IV		11,000 ± 140†	Charcoal	Pta-3003	G-M
		11,700 ± 140†	Charcoal	Pta-3690	G-M
Shunera XXI	1	12,100 ± 140†	Charcoal	OxA-2138	OxA
Natufian					
Ain Mallaha	III-House 51	11,310 ± 880	Charcoal	Ly-1662	W
	III-House 51	11,740 ± 570	Charcoal	Ly-1661	W
	IV-House 131	11,590 ± 540	Charcoal	Ly-1660	W
		330 ± 100‡	Bread wheat seed	OxA-543	OxA
El Wad	B2 Cave	11,920 ± 660	Bone	UCLA-?	B-Y
	B2 Terrace	11,475 ± 650	Bone	UCLA-?	B-Y
	B1	9795 ± 600	Bone	UCLA-?	B-Y
	--	12,950 ± 200	Charcoal	RT-1368	W-E
	--	12,620 ± 110	Charcoal	Pta-5435	W-E
	--	{10,740 ± 200	Charcoal	Pta-1367	W-E
		10,680 ± 190			
Hayonim Cave	H77 4 (9.7)	12,360 ± 160	*Lupinus* seeds	OxA-742	OxA
	H77 4 (5)	12,010 ± 180	*Lupinus* seeds	OxA-743	OxA
Hayonim Terrace	1648	17,420 ± 170‡	Charred bone	OxA-2568	OxA
	1719	11,220 ± 110	Charred bone	OxA-2569	OxA
	1894	6970 ± 80‡	Wild barley	OxA-1900	OxA
	2168	10,000 ± 100	Wild barley	OxA-1899	OxA
	2505	11,820 ± 120	Charred bone	OxA-2570	OxA
	3052	11,720 ± 120	Charred bone	OxA-2977	OxA
	3098	9640 ± 100‡	Charred bone	OxA-2571	OxA
	3101	14,050 ± 140‡	Charred bone	OxA-2976	OxA
	3143	11,460 ± 110	Charred bone	OxA-2572	OxA
	3143	11,790 ± 120	Charred bone	OxA-2975	OxA
	3185	10,100 ± 160	Charred bone	OxA-2573	OxA
	3186-87	16,810 ± 210‡	Charred bone	OxA-2974	OxA
	D	11,920 ± 90	Charcoal	SMU-231	B-Y
Jericho	E I,II,V phI.ii	9850 ± 240‡	Charcoal	GL-69	W
	E I,II,V phI.ii	10,800 ± 180	Charcoal	GL-70	W
	E I,II,V phI.ii	9800 ± 240‡	Charcoal	GL-72	W
	E I,II,V phI.ii	11,166 ± 107	Charcoal, ash	P-376	W
	E I,II,V phI.ii	11,090 ± 90	Charcoal	BM-1407	W
Kebara Cave	B	11,150 ± 400	Bone	UCLA-?	B-Y
Nahal Oren Terrace	LV	10,046 ± 318	Bone collagen	BM-764	W
Rakefet Cave		10,980 ± 260	Bone	I-7032	G-M
		10,580 ± 140	Bone	I-7030	G-M
		2760 ± 200‡	*Vicia ervila* seeds	OxA-541	OxA
Rosh Horesha	Midden 24–40cm	13,090 ± 200‡	Charcoal	I-5496	W
	Fea. 13	10,490 ± 430	Charcoal	SMU-9	W
	Fea. 15/16	10,880 ± 280	Charcoal	SMU-10	W
Salibiya I	Marsh	11,530 ± 550	Charcoal	RT-505A	G-M
Saflulim	J21c 145-150	10,930 ± 130	Charcoal	OxA-2136	OxA
	?	11,150 ± 100	Charcoal	OxA-2869	OxA
Shunera VII	--	4520 ± 60‡	Charcoal	Pta-3082	G-M

TABLE 1. (Continued)

Site	Provenience	¹⁴C age (BP)	Material	Lab no.*	Reference**
Harifian					
Abu Salem	15–20cm	9970 ± 150	Charcoal	I-5498	W
	25–30cm	10,230 ± 150	Charcoal	I-5499	W
	45–55cm	10,230 ± 150	Charcoal	I-5500	W
	L1 155–160	10,300 ± 100	Charcoal	Pta-3289	G-M
	L21 120–130	10,340 ± 90	Charcoal	Pta-3290	G-M
	L22	11,660 ± 90‡	Charcoal	Pta-3080	G-M
	L22 180–190	10,550 ± 90	Charcoal	Pta-3292	G-M
	L22 120–130	10,140 ± 80	Charcoal	Pta-3291	G-M
	L24 190–200	10,420 ± 100	Charcoal	Pta-3293	G-M
Ramat Harif	L3 280	10,500 ± 100	Charcoal	Pta-3009	G-M
	L3 275–280	10,380 ± 100	Charcoal	Pta-3284	G-M
	L3 220–225	10,300 ± 100	Charcoal	Pta-3001	G-M
	L3 210–220	10,390 ± 100	Charcoal	Pta-3285	G-M
	L7 220–225	10,250 ± 100	Charcoal	Pta-3288	G-M
	L7 180–185	10,100 ± 100	Charcoal	Pta-3286	G-M
Maaleh Ramon East	L1 30–35	10,530 ± 100	Charcoal	Pta-3371	G-M
	L1 25–30	10,430 ± 80	Charcoal	Pta-3483	G-M
Maaleh Ramon West	--	10,400 ± 100	Charcoal	Pta-3483	G-M
	--	10,000 ± 200	Charcoal	RT-1068N	G-M
EASTERN LEVANT					
Non-Natufian Microlithic					
Azraq 17, Tr. 2	Sq. 11, 11	13,260 ± 200†	Charcoal	OxA-869	OxA
Ein Gev I	L. 4	15,700 ± 415	Bone	GrN-5576	W
Jilat 6	Phase C Sq.1,14A	7980 ± 150‡	Charcoal	OxA-539	OxA
	Phase B Sq.4,12A	11,740 ± 80‡	Charcoal	OxA-522	OxA
	Phase B Sq.2,12A	11,450 ± 200‡	Bone	OxA-523	OxA
	Phase A Sq.4,8A	15,520 ± 200	Charcoal	OxA-524	OxA
	Phase A Sq.1,5A	16,010 ± 200	Charcoal	OxA-525	OxA
	Phase A Sq. 1,8A	15,470 ± 130	Charcoal	AA-5492	G
	Phase A Sq. 1,7B	16,575 ± 120	Charcoal	AA-5491	G
	Phase A Sq. 2,3A	16,695 ± 120	Charcoal	AA-5493	G
	Phase A Sq. 3,9A	16,700 ± 140	Charcoal	AA-5494	G
Jilat 8	Sq.3,4C	13,310 ± 120	Charcoal	OxA-521	OxA
	Sq.3,4D	10,540 ± 160‡	Charcoal	OxA-636	OxA
Jilat 22	Phase B Sq.1,6B	11,920 ± 180†	Charcoal	OxA-1770	OxA
Kharaneh IV	Ph. A, S-I, L-VIII	13,970 ± 150†	Bone	Q-3075	M2
	Ph. B, S-I, L-V	12,200 ± 140†	Bone	Q-3074	M2
	Ph. B, S-III, L-V	10,620 ± 125‡	Bone	Q-3073	M2
	Ph. B, S-III, L-III	9840 ± 120‡	Bone	Q-3072	M2
	Ph. D, A 19.37	15,200 ± 450	?	KN-4192	M3
	Ph. D, A 19.37	15,700 ± 160	?	KN-4193	M3
Madamagh	Lower layer	15,300 ± 600	Bone	KN-3594	S&U
	A2	14,300 ± 650	Bone	KN-3593	S&U
Tabaqat al-Buma	B.20-2S bag 22	11,170 ± 100‡	Gazelle bone	TO-987	B
	B.20-2S bag 26	13,110 ± 130†	Gazelle bone	TO-989	B
	B.20-2S bag 30	14,850 ± 160	Gazelle bone	TO-991	B
	519	12,660 ± 430†	Bone	TO-2116	B
Tor Hamar	Layer C	12,680 ± 320†	Charcoal	SMU-1399	H
Uwaynid 14	Sq.5, 18	18,400 ± 250	Charcoal	OxA-866	OxA
	Sq.10,15	18,900 ± 250	Charcoal	OxA-865	OxA

TABLE 1. (Continued)

Site	Provenience	^{14}C age (BP)	Material	Lab no.*	Reference**
Uwaynid 18	Sq.5, 15B	19,800 ± 350	Charcoal	OxA-864	OxA
	Sq.1, 3K	19,500 ± 250	Charcoal	OxA-868	OxA
Wadi Hammeh 26		19,500 ± 600	Charcoal	SUA-2101	E
Wadi Hasa 618	Test 1	20,300 ± 600	Charcoal	AA-4395	C+
Wadi Hasa 784X		19,000 ± 1300	Charcoal	AA-4396	C+
Wadi Hasa 1065	Test B, level 7	15,580 ± 250	Charcoal	AA-4392	C+
	Test B, level 8	15,860 ± 430	Charcoal	AA-4394	C+
	Test C, level 13	16,570 ± 380	Charcoal	AA-4390	C+
	Test C, level 13	16,790 ± 340	Charcoal	AA-4393	C+
	Test A, level 5	16,900 ± 500	Charcoal	AA-4391	C+
Non-Microlithic					
Jilat 10	Sq.7,11B	14,790 ± 200*	Charcoal	OxA-520	OxA
	Sq.8,11	13,120 ± 180	Charcoal	OxA-1000	OxA
	Sq.8,11	12,700 ± 300	Charcoal	OxA-918	OxA
Jilat 22	Phase C Sq.3,15B	13,040 ± 180	Charcoal	OxA-1771	OxA
	Phase C Sq.3,15B	12,840 ± 140	Charcoal	OxA-1772	OxA
	Phase E Sq.1,17A	13,490 ± 110	Charcoal	OxA-2409	OxA
	Phase E Sq.2,17A	13,540 ± 120	Charcoal	OxA-2410	OxA
Natufian and Related Northern Industries					
Abu Hureyra	E-326	10,820 ± 160	Humic fraction of OxA-468	OxA-470	OxA
	E-326	10,920 ± 140	Humic fraction of OxA-468	OxA-469	OxA
	E-326	11,090 ± 150	Repeat of OxA-387	OxA-468	OxA
	E-326	11,070 ± 160	Charred *Bos* bone	OxA-387	OxA
	E-326	10,900 ± 200	*Triticum boeoticum* seeds	OxA-172	OxA
	E-316	10,680 ± 150	Humic fraction of OxA-430	OxA-431	OxA
	E-316	11,020 ± 150	Charred gazelle bone	OxA-430	OxA
	E-313	10,600 ± 200	*Triticum boeoticum* seeds	OxA-171	OxA
	E-286	10,450 ± 180	Humic fraction of OxA-434	OxA-435	OxA
	E-286	10,490 ± 150	Charred gazelle bone	OxA-434	OxA
	E-286	10,420 ± 150	*Triticum boeoticum* seeds	OxA-397	OxA
	E-285	10,930 ± 150	Wild *Ovis* bone	OxA-474	OxA
	E-281	10,750 ± 170	Humic fraction of OxA-473	OxA-472	OxA
	E-281	10,000 ± 170	Charred wild *Ovis* bone	OxA-473	OxA
	E-276	10,800 ± 160	*Triticum boeoticum* seeds	OxA-386	OxA
	E-275	10,620 ± 150	Humic fraction of OxA-407	OxA-471	OxA
	E-275	10,300 ± 160	Humic fraction of OxA-407	OxA-408	OxA
	E-275	9980 ± 160	Charred wild *Ovis* bone	OxA-407	OxA
	E-261	10,600 ± 200	*Triticum boeoticum* seeds	OxA-170	OxA
	E-252	9060 ± 140	Charred gazelle bone	OxA-475	OxA
	E-303	11,160 ± 110	Charcoal	BM-1718	H

TABLE 1. (Continued)

Site	Provenience	^{14}C age (BP)	Material	Lab no.*	Reference**
Abu Hureyra	E-254	9100 ± 100	Charcoal	BM-1719	H
	E-264-307	10,792 ± 82	Charcoal	BM-1121	H
	E-E-326	11,450 ± 300	Charred seeds	OxA-883	OxA
	E-E-324	6100 ± 200‡	Charred seeds	OxA-882	OxA
	E-286	9600 ± 200	Fluvic acids from OxA-434	OxA-476	OxA
Beidha	C-01:4	12,910 ± 250	Charcoal	AA-1463	B
	C-00:4	12,450 ± 170	Charcoal	AA-1465	B
	C-01:4	12,130 ± 190	Charcoal	AA-1464	B
	C-01:2	10,910 ± 520	Charcoal	AA-1462	B
	C-00:2	8390 ± 390‡	Charcoal	AA-1461	B
Mureybet	IA-R34,B1a	10,030 ± 150	Charcoal	MC-733	C+
	IA-Q33,B4	10,170 ± 200	Charcoal	MC-635	C+
	IA-Q33,B4	10,090 ± 170	Charcoal	MC-674	C+
	IA-Q33,B4	10,230 ± 170	Charcoal	MC-731	C+
	IA-Q32,E1c	10,230 ± 170	Charcoal	MC-732	C+
	IA-Q33	10,350 ± 150	Charcoal	MC-675	C+
	IB-P32,B4	10,590 ± 140	Charcoal	Lv-607	H
	Phase I	10,590 ± 140	Charcoal	Lv-608	H
Wadi Hammeh 27	XX/D+/3/4	11,920 ± 150	Humic acid	OxA-393	OxA
	XX/D/4/1	12,200 ± 160	Charred seeds	OxA-394	OxA
	XX/D+/5/1	11,950 ± 160	Humic acids	OxA-507	OxA
Wadi Judayid 2	C	12,090 ± 800	Charcoal	SMU-805	H
	C	12,750 ± 1000	Charcoal	SMU-806	H
	C	12,780 ± 660	Charcoal	SMU-803	H

* SMU=Southern Methodist University; I=Teledyne Isotopes; OxA=Oxford Accelerator; Hv=Hannover; Pta=Pretoria; RT=Rehovot; UCLA=University of California, Los Angeles; QC=Queens College; MC=Monaco; Tx=Texas; Ly=Lyon; GL=Geochronological Laboratory; P=Pennsylvania; BM=British Museum; GrN=Groningen; AA=Arizona Accelerator; Q=Cambridge; KN=Köln; TO=Toronto; SUA=Sydney University; Lv=Louvain

** M=Marks (1976); OxA=Housley 1994; H&S=Henry and Servello (1974); R=Ronen (1984); G-M=Goring-Morris (1987); N,L&H=Noy, Legge and Higgs (1973); P=Jim Phillips, personal communication; B-Y&P=Bar-Yosef and Phillips (1977); W=Weinstein (1984); B-Y=Bar-Yosef (1981); W-E=Weinstein-Ebron (1991); G=Garrard and Byrd (1992); M2=Muheisen (1988a); M3=Muheisen, personal communication; S&U=Schyle and Uerpmann (1988); B=E. B. Banning, personal communication; H=Henry (1989); E=Edwards *et al.* (1988); C+=Clark *et al.* (1988); B=Byrd (1989b); C=Cauvin (1991)

† Probably unreliable date

‡ Certainly unreliable date

REFERENCES CITED

Aurenche, O., J. Cauvin, M. Cauvin, L. Copeland, F. Hours and P. Sanlaville
   1981   Chronologie et organization de l'espace dans le Proche Orient de 12000 à 5600 avant J.-C. In *Préhistoire du Levant*, edited by J. Cauvin and P. Sanlaville, pp. 571–602. Colloques Internationaux du CNRS 598, Paris.
Banning, E. B., R. R. Dods, J. Field, I. Kuijt, J. McCorriston, J. Siggers, H. Taani and J. Triggs
   1992   Tabaqat al-Bumma: 1990 excavations at a Kebaran and Late Neolithic site in Wadi Ziqlab. *Annual of the Department of Antiquities* 36:43–62.
Bar-Yosef, O.
   1970   The Epi-Paleolithic Cultures of Palestine. Ph.D. Dissertation, Hebrew University, Jerusalem.
   1975   The Epi-Paleolithic in Palestine and Sinai. In *Problems in Prehistory: North Africa and the Levant*, edited by F. Wendorf and A. E. Marks, pp. 363–378. Southern Methodist University Press, Dallas.
   1981   The Epi-Paleolithic complexes in the southern Levant. In *Préhistoire du Levant*, edited by J. Cauvin and P. Sanlaville, pp. 389–408. Colloques Internationaux du CNRS 598, Paris.

Bar-Yosef, O.
  1983   The Natufian in the southern Levant. In *The Hilly Flanks and Beyond*, edited by C. Young, Jr., P. E. L. Smith and P. Mortensen, pp. 11–42. Oriental Institute Studies in Ancient Oriental Civilization 36. The University of Chicago, Chicago.
  1987   Direct and indirect evidence for hafting in the Epi-Paleolithic and Neolithic of the southern Levant. In *La Main et l'Outil. Manches et Emmanchements Préhistoriques*, edited by D. Stordeur, pp. 155–164. Travaux de la Maison de L'Orient 15. Maison de L'Orient, CNRS, Lyon.
  1989   The PPNA in the Levant – An overview. *Paléorient* 15(1):57–63.
  1990   The last glacial maximum in the Mediterranean Levant. In *The World at 18,000 b.p.*, edited by C. Gamble and O. Soffer, pp. 58–77. Unwin Hyman, London.
  1991a   Stone tools and social context in Levantine prehistory. In *Perspectives on the Past: Theoretical Biases on Mediterranean Hunter-Gatherer Research*, edited by G. A. Clark, pp. 371–395. University of Pennsylvania Press, Philadelphia.
  1991b   The search for lithic variability among Levantine Epi-Paleolithic industries. In *25 Ans d'Etudes Technologiques en Préhistoire*, pp. 319–335. Editions APDCA, Juan-les-Pins.
  1991c   Raw material exploitation in the Levantine Epi-Paleolithic. In *Raw Material Economies Among Prehistoric Hunter-Gatherers*, edited by A. Montet-White and S. Holen, pp. 235–250. University of Kansas Anthropology Publications 19, Lawrence.
Bar-Yosef, O. and A. Belfer-Cohen
  1977   The Lagaman industry. In *Prehistoric Investigations in Gebel Maghara, Northern Sinai*, edited by O. Bar-Yosef and J. L. Phillips, pp. 42–88. Qedem 7. Hebrew University, Jerusalem.
  1989   The origins of sedentism and farming communities. *Journal of World Prehistory* 3(4):447–498.
  1991   From sedentary hunter-gatherers to territorial farmers in the Levant. In *Between Bands and States*, edited by S. A. Gregg, pp. 181–202. Center for Archaeological Investigations Occasional Paper 9. Southern Illinois University, Carbondale.
  1992   From foraging to farming in the Mediterranean Levant. In *Transitions to Agriculture in Prehistory*, edited by A. B. Gebaure and T. D. Price, pp. 21–48. Prehistory Press, Madison, Wisconsin.
Bar-Yosef, O. and J. L. Phillips (editors)
  1977   *Prehistoric Investigations in Gebel Maghara, Northern Sinai*. Qedem 7. Hebrew University, Jerusalem.
Bar-Yosef, O. and F. R. Valla
  1979   L'évolution du Natoufien–Nouvelles suggestions. *Paléorient* 5:145–151.
Bar-Yosef, O. and F. R. Valla (editors)
  1991   *The Natufian Culture in the Levant*. International Monographs in Prehistory, Ann Arbor.
Bar-Yosef, O. and J. C. Vogel
  1987   Relative and absolute chronology of the Epipaleolithic in the south of the Levant. In *Chronologies du Proche Orient*, edited by O. Aurenche, J. Evin and F. Hours, pp. 219–246. BAR International Series 379, British Archaeological Reports, Oxford.
Besançon, J., L. Copeland and F. Hours
  1975   Tableaux de préhistoire Libanaise. *Paléorient* 3:5–46.
Byrd, B. F.
  1988   Late Pleistocene settlement diversity in the Azraq Basin. *Paléorient* 14(2):257–264.
  1989a   The Natufian: Settlement variability and economic adaptations in the Levant at the end of the Pleistocene. *Journal of World Prehistory* 3(2):159–197.
  1989b   *The Natufian Encampment at Beidha: Late Pleistocene Adaptation in the Southern Levant*. Jutland Archaeological Society Publications 23, Aarhus.
  1991   The dispersal of food production across the Levant. In *Transitions to Agriculture in Prehistory*, edited by A. B. Gebaure and T. D. Price, pp. 49–62. Prehistory Press, Madison.
Byrd, B. F. and S. Colledge
  1991   Early Natufian occupation along the edge of the southern Jordanian steppe. In *The Natufian Culture in the Levant*, edited by O. Bar-Yosef and F. R. Valla, pp. 265–276. International Monographs in Prehistory, Ann Arbor.
Byrd, B. and A. Garrard
  1990   The last glacial maximum in the Jordanian desert. In *The World at 18,000 b.p.*, edited by C. Gamble and O. Soffer, pp. 78–96. Unwin Hyman, London.
Cauvin, M. C.
  1991   Du Natoufien au Levant Nord? Jabroud et Mureybet (Syrie). In *The Natufian Culture in the Levant*, edited by O. Bar-Yosef and F. R. Valla, pp. 295–314. International Monographs in Prehistory, Ann Arbor.

Cauvin, M. C. and E. Coqueugniot
1988　L'oasis d'El Kowm et le Kébarien Géométrique. *Paléorient* 14(2):270–282.
Calley, S.
1986　*Technologie du Débitage à Mureybet, Syrie.* In *Chronologies du Proche Orient*, edited by O. Aurenche, J. Evin and F. Hours, pp. 219–246. BAR International Series 396, British Archaeological Reports, Oxford.
Champion, T.
1989　Introduction. In *Centre and Periphery: Comparative Studies in Archaeology*, edited by T. C. Champion, pp. 1–19. Unwin Hyman, London.
Clark, G., J. Lindley, M. Donaldson, A. Garrard, N. Coinman, J. Schuldenrein, S. Fish and D. Olszewski
1988　Excavations at Middle, Upper, and Epipaleolithic sites in the Wadi Hasa, west-central Jordan. In *The Prehistory of Jordan*, edited by A. N. Garrard and H.-G. Gebel, pp. 209–285. BAR International Series 396, British Archaeological Reports, Oxford.
Close, A.
1989　Identifying style in stone artifacts: A case study from the Nile Valley. In *Alternative Approaches to Lithic Analysis*, edited by D. O. Henry and G. H. Odell, pp. 3–26. Archaeological Papers of the American Anthropological Association 1, Washington, DC.
Copeland, L. and J. Waechter
1968　The stone industries of Abri Bergy, Lebanon. *Bulletin of the Institute of Archaeology* 7:15–36.
Edwards, P. C.
1987　Late Pleistocene Occupation in Wadi al-Hammeh, Jordan Valley. Ph.D. Dissertation, University of Sydney, Sydney.
Edwards, P. C, S. J. Bourke, S. M. Colledge, J. Head and P. G. Macumber
1988　Late Pleistocene prehistory in the Wadi al-Hammeh, Jordan. In *The Prehistory of Jordan*, edited by A. N. Garrard and H.-G. Gebel, pp. 525–565. BAR International Series 396, British Archaeological Reports, Oxford.
Ferring, C. R.
1977　The Late Upper Paleolithic site of Ein Aqev East. In *Prehistory and Paleoenvironments in the Central Negev, Israel*, Vol. II, edited by A. E. Marks, pp. 81–111. Southern Methodist University Press, Dallas.
1980　Technological Variability and Change in the Late Paleolithic of the Negev. Ph.D. Dissertation, Southern Methodist University, Dallas.
Fujimoto, T.
1979　The Epi-Paleolithic assemblages of Douara Cave. *University of Tokyo Bulletin* 16:47–75.
Garrard, A. N.
1991　Natufian settlement in the Azraq Basin, eastern Jordan. In *The Natufian Culture in the Levant*, edited by O. Bar-Yosef and F. R. Valla, pp. 235–244. International Monographs in Prehistory, Ann Arbor.
Garrard, A. N., Baird and B. Byrd
1994　The chronological basis and significance of the Late Paleolithic and Neolithic sequence in the Azraq Basin, Jordan. This volume.
Garrard, A. N., A. Betts, B. Byrd, S. Colledge and C. Hunt
1988　Summary of paleoenvironmental and prehistoric investigations in the Azraq Basin. In *The Prehistory of Jordan*, edited by A. N. Garrard and H.-G. Gebel, pp. 311–337. BAR International Series 396, British Archaeological Reports, Oxford.
Garrard, A. N., A. Betts, B. Byrd and C. Hunt
1987　Prehistoric environment and settlement in the Azraq Basin: An interim report in the 1985 excavation season. *Levant* 19:5–25.
Garrard, A. N. and B. F. Byrd
1992　New dimensions to the Epipaleolithic of the Wadi Jilat in central Jordan. *Paléorient* 18(2):47–62.
Garrard, A. N., B. Byrd, A. Betts
1986　Prehistoric environment and settlement in the Azraq Basin: An interim report on the 1984 excavation season. *Levant* 18:5–24.
Garrod, D. A. E.
1932　A new Mesolithic industry: The Natufian of Palestine. *Journal of the Royal Anthropological Institute* 62: 257–270.
1958　The Natufian culture: The life and economy of Mesolithic people in the Near East. *Proceedings of the British Academy* 43:211–227.
Gilead, I.
1983　Upper Paleolithic occurrences in Sinai and the transition to the Epi-Paleolithic. *Paléorient* 9:39–53.
1984　Is the term "Epipaleolithic" relevant to Levantine prehistory? *Current Anthropology* 25(2):227–228.

Gilead, I.
  1988   The Upper Paleolithic to Epi-Paleolithic transition in the Levant. *Paléorient* 14(2):177–182.
  1991   The Upper Paleolithic period in the Levant. *Journal of World Prehistory* 5(2):105–154.
Goring-Morris, A. N.
  1980   Late Quaternary Sites in Wadi Fazael, Lower Jordan Valley. M. A. Thesis, Department of Prehistory, Institute of Archaeology, Hebrew University, Jerusalem.
  1987   *At the Edge: Terminal Pleistocene Hunter-Gatherers in the Negev and Sinai.* BAR International Series 361, British Archaeological Reports, Oxford.
  1988   Reply to reviews of "At the Edge." *Mitekufat Haeven* 21:79–86.
  1989   Developments in terminal Pleistocene hunter-gatherer cultural systems: A perspective from the Negev and Sinai deserts. In *People and Culture in Change*, edited by I. Hershkovitz, pp. 7–28. BAR International Series 508, British Archaeological Reports, Oxford.
  1991   The Harifian of the southern Levant. In *The Natufian Culture in the Levant*, edited by O. Bar-Yosef and F. R. Valla, pp. 173–216. International Monographs in Prehistory, Ann Arbor.
Henry, D. O.
  1974   The utilization of the microburin technique in the Levant. *Paléorient* 2:389–398.
  1982   The prehistory of southern Jordan and relationships with the Levant. *Journal of Field Archaeology* 9:417–444.
  1983   Adaptive evolution within the Epipaleolithic of the Near East. *Advances in World Archaeology* 2:99–160.
  1985   Preagricultural sedentism: The Natufian example. In *Prehistoric Hunter-Gatherers: The Emergence of Cultural Complexity*, edited by T. D. Price and J. A. Brown, pp. 365–381. Academic Press, New York.
  1988a   Review of "At the Edge." *Mitekufat Haeven* 21:53–58.
  1988b   Summary of prehistoric and palaeoenvironmental research in the northern Hisma. In *The Prehistory of Jordan*, edited by A. N. Garrard and H.-G. Gebel, pp. 7–37. BAR International Series 396, British Archaeological Reports, Oxford..
  1989   *From Foraging to Agriculture: The Levant at the End of the Ice Age.* University of Pennsylvania Press, Philadelphia.
Henry, D. O. and F. Servello
  1974   Compendium of ^{14}C determinations derived from Near Eastern prehistoric sites. *Paléorient* 2:19–44.
Housley, R. A.
  1994   Eastern Mediterranean chronologies: The Oxford AMS contribution. This volume.
Hovers, E. and O. Mardel
  1991   Typo-chronology and absolute dating of the Kebaran complex: Implications from the second season of excavations at Urkan e-Rub IIA. *Journal of the Israel Prehistoric Society* 24:34–58.
Jones, M. L.
  1983   The Qualkan and Hamran: Two Epipaleolithic industries from southern Jordan. Ph.D. Dissertation, Southern Methodist University, Dallas.
Kaufman, D.
  1988   New radiocarbon dates for the Geometric Kebaran. *Paléorient* 14(1):107–110.
Kirkbride, D.
  1958   A Kebaran rock shelter in Wadi Madamagh, near Petra, Jordan. *Man* 58:55–58.
Kuijt, I. and O. Bar-Yosef
  1994   Radiocarbon chronology for the Levantine Neolithic: Observations and data. This volume.
Kukan, J.
  1978   A Technological and Stylistic Study of Microliths From Certain Levantine Epi-Paleolithic Assemblages. Ph.D. Dissertation, University of Toronto, Toronto.
Macumber, P. J. and M. J. Head
  1991   Implications of the Wadi al-Hammeh sequences for the terminal drying of Lake Lisan, Jordan. *Palaeogeography, Palaeoclimatology, Palaeoecology* 84:163–173.
Marks, A. E.
  1976   Ein Aqev: A Late Levantine Upper Paleolithic site in the Nahal Aqev. In *Prehistory and Paleoenvironments in the Central Negev, Israel*, Vol. I., edited by A. E. Marks, pp. 227–291. Southern Methodist University Press, Dallas.
  1988   At the edge or over it: A critique of Goring-Morris' construct for Upper Paleolithic development. *Mitekufat Haeven* 1:59–67.
Marks, A. E. and T. R. Scott
  1976   Abu Salem: Type site of the Harifian industry of the southern Levant. *Journal of Field Archaeology* 3(1): 43–60.

Marks, A. E. and A. H. Simmons
 1977 The Negev Kebaran of the Har Harif. In *Prehistory and Paleoenvironments of the Central Negev, Israel*, Vol. I., edited by A. E. Marks, pp. 233–270. Southern Methodist University Press, Dallas.

Moore, A. M. T.
 1992 The impact of accelerator dating at the early village of Abu Hureyra on the Euphrates. *Radiocarbon* 34(3): 850–858.

Moore, A. M. T., J. A. J. Gowlett, R. E. M. Hedges, G. C. Hillman, A. J. Legge and P. A. Rowley-Conwy
 1986 Radiocarbon accelerator (AMS) dates for the Epipaleolithic settlement at Abu Hureyra, Syria. *Radiocarbon* 28(3):1068–1076.

Muheisen, M.
 1983 La Préhistoire en Jordanie. Recherches sur L'Épipaléolithique. L'exemple du Gisement de Kharaneh IV. Ph.D. Dissertation, L'Université de Bordeaux, Bordeaux.
 1988a The Epipaleolithic phases of Kharaneh IV. In *The Prehistory of Jordan*, edited by A. N. Garrard and H.-G. Gebel, pp. 353–367. BAR International Series 396, British Archaeological Reports, Oxford.
 1988b Le gisement de Kharaneh IV, note sommaire sur la Phase D. *Paléorient* 14(2):265–269.

Nadel, D. and I. Hershkovitz
 1991 New subsistence data and human remains from the earliest Levantine Epipaleolithic. *Current Anthropology* 32(5):631–635.

Noy, T, A. J. Legge and E. S. Higgs
 1973 Recent excavations at Nahal Oren, Israel. *Proceedings of the Prehistoric Society* 39:75–99.

Olszewski, D. I.
 1984 The Early Occupation at Tell Abu Hureyra in the Context of the Late Epipaleolithic of the Levant. Ph.D. Dissertation, The University of Arizona, Tucson.
 1991 The lithic evidence from Abu Hureyra I, in Syria. In *The Natufian Culture in the Levant*, edited by O. Bar-Yosef and F. R. Valla, pp. 433–444. International Monographs in Prehistory, Ann Arbor.

Olszewski, D. I., G. A. Clark and S. Fish
 1990 WHS 784 X (Yutil al-Hasa): A late Ahmarian site in the Wadi Hasa, west-central Jordan. *Proceedings of the Prehistoric Society* 56:33–49.

Perevolotsky, A. and D. Baharav
 1987 The abundance of "desert kites" in the Eastern Sinai – An ecological analysis. In *Sinai*, edited by G. Gvirtz-man, A. Shmueli, Y. Gradus and M. Har-El, pp. 595–603. Eretz, Tel-Aviv University.

Perrot, J.
 1966 Le gisement Natoufien de Mallaha (Eynam), Israel. *L'Anthropologie* 70(5):437–484.

Phillips, J. L.
 1994 The Upper Paleolithic chronology of the Levant and the Nile Valley. This volume.

Phillips, J. L. and E. Mintz
 1977 The Mushabian. In *Prehistoric Investigations in Gebel Maghara, Northern Sinai*, edited by O. Bar-Yosef and J. L. Phillips, pp. 149–163. Qedem 7, Hebrew University, Jerusalem.

Ronen, A.
 1984 *Sefunim Prehistoric Sites, Mount Carmel, Israel*. BAR International Series 230, British Archaeological Reports, Oxford.

Rust, A.
 1950 *Die Holenfunde von Jabrud (Syrien)*. Karl Wachholtz, Neumunster, Germany.

Schiffer, M.
 1986 Radiocarbon dating and the "Old Wood" problem: The case of the Hohokam chronology. *Journal of Archaeological Science* 13:13–30.

Schyle, D. and H. P. Uerpmann
 1988 Paleolithic sites in the Petra area. In *The Prehistory of Jordan*, edited by A. N. Garrard and H.-G. Gebel, pp. 39–65. BAR International Series 396, British Archaeological Reports, Oxford.

Scott, T. R.
 1977 The Harifian of the central Negev. In *Prehistory and Paleoenvironments in the Central Negev, Israel*, Vol. 2, edited by A. E. Marks, pp. 271–322. Southern Methodist University Press, Dallas.

Shennan, P. J.
 1989 Introduction: Archaeological approaches to cultural identity. In *Archaeological Approaches to Cultural Identity*, edited by P. J. Shennan, pp. 1–32. Unwin Hyman, London.

Sheppard, P. J.
 1987 *The Capsian of North Africa: Stylistic Variation in Stone Tool Assemblages*. BAR International Series 353, British Archaeological Reports, Oxford.

Turville-Petre, F.
  1932   Excavations in the Mugharet el-Kebarah. *Journal of the Royal Anthropological Institute* 62:271–276.
Valla, F. R.
  1975   *Le Natoufien: Une Culture Préhistorique en Palestine.* Cahiers de la Revue Biblique 15. Gabalda, Paris.
  1984   *Les Industries de Silex de Mallaha (Eynam).* Mémoires et Travaux du Centre de Recherche Français de Jerusalem 3. L'Association Paléorient, Paris.
Valla, F. R.
  1987   Chronologie absolue et chronologies relatives dans le Natoufien. In *Chronologies du Proche Orient*, edited by O. Aurenche, J. Evin and F. Hours, pp. 267–294. BAR International Series 379, British Archaeological Reports, Oxford.
  1988a   Epipaléolithic synthèse. *Paléorient* 14(2):316–320.
  1988b   La fin de l'Epipaléolithique au Levant: Les industries à microlithes géometriques. *L'Anthropologie* 92(3): 901–925.
  1988c   At the edge – Commentaire. *Mitekufat Haeven* 21:50–53.
Waterbolk, H. T.
  1987   Working with radiocarbon dates in southwestern Asia. In *Chronologies du Proche Orient*, edited by O. Aurenche, J. Evin and F. Hours, pp. 39–60. BAR International Series 379, British Archaeological Reports, Oxford.
Weinstein, J. M.
  1984   Radiocarbon dating in the southern Levant. *Radiocarbon* 26(3):297–366.
Weinstein-Ebron, M.
  1991   New radiocarbon dates for the early Natufian of El-Wad Cave, Mt. Carmel, Israel. *Paléorient* 17(1):95–98.
Wiessner, P.
  1989   Style and changing relations between the individual and society. In *The Meaning of Things: Material Culture and Symbolic Expression*, edited by I. Hodder. Unwin Hyman, London.

RADIOCARBON CHRONOLOGY FOR THE LEVANTINE NEOLITHIC: OBSERVATIONS AND DATA

IAN KUIJT and OFER BAR-YOSEF

Department of Anthropology, Harvard University, Cambridge, Massachusetts 02138 USA

INTRODUCTION

The Levantine Neolithic is among the most closely examined prehistoric periods through which archaeologists have sought to refine existing chronologies and develop a more detailed understanding of long- and short-term changes in human culture. This period, representing the first appearance of systematic food production in the world, is a turning point in human socio-economic systems and a crucial threshold in the emergence of social complexity. Despite the wealth of archaeological research into the Levantine Neolithic, questions still exist as to the representative nature of radiocarbon dates for this period. Although many local and inter-regional chronological syntheses have been constructed for this period (Mellaart 1975; Bar-Yosef 1981; Cauvin 1978, 1987; Gebel 1987; Moore 1985) the accumulation of new data from excavations or reports published following new excavations require regular evaluation and new syntheses.

In this paper, we aim to 1) provide a current compilation of all known ^{14}C dates from Levantine Neolithic sites, 2) briefly discuss current limitations of these data and 3) suggest further research to clarify obvious deficiencies. We avoid discussion of relations between specific chronological sequences and local or regional cultural entities, as they are examined in depth elsewhere (*e.g.*, Cauvin 1987; Rollefson 1989; Bar-Yosef 1991). We argue that traditional research on large, deeply stratified Neolithic sites, interlaboratory inconsistencies, and problems associated with conventional ^{14}C dating of old wood have led to certain biases in the chronological reconstruction of the Neolithic period. Although these biases are not believed to have fundamentally undermined the quality of existing cultural-historical sequences for the Levant and southern Anatolia, our confidence in these chronologies should increase with continued critical re-examination of the potential sources of biases, such as taphonomic processes and accelerator mass spectrometric (AMS) dating of seeds from stratified contexts.

CHRONOLOGY AND CULTURAL HISTORY FOR THE LEVANTINE NEOLITHIC

Until recently, the formulation of relative and absolute chronologies for the Neolithic of the Near East has been based on stratified mounds, representing several different periods, such as Jericho (Kenyon 1981), Mureybet (Cauvin 1978) and Abu Hureyra (Moore 1975). Dated layers and contexts in sites that were founded and abandoned during the Neolithic, such as 'Ain Ghazel (Rollefson and Simmons 1988) and Beidha (Kirkbride 1966), have furnished additional important chronologic and cultural information. During the past 15 years, an increasing number of archaeological field projects have focused on unicultural settlements from a variety of sub-regions that provide well-defined material assemblages, limited stratigraphic mixing and, ultimately, greater understanding of cultural and social variability during the Neolithic (*e.g.*, Bar-Yosef 1981, 1984; Betts 1988; Garrard *et al.* 1988a; Kuijt, Mabry and Palumbo 1991; Watkins, Baird and Betts 1989). These excavations provide us with a better understanding of small-site occupations for the early Aceramic Neolithic (PPNA and Harifian), the middle and late Aceramic Neolithic (PPNB) and the Ceramic Neolithic (PNA) (Figs. 1–3; Tables 1, 2).

Late Quaternary Chronology and Paleoclimates of the Eastern Mediterranean
Edited by O. Bar-Yosef and R. S. Kra. RADIOCARBON 1994, pp. 227–245

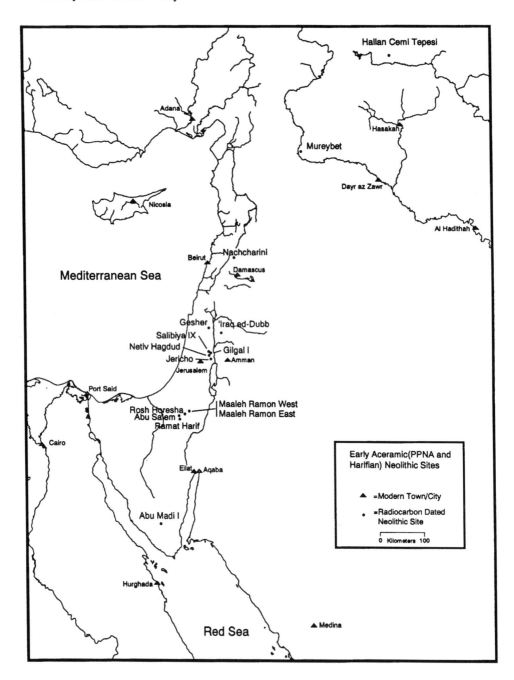

Fig. 1. ^{14}C-dated Levantine early Aceramic Neolithic sites

Dates are reported as before present (BP). Our compilation of dates (Table 3, which appears at the end of this article) from the literature and personal communications is probably incomplete. We have included some, but by no means all, ^{14}C dates from areas adjacent to the Levant; our list encompasses only some eastern Anatolian excavations. Readers seeking more information

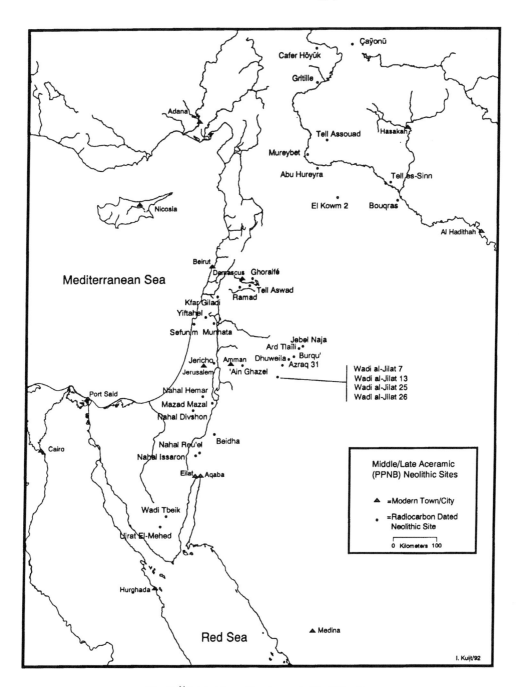

Fig. 2. ¹⁴C-dated Levantine Aceramic Neolithic sites

on this subject are referred to other sources (*e.g.*, Cauvin 1987). Finally, we have arranged the dates in stratigraphic order; however, the stratigraphic relations of some sites have not been clearly defined in the literature. Thus, readers are asked to treat the specific stratigraphic placement of individual dates with caution.

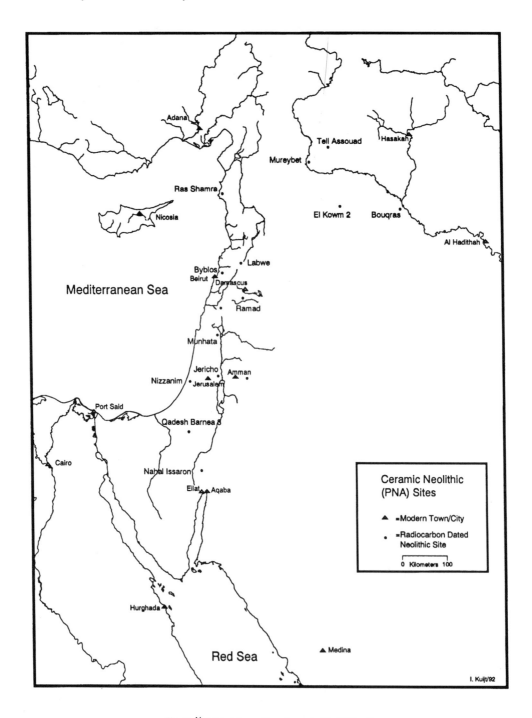

Fig. 3. ^{14}C-dated Levantine Ceramic Neolithic sites

TABLE 1. Generalized Chronological Divison of Early Aceramic, Middle/Late Aceramic and Ceramic Neolithic Archaeological Sites

---

Early Aceramic (PPNA and Harifian)
Abu Madi I, Abu Salem, Gesher, Gilgal I, Hallan Çemi Tepesi, 'Iraq ed-Dubb, Jericho, Maaleh Ramon East, Maaleh Ramon West, Mureybet, Nachcharini, Netiv Hagdud, Ramat Harif, Shunera VI Dune, Salibiya IX

Middle/Late Aceramic (PPNB)
Abu Hureyra, 'Ain Ghazel, Azraq 31, Beidha, Bouqras, Burqu', Çayönü, Cafer Höyük, Dhuweila, El Kowm 2, Ghoraifé, Gritille, Jebel Naja, Jericho, Kfar Giladi, Mazad Mazal, Munhata, Mureybet, Nahal Divshon, Nahal Hemar, Nahal Issaron, Nahal Reu'el, Ramad, Sefunim, Tell Assouad, Tell Aswad, Tell es-Sinn, Ujrat El-Mehed, Wadi al-Jilat 7, Wadi al-Jilat 13, Wadi al-Jilat 25, Wadi al-Jilat 26, Wadi Tbeik, Yiftahel

---

Ceramic Neolithic (PNA)
Ard Tlaïli, Bouqras, Byblos, El Kowm 2, Jericho, Labwe, Munhata, Mureybet, Nahal Issaron, Nizzanim, Qadesh Barnea 3, Ramad, Ras Shamra, Tell Assouad

---

TELL SAMPLING, OLD WOOD AND LABORATORY INCONSISTENCIES

In interpreting compiled ¹⁴C dates, one must examine carefully how sampling, analysis, excavation methods and interpretations of archaeological context may bias the reconstruction of cultural-historical chronologies (*e.g.*, Dean 1978; Waterbolk 1987). Specifically, we call attention to four issues of potential concern in ¹⁴C dating Neolithic sites: 1) sampling biases within the excavations of large, deeply stratified sites; 2) problems of biogenic and anthropogenic mixing and unclear contextual association often encountered in large, multicomponent sites; 3) biases introduced by old wood; and 4) interlaboratory inconsistencies.

Archaeological research in the Near East has traditionally focused on sites with intact domestic and public architecture, well-defined stratigraphy and great quantities of cultural material. As a byproduct of this trend, the majority of ¹⁴C dates has been obtained from sites between 4 and 10 ha in area. An example of this bias can be seen in the number of ¹⁴C dates from Early Neolithic sites along the Jordan River Valley (Table 2). A 100-km-long and 50-km-wide corridor between the Dead Sea and Lake Kinneret has yielded 65 ¹⁴C dates from the large (>1.5 ha) and deeply stratified sites of Jericho, 'Ain Ghazel and Yiftahel, and 25 dates from medium-sized sites (0.5–1.5 ha), such as Netiv Hagdud, Munhata and Gilgal I. The discrepancy in the representation of ¹⁴C dates is further demonstrated by the fact that only 13 ¹⁴C dates are available from sites measuring <0.5 ha (Fig. 4).

If chronological sequences based on materials excavated from large tell sites do represent a sampling bias, how has this modified our reconstruction of Neolithic economic and social behavior? The answer is at least partially linked to the type(s) of economic and settlement systems that existed in different geographic areas during the Neolithic. In areas adjacent to the Jordan Valley, PPNB agricultural villages of 4–10 ha² may have served as economic and social foci, with only a few peripheral hamlets between them. Most samples from these villages have been dated through conventional ¹⁴C methods. Arid areas, such as the Azraq Basin, the eastern desert of Jordan and the Sinai, appear to have been occupied by indigenous mobile hunter-gatherers/foragers living in small encampments, often covering <0.05 ha (Bar-Yosef 1984; Bar-Yosef and Belfer-Cohen 1992; Betts *et al.* 1991; Byrd 1992; Garrard *et al.* 1988b, and references therein). Samples from these small sites are usually AMS-dated (Table 4).

TABLE 2. Number of ^{14}C Dates for Aceramic Neolithic Sites *ca.*
50 km from the Dead Sea and Lake Tiberias

Size of site	Site	No. of ^{14}C dates	Total
Small (<0.5 ha)	'Iraq ed-Dubb	2	
	Nahal Hemar	8	
	Nahal Divshon	3	13
Medium (0.5–1.5 ha)	Gesher	4	
	Gilgal I	6	
	Netiv Hagdud	11	
	Salibiya IX	2	
	Munhata	2	25
Large (>1.5 ha)	Jericho	40	
	'Ain Ghazel	21	
	Yiftahel	4	65

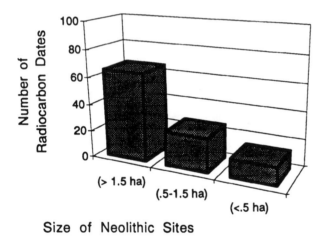

Fig. 4. Number of ^{14}C dates for Aceramic Neolithic sites, sorted by site size within the southern Levantine corridor.

It is reasonable to assume that there was interaction, exchange or trade among members of different communities in different geographic areas. If the majority of archaeological research focuses on larger sites, how can archaeologists understand the economic and social contributions made by the inhabitants of small sites within an interaction sphere? Ultimately, archaeologists must develop regional cultural-historical sequences based on data from single sites. We must recognize that, in reconstructing Neolithic economies and chronology, certain geographic regions do not receive the same amount of attention as others. Needless to say, the degree to which this trend has influenced general chronologic and social reconstructions of the Neolithic period has yet to be examined in detail and clearly requires further consideration.

Another issue centers on how factors of re-occupation, such as leveling, building, digging pits and burying trash, cause mixing of deposits, and weaken associations between individual samples and their original stratigraphic context (*e.g.*, Bar-Yosef 1991; or see Waterbolk 1987, for a very insightful essay). A characteristic example of such difficulties is the interpretation of conventional ¹⁴C dates and stratigraphy in the excavations of Jericho (Kenyon 1981; Farrand 1994). Repeated occupations, alternating with long intervals of abandonment from the late Natufian to the Iron Age, and the vertical and horizontal movement of archaeological materials, especially charcoal, are factors that contribute to serious chronological uncertainties. Charcoal is often charred wood, and if not uncovered in a fireplace, can be only broadly related to the cultural materials of a certain level. In this case, it is not the quality of dating that is at issue, but the original contextual association of the sample.

The "old wood" factor also has a potential impact on Neolithic chronologies. In its broadest application, old wood refers to dated charcoal material that, while stratigraphically associated with specific deposits or cultural materials, actually predates these deposits (Dean 1978; Schiffer 1986; Orme 1982). In semi-arid areas, old dead wood was used as fuel, or re-used as timber for construction. The sampling of wood charcoal from trees such as oak, which may have life cycles of several hundred years, may lead to dates older than their contexts. When combined with issues of interlaboratory inconsistencies, the re-use of timber for building and firewood, and weak contexts or associations, this source of potential error (<500 ¹⁴C yr) can be magnified. Because most ¹⁴C dates from the Neolithic derive from wood charcoal samples recovered from hearths, architectural features or fill deposits, we should be wary of old wood as a source of bias (Table 3).

TABLE 4. Levantine Neolithic Sites with AMS ¹⁴C Dates

Site	No. of AMS dates
Abu Hureyra	17
'Ain Ghazel	4
Azraq 31	3
Burqu'	8
Dhuweila	4
'Iraq ed-Dubb	1
Jebel Naja	1
Nahal Hemar Cave	3
Netiv Hagdud	1
Wadi al-Jilat 7	4
Wadi al-Jilat 13	3
Wadi al-Jilat 25	1
Wadi al-Jilat 26	2
Total no. of sites (26% of ¹⁴C dated sites)	13
Total no. of AMS dates (15% of total ¹⁴C dates)	52

A final concern is in laboratory processing. Several independent studies have addressed issues of systematic or random bias in ¹⁴C laboratories (see Scott, Long and Kra 1990, for general problems encountered in intercomparison studies; Waterbolk 1987 and Weinstein 1984 and references therein, for specific problems related to the Near East). The rationale behind the ongoing interlaboratory comparisons (Scott, Long and Kra 1990) is reduction of laboratory error and implementation of internal quality control. Split samples (*i.e.,* sending parts of the same sample to different laboratories) is a good measure with which to monitor interlaboratory bias. In the event of a marked discrepancy, this practice can lead to difficult decision-making for the archaeologist; however, it also helps the archaeologist to identify systematic differences among laboratories.

FUTURE DIRECTIONS

How can archaeologists minimize the biases introduced to cultural-historical sequences, and more importantly, how can future research be directed toward improving our confidence in the chronology of the Neolithic period? First, our understanding of Neolithic chronology would be strengthened by the excavation of small, single-component, stratified sites to complement our knowledge about large settlements, providing us with a finer resolution of both material culture and chronology. Since the early 1980s, several studies have begun to detail relations of smaller Neolithic sites with larger Neolithic villages. Among others, these include small hunting camps near 'Ain Ghazel (Simmons and Kafafi 1988), and small PPNA sites, such as 'Iraq ed-Dubb (Kuijt, Mabry and Palumbo 1991) and Hatoula (Lechevallier and Ronen 1985). Similarly, researchers working in areas such as the desert belt of the southern Levant have begun to study Neolithic sites in the region and their economic and social interactions (*e.g.*, Bar-Yosef 1984; Betts *et al.* 1991; Byrd 1992; Garrard *et al.* 1988a,b; Goring-Morris and Gopher 1983; Goring-Morris 1991). While producing our first detailed reconstructions of lifeways in small Neolithic settlements and special-purpose hunting sites, research on single-component stratified sites needs to be expanded.

Second, the chronology of the Neolithic would be improved by excavation of sites in areas beyond the fertile Levantine corridor. Several investigations have focused attention on more arid areas of the southern Sinai, the Negev desert (Bar-Yosef 1984; Dyan *et al.* 1986; Goring-Morris and Gopher 1983; Tchernov and Bar-Yosef 1982) and the east-central Levant, specifically from the Azraq Basin northward to the Palmyra and El-Kowm Basins (Betts 1988; Betts *et al.* 1991; Garrard *et al.* 1988a,b; Garrard, Baird and Byrd 1994), reviewed in greater detail elsewhere (Bar-Yosef and Belfer-Cohen 1989; Byrd 1992). These studies demonstrate that arid areas appear to have been occupied through much, if not all, of the Neolithic by groups that developed adaptations to local subsistence resources.

Finally, the increasing use of AMS dating will also improve cultural chronologies for the Neolithic. By selecting milligram-sized samples, such as identifiable seeds, one can directly monitor the development of domesticated plant species. Small samples can also be used to improve control over associations and increase confidence in the relative context of a sample with archaeological materials. Thus, AMS dating will enable archaeologists to place in time plants that have short-term growth cycles, split samples and individual seeds, and reduce the chance of erroneous dates as a result of old wood.

ACKNOWLEDGMENTS

Special thanks are due Michael Rosenberg, University of Delaware, for permission to include the latest ^{14}C dates from Hallan Çemi Tepesi. The writing of this article was made possible by a Doctoral Fellowship from the Social Sciences and Humanities Research Council of Canada to the senior author. Thanks are given to Meredith Chesson, Chris Rodning and Renee Kra for their editorial comments and suggestions. The considerable research on the Levantine Neolithic conducted over the past ten years has made it increasingly difficult to keep current with results of a number of field projects. Thus, we may have unintentionally omitted published ^{14}C dates, or more likely, listed incorrectly the contexts of specific ^{14}C samples. We apologize, in advance, for these inevitable errors, and ask that they be brought to our attention.

TABLE 3. Radiocarbon Dates for the Levantine Neolithic (Rounded to Nearest 5 yr)

Site	Date (BP)	Lab no.*	Sample**	Provenience	Reference
Abu Hureyra	10,700 ± 500	BM-1723	Ch	Aceramic	Moore (1975,1979)
Abu Hureyra	9375 ± 70	BM-1122	Ch	Early Aceramic	Hedges *et al.* (1990)
Abu Hureyra	8675 ± 70	BM-1423	Ch	Early Aceramic	Gowlett *et al.* (1987)
Abu Hureyra	8610 ± 50	BM-1722	Ch	Early Aceramic	
Abu Hureyra	21,940 ± 180	BM-1720	Ch	Early Aceramic	
Abu Hureyra	8410 ± 60	BM-1721	Ch	Early Aceramic	
Abu Hureyra	8665 ± 65	BM-1120	Ch	Mid-Aceramic	
Abu Hureyra	8395 ± 70	BM-1425	Ch	Late Aceramic	
Abu Hureyra	8190 ± 75	BM-1424	Ch	Late Aceramic	
Abu Hureyra	7900 ± 50	BM-1724	Ch	Late Aceramic	
Abu Hureyra	390 ± 60	OxA-2044	B	Tr.A	
Abu Hureyra	170 ± 60	OxA-2045	B	Tr.B	
Abu Hureyra	7310 ± 150	OxA-1232	B	Tr.B	
Abu Hureyra	8500 ± 120	OxA-1190	S	Tr.B	
Abu Hureyra	8640 ± 110	OxA-2169	S	Tr.B	
Abu Hureyra	8500 ± 90	OxA-876	B	Tr.D	
Abu Hureyra	8300 ± 150	OxA-877	B	Tr.D	
Abu Hureyra	8490 ± 110	OxA-878	B	Tr.D	
Abu Hureyra	8570 ± 130	OxA-879	B	Tr.D	
Abu Hureyra	14,920 ± 180	OxA-880	B	Tr.D	
Abu Hureyra	8870 ± 100	OxA-881	B	Tr.D	
Abu Hureyra	8330 ± 100	OxA-1190	Ch	Tr.E	
Abu Hureyra	8270 ± 100	OxA-2167	S	Tr.E	
Abu Hureyra	7890 ± 90	OxA-1931	S	Tr.G	
Abu Hureyra	8180 ± 100	OxA-1930	S	Tr.G	
Abu Hureyra	8320 ± 80	OxA-1227	Ch	Tr.G	
Abu Hureyra	9680 ± 90	OxA-1228	Ch	Tr.G	
Abu Madi I	10,110 ± 100	Pta-2699	Ch	Layer 8	Bar-Yosef (1981, 1991)
Abu Madi I	9970 ± 120	Pta-4568	Ch	Layer 10	
Abu Madi I	9790 ± 100	Pta-4572	Ch	Layer 10	
Abu Madi I	9920 ± 80	Pta-4552	Ch	Layer 11	
Abu Madi I	9790 ± 100	Pta-4551	Ch	Layer 11	
Abu Madi I	9870 ± 100	Pta-4577	Ch	Layer 12	
Abu Madi I	9800 ± 80	Pta-4580	Ch	Layer 12	
Abu Salem	10,550 ± 90	Pta-3292	Ch	L22/180-190	Goring-Morris (1991)
Abu Salem	10,420 ± 100	Pta-3293	Ch	L24/190-200	
Abu Salem	10,140 ± 80	Pta-3291	Ch	L22/120-130	
Abu Salem	11,660 ± 90	Pta-3080	Ch	L22	
Abu Salem	10,340 ± 90	Pta-3290	Ch	L21/120-130	
Abu Salem	10,300 ± 100	Pta-3289	Ch	L1/155-160	
Abu Salem	10,230 ± 150	I-5500	Ch	Trash Pit 45-55	
Abu Salem	10,230 ± 150	I-5499	Ch	Trash Pit 25-30	
Abu Salem	9970 ± 150	I-5498	Ch	Trash Pit 15-25	
'Ain Ghazel	7820 ± 240	AA-1165	Ch	IIa	Rollefson and Simmons
'Ain Ghazel	8950 ± 390	AA-1166	Ch	IIa	(1988)
'Ain Ghazel	8165 ± 50	GrN-12972	Ch	Ib	Hedges *et al.* (1989)
'Ain Ghazel	8460 ± 90	GrN-12971	Ch		Rollefson *et al.* (1992)
'Ain Ghazel	8810 ± 80	GrN-12969	Ch	VI	
'Ain Ghazel	8620 ± 320	UCR-1721	Ch	V	
'Ain Ghazel	8650 ± 200	GrN-12970	Ch	IVb	
'Ain Ghazel	9100 ± 140	AA-1164	Ch	IVa	
'Ain Ghazel	8470 ± 650	UCR-1718	Ch	II	
'Ain Ghazel	8070 ± 230	UCR-1722	Ch	--	

TABLE 3. (Continued)

Site	Date (BP)	Lab no.*	Sample**	Provenience	Reference
'Ain Ghazel	11,875 ± 650	UCR-1723	Ch	Loc 3076.159	
'Ain Ghazel	10,850 ± 610	UCR-1729	Ch	Loc 3076.294	
'Ain Ghazel	5130 ± 315	UCR-1725	Ch	Loc 3076.048	
'Ain Ghazel	8660 ± 80	OxA-1472	Ch	Statue Cache	
'Ain Ghazel	8700 ± 80	OxA-1473	Ch	Statue Cache	
'Ain Ghazel	9000 ± 90	GrN-12959	Ch	--	
'Ain Ghazel	8930 ± 60	GrN-12961	Ch	II	
'Ain Ghazel	9030 ± 80	GrN-12960	Ch	I/II	
'Ain Ghazel	8680 ± 190	GrN-12962	Ch	I	
'Ain Ghazel	8970 ± 80	GrN-12963	Ch	IV	
'Ain Ghazel	8970 ± 80	GrN-12964	Ch	III	
'Ain Ghazel	9050 ± 80	GrN-12965	Ch	III	
'Ain Ghazel	8930 ± 80	GrN-12967	Ch	IV	
'Ain Ghazel	8970 ± 110	GrN-12968	Ch	III	
'Ain Ghazel	9200 ± 110	GrN-12966	Ch	II	
'Ain Ghazel	8570 ± 180	AA-1167	Ch	--	
Ard Tlaïli	6660 ± ?	K-1431	Ch	Lower	Kirkbride (1969)
Ard Tlaïli	6870 ± 130	K-1432	Ch	Lower	
Ard Tlaïli	6850 ± 130	K-1433	Ch	Lower	
Ard Tlaïli	6790 ± 130	K-1434	Ch	Lower	
Azraq 31	8350 ± 120	OxA-870	Ch	Sq. 1, 10	Hedges *et al.* (1987, 1992)
Azraq 31	8275 ± 80	OxA-2414	Ch	C, 19b	
Azraq 31	1280 ± 90	OxA-871	B	Sq.14, 107	
Basta	8380 ± 100	GrN-14537	Ch	--	Nissen *et al.* (1987)
Basta	8155 ± 50	GrN-14538	Ch	Locus 7	
Beidha	8940 ± 160	K-1086	Ch	Level VI	Barker and Mackey (1968)
Beidha	8850 ± 100	K-1410	Ch	Level VI	Stuckenrath and Lawn (1969)
Beidha	8770 ± 150	K-1411	Ch	Level VI	Vogel and Waterbolk (1972)
Beidha	8720 ± 150	K-1412	Ch	Level VI	Weinstein (1984)
Beidha	8715 ± 130	P-1378	Ch	Level VI	
Beidha	8770 ± 160	K-1082	N	Level VI	
Beidha	8640 ± 50	GrN-5063	N	Level VI	
Beidha	8545 ± 100	P-1379	N	Level VI	
Beidha	8640 ± 160	K-1083	Ch	Level V	
Beidha	9130 ± 105	P-1380	Ch	Level IV	
Beidha	8810 ± 50	GrN-5136	Ch	Level IV	
Beidha	8790 ± 200	BM-111	Ch	Level IV	
Beidha	8765 ± 100	P-1381	Ch	Level IV	
Beidha	8730 ± 160	K-1084	Ch	Level IV	
Beidha	9030 ± 50	GrN-5062	Ch	Level II	
Beidha	8890 ± 115	P-1382	Ch	Level II	
Beidha	8550 ± 160	K-1085	Ch	Level II	
Bouqras	8115 ± 40	GrN-8258	Ch	0.5 mbs	Akkermans *et al.* (1983)
Bouqras	7860 ± 40	GrN-8264	Ch	0.5 mbs	
Bouqras	7925 ± 40	GrN-8259	Ch	2.5 mbs	
Bouqras	7905 ± 45	GrN-8260	Ch	2.6 mbs	
Bouqras	8155 ± 45	GrN-8261	Ch	2.4 mbs	
Bouqras	8380 ± 45	GrN-8262	Ch	4.5 mbs	
Bouqras	8330 ± 80	GrN-8263	Ch	5.0 mbs	
Bouqras	8240 ± 100	GrN-4852	Ch	Layer I	
Bouqras	8140 ± 60	GrN-4818	Ch	Layer I	
Bouqras	7960 ± 55	GrN-4819	Ch	Layer II	
Bouqras	7840 ± 60	GrN-4820	Ch	Layer III	

TABLE 3. (Continued)

Site	Date (BP)	Lab no.*	Sample**	Provenience	Reference
Bouqras	7465 ± 45	GrN-10589	Ch	Lev. 3–4	
Bouqras	12,230 ± 190	GrN-10590	Ch	Lev. 3–4	
Bouqras	7945 ± 50	GrN-10591	Ch	Lev. 3–4	
Bouqras	8110 ± 50	GrN-10592	Ch	Lev. 10	
Bouqras	7485 ± 50	GrN-13079	Ch	Lev. 3–4	
Bouqras	8365 ± 50	GrN-13080	Ch	Lev. 3–4	
Bouqras	7520 ± 50	GrN-13081	Ch	Lev. 3–4	
Bouqras	7530 ± 50	GrN-13082	Ch	Lev. 3–4	
Bouqras	7880 ± 60	GrN-13090	Ch	Lev. 3–4	
Bouqras	8025 ± 50	GrN-13099	Ch	Lev. 3	
Bouqras	8080 ± 50	GrN-13100	Ch	Lev. 3	
Bouqras	8230 ± 35	GrN-13101	Ch	Lev. 7	
Bouqras	8345 ± 35	GrN-13102	Ch	Lev. 8	
Bouqras	8285 ± 50	GrN-13103	Ch	Lev. 9	
Bouqras	8300 ± 50	GrN-13104	Ch	Lev. 9	
Burqu' 2	144.2 ± 1pMC†	OxA-2807	Ch	2 203	Betts *et al.* (1991)
Burqu' 3	6900 ± 100	OxA-2808	Ch	3 158	Hedges *et al.* (1992)
Burqu' 27	7930 ± 80	OxA-2766	Ch	27 142	
Burqu' 27	7350 ± 80	OxA-2765	Ch	27 141	
Burqu' 27	7270 ± 80	OxA-2764	Ch	27 132	
Burqu' 35	8180 ± 80	OxA-2769	Ch	27 132	
Burqu' 35	8140 ± 90	OxA-2768	Ch	35 208	
Burqu' 37	8270 ± 80	OxA-2770	Ch	37 112	
Byblos	7360 ± 70	GrN-1544	Ch	Level XLIII	Vogel and Waterbolk (1972)
Byblos	6550 ± 250	W-627	Ch	Néolithique Ancien	
Çayönü	5815 ± 65	GrN-5827	Ch	BN(NS), 5	Braidwood and Çambel (1982)
Çayönü	6100 ± 80	GrN-5952	Ch	BN(NS), 5	
Çayönü	8055 ± 75	GrN-5954	Ch	QC 5, 4	
Çayönü	8080 ± 90	GrN-8819	Ch	SE, 12-2	
Çayönü	8355 ± 50	GrN-8078	Ch	SA, 14-17	
Çayönü	8795 ± 50	GrN-6242	Ch	R, 8-2	
Çayönü	8865 ± 45	GrN-8820	Ch	HG, 14-0	
Çayönü	8980 ± 80	GrN-6244	Ch	EF, 2/1	
Çayönü	9175 ± 55	GrN-8821	Ch	HA, 25/-1/1	
Çayönü	9200 ± 60	GrN-4459	Ch	K 6-9, 4-5	
Çayönü	9250 ± 60	GrN-8079	Ch	HA, 24-1	
Çayönü	9275 ± 95	GrN-6241	Ch	R, 14-0	
Çayönü	9320 ± 55	GrN-6243	Ch	R, 18-1	
Çayönü	9520 ± 100	GrN-4458	Ch	K-12	
Çayönü	9795 ± 260	GrN-5953	Ch	SB 1-3	
Çayönü	10,430 ± 80	GrN-8103	Ch	S, 3-1	
Çayönü	9180 ± 80	GrN-10358	Ch	KE 6-1	
Çayönü	9050 ± 140	GrN-10354	Ch	KE 6-5	
Çayönü	9300 ± 140	GrN-10360	Ch	KW 8-1	
Çayönü	9290 ± 110	GrN-10361	Ch	KW 6-5	
Çayönü	8790 ± 250	M-1609	Ch	K 6-9	
Çayönü	8570 ± 250	M-1610	Ch	K 6-9	
Çayönü	8340 ± 250	UCLA-1703B	B	--	
Çayönü	7620 ± 140	UCLA-1703C	B	--	
Cafer Höyük	8450 ± 160	Ly-2181	Ch	Test 1, Bed E	Cauvin and Aurenche (1982)
Cafer Höyük	8980 ± 160	Ly-2182	Ch	Test 2, Bed A	
Cafer Höyük	8150 ± 210	Ly-3089	Ch	East, Level III	
Cafer Höyük	8980 ± 150	Ly-3091	Ch	East, Level IV	

TABLE 3. (Continued)

Site	Date (BP)	Lab no.*	Sample**	Provenience	Reference
Cafer Höyük	8920 ± 160	Ly-3090	Ch	East, Level V	
Cafer Höyük	8400 ± 220	Ly-2522	Ch	West, str 3	
Cafer Höyük	8600 ± 120	Ly-2523	Ch	West, MB84,3a	
Cafer Höyük	8480 ± 140	Ly-3772	Ch	Lev VI	
Cafer Höyük	7900 ± 190	Ly-3773	Ch	Lev VI	
Dhuweila	8350 ± 100	OxA-1637	Ch	2202/2133	Hedges *et al.* (1989)
Dhuweila	8190 ± 60	BM-2349	Ch	--	
Dhuweila	7450 ± 90	OxA-1729	Ch	4118	
Dhuweila	7140 ± 90	OxA-1728	Ch	4225	
Dhuweila	7030 ± 90	OxA-1636	Ch	2202/4217	
El-Kowm 1	7400 ± 45	GrN-6778	Ch	S67-3	Aurenche and Evin (1987)
El-Kowm 1	7290 ± 45	GrN-6777	Ch	S67-2	
El-Kowm 2	7760 ± 280	Ly-2521	Ch	B4a	Stordeur *et al.* (1982)
El-Kowm 2	7680 ± 200	Ly-2520	Ch	B7	
El-Kowm 2	23,500 ± 760	Ly-2519	Ch	A2b	
El-Kowm 2	>33,500	Ly-2575	Ch	A2b	
El-Kowm 2	>33,500	Ly-2576	Ch	A2b	
El-Kowm 2	4410 ± 130	Ly-2577	Ch	A2b	
Gesher	10,020 ± 100	Pta-4553	Ch	--	Garfinkel and Nadel (1989)
Gesher	9870 ± 80	Pta-4595	Ch	--	
Gesher	9820 ± 140	RT-868A	Ch	--	
Gesher	9790 ± 140	RT-868B	Ch	--	
Ghoraifé	8710 ± 190	Gif-3376	Ch	Level I	de Contenson (1976)
Ghoraifé	8460 ± 190	Gif-3375	Ch	Level I	Delibrias *et al.* (1982)
Ghoraifé	8400 ± 190	Gif-3374	Ch	Level I	
Ghoraifé	8150 ± 190	Gif-3372	Ch	Level II	
Ghoraifé	6940 ± 190	Gif-3371	Ch	Level II	
Gilgal I	9950 ± 150	RT-777	Ch	--	Noy (1989)
Gilgal I	9900 ± 220	RT-777	Ch	--	
Gilgal I	9950 ± 150	RT-777	Ch	--	
Gilgal I	9830 ± 80	Pta-4583	Ch	--	
Gilgal I	9710 ± 70	Pta-4585	Ch	--	
Gilgal I	9920 ± 70	Pta-4588	Ch	--	
Gritille	7950 ± 120	Beta-13218	Ch	Phase B/50	Voigt (1986)
Gritille	7770 ± 150	Beta-8240	Ch	Phase B/16	
Gritille	7860 ± 80	Beta-8241	Ch	Phase B/16	
Gritille	8610 ± 90	Beta-13216	Ch	Phase C/16	
Gritille	8000 ± 230	Beta-13215	Ch	Phase C/16	
Gritille	8460 ± 180	Beta-13217	Ch	Basal/48	
Hallan Çemi Tepesi (HÇT)	10,040 ± 160	Beta-46647	Ch	5H 18/19	Rosenberg (personal
HÇT	10,800 ± 220	Beta-46649	Ch	7F7-518-2	communication)
HÇT	10,060 ± 120	Beta-47211	Ch	6F7-518	
HÇT	11,700 ± 460	Beta-47252	Ch	6F9-244	
HÇT	9730 ± 300	Beta-47253	Ch	6G3-030	
Hayaz Höyük	8300 ± 60	GrN-12510	Ch	EG54/265	Cauvin and Aurenche (1982)
Hayaz Höyük	8040 ± 170	GrN-12512	Ch	FF25/324	
Hayaz Höyük	5600 ± 160	GrN-10686	Ch	FG314	
Hayaz Höyük	5530 ± 50	GrN-11654	Ch	EG83	
'Iraq ed-Dubb	9950 ± 100	OxA-2567	Ch	Struct. I, Loc. 7	Kuijt *et al.* (1991)
Jebel Naja	7430 ± 100	OxA-375	Ch	--	Gowlett *et al.* (1986)

TABLE 3. (Continued)

Site	Date (BP)	Lab no.*	Sample**	Provenience	Reference
Jericho (Proto-Neo)	10,300 ± 200	BM-106	Ch	VI/ A . x-xi	Burleigh (1981, 1983)
Jericho (PPNA)	9380 ± 85	BM1323	Ch	VI/ A . x-xi	
Jericho (PPNA)	10,300 ± 500	BM-250	Ch	IV. iva	
Jericho (PPNA)	9320 ± 150	BM-252	Ch	VIII A. xvia	
Jericho (PPNA)	9655 ± 85	P-379	Ch	VI A. x-xi	
Jericho (PPNA)	9200 ± 70	BM-1789	Ch	IX. xx-xxia	
Jericho (PPNA)	10,180 ± 200	BM-110	Ch	IX. xxii-xxiii	
Jericho (PPNA)	9390 ± 150	BM-251	Ch	VI. via	
Jericho (PPNA)	9580 ± 90	P-377	Ch	IV. viii	
Jericho (PPNA)	9430 ± 85	BM-1324	Ch	VI. xxvii	
Jericho (PPNA)	9560 ± 65	BM-1327	Ch	IV A. iiib	
Jericho (PPNA)	9230 ± 220	BM-1326	Ch	VIII A. xvib	
Jericho (PPNA)	9230 ± 80	BM-1321	Ch	VIII A. xvib	
Jericho (PPNA)	9280 ± 100	BM-1787	Ch	VIII A. xv	
Jericho (PPNA)	10,250 ± 200	BM-105	Ch	IV. iiib	
Jericho (PPNA)	9775 ± 110	P-378	Ch	IV A. iiib	
Jericho (PPNA)	9380 ± 85	BM-1322	Ch	IV A. iiib	
Jericho (PPNA)	8770 ± 150	GL-39	Ch	VIII B. xviia	
Jericho (PPNA)	8690 ± 150	GL-40	Ch	VIII B. xviia	
Jericho (PPNA)	8895 ± 150	GL-43	Ch	VIII B. xviia	
Jericho (PPNA)	7300 ± 200	GL-46	Ch	VIII B. xviia	
Jericho (PPNB)	8610 ± 75	P-380	Ch	XV A. xxxviiia	
Jericho (PPNB)	8660 ± 130	BM-1793	Ch	XIV. xxxvii	
Jericho (PPNB)	8390 ± 200	GL-36	Ch	XIII. li	
Jericho (PPNB)	8200 ± 200	GL-28	Ch	XIII. liv	
Jericho (PPNB)	8710 ± 150	BM-253	Ch	XIII. i	
Jericho (PPNB)	9170 ± 200	BM-115	Ch	XII. xlviia	
Jericho (PPNB)	8955 ± 105	P-382	Ch	XII. xlviia	
Jericho (PPNB)	8660 ± 100	P-381	Ch	X. x.lii	
Jericho (PPNB)	7800 ± 160	GL-38	Ch	XVII. xxx	
Jericho (PPNB)	8670 ± 150	GL-41	Ch	XVII. xxx	
Jericho (PPNB)	8700 ± 200	GL-42	Ch	XVII. xxx	
Jericho (PPNB)	9140 ± 70	GrN-942	Ch	XVII. xxx	
Jericho (PPNB)	9025 ± 100	GrN-963	Ch	XVII. xxx	
Jericho (PPNB)	8540 ± 65	BM-1320	Ch	XI. lv	
Jericho (PPNB)	8700 ± 110	BM-1769	Ch	XI. lvia	
Jericho (PPNB)	8680 ± 70	BM-1770	Ch	XI. lxa	
Jericho (PPNB)	8660 ± 260	BM-1771	Ch	XIII. lxxa	
Jericho (PPNB)	8810 ± 100	BM-1772	Ch	XIII. lxxiv-XIV.lxxv	
Jericho (PPNB)	8730 ± 80	BM-1773	Ch	XIV. lxxvi	
Kfar Gilad	8905 ± 320	--	Ch	VI	Gopher (1985)
Labwe	7990 ± 140	K-1430	Ch	I	Kirkbride (1969)
Labwe	7860 ± 140	K-1428	Ch	I	
Labwe	7850 ± 140	K-1429	Ch	I	
Maaleh Ramon E	10,530 ± 100	Pta-3371	Ch	L1/30-35	Goring-Morris (1991)
Maaleh Ramon E	10,430 ± 80	Pta-3483	Ch	L1/25-30	
Maaleh Ramon W	10,400 ± 100	Pta-3483	Ch	--	
Maaleh Ramon W	10,000 ± 200	RT-1068N	Ch	--	
Mazad Mazal	8480 ± 70	B-2737	Ch	Sample 1	Weinstein (1984)
Mazad Mazal	8440 ± 80	HV-9108	Ch	Sample 1	
Mazad Mazal	8350 ± 75	KN-2444	Ch	Sample 2	
Mazad Mazal	8330 ± 75	HV-9107	Ch	Sample 2	

TABLE 3. (Continued)

Site	Date (BP)	Lab no.*	Sample**	Provenience	Reference
Mazad Mazal	8240 ± 95	HV-9106	Ch	Sample 3	
Mazad Mazal	8070 ± 75	KN-2443	Ch	Sample 3	
Munhata	9160 ± 500	M-1793	Ch	IVB	Crane and Griffin (1970)
Munhata	7370 ± 400	M-1792	Ch	IVA	
Mureybet	10,215 ± 115	P-1217	Ch	Phase IB	Stuckenrath and Lawn (1969)
Mureybet	10,005 ± 95	P-1215	Ch	Phase IB	Cauvin (1987)
Mureybet	10,590 ± 140	Lv-607	Ch	Phase IB	
Mureybet	10,590 ± 140	Lv-605	Ch	Phase II	
Mureybet	10,460 ± 200	Lv-606	Ch	Phase II	
Mureybet	9970 ± 115	P-1220	Ch	Phase IIIa	
Mureybet	9675 ± 110	MC-616	Ch	Phase IIIa	
Mureybet	9730 ± 150	MC-735	Ch	Phase IIIa	
Mureybet	9950 ± 150	MC-734	Ch	Phase IIIa	
Mureybet	9905 ± 115	P-1222	Ch	Phase IIIb	
Mureybet	9490 ± 120	P-1224	Ch	Phase IIIb	
Mureybet	9840 ± 260	MC-611	Ch	Phase IIIb	
Mureybet	9520 ± 150	MC-612	Ch	Phase IIIb	
Mureybet	9620 ± 200	MC-613	Ch	Phase IIIb	
Mureybet	9570 ± 200	MC-614	Ch	Phase IIIb	
Mureybet	9540 ± 130	MC-615	Ch	Phase IIIb	
Mureybet	9730 ± 140	Lv-604	Ch	Q 32	
Mureybet	10,092 ± 118	P-1216	Ch	Lev I Base	
Mureybet	9280 ± 150	MC-736	Ch	--	
Mureybet	8910 ± 150	MC-737	Ch	--	
Mureybet	9600 ± 150	MC-861	Ch	--	
Mureybet	9130 ± 150	MC-862	Ch	--	
Mureybet	9030 ± 150	MC-863	Ch	--	
Nachcharini	8980 ± 275	I-9768	Ch	4d1	Schroeder (1977)
Nachcharini	7505 ± 140	I-9767	Ch	4a	
Nachcharini	7340 ± 165	I-9766	Ch	4c	
Nahal Divshon	8900 ± 180	SMU-3	Ch	Layer 6	Haynes and Haas (1974)
Nahal Divshon	8620 ± 140	I-5501	Ch	Layer 6	
Nahal Divshon	8170 ± 180	Tx-1125	Ch	Layer5/6	
Nahal Hemar	8100 ± 100	RT-650	Ch	Layer 3a	Hedges *et al.* (1987, 1990)
Nahal Hemar	8270 ± 80	Pta-3650	Ch	Layer 3a	
Nahal Hemar	8250 ± 70	BM-2298	Ch	Layer 3a	
Nahal Hemar	8600 ± 120	OxA-1014	Cordage	Layer 3/4	
Nahal Hemar	8500 ± 220	OxA-1015	Cordage	Layer 3/4	
Nahal Hemar	8810 ± 120	OxA-1016	Linen	Layer 4	
Nahal Hemar	8850 ± 90	Pta-3625	Linen	Layer 4	
Nahal Hemar	9210 ± 300	BM-2298	Linen	Layer 4	
Nahal Issaron	8460 ± 80	Pta-2999	Ch	Layer B	Weinstein (1984)
Nahal Issaron	8430 ± 80	Pta-3000	Ch	Layer C	
Nahal Issaron	8180 ± 80	Pta-3377	Ch	Layer C	
Nahal Issaron	8050 ± 80	Pta-3376	Ch	Layer C	
Nahal Issaron	6130 ± 70	Pta-3486	Ch	Layer C	
Nahal Reu'el	8670 ± 60	Pta-2848	Ch	--	Gopher (1985)
Nahal Reu'el	8620 ± 60	Pta-3137	Ch	--	
Nahal Reu'el	8550 ± 60	Pta-3202	Ch	--	
Netiv Hagdud	9700 ± 80	Pta-4590	Ch	Loc. 1007	Gowlett *et al.* (1986)
Netiv Hagdud	9780 ± 90	Pta-4557	Ch	Loc. 1001	Bar-Yosef (1991)

TABLE 3. (Continued)

Site	Date (BP)	Lab no.*	Sample**	Provenience	Reference
Netiv Hagdud	9680 ± 140	RT-762A	Ch	Loc. 1000	
Netiv Hagdud	9600 ± 170	RT-762B	Ch	Loc. 1002	
Netiv Hagdud	9970 ± 150	RT-762C	Ch	Loc. 1004	
Netiv Hagdud	9400 ± 180	RT-762D	Ch	Loc. 1001	
Netiv Hagdud	9790 ± 380	RT-502A	Ch	Section	
Netiv Hagdud	10,180 ± 300	RT-502C	Ch	1.5 m bs	
Netiv Hagdud	9750 ± 90	Pta-4555	Ch	Loc. 1012	
Netiv Hagdud	9660 ± 70	Pta-4556	Ch	Loc. 1006	
Netiv Hagdud	9700 ± 150	OxA-744	S	Loc. 1004	
Nizzanim	6790 ± 90	Hv-8509	B	--	Yeivin and Olami (1979)
Qadesh Barnea 3	7530 ± 100	SMU-662	Ch	--	Gopher (1985)
Qadesh Barnea 3	7350 ± 80	Pta-3662	Ch	--	
Ramad	8210 ± 50	GrN-4426	Ch	Level I	de Contenson (1977)
Ramad	8200 ± 80	GrN-4428	Ch	Level I	
Ramad	8090 ± 50	GrN-4821	Ch	Level I	
Ramad	7920 ± 50	GrN-4427	Ch	Level II	
Ramad	7900 ± 50	GrN-4822	Ch	Level II	
Ramad	7880 ± 55	GrN-4823	Ch	Level II	
Ramat Harif	10,500 ± 100	Pta-3009	Ch	L3/280	Goring-Morris (1991)
Ramat Harif	10,380 ± 100	Pta-3284	Ch	L3/275-280	
Ramat Harif	10,300 ± 100	Pta-3001	Ch	L3/220-225	
Ramat Harif	10,390 ± 100	Pta-3285	Ch	L3/210-220	
Ramat Harif	10,250 ± 100	Pta-3288	Ch	L7/220-225	
Ramat Harif	10,100 ± 100	Pta-3286	Ch	L7/180-185	
Ras Shamra	9030 ± 400	Gif-102	Ch	Vc	de Contenson (1977)
Ras Shamra	8365 ± 100	P-460	Ch	Vc	
Ras Shamra	8140 ± 100	P-459	Ch	Vc	
Ras Shamra	7185 ± 85	P-457	Ch	Vc	
Ras Shamra	7685 ± 110	P-458	Ch	Vb	
Ras Shamra	8000 ± 115	Pta-113	Ch	Va	
Ras Shamra	7480 ± 90	Pta-100	Ch	Va	
Ras Shamra	7185 ± 90	P-457	Ch	Va	
Ras Shamra	6100 ± 175	P-389	Ch	IIIc	
Shunera VI Dune	9500 ± 130	RT-?	Ca	--	Goring-Morris (1991)
Salibiya IX	18,500 ± 100	Pta-3385	Ch	--	Bar-Yosef (1991)
Salibiya IX	12,300 ± 470	Pta-3008	Ch	--	
Sefunim	9395 ± 130	Hv-3368	Ch	V Terrace	Gopher (1985)
Sefunim	9120 ± 85	KN-I 336	Ch	V Terrace	
Sefunim	7730 ± 115	Hv-2597	Ch	V Terrace	
Tell Assouad	12,500 ± 160	MC-607	Ch	--	J. Cauvin (1972)
Tell Assouad	8650 ± 120	MC-865	Ch	Level III	M. C. Cauvin (1972)
Tell Assouad	8450 ± 120	MC-864	Ch	Level VIII	
Tell Aswad	9730 ± 120	Gif-2633	Ch	Phase Ia	Delibrias *et al.* (1982)
Tell Aswad	9640 ± 120	Gif-2372	Ch	Phase Ia	de Contenson (1989)
Tell Aswad	9340 ± 120	Gif-2370	Ch	Phase Ib	
Tell Aswad	9270 ± 120	Gif-2371	Ch	Phase Ib	
Tell Aswad	8875 ± 55	GrN-6678	Ch	Phase Ib	
Tell Aswad	8865 ± 60	GrN-8865	Ch	Phase Ib	
Tell Aswad	8720 ± 75	GrN-6677	Ch	Phase II	
Tell Aswad	8650 ± 55	GrN-6676	Ch	Phase II	
Tell Aswad	8540 ± 110	Gif-2369	Ch	Phase II	

TABLE 3. (Continued)

Site	Date (BP)	Lab no.*	Sample**	Provenience	Reference
Tell es-Sinn	8170 ± 100	GrN-9831	Ch	Level XIII	Roodenberg (1981)
Tell es-Sinn	8280 ± 40	GrN-9832	Ch	Level XIV	
Tell es-Sinn	8650 ± 50	GrN-9833	Ch	Level XIV	
Ujrat El-Mehed	8220 ± 80	Pta-2703	Ch	Loc. 2	Weinstein (1984)
Wadi al-Jilat 7	8810 ± 110	OxA-526	Ch	6/28A	Gowlett *et al.* (1986)
Wadi al-Jilat 7	8520 ± 110	OxA-527	Ch	8/25A	Hedges *et al.* (1989; 1992)
Wadi al-Jilat 7	8390 ± 80	OxA-2413	Ch	A 34b	
Wadi al-Jilat 7	5840 ± 100	OxA-1799	Ch	A 34 a	
Wadi al-Jilat 13	7920 ± 100	OxA-1800	Ch	A 21a 19	Hedges *et al.* (1989; 1992)
Wadi al-Jilat 13	7900 ± 80	OxA-2411	Ch	C 24	
Wadi al-Jilat 13	7870 ± 100	OxA-1801	Ch	A 15a 9	
Wadi al-Jilat 25	8020 ± 80	OxA-2408	Ch	A a10a 7	Hedges *et al.* (1992)
Wadi al-Jilat 26	8690 ± 110	OxA-1802	Ch	Cb 7a 1	Hedges *et al.* (1989; 1992)
Wadi al-Jilat 26	8370 ± 100	OxA-2407	Ch	C 12a 3	
Wadi Tbeik	10,350 ± 100	Pta-2700	Ch	Struct. 13	Gopher (1985)
Yiftahel	8890 ± 120	RT-736b	S	Locus 710	Garfinkel *et al.* (1987)
Yiftahel	8720 ± 70	Pta-4245	S	Locus 710	
Yiftahel	8570 ± 130	RT-736a	S	Locus 719	
Yiftahel	8870 ± 90	Pta-4242	S	Locus 719	

* AA=NSF-Arizona Accelerator; B=Bern; Beta=Beta Analytic; BM=British Museum; Gif=Gif-sur-Yvette; GrN=Gron-ingen; GX=Geochron; Hv=Hannover; I=Teledyne Isotopes; K=Copenhagen; KN=Köln; Lv=Louvain-La-Neuve; Ly= Lyon; M=Michigan; MC=Monaco; OxA=Oxford Accelerator; P=Pennsylvania; Pta=Pretoria; RT=Rehovot; SMU= Southern Methodist University; Tx=Texas; UCR=University of California, Riverside; W=USGS

** S=seeds; B=bone; Ch=charcoal; N=nuts

† pMC=percent modern carbon

REFERENCES CITED

Akkermans, P. A., J. A. K. Boerma, A. T. Clason, S. G. Hill, E. Lohof, C. Meiklejohn, M. Le Miere, G. M. F. Molgat, J. J. Roodenberg, W. Waterbolk van Rooyen and W. van Zeist
1983   Bouqras revisited: Preliminary report on a project in eastern Syria. *Proceedings of the Prehistoric Society* 49:335–372.
Bar-Yosef, O.
1981   Neolithic sites in Sinai. In *Contributions to the Environmental History of Southwest Asia*, edited by W. Frey and H. P. Uerpmann, pp. 217–235. In Kommission bei Reichert, Wiesbaden.
1984   Seasonality among Neolithic hunter-gatherers in southern Sinai. In *Animals and Archaeology: Herders and Their Flocks*, edited by J. Clutton-Brock and C. Grigson, pp. 145–160. BAR International Series 202, British Archaeological Reports, Oxford.
1991   The Early Neolithic of the Levant: Recent advances. *The Review of Archaeology* 12(2) 1–18.
Bar-Yosef, O. and A. Belfer-Cohen
1989   The origins of sedentism and farming communities in the Levant. *Journal of World Prehistory* 3:447–498.
1992   From foraging to farming in the Mediterranean Levant. In *Transitions to Agriculture in Prehistory*, edited by A. B. Gebauer and T. D. Price, pp. 21–48. Monographs in World Archaeology No. 4, Prehistory Press, Madison.
Barker, H. and J. Mackey
1968   British Museum natural radiocarbon measurements V. *Radiocarbon* 10:1–7.
Betts, A.
1988   The Black Desert survey. In *The Prehistory of Jordan, the State of Research in 1986*, edited by A. N. Garrard and H.-G. Gebel, pp. 369–91. BAR International Series 396, British Archaeological Reports, Oxford.
Betts, A., S. Helms, W. Lancaster and F. Lancaster
1991   The Burqu'/Ruweishid Project: Preliminary report on the 1989 field season. *Levant* 23: 7–28.

Braidwood, R. J. and H. Çambel
 1982   The Çayönü excavations. In *Prehistoric Village Archaeology in South-Eastern Turkey*, edited by L. S. Braidwood and R. J. Braidwood, pp. 1–15. BAR International Series 138, British Archaeological Reports, Oxford.

Burleigh, R.
 1981   Radiocarbon dates: Appendix C. In *The Architecture and Stratigraphy of the Tell. Excavations at Jericho*, Vol. III, edited by K. M. Kenyon, British School of Archaeology in Jerusalem, London.
 1983   Additional radiocarbon dates for Jericho. In *Excavations at Jericho*, Vol. V, edited by K. M. Kenyon and T. A. Holland, pp. 760–765. Oxford University Press, Oxford.

Byrd, B.
 1992   The dispersal of food production across the Levant. In *Transitions to Agriculture in Prehistory*, edited by A. B. Gebauer and T. D. Price, pp. 49–62. Monographs in World Archaeology No. 4. Prehistory Press, Madison.

Cauvin, J.
 1972   Sondage à Tell Assouad (Djezireh, Syrie). *Annales Archéologiques Arabes Syriennes* 22:86–89.
 1978   *Les Premiers Villages de Syrie-Palestine du IXe au VIIIe Millénaire avant J. C.*. Maison de L'Orient, CNRS, Lyon.
 1987   Absolue dans le Néolithique du Levant Nord et d'Anatolie entre 10,000–8,000 B.P. In *Chronologies du Proche Orient*, edited by O. Aurenche, J. Evin and F. Hours, pp. 325–342. BAR International Series 379, British Archaeological Reports, Oxford.

Cauvin, J. and O. Aurenche
 1982   Le Néolithique de Cafer Höyük (Malatya, Turquie). Fouilles 1979–1980. *Cahiers de l'Euphrates* 3:123–138.

Cauvin, M. C.
 1972   Note préliminaire sur l'outillage lithique de Tell Assouad, Djézireh. *Annales Archéologiques Arabes Syriennes* 22:90–94.

Contenson, H. de
 1976   Nouvelles données sur le Néolithique précéramique dans la région de Damas (Syrie) d'après les Fouilles de Ghoraifé en 1974. *Bulletin de la Société Préhistorique Française, Comptes Rendus des Séances Mensuelles* 73(3):80–82.
 1977   Le Néolithique de Ras Shamra Vc d'après les campagnes 1972–1976 dans le sondage SH. *Syria* 54(1–2):1–23.
 1989   L'Aswadien, un nouveau faciès du Néolithique Syrien. *Paléorient* 15:259–262.

Crane, H. R. and J. B. Griffin
 1970   University of Michigan radiocarbon dates XIII. *Radiocarbon* 12(1):161–180

Dean, J. S.
 1978   Independent dating in archaeological analysis. In *Advances in Archaeological Method and Theory*, Vol. 1, edited by M. B. Schiffer, pp. 223–255. Academic Press, New York.

Delibrias, G., M-T. Guillier, and J. Labeyrie
 1982   Gif natural radiocarbon measurements IX. *Radiocarbon* 24(3):291–343.

Dyan, T., E. Tchernov, O. Bar-Yosef and Y. Tom-Tov
 1986   Animal exploitation in Ujrat el Mehed, a Neolithic site in southern Sinai. *Paléorient* 12(2):105–116.

Farrand, W.
 1994   Confrontation of geological stratigraphy and radiometric dates from upper Pleistocene sites in the Levant. This volume.

Garfinkel, Y., I. Carmi and J. C. Vogel
 1987   Dating of horsebean and lentil seeds from the Pre-Pottery Neolithic B village of Yiftah'el. *Israel Exploration Journal* 37:40–42.

Garfinkel, Y. and D. Nadel
 1989   The Sultanian flint assemblage from Gesher and its implications for recognizing early Neolithic entities in the Levant. *Paléorient* 15:139–151.

Garrard, A., D. Baird and B. F. Byrd
 1994   The chronological basis and significance of the Late Paleolithic and Neolithic sequence in the Azraq Basin, Jordan. This volume.

Garrard, A. N., A. Betts, B. Byrd, S. Colledge and C. Hunt
 1988a   Summary of the paleoenvironmental and prehistoric investigations in the Azraq Basin. In *The Prehistory of the Jordan*, edited by A. N. Garrard and H.-G. Gebel, pp. 311–337. BAR International Series 396, British Archaeological Reports, Oxford.

Garrard, A. N., S. Colledge, C. Hunt and R. Montague
   1988b   Environment and subsistence during the Late Pleistocene and Early Holocene in the Azraq Basin. *Paléorient* 14(2):40–49.
Gebel, H.-G.
   1987   Relative and absolute chronologies of the southern Levant between 10,000 and 8,000 BP. In *Chronologies du Proche Orient,* edited by O. Aurenche, J. Evin and F. Hours, pp. 343–352. BAR International Series 379, British Archaeological Reports, Oxford.
Gopher, A.
   1985   Flint Tool Industries of the Neolithic Period of Israel. Ph.D. Dissertation, Hebrew University, Jerusalem.
Goring-Morris, A. N
   1991   The Harifian of the southern Levant. In *The Natufian Culture in the Levant.* Edited by O. Bar-Yosef and F. R. Valla, pp. 173–216. International Monographs in Prehistory, Ann Arbor.
Goring-Morris, A. N. and A. Gopher
   1983   Nahal Issaron: A Neolithic settlement in the southern Negev. *Israel Exploration Journal* 33(3):149–162.
Gowlett, J. A. J., R. E. M. Hedges, I. A. Law, and V. C. Perry
   1986   Radiocarbon dates from the Oxford AMS system: Archaeometry datelist 4. *Archaeometry* 28(2):206–221.
   1987   Radiocarbon dates from the Oxford AMS system: Archaeometry datelist 5. *Archaeometry* 29:125–155.
Haynes, V. and H. Hass
   1974   Southern Methodist University Radiocarbon datelist I. *Radiocarbon* 16(3):368–380.
Hedges, R. E. M., R. A. Housley, C. R. Bronk, and G. J. van Klinken
   1990   Radiocarbon dates from the Oxford AMS system: Archaeometry datelist 11. *Archaeometry* 32(2):211–237.
   1992   Radiocarbon dates from the Oxford AMS system: Archaeometry datelist 14. *Archaeometry* 34(1):141–159.
Hedges, R. E. M., R. A. Housley, I. A. Law, and C. R. Bronk
   1989   Radiocarbon dates from the Oxford AMS system: Archaeometry datelist 9. Archaeometry 31(2):207–234.
Hedges, R. E. M., R. A. Housley, I. A. Law, C. Perry, and J. A. Gowlett
   1987   Radiocarbon dates from the Oxford AMS system: Archaeometry datelist 6. *Archaeometry* 29(2):289–306.
Kenyon, K. M.
   1981   *The Architecture and Stratigraphy of the Tell. Excavations at Jericho,* Vol. III. British School of Archaeology in Jerusalem, London.
Kirkbride, D.
   1966   Five Seasons at the Pre-Pottery Neolithic Village of Beidha in Jordan. *Palestine Exploration Quarterly* 98:5–61.
   1969   Early Byblos and the Beqa'a. *Mélanges de l'Université Saint-Joseph* 45:45–60.
Kuijt I., J. Mabry and G. Palumbo
   1991   Early Neolithic use of upland areas of Wadi El-Yabis: Preliminary evidence from the excavations of 'Iraq ed-Dubb, Jordan. *Paléorient* 17(1):99–108.
Lechevallier, P. M. and A. Ronen
   1985   Le site Natufien-Khiamien de Hatoula, près de Latroun. Fouilles 1980–82. Rapport préliminaire. *Cahiers du Centre de Recherches Français de Jerusalem* 1. Jerusalem.
Mellaart, J.
   1975   *The Neolithic of the Near East.* Thames and Hudson, London.
Moore, A.
   1975   The excavation of Tell Abu Hureyra in Syria: A preliminary report. *Proceedings of the Prehistoric Society* 41:50–77.
   1979   A pre-Neolithic farmers' village on the Euphrates. *Scientific American* 241(2):62–70.
   1985   The development in Neolithic societies in the Near East. *Advances in World Archaeology,* edited by F. Wendorf and A. E. Close, pp. 1–69. Academic Press, New York.
Nissen, H. J., M. Muheisen, and H.-G. Gebel
   1987   Report on the first two seasons of excavations at Basta. *Annual of the Department of Antiquities of Jordan* 31:79–119.
Noy, T.
   1989   Gilal I. A Pre-Pottery Neolithic site, Israel. The 1985–1987 seasons. *Paléorient* 15 (1):11–18.
Orme, B.
   1982   The use of radiocarbon dates in the Somerset Levels. In *Problems and Case Studies in Archaeological Dating,* edited by B. Orme, pp. 5–34. Exeter Studies in Archaeology 1.
Rollefson, G. A
   1989   The Late Aceramic Neolithic of the Levant: A synthesis. *Paléorient* 15:168–173.

Rollefson, G. A. and A. Simmons
  1988   The Neolithic village of 'Ain Ghazal, Jordan: Preliminary report of the 1985 season. *BASOR Supplement* 25:93–106.

Rollefson, G. A., A. H. Simmons, and Z. Kafafi
  1992   Neolithic cultures at 'Ain Ghazal, Jordan. *Journal of Field Archaeology* 19:443–470.

Roodenberg, J. J.
  1981   Premiers résultats des recherches archéologiques à Hoyaz Höyük. *Anatolica* 7:21–34.

Schiffer, M. B.
  1986   Radiocarbon dates and the "old wood" problem: The case of Hohokam chronology. *Journal of Archaeological Science* 13:13–30.

Schroeder, H. B.
  1977   Nachcharini, a stratified post-Natufian camp in the Anti-Lebanon Mountains. Paper presented at the Annual Meeting of the Society for American Archaeology, May 1977.

Scott, E. M., A. Long and R. S. Kra
  1990   Cross check ¹⁴C: Proceedings of the International Workshop on Intercomparison of Radiocarbon Laboratories. *Radiocarbon* 32(3): 253–397.

Simmons, A. H. and Z. Kafafi
  1988   Preliminary report on the 'Ain Ghazel Archaeological Survey, 1987. *Annual of the Department of Antiquities of Jordan* 32:27–39.

Stordeur, D., C. Maréchal and M. Molist
  1982   El Kowm 2–Caracol: Campagnes 1978, 1979 et 1980. Stratigraphie et architecture. *Cahiers de l'Euphrate* 3:33–49.

Stuckenrath, R. Jr. and B. Lawn
  1969   University of Pennsylvania radiocarbon dates XI. *Radiocarbon* 11(1):150–162.

Tchernov, E. and O. Bar-Yosef
  1982   Animal exploitation in the Pre-Pottery Neolithic B period at Wadi Tbeik, southern Sinai. *Paléorient* 8(2): 17–37.

Voigt, M. M.
  1986   Review article on *The Hilly Flanks and Beyond*, edited by T. C. Young, Jr., P. Smith and P. Mortensen. *Paléorient* 12(1):103–113.

Vogel, J. C. and H. T. Waterbolk
  1972   Groningen Radiocarbon dates X. *Radiocarbon* 14(1):6–110.

Waterbolk, H. T.
  1987   Working with radiocarbon dates in southwestern Asia. In *Chronologies du Proche Orient,* edited by O. Aurenche, J. Evin and F. Hours, pp. 39–60. BAR International Series 379, British Archaeological Reports, Oxford.

Watkins, T., D. Baird and A. Betts
  1989   Qermez Dereh and the early Aceramic Neolithic of northern Iraq. *Paléorient* 15(1):19–24.

Weinstein, J.
  1984   Radiocarbon dating in the southern Levant. *Radiocarbon* 26(3):297–366.

Yeivin, E. and Y. Olami
  1979   Nizzanim–A Neolithic site in Nahal Evtah: Excavations of 1968–1970. *Tel Aviv* 6:99–135.

ASSESSING THE RADIOCARBON DETERMINATIONS FROM AKROTIRI *AETOKREMNOS*, CYPRUS

ALAN H. SIMMONS

Department of Anthropology, University of Nevada at Las Vegas, Las Vegas, Nevada 89154-5012 USA

and

PETER E. WIGAND

Quaternary Sciences Center, Desert Research Institute, University of Nevada System Reno, Nevada 89506 USA

INTRODUCTION

Recent excavations along the southern coast of Cyprus have created a stir among usually placid Mediterranean archaeologists. Akrotiri *Aetokremnos* ("Eagle Cliff" or "Site E") is a collapsed rockshelter that is significant for at least two reasons. First, it is the most ancient archaeological locality in Cyprus, and indeed, among the best-documented oldest sites on any of the Mediterranean Islands. Second, it is associated with extinct endemic island fauna, notably pygmy hippopotami (*Phanourios minutus*). Such an association has never before been demonstrated, and suggests that humans may have been partially responsible for the Early Holocene extinction of these unique animals (Simmons 1988, 1991a). Needless to say, claims such as these have resulted in some controversy (Simmons 1991b).

In this contribution, we examine the radiocarbon dating of *Aetokremnos*. Presently, a series of 31 determinations are available from *Aetokremnos* (Table 1). Figure 1 illustrates the range of these dates, at one standard deviation. We focus here on three aspects of the dating of the site. The first relates to the actual date of the site, the second to the stratigraphy of the site, and the third to *Aetokremnos*'s significance in helping to establish an eastern Mediterranean correction factor for the reservoir effect, which is a 400-yr estimated correction for the surface ocean water effect on atmospheric ^{14}C concentration.

THE RADIOCARBON DATES

Much of the controversy surrounding *Aetokremnos* comes from its chronology. We have dated marine shell, hippopotamus bone, sediment from a feature and charcoal. Both bone and shell, of course, are notoriously difficult to date, and some researchers have questioned the *Aetokremnos* dates because of the unreliability of these materials. However, it is our belief that the quantity and overall consistency of the dates of all samples exceeds the usual requirements for archaeological acceptance.

In most cases, uncorrected ^{14}C determinations were provided with δ^{13}C values and corrected ^{14}C ages. However, in some cases, only the uncorrected determination, in years before present (BP), was provided (*e.g.*, the UCL shell dates (Tables 1 and 2)). We used an estimated δ^{13}C correction factor to calculate weighted averages (following Ward and Wilson 1978). We took a value of +2.72 (the average δ^{13}C correction factor of the six ^{13}C-corrected shell dates) as the correction factor for shell determinations, and applied it in a formula derived from Stuiver and Polach (1977) (Table 2). The formula was tested against samples that had uncorrected and δ^{13}C-corrected determinations

Late Quaternary Chronology and Paleoclimates of the Eastern Mediterranean
Edited by O. Bar-Yosef and R. S. Kra. RADIOCARBON 1994, pp. 247–264

TABLE 1. Radiocarbon Dates from Akrotiri Aetokremnos* (Note that for shell dates, this table does not include a correction for the reservoir effect; such a correction was included in earlier publications [*e.g.*, Simmons 1988a,b; 1989]; see text for additional discussion.)

Date (BP)	Lab no.	Material	Provenience/Comments
3700 ± 60	Pta-3435	Bone collagen	Surface
6310 ± 160	Beta-3412	Burned bone	Surface
7150 ± 140	Beta-43174	Burned bone	N96E91, Stratum 4B
7900 ± 500	UCLA-304	Shell	N97E87-88, Stratum 4B
8330 ± 100	Pta-3281	Burned bone	Surface
9040 ± 160	Tx-5976A	Bone apatite	N95E88, Stratum 2/4
9100 ± 790	ISGS-1743	Total organics from bone	N95E88, Stratum 2/4
9240 ± 420	Tx-5833C	Humin fraction	Feature 1, N98E88-87, Stratum 2A
9250 ± 150	Pta-3128	Burned bone	Partially exposed beneath shell layer, Stratum 2/4
9420 ± 550	Tx-5976B	Bone collagen	N95E88, Stratum 2/4; same sample as Tx-5976A
9490 ± 120	Tx-5833A	Bulk organic carbon	Feature 1, N98E88-87, Stratum 2A
10,100 ± 370	UCLA-203	Shell	N97E86, Stratum 4B
10,150 ± 130	Tx-5833B	Humic acid fraction	Feature 1, N98E87-88, Stratum 2A
10,190 ± 230	Beta-41405	Charcoal	N97E88, Stratum 2A
10,420 ± 85	{ Beta-41000 ⎨ ETH-7188**	Charcoal	N97E89, Stratum 2A
10,480 ± 300	Beta-41407	Charcoal	N96E89, Stratum 2A
10,485 ± 80	{ Beta-41406 ⎨ ETH-7331	Charcoal (Paired with Beta-41405)	N97E88, Stratum 2A
10,560 ± 90	{ Beta-40382 ⎨ ETH-7160	Charcoal	N97E89, Stratum 4C
10,575 ± 80	{ Beta-41408 ⎨ ETH-7332	Charcoal (Paired with Beta-41407)	N96E89, Stratum 2A
10,770 ± 90	{ Beta-41002 ⎨ ETH-7189	Charcoal	N96E89, Stratum lower 2A
10,770 ± 160	Beta-43176	Burned bone	N96E90, Stratum 4B
10,800 ± 550	UCLA-201	Shell	N97E90, Stratum lower 2A
10,810 ± 110	Beta-22811	Shell	N95E88, Stratum 2/4; in dark midden-like matrix containing bone and artifacts below exposed shell layer
10,840 ± 60	SMU-1991	Shell	N98E88/87, Stratum 2/4; associated with bone, artifacts and Feature 1
10,840 ± 270	Beta-40655	Charcoal	N96E90, Stratum lower 2A
10,970 ± 100	Pta-3322	Shell	Exposed shell layer; Stratum 2A
11,000 ± 100	Pta-3112	Shell	Exposed shell layer; Stratum 2A
11,030 ± 130	Beta-28795	Shell	N98E89, Stratum 2A
11,200 ± 500	UCLA-194	Shell	N96E87, Stratum 4B
11,700 ± 500	UCLA-192	Shell	N98E90, Stratum 2A
11,720 ± 240	Beta-40380	Charcoal	N97E89, Stratum 2A; Feature 10

*All of the Pta dates, as well as Beta-3412, were obtained prior to the 1987 test excavations; thus, exact provenience information is not known. The exposed surface specimens are likely to have been contaminated due to their long exposure; this may well account for the wide range in dates.

**ETH numbers are for AMS dates.

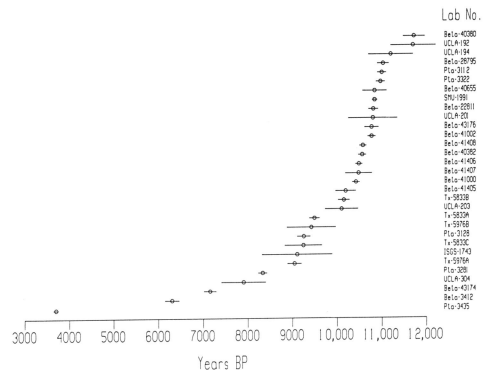

Fig. 1. Distribution of the 31 Akrotiri *Aetokremnos* [14]C determinations, as reflected in Table 1

and for which the correction factor was known. We used the average $\delta^{13}C$ correction of the other bone dates, −22.75, for the bone dates for which corrections had not been provided (Table 2). These newly generated values were used in conjunction with those already available to calculate the weighted averages presented in Table 2.

Despite the problematic nature of the dated materials, there is a remarkable clustering of the determinations (see Fig. 1), regardless of material type. The three surface dates, all on bone, were rejected because of possible contamination from long exposure. The weighted average of the remaining 28 determinations is 10,465 ± 25 BP. We suggest that this is a minimal date for the site. Manning (1991), with fewer dates, arrived at a somewhat older age for the site.

Let us consider these determinations in more detail by examining them according to material. For shell, the weighted average (10 samples) is 10,900 ± 40 BP; for charcoal (9 samples), it is 10,575 ± 35 BP; for bone (6 samples, omitting the surface specimens), it is 8955 ± 75 BP; and for sediment (3 samples), it is 9770 ± 85 BP. The charcoal and shell determinations are very close. The bone and sediment determinations, however, differ considerably. Almost 2000 yr separate the weighted averages of shell and bone determinations, with the weighted average of the sediment determinations lying midway between the two.

We have received some criticism on the bone determinations, and indeed, they represent the most problematic of the *Aetokremnos* dates. If these were our only data, we would be more skeptical of the site's true age. We are, however, impressed by the relative clustering of these determinations when the surface samples are disregarded. Although seemingly well preserved, the *Aetokremnos* bones contain only minimal amounts of collagen, which is what we would prefer to date. Ideally,

TABLE 2. *Aetokremnos* Radiocarbon Samples Showing δ^{13}C Correction Factors and Corrected and Uncorrected Determinations

Laboratory no.	Uncorrected date	Corrected date	δ^{13}C(‰)
Pta-3435	3655 ± 60	3700 ± 60	−22.3
Beta-3412	6310 ± 160	6350 ± 160	−22.75*
Beta-43174	7150 ± 140	7190 ± 140	−22.75*
UCLA-304	7900 ± 500	8350 ± 500	2.72*
Pta-3281	8295 ± 100	8330 ± 100	−23.0
Tx-5976A	8875 ± 160	9040 ± 160	−15.03
ISGS-1743	9095 ± 790	9100 ± 790	−24.7
Tx-5833C	9250 ± 420	9240 ± 420	−25.47
Pta-3128	9210 ± 150	9250 ± 150	−22.5
Tx-5976B	9270 ± 550	9420 ± 550	−16.0
Tx-5833A	9485 ± 120	9490 ± 120	−24.56
UCLA-203	10,100 ± 370	10,550 ± 370	2.72*
Tx-5833B	10,130 ± 130	10,150 ± 130	−23.65
Beta-41405	10,180 ± 230	10,190 ± 230	−24.4
Beta-41000 } ETH-7188	--	10,420 ± 85	**
Beta-41407	10,480 ± 300	10,480 ± 300	−25.1
Beta-41406 } ETH-7331	--	10,485 ± 80	**
Beta-40382 } ETH-7160	--	10,560 ± 90	**
Beta-41408 } ETH-7332	--	10,575 ± 80	**
Beta-41002 } ETH-7189	--	10,770 ± 90	**
Beta-43176	10,770 ± 160	10,805 ± 160	−22.75*
UCLA-201	10,800 ± 550	11,250 ± 550	2.72*
Beta-22811	10,350 ± 110	10,810 ± 110	2.7
SMU-1991	10,380 ± 60	10,840 ± 60	3.2
Beta-40655	10,850 ± 270	10,840 ± 270	−25.2
Pta-3322	10,520 ± 100	10,970 ± 100	2.7
Pta-3112	10,555 ± 100	11,000 ± 100	2.3
Beta-28795	10,570 ± 130	11,030 ± 130	2.7
UCLA-194	11,200 ± 500	11,650 ± 500	2.72*
UCLA-192	11,700 ± 500	12,150 ± 500	2.72*
Beta-40380	11,710 ± 240	11,720 ± 240	−24.1

*Estimated δ^{13}C correction factor; see text for explanation.
**AMS date; δ^{13}C value is automatically calculated.

we had hoped to obtain dates on the bones' amino acids (*cf.* Stafford *et al.* 1988). With this in mind, we sent a small sample to Dr. T. Stafford, University of Colorado. Unfortunately, the amount of nitrogen preserved was far below the minimum required for such analysis, so Stafford (personal communication) considered it unlikely that accurate amino-acid dates could be obtained on these samples.

Let us illustrate how "bad" the carbon contents are on some of these bones. On one of the most recent determinations, a sample that weighed *ca.* 3.6 kg yielded only *ca.* 0.5 g of organic carbon.

This translates to a total organic carbon content of <0.1 of 1%. Normally, bone contains *ca.* 12%. This suggests extremely poor organic preservation of the bones, and certainly would lead to caution in their use as a reliable indicator of age. The clustering of these dates with non-bone determinations, however, bolsters our confidence in their accuracy. It is clear that these results are based on some organic residue.

Figure 1 shows two clusters of dates, based on the type of material that was dated. The older group comprises charcoal (weighted mean of 10,575 BP) and shell determinations (weighted mean of 10,900 BP). If the shell determinations are corrected for reservoir effect, they also would cluster *ca.* 10,575 BP. The younger group comprises bone (weighted mean of 8955 BP) and sediment determinations (weighted mean of 9770 BP).

All three sediment determinations are from the same sample. The results are skewed toward older values by the two fractions that are composed of alkali-soluble carbon (humic acid and humins). These are easily mobilized by high-pH groundwater, and can migrate up or down in the sediment profile with the groundwater. These two fractions could reflect decomposition products from organics higher in the profile, *i.e.*, decaying bone, rootlets or wood, or charcoal that was incompletely carbonized. The solid carbon fraction of the sediment sample dated to 9490 ± 120 BP.

The bone determinations are highly variable, reflecting differing degrees of contamination. Two determinations, Pta-3128 (9250 ± 150 BP) and Pta-3281 (8330 ± 100 BP), are on soluble carbon humate fractions that could reflect mobilized carbon from the decay of materials other than the bone itself. Sample TX-5976 (9040 ± 160 BP) is on bone apatite from a sample whose "collagen" had dated to 9420 ± 550 BP (TX-5976B). Bone apatite is notoriously poor for dating bone (Polach 1971; compare carbonate, apatite and collagen fraction determinations from the same bone). Collagen is the only fraction that does not exchange carbon during diagenesis. Therefore, we also question the reliability of this sample. Further, once these samples are rejected and the new weighted average is calculated, the Beta-43174 determination of 7190 ± 140 BP is rejected as an outlier, according to Chavenet's criteria of rejecting samples differing, by more than 1.65 standard deviations, from the average of five samples (Long and Rippeteau 1974). The result is a weighted average for the bone determinations of 10,640 ± 150 BP. This closely compares with the weighted averages calculated for the charcoal and shell determinations.

Conceivably, one could use the range in dates to argue for two separate occupations. However, we do not believe this to be the case, as explained below.

SITE STRATIGRAPHY

The site has two major strata, both of which are cultural (see Simmons 1991a for more details). The strata are sometimes separated by a thin, sterile layer of sediment, which may suggest a brief hiatus. The upper stratum (Stratum 2) contains *ca.* 75% of the chipped stone artifacts and <1% of the hippopotamus bones (although this still constitutes >1500 individual pieces). We interpret the lower stratum (Stratum 4) to be a "midden." This deposit contains the majority of the hippopotamus bones, but nearly 12% of the chipped stone were also found here. In areas where the intervening sterile stratum (Stratum 3) is not present, Strata 2 and 4 directly adjoin.

Seventeen samples are from Stratum 2, 5 are from the Strata 2/4 articulation, 6 are from Stratum 4, and the remaining 3 are from surface contexts. The last three were rejected for reasons explained above. From the 28 remaining results, the weighted average from Stratum 2 is 10,640 ± 30 BP; from Stratum 2/4, it is 9960 ± 75 BP, and from Stratum 4, it is 9835 ± 70 BP. This presents us with an interesting case of reversed stratigraphy. There is a *ca.* 800-^{14}C-yr difference between the two major strata. However, the difference between the lower stratum (4) and the "mixed" stratum (2/4) is minuscule. Given the similarity of the Stratum 2 determinations and those of the charcoal (from all strata), which may be the most reliable, we should, perhaps, consider that the Stratum 2 dates are the most accurate, and that post-depositional diagenetic processes may have slightly affected the ages of the stratigraphically lower dates. Further, Stratum 2 dates very closely mirror the average of all dates from the site, being separated by only 175 ^{14}C yr.

However, if we take into consideration the previous discussion, rejecting questionable bone and sediment dates, the resulting weighted averages for each of the strata agree much more. The weighted average of the remaining samples without reservoir-effect correction from Stratum 2 is 10,670 ± 30 BP; from Stratum 2/4, it is 10,725 ± 110 BP; and from Stratum 4, it is 10,600 ± 75 BP (Table 3). The average of all ^{14}C determinations excluding the rejected bone and sediment samples becomes 10,665 ± 25 BP.

TABLE 3. Weighted Averages of δ^{13}C-Corrected Determinations from Akrotiri *Aetokremnos*

Sample	No reservoir correction*	Rejected**	Reservoir correction†
All	10,119 ± 18	10,665 ± 26	10,529 ± 26
Charcoal	10,577 ± 36	10,577 ± 36	10,577 ± 36
Shell	10,898 ± 39	10,898 ± 39	10,577 ± 39
Bone	6228 ± 41	10,639 ± 151	10,639 ± 151
Sediment	9770 ± 86	9490 ± 120	9490 ± 120
All 2	10,641 ± 28	10,671 ± 28	10,508 ± 28
All 4	9835 ± 66	10,597 ± 75	10,571 ± 75
All 2/4	9958 ± 76	10,726 ± 107	10,423 ± 107
2 charcoal	10,581 ± 40	10,581 ± 40	10,581 ± 40
4 charcoal	10,560 ± 90	10,560 ± 90	10,560 ± 90
2 shell	10,926 ± 43	10,926 ± 43	10,605 ± 43
4 shell	10,353 ± 262	10,353 ± 262	10,032 ± 262
2/4 shell	10,810 ± 110	10,810 ± 110	10,489 ± 110
4 bone	8758 ± 105	10,805 ± 160	10,805 ± 160
2/4 bone	9161 ± 106	9316 ± 451	9316 ± 451

*Weighted averages, including surface samples, which have not been corrected for reservoir effect
**Weighted averages after several determinations were rejected, as outlined in the text. The reservoir effect was not calculated.
†Weighted averages after rejected determinations were removed and the newly determined reservoir effect was calculated (see text for details).

An additional argument that supports the lack of a major chronological hiatus between the strata is the similarity of the lithic assemblages. Typologically and technologically, there is no difference in materials; chi-square tests show no distinction between the strata. We believe that this strongly suggests a very minimal separation in time between the two strata.

RESERVOIR EFFECT

^{14}C activity levels can vary significantly in large bodies of water, such as the Mediterranean Sea, from those in the contemporaneous atmosphere. Reservoir activity values vary significantly through time due to a multitude of conditions: 1) lag in the exchange of ^{14}C between the atmosphere and the ocean surface waters; 2) changes in ocean circulation; 3) incorporation of waters previously outside the basin (for the Mediterranean Sea, these could include glacial meltwaters from Russia spilling through the Black Sea, and from the glaciated Alps). This is particularly crucial for the ^{14}C determinations from *Aetokremnos*, because they are from the period during which dramatic changes occurred in atmospheric and the oceanic ^{14}C composition (Stuiver *et al.* 1991). In order to correct for such factors, we would need paired dates on shells and other materials (preferably charcoal). *Aetokremnos* offers such comparisons. The local Mediterranean reservoir correction, which compensates for upwelling and evaporation effects, has previously had only one point listed for the Mediterranean Sea, off the coast of Algeria; this figure is −135 ± 85 from a single shell sample, dating to 357 BP (Stuiver, Pearson and Braziunas 1986, Table 1:1019). Thus, we have very little baseline information from which to interpret the *Aetokremnos* dates.

All the weighted averages of the δ^{13}C-corrected shell dates were compared with the weighted average of δ^{13}C-corrected charcoal dates from both Strata 2 and 4. The correction factor that must be added to the shell dates to make them equivalent to the charcoal dates is 321 yr. If the same comparison is made among the weighted averages of 8 δ^{13}C-corrected charcoal dates and 6 δ^{13}C-corrected shell determinations from Stratum 2, the result is 345 yr. Although the method of calculation is the same, this result differs from Manning's (1991:871,Table 1) calculation of 481 ± 56 for two reasons: 1) we did not incorporate sediment dates, because the possibility of mobile carbon contamination in an alkali-rich soil was too great; 2) we obtained two additional shell determinations from Stratum 2A. For Stratum 4, the same comparison between the single δ^{13}C-corrected charcoal and single δ^{13}C-corrected shell determinations results in a difference of 207 yr. We reject the latter result, because only two samples are compared with the charcoal sample that came from the bottom of the unit and with the shell date that came from the top of the unit. The amount of real time separating the top and bottom of the unit is unknown. We have not attempted to correct our ^{14}C determinations to calendar years as Manning (1991) has done. Until the tree-ring calibrations are extended into the Late Glacial, we believe the exercise is premature.

CONCLUSION

Even though more paired dates are needed from this region, the *Aetokremnos* specimens provide crucial information on an area whose chronology has not been well studied. The present results should also help to interpret marine shell dates from other archaeological contexts in the eastern Mediterranean for the Early Holocene.

In summary, the ^{14}C chronology from Akrotiri *Aetokremnos* has added substantial new information to a sparse database. These data strongly suggest a mid-to-late eleventh millennium BP occupation at Akrotiri. Although critics have voiced concern about these dates, we need to consider these not in isolation, but in their proper archaeological context. We remain convinced that the ^{14}C dates are an accurate reflection of the site's true age.

ACKNOWLEDGMENTS

Several individuals and institutions have been involved in the interpretation of the ^{14}C determinations from Akrotiri *Aetokremnos*. Many have provided dates free of charge. We would like to thank Claudio Vita-Finzi, University College, London, Salvatore Valastro, Jr., University of Texas, San Antonio, Chao-li Liu and Dennis D. Coleman, Illinois State Geological Survey, Urbana, J. J. Stipp and Murry Tamers, Beta Analytic, Inc., Miami, Florida, Herbert Haas, Desert Research Institute, Las Vegas, John C. Vogel, National Physical Research Laboratory, Pretoria, South Africa and ETH/AMS Facility, Zurich, Switzerland (*via* Beta Analytic, Inc.) for providing ^{14}C dates.

Among those who have commented extensively on the dates are Steven Held, Stuart Swiny, Paul S. Martin, Donald Grayson, Sturt Manning, R. Mandel and Thomas W. Stafford, Jr. Although not all may be in agreement with our interpretations, we appreciate their instructive observations. I would also like to acknowledge Don Graybill for his good counsel on dating matters as well as his friendship; he will be sorely missed.

The excavations at Akrotiri *Aetokremnos* were funded by grants from the National Geographic Society, the National Science Foundation, the Leakey Foundation, the National Endowment for the Humanities, the Lindley Foundation, the Institute for Aegean Prehistory and the Desert Research Institute. The project was affiliated with the American Schools of Oriental Research and their Cypriot organization, the Cyprus American Archaeological Research Institute. This project could not have been undertaken without the enthusiastic support of the Republic of Cyprus Department of Antiquities and the Royal Air Force Western Sovereign Base Area.

REFERENCES CITED

Long, A. and B. Rippeteau
  1974   Testing contemporaneity and averaging radiocarbon dates. *American Antiquity* 39:205–215.
Manning, S.
  1991   Approximate calendar date for the first human settlement of Cyprus. *Antiquity* 65:870–878.
Polach, H.
  1971   Radiocarbon dating of bone organic and inorganic matter. *Proceedings of the Radiocarbon Users Conference, 1971*, pp. 180–211. Institute of Nuclear Sciences, Wellington, New Zealand.
Simmons, A.
  1988   Extinct Pygmy Hippopotamus and Early Man in Cyprus. *Nature* 333:554–557.
  1991a   Humans, island colonization and Pleistocene extinctions in the Mediterranean: The View from Akrotiri *Aetokremnos*, Cyprus. *Antiquity* 65:857–869.
  1991b   One flew over the hippo's nest: Extinct Pleistocene fauna, Early Man, and conservative archaeology in Cyprus. In *Perspectives on the Past*, edited by G. Clark, pp. 282–304. University of Pennsylvania Press, Philadelphia.
Stuiver, M., T. F. Braziunas, B. Becker and B. Kromer
  1991   Climatic, solar, oceanic and geomagnetic influences on late-Glacial and Holocene atmospheric $^{14}C/^{12}C$ change. *Quaternary Research* 35(1):1–24.
Stuiver, M., G. W. Pearson, and T. Braziunas
  1986   Radiocarbon age calibration of marine samples back to 9000 cal yr BP. *Radiocarbon* 28(2B):980–1021.
Ward, G. K. and S. R. Wilson
  1978   Procedures for comparing and combining radiocarbon age determinations: A critique. *Archaeometry* 20:19–34.

RADIOCARBON DATES FROM ACERAMIC IRAQ

STEFAN KAROL KOZŁOWSKI

Archaeological Institute, Warsaw University, ul. Zwirki i Wigury 97/99, PL-02089 Warsaw, Poland

INTRODUCTION

In this paper, I briefly discuss the radiocarbon dates from sites in Iraq dating from the Epipaleolithic to the early Neolithic periods. More than 90 new dates from Nemrik and M'lefaat are reported and previously published data from Jarmo and Zewi-Chemi Shanidar are reinterpreted. I also give a brief overview of the cultural characteristics of major archaeological entities to clarify the cultural context of the ^{14}C chronology.

THE EPIPALEOLITHIC

Garrod (1930) described the typical lithic industry of this period as Zarzian following her excavations in Zarzi Cave in Iraqi Kurdistan. Since that time, several other Epipaleolithic sites have been excavated and dated (Shanidar Cave, Zewi-Chemi Shanidar and Pelegawra). Some of these sites, from Shanidar in Iraq to Warwasi in Iran, provided overlapping dates. The ^{14}C chronology covers the 15th through the 11th millennia BP, a period contemporaneous with the Geometric Kebaran and the Natufian in the Levant, as well as the upper sequence of Karain cave and the deposits in Öküzini cave in southwest Turkey (Albrecht 1992).

Lithic assemblages of this period are characterized by the presence of geometric and microlithic, backed points and small, short endscrapers made from flakes. Most of the sites along the Taurus-Zagros belt are notable for the absence of Helwan retouch on Zarzian lunates, in contrast with finds from this period in the Levant. This characteristic lithic industry spread throughout the region to Caucasian sites, Belt and Hotu caves in Iran, and sites in central Asia. Similar assemblages appear later in the Crimea and in the Balkans (*e.g.,* Franchthi cave). Geographic distribution of the Zarzian industry is bordered in the west by the Mesopotamian plain and in the east by the Zagros Mountains. Sites on the northern slopes provide evidence of a different industry that includes trapezes, indicating Caucasian-Caspian connections. A brief review of the major sites in this region follows.

Zewi-Chemi Shanidar

The Zarzian time span corresponds to the terminal Pleistocene, perhaps with the exception of some mountainous areas (*e.g.,* near Shanidar), where it could have lasted longer. This may be true for the multilayer Proto-Neolithic site of Zewi-Chemi Shanidar (Solecki 1981). A single ^{14}C date comes from the base of a thick layer (110–150 cm). The Zarzian chipped stone industry appears in its upper levels together with polished axes and a late ground-stone industry, including bracelets (Mazurowski, in press).

THE PROTO-NEOLITHIC/EARLY NEOLITHIC

Following (or in some regions contemporary with) the Zarzian industry are two new assemblages—the Nemrikian in the west and the Mlefatian in the east. Both yielded a long series of ^{14}C dates. At their initial stages, both tool complexes share Proto-Neolithic characteristics, namely village sites with clay architecture, ground-stone industry and evidence of subsistence based on hunting, fishing and gathering. These entities gradually give way to more typical Neolithic adaptations, which include animal husbandry and agriculture. However, the chipped-stone industries

Late Quaternary Chronology and Paleoclimates of the Eastern Mediterranean
Edited by O. Bar-Yosef and R. S. Kra. RADIOCARBON 1994, pp. 255–264

of Neolithic groups do not demonstrate major techno-typological change during this revolutionary economic transformation. The same is true for the ground-stone industry, which includes stone vessels and elaborate jewelry. The domestic architecture of the Nemrikian and the Mlefatian shifts from circular to rectangular houses at the end of the 10th and the beginning of the 9th millennium BP (Hole, Flannery and Neely 1969; Kozłowski and Kempisty 1990). Both entities bear evidence of a stable cultural tradition and merge into the Pre-Pottery Neolithic (PPN) in the 10th millennium BP. Ceramic production appears at *ca.* 8000 BP, including Proto-Hassuna in the west and Jarmoan in the east (*cf.* Bader 1989; Mortensen 1964).

A true technological and stylistic break occurred between the Zarzian and the Nemrikian and Mlefatian. The major change is marked by the introduction of a new core technology that included preformed single-platform cores for the removal of regular blades and bladelets. Detaching techniques involve percussion and/or pressure flaking accompanied by the sectioning of blades. This also resulted in several additions to the tool kit, such as blade endscrapers, retouched blades and perforators. A few elements of the old tradition persisted, such as backed pieces, lunates and triangles, which developed over time into more delicate or elegant forms (Hole, Flannery and Neely 1969).

The Nemrikian

Of the two well-dated Proto-Neolithic/Neolithic industries of Iraq, the Nemrikian provides good chronological information. Samples from the site of Nemrik, analyzed by M. F. Pazdur of Poland's Gliwice Laboratory, have yielded 81 dates. Five dates are known from Telul-eth-Talathat, and several from Qermez Dare. The Nemrikian tradition in northern Iraq persisted from the end of the 11th to the end of the 9th millennium BP. It is associated with Proto-Neolithic villages with circular houses (Nemrik, lower layers) and with later Neolithic villages that had circular (Nemrik 3-4) and rectangular (Nemrik 5) houses. The Nemrikian tradition features a rich ground-stone industry (Mazurowski, in press) and, at a later phase, *ca.* 8000 BP, Proto-Hassuna ceramics. The Nemrikian core technology, blanks and much of the rest of the tool kit described above corresponds to the Levantine Neolithic and includes arrowheads (rhomboidal and leaf-shaped points), backed bladelets, Khiamian points and heavy-duty tools such as picks (Kozłowski 1990).

The multilayer site of Nemrik indicates continuous occupation over an extended period of time. Samples provided 81 ^{14}C dates, but only one-third of them are acceptable (see Table 3 at the end of this chapter for notes on confidence in the values of the ^{14}C dates). Most of these dates come from stratified houses, either from their floors or levels overlying the lower part of the fill. No fireplaces were found, and the floors had been cleaned. Other samples come from the main section, 80 m long, which transects the site along the N-S axis (Kozłowski 1992). With well-dated stratified deposits that accumulated over a long-term occupation, Nemrik represents a standard for the study of Mesopotamian prehistory preceding the period associated with the Jarmo sequence.

Telul-eth-Talathat

A Nemrikian industry together with Proto-Hassuna ceramics appear in Layers XVI and XV, ^{14}C-dated to the 8th millennium BP. At both Telul-eth-Talathat and Jarmo (Hole 1983), high percentages of obsidian and presence of broad blades are evidence of roughly contemporaneous assemblages, whereas Çayönü knives and arrowheads with covering retouch show affinities to Pre-Pottery Neolithic B (PPNB) assemblages (see below).

THE MLEFATIAN

The Mlefatian is also a well-dated Proto-Neolithic/Neolithic industry of eastern Iraq and western Iran, dating from the 10th to the 8th or 7th millennium BP. Known from villages with circular

(M'lefaat) and rectangular (Jarmo, Ali-Kosh) houses, the Mlefatian industry developed as a material culture in transition from hunter-gatherer (M'lefaat) to Neolithic economy (aceramic Ali-Kosh and Jarmo). The Mlefatian is characterized by a rich ground-stone industry; ceramics appeared during the Late Mlefatian or Jarmoan stage. Included in an interregional PPN/PN standard of a chipped-stone tool kit, the Mlefatian tradition maintained its typical features, especially among microlithic forms such as bladelets, backed truncated blades, scalene triangles and nibbed bladelets. Geometrics appeared *ca.* 8000 BP, and disappeared later during the advanced ceramic phase (Hole 1977).

Jarmo

Twenty-two ^{14}C samples were dated from Jarmo (Fig. 1). Some dates were based on samples from soundings and do not have reliable stratigraphic associations. Both these dates and those that came from the main excavation have caused some confusion. R. Braidwood proposed a date of *ca.* 6400 BC (*ca.* 8400 BP). Table 1 suggests a stratigraphic correlation between the two main Jarmo trenches (Operations I and II), taking into consideration the presence/absence of ceramics, type of architecture and development of stone vessels. This stratigraphy is asymmetrical. The lower layers of Operation I have no equivalent in Operation II, and the uppermost layers from Operation II have no equivalent in Operation I.

According to existing ^{14}C determinations, one can date the aceramic layers to about the 9th millennium BP, and those with ceramics to 7000 BP and later. However, these dates do not fit well with the archaeological material found on the site. Some elements, especially the earliest ceramics, as well as geometrics such as trapezes and broad lunates, are similar to those known from other well-dated sites (*e.g.,* Ali Kosh and Chaga Sefid in Iran) (*cf.* Hole, Flannery and Neely 1969; Hole 1977), where they first appear at *ca.* 8000 BP. Similar geometrics are also known from several sites in Iraq, including Magzalia, Umm Dabaghiya and Choga Mami, which also dates to *ca.* 8000 BP (Mortensen 1973, 1983) or later.

Given the regional evidence, the Jarmo material demonstrates either that retardation was a local cultural phenomenon or that most of its ^{14}C dates are wrong. In my view, the second hypothesis is more probable. This possibility corresponds well to the scarcity of numerous stone vessels and absence of obsidian in the well-dated 5th phase of Nemrik (*ca.* 8500 BP), as well as to the presence of late ground-stone pieces in Jarmo that are absent from Nemrik. Obsidian appeared in massive amounts in the area at the end of the 9th and the beginning of the 8th millennium BP, for example, at Magzalia and Telul-eth-Talathat Layers XVI–XV.

M'lefaat

Eight dates from M'lefaat fall within two chronological horizons, from 13,500–12,500 BP and 10,600–10,500 BP. The second horizon is much more acceptable than the first, as indicated by the

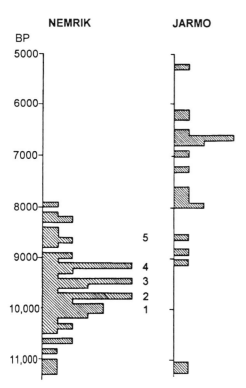

Fig. 1. [14]C dates from Nemrik and Jarmo, 100-yr intervals. Numbers 1–5 signify settlement phases.

TABLE 1. Jarmo Sequence

ARCHITECTURE	CERAMICS	STONE VESSELS TYPES					OPERATIONS		DATES BP
		A	B	C	D	E	I LAYERS	II LAYERS	
STONE	PRESENT	LESS NUMEROUS	NUMEROUS	NUMEROUS		NUMEROUS		1	7650(?)
								2	
								3	
							1	4	8850(?)
							2	5	6300–6900
							3	6	
CLAY	ABSENT	MANY	MEDIUM	MEDIUM	FEW	FEW	4		
							5		
							6		
							7		6600–(8500?)
							8		6650–6750
							9		
							Virgin soil		

dates for the Zarzian, especially in Pelegawra, where it is followed by the Mlefatian. However, four recent accelerator mass spectrometric (AMS) dates suggest a later time frame for the site, from 9800–9600 BP (Table 3).

Karim-Shahir

Many elements of the Mlefatian (also earlier?) are present at Karim-Shahir. Mlefatian components have no stratigraphic associations and are in mixed layers. Late bracelets and axes, as well as one geometric microlith, may represent a composite of many occupations.

Pelegawra

A well-dated Zarzian component precedes an undated Mlefatian component.

Iranian Sites

The same Mlefatian industry was found at many Iranian sites, including Ali-Kosh, Chaga Sefid, Ganj-Dareh, Guran, Sarab and Asiab, all of which date to the Aceramic Neolithic of the 9th millennium and later (Hole 1987).

CLASSICAL PPNB

The PPNB is typical for the Levant and eastern Anatolia. It is represented at the poorly dated stratified site of Magzalia in northern Jezireh and at the Umm-Dabaghiya site, where it is associated with Proto-Hassuna pottery. The architecture is characterized by rectangular houses, chipped industry by large-size obsidian, typical single-platform pressure-core technology, large arrowheads, Çayönü knives and side-blow flakes. The old Nemrikian tradition is still represented by a few Nemrik points. All PPNB material culture is a marginal phenomenon in Mesopotamia.

KHIAMIAN

Qermez Dare manifests this industry in the middle phase.

DATES TOO OLD OR TOO YOUNG

All the stratified sites mentioned here yielded a series of dates (M'lefaat-12, Nemrik-81, Telul-5, Pelegawra-6, Jarmo-22), but none gave a satisfactory sequence of coherent clusters of dates. These sites have also yielded anomalous dates, especially those with extensive architectural remains, such as houses, trenches and pits, which may have been subject to intrusions resulting from such activities as digging, leveling and filling. Most of the aberrant results are older than expected, as at Nemrik and M'lefaat, probably due to taphonomic disturbances of digging into older cultural layers during construction of pits and houses sunk into the soil. Older material could have been redeposited in more recent layers, or foreign organic material could have been imported during construction. Possibilities include the mixture of imported clay with old charcoal, the reuse of old wood by later dwellers (a practice still known in the Near East), and the use of very old organic material such as bitumen for covering a roof, plastering pits, or hafting sickle blades to handles. In the foothills of the Zagros Mountains, wood can be washed down from the mountains during floods or trees can be cut down long before they are collected and eventually used, a common practice among Near Eastern populations of today. Also, ^{14}C age differences between oldest and youngest tree rings, especially for long-lived species, are noticeable. Most typical charcoal samples are too small to be placed in the tree-ring sequence of the dated tree; thus, the date may be older than the actual date of death and provides the earliest possible date for the tree's importation and use on the site—for practical purpose, a wrong date. Finally, taking into account the average age of trees growing in the region at the time (*e.g.* oaks up to 600 yr; olives or junipers up to *ca.* 1000 yr), it is easy to imagine how large the error can be. The error is multiplied when part of a trunk dies before the whole tree does.

Younger-than-expected ^{14}C dates also occur, although much less frequently, except for the well-known case of Jarmo. Several explanations have been offered for this phenomenon, which is due to contamination by younger organic material before, during or after excavation. During excavation, contamination may occur when features with younger material sunk into older layers (*e.g.,* pits or trenches) have not been properly identified. If sampling is done properly and laboratory methods are sound, the only valid explanation of excessively young dates must be related to uncontrolled microphenomena (excluding roots, which can be eliminated by chemical treatment) leading to penetration of younger material *via* vertical fissures or burrowing animals. Finally, it is also possible that unexpected or locally increased radiation can influence the ^{14}C date.

DIFFICULTIES IN RELATING SAMPLES TO THEIR ORIGINAL POSITION

Samples have been collected from two different contexts in Early Neolithic sites: 1) houses and 2) layers outside houses. Houses provide an opportunity to date each structure precisely. It is usually expected that every house has a fireplace or kiln containing charcoal, but this may not be the case. Early Neolithic villagers usually cleaned their houses very carefully. No fire installations with charcoals were found in *ca.* 30 buildings in Nemrik and M'lefaat. In such a case, we may be left with the possibility of dating house fills, which are not necessarily chronologically homogeneous. Usually, the best source of samples from these fills are layers directly overlying house floors. These layers may represent cultural contexts surrounding the houses at the time of their use and abandonment. Thus, when sampling charcoal in direct contact with a house floor, one may expect to collect charcoal related to human occupation of the house.

At Houses 1A and 2A at Nemrik, the house floor was covered by the remains of a burned and collapsed roof, from which we were able to obtain the date of the last use of wood (construction of the roof) and possibly also an *ante quem* date of the house (including the time of the house's existence plus a small but unknown amount of time based on the age of the tree), provided that the wood was not used several times. Layers outside houses are less prone to contamination by younger materials, because they are sealed by younger deposits. The most difficult task is determining the exact spatial or temporal relation of the sample with its associated layer, phase and age. AMS dates for single seeds or pieces of charcoal from known stratigraphic contexts are the most valuable, such as the dates for M'lefaat.

Because of the uncertainty in ^{14}C dates, a single ^{14}C date or even several are of little value; only a series of dates provides a reliable age determination after statistical analysis. Thus, only 40% of the dates from Nemrik and M'lefaat are acceptable. AMS dates for seeds are often younger than dates for charcoal, which need to be corrected for this discrepancy.

CULTURAL SEQUENCE

A summary of the results of ^{14}C dating of the main units of the Epipaleolithic/Early Neolithic of Iraq suggests a model such as is given in Table 2.

TABLE 2. Cultural Sequence in Iraq

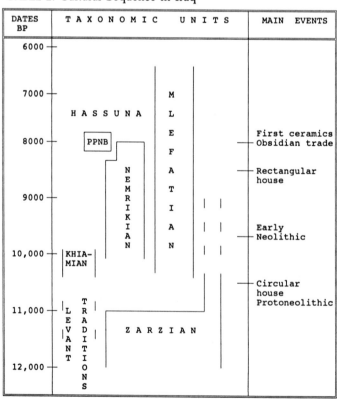

TABLE 3. ^{14}C Dates from Aceramic Iraq

Site	Feature, context	Material	Lab*	Date (BP)
ZARZIAN				
Pelegawra	120cm	Charcoal	GrN-6358	14,350 ± 280
	120–100cm	Charcoal	UCLA-1703D	14,210 ± 80
	100–80cm	Charcoal	GrN-6357	14,480 ± 75**
	100–80cm	Charcoal	UCLA-1714D	13,600 ± 460
	80–60cm	Charcoal	GrN-6356	13,060 ± 110
	<60cm	Charcoal	GrN-6415	11,590 ± 95
Shani-Dar	B$_2$	Charcoal	W-179	12,400 ± 400
	B$_1$	Charcoal	W-667	10,600 ± 300
Zawi-Chemi		Charcoal	W-681	10,870 ± 300
NEMRIKIAN				
Nemrik 9				
Phase 1	Below house 6	Charcoal	Gd-2969	13,000 ± 2400**
	On virgin soil	Charcoal	Gd-6128	9870 ± 160
Phase 1/2	House 8B	Charcoal	Gd-4469	11,090 ± 190**
Phase 2	Near house 6	Charcoal	Gd-?	33,300 ± 1100†
	Near house 6	Charcoal	Gd-4215	>26,000†
	Near house 6	Charcoal	Gd-2775	25,200 ± 670†
	Near house 6	Charcoal	Gd-4223	20,800 ± 550†
	House 9A, pit 1	Charcoal	Gd-4477	11,150 ± 560†
	Near house 6	Mollusk shell	Gd-2714	10,900 ± 140†
	House 6, floor	Charcoal	Gd-2973	10,400 ± 190†
	Floor below h 7A	Charcoal	Gd-4475	10,370 ± 330**
	House 9A, pit 3	Charcoal	Gd-6111	10,130 ± 180**
	House 6, wall	Charcoal	Gd-2970	10,070 ± 120
	Floors near house 8	Charcoal	Gd-6143	9990 ± 140
	House 9A, fill	Charcoal	Gd-6110	9970 ± 170
	Floors near house 7	Charcoal	Gd-6127	9800 ± 160
	Floors below h 7A	Charcoal	Gd-6121	9780 ± 180
	Near house 6	Charcoal	Gd-2963	9780 ± 130
	Near house 6	Charcoal	Gd-4371	9770 ± 520
	House 9A, fill	Charcoal	Gd-4372	9770 ± 240
	Near house 6	Charcoal	Gd-5443	9420 ± 90†
	House 6, floor	Charcoal	Gd-4364	9030 ± 400†
	House 6, fill	Charcoal	Gd-4205	9000 ± 150†
	House 7A, fill	Charcoal	Gd-4463	8910 ± 220†
	Near house 2A	Charcoal	Gd-4204	7980 ± 140†
Phase 3	H 2A, lower floor	Charcoal	Gd-4370	12,550 ± 1000†
	Below house 3	Charcoal	Gd-4473	12,240 ± 340†
	House 1A, pit 18	Charcoal	Gd-5249	11,180 ± 90†
	Below house 3	Charcoal	Gd-4478	10,700 ± 190†
	H 2A, upper floor	Charcoal	Gd-5451	10,700 ± 120†
	House 1A, roof	Charcoal	Gd-4212	10,480 ± 180†
	H 2A, lower fill	Charcoal	Gd-2971	10,330 ± 150†
	House 1A, roof	Charcoal	Gd-4211	10,260 ± 170†
	H 2A, upper fill	Charcoal	Gd-4209	10,040 ± 130†
	H 2A, lower floor	Charcoal	Gd-5257	10,020 ± 80†
	H 2A, upper fill	Charcoal	Gd-4208	10,100 ± 130†
	Structure 15	Charcoal	Gd-4224	9930 ± 230†
	House 4A, fill	Charcoal	Gd-4474	9640 ± 300
	House 8A, floor	Charcoal	Gd-4453	9630 ± 160
	House 1A, roof	Charcoal	Gd-2766	9570 ± 130
	House 8A, floor	Charcoal	Gd-6120	9530 ± 140
	House 8A, fill	Charcoal	Gd-6129	9510 ± 150
	House 1A, roof	Charcoal	Gd-4193	9500 ± 130

Table 3. (Continued)

Site	Feature	Material	Lab*	Date (BP)
	H 2A, lower fill	Charcoal	Gd-2972	9490 ± 170
	House 1A, roof	Charcoal	Gd-2773	9480 ± 170
	H 2A, lower floor	Charcoal	Gd-2966	9440 ± 160
	House 4A, fill	Charcoal	Gd-6131	9370 ± 120
	H 2A, upper fill	Charcoal	Gd-5421	9250 ± 70
	House 4A, fill	Charcoal	Gd-6130	9230 ± 160
	H 2A, lower fill	Charcoal	Gd-4365	9140 ± 150**
	H 2A, lower fill	Charcoal	Gd-5425	9140 ± 90†
	H 2A, upper fill	Charcoal	Gd-5240	9130 ± 60†
	House 1A, roof	Charcoal	Gd-2778	9010 ± 170†
	House 7, floor	Charcoal	Gd-6119	8300 ± 150†
Phase 3/4	H 1/1A, base pillar	Charcoal	Gd-4210	10,180 ± 190†
	H 1/1A, base pillar	Charcoal	Gd-4207	8700 ± 110†
Phase 4	Cemetery	Charcoal	Gd-5237	>40,000†
	Grave 2	Charcoal	Gd-2967	>37,700†
	House 1, fill	Charcoal	Gd-4214	>27,000†
	House 4, fill	Charcoal	Gd-5440	18,250 ± 220†
	House 8, pillar	Charcoal	Gd-5595	9950 ± 100†
	House 8, fill	Charcoal	Gd-6152	9800 ± 130†
	House 4, fill	Charcoal	Gd-2937	9740 ± 150†
	Cemetery	Charcoal	Gd-4213	9410 ± 550
	House 4, roof	Charcoal	Gd-2936	9170 ± 130
	House 4, fill	Charcoal	Gd-5186	9170 ± 90
	House 4, roof	Charcoal	Gd-5424	9140 ± 90
	House 4, roof	Charcoal	Gd-5422	8750 ± 80†
	House 8, fill	Charcoal	Gd-6113	8570 ± 150†
	House 1, fill	Charcoal	Gd-2637	8440 ± 130†
	House 8, fill	Charcoal	Gd-6108	8300 ± 130†
	House 4, fill	Charcoal	Gd-2935	7640 ± 110†
	Cemetery	Charcoal	Gd-4194	5200 ± 450†
Phase 4/5	Near house 3	Mollusk shell	Gd-2713	9470 ± 140†
	Near house 3, pit 2	Charcoal	Gd-8180	8180 ± 120†
Phase 5	House 5, pit 10	Charcoal	Gd-4476	13,600 ± 900†
	House 2, fill	Charcoal	Gd-4118	11,300 ± 200†
	House 2, fill	Charcoal	Gd-2777	10,180 ± 130†
	House 5, pit 4	Charcoal	Gd-6148	9720 ± 130†
	House 2, fill	Mollusk shell	Gd-5111	8630 ± 70
	Stone pavement	Mollusk shell	Gd-5110	7470 ± 60†
Tell-eth-Talathat	XVI	Charcoal	TK-23	7360 ± 100**
	XVI	Charcoal	TK-199b	6680 ± 290†
	XVI	Charcoal	TK-199a	6340 ± 390**
	XV	Charcoal	TK-198	7800 ± 80
	XV	Charcoal	TK-24	7520 ± 120**
CLASSICAL PPNB				
Magzalya	Layer 10	Charcoal	IGAN-772	8010 ± 50**
	Layer 10	Charcoal	IGAN-772	7490 ± 50**
MLEFATIAN				
M'lefaat				
Lower layer	House 8, foundation	Charcoal	Gd-4658	12,360 ± 280**
	House 8, floor	Charcoal	Gd-6356	9630 ± 130†
	House 8, fill	Charcoal	Gd-4652	13,860 ± 300†
	House 4, fill	Charcoal	Gd-4483	12,810 ± 660**
	House 3A, fill	Charcoal	Gd-6149	10,290 ± 180**
Upper layer	House 3, fill	Charcoal	Gd-6363	13,540 ± 180†
	Hearth B	Charcoal	Gd-6150	10,890 ± 140

Table 3. (Continued)

Site	Feature	Material	Lab*	Date (BP)
	Hearth A	Charcoal	Gd-4465	10,850 ± 200
	Houses 3 and 8, fill	Grain	OxA-3747	9870 ± 1140
	Houses 3 and 8, fill	Grain	OxA-3748	9890 ± 120
	Houses 3 and 8, fill	Grain	OxA-3749	9660 ± 250
	Houses 3 and 8, fill	Grain	OxA-3819	9680 ± 100
Jarmo, stratified				
Operation I	8	Charcoal	GL-50	6750 ± 120
	8	Charcoal	GL-45	6670 ± 120
	7/8	Mollusk shell	C-113	6710 ± 320
	7/8	Charcoal	C-742	6605 ± 330
	7a	Charcoal	W-652	7950 ± 200†
	7	Charcoal	H-55/491	8520 ± 175†
	7	Bone	UCLA-1714E	7980 ± 140†
Operation II	5	Charcoal	C-743	6690 ± 360
	5	Charcoal	GL-44	6650 ± 120
	5	Charcoal	GL-48	6930 ± 120**
	5	Charcoal	GL-49	6300 ± 180
	4	Charcoal	W-651	8830 ± 200†
	2	Charcoal	C-744	5265 ± 450
	1	Pottery	GrN-6353	7655 ± 75†
Jarmo, soundings	PQ 14-2.5m	Ash	W-607	9040 ± 250†
	PQ 14-2.5m	Humic acids	W-608	7750 ± 250**
	PQ 14-2.25m	Soil	W-657	11,240 ± 300†
	PQ 14-5a	Bone	UCLA-1723A	7800 ± 120**
	PQ 14-2	Bone	UCLA-1723B	7270 ± 200**
	N 18-2m	Soil	W-665	11,200 ± 200†
	K 21-3	Bone	UCLA-1723D	6550 ± 200**
	K 21-1	Bone	UCLA-1723C	6180 ± 300**

*GrN=Groningen; UCLA=University of California, Los Angeles; W=USGS, National Center; Gd=Gdansk; TK= University of Tokyo; IGAN=Institute of Geography; GL=Geochronological Laboratory; C=Chicago; H=Heidelberg; OxA=Oxford Accelerator
**Questionable date
†Unacceptable date

REFERENCES CITED

Albrecht, G., B. Albrecht, H. Berke, D. Burger, J. Moser, W. Rahle, W. Schoch, G. Storch, H. P. Uerpmann and B. Urban.
    1992   Late Pleistocene and Early Holocene finds from Öküzini. *Paléorient* 18(2):123–141.
Bader, N. O.
    1989   *Drevneichie Zemledeltsy Severnoi Mesopotamii* (Earliest cultivators in Northern Mesopotamia). Nauka, Moscow.
Garrod, D.
    1930   The Palaeolithic of southern Kurdistan: Excavations of Zarzi and Hazar Merd. *Bulletin of the American School of Prehistoric Research* 6:8–43.
Hole, F.
    1977   *Studies in the Archaeological History of the Deh Luran Plain.* Museum of Anthropology, University of Michigan, Ann Arbor.
    1983   The Jarmo chipped stone. In *Prehistoric Archaeology along the Zagros Flank,* edited by L. S. Braidwood, B. Howe, C. A. Reed and P. J. Watson, pp. 235–287. Oriental Institute of the University of Chicago, Chicago.
    1987   Chronologies in the Iranian Neolithic. In *Chronologies du Proche Orient,* edited by O. Aurenche, J. Evin and F. Hours, pp. 353–379. BAR International Series 379, British Archaeological Reports, Oxford.
Hole, F., K. V. Flannery and J. A. Neely.
    1969   *Prehistory and Human Ecology of the Deh Luran Plain.* University of Michigan, Ann Arbor.
Kozłowski, S. K. (editor)
    1990   *Nemrik 9: Pre-Pottery Neolithic Site in Iraq. General Report, Seasons 1985–1986.* Warsaw University Press, Warsaw.

Kozłowksi, S. K. (editor)
  1992   *Nemrik 9: Pre-Pottery Neolithic Site in Iraq. House 1, 1A, 1B.* Warsaw University Press, Warsaw.
Kozłowski, S. K., and A. Kempisty
  1990   Architecture of the Pre-Pottery Neolithic settlement in Nemrik 9, Iraq. *World Archaeology* 21(8):248–262.
Kozłowski, S. K. and K. Szymczak
  1989   Flint industry from House 1, 1A, 1B at the Pre-Pottery Neolithic site in Nemrik 9, northern Iraq. *Paléorient* 15(1):32–42.
Mazurowski, R.
          Ground and Pecked Stone Industry in the Pre-Pottery Neolithic of Northern Iraq. Warsaw University Press, Warsaw, in press.
Mortensi, P.
  1964   Additional remarks on the chronology of early village farming communities in Zagros. *Sumer* 20:29–34.
  1973   A sequence of flint and obsidian tools from Choga Nami. *Iraq* 20:37–56.
  1983   Patterns of interaction between seasonal settlements and early villages in Mesopotamia. In *The Hilly Flanks and Beyond: Essays on the Prehistory of Southwestern Asia*, edited by T. C. Young, P. E. L. Smith, P. Mortensen and R. J. Braidwood, pp. 207–229, Oriental Institute of the University of Chicago, Chicago.
Solecki, R. S.
  1981   *An Early Village Site at Zawi Chemi Shanidar.* Undena Publications, Malibu, California.

NEOLITHIC TO BRONZE AGE SETTLEMENT OF THE NEGEV AND SINAI IN LIGHT OF RADIOCARBON DATING: A VIEW FROM THE SOUTHERN NEGEV

UZI AVNER[1], ISRAEL CARMI[2] and DROR SEGAL[1]

INTRODUCTION

In the past two decades, numerous archaeological studies have been made in the deserts of the Negev, Sinai and neighboring lands, some of which have attempted to draw the historical outline of the southern Levant's desert. *Ca.* 150 ^{14}C dates available today (over 100 from the southern Negev and nearly 50 from neighboring areas) shed new light on the desert's past. Here, we summarize and discuss the present state of research and the settlement history of the desert from the 8th to 3rd millennia BC, in light of ^{14}C dating, focusing on the southern Negev, from which most of the ^{14}C dates were obtained.

The southern Negev encompasses the area south of the Ramon Crater to the Gulf of Aqaba, bordered by the Arabah Valley in the east and Egypt in the west (Fig. 1). This is an extreme desert, with *ca.* 30 mm average annual precipitation and *ca.* 3500 mm annual evaporation. This negative water balance causes the area to be poor in water sources and limits Saharo-Arabian vegetation almost totally to wadi beds. The significance of these conditions is better understood when one compares them to conditions in the Negev Highlands to the north, with 100 mm annual average precipitation and 2000 mm annual evaporation; vegetation there is Irano-Turanian and often covers the hillsides. Most of the southern Negev is limestone mountain, whereas igneous rock and sandstone are exposed from Timna Valley to Eilat. Considering its environmental conditions, one would not expect the southern Negev to be rich in remains of ancient human presence and activity.

The research of N. Glueck led him to describe the occupational history of the Negev as a series of short settlement periods separated by long intervals of abandonment (Glueck 1959, 1961, 1968, 1970). Glueck identified the periods of settlement as Chalcolithic (found almost exclusively in the Beer Sheva Basin), Middle Bronze I (MB I), Iron Age II and Hellenistic-Roman-Byzantine, with some continuation to the Ummayad period. Gaps occurred during the Early Bronze Age, Middle Bronze, Late Bronze, Iron Age I, Persian and the 8th century AD to the present. According to Glueck, occupation during the settlement periods was permanent and agricultural, whereas during the gaps, Bedouins roamed the area, destroying existing cultural remains and leaving no traces of their own (Glueck 1968:11–12, 127; 1970:11–12, 65).

In numerous subsequent studies, scholars adopted Glueck's "up and down" pattern (*e.g.,* Reifenberg 1955; Rothenberg 1967; Evenari, Shana and Tadmor 1971; Baron 1981). A new and intensive stage of research began in the late 1970s when the Israel Antiquities Authority (formally the Department of Antiquities) and other archaeological institutes were organized for an emergency survey in preparation for the redeployment of Israeli military forces from Sinai. Although the survey covered only 25% of the Negev area, some 10,000 previously unknown sites were found, of which *ca.* 100 were excavated (Eitan 1979; Cohen 1988, and in press). The survey brought to light much new data but did not alter the basic perception of alternating periods of settlement and abandonment (Cohen 1985, 1986, 1988, in press; Rosen 1987b; Haiman 1986, 1991; Lender 1990; Avni 1992).

[1]Israel Antiquities Authority, P.O.B. 586, Jerusalem 91004 Israel
[2]Department of Environmental Science and Energy Research, Weizmann Institute of Science 76100 Rehovot, Israel

Late Quaternary Chronology and Paleoclimates of the Eastern Mediterranean
Edited by O. Bar-Yosef and R. S. Kra. RADIOCARBON 1994, pp. 265–300

265

Of the various explanations suggested for the phenomenon, one relates periods of settlement to the initiative of a strong political regime in the nearby fertile country (Cohen, 1985, 1986, 1988; Glueck 1961, 1968, 1970; Rothenberg 1970:21 *etc.*; Amiran *et al.* 1973; Beit-Arieh 1974, 1981b, 1983; Baron 1981; Rosen 1987b; Haiman 1988, 1989a, b; Finkelstein 1988), while a contrary one claims that settlement in the desert flourished simultaneously with crises in the fertile lands (Finkelstein 1989; Finkelstein and Perevolotsky 1990). The dearth of archaeological remains during the intervening periods has been attributed by some scholars to nomads' failure to leave traces of their presence (Rothenberg 1970:22; Finkelstein 1984:198; Cohen 1986:433; Finkelstein and Perevolotsky 1990:67–68, 77; for opposing views, see Cribb 1991 and, for the Negev, Rosen 1993). Most scholars agree that during the settlement periods, the dominant population penetrated the desert from neighboring regions.

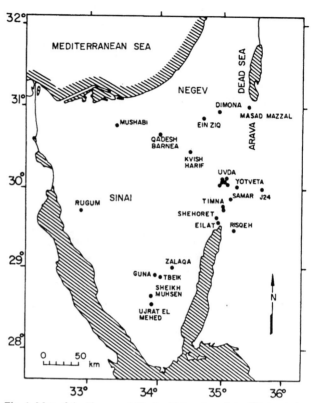

Fig. 1. Map of the Negev and Sinai with location of the ^{14}C-dated sites

There are still unanswered questions about settlement in the Negev and Sinai deserts. What are the precise dates of each period or culture? How can the lifetime of a site be determined? And what actually occurred during the periods of gaps? Archaeology alone cannot provide satisfactory answers, since datable artifacts are not always available in desert sites, and until recently, there were only a few ^{14}C dates from this area.

A comprehensive survey of the Arabah and Eilat Mountains in the southern Negev was undertaken by Rothenberg during the 1960s. This survey resulted in 48 Chalcolithic sites, 51 Iron Age I sites (mainly related to copper production), 3 Nabatean, 6 Roman, 48 Byzantine, 11 Medieval-Islamic, 16 Late Islamic, and 49 undated sites: 220 sites altogether, including those discovered by A. Musil, F. Frank and others (Rothenberg 1967, 1970:7; Rothenberg and Cohen 1968). The unoccupied periods that emerge from this list form a pattern similiar to Glueck's, but with four major differences: 1) the Chalcolithic period, almost absent south of the Beer Sheva Basin in Glueck's survey, is one of the most intensive settlement periods in Rothenberg's survey. Indeed, the same type of site was identified by both scholars as belonging to different periods; 2) from the MB I, one of the most intensive periods in Glueck's survey, Rothenberg found only 1 site (and 2 doubtful sites); 3) the Iron Age I period (later found to begin at the end of Late Bronze) was not identified by Glueck; 4) Rothenberg did not relate any site to the Early Islamic period, while Glueck argued for some continuity from the Byzantine to the Ummayad period. Rothenberg has published several corrections to his survey, but still concludes that the southern Negev was uninhabited during most of prehistory and history.

Within the past decade, however, surveys have produced evidence that the settlement history of the area does not conform to expectations based on its harsh environmental conditions. We now know of 1400 ancient sites within the 1200 km^2 extending from the Uvda Valley southward toward Eilat, although only 7% of the area has been intensively resurveyed.[3] In addition, ^{14}C dates now demonstrate a complete sequence of human presence and activity in the southern Negev from the 8th millennium BC to the modern era.

We base our discussion here on 84 ^{14}C dates (Table 1) from 37 sites obtained by 9 different laboratories, collected from Uvda Valley (40 dates),[4] Sinai (12), Eilat (10), other sites in the Eilat area (5), Timna (3), the Negev Highlands (6), the northern Arabah (6), and southern Jordan (2). Most samples were charcoal with the exception of Nos. 31, 83, 84 (unburned wood), 57 (goat dung), and 54 (ostrich eggshell). Calendric ages in Table 1 were obtained using the accepted conversion based on the calibrations in Stuiver and Kra (1986) and the CalibETH program (Niklaus 1991). For dates that extended beyond the range of calibration, an approximation method was used (Carmi, Sirkes and Magaritz 1984). Figure 1 is a map of the dated sites; Figure 2 is a graph of the dates; Table 1 shows the range of calendric ages. Within the text, the dates are calibrated, averaged, and rounded to the nearest ten. Dates without references are published here for the first time.

THE NEOLITHIC – DESCRIPTION OF INVENTORY AND DISCUSSION

Remains from the Sultanian and Khiamian cultures of the Pre-Pottery Neolithic A (PPNA, *ca.* 9300–8000 BC) are almost totally absent in the Negev; in only one site, Nahal Lavan 109 in the western Negev, "El Khiam" points were found (Gopher 1985:176–180, 1989:47). A single PPNA site, Abu Maadi I, was excavated in southern Sinai (Bar-Yosef 1989:59) and no sites of the period have been discovered to date in the southern Negev. The Harifian culture of the Negev Highlands is sometimes described as continuing into this stage, but ^{14}C dates show that it is restricted to the Epipalaeolithic (Goring-Morris 1991).

Sites of the Pre-Pottery Neolithic B (PPNB, *ca.* 8000–6500 BC) are known from all desert areas of the Levant: the Negev Highlands (Noy and Cohen 1974; Servello 1976; Burian, Friedman and Mintz 1976; Goring-Morris and Gilead 1981; Goring-Morris and Gol 1982; Bar-Yosef and Gopher 1982; Simmons 1981; Rosen 1988; Lender 1990);[5] the northern Arabah (Taute 1981); eastern Jordan (Garrard and Stanley-Price 1975a,b; Garrard, Harvey and Switsur 1981; Garrard *et al.* 1981, 1985, 1987a,b, 1988; Garrard, Byrd and Betts 1986; Betts 1982, 1983, 1984a,b, 1985); and southern Jordan (Kirkbride 1960, 1966; Henry 1982:438–440; Raikes 1980; Nissen, Muheisen and Gebel 1991). In southern Sinai, one site was already excavated by Currelly (Petrie 1906:240) and an extensive study of the sites in southern Sinai began in 1975 (Goring-Morris and Mintz 1976;

---

[3]The surveys in the southern Negev have not yet been published. For preliminary reports, see Avner (1979–1989) and Kaminer (1982). It should be noted that most of the sites included in the count are not large, and the total of 1400 consists of dwelling sites (usually suited to one extended family), tent camps, villages, fortresses, burial and cult sites, agricultural installations, copper production and other industrial sites.

[4]Excavations of most of the Uvda Valley sites took place during a special excavation operation in February 1980, headed by Eitan and Cohen. The results have not yet been published, with the exception of those for Sites 11 and 15 (Reich 1990) and preliminary publication of Site 14 (Goring-Morris and Gopher 1983, 1987) and Site 6 (Yogev 1983). For short preliminary reports, see *Hadashot Archeologiot* 74/75 (1981:35–49). Sites 1, 3 and 13 were excavated by R. Cohen; Site 2 by G. Mazor; Sites 4, 5, 12, 19 and 21 by E. Eisenberg; Sites 6 and 16 by O. Yogev; Site 7 by B. Sass and A. Goren; Sites 9 and 124 by R. Amiran, C. Cohen, O. Ilan and U. Avner; Sites 10 and 18 by A. Eitan; and Site 20 by A. Ronen. For a general description of settlement in Uvda Valley, see Avner (1990b).

[5]A total of 12 sites in the Negev Highlands, 3 in northern Sinai and 5 in southern Sinai, are discussed by Gopher (1985: 144–185), with further bibliography.

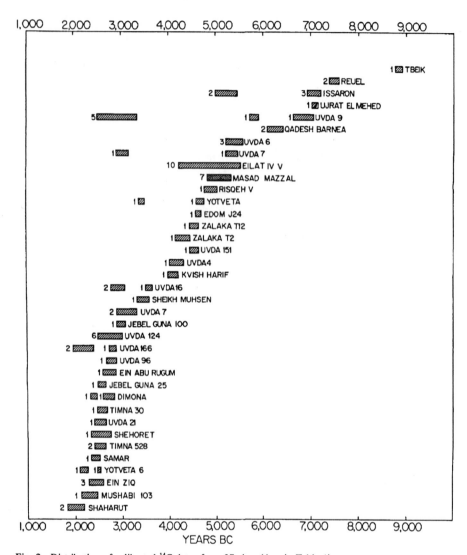

Fig. 2. Distribution of calibrated ^{14}C dates from 37 sites (data in Table 1)

Bar-Yosef 1981a,b, 1984,1987a; Gopher 1981; Tchernov and Bar-Yosef 1982; Dayan *et al.* 1986); in Table 1, *cf.* Nos. 1 (considerably older than the finds) and 14.

In the southern Negev, the first PPNB site was discovered in 1977 near Ein Qtura (Avner and Naor 1978); 7 additional sites were found during the emergency survey of the eastern Uvda Valley; 3 were stone-built habitation sites, the other 4 industrial and camp sites (Avner 1990b). Neolithic material was found in two caves in the Eilat Mountains (Avner 1979, 1982a,b) and in Timna Valley (Eshel 1990). Two of the Uvda Valley sites were excavated, one in Nahal Re'uel (Site 20, Ronen 1980) and the other at the mouth of Nahal Issaron (Site 14, Goring-Morris and Gopher 1983, 1987). Both revealed a concentration of circular rooms, with only limited open spaces, each covering a 400-m area (Fig. 3). The inhabitants probably lived in the sites during the autumn, winter and spring, and subsisted on hunting and gathering, like the inhabitants of southern

TABLE 1. ^{14}C Dates of Sites in the Southern Negev and Vicinity

No.	Lab no.	Site	^{14}C age (yr BP)	^{14}C age range (cal BC)	References*
1	Pta-2700	W. Tbeik	10,350 ± 100	10,350–8740	1
2	Pta-3137	N. Reuel	8720 ± 70	7540–7420	2
3	Pta-2848	N. Reuel	8670 ± 50	7480–7390	3, 2
4	Pta-3202	N. Reuel	8650 ± 90	7490–7340	2
5	B-2373	Masad Mazzal	8480 ± 70	7330–7210	4
6	Hv-9108	Masad Mazzal	8440 ± 80	7310–7210	4
7	KN-2444	Masad Mazzal	8350 ± 75	7225–7095	4
8	Hv-9107	Masad Mazzal	8330 ± 75	7210–7080	4
9	Hv-9106	Masad Mazzal	8240 ± 95	7145–6980	4
10	KN-2443	Masad Mazzal	8070 ± 75	6980–6850	4
11	Pta-3000	N. Issaron(C)	8430 ± 80	7211–7080	5
12	Pta-3376	N. Issaron(C)	8180 ± 80	7080–6814	5
13	Pta-3377	N. Issaron(C)	8180 ± 80	7080–6814	5
14	Pta-2703	Ujrat el Mehed	8220 ± 80	7120–6980	6
15	RT-670D	B. Uvda 9	7960 ± 200	7066–6622	7
16	SMU-662	Kadesh Barnea 3	7530 ± 80	6445–6233	8
17	Pta-3662	Kadesh Barnea 3	7350 ± 80	6370–6090	9
18	Pta-3646	B. Uvda 9	6960 ± 70	5955–5740	10
19	RT-628A	B. Uvda 6	6560 ± 200	5640–5315	11, 12
20	RT-628B	B. Uvda 6	6400 ± 70	5416–5244	11, 7
21	Pta-3621	B. Uvda 6	6400 ± 60	5416–5244	13
22	Pta-2999	N. Issaron(B)	6460 ± 70	5475–5343	5
23	Pta-3486	N. Issaron(C)	6130 ± 70	5208–5000	5
24	RT-724B	B. Uvda 7	6410 ± 120	5474–5242	14, 15
25	RT-989	Eilat IV/16	6470 ± 80	5480–5338	14, 16
26	RT-1215	Eilat V/27	6400 ± 210	5549–5139	14, 16
27	RT-926A	Eilat IV/3	6340 ± 60	5342–5236	14, 16
28	RT-1216	Eilat V/28	6060 ± 65	5133–4900	14, 16
29	RT-1214	Eilat V/22	5980 ± 130	5063–4728	14, 16
30	RT-1212	Eilat V/18	5930 ± 80	4937–4729	14, 16
31	RT-1210	Eilat IV/8	5710 ± 75	4678–4489	14, 16
32	RT-1211	Eilat V/16	5640 ± 60	4578–4396	14, 16
33	RT-1213	Eilat V/19	5490 ± 60	4455–4248	14, 16
34	RT-926B	Eilat IV/I	5400 ± 100	4353–4146	14, 16
35	K-1467	Risqeh	6010 ± 120	5067–4784	17
36	RT-1547	Yotvata hill	5800 ± 45	4773–4606	18
37	SMU-804	Edom J24	5770 ± 40	4719–4586	19
38	Pta-3645	W. Zalaqa T12	5690 ± 50	4660–4473	10
39	Pta-3633	W. Zalaqa T2	5590 ± 70	4495–4360	10
40	RT-648E	W. Zalaqa T2	5440 ± 80	4346–4158	10, 11
41	RT-648A	B. Uvda 151	5670 ± 85	4669–4456	10, 11
42	RT-724D	B. Uvda 4	5400 ± 110	4355–4047	14, 20
43	Pta-3374	Kvish Harif	5260 ± 60	4222–4002	21
44	RT-640A	B. Uvda 16	4800 ± 70	3690–3516	11, 22
45	Hv-5296	Sheikh Muhsen	4710 ± 50	3613–3378	23
46	RT-1556	Dimona	4658 ± 55	3508–3400	24
47	RT-1546	Yotvata hill	4650 ± 75	3518–3345	18

TABLE 1. (Continued)

No.	Lab no.	Site	^{14}C age (yr BP)	^{14}C age range (cal BC)	References*
48	RT-724C	B. Uvda 7	4540 ± 100	3374–3093	14, 15
49	RT-899A	B. Uvda 9	4530 ± 50	3239–3107	14, 7
50	RT-899B	B. Uvda 9	4520 ± 60	3244–3103	14, 7
51	RT-864B	B. Uvda 9	4440 ± 180	3359–2912	14, 7
52	RT-1436	B. Uvda 9	4440 ± 180	3109–3028	25, 7
53	RT-864A	B. Uvda 9	4310 ± 90	3093–2876	14, 7
54	RT-714A	B. Uvda 9	4070 ± 100	2896–2497	25, 7
55	SMU-659(?)	Jebel Guna 100	4373 ± 64	3093–2917	26
56	RT-1452	B. Uvda 124/IV	4370 ± 50	3039–2920	25, 27
57	RT-1451	B. Uvda 124/IV	4370 ± 50	3095–2914	25, 27
58	RT-1419	B. Uvda 124/IV	4370 ± 100	3106–2901	25, 27
59	RT-1449	B. Uvda 124/IV	4285 ± 60	3028–2780	25, 27
60	RT-1448	B. Uvda 124/IV	4120 ± 60	2870–2612	25, 27
61	RT-1450	B. Uvda 124/IV	4075 ± 55	3632–3502	25, 27
62	RT-640B	B. Uvda 16	4400 ± 60	3099–2922	11, 22
63	RT-640C	B. Uvda 16	4280 ± 80	3033–2775	11, 22
64	RT-1420	B. Uvda 166	4210 ± 60	2912–2697	25, 27
65	RT-648B	B. Uvda 96/III	4250 ± 50	2919–2777	25, 27
66	RT-447A	Ein Abu Rugum	4180 ± 300	3430–2365	28
67	RT-1557	Dimona	4127 ± 52	2871–2614	24
68	SMU-659(?)	Jebel Guna 25	4056 ± 72	2664–2494	26
69	HAM-215	Timna 30	4020 ± 100	2696–2458	28
70	RT-724F	B. Uvda 21	4015 ± 80	2661–2461	14, 20
71	RT-591	Shehoret hill	4010 ± 150	2772–2355	25, 27
72	BONN-2363	Timna S28/2	4000 ± 90	2663–2398	29
73	BONN-2632	Timna S28	3890 ± 70	2477–2286	29
74	Pta-3627	Samar	3940 ± 60	2570–2352	27
75	RT-1558	Dimona	3914 ± 52	2486–2339	24
76	RT-1439	Yotvata south	3980 ± 60	2598–2455	30
77	RT-1438	Yotvata south	3770 ± 50	2292–2137	30
78	RT-885A	Ein Ziq	3960 ± 90	2659–2360	31
79	RT-885B	Ein Ziq	3850 ± 50	2464–2300	31
80	RT-714B	B. Uvda 166	3850 ± 80	2459–2206	32, 27
81	RT-1421	B. Uvda 166	3680 ± 50	2176–1982	25, 27
82	RT-447B	Mushabi 103	3800 ± 330	2687–1833	28
83	RT-899C	Shaharut IV	3700 ± 55	2196–2031	14, 27
84	RT-771B	Shaharut IV	3580 ± 130	2134–1763	14, 27

*References: 1=Tchernov and Bar-Yosef (1982); 2=Gopher (1985); 3=Ronen (1980); 4=Taute (1981); 5=Goring-Morris and Gopher (1983); 6=Bar-Yosef (1981a); 7=Excavated by Avner and Ilan; 8=Bar-Yosef (1987); 9=Excavated by Bar-Yosef; 10=Avner (1984); 11=Carmi (1987); 12=Yogev (1983); 13=Excavated by Yogev; 14=Carmi and Segal (1992); 15=Excavated by Sass and Goren; 16=Avner (in press); 17=Kirkbride (1969); 18=Excavated by Meshel; 19=Henry (1982); 20=Excavated by Eisenberg; 21=Rosen (1984a); 22=Excavated by Yogev; 23=Beit-Arieh (1977); 24=Nahlieli and Tahal (unpublished); 25=Carmi and Segal (unpublished); 26=Bar-Yosef *et al.* (1986); 27=Excavated by Avner; 28=Scharpenseel, Pietig and Schiffmann (1976); 29=Conrad and Rothenberg (1980); 30=Excavated by Meshel and Sass; 31=Excavated by Cohen; 32 = Carmi (in preparation)

Fig. 3. Nahal Issaron site (Uvda 14) from the west, excavated by Goring-Morris and Gopher

Sinai.[6] From the published ^{14}C dates, it seems that both sites were short-lived and that N. Reu'el (Nos. 2–4, Table 1) preceded N. Issaron by 300 yr (Nos. 11–13, 23). However, 35 new, unpublished dates from N. Issaron indicate a much longer time span for Stratum C, from *ca.* 8000–6500 BC (Goring-Morris and Gopher, personal communication).

A single Late Neolithic[7] (6500–4500 BC) site in the Negev Highlands (within Sinai), Kadesh Barnea 3, was ^{14}C-dated (Nos. 16, 17, Table 1)(Bar-Yosef 1987a). The Kvish Harif site is either late Neolithic or early Chalcolithic (No. 43)(Rosen 1984a), and another Late Neolithic site (349) was identified on the Nafha ridge (Lender 1990). Only one Late Neolithic site, Wadi Jiba', has been recorded for the southern Sinai (Gopher 1985:166–168). However, six sites from the southern Negev ^{14}C-dated to the Late Neolithic. One is Stratum B of N. Issaron, featuring scant remains of circular rooms surrounding a circular open space (Goring-Morris and Gopher 1987:18).[8] Only a

---

[6]The occupation seasons are suggested by the excavators, who also suggest that animal husbandry was already established here during in the PPNB, based on the high percentage of *Capra* (ibex) bones and the fact that domestication in that period may also have existed in Beida (Hecker 1975), only 70 km northeast of Uvda Valley. Recent studies also suggest the beginning of domestication in 'Ain Ghazal in the PPNC (Kohler-Rollefson 1989) and in Basta already in the late PPNB (Becker, in Nissen *et al.* 1991). In the Negev and Sinai, however, domestication probably appeared only later. In the Ujrat el Mehed site in southern Sinai, the fact that *Capra* <1 yr old were not hunted has been explained as only a first step toward domestication, which did not continue (Dayan *et al.* 1986). Nor have any signs of domestication been found in the W. Tbeik site (Tchernov and Bar-Yosef 1982). The large quantity and high percentage of arrowheads in N. Issaron (Gopher 1985: 154–156) testify to the importance of hunting to the economy of the inhabitants.

[7]We prefer to use this term instead of the commonly used "Pottery Neolithic", because pottery is still rare in the desert sites of that period. (Exceptional, for example, are a few sherds of a jar from the Eilat burial site that resemble "W. Rabah" pottery.)

[8]In this Hebrew publication, "several circular structures surrounding central courtyards" are mentioned, whereas in the English version (Goring-Morris and Gopher 1983), this pattern was not noted. In recent oral discussion, the excavators preferred the term "open space" for the central part of Stratum B.

Fig. 4. Uvda site 18, consisting of courts and rooms, from the west, excavated by A. Eitan

single ^{14}C date has been published from that stratum (No. 22, Table 1), but the new series of unpublished dates indicates an occupation from the mid-6th to early 4th millennium BC. Early strata were dated to the 6th millennium in two other sites, Uvda Site 9 (No. 18) with *Haparsah* and *transversal* arrowheads, and Uvda Site 7 (No. 24). No architecture was attributed to these strata due to limited probes.

The open-space structure of N. Issaron Stratum B may be important for marking the appearance of the built courtyard, a notable innovation for the desert, and probably connected with emerging animal domestication. No evidence exists as yet for the beginning of grazing in the Negev and Sinai; in the Transjordan desert, grazing probably started at the beginning of the Late Neolithic (Garrard *et al.* 1987a; Betts 1988; Baird *et al.* 1992; McCartney 1992). The earliest built courtyard is possibly in Dhuweila, ^{14}C-dated to the Late Neolithic (Betts 1988). In Uvda Valley, other sites of this type were dated to the 5th–3rd millennia BC (Figs. 3, 4). Caprid bones were found in all the sites, and layers of dung were unearthed in several courtyards, making the association between the courtyards and animal domestication (Rosen 1984a, 1988; Bar Yosef 1987b; Avner 1990b). Consequently, a new type of dwelling site, consisting of circular courtyards with attached circular rooms became a dominant architectural feature in the desert for several millennia.

Late Neolithic remains were also found in three cult sites in Uvda Valley. Two ^{14}C dates were derived from a hearth at the foot of a broad *Massebah*[9] or standing stone located 5 m south of Site 9; No. 15 (Table 1) is probably incorrect; No. 18 correlates with *Haparsa* points from the nearby probes. The hearth was 75 cm below the surface; overlying layers contained artifacts from later periods, with EB IV sherds at the top. Thus, it appears that the shrine was in almost constant use for four millennia, as was nearby dwelling Site 9. Similar is an open sanctuary (Site 6, Figs. 5, 6)

---

[9]The biblical Hebrew term, *Massebah*, plural *Masseboth*, is commonly used in English literature. *Masseboth*, unlike *Stelae*, are not decorated or inscribed and are generally unworked.

Fig. 5. Neolithic open sanctuary (Uvda 6) after minor restoration, from the east, excavated by Yogev

where three samples (Nos. 19–21) dated a sunken altar to the mid-6th millennium BC. Both surface and excavation finds indicate continual use during the 5th–3rd millennia BC. Another *Masseboth* shrine (Site 151, Table 1 No. 41, Fig. 7) was dated to the end of the Late Neolithic (for the last three sites, and on cult sites in general, see Yogev 1983; Avner 1983, 1984, 1990b, 1993a).

A series of 10 ^{14}C dates were obtained from a burial site in Eilat, which included 20 tumuli tombs and 2 open sanctuaries (Avner 1990a, 1991). Nine charcoal samples were collected from hearths discovered around 2 of the tombs (Table 1, Nos. 25–30, 32–34; Fig. 8) and 1 from the remains of unburned sacred wood, *Asherah*, found in a stone-built installation (No. 31; Fig. 9). The dates indicate 1200 yr of occupation, from mid-6th to the second half of the 5th millennium BC. Tumuli tombs are commonly dated to EB IV (MB I), without justification. Chalcolithic tumuli were excavated as early as the 1930s (Stekelis 1935), and later near Bab edh Dhra' (Clark 1979), whereas an EB II date was assigned to tumuli in the Negev Highlands (Haiman 1989a,b). ^{14}C dates of the 5th millennium BC were measured from tumuli in W. Zalaqa, Eastern Sinai (Nos. 38–40); dates from Eilat show that this type of burial appeared in the desert during the 6th millennium BC.

Until recently, scholars believed that there was a profound hiatus in settlement in the southern Levant during much of the Late Neolithic (Moore 1973:37–41, 1982:16, 25; Mellaart 1975:67–69), and a severe crisis in settlement at the end of PPNB is still accepted today (Rollefson 1989:169). However, the six excavated Late Neolithic sites in the Eilat area, previously thought to be younger, call this idea into question. This, with the knowledge that younger levels may superimpose Late Neolithic strata, suggests that our understanding of Late Neolithic settlement distribution in the Negev and Sinai may be significantly enriched in the future.

THE CHALCOLITHIC AND EARLY BRONZE AGE – DESCRIPTION OF INVENTORY

Near Eastern archaeology clearly distinguishes the Chalcolithic from the Early Bronze Age. Because it is often difficult to separate these periods in the desert, however, we treat the remains as one unit. The intensive settlement of the Beer Sheva Basin dates to between *ca.* 4500 and 3500 BC (Levy 1986; Weinstein 1984; Gilead 1988). South of Beer Sheva, Chalcolithic sites are few and small,[10] and the general view is that the "Beer Sheva culture" hardly penetrated the Negev Highlands. However, the Negev and Sinai were not at all deserted at this time. Rothenberg (1967, 1969, 1970, 1971, 1973, 1974, 1978, 1979) identified 48 Chalcolithic sites in the southern Negev, with many more in southern and central Sinai, although their identification was later challenged. In the Har Karkom area, several hundred sites were dated to the 4th–3rd millennium BC, which Anati (1986) called the "Bronze Age Complex".

Archaeological remains and ^{14}C dates indicate that many sites in the southern Negev and Sinai belong to the Chalcolithic. In Uvda Valley, dates from Sites 4 and 16 (No. 42, 44, Table 1) and two dates (Nos. 36 and 47) of the 5th–4th millennia BC from the Yotvata Hill are within the Chalcolithic time frame. These samples were taken from an occupation level attached to the core of a rampart previously attributed to an Iron Age fortress (Meshel 1990), but should now be related to an earlier settlement. There are also two large Chalcolithic

Fig. 6. "Leopard drawings" near the Neolithic open sanctuary after being damaged and restored (the small stones denote restoration), from the south, excavated by Yogev and Avner

sites north of Aqaba: Tel Maqus, 3000 m², and Hujeirat el-Ghuzlan, 9000 m² (Khalil 1987; Khouri 1988:130–131).

In W. Zalaqa, eastern Sinai, a complex consisting of a dwelling site, 15 tumuli tombs, 2 open sanctuaries and 2 *Masseboth* shrines was dated to the mid-5th millennium (Nos. 38–40). Many other sites were found in close proximity, including tent camps, stone-built dwellings, and cult and

[10]Sites 25, 90, 147, 272 (Haiman 1986:14); Sites 15, 326, 349 (Lender 1990:xix). Cohen described 16 additional sites (1986:1–13, 199–214), and one other site from the northern Aravah Valley has been published (Beit-Arieh and Gophna 1981). Almost all are temporary campsites with only a few finds (*cf.* Haiman 1989b:178).

Fig. 7. Uvda site 151 (near Ma'ale Shaharut) with circle of *Masseboth,* from the northeast, after restoration

burial sites. Similar sites were found in other parts of the peninsula (Avner 1984). The numerous *Nawamis* tombs and adjacent dwelling sites were dated to the Chalcolithic and EB I (Bar-Yosef *et al.* 1977, 1983, 1986). As mentioned, Rothenberg dated many sites in central and southern Sinai to this period. Ronen (1970), Kozloff (1973), Rothenberg (1979) and Rothenberg and Ordentlich

Fig. 8. Eilat burial site, Tomb V, from the northeast, with *Masseboth* inside and outside the burial cells

(1979) later attributed these dates to two different cultures, the *Eilatian* and *Timnian*, terms recently replaced by *Copper Age, Early, Middle and Late Phases* (Rothenberg 1990a:xiv). A site near Serabit el-Khadim was archaeologically dated by finds to the Chalcolithic (Beit-Arieh 1980), and >50 *desert kites* discovered in eastern Sinai (Meshel 1980; Perevolotsky and Baharav 1987) should generally be attributed to the 5th–3rd millennia BC. Several desert kites were also found in the Eilat area (Meshel 1974; Avner 1987) and a kite near Kibbutz Samar was overlain by a later EB site (Avner 1982c, No. 68, Table 1).

Agriculture, copper production and trade are key cultural characteristics of the Chalcolithic. Adzes, hoes, sickle blades and countless grinding stones testify to the importance of agriculture in the Uvda Valley. Thirty threshing floors were located within an area of 1 km². Excavation of a threshing floor (Fig. 10) demonstrated their emergence and evolutionary development during the 4th millennium BC (Avner 1990b).

Fig. 9. Eilat burial site; the sacred wood remains inside a stone-built installation, from the west

Copper mines and smelting sites in the Feinan area were identified as Chalcolithic (Hauptmann 1989; Hauptmann and Weisberger 1987; Hauptmann, Wiesberger and Bachmann 1989). Although dates from Timna Valley mines and smelting sites are Chalcolithic, they are problematic. In dwelling and industrial Site 39, suitable flint core implements were collected (Bercovici 1978), but the adjacent furnace thought to be Chalcolithic (Rothenberg 1978, 1990a:4–7, 1990b) yielded a very late date: 1945 ± 309 (BM-1116: Burleigh and Hewson 1979:349). Mine G was dated to the Chalcolithic by association with smelting Site F 2 (Conrad and Rothenberg 1980:169–170, 183; Rothenberg 1990a:4–7), but a ^{14}C date of 3030 ± 50 BP was obtained from the latter (BM-1368: Burleigh and Matthews 1982:165). Mine T has been dated archaeologically to the Chalcolithic or EB I (Conrad and Rothenberg 1980:183).

In N. Roded near Eilat, flint-digging tools of the 5th–4th millennia BC were recently found in copper-digging trenches in white sandstone and in nearby dwelling sites (Avner 1993b). Copper production deposits have been found on Yotveta Hill (No. 36, Table 1), and remains from a rich copper industry have been reported from Tel Maqus. A small copper bead found in the Eilat burial site may be the earliest copper object found in Israel, and suggests the possible emergence of metallurgy in the 5th millennium BC (Avner 1990a, 1991). (It has not yet been determined whether the bead was made from native-metallic copper or by smelting. If it was native copper, current hypotheses on the beginning of smelting remain unchanged.) Studies show that, during the

Fig. 10. An aerial photograph of the excavated threshing floor (Uvda 96 III), from the east. The floor was cut into an earlier and larger one by the end of the 4th millennium BC. The smallest circles are granaries; the larger one is a flint workshop.

Chalcolithic and EB I, copper objects and industry remains were almost totally restricted to the Negev, and only during EB II did they become more common in the north (Ilan and Sebbane 1989; Levy and Shalev 1989). Along with the evidence presented here, this implies that the desert population was thoroughly involved in copper mining and production.

EB I sites (3500–3100 BC) (Joffe 1991:185–189) were almost unknown in the Negev and Sinai, but remains have recently been identified, mainly in the Eilat area. Meshel (1990) and Sass excavated a settlement site south of Yotvata, which they dated to this period by pottery and a sherd of an Egyptian alabaster jar. Next to the excavated threshing floor in Uvda Valley was a flint workshop that produced sledge blades, suggesting the invention of the sledge during this period. Another important find from this site was a large, hard limestone tool, which is probably a plow head (Avner 1982d, 1990b). The dating of this rare implement to EB I is based on crescent-shaped arrowheads found with it (*cf.* Rosen 1983b) and concurs with the belief that the plow appeared during the 4th millennium BC (Sherratt 1981). In a rockshelter in Maa'leh Shaharut, east of Uvda Valley, a tomb was excavated whose walls were built by a technique similar to that used for *Nawamis* tombs (Avner 1986). Part of a jug with close parallels to EB I jugs of Bab edh Dhra tombs was found inside (*cf.* Schaub 1981: Fig. 19:3,11). An EB I jar was found in Uvda Valley Site 10 (Eitan 1979), and a larger one with a cup in a rockshelter tomb in Nimra Valley, south of Timna; both date to the very beginning of EB I (Sebbane and Avner 1993). This tomb is probably associated with a nearby copper production site (and mine T in Timna may belong to this period as well; see above). Dates Nos. 48–51 (Table 1) from Uvda sites, along with ones from Dimona (46) and Yotvata Hill (47) are also within this time frame. Rimsherds of an Egyptian jar from a site comprised of a courtyard and rooms, 15 km northwest of Eilat in Sinai, were dated to EB I by R. Amiran (Avner and Naor 1978). In W. Jenah, eastern Sinai, a desert kite was dated to EB I, on the basis of a few dozen crescent-shaped arrowheads (Goren, personal communication).

EB II (3100–2700 BC) (Joffe 1991:253–254) probably was the climax of settlements and copper production among the periods discussed here. *Ca.* 600 EB II sites have been recorded for the Negev; 14 EB II dates were obtained from Uvda Valley (Nos. 52–54, 56–65, Table 1) from 6 sites. Agriculture dominated the economy of Uvda Valley, judging, for example, from the high percentage of sickle blades (*ca.* 10.7%) (Rosen 1983a:138–238), and many of the settlements in the valley were sedentary (Avner 1990b). In southern Sinai, comparatively large villages were inhabited, and a few sites in both southern and northern Sinai were ^{14}C-dated to EB II (Nos. 55, 66, 68; the latter is culturally assigned to the period but the date is EB III).

Copper production intensified during EB II in the Feinan area (Hauptmann 1989; Hauptmann and Weisberger 1987; Hauptmann, Weisberger and Bachmann 1989). Two mining shafts, *ca.* 1 m in diameter, in Timna Valley were ^{14}C-dated to the mid-3rd millennium BC (Nos. 72, 73)(Conrad and Rothenberg 1980:179), suggesting that other shafts of this type are similarly dated. These dates are significant for understanding the history of copper mining.[11]

Another related date from Timna (Site 30) suggests that industrial activity was already taking place during the 3rd millennium BC in smelting camps otherwise dated only to the late 2nd millennium BC. Rothenberg (1978) excavated an EB industrial site outside Timna Valley, and Davis and Avner excavated the remains of a smelting furnace of the mid-3rd millennium on Shehoret Hill, north of Eilat (No. 71, Table 1).[12]

THE CHALCOLITHIC AND EB, A DISCUSSION

EB II was first identified in the early 1970s among the "Chalcolithic" sites in southern Sinai (Amiran, Beit-Arieh and Glass 1973; Beit-Arieh 1974, 1977, 1980, 1981a,b, 1982, 1983, 1984a,b, 1986, 1989). EB II remains were then retrieved from the Chalcolithic stratum of Tel Esdar in the northeastern Negev and in MB I sites in the Negev (Cohen 1978, 1981:ix, 1985:ix, 1986:119, 215). However, the overall distribution of the sites was very limited initially. When additional sites were found near Kadesh Barnea and in Uvda Valley, they were marked as isolated spots on the map and interpreted as road stations connecting the city of Arad with its related settlements in southern Sinai (Cohen 1978, 1985:ix, 1986:277–278; Beit-Arieh and Gophna 1981; Beit-Arieh 1984b).

The full intensity of EB II settlement was first revealed through the emergency survey, when hundreds of sites were dated to this period and many were excavated (Cohen 1986:215–245; Haiman 1986:15–16, 1989a,b, 1991:xix–xx; Rosen 1987b; Lender 1990:xix–xx). A comprehensive settlement model relates the period to the florescence of Arad as the political administrative center, colonizing southern Sinai to monopolize the copper sources of the region (Amiran, Beit-Ariah and Glass 1973; Beit-Arieh 1974, 1981a,b, 1983). Thus, the abandonment of the desert sites at the end of EB II, after 350 yr of prosperity, was related to the fall of Arad (Beit-Arieh 1981b:134, 1983:48; Amiran 1986; Haiman 1986:16; Amiran and Gophna 1989), or to an Egyptian conquest of Sinai

---

[11]The shafts, excavated by stone digging axes, represent one of the early stages in development of mining technology. Similar, but more advanced ones, excavated by hard metal chisels, are termed by Rothenberg "Egyptian", late 2nd millennium BC. However, since the course of development from the earlier to the later shafts is obvious, it seems incorrect to interpret the latter as a result of imported technology. Instead, an indigenous development dependent on available digging implements is more acceptable.

[12]The location of the furnace high on the northern side of the hill was probably an attempt to exploit the prevailing north wind for fanning the forge-fire. Furnace remains are found on almost all hills in the southern Aravah Valley and on several hilltops in the northern Aravah. Although each furnace of this type was related to small-scale activity, the general phenomenon is important in the overall picture of copper production.

(Rothenberg and Ordentlich 1979; Cohen 1986:244). The discovery of an EB III settlement at Tel Ira, in the Beer Sheva Basin, the "southernmost in the country" (Beit-Arieh 1991), emphasizes the emptiness of the Negev and Sinai at that time. EB III (2700–2300 BC) is often considered totally devoid of habitation in the Negev and Sinai.

Scholars have used geographic-social reconstruction to account for exceptional settlement intensity in the desert during a given period. However, a closer look at their models reveals several problematic issues.

Determining the Life Span of Individual Sites. Desert sites are commonly believed to be seasonal and short-lived (Haiman 1986:16, 1989b:185; Beit-Arieh 1982:155, 1986:51). Detailed ^{14}C data sets are necessary to demonstrate the full occupational sequence of a site; as yet, such data exist only for N. Issaron. Nevertheless, the dates available from Uvda Valley point to a much longer period of settlement than previously suspected. From Site 124/IV, 6 dates from a single room (Nos. 56–61, Table 1) range from 3000 to 2600 BC, a span of 400 yr; from Site 9, 6 dates from the 2 upper strata (49–54) range from 3170 to 2700 BC, a span of 470 yr; from Site 16, 3 dates (44, 62, 63) range from 3600 to 2900 BC, a span of 700 yr. The best example is the N. Issaron site with 40 dates, indicating almost a complete sequence of 4500 yr. No occupational gaps could be identified in the sections excavated at these sites; instead, most showed a continuous living level that had undergone some repairs and changes in architecture.

Since these results were unexpected, scholars questioned the reliability of the ^{14}C dates for the sites. They argued that, because wood is well preserved in a desert environment, the wood samples could have been from trees that had died decades before use, and the construction wood could have been used repeatedly. In our opinion, such preservation was rare, because wood is comparatively scarce in the desert and would have been consumed quickly for heating and cooking. Combustible materials were necessary throughout the year, especially during cold winter nights. In addition, most of our charcoal samples from Uvda Valley and other sites in the area were selected from bushes or tree twigs. In any case, an error of a few decades cannot change the overall history, and only large deviations should be suspect. Only two of the results listed here are questionable (Nos. 1 and 15, Table 1; the dates on 5–10 may also have been affected by the presence of bitumen (Goring-Morris, personal communication)). One must not underestimate the reliability of ^{14}C dates as a tool for reconstructing the past. Although the sites were not necessarily inhabited every year during the long periods covered by the date series, their prolonged use over hundreds or thousands of years has great cultural significance.

Dating Negev and Sinai Sites Exclusively to the EB II. Whereas southern Sinai dates are well based on Aradian pottery, Negev Highlands sites are not. The identification of this pottery with EB II is based mainly on holemouth sherds and fan scrapers, even though some finds represent other periods.[13] Uvda Valley EB II dates are also based on the same artifacts (Reich 1990; Goring-Morris and Gopher 1983, 1987; Yogev 1983; Avner 1990b). The first reservations about EB II dating occurred when Dever (1980:3), Cohen and Dever (1981:74) and Cohen (1986:240) suggested continuous occupation from EB II to EB IV in the Negev Highlands. Cohen (1986:244) also suggested that settlement in the Negev Highlands began as early as EB I. However, these ideas were based more on parallelism with the evolution of Arad and Tel Halif than on unequivocal finds. The issue

---

[13]For example, see the identification of flint adzes and axeheads as "EB II" (Haiman 1986, Nos. 127, 134, 172, 383, 384). Others restrict this type to the Chalcolithic (McConaughy 1979:217; Rosen 1984b, 1987a:300).

also arose during the Uvda Valley survey[14] and substantial support for broader dating was provided when Rosen analyzed the flint from the excavated sites. Based on statistical rather than typological criteria, he established three main age groups of flint industry: 1) Chalcolithic and EB I; 2) EB I–III; and 3) EB/MB or MB I (Rosen 1983a:138–143, 206–238).

Sufficient evidence shows that the two principal artifacts used in dating these sites have a longer range than previously thought, and emphasis only on EB II is unjustified. Based on ^{14}C dates, holemouth cooking pots appeared in Uvda Valley as early as 4200 BC (No. 42), and with a lower probability, from 5360 BC (No. 24). Holemouth sherds were found in southern Jordan (Site J 24) with ^{14}C dates of 4650 BC (No. 37) and with 21 similar ^{14}C dates from Jebel Khashem-Tareff sites in Sinai west of Eilat (Henry 1982:443).[15] Typical "EB II" holemouth rim shapes show dates as early as 3600 BC (No. 44, Table 1; Nos. 1, 2, Fig. 11).

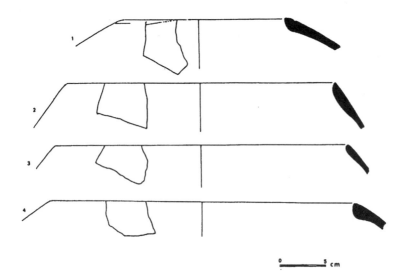

Fig. 11. Holemouth rims from Uvda Valley: Nos. 1, 2 from Site 16; Nos. 3, 4 from Site 166

The same "EB II" rim shapes are found in EB III contexts (Beit Arieh 1991), and even into EB IV, often, but not always, with changes in shape (*e.g.,* Cohen and Dever 1981, Fig. 11). Their petrographic composition and manufacturing techniques, however, continued without change (Porat 1989:180). In Uvda Valley, the same holemouth rims correspond to ^{14}C dates of 2330 and 2080 BC (Nos. 80, 81, Table 1; Nos. 3, 4, Fig. 11)[16] with no sign of later penetration or contamination of the site. Thus, the holemouth jar, as the dominant or only type in desert sites, was in use for more than 2500 yr, and the so-called "EB II" holemouth cooking pot, for nearly 1500 yr. A few Chalcolithic "Beer Sheva", EB "Aradian" or EB IV "Southern family" sherds are sometimes found

[14]At the beginning of the survey, Avner (1979) also dated many sites to EB II, but shortly thereafter, he preferred a general label of "4th–3rd millennia" (Avner 1982a,b, 1990b). This term has been adopted by Reich and Eisenberg, although other excavators still maintain EB II dates. See note 4.

[15]These sites, mentioned by Henry, were excavated by Kozloff (1981). The ^{14}C dates were published by Rothenberg and Glass (1992), after this paper was written. See also the postscript.

[16]Petrographic examination made recently by Y. Goren showed that all four pieces presented in Fig. 11 were made of the same Sinaitic clay with Arkose temper; the full results will be published elsewhere.

in the same levels as younger sherds, indicating that pottery use may extend beyond typological time frames (*cf.* Sebbane *et al.* 1993).

The life span of fan scrapers was even longer. They appeared at the beginning of the Late Neolithic (PNA) (Yeivin and Olami 1979, Fig. 14; Noy 1977, Figs. 7.12, 8.7, 8.8; Garrard *et al.* 1985, Fig. 13a, 1987, Fig. 12c; Betts 1988, Fig. 15.2; McCartney 1992, Figs. 14, 15), and all types known in EB have been found in the Chalcolithic (McConaughy 1979:216; Rosen 1984a, 1986, 1987a, 1989). In conjunction with ^{14}C dates, fan scrapers are found in sites dated to the 5th or even 6th millennium BC, such as the burial site in Eilat, where more than 40 well-shaped examples were dated between 5410 and 4250 BC (Nos. 19–28, Table 1). They are dated to *ca.* 4930 BC (No. 35) in the Risqeh site, east of Aqaba, and to *ca.* 4670 BC (No. 37) in south Jordan Site J 24. Fan scrapers, and flint assemblages in general, continued a Neolithic tradition that prevailed until the end of the 3rd millennium.[17] Only the random presence of core tools in an assemblage can indicate a Chalcolithic time frame, and the rare "Canaanean blades" indicate an EB period.[18]

This description of Uvda Valley sites prompts a re-evaluation of southern Sinai sites. While their coexistence with Arad II–III (3000-2650 BC) is unquestioned, they may have existed earlier and later, for the following reasons:

1. Layers of ash in the rooms penetrated under the walls (Beit-Arieh 1977:9, 50, 83). Similar layers were also found under several Uvda Valley sites, three of which (Sites 4, 7, 9) were ^{14}C-dated to the 6th and 5th millennia BC (Nos. 18, 24, 42). The resemblance between the two is remarkable, and hence the possibility of older living levels in Sinai as well.
2. The ^{14}C date from Sheikh Muhsen (No. 45), the only one from a southern Sinai site, is 500 yr earlier than the establishment of the city of Arad.
3. The fact that holemouth cooking pots from Sinai, the Negev and Arad were all manufactured with the same specially selected Sinaitic clay was considered evidence for the connection between Arad and southern Sinai (Amiran, Beit-Ariah and Glass 1973). However, the same clay had already been used during EB I (Porat 1989:183), suggesting earlier relations and occupation of the southern Sinai before EB II.
4. Several holemouth rim types (Beit-Arieh 1977, Figs. 1.5–6, 5.14, 5.18, 6.7, 6.17–18, 7.7, 7.10–11, 7.19, 7.25; 1986, Figs. 12.5, 12.6) are unparalleled in other stratified EB II sites, and seem to belong to EB III–IV (*cf.* Cohen 1986, Figs. 22, 26, 43, 55, 71; Richard and Boraas 1984, Fig. 18.1–4; Beit-Arieh 1991, Figs. 7.16, 8.5). Another possible sign of later use of the sites is a bronze awl with a circular section from the Nebi Salah site.[19]

---

[17]The flint assemblages from Uvda Valley are very similar to those of Bab edh Dhra, which also demonstrate great continuity from the Chalcolithic to EB. "All of the lithic types found at Bab edh Dhra have Ghassulian antecedents...if they were mixed together one would be hard pressed to separate the Early Bronze tools from Ghassulian forms" (McConaughy 1979:214). Noteworthy are *crescent-shaped* blades, a few hundred of which were found in Uvda Valley, although extremely rare in other sites in the country. One can consider this implement a cultural characteristic unique to Uvda Valley settlements (Avner 1990b).

[18]The disappearance of core tools during the transition from Chalcolithic to EB is interpreted as a result of the introduction of copper (McConaughy 1979:217; Rosen 1984b; Ilan and Sebbane 1989). For the Canaanean sickle blade, see Rosen (1982, 1983c).

[19]Beit-Arieh uses the term, "bronze pick", but he must mean "awl". Round cut awls are known in EB IV sites (*e.g.*, Cohen 1986, Figs. 42.14-16); see also Ilan and Sebbane (1989) for awl typology and chronology. Bronze first appeared in the Levant in EB IV (Eisenberg 1985; Stech, Muhly and Maddin 1985; Merkel and Dever 1989). The possibility of continuation of settlement in southern Sinai after the fall of Arad has been suggested, but on theoretical grounds (Beit-Arieh 1983:48).

These considerations point to a longer duration of southern Sinai sites then previously believed, probably similar to that of Uvda Valley sites. Thirteen ^{14}C dates from our list fall within EB III (Nos. 68–80), indicating that settlement in the Negev and Sinai did not cease with the fall of Arad, that EB III culture in these areas was a direct continuation of the preceding periods, and that it cannot be defined separately. No settlement crisis or gap is apparent during this period.

Attribution of Southern Sinai Sites to Aradian Colonization. The presence of many "Aradian" broad rooms from south Sinai sites led scholars to believe that the architecture and population of this region originated in Arad. However, all characteristics of this type of house had already appeared during the Chalcolithic in the Near East, and only reached their final stage of evolution in the EB II urban culture. Thus, the term "Aradian" may be misleading. A closer look shows that the architecture of south Sinai sites is based on curved lines, which point to local origin. This tradition long preceded the orthogonal rooms (see Fig. 3), existed simultaneously with them (see Fig. 4), and persisted during later periods. Circular architecture is primary and natural for any human society, whereas the orthogonal design results from constraints imposed by transition to large, permanent settlement (Wachman 1959; Flannery 1972). Thus, Beit-Arieh's (1981b, Fig. 3) examples of resemblances between Aradian and south Sinai rooms underscore their differences and highlight the local-indigenous nature of the Sinai sites. Even if there were an "Aradian" influence on southern Sinai architecture, it would not necessarily mean an Aradian population. Similarly, a typical Aradian house, again with rounded corners, excavated in a 3rd millennium site in southern Yemen (di Maigret, Fedele and di Mario 1988) does not imply Aradian colonization in that country.

Identifying Copper Sources as the Incentive for Both Settlement and the Arad–Sinai Connection. The copper source of southern Sinai is considered to be the stimulus for the growth of EB sites and Aradian settlement in the area, but there is no confirming evidence for this. Although copper objects and industrial remains were found in some of the sites, the copper ore of the area is poor compared to that of Arabah Valley and western Sinai. Two veins of copper exist in W. Rimti (in igneous rocks, 4.5 km long and nearly 1 m wide), and a smelting site was found nearby in W. Riqitia. On the basis of chemical analysis, scholars believed these veins were the source of the copper objects (Beit-Arieh 1977:157–172, 1981a:113) but the published data are inconclusive. Of the 61 samples that were analyzed by the Israeli Geological Institute, only 2 contained sufficient proportions of copper (38% and 49%) to have enabled production by smelting; 13 samples showed 1–7%, far less than required; all others showed <1% copper (Bogoch and Zilberfarb 1979). However, the percentage of copper in ore discovered in southern Sinai EB sites is much higher: 22%–67% in 8 of 12 samples, and 7–12% in the remaining 4 (Beit-Arieh 1977:169). These results show that all nodules analyzed from the sites originated from a sandstone deposit, not from magmatic rocks, *i.e.*, from Timna (*cf.* Leese *et al.* 1986:94) or from western Sinai, from which no analysis has been published. A comparison of the chemical analysis of copper objects from the sites with the W. Rimti ores resulting in similar difficulties. Therefore, the copper connection between Arad and southern Sinai is not convincing.

We believe that southern Sinai sites were permanent pastoral-agricultural villages, which explains, for example, why domesticated cereal reached 12% of the pollen profile (Beit-Arieh 1977:148, 1983:46). The population was indigenous, not migrant, and the *raison d'être* of these sites was people, not copper.

EARLY BRONZE IV (MB I, 2300–2000 BC)

While previous theories posited invasions of Amorites or others into the Levant (*e.g.,* Kenyon 1979), recent studies emphasize indigenous processes and cultural continuity during EB IV (Prag

1974; Dever 1980, 1985; Richard 1980, 1987a,b, 1990). *Ca.* 400 sites in the Negev Highlands have been attributed to this period and several have been excavated (Cohen 1986:41–106, 246–313; Cohen and Dever 1981; Haiman 1986, 1989a,b, 1991; Lender 1990). Several hundred additional sites from central and northern Sinai were dated to this period (Rothenberg 1969:38, 1970:22, 1973:32–34, 1979:120; Clamer and Sass 1977; Oren and Yekutieli 1990). Beit-Arieh (1981:134) noted a single EB IV site in southern Sinai, which ostensibly emphasizes the emptiness of that region at the end of the 3rd millennium BC. In light of the discussion above, this site may now be better understood as the only one in southern Sinai where recognizable EB IV sherds have been found. The large number of sites in the Negev Highlands, northern and central Sinai and Uvda Valley stands out against the desolation of EB cities and the shrinking settlements in the fertile land to the north. This is especially so in southern Jordan, where permanent and even fortified settlements were established on the desert fringe during EB IV (Richard 1986, 1987a,b, 1990).

Settlements of the Negev Highlands are varied, ranging from small ephemeral sites to large permanent villages covering up to *ca.* 2 ha. (A similar site discovered in central Sinai has been interpreted as protodynastic Egyptian (Rothenberg 1979:117–119).) The large villages probably served as base camps for the smaller sites (Cohen 1986:255).[20] The material culture is primarily that of sheperds who were also engaged in agriculture and trade. Copper ingot hoards discovered in three Negev sites (Kochavi 1967:108–118; Cohen 1986:295–296), in Lachish and near Dahariah (Dever and Tadmor 1976) suggest extensive trade in copper. This corresponds with the large quantity of copper weapons discovered (mainly in tombs).

Little is known about EB IV copper production in the Feinan areas (Hauptmann and Weisberger 1987; Hauptmann 1989; Hauptmann, Wiesberger and Bachmann 1989) and in Timna Valley (Rothenberg and Shaw 1990). However, because all five copper hoards mentioned above were in the south, we expect that the remains of more intensive mining and metallurgical activity will be found in the future. Lead isotope analysis of one copper ingot from Be'er Resisim suggests Timna or Feinan as the source of the metal and supports this view (Merkel and Dever 1989).[21]

In Uvda Valley, remains of this period were identified in 9 out of 22 excavated habitation sites; all were continuations of earlier occupations (*contra* Beit-Arieh 1989:195), as was the excavated threshing floor (Avner 1982d, 1990b). It is difficult to study the transition from EB I–III to EB IV because recognizable EB IV sherds are usually scarce and sometimes mixed with earlier layers and Aradian sherds.[22] Deterioration in masonry quality may distinguish EB IV from earlier sites, but this criterion alone is not reliable. Although flint assemblages might provide another identification tool, little is known about EB IV flint (Gilead 1973). Fan scrapers do not seem to continue into EB IV (Gilead 1973; Rosen 1983a:141), yet their presence is pronounced in so-called EB IV

---

[20]See Dever (1980) for a different view, that the Negev sites in general served as winter camps for the inhabitants of the southern Judaean Hills who practiced transhumance.

[21]As mentioned above, the early mining shafts of the 3rd millennium were dug by stone digging axes, whereas metal chisels were used during the late 2nd millennium. Digging in sandstone demands a metal resistant to the hardness of the quartz (grade 7 in Mohs' scale) and the first was bronze, which emerged during EB IV (see note 18). It is possible that many of the advanced shafts in Timna and elsewhere had already been dug during this period.

[22]For example, in the southern courtyard of Site 9, within a layer of crushed goat dung mixed with soil, were crescent-shaped EB I arrowheads, along with EB II and EB IV sherds, representing >1000 yr, in a deposit of only 40 cm. The only case of clearly marked stratigraphy between EB IV and the preceding periods was found in Uvda Valley Site 17, excavated by Beit-Arieh (1989:195). There, a typical broad room was overlain by circular courtyards and circular rooms dated to EB IV. However, sites with plans similar to this upper layer are also dated to previous periods, such as Site 16 (Nos. 44, 62, 63, Table 1). Thus, the precise date of construction of the upper layer of Site 17 is still in question. Two unpublished ^{14}C dates on charcoal from Site 17 are earlier than EB IV (Beit-Arieh, personal communication).

central Sinai sites (Kozloff 1973:40; Rothenberg 1974:19).[23] An attempt to distinguish between the flint assemblages in the Uvda sites was based on statistical differentiation, on the general decrease in the quantity of flint, and on associated sherds. However, since no site provided a "clean" EB IV assemblage, no clear separating criteria were discerned; on the contrary, EB IV flint technology continued the traditions of previous periods (Rosen 1983a:138–143). Even more so in Transjordan, where Richard (1980:12, 22, 1987a:38) and Richard and Boraas (1984:83) reported complete continuity in lithic technology from EB III–EB IV.

Continuity was also found in cult and burial sites. In Uvda Valley Site 9, a broad *Massebah* was erected in the early 6th millennium BC (No. 18, Table 1); stratigraphically associated artifacts testify to its continued use into EB IV. No gaps were observed in this section, so one may assume that the site and shrine were in use for 4000 yr. Similarly, three ^{14}C dates (Nos. 19–21) from the open sanctuary, Site 6, point to its origin in the mid-6th millennium, whereas retrieved objects include Chalcolithic, EB and EB IV sherds. Also, tumuli tombs from the Negev Highlands are attributed to both EB II and EB IV (Haiman 1989b).

The ^{14}C dates from EB IV sites do not eliminate the difficulty in distinguishing EB III and IV, since only some correlate well with the period and finds. In W. Mushabi 103 (No. 82, Table 1) a single date concurs with expectations; in Yotvata South, 1 of 2 dates (No. 77) also agrees, as does 1 of 2 dates in Ein Ziq (No. 79). One of 3 dates in Dimona (No. 75) and 1 date from Uvda Site 17 are close to the period (see note 22). In Uvda Valley Site 9, the upper stratum is attributed to EB IV, but 3 dates (Nos. 52–54) are at least 400 yr earlier. From Uvda Valley Site 166, 2 dates (Nos. 80, 81) fall within the period, but the artifacts (fan scrapers, crescent-shaped blades and holemouth sherds) were not diagnostic of EB IV. The limited number of ^{14}C dates, undifferentiated stratigraphy, continuity of holemouth shapes and flint, as well as architecture and installation, reinforce the notion of an undefined transition from EB III to EB IV.

Despite this, we attempt a cautious reconstruction of the transition: fewer sites were inhabited; most square and rectangular rooms were abandoned. Outside contact probably decreased, so that pottery typical of the Negev Highlands, the "southern family", is rare in the southern Negev and almost totally absent in southern Sinai. Flint use decreased, probably due to the increased use of metal and the emergence of bronze. (There is a contradiction between the increased trade in metal and the rarity of the EB IV southern family pottery in the southern Negev and southern Sinai.) The decrease in the percentage of sickle blades may be linked to the decline in agriculture and the increased importance of grazing. Such changes are compatable with socio-economic changes in other parts of the country. However, the overall picture of settlement and continuity is remarkable in comparison with the general decline that overtook the fertile country to the north. Climate fluctuation could be one cause for these changes.

Here, at *ca.* 2000 BC, we conclude the description of the settlement sequence in the desert, but note that archaeological remains and ^{14}C dates show continuous occupational sequences up to modern times. The Middle and Late Bronze Ages, generally considered to be absent in the Negev, are covered by 18 dates from the southern Negev, and the first millennium BC is represented by 15 dates, many of them from the 10th–9th centuries BC (see Scharpenseel, Pietig and Schiffmann 1976; Burleigh and Hewson 1979; Burleigh and Matthews 1982; Conrad and Rothenberg 1980; Rothenberg 1990a; Carmi 1987; Carmi and Segal 1992). Evidence from MB II is limited, but the

---

[23]Surface collection only was done at these sites and the possibility that they were settled during more then one period was not considered by Kozloff and Rothenberg.

remains from the Late Bronze and Iron Age are numerous, primarily around copper production sites. Only a few ^{14}C dates in the range of 500 BC to AD 500 exist, but the interval has yielded archaeological remains and historical sources. For the last 10,000 yr, there are no missing links in human cultural remains from the area.

THE PALEOCLIMATE OF THE DESERT

Traditionally, most scholars assumed that climate·did not change significantly in the desert and that change in settlement systems was anthropogenically induced (Albright 1951:250–252; Reifenberg 1955:22–23; Glueck 1968:7–12, 209–210; 1970:33–44, 184; *cf.* Finkelstein and Perevolotsky 1990: 80). However, current research implicates climate change as a possible cause for changing settlement patterns (*e.g.*, Issar 1990). (We report paleoclimatic data as cal BC instead of BP.)

The climate between the PPNB and Chalcolithic periods is generally considered to have been more humid than today. Oxygen isotopes from Mediterranean sediments near the Israeli coast show ^{18}O depletion from the 8th to the end of 6th millennia and *ca.* 4000 BC. This indicates lower air temperature and/or more contribution of freshwater from rain and rivers. The Red Sea also contributed a considerable amount of freshwater *ca.* 7000 BC (Luz 1982). Analyses of oxygen isotopes and amino acids of land snails show ^{18}O depletion from 8000–2000 BC. The inference is that the isohyets of 240–280 mm were *ca.* 30 km south of their present location, and the northern Negev received double the present-day annual precipitation. Increased ^{18}O after 1800 BC implies desiccation to present conditions (Goodfriend 1988, 1991; Goodfriend, Magaritz and Carmi 1986). Vegetation of a wetter climate is indicated by pollen from PPNB site, D.1, and Chalcolithic sites, D.60, D.62, in the Negev Highlands where arboreal pollen registered *ca.* 8% and 3%, respectively, and included olive, oak, pine, almond and juniper, all absent from contemporary pollen samples (Horowitz 1976:66, 1979:248). A study of Chalcolithic alluvial terraces in southern Shefelah, northern Negev and western Sinai demonstrates sedimentation processes indicative of moisture. However, erosion throughout most of the Holocene signifies aridity (Goldberg and Bar-Yosef 1982; Goldberg 1986; A. Rosen 1986), contrary to most studies from other fields.

Early studies on sea-level fluctuations showed that the Dead Sea was much higher from 8500–5000 and 2500–1500 BC than today (Neev and Hall 1977). More recently, Frumkin *et al.* (1991) found that the Dead Sea was at a higher level until 5500 BC and from 4000–2500 BC, with a maximum of 120 m higher than today. The level was relatively low at *ca.* 5500–5000 and 2300–1500 BC.

Weathering patterns on endolithic lichens on rocks at ancient sites show that species of a wetter climate lived in the Negev from the 8th–5th millennia BC, and are absent from Chalcolithic and later sites. Unlike other studies, this evidence implies an unchanging climate from the 4th millennium to the present (Danin 1985).

A faunal study of various sites also shows a more humid period between the 8th and 3rd millennia BC (Davis 1982). In Sinai, most of the desert kites of the 5th–3rd millennia BC are from areas with almost no vegetation today. However, they were built originally in areas of rich vegetation where gazelle grazed (Perevolotsky and Baharav 1987). A desert kite from W. Jenah, eastern Sinai, dated by crescent-shaped arrowheads to the second half of the 4th millennium BC, revealed the bones of wild ass, which indicates steppic vegetation richer than at present (Goren and Tchernov, personsal communication).

From the southern Negev, 23 out of 25 charcoal samples from hearths surrounding the 6th–5th millennia BC tombs of Eilat were tamarisk, which is not native today near the site, and 2 were acacia, almost the only tree species currently growing in the area. The sacred wood found at this site was juniper, which also does not grow in the region today, but could have been brought from the Edom Mountains. Sixteen charcoal samples were examined from 4th–3rd millennia BC Uvda Valley sites, including acacia, tamarisk, persian haloxylon and desert broom, members of typical desert species present today. However, one sample from Site 17 was pistacia (*P. khinjuk*).[24] In general, the vegetation profile from the southern Negev during the 6th–3rd millennia BC was still desertic, but with indications of conditions somewhat better than today's.

Because the data from the Negev and Sinai are limited, it is useful to briefly survey some paleo-climatic studies from neighboring deserts. These do not necessarily correlate directly with the Negev and Sinai data, although similarities cannot be ignored. In the Rub al Khali, a sterile sand desert in modern Saudi Arabia, are relics of fossil lakes. ^{14}C-dated organic sediments and shells from these fossil lakes show flooding between the 8th and 6th millennia BC (McClure 1976). Hunting, grazing and agriculture were practiced at the Neolithic sites surrounding the lakes, and bones including those of wild cows, ostriches, antelopes provide evidence of savannah vegetation (Zarins *et al.* 1980:19–21; Zarins, Murad and Al-Yish 1981:20; Edens 1982). These and other "Neolithic" sites throughout the peninsula existed until the end of the 3rd millenniun BC.[25] Further evidence of a wetter climate during the 8th–5th millennia BC derives from dating alluvial terraces of W. Dawasir, central Arabia, from swamp sediments in Jubba and W. Lahi and travertine sediments in Ein Qanas in the El Hesa oasis (Oates 1982; Garrard, Harvey and Switsur 1981). In the southern Tihama plain, a *sabkha* (playa) existed during the 5th–3rd millennia BC with Neolithic sites nearby (Zarins and Al-Badr 1986). Penetration of the Ubaid culture into the eastern Arabian Peninsula also points to a better climate during the mid-5th to mid-4th millennia BC (Zarins, Rahbini and Kamal 1982; Oates 1982). (On ^{14}C-dating of the Ubaid culture, see Akkermans (1988).)

In the Persian Gulf, argonitic mud and clay sediments resulting from pluvial conditions are dated *ca.* 7000 BC, and microfaunal remains in these sediments suggest decreased salinity and increased freshwater (Luz 1982). In Abu Dhabi and Qatar, a series of Persian Gulf rises of 2.5 m were dated between 5900 and 2400 BC, and attributed to increased affluence of the Euphrates and Tigris Rivers (Al Asfour 1978; Wilkinson 1978; Luz 1982). (The rise of the Gulf's level could also have been affected by a global rise in sea level, as measured elsewhere (Zarins and Al-Badr 1986). This may have been caused by a global increase in temperature and melting ice at the poles.) The Tigris and Euphrates also caused floods and clay sedimentation during the 4th to 3rd millennia BC, which affected the lower Euphrates Valley (Mallowan 1964; Raikes 1966).

In upper Egypt, playa lakes existed from the end of the 8th to the end of the 6th millennia, with some decrease in their water levels between 6500 and 6000 BC (Roberts 1982). An interdisciplinary study based on geomorphology, floral, faunal and archaeological remains, and 43 ^{14}C dates in the Gilf Kebir Plateau, shows that this region was extremely arid only between 10,500 and 5000 BC. From 5000–4000 BC, conditions were semi-arid and lake levels were at their highest; flora and fauna were richer and Neolithic settlement existed in an area that is totally uninhabited today. Shortly after 4000 BC, the sand dune that dammed the lake in W. el Akhdar was breached, the lake ceased to exist, but settlement of the plateau continued until *ca.* 2500 BC (Kropelin 1987). In the Nile Delta, two episodes of decreased sedimentation were detected at *ca.* 6300 and 5400 BC;

---

[24]Charcoal analyses from Uvda and Eilat were made by E. Verker and U. Baruch (unpublished), whom we thank for permission to report their data. The sample from Uvda Site 17 was identified by N. Liphschitz (1986:87).
[25]Vast information on the Neolithic of the Arabian Peninsula can be found in *Atlal: The Journal of Saudi Arabian Archaeology* 1978–1988. Because of space limitations, these data are not presented here in detail.

however, red paleosol developed during this interval, testifying to increased rainfall in lower Egypt (Butzer 1975).

Throughout the Sahara, many Neolithic sites are dated between the 8th and the end of the 3rd millennia BC, with a climax of settlement during the 4th millennium BC. Pollen studies in the ancient sites of the Hoggar Highlands, central Sahara, an extremely arid area today, show rich Mediterranean and tropical vegetation *ca.* 6000–2300 BC (Hays 1975; Camps 1975; Aliman 1982). Pollen studies from fossil lakes in the Sudan desert show a 500-km northward shift of the monsoonal belt relative to its present location *ca.* 10,000–3000 BC (Ritchie and Haynes 1987). Another study shows that the Sahara lakes, as well as others in the northern hemisphere desert belt, reached their peak between 10,000 and 5000 BC, correlating to the Milankovitch fluctuation of sun radiation (Kutzbach and Street-Perrott 1985).

Virtually no evidence exists for wetter climate during the 3rd millennium BC; desiccation was probably gradual. The Dead Sea level fell and reached its lowest point at *ca.* 2300 BC (Frumkin *et al.* 1991); an excavation in Tel Aviv revealed sand overlying EB deposits (Ritter-Kaplan 1984). A concurrent decline in Nile sedimentation was also detected (Butzer 1975); in the northern Near East, lake levels fell (Roberts 1982). More signs of desiccation are found both in and beyond the Near East (Crown 1972). Toward the end of the 3rd millennium BC, centralized regimes and urban systems collapsed throughout most of the region (Bell 1971; Richard 1980, 1987a,b; Dever 1985). Cultural behavior also changed in the Sahara desert (Hays 1975; Camps 1975; Aliman 1982) and the Arabian Peninsula (Zarins *et al.* 1980:20–23), where "Neolithic" agricultural cultures were replaced by more nomadic ones.

Signs of a wetter climate soon reappeared. Sweetwater swamps developed in Israel's coastal plain and in the Jordan Valley (Neev 1980); upper Egypt lakes experienced a new pluvial stage (Roberts 1982), and in Qatar, the Persian Gulf rose at *ca.* 2350 BC (Al Asfour 1978). These data may attest a severe but short climatic crisis toward the end of the 3rd millennium BC.

Correlation between the studies' results is not absolute, but the general trend seems clear (*cf.* Goldberg and Rosen 1987): between 8000 and *ca.* 3000 BC, the Negev, Sinai and neighboring deserts experienced higher precipitation than today. The period between 6000–4300 BC was somewhat drier but still wetter than at present. One explanation is a northward shift of the monsoonal belt during the Neolithic and Chalcolithic (Gat and Magaritz 1980; Roberts 1982; Kutzbach and Street-Perrott 1985; Goldberg and Rosen 1987; Goodfriend 1991). If this is the case, a single summer rain could greatly alter the region's carrying capacity, and any minor change in the precipitation/evaporation rate would affect the living conditions in the Negev and Sinai. Thus, in general, there seems to be no climatic cause for significant gaps in settlement patterns. It should also be noted that Bedouins living in the southern Negev until the mid-20th century carried on fairly extensive agriculture, although less sophisticated and productive than in earlier periods (Avner 1990b).

CONCLUSIONS

From the data outlined above, we draw these general conclusions:

1. Despite the environmental conditions of the area, and previous beliefs, there were no gaps in settlement in the southern Negev from the Neolithic to EB IV (and beyond) but rather a complete occupational sequence. There is no evidence of any significant immigration to the area. Physio-anthropological research indicates that the desert population remained indigenous

and homogenous from the Neolithic to the end of EB IV (Arensburg 1973; Hershkovitz *et al.* 1987; Arensburg and Hershkovitz in Bar-Yosef and Alon 1988; Smith 1989).

To date, the complete settlement sequence derives mainly from the southern Negev, but with ongoing research, gaps in other desert areas may be eliminated as well. Also to be considered is the possibility that during these periods the southern Negev enjoyed monsoonal trajectories that increased the carrying capacity of the area. This might explain, for example, why the settlement density in Uvda Valley was higher than in the Negev Highlands.

2. ^{14}C is a reliable and vital method for dating desert sites, specifically when material remains are insufficient or represent a broad time span. Desert settlement in the periods parallel to Late Neolithic, Chalcolithic, EB I and EB III were determined by ^{14}C dates rather than by recognized artifacts. Discrepancies emerged between settlement patterns based on archaeological surveys and excavations, and those based on ^{14}C dating. One may conclude that survey results should be used cautiously and need to be supported by meticulous excavations and detailed series of ^{14}C dates before they are used for reconstruction of the past. Various models offered to explain the "ups and downs" in desert settlement history should be repudiated, and before further models are presented a vast amount of fieldwork is still necessary.

3. ^{14}C dating revealed that the life spans of habitation, cult and burial sites in the desert were often far longer than expected by hundreds or even thousands of years.

4. Since the desert was less affected by military and political events, cultural changes occurred in different ways and with different rhythms than in the fertile country. Thus, it is difficult to apply to the desert the chronological framework commonly used in archaeology of the Near East. Attempts have already been made to construct a separate chronology for the desert (Ronen 1970; Kozloff 1973; Rothenberg 1979 *etc.*; Anati 1986), but as yet they are insufficient. At this stage, it is more correct to use unspecified terms such as "4th–3rd millennia". In the future, a more accurate dating of processes and innovations, and a better definition of cultures and subcultures, will be possible.

5. In spite of the limited knowledge at hand, it is still worthwhile to offer a general guideline of cultural evolution in the desert as a base for future amendment. A tentative reconstruction is as follows:

During the 8th–7th millennia BC, PPNB culture covered the entire desert zone of the Near East, though low in density. Most sites of this culture were suited for one extended family, characterized by a concentrated "beehive" pattern of circular rooms, void of large built courtyards. In some locations, especially on the desert fringe where environmental conditions permitted, large villages developed, such as Beida, Basta and 'Ain Ghazel. The economy of the desert population was based on hunting and gathering, with intensive collection of wild cereals. This population maintained a wandering cycle of *ca.* 6 months, following animal and vegetational food resources, and returning to their dwellings seasonally. People of the Arabah Valley and southern Negev also traded in copper ore used for artistic and cosmetic purposes, and in sea shells; those living in western Sinai traded in turquoise as well.[26]

During the 6th (or even 7th) millennium BC, goat and sheep grazing emerged in the desert, and with it "courtyard sites", corrals, tent camps and fan scrapers. Agriculture was introduced

---

[26]For artistic use of copper ore and trade in Red Sea shells, see Bar-Yosef and Alon (1988). For the occurrence of turquoise, see Goring-Morris and Gopher (1983:156).

during the 6th–5th millenna BC, linked to the appearance of holemouth vessels. From this period on, pastoral, semi-nomadic societies, not fully nomadic,[27] populated the desert, combining herding and crop agriculture. The relative importance of each differed from place to place, and this is probably the stage at which the desert population began to diverge into a number of societies or subcultures (Ronen 1970; Kozloff 1973; Beit-Arieh 1986). In some areas, such as Uvda Valley and southern Sinai, where the environment permitted emphasis on agriculture, permanent settlement evolved and a rural culture developed.

An important role should also be attributed to the "secondary product revolution" of the 4th millennium BC that witnessed the introduction of the use of wool, the processing of milk into preservable products, the harnessing of animals for transport and draft and the invention of the plough (Sherrat 1981). To these we can now add the appearance of the circular threshing floor and sledge (Avner 1990b). Agriculture probably grew progressively important with developing technology, and the creation of a "law of living" compatible with life in the desert. This process reached its zenith in the 3rd millennium BC, resulting in a dramatic expansion of the desert population. In Uvda Valley, for example, within an area of 40 km^2 the number of habitation sites increased from only 3 in the PPNB to >150 during the 5th–3rd millennium BC.[28]

Copper mining and production were other innovations of the 4th, or even 5th millennium BC. The desert population, previously well-acquainted with sources of copper ore, became expert in exploration, mining and smelting, and benefited from the commercial value of the metal.

These technological and cultural advances, shared by the entire Near East, encouraged population growth and paved the way for the next stage, the emergence of urbanism. Arad was in the southernmost environmental boundary that still permitted the evolution of the EB I village to an EB II town, whereas the desert areas to the south only permitted organization of a smaller-scale social framework. Hence, the population climax in the desert during the 3rd millennium is best understood as an indigenous process. In this light, it is no longer necessary to attribute the EB desert settlement to the rise of Arad (Haiman 1989a:28–30), to assign the population of Sinai as migrants from Arad (Amiran *et al.* 1973; Beit-Arieh 1974, 1981a,b; 1983), the Arad and the Negev Highlands population as migrants from Sinai (Govrin 1990), or the population of Sinai as migrants from Arabia (Beit-Arieh 1986:52).

It is interesting to note that the EB settlement climax coincided with a period of gradual desiccation. Probably, previous cultural development enabled the desert population to find appropriate solutions for the difficulties of living. The climatic crisis of the late 3rd millennium could not be overcome without changes in mode of life, and it primarily influenced the agricultural settlements.

Since the crisis was short, the desert population revived and evolved into the EB IV culture, continuing to emphasize grazing, but also incorporating agriculture, trade and industry. This may explain the continuity from "EB I–III" to "EB IV".

Material remains from the desert cannot be fully appreciated without considering spiritual culture, since cult sites in the desert are numerous and indicative of a well-established region.

---

[27]Semi-nomadism, or "enclosed nomadism" (Rowton 1974) clearly differs economically, culturally and technologically from true nomadism. In the Near East, true nomadism could not appear before the domestication of the camel at the end of the 2nd millennium BC and even then it is doubtful whether it was ever practiced here. For a full account, see Khazanov (1984).
[28]Because of the geomorphological situation of N. Issaron Site Stratum C, it is possible that only parts of the PPNB sites could be detected. Even so, the increase in number of sites remains dramatic.

Masseboth shrines had already appeared in the desert during the Natufian culture, and they became abundant from the 5th millennium BC on. However, in the fertile zones they became an integral part of the cult practice only from the 2nd millennium, with an affinity for the characteristics of desert shrines. Open sanctuaries, also abundant in the desert, first appeared in the 6th millennium BC and their essential concepts were adopted in the 4th–3rd millennia BC sanctuaries of the fertile country. An especially rich spiritual world comes to light through the burial sites. We shall only note the occurrence of tumuli tombs as early as the 6th millennium BC and the sacred wood, *Asherah,* the earliest example in the Near East. Although inferior in material culture, the desert population influenced the spiritual culture of the fertile countries.

Altogether, the desert population was an indigenous society that developed and retained its own culture, and retained continuity in material and spiritual culture for several millennia. The many remains in the desert are not those of "nomads who do not leave remains", who "left behind only devastation", and there is no reason why they should "escape the archaeologists' eye".

POSTSCRIPT

Following delivery of this paper, several related articles were published. One with similar intent is by Rothenberg and Glass (1992), with Kozloff's ^{14}C dates from Khashem-Tareff and Thamed. Although we agree with their basic conclusions of the indigenous nature of the desert population and cultural process, their "database" and chronological sequence need serious criticism. This will be addressed in Ilan *et al.* (in press). In addition, many new ^{14}C dates were received from sites in the Sinai and the Negev, and they fully confirm the above discussion and conclusions.

ACKNOWLEDGMENTS

We thank Amir Drori, Director of the Israel Antiquities Authority for permission to publish this material. We are grateful to our friends and colleagues who read the draft and offered valuable comments: Rudolph Cohen, Avi Gopher, Nigel Goring-Morris, David Ilan, Alex Joffe, Steve Rosen and Michael Sebbane. The dates from Pretoria were provided by J. Vogel through the efforts of O. Bar-Yosef, for which we thank both. We also thank R. Cohen, D. Nahlieli and Z. Meshel for their permission to publish the dates from Ein Ziq, Dimona and Yotvata, respectively. We thank R. Cohen and M. Sebbane for their advice on dating holemouth rim shape pottery, and Rina Avner for assisting in the preparation of this paper.

REFERENCES

Akkermans, P. M. M. G.
    1988   An updated chronology for the northern Ubaid and Late Chalcolithic periods in Syria: New evidence from Tell Hammam et-Turkman. *Iraq* 50:109–144.
Al Asfour, T.
    1978   The marine terraces of the Bay of Kuwait. In *The Environmental History of the Near and Middle East Since the Last Ice Age,* edited by W. C. Brice, pp. 245–254. Academic Press, London, New York.
Albright, W. F.
    1951   *The Archaeology of Palestine.* Penguin Books, Ltd., Harmondsworth, Middlesex.
Aliman, M. H.
    1982   Le Sahara: Grande zone désertique Nord-Africaine. In *The Geological Story of the World's Desert, Striae 17,* edited by T. L. Smiley, pp. 35–51. Societas Upsaliensis pro Geologia Quaternaria, Uppsala.
Amiran, R.
    1986   The fall of the Early Bronze Age city of Arad. *Israel Exploration Journal* 36:74–76.

Amiran, R., I. Beit-Arieh and J. Glass
    1973   The interrelationship between Arad and sites in southern Sinai in the Early Bronze Age II. *Israel Exploration Journal* 23:193-197.

Amiran, R. and R. Gophna
    1989   Urban Canaan in the Early Bronze II and III periods – Emergence and structure. In *L'Urbanisation de la Palestine à l'Age du Bronze Ancien,* edited by P. de Miroschedji, pp. 109-116. BAR International Series 527, British Archaeological Reports, Oxford.

Anati, E.
    1986   *Har Karkom, the Mountain of God.* Rizzoli, New York.

Arensburg, B.
    1973   The People in the Land of Israel from the Epipaleolithic to Present Times. Ph. D. Dissertation, Tel Aviv University.

Avner, U.
    1979   A survey in the Uvda Valley. *Hadashot Archeologiot* 69–71:1-2 (in Hebrew).
    1982a   Biq'at 'Uvda survey. *Excavations and Surveys in Israel* 1:79-81.
    1982b   Survey of Biq'at 'Uvda–Eilat Road. *Excavations and Surveys in Israel* 1:81-82.
    1982c   Excavation of a desert kite near Kibbutz Samar. *Excavations and Surveys in Israel* 1:103-104.
    1982d   Excavation of a threshing floor in Biq'at 'Uvda. *Excavations and Surveys in Israel* 1:80-81.
    1983   Excavation of cult sites in Biq'at 'Uvda. *Excavations and Surveys in Israel* 2:14-15.
    1984   Ancient cult sites in the Negev and Sinai Deserts. *Tel Aviv* 11:115-131.
    1986   Excavation of tombs in a rock shelter near Ma'ale Shaharut. *Excavations and Surveys in Israel* 5:62-63.
    1987   Desert kites. In *The Gazelles in Israel,* edited by B. Shalmon, pp. 20-27. The Society for the Protection of Nature, Tel Aviv (in Hebrew).
    1989a   Ma'ale Shaharut, survey. *Excavations and Surveys in Israel* 7/8:114-116.
    1989b   Mispe Sayyarim Area, Survey. *Excavations and Surveys in Israel* 7/8:134-135.
    1990a   Excavation of Tumuli in Eilat. *Excavations and Surveys in Israel* 9:76-78.
    1990b   Ancient agricultural settlement and religion in the Uvda Valley in southern Israel. *Biblical Archaeologist* 53:125-141.
    1991   A note on Late Neolithic burial site in Eilat. *American Journal of Archaeology* 95:496-497.
    1993a   Masseboth sites in the Negev and their significance. In *Biblical Archaeology Today, 1990, Proceedings of the Second International Congress on Biblical Archaeology,* edited by J. Aviram, pp. 166-181. Israel Exploration Society, Jerusalem.
    1993b   A Survey in Nahal Roded. *Hadashot Archeologiot* 99:98.

Avner, U. and A. Naor
    1978   A survey in the Eilat area. *Hadashot Archeologiot* 67/68:66-68 (in Hebrew).

Avni, G.
    1992   *Archaeological Survey of Israel: Map of Har Saggi Northeast* (225). Israel Antiquities Authority, Jerusalem.

Baird, D., A. Garrard, L. Martin and K. Wright
    1992   Prehistoric environment and settlement in the Azraq Basin: An interim report on the 1989 excavation season. *Levant* 24:1-30.

Baron, A.
    1981   Adaptive strategies in the archaeology of the Negev. *Bulletin of the American Schools of Oriental Research* 242:51-81.

Bar-Yosef, O.
    1981a   The "Pre-Pottery Neolithic" period in the southern Levant. In *Préhistoire du Levant,* edited by J. Cauvin and P. Sanlaville, pp. 555-569. Editions du Centre National de la Recherche Scientifique, Paris.
    1981b   Pre-Pottery Neolithic sites in southern Sinai. *Biblical Archaeologist* 45:9-12.
    1984   Seasonality among Neolithic hunter-gatherers in southern Sinai. In *Animals and Archaeology,* Vol. 3, *Early Herders and Their Flocks,* edited by J. Clutton-Brock and C. Grigson, pp. 145-160. BAR International Series 202, British Archaeological Reports, Oxford.
    1987a   The prehistory of the Sinai Peninsula. In *Sinai,* Project of the Advancement of Knowledge of Eretz Israel, Tel Aviv University, edited by G. Gvirtzman, A. Shmueli, Y. Gradus, I. Beit-Arieh and M. Har-El, pp. 559-578. Ministry of Defense, Tel Aviv (in Hebrew).
    1987b   The origin and emergence of pastoral societies in the Levant. In *Israel, Land and People,* Vol. 4, edited by R. Ze'evi, pp. 85-99. Ha'aretz Museum, Tel Aviv (in Hebrew).
    1989   The PPNA in the Levant – An overview. *Paléorient* 15:57-63.

Bar-Yosef, O., A. Belfer-Cohen, A. Goren, I. Hershkovitz, O. Ilan, H. K. Mienis and B. Sass
1986   Nawamis and habitation sites near Gebel Gunna, southern Sinai. *Israel Exploration Journal* 36:121–167.
Bar-Yosef, O., A. Belfer, A. Goren and P. Smith
1977   The Nawamis near 'Ein Huderah (eastern Sinai). *Israel Exploration Journal* 27:65–88.
Bar-Yosef, O. and A. Gopher
1982   Nahal Lavan 104, a PPNB site. *Mitskutat Haeven, Journal of the Israel Prehistoric Society* 17:71–78 (in Hebrew).
Bar-Yosef, O., I. Hershkovitz, G. Arbel and A. Goren
1983   The orientation of Nawamis entrances in southern Sinai: Expressions of religious belief and seasonality? *Tel Aviv* 10:52–60.
Becker, C.
1991   Faunal remains. *Annual of the Department of Antiquities of Jordan* 35:29–32.
Beit-Arieh, I.
1974   An Early Bronze Age II site at Nabi Salah in southern Sinai. *Tel Aviv* 1:144–156.
1977   South Sinai in the Early Bronze Age. Ph.D. Dissertation, Tel Aviv University (in Hebrew, English summary).
1980   A Chalcolithic site near Serabit El-Khadim. *Tel Aviv* 7:45–64.
1981a   An Early Bronze Age II site near Sheikh 'Awad in southern Sinai. *Tel Aviv* 8:95–127.
1981b   A pattern of settlement in southern Sinai and southern Canaan in the third millennium B.C. *Bulletin of the American Schools of Oriental Research* 243:31–55.
1982   An Early Bronze Age II site near the Feiran Oasis in southern Sinai. *Tel Aviv* 9:146–156.
1983   Central southern Sinai in the Early Bronze Age II and its relations with Palestine. *Levant* 16:39–48.
1984a   Fifteen years in Sinai. *Biblical Archaeology Review* 10:26–54.
1984b   New evidence of the relations between Canaan and Egypt during the Proto-Dynastic period. *Israel Exploration Journal* 34:20–23.
1986   Two cultures in southern Sinai in the third millennium B.C. *Bulletin of the American Schools of Oriental Research* 263:27–54.
1989   The Early Bronze Age pattern of settlement in the Sinai. In *L'Urbanisation de la Palestine à l'Age du Bronze Ancien,* edited by P. de Miroschedji, pp. 189–197. BAR International Series 527, British Archaeological Reports, Oxford.
1991   An Early Bronze Age III settlement at Tel 'Ira in the northern Negev. *Israel Exploration Journal* 41:1–18.
Beit-Arieh, I. and R. Gophna
1981   The Early Bronze Age II settlement at 'Ain El-Qudeirat (1980–1981). *Tel Aviv* 8:128–135.
Bell, B.
1971   The Dark Ages in ancient history. *American Journal of Archaeology* 75:1–75.
Bercovici, A.
1978   Flint implements from Timna Site 39. In *Chalcolithic Copper Smelting, Archaeo-Metallurgy 1,* edited by B. Rothenberg, R. F. Tylecote and P. J. Boydell, pp. 16–20. Institute for Archaeo-Metallurgical Studies, London.
Betts, A.
1982   Prehistoric sites at Qa'a Mejalla, Eastern Jordan. *Levant* 14:1–34.
1983   Black Desert survey, Jordan: First preliminary report. *Levant* 15:1–10.
1984a   Black Desert survey, Jordan: Second preliminary report. *Levant* 16:25–34.
1984b   Black Desert survey, 1983. *Palestine Exploration Quarterly* 116:78.
1985   Black Desert survey, Jordan: Third preliminary report. *Levant* 17:29–52.
1988   1986 excavations at Dhuweila, eastern Jordan: A preliminary report. *Levant* 20:7–21.
Bogoch, R. and A. Zilberfarb
1979   Re-evaluation of the Wadi Rimthi copper prospect. Geological Survey of Israel Report No. M.P.B.K. 417/79 (unpublished), Jerusalem.
Burian, F., E. Friedman and E. Mintz
1976   An Early PPNB site in Nahal Lavan region – Site No. 109. *Mitekufat Haeven, Journal of the Israel Prehistoric Society* 40:50–60 (in Hebrew).
Burleigh, R. and A. Hewson
1979   British Museum natural radiocarbon measurements XI. *Radiocarbon* 21(3):349.
Burleigh, R. and K. Matthews
1982   British Museum natural radiocarbon measurements XIII. *Radiocarbon* 24(2):165.
Butzer, K. W.
1975   Patterns of environmental change in the Near East during Late Pleistocene and Early Holocene time. In *Problems in Prehistory: North Africa and the Levant,* edited by F. Wendorf and A. Marks, pp. 389–410. Southern Methodist University Press, Dallas.

Camps, C.
1975   The prehistoric cultures of North Africa radiocarbon chronology. In *Problems in Prehistory: North Africa and the Levant,* edited by F. Wendorf and A. Marks, pp. 181–204. Southern Methodist University Press, Dallas.

Carmi, I.
1987   Rehovot radiocarbon measurements III. *Radiocarbon* 29(1):100–114.

Carmi, I. and D. Segal
1992   Rehovot radiocarbon measurements IV. *Radiocarbon* 34(1):115–132.

Carmi, I., Z. Sirkes and M. Magaritz
1984   Radiocarbon – A direct calculation of the period of the grand trend. *Radiocarbon* 26(1):149–151.

Clamer, C. and B. Sass
1977   Middle Bronze I. In *Prehistoric Investigations in Gebel Maghara, Northern Sinai,* edited by O. Bar-Yosef and J. L. Phillips, pp. 245–264. Qedem 7, Hebrew University, Jerusalem.

Clark, V.
1979   Investigations in a prehistoric necropolis near Bab Edh-Dhra'. *Annual of the Department of Antiquities of Jordan* 23:57–77.

Cohen, R.
1978   Tel Esdar, Stratum IV. *Israel Exploration Journal* 28:185–189.
1981   *Archaeological Survey of Israel: Map of Sede Boqer–East* (168). Archaeological Survey of Israel, Jerusalem (in Hebrew).
1985   *Archaeological Survey of Israel: Map of Sede Boqer–West* (167). Archaeological Survey of Israel, Jerusalem (in Hebrew).
1986   The Settlement of the Central Negev in the Light of Archaeology and Literary Sources During the 4th–1st Millennia BCE. Ph.D. Dissertation, Hebrew University, Jerusalem (in Hebrew, English summary).
1988   Settlement in the Negev Highlands from the Fourth Millennium BCE to the Fourth Century BCE. *Qadmoniot* 22:62–81 (in Hebrew).
        Negev Rescue Survey 1978–1988. *Biblical Archaeologist,* in press.

Cohen, R. and W. G. Dever
1981   Preliminary report of the third of final season of the "Central Negev Highlands Project". *Bulletin of the American Schools of Oriental Research* 243:57–77.

Conrad, H. G. and B. Rothenberg
1980   *Antikes Kupfer im Timna-Tal.* Laupenmuhlen Druck, Bochum, Germany.

Cribb, R.
1991   *Nomads in Archaeology.* Cambridge University Press, Cambridge.

Crown, A. D.
1972   Toward a reconstruction of the climate of Palestine 8000–0 B.C. *Journal of Near Eastern Studies* 31:312–330.

Danin, A.
1985   Palaeoclimates in Israel: Evidence from weathering patterns of stones in and near archaeological sites. *Bulletin of the American Schools of Oriental Research* 259:33–43.

Davis, S. J. M.
1982   Climatic change and the advent of domestication: The succession of ruminant artiodactyls in the Late Pleistocene-Holocene in the Israel region. *Paléorient* 8:5–15.

Dayan, T., E. Tchernov, O. Bar-Yosef and Y. Yom-Tov
1986   Animal exploitation in Ujrat El-Mehed, a Neolithic site in southern Sinai. *Paléorient* 12:105–116.

Dever, W. G.
1980   New vistas on the EB IV ("MBI") horizon in Syria-Palestine. *Bulletin of the American Schools of Oriental Research* 237:35–64.
1985   From the end of the Early Bronze Age to the beginning of the Middle Bronze. In *Biblical Archaeology Today, Proceedings of the International Congress on Biblical Archaeology,* edited by J. Aviram, A. Biran, J. C. Greenfield, M. Kochavi, A. Malamat, B. Mazar and E. E. Urbach, pp. 113–135. Israel Exploration Society, American Schools of Oriental Research and the Israel Academy of Sciences and Humanities, Jerusalem.

Dever, W. G. and M. Tadmor
1976   A copper hoard of Middle Bronze I. *Israel Exploration Journal* 26:163–169.

Di Maigret, A., F. Fedele and F. Di Mario
1988   Lo Yemen prima del regno di Saba. *Le Scienze-Scientific American* 40:12–23.

Edens, C.
1982   Towards a definition of the western ar-Rub' al-Khali "Neolithic". *Atlal, Journal of Saudi Arabian Archaeology* 6:109–124.

Eisenberg, E.
    1985   A burial cave of the Early Bronze Age IV (MB I) near 'Enan. *Atiqot* 17:59–73.
Eitan, A.
    1979   The emergency archaeological operation in the Negev. *Qadmoniot* 12:13 (in Hebrew).
Eshel, I.
    1990   Timna. *Excavations and Surveys in Israel* 9:171–172.
Evenari, M., L. Shanan, and N. Tadmor
    1971   *The Negev.* Harvard University Press, Cambridge, Massachusetts.
Finkelstein, I.
    1984   The Iron Age "Fortresses" of the Negev Highlands: Sendentarization of the nomads. *Tel Aviv* 11:189–209.
    1988   Arabian trade and socio-political conditions in the Negev in the twelfth–eleventh centuries B.C.E. *Journal of Near East Studies* 47:241–252.
    1989   Further observations on the socio-demographic structure of the Intermediate Bronze Age. *Levant* 21:129–140.
Finkelstein, I. and A. Perevolotsky
    1990   Processes of sedentarization and nomadization in the history of Sinai and the Negev. *Bulletin of the American Schools of Oriental Research* 279:67–88.
Flannery, K. V.
    1972   The origin of the village as settlement types in Mesoamerica and the Near East, a comparative study. In *Man, Settlement and Urbanism,* edited by P. J. Ucko, R. Tringham and G. W. Dimbleby, pp. 23–53. Duckworth, London.
Frumkin, A., M. Magaritz, I. Carmi and I. Zak
    1991   The Holocene climatic record of the salt caves of Mount Sedom, Israel. *Holocene* 1:191–200.
Garrard, A. N., A. Betts, B. Byrd and C. Hunt
    1987a   Prehistoric environment and settlement in the Azraq Basin: An interim report on the 1985 excavation season. *Levant* 19:5–25.
Garrard, A. N., B. Byrd and A. Betts
    1986   Prehistoric environment and settlement in the Azraq Basin: An interim report on the 1984 excavation season. *Levant* 18:5–24.
Garrard, A. N., B. Byrd, P. Harvey and F. Hivernel
    1985   Prehistoric environment and settlement in the Azraq Basin. A report on the 1982 survey season. *Levant* 17:1–28.
Garrard, A. N., S. Colledge, C. Hunt and R. Montague
    1988   Environment and subsistence during the Late Pleistocene and Early Holocene in the Azraq Basin. *Paléorient* 4:40–49.
Garrard, A. N., P. Harvey, F. Hivernel and B. Byrd
    1987b   The environmental history of the Azraq Basin. In *Studies in the History and Archaeology of Jordan II,* edited by A. Hadidi, pp. 109–115. Amman, Jordan.
Garrard, A. N., C. P. D. Harvey and V. R. Switsur
    1981   Environment and settlement during the Upper Pleistocene and Holocene at Jubba in the Great Nefud, northern Arabia. *Atlal, Journal of Saudi Arabian Archaeology* 5:137–148.
Garrard, A. N. and N. P. Stanley-Price
    1975a   A survey of prehistoric sites in the Azraq Basin, eastern Jordan. *Paléorient* 3:109–126.
    1975b   A survey of prehistoric sites in the Azraq Desert National Park, in eastern Jordan. *Annual of the Department of Antiquities of Jordan* 20:83–90.
Gat, J. R. and M. Magaritz
    1980   Climatic variations in the eastern Mediterranean Sea area. *Naturwissenschaften* 67:80–87.
Gilead, D.
    1973   Middle Bronze flint tools from Har Yeruham and Tel Najila. In *Excavations and Studies,* edited by Y. Aharoni, pp. 133–141. Tel Aviv University (in Hebrew).
Gilead, I.
    1988   The Chalcolithic period in the Levant. *Journal of World Prehistory* 2:397–443.
Glueck, N.
    1959   The Negev. *Biblical Archaeologist* 22:82–97.
    1961   The archaeological history of the Negev. *Hebrew Union College Annual* 32:11–18.
    1968   *Rivers in the Desert,* revised edition. Grove Press, New York.
    1970   *The Other Side of the Jordan,* revised edition. American Schools of Oriental Research, Cambridge, Massachusetts.

Goldberg, P.
1986   Late Quaternary environmental history of the southern Levant. *Geoarchaeology* 1:225–244.
Goldberg, P. and O. Bar-Yosef
1982   Environmental and archaeological evidence for climatic change in the southern Levant. In *Palaeoclimates, Palaeoenvironments and Human Communities in the Eastern Mediterranean Region in Later Prehistory,* edited by J. L. Bintliff and W. van Zeist, pp. 399–418. BAR International Series 133, British Archaeological Reports, Oxford.
Goldberg, P. and A. M. Rosen
1987   Early Holocene palaeoenvironments of Israel. In *Shiqmim I, Studies Concerning Chalcolithic Societies in the Northern Negev Desert, Israel (1982–1984),* edited by T. E. Levy, pp. 23–33. BAR International Series 356, British Archaeological Reports, Oxford.
Goodfriend, G. A.
1988   Mid-Holocene rainfall in the Negev Desert from ^{13}C of land snail shell organic matter. *Nature* 333:757–760.
1991   Holocene trends in ^{18}O in land snail shells from the Negev Desert and their implications for changes in rainfall source areas. *Quaternary Research* 35:417–426.
Goodfriend, G. A., M. Magaritz and I. Carmi
1986   A high stand of the Dead Sea at the end of the Neolithic period: Paleoclimatic and archeological implications. *Climatic Change* 9:349–356.
Gopher, A.
1981   The Stratigraphy and Flint Industry in Wadi Tbeik, a PPNB Site in southern Sinai. M.A. Thesis, Hebrew University, Jerusalem (in Hebrew).
1985   Flint Tool Industries of the Neolithic Period in Israel. Ph.D. Dissertation, Hebrew University.
1989   Neolithic arrowheads of the Levant: Results and implications of a seriation analysis. *Paléorient* 15:43–56.
Goring-Morris, A. N.
1987   *At the Edge: Terminal Pleistocene Hunter-Gatherers in the Negev and Sinai.* BAR International Series 361, British Archaeological Reports, Oxford.
1991   The Harifian of the southern Levant. In *The Natufian Culture in the Levant,* edited by O. Bar-Yosef and F. R. Valla, pp. 173–216. International Monographs in Prehistory, Ann Arbor.
Goring-Morris, A. N. and I. Gilead
1981   Prehistoric survey and excavations at Ramat Matred, 1979. *Israel Exploration Journal* 31:132–133.
Goring-Morris, A. N. and S. Gol
1982   Holot Shunra, Nahal Sekher. *Hadashot Archeologiot* 80/81:57–58 (in Hebrew).
Goring-Morris, A. N. and A. Gopher
1983   Nahal Issaron: A Neolithic settlement in the southern Negev. *Israel Exploration Journal* 33:149–162.
1987   Nahal Issaron: A Neolithic site in the southern Negev. *Qadmoniot* 20:18–21 (in Hebrew).
Goring-Morris, A. N. and E. Mintz
1976   Surveys in southern Sinai. *Israel Exploration Journal* 26:137–138.
Govrin, Y.
1990   The question of the origin of early Arad's population. In *Eretz-Israel,* Vol. 21, edited by A. Eitan, R. Gophna and M. Kochavi, pp. 107–110. Israel Exploration Society, Jerusalem (in Hebrew with English summary).
Haiman, M.
1986   Archaeological Survey of Israel: *Map of Har Hamran – Southwest* (198). Israel Antiquities Authority, Jerusalem.
1988   The Iron Age Sites of the Negev Highland. M.A. Thesis, Hebrew University, Jerusalem.
1989a   *Shepherds and Farmers in Kadesh Barnea Zone,* edited by E. Orion, Sede Boqer (in Hebrew).
1989b   Preliminary report of the western Negev Highlands emergency survey. *Israel Exploration Journal* 39:173–191.
1991   *Archaeological Survey of Israel: Map of Mizpe Ramon – Southwest* (200). Israel Antiquities Authority, Jerusalem.
Hauptmann, A.
1989   The earliest periods of copper metallurgy in Feinan, Jordan. In *Old World Archaeometallurgy: Proceedings of the International Symposium.* Selbstverlag des Deutschen, Bergbau Museums, Bochum, Germany.
Hauptmann, A. and G. Weisberger
1987   Archaeometallurgical and mining – Archaeological investigations in the area of Feinan, Wadi Arabah (Jordan). *Annual of the Department of Antiquities of Jordan* 31:419–435.
Hauptmann, A., G. Weisberger and H. G. Bachmann
1989   Ancient copper production in the area of Feinan, Khirbet en-Nahas, and Wadi el-Jariye, Wadi Arabah, Jordan. In *MASCA Research Papers in Science and Archaeology, History of Technology: The Role of Metals,* Vol. 6, edited by S. J. Fleming and H. R. Schenck, pp. 7–16. The University Museum, Philadelphia.

Hays, T. R.
  1975   Neolithic settlement of the Sahara as it relates to the Nile Valley. In *Problems in Prehistory: North Africa and the Levant*, edited by F. Wendorf and A. Marks, pp. 193–201. Southern Methodist University Press, Dallas.
Hecker, H.
  1975   *The Faunal Analysis of the Primary Food Animals from Pre-Pottery Neolithic Beidha (Jordan)*. University Microfilms International, Ann Arbor and London.
Henry, D. O.
  1982   The prehistory of southern Jordan and relationships with the Levant. *Journal of Field Archaeology* 9:417–444.
Hershkovitz, I., Y. Ben-David and B. Arensburg
  1987   Neolithic populations of southern Sinai, the Levant, southern Europe and North Africa: Craniometric multi-variate analysis: Israel. In *Sinai*, edited by G. Gvirtzman, A. Shmueli, Y. Gradus, I. Beit-Arieh and M. Har-El, pp. 589–594. Ministry of Defense, Tel Aviv (in Hebrew).
Horowitz, A.
  1976   Late Quaternary paleoenvironments of prehistoric settlements in the Avdat/Aqev area. In *Prehistory and Paleoenvironment in the Central Negev, Israel I*, edited by A. Marks, pp. 57–72. Southern Methodist University Press, Dallas.
  1979   *The Quaternary of Israel*. Academic Press, New York.
Ilan, O. and M. Sebbane
  1989   Copper metallurgy, trade and the urbanization of southern Canaan in the Chalcolithic and Early Bronze Age. In *L'Urbanisation de la Palestine à l'Age du Bronze Ancien*, edited by P. de Miroschedji, pp. 139–162. BAR International Series 527, British Archaeological Reports, Oxford.
Ilan, D., M. Sebbane, N. Porat and U. Avner
          Some comments on Rothenberg and Glass's "The Beginning and the Development of Early Metallurgy and the Settlement and Chronology of Western Arabia, from the Chalcolithic to the Early Bronze Age IV". *Levant* 25, in press.
Issar, A. S.
  1990   *Water Shall Flow from the Rock*. Springer-Verlag, Berlin.
Joffe, A.
  1991   Settlement and Society in Early Bronze I and II Canaan. Ph.D. Dissertation, The University of Arizona, Tucson.
Kaminer, O.
  1982   Biq'at Sayyarim Survey. *Excavations and Surveys in Israel* 1:79.
Kenyon, K.M.
  1979   *Archaeology in the Holy Land*, 4th edition. Ernest Benn Limited, London.
Khalil, L.
  1987   Preliminary report on the 1985 season of excavation at el-Maqass-'Aqaba. *Annual of the Department of Antiquities of Jordan* 31:481–483.
Khazanov, A. M.
  1984   *Nomads and the Outside World*. Cambridge University Press, Cambridge.
Khouri, R. G.
  1988   *The Antiquities of the Jordan Rift Valley*. Al Kutba, Amman, Jordan.
Kirkbride, D.
  1960   The excavation of a Neolithic village at Seyl Aqlat, Beidha, near Petra. *Palestine Exploration Quarterly* 92:136–145.
  1966   Five seasons at the Pre-Pottery Neolithic village of Beidha in Jordan, a summary. *Palestine Exploration Quarterly* 98:8–72.
Kochavi, M.
  1967   The Settlement of the Negev in the Middle Bronze (Canaanite) I Age. Ph.D. Dissertation, Hebrew University, Jerusalem (in Hebrew, English summary).
Kohler-Rollefson, I.
  1989   Changes in goat exploitation at 'Ain Ghazal between the Early and Late Neolithic: A metrical analysis. *Paléorient* 15:141–146.
Kozloff, B.
  1973   A brief note on the lithic industries of Sinai. *Museum Ha'aretz Yearbook* 15/16:35–49.
  1981   An ethno-archaeological study of pastoral nomadism in the Sinai. Paper presented at the 1981 Annual Meeting of the American Anthropological Association, December 4, 1981, Los Angeles.
Kropelin, S.
  1987   Palaeoclimatic evidence from Early to Mid-Holocene playas in the Gilf Kebir (southwest Egypt). In *Palaeo-*

ecology of Africa and the Surrounding Islands, edited by J. A. Coetzee, pp. 189–208. A. A. Balkema, Rotterdam.

Kutzbach, J. E. and F. A. Street-Perrott
1985   Milankovitch forcing of fluctuations in the level of tropical lakes from 18 to 0 kyr BP. *Nature* 317:130–134.

Leese, M. N., P. T. Craddock, I. C. Freestone and B. Rothenberg
1986   The composition of ores and metal objects from Timna, Israel. In *Wiener Berichte über Naturwissenschaft in der Kunst,* edited by Al Vendl, B. Pichler and J. Weber, pp. 90–120. Technische Universität, Vienna.

Lender, Y.
1990   *Archaeological Survey of Israel: Map of Har Nafha* (196). Israel Antiquities Authority, Jerusalem.

Levy, T. E.
1986   The Chalcolithic period. *Biblical Archaeologist* 49:82–108.

Levy, T. E. and S. Shalev
1989   Prehistoric metalworking in the southern Levant: Archaeometallurgical and social perspectives. *World Archaeology* 20:352–372.

Liphschitz, N.
1986   The vegetational landscape and the macroclimate of Israel during prehistoric and protohistoric periods. *Mitekufat Haeven* 19:80–90.

Luz, B.
1982   Paleoclimatic interpretation of the last 20,000 years. Record of deep sea cores around the Middle East. In *Palaeoclimates, Palaeoenvironments and Human Communities in the Eastern Mediterranean Region in Later Prehistory,* edited by J. L. Bintliff and W. van Zeist, pp. 41–61, BAR International Series 133, British Archaeological Reports, Oxford.

Mallowan, M. E. L.
1964   Noah's flood reconsidered. *Iraq* 26:62–82.

McCartney, C. J.
1992   Preliminary report of the 1989 excavations at Site 27 of the Burqu'/Ruweishid Project. *Levant* 24:33–54.

McClure, H. A.
1976   Radiocarbon chronology of Late Quaternary lakes in the Arabian Desert. *Nature* 263:755–756.

McConaughy, M. A.
1979   Formal and Functional Analyses of the Chipped Stone Tools from Bab Edh-Dhra, Jordan. Ph.D. Dissertation, University of Pittsburgh, Pennsylvania.

Mellaart, J.
1975   *The Neolithic of the Near East.* Thames and Hudson, London.

Merkel, J. F. and W. G. Dever
1989   Metalworking technology at the end of the Early Bronze Age in the southern Levant. *Institute for Archaeo-Metallurgical Studies*:1–4.

Meshel, Z.
1974   New data about the "desert kites". *Tel Aviv* 1:129–143.
1980   Desert kites in Sinai. In *Sinai in Antiquity,* edited by Z. Meshel and I. Finkelstein, pp. 265–288. The Society for Protection of Nature and Israel Exploration Society, Tel Aviv (in Hebrew).
1990   *Yotvata Oasis.* Eilot Municipality.

Moore, A. M. T
1973   The Late Neolithic in Palestine. *Levant* 5:36–68.
1982   A four stage sequence for the Levantine Neolithic, *ca.* 8500–3750 BC. *Bulletin of the American Schools of Oriental Research* 246:1–34.

Neev, D.
1980   A correlation between four Holocene tectonic and pluvial phases in Israel. In *Approaches and Methods in Paleoclimatic Research with Emphasis on Aridic Areas,* Bat Sheva Seminar 37, pp. 55–56. Jerusalem.

Neev, D. and J. K. Hall
1977   Climatic Fluctuations During the Holocene as Reflected by the Dead Sea Levels. Paper presented at the International Conference on Terminal Lakes, Weber State College, Ogden, Utah.

Niklaus, Th. R.
1991   *CalibETH Version 1.5,* pp. 1–150. ETH, Zurich.

Nissen, H. J., M. Muheisen and H.-G. Gebel.
1991   Report on the excavations at Basta 1988. *Annual of the Department of Antiquities of Jordan* 35:13-34.

Noy, T.
1977   Neolithic sites in the western coastal plain. *Eretz Israel* 13:18–33 (in Hebrew with English summary).

Noy T. and R. Cohen
1974   Nahal Boqer: An Early Pre-Pottery Neolithic B site. *Mitekufat Haeven, Journal of the Israel Prehistoric Society* 12:15–25 (in Hebrew).

Oates, J.
1982   Archaeological evidence for settlement patterns in Mesopotamia and eastern Arabia. In *Palaeoclimates, Palaeoenvironments and Human Communities in the Eastern Mediterranean Region in Later Prehistory*, edited by J. L. Bintliff and W. van Zeist, pp. 359–398. BAR International Series 133, British Archaeological Reports, Oxford.

Oren, E. D. and Y. Yekutieli
1990   North Sinai during the MBI period – Pastoral nomadism and sedentary settlement. *Eretz Israel* 21:6–22 (in Hebrew with English summary).

Perevolotsky, A. and D. Baharav
1987   The abundance of desert kites in eastern Sinai – An ecological analysis. In *Sinai*, edited by G. Gvirtzman, A. Shmueli, Y. Gradus, I. Beit-Arieh and M. Har-El, pp. 595–604. Ministry of Defense, Tel Aviv (in Hebrew).

Petrie, W. M. F.
1906   *Researches in Sinai.* John Murray, London.

Porat, N.
1989   Petrography of pottery from southern Israel and Sinai. In *L'Urbanisation de la Palestine à l'Age du Bronze Ancien*, edited by P. de Miroschedji, pp. 169–188. BAR International Series 527, British Archaeological Reports, Oxford.

Prag, K. W.
1974   The intermediate Early Bronze–Middle Bronze Age: An interpretation of the evidence from Transjordan, Syria and Lebanon. *Levant* 6:69–116.

Raikes, R. L.
1966   The physical evidence for Noah's flood. *Iraq* 28:42–63.

Raikes, T. D.
1980   Notes on some Neolithic and later sites in Wadi Araba and the Dead Sea Valley. *Levant* 12: 40–60.

Reich, R.
1990   Two sites in Biq'at 'Uvda. *Atiqot* 10:13–19 (in Hebrew with English summary).

Reifenberg, A.
1975   *The Desert and the Sown.* Jewish Agency, Jerusalem.

Richard, S.
1980   Toward a consensus of opinion on the end of the Early Bronze Age in Palestine-Transjordan. *Bulletin of the American Schools of Oriental Research* 237:5–34.
1986   Excavations at Khirbet Iskander, Jordan. *Expedition* 28:3–12.
1987a   The Early Bronze, the rise and collapse of urbanism. *Biblical Archaeologist* 50:22–42.
1987b   Questions of nomadic incursions at the end of the 3rd millennium B.C. In *Studies in the History and Archaeology of Jordan*, Vol. 3, edited by A. Hadidi, pp. 241–246. Department of Antiquities, Hashemite Kingdom of Jordan, Amman, Jordan.
1990   The 1987 expedition to Khirbet Iskander and its vicinity: Fourth preliminary report. *Bulletin of the American Schools of Oriental Research Supplement* 26:33–58.

Richard, S. and R. Boraas
1984   Preliminary report of the 1981–82 seasons of the expedition to Khirbet Iskander and its vicinity. *Bulletin of the American Schools of Oriental Research* 254:63–87.

Ritchie, J. C. and C. V. Haynes
1987   Holocene vegetation zonation in the eastern Sahara. *Nature* 330:645–647.

Ritter-Kaplan, H.
1984   The impact of drought on the third millennium B.C.E. cultures on the basis of excavations in the Tel Aviv exhibition grounds. *Eretz Israel* 17:333–338 (in Hebrew, English summary).

Roberts, N.
1982   Lake levels as an indicator of Near Eastern paleoclimate. In *Palaeoclimates, Palaeoenvironments and Human Communities in the Eastern Mediterranean Region in Later Prehistory*, edited by J. L. Bintliff and W. van Zeist, pp. 235–271. BAR International Series 133, British Archaeological Reports, Oxford.

Rollefson, G. O.
1989   The Late Aceramic Neolithic of the Levant: A synthesis. *Paléorient* 15:168–173.

Ronen, A.
1970   Flint implements from south Sinai preliminary report. *Palestine Exploration Quarterly* 102:30–41.
1980   Biqat Uvda 20 (N. Reuel). *Hadashot Archeologiot* 74/75:47–48 (in Hebrew).

Rosen, S.
1982 Flint sickle blades of the Late Protohistoric and Early Historic periods in Israel. *Tel Aviv* 9:139–145.
1983a Lithics in the Bronze and Iron Ages in Israel. Ph.D. Dissertation, University of Chicago, Chicago.
1983b The microlithic lunate: An old-new tool type from the Negev, Israel. *Paléorient* 9:81–83.
1983c The Canaanean blade and the Early Bronze Age. *Israel Exploration Journal* 33:15–29.
1984a Kvish Harif: Preliminary investigation at a Late Neolithic site in the central Negev. *Paléorient* 10:111–121.
1984b The adoption of metallurgy in the Levant: A lithic perspective. *Current Anthropology* 25:504–505.
1986 The analysis of trade and craft specialization in the Chalcolithic period: Comparisons from different realms of material culture. *Michmanim* 3:21–31.
1987a The potentials of lithic analysis in the Chalcolithic of the northern Negev. In *Shiqmim I: Studies Concerning Chalcolithic Societies in the Northern Negev Desert, Israel (1982–1984)*, edited by T. E. Levy, pp. 295–309. BAR International Series 356, British Archaeological Reports, Oxford.
1987b Demographic trends in the Negev Highlands: Preliminary results from the emergency survey. *Bulletin of the American Schools of Oriental Research* 266:45–58.
1988 Notes on the origins of pastoral nomadism: A case study from the Negev and Sinai. *Current Anthropology* 29:498–506.
1989 The analysis of Early Bronze Age chipped stone industries: A summary statement. In *L'Urbanisation de la Palestine à l'Age du Bronze Ancien,* edited by P. de Miroschedji, pp. 199–222. BAR International Series 527, British Archaeological Reports, Oxford.
1992 Nomads in archaeology: A response to Finkelstein and Perevolotsky. *Bulletin of the American School for Oriental Research* 287:75–85.
Rothenberg, B.
1967 *Negev. Archaeology in the Negev and the Arabah.* Masada, Ramat Gan (in Hebrew).
1969 An archaeological survey of south Sinai, first season 1967/68, preliminary report. *Museum Ha'aretz Bulletin* 11:22–38.
1970 An archaeological survey of south Sinai, first season 1967/1968. *Palestine Exploration Quarterly* 102:4–29.
1971 The Sinai Archaeological Expedition (1967–1970). *Ariel* 28:59–64.
1973 Sinai explorations 1967–1972. *Museum Ha'aretz Bulletin* 14:31–46.
1974 Sinai explorations III. *Museum Ha'aretz Bulletin* 15/16:16–34.
1978 Site 201 in the southern Arabah. *Hadashot Archeologiot* 65/66:57–58 (in Hebrew).
1979 *Sinai.* Kummerly und Frey, Bern.
1990a *The Ancient Metallurgy of Copper.* The Institute for Archaeo-Metallurgical Studies, London.
1990b The Chalcolithic copper smelting furnace in the Timna Valley – Its discovery and the strange argument surrounding its dating. *Institute for Archaeo-Metallurgical Studies* 15/16:9–12.
Rothenberg, B. and E. Cohen
1968 An archaeological survey of the Eloth district and the southernmost Negev. *Museum Ha'aretz* 10:25–35.
Rothenberg, B. and I. Ordentlich
1979 A comparative chronology of Sinai, Egypt and Palestine. *Bulletin of the Institute of Archaeology University of London* 16:233–237.
Rothenberg, B. and C. T. Shaw
1990 The discovery of a copper mine and smelter from the end of the Early Bronze Age (EB IV) in the Timna Valley. *Institute for Archaeo-Metallurgical Studies* 15/16:1–8.
Rowton, M. B.
1974 Enclosed Nomadism. *Journal of the Economic and Social History of the Orient* 17:1–30.
Scharpenseel, H. W., F. Pietig and H. Schiffmann
1976 Hamburg University radiocarbon dates I. *Radiocarbon* 18(3):286–287.
Schaub, R. T.
1981 Ceramic sequences in the tomb groups at Bab edh Dhra. *Annual of the American Schools of Oriental Research* 46:69–118.
Sebbane, M. and U. Avner
1993 Biq'at Nimra: A site from the beginning of the Early Bronze Age I. *'Atiqot* 12:33–40.
Sebbane, M., O. Ilan, D. Ilan and U. Avner
1993 The dating of Early Bronze Age settlement in the Negev and Sinai. *Tel Aviv:* 20:41–54.
Servello, A. F.
1976 Nahal Divshon: A Pre-Pottery Neolithic B hunting camp. In *Prehistory and Paleoenvironment in the Central Negev, Israel 1*, edited by A. Marks, pp. 349–369. Southern Methodist University Press, Dallas.

Sherratt, A.
    1981   Plough and pastoralism: Aspects of the secondary products revolution. In *Pattern of the Past: Studies in Honour of David Clarke*, edited by I. Hodder, G. Isaac and N. Hammond, pp. 261– 305. Cambridge University Press, Cambridge.

Simmons, A. H.
    1981   A paleosubsistence model for Early Neolithic occupation of the western Negev Desert. *Bulletin of the American Schools of Oriental Research* 242:31–50.

Smith, P.
    1989   The skeletal biology and paleopathology of Early Bronze Age populations in the Levant. In *L'Urbanisation de la Palestine à l'Age du Bronze Ancien*, edited by P. de Miroschedji, pp. 297–313. BAR International Series 527, British Archaeological Reports, Oxford.

Stech, T., J. D. Muhly and R. Maddin
    1985   Metallurgical studies on artifacts from the Near 'Enan. *'Atiqot* 17:75–82.

Stekelis, M.
    1935   *Les Monuments Mégalithiques de Palestine*. Mémoire 15, Archives de l'Institut de Paleontologie Humaine, Paris.

Stuiver, M. and R. S. Kra (editors)
    1986   Calibration Issue. *Radiocarbon* 28(2B):805–1030.

Taute, W.
    1981   Masad Mazzal, ein Siedlungsplatz des Prekeramischen Neolithikume Südlich des Toten Meers (Vorbericht). In *Beitrage zur Umweltgeschichte des Vorderen Orients*, edited by W. Frey and H. P. Uerpmann, pp. 236–256. Wiesbaden.

Tchernov, E. and O. Bar-Yosef
    1982   Animal exploitation in the Pre-Pottery Neolithic B period at Wadi Tbeik, southern Sinai. *Paléorient* 8:17–37.

Wachman, A.
    1959   Circular and Orthogonal Building. M.A. Thesis, Israel Institute of Technology, Haifa.

Weinstein, J. M.
    1984   Radiocarbon dating in the southern Levant. *Radiocarbon* 26(3):297–366.

Wilkinson, T. J.
    1978   Erosion and sedimentation along the Euphrates Valley in north Syria. In *The Environmental History of the Near and Middle East Since the Last Ice Age*, edited by W. C. Brice, pp. 215–226. Academic Press, London, New York.

Yeivin, E. and Y. Olami
    1979   Nizzanim – A Neolithic site in Nahal Evtah: Excavations of 1968–1970. *Tel Aviv* 6:99–135.

Yogev, O.
    1983   A fifth millennium B.C. sanctuary in the Uvda Valley. *Qadmoniot* 16:118–122 (in Hebrew).

Zarins, J. and H. Al-Badr
    1986   Archaeological investigation in the southern Tihama Plain II (including Sihi, 217–107 and Sharja, 217–172) 1405/1985. *Atlal, Journal of Saudi Arabian Archaeology* 10:36–57.

Zarins, J., A. Murad and Kh. Al-Yish
    1981   The comprehensive archaeological survey program: The second preliminary report on the southwestern province. *Atlal, Journal of Saudi Arabian Archaeology* 5:9–42.

Zarins, J., A. Rahbini and M. Kamal
    1982   Preliminary report on the archaeological survey of the Riyadh Area. *Atlal, Journal of Saudi Arabian Archaeology* 6:25–38.

Zarins, J., N. Whalen, M. Ibrahim, A. Mursi and M. Khan
    1980   Comprehensive archaeological survey program: Preliminary report on the central and southwestern provinces survey: 1979. *Atlal, Journal of Saudi Arabian Archaeology* 4:9–36.

COMPARATIVE CHRONOLOGY OF CLIMATE AND HUMAN HISTORY IN THE SOUTHERN LEVANT FROM THE LATE CHALCOLITHIC TO THE EARLY ARAB PERIOD

HENDRIK J. BRUINS

Ben-Gurion University of the Negev, Jacob Blaustein Institute for Desert Research
Sede Boker Campus 84993 Israel

INTRODUCTION

In this chapter, I link the chronology of climate history in the southern Levant to the chronology of archaeological history, with emphasis on the central Negev. The radiocarbon time scale, used in relation to paleoclimate data from Dead Sea-level changes during the Holocene (Frumkin *et al.* 1991), has been related to archaeo-historical time scales with the help of computerized calibration (van der Plicht 1991, 1993). A distinction must be made between climate history and climate impact assessment. The former sphere of research is mainly directed at acquiring paleoclimate data through proxy indicators. The latter is particularly concerned with analyzing the effect of climate change on human society. Climate change may have a more straightforward impact on the environment, but the possible effect on economic activities and society is far more complex. Pollen data are important in the reconstruction of vegetational history, though the relation with paleoclimate in historical times may be uncertain, as a result of human interaction (Baruch 1983). The correlation between tree rings and paleoclimate (Waisel and Liphschitz 1968; Liphschitz, Lev-Yadun and Waisel 1987; Lev-Yadun 1987) is valuable but complex. Hence, the comprehensive record from Dead Sea-level changes has been preferred as the paleoclimate master curve. I present here a juxtaposition of climate and human history from the Late Chalcolithic until the end of the Early Arab period. Such a chronological framework may provide a basis for more detailed studies about climate impact assessment and relations between climate and local resource management. Although climate patterns discussed here seem generally valid for the entire Levant, discussion about their relation to archaeological history has been targeted mainly at the central Negev.

THE DEAD SEA AS A PRIMARY INDICATOR OF PALEOCLIMATE FOR THE SOUTHERN LEVANT

Lake-level changes of terminal lakes such as the Dead Sea are good indicators of past climate variations, as they reflect the combined effect of precipitation and evaporation. However, since the 1960s, the Dead Sea is no longer a valid indicator of climatic fluctuations. Much of the water that formerly flowed to the Dead Sea is now diverted for human use by both Israel and Jordan, and its level has fallen to below −400 m (400 m below mean ocean level) (Anati and Shasha 1989). The equilibrium level under current water-diversion practices and climate conditions has been estimated by Klein (1990) at −680 m, which would be reached in *ca.* 360 yr. Geographical, historical and archaeological data compiled by Klein (1961, 1981, 1982, 1986) yielded the most detailed consecutive curve of Dead Sea levels from AD 930 to the present. For this period, Dead Sea levels varied from −350 m at *ca.* AD 1050, to below −406 m at present. Data sources become scanty for earlier periods, except 100 BC to AD 40, for which time, Klein (1982, 1986) reported a dramatic rise from −400 m to −330 m and subsequent decline to −395 m.

Stratigraphic data of Dead Sea deposits were obtained by Neev and Emery (1967), who associate clay sediments with humid periods, and salt deposits with dry periods. The Late Pleistocene Lisan sediments were deposited when the lake level of the Dead Sea was much higher than at present

Late Quaternary Chronology and Paleoclimates of the Eastern Mediterranean
Edited by O. Bar-Yosef and R. S. Kra. RADIOCARBON *1994, pp. 301–314*

(Begin, Ehrlich and Nathan 1974). Bowman (1971) studied the geomorphology of former shore terraces associated with these high water levels. Begin *et al.* (1985) published a comprehensive account of Dead Sea fluctuations during the past 30,000 yr. The highest levels reached *ca.* –200 m during the Late Pleistocene, whereas the lowest level of –700 m occurred, *ca.* 11,000 BP, toward the end of the Pleistocene.

Goodfriend, Magaritz and Carmi (1986) investigated land snail (*Trochoidea seetzeni*) shells covered by salt near Qumran, at an elevation of –280 m. The shells gave a ^{14}C date of 6660 ± 400 BP (RT-725), corrected for reservoir effects and fractionation. The authors suggested that the salt deposit represents a Dead Sea level of –280 m, at some time between *ca.* 7100 and 6400 BP. Frumkin *et al.* (1991) presented a comprehensive Holocene climate record (Fig. 1), derived from the salt caves of Mount Sedom, which is an 11 × 1.5-km north-south ridge near the southwestern boundary of the Dead Sea, reaching an elevation of *ca.* –160 m, 240 m above the present lake level (see Frumkin *et al.* 1994). Mount Sedom is the exposed head of a salt diapir with the longest salt caves in the world, 5500 m long (Frumkin 1982; Frumkin *et al.* 1991). Their Holocene record (Fig. 1) is based on the elevation of corresponding cave passages, the ratio of their width in relation to the present width, and associated floral and wood remains. The authors distinguish 10 climate stages; the chronology of the curve is based on 33 ^{14}C dates on wood, derived from flood sediments deposited in the various cave passages.

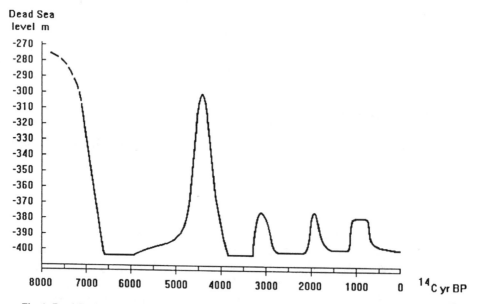

Fig. 1. Dead Sea level changes during the Holocene (from Fig. 8, Frumkin *et al.* 1991). Reprinted by permission of Edward Arnold, Ltd.

DATING CLIMATE AND HUMAN HISTORY

In order to link human and climate history in time, reliable and corresponding chronologies are needed. Bruins and Mook (1989) discussed the need to establish a calibrated ^{14}C chronology of Near Eastern archaeology. Weinstein (1984), Hassan and Robinson (1987) and Haas *et al.* (1987) undertook studies in that field. Dendrochronological calibrations linking tree-ring dates to high-precision ^{14}C dates provide reliable chronologies for the Holocene (Stuiver and Kra 1986; Stuiver,

Long and Kra 1993). Several ^{14}C calibration programs are now readily available (van der Plicht 1993; Stuiver and Reimer 1993). Calibrated (cal) years are conventionally expressed in BC and AD calendar years. The cal BC/AD values in Figure 2 (time scale B) represent "averages" with certain statistical uncertainties. Dehling and van der Plicht (1993) most recently discussed the statistical problems involved in ^{14}C calibration. A calibration result should be expressed as age ranges or as point dates with ± age ranges (if justified). The width of the calibrated age range is determined by the precision of the original ^{14}C date, calibrated to 1 or 2 standard deviations (σ).

I use the Frumkin *et al.* (1991) data to relate climate history to historical archaeological periods (Fig. 2). Figure 2 also includes Klein's (1961, 1981, 1982, 1986) more detailed curves, although their time range is confined mainly to the last 1000 yr. The C and D time scales denote two versions (Mazar 1990 and Negev 1972, respectively) of both archaeological and historical periods, to facilitate comparison between climate and human history. Comparing the curves of Frumkin *et al.* (1991) and Klein (1986) shows that the sensitivity of the former is less than the actual changes of the Dead Sea level, and appears to be a moving average.

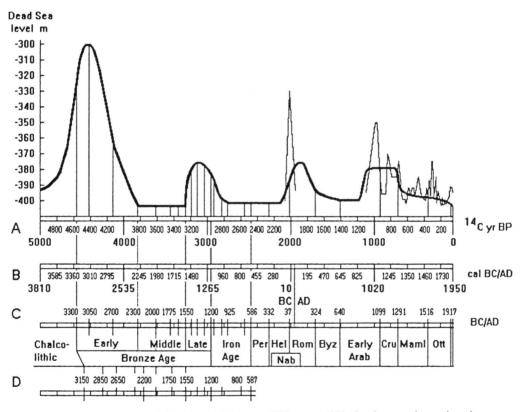

Fig. 2. Dead Sea-level changes during historical times, *ca.* 3800 BC–AD 1950, showing a continuous (——) curve (Frumkin *et al.* 1991) and more detailed (——) curves (Klein 1961, 1981, 1982, 1986). The curves are related to three different time scales: A. ^{14}C years; B. calibrated ^{14}C years; C. and D. historical periods (C=Mazar 1990; D=Negev 1972).

CHALCOLITHIC – EARLY BRONZE AGE TRANSITION

At *ca.* 3800 BC (Fig. 2), the climate of the Chalcolithic period was still dry, with an average Dead Sea level of *ca.* −395 m, according to the curve of Frumkin *et al.* (1991). However, climate became progressively wetter during the 4th millennium BC. The average Dead Sea level had risen to *ca.* −370 m by 3500 BC and continued to rise. At the Chalcolithic–Early Bronze Age transition, *ca.* 3300 BC, the Dead Sea reached a level of −330 m. Cohen (1986) believes that human migration took place in the Chalcolithic from the north into the Negev and Sinai. Pastoralism and hunting appear to have been the main forms of land use, with habitation in small open villages and natural caves. Settlement extended along the edge of the very dry Arabah rift valley (Cohen 1986). A possible permanent Chalcolithic settlement in Nahal Mitnan in the western central Negev shows wide courtyards, which "could be the most ancient architectural expression of sheep and goat husbandry in the Negev highlands" (Haiman 1989:178). Archaeological finds in the Negev and Sinai appear compatible, with an increasingly wetter climate in the second half of the Chalcolithic period.

EARLY BRONZE AGE

The wettest period of the Middle and Late Holocene, with average Dead Sea levels between −370 and −300 m, lasted for almost a millennium, from *ca.* 3500–2600 BC. The climate trend at the onset of the Early Bronze (EB) Age was from humid to even more humid. *Ca.* 3000 BC, during the transition from EB I to EB II, the average Dead Sea level peaked at *ca.* −300 m (Fig. 2). The wet climate became gradually drier during EB II, but remained humid. Average Dead Sea levels declined during EB II from *ca.* −300 to −370 m (Fig. 2). Progressive desiccation of the climate continued throughout EB III, as average Dead Sea levels declined from *ca.* −370 m to −404 m. Maximum aridity was reached at the beginning of EB IV/MB I. An investigation of wadi sediments near Tel Lachish (Rosen 1986a, 1989) uncovered evidence for a higher water table during most of the Early Bronze Age, but a clear decline during EB IV; this corresponds to Frumkin *et al.*'s (1991) paleoclimate curve.

Settlements in the Negev and Sinai (Beit Arieh 1982; Cohen 1986) are usually assigned to EB II, but probably existed during EB III (Cohen 1986). Numerous settlements were found in the comparatively dry Biqat Uvda area of the southern Negev (Avner 1990; Avner, Carmi and Segal 1994). Large EB settlements in the southern Levant were established near permanent water sources, with an economy based on agriculture, pastoralism and hunting (Cohen 1986). Haiman (1989) found that land was used principally for sheep and goat husbandry in the western central Negev, as most sites had large animal pens. Haiman (1989) also noted grain cultivation. The more arid Biqat Uvda region in the southern Negev (Avner 1990; Avner, Carmi and Segal 1994) showed a proportion of 7–10% sickle blades of total lithic tools, as compared to *ca.* 1% in the Negev highlands. The Jawa site in northeast Jordan (Helms 1981), which relied on runoff water for its agricultural economy and existence, was apparently established at the beginning of the Early Bronze Age. The wettest period in historical times undoubtedly served as a basis for successful rainwater harvesting.

MIDDLE BRONZE AGE

The entire Middle Bronze (MB) Age, *ca.* 2300–1550 BC, including the transitional EB IV/MB I period, appears to have coincided with the driest period in historical times (Fig. 2). Aridity seems to have persisted throughout the Middle Bronze Age, according to the curve by Frumkin *et al.* (1991), as the average Dead Sea level remained at *ca.* −404 m. Archaeological opinion and terminology differ considerably on the end of the Early Bronze Age and the beginning of the Middle Bronze Age. Settlement in the Negev during the Middle Bronze Age appears to have been restricted to EB IV/MB I. The pattern of settlement appears similar to the (early) Early Bronze Age, and also reaches the Biqat Uvda area (Avner 1990; Avner, Carmi and Segal 1994) in the southern Negev (Cohen 1986). During an extensive survey in the western central Negev (Haiman 1989), 70 small EB IV/MB I sites were found, contrasting with 180 EB sites discovered in the same area, which may also reflect the drier climate during EB IV/MB I.

From archaeological finds in the central Negev, Cohen (1986) deduced that most EB IV/MB I settlements were occupied only seasonally by groups engaging in pastoralism, hunting and sporadic agriculture. The presence of animal pens characterizes the small sites. Several large, densely populated villages were also found near permanent sources of water. These "central" settlements, located in the north-central Negev, were probably inhabited throughout the year. Copper ingots were found in the central sites, but no animal pens were present at Nahal Nizzana (Cohen 1986). Following EB IV/MB I settlement, architectural remains are not apparent in the central Negev for the next 1000 yr, until the Iron Age (Cohen 1986). Figure 2 shows a steady arid climate throughout the MB. Pollen data (Horowitz 1978) point to drying at the beginning of the MB. Evidence from wadi sediments near Tel Lachish (Rosen 1986a, 1989), suggests aridification during EB IV/MB I, as do Dead Sea deposits (Neev and Emery 1967).

Controversy exists in archaeological terminology and age assignment of the middle and late MB in the Levant (Mazar 1986; Kempinski 1983; Bietak 1984; Bienkowski 1989). Remains of an aqueduct in the valley of Ein el Qudeirat in northeastern Sinai yielded a ^{14}C date of 3270 ± 100 BP (GrN-12327) from small charcoal pieces in the mortar of the aqueduct (Bruins 1986). The highest relative probability in the calibrated 1 σ age range centers *ca.* 1580 and 1530 cal BC, *i.e.*, to the MB–LB transition.

LATE BRONZE AGE

The beginning of the Late Bronze Age seems to coincide with a sharp climate change to moister conditions, which peaked *ca.* 1350 BC, when the average Dead Sea level stood at *ca.* −375 m. No Late Bronze Age settlements were reported for the central Negev, but Oren (1979) found many LB Egyptian sites in northern Sinai. Moreover, Rothenberg (1972, 1989) excavated LB sites related to copper mining in the Timna area in the southern Negev. The climate seems to have been favorable during this period; average Dead Sea levels ranged from −375 to −383 m. The natural biomass production must have been higher than today, and more fuel wood, necessary for copper smelting, would have been available.

IRON AGE

Oren (1985) discussed chronological problems in the transition from the Late Bronze to the Iron Age, *ca.* 1200 BC, when the climate was already drying in the southern Levant (Fig. 2). Aridity increased progressively during Iron Age I (1200–1000 BC), with average Dead Sea levels declining from *ca.* −383 m to −397 m. During Iron Age II, the climate became drier (Fig. 2), as average Dead Sea levels dropped to *ca.* −400 m. Aridity was only slightly less severe than during the Middle Bronze Age. Many Iron Age settlements, with numerous agricultural villages and fortresses (Cohen 1976, 1980, 1986), were discovered in central Negev and northeastern Sinai. Cohen (1986) dated virtually all these settlements, on archaeological-historical grounds, to the 10th century BC. However, Haiman (1989) noted that the architecture of the Iron Age sites in the central Negev is not uniform. He recorded *ca.* 160 Iron Age sites in the west-central Negev, compared to 180 EB and 70 MB I sites. Animal pens and abundant sickle blades in many Iron Age settlements provide evidence for sheep and goat husbandry, and agriculture (Haiman 1989).

Cohen (1981a,b, 1983, 1986) conducted extensive excavations in northeastern Sinai at Tel el Qudeirat, and, on the basis of pottery, assigned the earliest fortress at the site to the 10th century BC. In Square K-67, which shows most of the tell stratigraphy, a sample was taken from the lowermost ash layer. This layer is associated with the destruction of the Early Fortress (Cohen, personal communication 1981), and overlies loess soil (0–20 cm below the ash layer) and "virgin" gravel mixed with sandy loam (20–40+ cm below the ash layer) (Bruins 1986). The sample yielded a highest probability calibrated ^{14}C age centered *ca.* 1150 cal BC (GrN-12330), *ca.* 200 yr older than the archaeological age assessed from pottery. It seems clear from Figure 2 that the 12th and 11th centuries BC would have been more favorable for settlement in the arid Negev desert than the later Iron Age. However, as will be seen also in later periods, climate is not necessarily the main determining factor.

The site of Horvat Haluqim in the central Negev, excavated by Cohen (1976), exhibits an oval-shaped fortress similar in shape and size to the Early Fortress at Tel el Qudeirat. A small village also existed at Horvat Haluqim along three terraced wadis (Cohen 1976). Bruins (1986) investigated environmental and agricultural aspects of this site. Rainwater harvesting constituted a significant economic support activity. Excavation in a terraced wadi soil revealed Iron Age pottery in a former A-horizon, at a depth of 75 cm. Evidence for temporary waterlogged conditions in the terraced fields as a result of runoff farming was provided when iron (hydro)oxide nodules were found in the Iron Age soil horizon (Bruins 1986). Unfortunately, no samples from Horvat Haluqim have been ^{14}C dated.

Remains of later phases of the Iron Age, when the climate was dry, appear to be rare or absent in the central Negev (Cohen 1986), except for the Middle and Upper Fortresses at Tel el Qudeirat in northeastern Sinai, situated next to a perennial spring. On the basis of wheel-thrown pottery, Cohen (1981a) assigned the Middle Fortress to the 8th–7th centuries BC. Two *ostraca* (potsherds) showing Hebrew script were found in the Middle Fortress (Cohen 1983). A sample from a black ash layer was ^{14}C-dated. The layer had been a surface layer at the tell, touching the retaining wall of the Middle Fortress 60 cm above its base. Hence, the retaining wall must be older than the black layer. The sample, GrN-11948 (Bruins and Mook 1990), dated to 2740 ± 110 BP. The calibrated age range, at 1 σ (68.3% confidence level), is 1030–800 cal BC; the highest relative probability is centered *ca.* 900 cal BC. Again, this result might indicate a date *ca.* 200 yr older than archaeological age assignment related to ceramics.

Cohen (1981) dated the Upper Fortress at Tel el Qudeirat to the 7th–6th centuries BC on the basis of wheel-thrown pottery. Cohen (1981a, 1983) also found several *ostraca* with Hebrew script in the Upper Fortress. Two ^{14}C samples were collected from layers associated with the destruction of the Upper Fortress. One sample was taken from the uppermost black ash layer in Square K-67, (Bruins and Mook 1990), and yielded a date of 2535 ± 50 BP (GrN-12329). The calibrated age ranges, in calendar years at 1 σ, are 800–760, 686–656, 636–592 and 586–550 cal BC. The second sample, charred cereals (barley and wheat) (Kislev, personal communication 1990) that came from a complete storage jar (Cohen, personal communication 1987) was also associated with the destruction of the Upper Fortress. This sample yielded a date of 2515 ± 15 BP (GrN-15551), for which the calibrated age ranges, at 2 σ (95.4% confidence level), are 791–760, 684–658, 634–595 and 580–552 cal BC. Both of these dates fall in a time range over which the calibration curve is horizontal, yielding calibrated dates with a broad age range (Bruins, van der Plicht and Mook 1991). A date of 586 BC, which Cohen assigned to the destruction of the Upper Fortress, on archaeological-historical grounds, falls within the calibrated age range. The four calibrated dates from Tel el Qudeirat associated with the three fortresses are internally consistent, in relative chronological order, based on archaeological stratigraphy, but the earliest dates (GrN-12330 and GrN-11948) from the Early and Middle Fortresses seem consistently *ca.* 200 yr older than ages based on pottery.

BABYLONIAN-PERSIAN AND HELLENISTIC PERIODS

The dry climate of Iron Age II and III appears to have continued during the Babylonian-Persian period and the first half of the Hellenistic period, until *ca.* 190 BC. The average Dead Sea level stood at *ca.* −400 m (Fig. 2). A few remains of the Persian period are known from the Negev and northeastern Sinai (Cohen 1986; Haiman 1989). An unfortified Persian village existed on Tel el Qudeirat during a relatively dry climate, which may be the reason for its establishment near the perennial spring of Ein el Qudeirat (Bruins 1986). A charcoal sample, collected from a black ash layer, dated to 2400 ± 60 BP (GrN-12334), which was calibrated at 1 σ to the age ranges of 754–698 and 534–400 cal BC. The second range seems to fit the archaeological evidence. Climate was quite dry at the beginning of the Early Nabatean period, as the average Dead Sea level stood at *ca.* −400 m (Fig. 2). It is important to note that, during this dry phase, rainfall must have been adequate for Nabatean occupation in the southern Levant. Beginning in the early second century BC, climate became more moist.

ROMAN PERIOD

The change toward increasing humidity, which began during the second half of the Early Nabatean period (*ca.* 190 BC), continued during the first half of the Roman period, beginning 37 BC. Figure 2 shows that, in the southern Levant, the Roman period coincided with a relatively wet phase, comparable to the Late Bronze–Early Iron Age wet period. Issar (1990) compared the Roman period with a miniglacial. The Middle Nabatean period, which lasted from the last quarter of the 1st century BC to the middle of the 1st century AD (Negev 1982), was coeval with this wet period. Important innovations occurred in Nabatean culture during Middle Nabatean times: pottery production; permanent road stations along the commercial routes from the Arabian and Edomite regions to the Mediterranean; and the construction of most Nabatean temples, military camps and caravanserais. Yet, most Nabateans continued to live in tents, and apparently, did not engage in agriculture (Negev 1982), despite the favorable climate, as the Dead Sea reached a level of −330 m by 30 BC (Klein 1982, 1986; Fig. 2).

The overall wet period during Roman times reached its average peak *ca.* AD 90, according to the curve of Frumkin *et al.* (1991). The important question is, when did the Nabateans begin to farm using runoff rainwater for irrigation? If agriculture was adopted by the Nabateans *ca.* AD 90 (Negev 1981, 1982), they started shortly before the kingdom lost its independence, in AD 106, when it was incorporated into the Roman empire. It is apparent that the climate alone cannot account for the beginning of Nabatean agriculture. Admittedly, the climate was dry during the Early Nabatean period, when no agriculture was practiced. However, the wet climate in the 1st century BC and beginning of the 1st century AD (Klein 1982, 1986) did not lead to agriculture during Middle Nabatean times. Early Nabatean customs, in which agriculture was unacceptable socially, may have played an overriding role. Both Haiman (1989) and Nevo (1991) have questioned the existence of Nabatean agriculture in the area, because they found no firm evidence for it.

In the wetter part of the Levant, Feliks (1963) and Sperber (1978) noted that crop yields were very high during the 1st century AD according to rabbinical sources in the Mishna and Talmud. However, in the 2nd century AD, the climate began its drier trend, according to the curve of Frumkin *et al.* (1991). Sperber's (1978) investigation based on literary sources attests to gradual desiccation and a sharp drop in crop yields during the 3rd century, which fits well with the paleoclimate curve of the Dead Sea (Fig. 2).

BYZANTINE PERIOD

The Byzantine period began in AD 324, when the climate was significantly drier than during the 1st century BC and 1st century AD. The climate gradually became more arid in the course of the Byzantine period (Fig. 2). The average Dead Sea level *ca.* AD 324 stood at *ca.* −393 m, and, at the end of Byzantine rule, AD 640, at *ca.* −398 m (Fig. 2). Sperber (1978) refers frequently to drought in the 4th century; apparently, increasing desiccation caused the dunes to become more active and shift eastward (Mayerson 1983). However, most researchers (Mayerson 1955, 1960; Kedar 1967; Evenari, Shanan and Tadmor 1971, 1982; Bruins 1986; Bruins, Evenari and Rogel 1987; Bruins 1990a, 1990b; Nevo 1991) agree that the peak of rainwater harvesting, both for runoff farming and domestic water use in the Negev Highlands, was reached during the Byzantine period. A surprising correlation exists between a prevailing dry climate and the peak of this impressive desert civilization. Reconstructing ancient runoff farms in the Negev, Evenari, Shanan and Tadmor (1971, 1982) demonstrated that this system can function in the present climate, which appears similar to the Late Byzantine climate.

In the Makhtesh Ramon region, Rosen (1987) found evidence for Byzantine pastoral nomadism in the more arid southern Negev highlands. Haiman's (1989) archaeological survey in the western Negev highlands located 220 Byzantine campsites. He found large animal pens in virtually all the sites, and concluded that nomads populated the southern and west-central Negev highlands during the Byzantine period, whereas cities and agriculture flourished in other parts of the central Negev.

The Nizzana papyri, dating to the 6th and 7th centuries AD, attest to crops of wheat and barley, despite the dry climate. Archaeological evidence also exists for wine and oil presses, which infers olive trees and grapevines. Bruins (1986) suggested that drought must have caused occasional problems in crop yields, which were insufficient for the estimated population of at least 30,000 (Broshi 1980). Bruins (1986) calculated that local wheat production could support a maximum of 8000 people, whereas Nevo (1991) estimated an even lower figure, 2500 people.

In view of the convincing evidence of aridity, relatively large population and inevitable drought, 1) imperial subsidies must have played a role in maintaining the local agricultural economy, 2) runoff farming could not have matched the direct food requirements of this sedentary population, and 3) a supplementary food supply from outside the region must have been integral in the political and economic regime of Byzantine times (Bruins 1986).

EARLY ARAB PERIOD

Dry conditions prevailed throughout the first half of the Early Arab period until *ca.* AD 850, as indicated by the average Dead Sea level of *ca.* −399 m (Fig. 2). Erosion in Wadi el Qudeirat also suggests a dry phase in Early Arab times (Bruins 1986). In comparing this climate phase with long-term previous lows in the level of the Dead Sea, the dry Early Arab period appears to have been slightly less arid than the long dry period from Iron Age II into Hellenistic times, and also less dry than during the Middle Bronze Age.

The Negev was the first area outside the Arabian peninsula to be conquered by the Muslim Arabs in AD 634, which marked the beginning of their drive against the Byzantine empire (Mayerson 1964) and subsequent rapid expansion into Asia and Africa. The prevailing dry climate during Late Byzantine times and the first half of the Early Arab period has raised speculation that aridity may have been a factor in the Muslim Arab conquest. However, more detailed climate impact assessment is necessary to understand whether climate influenced political decision-making through its effect on agricultural yields, livestock production, and village and regional economics. The dry period ended *ca.* AD 850 (Fig. 2). Klein's (1986) curve shows a sharp rise to wetter conditions, beginning at AD 930. The wet climate in the second half of the Early Arab period peaked *ca.* AD 1050, when the Dead Sea level reached −350 m, dropping again to −386 m *ca.* AD 1099. This date marks the end of the Early Arab period.

Bruins (1986) studied two hydraulic installations in northeastern Sinai. A dam once blocked the valley of Ein el Qudeirat to raise the level of the water from the spring for irrigation agriculture (Porath 1986; Bruins 1986). Fine pieces of charcoal, dispersed in the mortar of the dam, were extracted and ^{14}C dated (Bruins 1986; Bruins and Mook 1990). The charcoal yielded a date of 1380 ± 90 BP (GrN-12326); the calibrated 1 σ ranges are cal AD 560–584, 588–718, 740–764, with the highest relative probability *ca.* cal AD 655. Charcoal from the mortar of an aqueduct situated downstream yielded a date of 1395 ± 50 BP (GrN-12328). The calibrated age range at 1 σ is cal AD 608–666, with the highest relative age probability *ca.* cal AD 650. Thus, it appears that both the dam and aqueduct date approximately to the same time, with the highest relative probability of the calibration falling at the beginning of the Early Arab period. Further, if wood from trees had been used in the preparation of the mortar for the dam and the aqueduct, the "old wood" factor might render the actual times of construction somewhat younger than the respective ^{14}C dates, making an association with the Early Arab period even more likely. The Arabs introduced innovations of irrigation agriculture in several areas (Watson 1983). The copious spring of Ein el Qudeirat was a choice location during the dry climate of both Late Byzantine times and the beginning of the Early Arab period.

Rothenberg (1988) studied an Early Arab copper smelting site in the southern Arabah, at Beer Ora. The large slag heap yielded well-stratified charcoal samples, which all dated to the Early Arab period. The lowermost sample dated to 1390 ± 50 BP (Pta-4117), which is virtually identical to the two dates from Ein el Qudeirat described above: 1380 ± 90 BP (GrN-12326) and 1395 ± 50 BP (GrN-12328). These three synchronous ^{14}C dates suggest coordinated resource exploitation at suitable spots in this desert region (irrigation agriculture and copper smelting) at the very beginning of the Early Arab period.

Haiman's (1989) archaeological survey in the western Negev Highlands revealed some 70 farms in an area of 450 km^2. The farm houses were usually built on the lower hillside near terraced wadis. The number of structures in the farms varied from 1 to 25. Haiman (1989) found very few animal pens, and assigned an Early Arab age to the farms. However, problems with dating, based on pottery, in the transition from the Late Byzantine to Early Arab period are not yet resolved (Nevo 1991). Bruins (1986, 1990) excavated two adjacent fields of the terraced wadi of Nahal Mitnan, near a large farm house. The dam separating the two fields arrested the runoff floodwaters for ponding, enabling farming in the desert. The dam was one of many in the terraced wadi, and was built of limestone blocks in at least three stages, which suggests a relatively long history of agricultural use. The runoff floodwaters added new sediment to the soil, and new stone layers had to be added to the dam over the years. If, according to Haiman (1989), the fields were established in the Early Arab period, *ca.* AD 640–650, and abandoned *ca.* AD 750, they would have been used only for 100 yr. Whether this period is long enough to account for gradual silting of the soils and accompanying development of the dam seems questionable. Independent dates are available neither for the dam, measuring 140 cm high, nor for the rate of soil accumulation. It appears unlikely that both the 140-cm-high composite dam and the 110-cm-deep soil could have developed in only 100 yr. Thus, check-dams in Nahal Mitnan may have been first constructed for runoff farming during the Byzantine period, when Nevo (1991) believes most wadis in the central Negev were terraced.

Only 20 nomadic campsites with animal pens were found in the area surveyed by Haiman (1989), who noted that nomadic sites from the Early Arab period expanded to include the southern slopes of the Negev Highlands, as well as Biqat Uvda (Avner 1990; Avner, Carmi and Segal 1994) in the southern Negev. Haiman (1989) concluded that the nomadic campsites, runoff farms and the last cities in the Negev were all abandoned in the middle of the 8th century.

What caused the termination in Early Arab times, *ca.* AD 750 (Nevo 1985, 1991; Haiman 1989), of settlement, agriculture and pastoralism in the central Negev? According to the curve of Frumkin *et al.* (1991), there was no change in the average Dead Sea level, which stood at *ca.* −399 m (Fig. 2), throughout the first half of the Early Arab period. If climate conditions made runoff farming possible at *ca.* AD 650, there is no obvious reason why it might have been more difficult *ca.* 100 yr later. However, Frumkin *et al.*'s (1991) curve records the moving average rather than annual variations of the Dead Sea level. This is clearly seen for the last 1000 yr, in comparison with the detailed Klein curve (Fig. 2). The possibility of a drier phase during the mid-8th century should not be ruled out as a terminating factor to Byzantine–Early Arab runoff irrigation in the Negev Highlands. On the other hand, religious, economic, social or political factors may just as well have caused the eventual demise of this sedentary settlement system.

CONCLUSION

The importance of ^{14}C dating for comparisons between climate and human history cannot be over-emphasized. Assessing possible interactions between climate and history is a complex matter, and should be studied as systems analyses in relation to biophysical, economic and social models on different hierarchical levels. My conclusions are more a juxtaposition based on comparative chronology, than an impact assessment. However, it is already apparent from this analysis that a simple relation between climate and human history, *i.e.*, climatic determinism, is not manifest in many cases. Human determination may clearly override negative climate trends.

The transition from the Late Chalcolithic to the Early Bronze Age occurred during the most humid period of the past 7000 yr, which lasted for nearly a millennium from *ca.* 3500–2600 BC. The wettest climate phase occurred *ca.* 3000 BC. EB I and, to a lesser extent, EB II coincided with a climate optimum. Progressive desiccation during EB II and EB III may have influenced the abandonment of sites in the Negev and Sinai. However, the existence of settlements in these areas during the very dry EB IV/MB I seems a paradox, ruling out the argument for climatic determinism. The Middle Bronze Age, including the transitional EB IV/MB I period, seems to have been contemporaneous with the driest phase in historical times, which lasted chronologically in climatic terms from *ca.* 2300 to 1550 BC. The Late Bronze Age and Early Iron Age coincided with a more humid period, which lasted for *ca.* 600 yr until 950 BC. Progressive desiccation during Iron Age I led to aridity, which lasted from *ca.* 950–200 BC. Settlement in the central Negev during the 11th and/or 10th century BC thus occurred at the end of a wet phase, when the climate became increasingly drier. The next humid period began during Late Hellenistic times and peaked *ca.* AD 90. The Roman period was coeval with this humid period, which ended *ca.* AD 300.

Progressive desiccation that began in the 2nd century AD continued throughout the Byzantine and first half of the Early Arab period. The peak of development of the rainwater-harvesting civilization in the Negev Highlands during Byzantine times occurred, surprisingly, during a dry period. Human determination, including political factors and economic subsidies, were apparently more influential than the negative climatic trend. The eventual demise of runoff farming in the central Negev during the Early Arab period could have been affected by drought. However, the decline of the Umayyads and the rise of the Abbasids in AD 750, with the accompanying shift in emphasis from Damascus to Baghdad, may have been the dominant cause. The humid period that began *ca.* AD 850 did not lead to resettlement of the central Negev during the second half of the Early Arab period and subsequent Middle Ages.

REFERENCES CITED

Amiran, D. H. K.
   1991   The climate of the ancient Near East: The early third millennium BC in the northern Negev of Israel. *Erdkunde* 45(3):153–162.
Amiran, R. (editor)
   1978   *Early Arad I. The Chalcolithic Settlement and Early Bronze City.* Israel Exploration Society, Jerusalem.
Anati, D. A. and S. Shasha
   1989   Dead Sea surface-level changes. *Israel Journal of Earth Sciences* 38:29–32.
Avner, U.
   1990   Ancient agricultural settlements and religion in the Uvda valley in southern Israel. *Biblical Archeologist*: 125–141.
Avner, U., I. Carmi and D. Segal
   1994   Neolithic to Bronze Age settlement of the Negev and Sinai in light of radiocarbon dating: A view from the southern Negev. This volume.
Baruch, U.
   1983   The Palynology of a Late Holocene Core from Lake Kinneret. M.A. Thesis, The Hebrew University of Jerusalem, Institute of Archaeology.
Begin, Z. B., A. Ehrlich and Y. Nathan
   1974   Lake Lisan, the Pleistocene precursor of the Dead Sea. *Geological Survey of Israel, Jerusalem, Bulletin* 63.
Begin, Z. B., W. Broecker, B. Buchbinder, Y. Druckman, A. Kaufman, M. Magaritz and D. Neev
   1985   Dead Sea and Lake Lisan levels in the last 30,000 years, a preliminary report. *Geological Survey of Israel, Jerusalem, Report* GSI/29/85.
Beit-Arieh, I.
   1982   An Early Bronze Age II site near the Feiran oasis in southern Sinai. *Tel Aviv* 9:145–156.
Bienkowski, P.
   1989   The division of Middle Bronze IIB-C in Palestine. *Levant* 21:169–179.
Bietak, M.
   1984   Problems of Middle Bronze chronology: New evidence from Egypt. *American Journal of Archaeology* 88:471–485.
Bowman, D.
   1971   Geomorphology of the shore terraces of the Late Pleistocene Lake Lisan, Israel. *Palaeogeography, Palaeoclimatology, Palaeoecology* 9:183–209.
Broshi, M.
   1980   The population of Western Palestine in the Roman-Byzantine period. *Bulletin of the American Schools of Oriental Research (BASOR)* 236:1–10.
Bruins, H. J.
   1986   *Desert Environment and Agriculture in the Central Negeb and Kadesh-Barnea During Historical Times.* Ph.D. Dissertation, The Agricultural University of Wageningen. Midbar Foundation, Nijkerk, The Netherlands.
   1990a Ancient agricultural terraces at Nahal Mitnan. *Atiqot* 10:127–128 (Hebrew), 22*–28* (English).
   1990b The impact of man and climate on the central Negev and northeastern Sinai deserts during the Late Holocene. In *Man's Role in the Shaping of the Eastern Mediterranean Landscape,* edited by S. Bottema, G. Entjes-Nieborg and W. van Zeist, pp. 87–99. Balkema, Rotterdam.
Bruins, H. J., M. Evenari and A. Rogel
   1987   Run-off farming management and climate. In *Progress in Desert Research,* edited by L. Berkofsky and M. G. Wurtele, pp. 3–14. Roman and Littlefield, Totowa, New Jersey.
Bruins, H. J. and W. G. Mook
   1989   The need for a calibrated ^{14}C chronology of Near Eastern archaeology. *Radiocarbon* 31(3):1019–1029.

Bruins, H. J. and W. G. Mook
   1990   Radiocarbon dating in the northeastern Sinai desert: Ein el Qudeirat, Kadesh-Barnea. In *Proceedings of the Second International Symposium on ^{14}C and Archaeology Groningen*, edited by W. G. Mook and H. T. Waterbolk, pp. 311–334. PACT 29, Strasbourg.

Bruins, H. J., J. van der Plicht and W. G. Mook
   1991   Establishing calibrated ^{14}C chronologies: Problematic time zones and high precision dating, with reference to Near Eastern archaeology (Abstract). *Radiocarbon* 33(2):183–184.

Cohen, R.
   1976   Excavations at Horvat Haluqim. *Atiqot* 11:34–50.
   1980   The Iron Age fortresses in the central Negev. *Bulletin of the American Schools of Oriental Research* 236:61–79.
   1981a   Excavations at Kadesh-Barnea, 1976–1978. *Biblical Archeologist* 44:93–107.
   1981b   Did I excavate Kadesh-Barnea? *Biblical Archaeology Review* 7:20–33.
   1983   *Kadesh-Barnea. A Fortress from the Time of the Judaean Kingdom.* The Israel Museum, Jerusalem.
   1986   The Settlement of the Central Negev in the Light of Archaeology and Literary Sources During the 4th–1st Millennia B.C.E. Ph.D. Dissertation, The Hebrew University of Jerusalem.

Dehling, H. and J. van der Plicht
   1993   Statistical problems in calibrating radiocarbon dates. *Radiocarbon* 35(1):239–244.

Evenari, M., L. Shanan and N. H. Tadmor
   1971   *The Negev: The Challenge of a Desert.* Harvard University Press, Cambridge, Massachusetts.
   1982   *The Negev: The Challenge of a Desert,* Second edition. Harvard University Press, Cambridge, Massachusetts.

Feliks, J.
   1963   *Agriculture in Palestine in the Period of the Mishna and Talmud.* Magnes Press, Jerusalem (in Hebrew).

Frumkin, A.
   1982   Formation of potholes and caves in rocksalt, Mount Sedom. *Niqrot Zurim, Journal of the Israel Cave Research Center* 6:15–38 (in Hebrew).

Frumkin, A., I. Carmi, I. Zak and M. Magaritz
   1994   Middle Holocene environmental change determined from the salt caves of Mount Sedom, Israel. This volume.

Frumkin, A., M. Magaritz, I. Carmi and I. Zak
   1991   The Holocene climatic record of the salt caves of Mount Sedom, Israel. *The Holocene* 1:190–200.

Goodfriend, G. A., M. Magaritz and I. Carmi
   1986   A high stand of the Dead Sea at the end of the Neolithic period: Paleoclimatic and archeological implications. *Climatic Change* 9:349–356.

Haas, H., J. M. Devine, R. Wenke, M. Lehner, W. Wolfli and G. Bonani
   1987   Radiocarbon chronology and the historical calendar in Egypt. In *Chronologies du Proche Orient*, edited by O. Aurenche, J. Evin and F. Hours, pp. 585–606. BAR International Series 379. British Archaeological Reports, Oxford.

Haiman, M.
   1989   Preliminary report of the western Negev Highlands emergency survey. *Israel Exploration Journal* 39:173–191.

Hassan, F. A. and S. W. Robinson
   1987   High-precision radiocarbon chronometry of ancient Egypt, and comparisons with Nubia, Palestine and Mesopotamia. *Antiquity* 61:119–135.

Helms, S. W.
   1981   *Jawa. Lost City of the Black Desert.* Methuen, London.

Horowitz, A.
   1978   Human settlement patterns in Israel. *Expedition* 20:55–58.

Ingram, M. J., G. Farmer and T. M. L. Wigley
   1981   Past climates and their impact on man: A review. In *Climate and History*, edited by T. M. L. Wigley, M. J. Ingram and G. Farmer, pp. 3–50. Cambridge University Press, Cambridge.

Issar, A. S.
   1990   *Water Shall Flow from the Rock.* Springer-Verlag, Berlin.

Kedar, Y.
   1967   *The Ancient Agriculture in the Negev Mountains.* Bialik Institute, Jerusalem (in Hebrew).

Kempinski, A.
   1983   *Syrien und Palastina (Kanaan) in der letzten Phase der Mittelbronze IIB-Zeit (1650–1570 v. Chr.).* Otto Harrassowitz, Wiesbaden.

Klein, C.
1961   On the fluctuations of the level of the Dead Sea since the beginning of the 19th century. *Hydrological Paper 7*. Ministry of Agriculture, Hydrological Service, Jerusalem.
1981   The influence of rainfall over the catchment area on the fluctuations of the level of the Dead Sea since the 12th century. *Israel Meteorological Research Papers* 3:29–57.
1982   Morphological evidence of lake level changes, western shore of the Dead Sea. *Israel Journal of Earth Sciences* 31:67–94.
1986   Fluctuations of the Level of the Dead Sea and Climatic Fluctuations in Erez-Israel during Historical Times. Ph.D. Dissertation, The Hebrew University of Jerusalem.

Klein, M.
1990   Dead Sea level changes. Letter to the editor. *Israel Journal of Earth Sciences* 39:49–51.

Lev-Yadun, S.
1987   Annual rings in trees as an index to climate changes intensity in our region in the past. *Rotem* 22:6–17, 113 (in Hebrew, English abstract).

Liphschitz, N., S. Lev-Yadun and Y. Waisel
1987   A climatic history of the Sinai peninsula in the light of dendrochronological studies. In *Sinai*, edited by G. Gvirtzman, A. Shmueli, Y. Gradus, I. Beit-Arieh and M. Har-El, pp. 525–531. Eretz, Tel-Aviv University and Publishing House, Ministry of Defense (in Hebrew).

Mayerson, P.
1955   Arid Zone Farming in Antiquity: A Study of Ancient Agricultural and Related Hydrological Practices in Southern Palestine. Ph.D. Dissertation, New York University.
1960   *The Ancient Agricultural Regime at Nessana and the Central Negeb.* Colt Archaeological Institute. The British School of Archaeology in Jerusalem, London.
1964   The first Muslim attacks on southern Palestine according to Byzantine sources. *Transactions and Proceedings of the American Philological Association* 95:155–199.
1983   The city of Elusa in the literary sources of the fourth–sixth centuries. *Israel Exploration Journal* 33:247–253.

Mazar, A.
1990   *Archaeology of the Land of the Bible - 10,000–586 B.C.E.* Doubleday, New York.

Mazar, B.
1986   The Middle Bronze Age in Canaan. In *The Early Biblical Period*, edited by B. Mazar, pp. 1–34. Israel Exploration Society, Jerusalem.

Neev, D. and K. O. Emery
1967   The Dead Sea. Depositional processes and environments of evaporites. *Geological Survey of Israel, Jerusalem, Bulletin* 41.

Negev, A.
1981   Les Nabateans au Negev. Le Christianisme au Negev. La vie économique et sociale à l'époque Byzantine. *Le Monde de la Bible* 18:4–46.
1982   Numismatics and Nabatean chronology. *Palestine Exploration Quarterly* 114:119–128.

Negev, A. (editor)
1972   *Archaeological Encyclopedia of the Holy Land.* Jerusalem: The Jerusalem Publishing House and Steimatzky.

Nevo, Y. D.
1985   Sede Boqer and the central Negev: 7th-8th century AD. In *Third International Colloquium: From Jahiliyya to Islam*, The Hebrew University of Jerusalem.
1991   *Pagans and Herders. A Re-examination of the Negev Runoff Cultivation Systems in the Byzantine and Early Arab periods.* IPS Ltd., Midreshet Ben-Gurion.

Oren, E. D.
1979   North Sinai before the Classical period. In *Sinai, Pharaohs, Miners, Pilgrims and Soldiers*, edited by B. Rothenberg, pp. 181–191. Kümmerly and Frey, Bern.
1985   Respondent. In *Biblical Archaeology Today*. Proceedings of the International Congress on Biblical Archaeology, pp. 223–226. Israel Exploration Society, Jerusalem.

Parry, M. L. and T. R. Carter
1987   Climate impact assessment: a review of some approaches. In *Planning for Drought*, edited by D. A. Wilhite and W. E. Easterling with D. A. Wood, pp. 165–187. Westview Press, Boulder and London.

Porath, Y.
1985   Ancient Irrigation Agriculture in the Arid Zones of Eretz Israel. Ph.D. Dissertation, Institute of Archaeology, Tel-Aviv University.

314   *H. J. Bruins*

Rosen, A. M.
   1986a   Quaternary stratigraphy and paleoenvironments of the Shephela, Israel. *Geological Survey of Israel, Jerusalem, Report* 25/86.
   1986b   *Cities of Clay: The Geoarcheology of Tells.* The University of Chicago Press, Chicago.
   1989   Environmental change at the end of Early Bronze Age Palestine. In *L'Urbanisation de la Palestine à l'Age du Bronze Ancien,* edited by P. de Miroschedji, pp. 247–255. BAR International Series 527, British Archaeological Reports, Oxford.
Rosen, S. A.
   1987   Byzantine nomadism in the Negev: Results from the emergency survey. *Journal of Field Archaeology* 14:29–42.
Rothenberg, B.
   1972   *Timna.* Thames and Hudson, London.
   1988   Early Islamic copper smelting – and worship – at Beer Ora, southern Arabah (Israel). *Newsletter of the Institute for Archaeo-Metallurgical Studies* 12:1–4.
Rothenberg, B. (editor)
   1989   *The Egyptian Mining Temple at Timna: Researches in the Arabah 1959–1984,* Vol. 1. Institute for Archaeo-Metallurgical Studies, University of London.
Sperber, D.
   1978   *Roman Palestine 200–400 – The Land: Crisis and Change in Agrarian Society as Reflected in Rabbinic Sources.* Bar-Ilan University, Ramat Gan.
Stuiver, M. and R. S. Kra (editors)
   1986   Calibration Issue. *Radiocarbon* 28(2B):805–1030.
Stuiver, M., A. Long, and R. S. Kra (editors)
   1993   Calibration 1993. *Radiocarbon* 35(1):1–244.
Stuiver, M. and P. J. Reimer
   1993   Extended ^{14}C data base and revised CALIB 3.0 ^{14}C age calibration program. *Radiocarbon* 35(1):215–230.
van der Plicht, J.
   1991   Automatic calibration of radiocarbon dates. *Radiocarbon* 33(2):252.
   1993   The Groningen Radiocarbon Calibration Program. *Radiocarbon* 35(1):231–237.
van der Plicht, J. and W. G. Mook
   1987   Automatic ^{14}C calibration: Illustrative examples. *Palaeohistoria* 29:173–182.
   1989   Calibration of radiocarbon ages by computer. *Radiocarbon* 31(3):805–816.
Waisel, Y. and N. Liphschitz
   1968   Dendrochronological studies in Israel. II. *Juniperus phoenicea* of north and central Sinai. *La-Yaaran* 18:63–67.
Watson, A. M.
   1983   *Agricultural Innovation in the Early Islamic World. The Diffusion of Crops and Farming Techniques, 700–1100.* Cambridge University Press, Cambridge.
Weinstein, J. M.
   1984   Radiocarbon dating in the Southern Levant. *Radiocarbon* 26(2):297–366.

MIDDLE HOLOCENE ENVIRONMENTAL CHANGE DETERMINED FROM THE SALT CAVES OF MOUNT SEDOM, ISRAEL

AMOS FRUMKIN[1], *ISRAEL CARMI*[2], *ISRAEL ZAK*[3] and *MORDECKAI MAGARITZ*[4]

INTRODUCTION

Several researchers have suggested that climate change was one of the causes of the rise and fall of the Early Bronze Age culture in Israel (*e.g.* Neev and Emery 1967; Goldberg and Bar-Yosef 1980; Richard 1980; Amiran 1986; Rosen 1989; Issar 1990). Others suggest that environmental changes were subordinate to political and social/economic factors (Crown 1972; Dever 1989). They agree that archaeological data alone do not suffice as paleoclimate indicators. However, other kinds of natural evidence, such as pollen or paleomorphology, may also suffer from such human interference as deforestation and agriculture, and do not always record pure climatic events. The interpretation of paleoclimates and paleocultures should be based on multidisciplinary studies. In this chapter, we discuss new data from Mount Sedom, which is located far from human interference. In our interpretation of Middle Holocene climate change, we also consider other evidence gathered in Israel mainly during the last decade. Finally, we correlate our data with African climate fluctuations.

Only a few karst salt caves are known from the non-arid areas of the world (Spain, Romania, Russia). Such caves are more common in arid climates where rock-salt outcrops may escape complete dissolution and cave destruction. Mount Sedom is a salt diapir on the southwestern shore of the Dead Sea, one of the most arid parts of Israel. In this region, a climate change occurred from semi-arid to extremely arid during the Late Pleistocene and Holocene. Mount Sedom broke through the bottom of the Late Pleistocene Lake Lisan (Begin, Nathan and Ehrlich 1980). In the course of the Holocene, after the lower-level Dead Sea succeeded Lake Lisan, an active karst system developed within the continually rising diapir.

[14]C ages of plant remains that were found within flood sediments at various levels of the cave systems, together with the corresponding cave geometry, were used to reconstruct Holocene Dead Sea levels, and deduce stages in regional climate history (Frumkin *et al.* 1991). The Dead Sea, a highly saline closed lake (Fig. 1), occupies the depositional center of an extensional basin within the Dead Sea Rift Valley, formed along the sinistral transform of the Levant (*e.g.*, Zak and Freund 1981). The 1993 elevation of the Dead Sea surface is 410 m below mean ocean level (−410 m). The area is extremely arid, with an average yearly rainfall of 50 mm.

The Dead Sea basin is filled by a thick sequence of detrital sediments and evaporites that give rise to subsurface salt diapirs (Neev and Hall 1979). Of these, Mount Sedom, an exposed head of salt diapir on the southwestern shore of the lake, is the only one to have broken surface. Mount Sedom forms an elongated ridge, 11 km x 1.5 km, rising up to 250 m above the present Dead Sea level (Fig. 1). It consists of Plio-Pleistocene (?) beds of rock salt of marine origin, piercing through tilted strata of younger lake evaporites and clastics. Before its subaerial extrusion, the top of the rising diapir underwent dissolution by groundwater and residual insoluble matter accumulated to form a cap rock up to 50 m thick (Zak 1967; Zak and Bentor 1968). The flat, near-horizontal contact

[1]Israel Cave Research Center, 90906 Ofra, Israel
[2]Department of Environmental Sciences and Energy Research, Weizmann Institute of Science, 76100 Rehovot, Israel
[3]Department of Geology, The Hebrew University of Jerusalem, 91904 Jerusalem, Israel
[4]Deceased 1993

Late Quaternary Chronology and Paleoclimates of the Eastern Mediterranean
Edited by O. Bar-Yosef and R. S. Kra. RADIOCARBON 1994, pp. 315–332

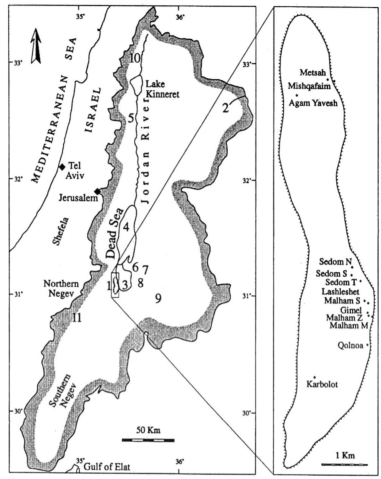

Fig. 1. Location map. 1. Mount Sedom; 2. Boundary of Dead Sea catchment area; 3. South Dead Sea basin; 4. North Dead Sea basin; 5. Bet She'ean basin; 6. Wadi Kerak; 7. Bab edh-Dhra; 8. Numeira; 9. Wadi Hasa; 10. Hula basin; 11. Avedat

between the almost vertical salt layers and the cap rock is referred to as the "salt table" or "salt mirror". The top of Mount Sedom is roughly tabular, with many small watersheds up to 0.7 km^2 (Gerson 1974). The relatively insoluble cap rock overlying the highly soluble rock salt has favored the development of allogenic karst (Frumkin *et al.* 1991).

During infrequent rainstorms, runoff collects on the somewhat impervious cap rock and flows into fissures, which offer a higher gradient than the subaerial routes. Ultimately, an allogenic vadose cave system develops, acting as an underground watercourse (Frumkin 1992). A salt cave consists generally of a vertical shaft, through which water and detritus enter the cavity, and a subhorizontal passage. Nearly all caves have active passages as well as relict passages at higher levels. Some cave passages join underground, forming a branchwork cave system, *e.g.*, Malham Cave, whose tributaries are termed Malham Z, Malham S and Malham M, or Sedom Cave, whose tributaries are Sedom N, Sedom S and Sedom T (for symbols, see Table 1 and Fig. 1). Mount Sedom possesses the longest salt caves known in the world, over 5500 m long.

TABLE 1. Dates of wood fragments from measured cave passages of Mount Sedom. Some samples could be identified to genus level only. Calibration of ¹⁴C to calendrical dates (cal ages) is by the standard conversion method (Stuiver and Pearson 1986; Pearson *et al.* 1986). Passage width was measured close to the sampling site, and normalized to presently active passage width (percent of present width).

Cave name	Field no.	Lab no. (RT-)	Species	¹⁴C date (yr BP)	Calibrated age (1 σ range)	Passage width ratio (%)	Proposed climate stage
Lashleshet	La1	886H	*Anabasis setifera* Moq.	7090 ± 175	6089–5760 BCE*	370	1
Malham Z	MZ5	886A	*Tamarix* sp.	5940 ± 80	4940–4730 BCE	85	
Malham S	MS2	848E	*Anabasis setifera* Moq.	5570 ± 110	4576–4336 BCE	Nondet.	2b
Malham Z	MZ3	1205	*Tamarix* sp.	5220 ± 50	4218–3983 BCE	85	
Malham S	MS3	886D	*Anabasis setifera* Moq.	5070 ± 90	3972–3788 BCE	185	
Malham Z	MZ2	848G	*Tamarix* sp.	4960 ± 180	3980–3534 BCE	248	
Malham M	MM3	886B	*Quercus calliprinos* Webb.	4580 ± 90	3497–3105 BCE	290	
Gimel	Gi1	886E	*Quercus calliprinos* Webb.	4500 ± 75	3339–3098 BCE	Nondet.	
Malham S	MS1	848D	Nondet.	4440 ± 120	3330–2927 BCE	358	
Qolnoa	Qo1	810E	*Quercus calliprinos* Webb.	4360 ± 140	3323–2882 BCE	327	3
Metsah	Me3	886F	*Anabasis setifera* Moq.	4350 ± 75	3093–2904 BCE	437	
Malham M	MM2	886C	*Quercus calliprinos* Webb.	4250 ± 95	3028–2662 BCE	289	
Sedom N	SN1	810A	*Anabasis setifera* Moq.	4050 ± 75	2694–2490 BCE	106	
Sedom N	SN3	810C	*Tamarix* sp.	3970 ± 100	2654–2336 BCE	106	
Sedom N	SN2	810B	*Nitraria retusa* Asch.	3900 ± 90	2562–2280 BCE	106	
Sedom N	SN5	810D	*Tamarix* sp.	3580 ± 80	2112–1819 BCE	37	4
Mishqafaim	Mi15	982G	Nondet.	3100 ± 55	1436–1312 BCE	185	
Mishqafaim	Mi12	982E	*Haloxylon persicum*	3030 ± 50	1393–1258 BCE	111	5
Agam Yavesh	AY4	943B	*Anabasis setifera* Moq.	2880 ± 50	1159–993 BCE	Nondet.	
Agam Yavesh	AY1	943A	*Anabasis setifera* Moq.	2750 ± 50	976–838 BCE	Nondet.	6
Mishqafaim	Mi14	982F	*Haloxylon persicum*	1990 ± 50	54 BCE–66 CE**	259	
Mishqafaim	Mi13	1236	*Salsola* sp.	1890 ± 40	60–180 CE	259	
Malham M	MM1	848F	*Tamarix* sp.	1860 ± 90	29–249 CE	190	7
Mishqafaim	Mi10	1235	*Salsola* sp.	1690 ± 50	259–408 CE	221	
Agam Yavesh	AY6	943C	*Anabasis setifera* Moq.	1320 ± 50	654–767 CE	Nondet.	8
Malham Z	MZ16	982C	Nondet.	1100 ± 45	895–979 CE	150	
Mishqafaim	Mi2	982D	*Anabasis setifera* Moq.	930 ± 50	1033–1158 CE	177	
Mishqafaim	Mi1	848C	*Anabasis setifera* Moq.	885 ± 95	1043–1217 CE	177	9
Malham Z	MZ15	982B	Nondet.	830 ± 60	1127–1266 CE	150	
Metsah	Me2	1204	*Salsola* sp. or *Suaeda* sp.	720 ± 40	1256–1289 CE	250	
Karbolot	Ka1	982A	*Tamarix* sp.	480 ± 40	1411–1444 CE	Nondet.	
Sedom S	SS1	848A	*Anabasis setifera* Moq.	260 ± 85	1504–1799 CE	Nondet.	10
Sedom S	SS2	848B	*Anabasis setifera* Moq.	200 ± 90	1639–1878 CE	Nondet.	

*BCE=before Christian era; **CE=Christian era. From Table 1, Frumkin *et al.* 1991; reprinted by permission of Edward Arnold, Ltd.

DOWNCUTTING RATES AND BASE-LEVEL CHANGES

The incision rate of the caves varies according to time scale involved (Frumkin 1992). A momentary rate of 0.2 mm/sec (averaged along the passage) was recorded, by mass balance calculation, along the Sedom T passage during a flood. The entrenchment of the same cave passage was measured directly several times from 1986 to 1991, using 75 plastic pegs as datum. The mean incision into the rock salt along the passage bottom during these years was 4.4 cm (average 0.88 cm/yr). These recorded incision rates are at least one order of magnitude higher than the maximum incision rates in limestone caves (Gascoyne, Ford and Schwarz 1983; Palmer 1991). The high incision rates are attributed to the high solubility of the rock salt, which is only partly balanced by the scarcity of water. These rates cannot be extrapolated reliably in time because of the large variance of flood distribution in this extremely arid zone, and possible climate change (Gerson 1972).

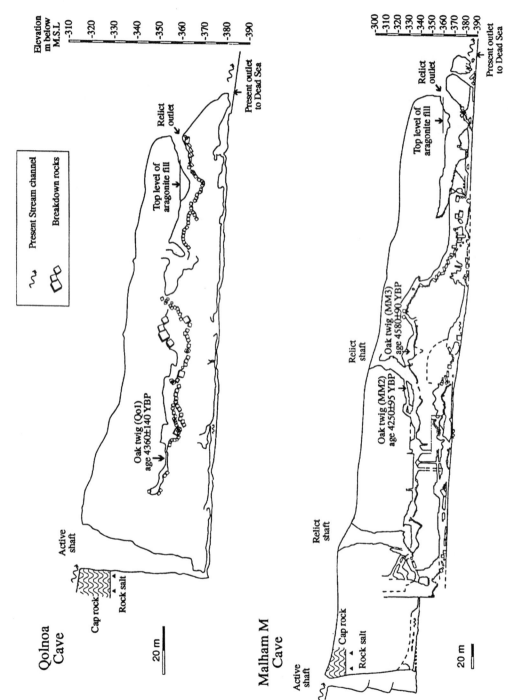

Fig. 2. Longitudinal profiles of two caves in Mount Sedom with ^{14}C ages of driftwood and major morphological elements

The slope of the Sedom T passage (excluding the shaft) is 22°. However, most cave passages in Mount Sedom slope at gradients of only a few degrees toward the base level (Fig. 2). The passage bottom is usually shielded by alluvial clastic deposits, fine-grained to pebbly, which include anhydrite, dolomite and quartz, all locally derived from Mount Sedom. This prevents dissolution of the bed and lower walls of the passage. In some passages, aggradation was accompanied by upward solution of the ceiling. These passages are wide and flat-roofed.

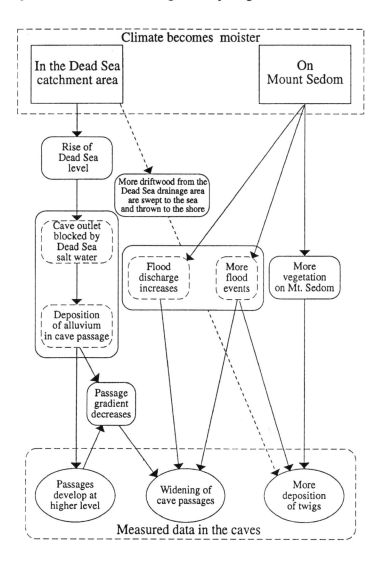

Fig. 3. Some effects of moister climate on cave evolution in Mt. Sedom (from Fig. 5, Frumkin *et al.* 1991). Reprinted by permission of Edward Arnold, Ltd.

Our observations suggest that the Mount Sedom cave system is highly responsive to flow regime and base-level changes. After such a change, the passage soon attains a graded sub-horizontal longitudinal profile, sloping asymptotically to the new base level. The local base level that influences the cave levels is the Dead Sea, or, during periods of lake retreat, the low areas surrounding the diapir. During phases of rapid changes in base level, downcutting or ceiling dissolution adjust the cave passage elevation to the new base level (Fig. 3). Thus, the topographic elevation of a relict horizontal cave passage can be used as an indicator for the Dead Sea level. The apparent Dead Sea level history, as indicated by cave levels, should be separated into two components: the true lake level change and the diapir uplift. We took into account an estimated 4-mm/yr rising diapir rate (Frumkin 1992) in the reconstructed lake-level curve presented in this study.

DATING RELICT TERRACES AND CAVE LEVELS

Regression levels of Lake Lisan and fluctuating Dead Sea levels have left terraces on the sloping shores (Bowman 1971). Zak (1967) noticed that, on Mount Sedom, vertical distances between terraces are somewhat greater than along nearby (and more northern) shores of the lake, most probably as a result of continuous uplift of the mountain. Datable material is rarely found along these terraces. Within the karst system of the mountain, on the other hand, ancient base levels are preserved by the subhorizontal cave passages, today left high and dry. In cases where their ages can be determined by datable remnants (such as fossil plant material), and the estimated or assumed rate of the diapir's rising, the approximate lake level at the time of passage formation may be evaluated. A similar method was used by Gascoyne *et al.* (1983) in limestone terrain.

Datable materials were indeed found in alluvial clastic sediments within the Mount Sedom caves (Fig. 4), consisting of wood fragments left behind by flood waters, and which—since they were not flushed out—evidently represent the latest floods in the passage. The different plant species to which the wood belongs are probably indicative of the plant community which existed on Mount Sedom at the time of flood, since even today, with highly arid conditions, Mount Sedom sustains some shrubs whose twigs occasionally drift into the stream sinks.

Fig. 4. Piece of wood (Sample ME3), *ca.* 12 cm long, embedded on alluvial flood sediment lining a cave passage

Reconstructing the local climate by the amount and composition of plant remains from the immediate vicinity is more straightforward than the use of pollen, which, in this area, may be heavily wind-contaminated. The relation between the plant ages and the time of formation of the cave passage is subject to two uncertainties. One is the residence time of the plant remains on the surface, before they are carried into the cave; the other is the age of the cave before the wood was deposited in it. As to the first factor, Yechieli and Carmi (unpublished ^{14}C results, Weizmann Institute of Science) found an average 100-yr time lag in driftwood found in present-day wadis of the Dead Sea. As to the second factor, downcutting rates presented here suggest that, during periods of non-stable base level, active passages are abandoned quickly and new passages are formed at a higher or lower level. For the present study, we assume that the age of a passage level is approximated by the age of driftwood found in it.

CAVE MORPHOMETRY AS A PALEOCLIMATE INDICATOR

Data from active stream passages in Mount Sedom suggest that passage width may be increased by 1) increase of discharge; this could be caused by an increase in intensity or number of rain storms over Mount Sedom; 2) decrease of hydraulic gradient; this could be caused by a rise of Dead Sea level relative to Mount Sedom. A higher rate of Dead Sea rising would cause ceiling dissolution and widening; 3) duration of water flow in a single level. If the Dead Sea level rises at the same rate as the diapir, the net effect would be a relative base-level stability and cave widening.

We define the width ratio of a relict cave passage as the ratio (in %) of its width to the width of the presently active passage in the same cave tributary. From the discussion above, it follows that passage width and morphology can be used as a paleoclimate indicator for the amount or the intensity of rainfall over Mount Sedom, and also as an indicator for changes in the Dead Sea level. During moist periods, the Dead Sea level rises, cave passage width increases and more plant remains are deposited with the alluvium (Fig. 3). However, it should be noted that not all the cave parameters respond synchronously to climate change; while passage width responds almost instantaneously, the rise of lake level may take longer and changes of vegetation may take many years. Additional climate data should be used to differentiate between the regional (Dead Sea catchment area) and local (Mount Sedom) climate changes. The level of the Dead Sea had been used before as a paleoclimate indicator for the whole catchment area (*e.g.*, Neev and Hall 1977; Begin *et al.* 1985; Klein 1986), being a product of the precipitation/evaporation ratio. We define a ratio higher than today's as "moist" and lower than today's as "dry".

DATING PLANT REMAINS FROM THE CAVES BY [14]C

[14]C measurements were made on cellulose extracted from the wood samples by soxhlet apparatus. The cellulose was oxidized in a calorimetric bomb. The product CO_2 was next converted to lithium carbide, then to acetylene, and finally, to ethane. The ethane was used for counting gas in proportional counters (Carmi 1987). Samples were counted to a precision of *ca.* 0.5%. The conventional date calculation is based on the Libby half-life (5570 yr), and includes a correction for fractionation, based on ^{13}C measurements. The uniformity of ages in one location was tested on samples from three tree species from the same passage level in Sedom Cave (SN-1,2,3). The ages obtained were 4050 ± 75, 3970 ± 100 and 3900 ± 90 BP. These are quite close and suggest an age of *ca.* 4000 BP for this cave passage. Another piece of wood (SN5), from a passage 6 m lower, yielded a significantly younger age of 3580 ± 80 BP.

RESULTS

Ages of wood samples collected from the Mount Sedom caves range from nearly 7100 BP to *ca.* 200 BP. Table 1 presents conventional ^{14}C ages (BP), measured on 33 pieces of wood from 12 caves (Fig. 1). Here, we use conventional ^{14}C ages (BP) as suggested by Mangerud, Birks and Jäger (1982), unless mentioned otherwise. Calendric ages of the 33 samples were also calculated (Table 1) to enable comparison with historical data. Ages were calculated using dendrochronological calibration data (Stuiver and Pearson 1986; Pearson *et al.* 1986), and the CalibETH program (Niklaus 1991). Age distribution shows the absence of samples from 7000–6000 BP, followed by gradual increase to nine samples clustered within a 700-yr period, 4600–3900 BP, with a maximum from 4600–4200 BP. This is followed by gradual decrease (Table 1 and Fig. 5).

The plant species to which the wood fragments belong were identified by Prof. N. Lifshitz of Tel Aviv University and Dr. E. Werker of the Hebrew University. The defined species include *Anabasis setifera* Moq., *Tamarix* sp., *Nitraria retusa* Asch., *Phragmites australis* sp., *Haloxylon*

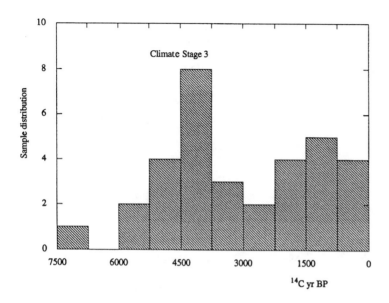

Fig. 5. Frequency distribution of ^{14}C dates of driftwood in Mount Sedom caves

persicum sp., *Salsola* sp., *Suaeda* sp. and *Quercus calliprinos* Webb. All these shrub and tree species, except *Quercus*, are found today in a neighboring area south of the Dead Sea (Danin, Orshan and Zohary 1975) or in small watersheds on Mount Sedom itself. Four fossil oak samples that were found are from three different caves and from the short interval, 4600–4200 BP. Oak does not grow today in the Dead Sea area, as it needs >400 mm annual precipitation. The soil profile on Mount Sedom does not support such a dramatic change of conditions, leading us to assume that the oak was transported by some agent from a nearby Mediterranean environment. Altogether, most of the Holocene arboraceous flora from the caves are similar to the present-day plant community in the area.

Temporal changes in cave passage width ratios fall between 37% and 437% (Table 1). A time-width ratio curve was drawn using the sampling points whose width ratio could be determined (Fig. 6). Using all data, we divided the period represented by the salt caves into ten climate stages. At the levels belonging to some of these periods, a relatively large quantity of wood fragments was found. The intervals between these periods, as well as the present, represent dry phases during which the rate of cave widening was diminished, as was the number of wood fragments. Dead Sea levels in the southern basin were calculated from the elevations of cave outlets, taking into account diapir uplift (Fig. 7) and other considerations (see discussion below).

Frumkin *et al.* (1991) discussed the general climate scheme inferred from the Mount Sedom caves. A good correlation was found between cave-passage elevation, width ratio and driftwood distribution. These data correlate fairly well with other Dead Sea fluctuation data, such as sediment succession in the south basin. All data point to climate as a regional controlling factor. The period from *ca.* 6000 to 5200 BP (Stage 2b) is the transition between the arid Stage 2a to the moist Stage 3. At this time, two tributaries of the Malham Cave system (MZ and MS) developed, as indicated by three wood samples. The proximity of stream sinks of the two earliest cave systems (Malham and Lashleshet) indicates the limited area of diapir emergence above base level during this period. Malham Cave was first to break through the foot of the eastern cliff of Mount Sedom.

Although the Stage 3 passages are partly altered by breakdown (Fig. 2), their principal morphology can be determined easily. Passage widening during this stage is the most pronounced in the whole

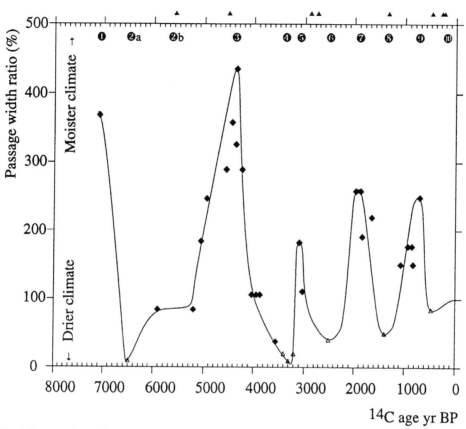

Fig. 6. Passage width ratio *vs.* age in Mount Sedom caves. Time-width ratio curve is drawn through analyzed and interpolated data points. Note that the narrow passages that developed during the drier stages (2a, 4, 6 and 8) did not yield any wood. ◆=¹⁴C date; △=dated by interpolation; ▲=¹⁴C dated but undefined passage width; ❸=proposed climate stage

cave system of Mount Sedom (Fig. 8A–E); the width ratio reaches 185–437% (Table 1). Some of these passages are 10–20 m wide and 10 m high. Their outlets on the southeastern face of the mountain are the only relict outlets not to become clogged by talus, and are clearly distinguished from a distance (Figs. 9, 10). Fossil wood is more common than in any other period (Fig. 5). Seven large cave passages were dated to 5200–3900 BP using 12 wood samples (Table 1), 4 of them oak (*Quercus calliprinos*). Six (including the 4 oak twigs) were dated to 4600–4200 BP, a period when width ratio reached maximal value. The oak samples were found in three caves with separate watersheds. This suggests that oaks either grew at several localities on the mountain, or were scattered there by some local transporting agent. However, the possibility that oaks grew on Mount Sedom during this period is unlikely, considering oak distribution in adjacent areas and the absence of significant soil profile on Mount Sedom. The oak could have been brought to Mount Sedom by humans, but no archaeological remains are known from the mountain. In a preliminary report of the present study (Frumkin *et al.* 1991), we suggested the Dead Sea as a possible trans-porting agent. The remote points in the caves where oak twigs were found prove that no direct deposition by the Dead Sea is possible (Fig. 2). The Dead Sea could only transport the twigs to the catchment area of the caves, from where they would have been swept into the caves by flood

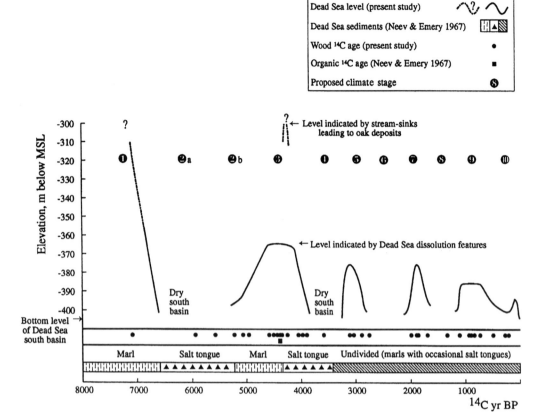

Fig. 7. Fluctuations of Dead Sea level and sediment types of the south basin. Calculated lake levels take into account diapir uplift of 4 mm/yr.

water. This scenario suggests a rising of the Dead Sea level up to *ca.* −300 m (assuming a diapir uplift of 4 mm/yr). However, there is no other indication of such a high level during Stage 3.

The caves' morphology does prove that the lake rose during this stage by several tens of meters, up to *ca.* −360 m. This level is indicated by Dead Sea solution features found at −345 m level in Stage 3 passage of Malham Cave (assuming a diapir uplift rate of 4 mm/yr). These features resemble some phreatic solution features in limestone caves, as opposed to flood solution features in salt caves, which resemble vadose solution features in limestone caves (Bretz 1942). Such Dead Sea solution features were first identified along the eastern escarpment of Mount Sedom, on rock salt outcrops flooded by the Dead Sea at the beginning of the 20th century.

The ceilings of Stage 3 passages are usually flat (if not disturbed by breakdown), and the bottom is usually covered by alluvial deposits, which become fine-grained toward the upper part of the exposed sections. These features indicate paragenesis—upward solution of the ceiling (Renault 1967). Aragonite fill (determined by X-ray diffraction) was deposited up to the ceiling of three cave passages near the outlets, up to present level of −359 m (Fig. 10). This deposit was found only in Stage 3 passages, and was determined to be ^{14}C free, indicating redeposition of older sediment. We suggest that a secondary detrital sediment settled from flood water and reached the caves' outlets while they were flooded by the Dead Sea. The sediment was probably derived from the Lisan formation that covers the mountain.

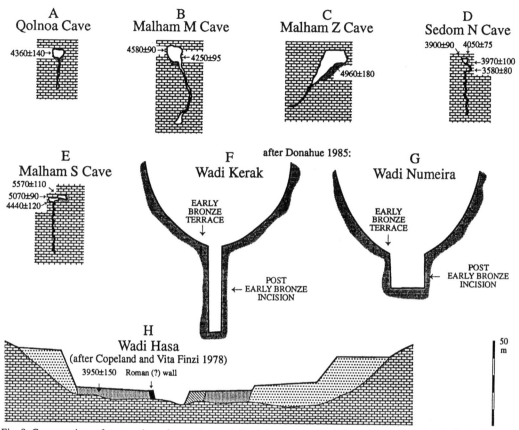

Fig. 8. Cross-sections of stream channels near the south Dead Sea basin, with dating evidence. Numbers indicate ^{14}C ages. A, B, C, D, E – Mount Sedom caves: Qolnoa, Malham M, Malham Z, Sedom N, Malham S, respectively. F, G, H – surficial streams on the eastern side of the Dead Sea. Text indicates dating by archaeology: Wadi Kerak, Wadi Numeira (both after Donahue 1985), Wadi Hasa (after Copeland and Vita-Finzi 1978), respectively.

The morphological evidence indicates that passages became completely filled with water and sediment during the climax of Stage 3, when the Dead Sea level reached *ca.* –360 m (taking into account 4 mm/yr diapir uplift). This level was maintained long enough for the passages to become wide and filled with sediment.

At the end of Stage 3, passage widths become narrower throughout the cave system, associated with deeper incision and base-level lowering (Fig. 8A–E). Fewer wood fragments were deposited in the caves. The end of the moist stage was dated to *ca.* 4000 BP by three twigs from the upper level of Sedom Cave (SN1-SN3, width ratio 106%). Soon after their deposition, passage width diminished dramatically (Fig. 8D). A fourth large twig (SN5), deposited in the lower narrow passage (width ratio 37%), was dated to 3580 ± 80 BP, which fixes the time of incision. The downstream part of this relict passage stands today at *ca.* –380 m. Thus, the Dead Sea lowered to this level or farther after Stage 3.

Stage 3 is the most pronounced moist stage in the cave morphology of Mount Sedom, which covers the last 7000 yr. A comparison between the ^{14}C dates reported here for Stage 3 and dates from archaeological excavations of the Early Bronze Age throughout Israel and Jordan (Weinstein 1984) indicates that the moist Stage 3 is roughly synchronous with Early Bronze Age (EB I, II,

Fig. 9. East face of Mount Sedom with outlets of Malham Cave on the right. The lowest outlet is active today. The highest outlet was dated to climate Stage 3.

Fig. 10. The Stage 3 relict outlet of Malham Cave. Rock salt layers dip *ca.* 70° to the left. Horizontal line (−359 m level) in the center is a solution notch and top of detrital aragonite sediment indicating Stage 3 Dead Sea level. Person in lower left for scale.

III). However, climate amelioration started during the Chalcolithic period, and desiccation that started during EB III continued into the Middle Bronze Age (MB). Here, we refer to the general trend of climate change in terms of ^{14}C results, without discussing the archaeological chronology in detail.

COMPARISON WITH OTHER PALEOCLIMATE RECORDS

During Stage 3, laminated clay was deposited in the south basin of the Dead Sea. Neev (1964) reported a ^{14}C date of 4410 ± 310 BP for disseminated organic carbon in Core CA−27 from a −403-m level, 3.4–4.0 m beneath lake bottom, at the southernmost part of the Dead Sea basin. The upper 6 m of this core consisted of clay and silt. However, rock salt was found in nearby cores further to the north. Projecting this upper salt tongue to the time-depth scale of CA−27 indicated that the salt was deposited between 4300 and 3500 BP. On the basis of this evidence, Neev and Emery (1967) suggested that a humid period prevailed between *ca.* 5500 and 4300 BP, when laminated clay was deposited. It was followed by desiccation represented by the upper salt tongue. Two ^{14}C dates, 5050 and 4500 BP (analytical standard deviation was not reported), were determined for freshwater gastropods from a bioturbated marl sequence found above the Lisan formation in the Beit She'an Basin (Neev and Emery 1967; Neev and Hall 1977). It was deposited in a lake, later to be drained through developing headward erosion of the Jordan River. Considering the available ^{14}C dates from the Dead Sea and Beit She'an sediments, a correlation seems to exist between Stage 3 in Mount Sedom caves and the moist period indicated by the lakes' sediments. However, sedimentary analysis cannot provide the lake level, which is needed for climate calibration techniques (Street-Perrott and Harrison 1985). On the other hand, geomorphological evidence attributed to the paleolake shore can yield precise lake level data. Klein (1982) reports some morphological evidence from the western shore of the Dead Sea, indicating steady paleo-Dead Sea level between −359 and −355 m. These include a bar of rounded boulders and a shingle beach, a notch and an abrasion cave at the northern corner of the Samar delta, a cliff with caves in the talus north of Ein Gedi, and a line of cliffs cutting most of the Lisan outcrops. A wooden coffin of the first century BC found in one of the caves near Ein Gedi (Yossi Feldman, personal communication), indicates that the cliff and caves are older.

Archaeological data from the southeastern Dead Sea area provides further evidence on Dead Sea levels. The lowest level Early Bronze Age site (probably a farmstead or working area) is BDS-18 at −351 m in the alluvial fan of Wadi Kerak (McConaughy 1981). This suggests a maximum Dead Sea level below −351 m during the Early Bronze Age, although it does not totally exclude a short phase of higher level. The excavated Early Bronze Age cities of Bab edh-Dhra and Numeira, located on higher parts of the alluvial fans, yielded ^{14}C dates (Rast and Schaub 1980; Weinstein 1984) comparable to those from Stage 3 in Mount Sedom caves. During the same expedition, Donahue (1985) recorded some terraces and incision features related to these sites. He found that both Wadi Kerak and Wadi Numeira had gentle bowl-shaped cross-sections during the Early Bronze Age (Fig. 8F–G). Below this terrace, they form narrow, deeply cut valleys with vertical walls (28–50 m below the Early Bronze Age terrace). The downcutting was attributed to a lowering of base level that increased the stream gradient and initiated rapid incision in the wadis after the Early Bronze Age occupation of the sites. Donahue (1985) stated that, "Although no specific data have yet to come to light documenting fault movement, the change from an aggradational to a degradational or erosional regime was most likely caused by a fault movement and uplift of the area." However, good morphological and dating correlation exists between phenomena in the two wadis and in the Mount Sedom caves, suggesting that all are controlled by Dead Sea level fluctuations rather than by local tectonics. Thus, the wide cross-sections of the channels during the Early Bronze Age correspond to the higher Dead Sea level, whereas the rapid incision after the Early Bronze Age reacts to the Dead Sea decline during the following desiccation.

Vita-Finzi (1964) described another distinctive terrace in the nearby Wadi Hasa. The terrace surface forms the wide floor of the valley from Qa'lat el-Hasa to the gorge (Fig. 8H). Copeland and Vita-Finzi (1978) determined a ^{14}C date of 3950 ± 150 BP on charcoal at a depth of 1 m in this 5-m-thick terrace. A protecting wall, presumed to be of Roman age, borders the incised terrace. It indicates that incision of the terrace took place before the Roman period. Base level that was suggested to control Mount Sedom caves, Wadi Kerak and Wadi Numeira is not likely to be dominant in the Wadi Hasa section, because of its large distance, 70 km (along the watercourse) from the river outlet to the Dead Sea rift. Unlike the other channels discussed here, Wadi Hasa reaches the Dead Sea from the south over a gently sloping fan, thus eliminating base-level regulation of its morphology (Bowman 1988). Local hydromorphological processes were probably dominant in controlling its cross-section.

Rosen (1986a) described the "Erani terrace" in several wadi channels in the southern Shefela region and dated it by pottery fragments to Chalcolithic/Early Bronze Age. Rosen suggested that it represents a moist period, whereas the following incision was caused by desiccation. Goodfriend (1987) dated some fluvial deposits in the northern Negev by amino acid epimerization analysis of land-snail shells. He showed that maximum Holocene fluvial sedimentation occurred during the period, *ca.* 6200–3700 BP, noting that age mixtures in some of these deposits tend to bias the apparent time of deposition toward older ages.

The factors controlling fluvial response to climate change are complex, especially in arid environments (*e.g.,* Bull 1991:120). The Mount Sedom cave data suggest some climate fluctuations during the Middle Holocene, which might explain the maximum fluvial sedimentation and terrace building. A possible sequence is a decrease in vegetation cover during the dry Stage 2a (*ca.* 7000–6000 BP), followed by moist Stages 2b and 3. Heavy rains and the long recovery rate of the vegetation caused an increase in sediment yield and valley backfilling. This was followed by incision of valley fill during dry Stage 4.

Goodfriend (1990) used stable carbon isotope ratios in land-snail shells to infer middle Holocene rainfall amounts. He suggested a stable geographic pattern in the northern Negev from *ca.* 6500 –3000 BP, when the annual rainfall isohyets were located some 20 km south of their present position. However, his conclusive data of rainfall shift are concentrated on ^{14}C dates of three distinct periods: 1) *ca.* 3100 BP (2790 ± 210, 3120 ± 210, 3130 ± 270, 3380 ± 250 BP); 2) *ca.* 4800 BP (4690 ± 230, 4840 ± 280, 4850 ± 220 BP); 3) *ca.* 6200 BP (6160 ± 220, 6240 ± 320 BP). All data from intermediate periods (6000–5100 and 4400–3600 BP) are not indicative of either the present climate pattern or of a rainfall shift. Thus, land snail data appear compatible with other evidence for the period, *ca.* 6000–3000 BP, whereas a discrepancy exists for the period, *ca.* 6200 BP. Pollen diagrams of cores from northern Israel yielded only one reliable date of the period discussed here, 4565 ± 75 BP, from Borehole U.P. 15 in the Hula basin, investigated by Horowitz (1979). The palynological information of this core suggested climate deterioration at *ca.* 4500 BP, from warm and humid vegetation to the present Mediterranean-type vegetation. The lake shrank concurrently, as shown by pollen data as well as by diatom study of the same core (Ehrlich 1973).

The general trend of decreasing arboreal pollen is indicated in the Hula pollen diagram analyzed by Tsukada (van Zeist and Bottema 1982) and in a Kinneret pollen diagram analyzed by Baruch (1983), who noted that the decreasing tree pollen might have resulted from anthropogenic deforestation and cultivation activities as well as from climate desiccation. Issar *et al.* (ms.) compare the $\delta^{18}O$ curve (Stiller *et al.* 1984) of the same Kinneret core (KIND-4) to $\delta^{18}O$ curve of speleothems from Galilee, northern Israel. They suggested a relatively cold period from *ca.* 4600–4200 BP, followed by a warming that started at *ca.* 4200 BP, which was reflected by the speleothems somewhat earlier.

In central Israel, some stratigraphic sections imply a moist Early Bronze Age, followed by desiccation. Ritter-Kaplan (1984) described a clay stratum from Tel Aviv dated to the EB by archaeological remains, covered by a sand stratum containing MB I encampment remains. The clay contained oak pollen, whereas the sand was barren. Ritter-Kaplan (1984) suggested that this sequence accumulated during a wetter and warmer EB, followed by extreme desiccation. However, the location of the section in the Yarkon River floodplain near the Mediterranean Sea allows also a nonclimate interpretation, involving the present common competition between channel shifting, swamps and sand dunes. Rosen (1986b) studied an alluvial section in the Shefela region, which was also dated by archaeological remains. She reported EB clayey floodplain sediments with a buried organic A horizon, and small carbonate nodules. It was attributed by Rosen to moister climate with a higher water table than at present. This was followed by unstable conditions during MB I and general desiccation beginning around MB II. Donahue (1985) suggested that higher water level during the EB existed also in Bab edh-Dhra, but here, the dominant cause was probably the high Dead Sea level.

During the last decade, the Negev Emergency Survey was conducted to record all sites in the areas that the Israel Defense Force was to occupy after the evacuation of the Sinai Peninsula. The temporal change in settlement pattern is particularly recognizable in the southern and central Negev (south of Avedat), where no large permanent water source exists, thus making the climate a most important factor in settlement distribution. The number of sites was generally small during the Chalcolithic, increased considerably during the EB, and decreased again toward the following MB and Late Bronze Age (LB) periods (Avner 1979; Avni 1982, 1985; Haiman 1986, 1991a,b; Lender 1990; Rosen 1982, 1985). We caution the reader, however, that this general treatment does not consider changes in type, size or location of individual sites. It is beyond the scope of this chapter to discuss all the complex political and social/economic factors that might have contributed to the changing settlement pattern. Such a change, by itself, is not considered here as evidence of climate change.

There seems to be a correlation between post-EB desiccation and similar evidence from the Sahara and eastern Africa; lakes fed from the Ethiopian highlands were high until *ca.* 4000 BP, when their levels fell rapidly until they reached their present levels (Gasse 1980). The shift to lower levels at *ca.* 4000 BP was the most important general trend for lakes across the entire African tropics (Hamilton 1982). The belt of high lake levels in Africa and Arabia appears to have migrated northward from 10,000–4500 BP (Street and Grove 1979). Nicholson and Flohn (1980) reviewed various paleoclimate data from dozens of sites in the Sahara and eastern Africa. They concluded that wetter-than-present conditions prevailed in these areas until *ca.* 4000 BP, followed by the dry Late Holocene.

CONCLUSION

The Mount Sedom data seem to be relatively free of human interference, and are concordant with other evidence discussed here. Our evidence suggests that the EB in Israel (Stage 3 in the Mount Sedom sequence) was the moistest period during the last 6000 yr, which allowed for developing agriculture, urbanization and desert occupation. Considerable desiccation followed, which led to arid conditions similar to the present (or even more arid) causing cultural deterioration and gradual abandonment of the evolving desert during the MB. The data presented here from Israel indicate that desiccation at *ca.* 4000 BP reached the Levant and played an important role in its developing cultures. The precipitation/evaporation ratio influenced lake levels, agriculture, natural flora and some geomorphological processes. The Mount Sedom data, as well as other evidence presented here, indicate higher precipitation amounts during the EB. However, the temperature fluctuations cannot yet be reconstructed reliably. Evidence from Africa suggests that the desiccation after Stage 3 was a global process.

ACKNOWLEDGMENTS

Our work was supported by the research fund of the Society for the Protection of Nature in Israel (SPNI).We wish to thank the team of the Israel Cave Research Center of the SPNI and its volunteers for their devoted help, during hundreds of days and nights in underground cave exploration and survey. S. Kazes of the Weizmann Institute of Science assisted with the ^{14}C measurements. Prof. N. Lifshitz, of Tel Aviv University and Dr. E. Werker, of the Hebrew University, identified the highly fragmentary plant material, often to the species level.

REFERENCES CITED

Amiran, R.
    1986   The fall of the Early Bronze Age II city of Arad. *Israel Exploration Journal* 36:74–76.
Avner, U.
    1979   Biq'at Uvda (in Hebrew). *Archaeological News* 69–71:17.
Avni, G.
    1982   Survey of Har Sagi (in Hebrew). *Archaeological News* 80–81:65.
    1985   Survey of Maps 206–207 – Har Lotz and Har Hame'ara (in Hebrew). *Archaeological News*
            86:40–41.
Baruch, U.
    1983   *The Palynology of a Late Holocene Core From Lake Kinneret.* M.A. Thesis, The Hebrew University of
            Jerusalem (in Hebrew with English summary).
Begin, Z. B., W. Broecker, B. Buchbinder, Y. Druckman, A. Kaufman, M. Magaritz and D. Neev
    1985   Dead Sea and Lake Lisan levels in the last 30,000 years: A preliminary report. *Geological Survey of Israel,*
            Report GSI/29/85.
Begin, Z. B., Y. Nathan and A. Ehrlich
    1980   Stratigraphy and facies distribution in the Lisan Formation – New evidence from the area south of the Dead
            Sea, Israel. *Israel Journal of Earth Sciences* 29:182–189.
Bowman, D.
    1971   Geomorphology of the shore terraces of the Late Pleistocene Lisan Lake, Israel. *Palaeogeography, Palaeo-*
            climatology, Palaeoecology 9:183–209.
    1988   The declining but non-rejuvenating base level of the Lisan Lake, the Dead Sea area, Israel. *Earth Surface*
            Processes and Landforms 13:239–249.
Bretz, J. H.
    1942   Vadose and phreatic features of limestone caverns. *The Journal of Geology* L(6):675–811.
Bull, W. B.
    1991   *Geomorphic Responses to Climatic Change.* Oxford University Press, New York.
Carmi, I.
    1987   Rehovot radiocarbon measurements III. *Radiocarbon* 29(1):100–114.
Copeland, L. and C. Vita-Finzi
    1978   Archaeological dating of geological deposits in Jordan. *Levant* 10:10–25.
Crown, A. D.
    1972   Toward a reconstruction of the climate of Palestine 8000 BC–0 BC. *Journal of Near Eastern Studies* 31:
            312–330.
Danin, A., G. Orshan and M. Zohary
    1975   The vegetation of the Northern Negev and Judean Desert of Israel. *Israel Journal of Botany* 24:118–172.
Dever, W. G.
    1989   The collapse of the urban Early Bronze Age in Palestine: Toward a systematic analysis. In *L'Urbanisation de*
            la Palestine à l'Age du Bronze Ancien, edited by P. Miroschedji, pp. 225–246. BAR International Series 527,
            British Archaeological Reports, Oxford.
Donahue, J.
    1985   Hydrologic and topographic change during and after Early Bronze occupation at Bab edh-Dhra and Numeira.
            In *Studies in the History and Archaeology of Jordan,* edited by A. Hadidi, pp. 131–140. Department of
            Antiquities and Routledge & Kegan Paul, Amman.
Ehrlich, A.
    1973   Quaternary diatoms of the Hula Basin (Northern Israel). *Geological Survey of Israel Bulletin* 58.
Frumkin, A.
    1992   The Karst System of the Mount Sedom Salt Diapir. Ph.D. Dissertation, The University of Jerusalem (in
            Hebrew with English summary).
Frumkin, A., M. Magaritz, I. Carmi and I. Zak
    1991   The Holocene climatic record of the salt caves of Mount Sedom, Israel. *The Holocene* 1(3):191–200.
Frumkin, A. and I. Zak
    1991   Holocene evolution of Mount Sedom Diapir based on karst evidence (abstract). Paper presented at the 35th
            Annual Israel Geological Society Meeting, Akko.
Gascoyne, M., D. C. Ford and H. P. Schwarcz
    1983   Rates of cave and landform development in the Yorkshire dales from speleothem age data. *Earth Surface Pro-*
            cesses and Landforms 8:557–568.

Gasse, F.
   1980   Late Quaternary changes in lake-levels and diatom assemblages on the southeastern margin of the Sahara.
            Palaeoecology of Africa 12:333–350.
Gerson, R.
   1972   Geomorphic Processes of Mount Sedom. Ph.D. Dissertation, The Hebrew University of Jerusalem (in Hebrew
            with English summary).
   1974   Geomorphic processes of Mount Sedom. *Zeitschrift für Geomorphologie Supplementband* 21:7–11.
Goldberg, P., and O. Bar-Yosef
   1980   Environmental and archaeological evidence for climatic change in the Southern Levant and adjacent areas.
            Paper presented at the INQUA Symposium, Environmental Evidence for Climatic Change in the Eastern
            Mediterranean and the Near East During the Last 20,000 Years, Groningen.
Goodfriend, G. A.
   1987   Chronostratigraphic studies of sediments in the Negev Desert, using amino acid epimerization analysis of land
            snail shells. *Quaternary Research* 28:374–392.
   1990   Rainfall in the Negev Desert during the Middle Holocene, based on ^{13}C of organic matter in land snail shells.
            Quaternary Research 34:186–197.
Haiman, M.
   1986   *Map of Har Hamran–Southwest*. The Department of Antiquities and Museums, The Archaeological Survey
            of Israel. Jerusalem.
   1991a   *Map of Mizpé Ramon–Southwest*. Israel Antiquities Authority, The Archaeological Survey of Israel. Jerusalem.
   1991b   Survey of Har Lotz Map Northeast (in Hebrew). *Archaeological News* 96:40–41.
Hamilton, A. C.
   1982   *Environmental History of East Africa, A Study of the Quaternary*. Academic Press. London.
Horowitz, A.
   1979   *The Quaternary of Israel*. Academic Press. New York.
Issar, A. S.
   1990   *Water Shall Flow from the Rock*. Springer-Verlag, Heidelberg.
Issar, A. S., Y. Govrin, M. E. Geyh, E. Wakshal and M. Wolf
            Climate changes during the Upper Holocene in Israel. Ms. in preparation.
Klein, C.
   1982   Morphological evidence of lake level changes, western shore of the Dead Sea. *Israel Journal of Earth-Sciences*
            31:67–94.
   1986   Fluctuations of the Level of the Dead Sea and Climatic Fluctuations in Israel During Historical Times. Ph.D.
            Dissertation, The University of Jerusalem (in Hebrew with English summary).
Lender, Y.
   1990   *Map of Har Nafha*. Israel Antiquities Authority, The Archaeological Survey of Israel. Jerusalem.
Mangerud, J., H. J. B. Birks and K. D. Jäger
   1982   Chronostratigraphical subdivisions of the Holocene: A review. Paper presented at the Striae 16 Congress,
            INQUA 1–16. Moscow.
McConaughy, M. A.
   1981   A preliminary report on the Bab edh-Dhra site survey. *Annual of the American Schools of Oriental Research*
            46:187–190.
Neev, D.
   1964   The Dead Sea. *Geological Survey of Israel, Report* Q/2/64.
Neev, D. and K. O. Emery
   1967   The Dead Sea, depositional processes and environments of evaporites. *Geological Survey of Israel Bulletin*
            41:1–147.
Neev, D. and J. K. Hall
   1977   Climatic fluctuations during the Holocene as reflected by the Dead Sea levels. Paper presented at the Inter-
            national Conference on Terminal Lakes, Ogden.
   1979   Geophysical investigations in the Dead Sea. *Sedimentary Geology* 23:209–238.
Nicholson, S. E. and H. Flohn
   1980   African environmental and climatic changes and the general atmospheric circulation in Late Pleistocene and
            Holocene. *Climatic Change* 2:313–348.
Niklaus, Th. R.
   1991   *CalibETH User's Manual*. ETH, Zürich.
Palmer, A. N.
   1991   Origin and morphology of limestone caves. *Geological Society of America Bulletin* 103:1–21.

Pearson, G. W., J. R. Pilcher, M. G. L. Baillie, D. M. Corbett and F. Qua
  1986   High-precision ^{14}C measurement of Irish oaks to show the natural ^{14}C variations from AD 1840 to 5210 BC. *Radiocarbon* 28(2B):911–934.

Rast, W. E. and R. T. Schaub
  1980   Preliminary report of the 1979 expedition to the Dead Sea Plain, Jordan. *Bulletin of the American Schools of Oriental Research* 240:21–61.

Renault, P.
  1967   Le problème de la spéléogenèse. *Annales de Spéléologie* 22:5–21.

Richard, S.
  1980   Toward a concensus of opinion on the end of the Early Bronze Age in Palestine-Transjordan. *Bulletin of the American Schools of Oriental Research* 237:5–34.

Ritter-Kaplan, H.
  1984   The impact of drought on third millennium B.C. cultures on the basis of excavations in the Tel Aviv exhibition grounds. *Zeitschrift des Deutschen Palastina-Vereins* 100:1–8.

Rosen, A. M.
  1986a   Quaternary alluvial stratigraphy of the Shephela and its paleoclimatic implications. *Geological Survey of Israel, Report GSI/25/86*.

  1986b   Environmental change and settlement at Tel Lachish, Israel. *Bulletin of the American Schools of Oriental Research* 263:55–60.

  1989   Environmental change at the end of Early Bronze Age Palestine. In *L'Urbanisation de la Palestine à l'Age du Bronze Ancien*, edited by P. Miroschedji, pp. 247–255. BAR International Series 527, British Archaeological Reports, Oxford.

Rosen, S.
  1982   West Makhtesh Ramon. *Archaeological News* 80/81:64–65 (in Hebrew).

  1985   Survey of Map 201–Mizpé Ramon. *Archaeological News* 86:40 (in Hebrew).

Stiller, M., A. Ehrlich, U. Pollingher, U. Baruch and A. Kaufman
  1984   The late Holocene sediments of Lake Kinneret (Israel) – Multidisciplinary study of a five meter core. In *Geological Survey of Israel Current Research 1983–1984*, edited by A. Ehrlich, pp. 83–90. Geological Survey of Israel, Jerusalem.

Street, F. A. and A. T. Grove
  1979   Global maps of lake-level fluctuations since 30,000 years BP. *Quaternary Research* 12:83–118.

Street-Perrott, F. A. and S. P. Harrison
  1985   Lake levels and climate reconstruction. In *Paleoclimate Analysis and Modeling*, edited by A. D. Hecht, pp. 291–340. John Wiley & Sons, New York.

Stuiver, M. and G. W. Pearson
  1986   High-precision calibration of the radiocarbon time scale, AD 1950–500 BC. *Radiocarbon* 28(2B):805–838.

van Zeist, W. and S. Bottema
  1982   Vegetation history of the Eastern Mediterranean and the Near East during the last 20,000 years. In *Paleoclimates, Paleoenvironments and Human Communities in the Eastern Mediterranean Region in Later Prehistory*, edited by J. L. Bintliff and W. van Zeist, pp. 277–321. BAR International Series 133, British Archaeological Reports, Oxford.

Vita-Finzi, C.
  1964   Observations on the late Quaternary of Jordan. *Palestine Exploration Quarterly* 1964(1):19–31.

Weinstein, J. M.
  1984   Radiocarbon dating in the Southern Levant. *Radiocarbon* 26(3):297–366.

Zak, I.
  1967   *The Geology of Mount Sedom*. Ph.D. Dissertation, The Hebrew University of Jerusalem (in Hebrew with English summary).

Zak, I. and Y. K. Bentor
  1968   Some new data on the salt deposits of the Dead Sea area, Israel. In *UNESCO Symposium on the Geology of Saline Deposits* 7, pp. 137–146. UNESCO, Hannover.

Zak, I. and R. Freund
  1981   Asymmetry and basin migration in the Dead Sea Rift. *Tectonophysics* 80:27–38.

NEW COMMENTS ON THE BIOSTRATIGRAPHY OF THE MIDDLE AND UPPER PLEISTOCENE OF THE SOUTHERN LEVANT

EITAN TCHERNOV

Department of Evolution, Systematics and Ecology, The Hebrew University of Jerusalem Jerusalem 91 904 Israel

THE LEVANT DURING THE PLIO-PLEISTOCENE

Since the Miocene, the southern Levant has witnessed intense geologic events that had long-ranging biogeographic and ecologic consequences. Because of its location, the Levant was intermittently used as a land bridge between Eurasia and Africa. Extensive tectonic activity and Quaternary climatic fluctuations modified the internal biotic configuration of the region. Alternately opened and closed barriers cleared the way for biotic and hominid immigrations from the north, east and south.

Progressive desiccation has been the principal climatic trend in the Levant (Tchernov 1968a). The shift toward aridity was a major factor in the extinction of many tropical African and Palearctic species and the separation between tropical African and Eurasian biota. The impact of the glacial period and the proximity to a large desert played a complex role in the distribution of Levantine flora and fauna, and reshaped the biotic gradients between Palearctica and the eremian belt (Tchernov 1988a).

Early Pliocene rifting in the Red Sea caused abrupt change in its sedimentary record. The southern Levant became isolated, free biotic connections with the north were hampered by the Taurus-Zagros orogeny, and the widening Red Sea and collapse of the Bab-el-Mandab Afro-Arabian land bridge caused disjunction with the African continent. Mediterranean sea level rose and deeply penetrated the lower Nile (Messinian) canyon to Aswan, some 1200 km inland (Said 1975; Williams and Williams 1976). Thus, Israel, Sinai and part of eastern Egypt became peninsular-like, and remained biogeographically isolated for the rest of the Pliocene.

Later Pliocene Mediterranean regression left behind a veil of freshwater bodies. From this later Pliocene period (probably lower Villafranchian) derives the bone-bearing-bed of Bethlehem, characterized by open-country species, and suggests a lowland African savanna regime (Tchernov 1986b, 1988a), with some fresh water nearby. At this time, cervids and other Palearctic species had not yet arrived in the southern Levant and North Africa (Bar-Yosef and Tchernov 1972; Tchernov 1981a; Geraads and Tchernov 1983; Tchernov and Guerin 1986).

The advent of the Pleistocene is distinguished by a combination of simultaneous natural events, for example, severe climatic fluctuations and eustatic sea-level changes, which were part of a global trend. Large-scale tectonism, mainly faulting and upwarping, of the Plio-Pleistocene transition molded the contemporary topographic, climatic and biotic configuration of southwest Asia. Later tectonic, geographic and climatic events continued to reshape the area and changed abundance and dispersal behavior of plant and animal groups.

During the Quaternary, fragmentation of the region into smaller biotic units and diversified climatic-ecologic belts created abrupt transitions in plant and animal lives over short distances. The Jordan Valley, part of the Syro-African Rift, was a main corridor for biotic exchange between Africa and Eurasia. The developing Red Sea later closed this corridor.

Late Quaternary Chronology and Paleoclimates of the Eastern Mediterranean
Edited by O. Bar-Yosef and R. S. Kra. RADIOCARBON 1994, pp. 333–350

Early Pleistocene faunal communities are extremely rare in the southern Levant. An exception is the rich fossiliferous beds of the 'Ubeidiya Formation in the Jordan Valley, 3 km south of Lake Kinneret. The 'Ubeidiya Formation represents one of the oldest known lithic cultures of *Homo erectus* outside Africa, and its archaeological finds reflect the earliest diffusion of man into Eurasia. Plio-Pleistocene lithologic and geophysical events in the central Jordan Valley set both upper and lower age limits on the 'Ubeidiya Formation, which are within the Matuyama reversed polarity chron. Additional dates, based on biostratigraphic and cultural evidence, fall within these limits. The 'Ubeidiya fossil mammalian assemblage is strongly correlated to the Lower Biharian of Europe, being somewhat younger than the 1.7 Myr of Sénèze, France, and to the Tamanian Faunal Complex, Russia, Aïn-Hanech, North Africa and Olduvai Upper Bed II, East Africa. Considering the geologic age constraints, the concurrence with well-dated fossils in Eurasia and East Africa and the strikingly similar lithic assemblage of Olduvai Upper Bed II, 'Ubeidiya can be dated to 1.4 Myr (Tchernov 1987, 1988a).

The Acheulean site of Gesher Benot Ya'akov exposed rich assemblages of lithic industry, which show strong affinities with African lithic traditions, namely, high frequencies of cleavers manufactured by "block on block" technique, and basalt as the preferred raw material despite the availability of abundant flint sources (Goren-Inbar and Belitzky 1989). The faunal assemblage also bears African parallels, suggesting Middle Pleistocene biotic expansion from tropical Africa (Hooijer 1959, 1960; Geraads and Tchernov 1983; Tchernov 1973, 1986a,b, 1988a). The date of the Benot Ya'akov Formation (Goren-Inbar and Belitzky 1989) has been placed between 800,000 and 500,000 yr (Tchernov and Guerin 1986). A second wave of Afro-tropical species and humans entered Eurasia during this period.

There is a large stratigraphic hiatus in the faunal sequence of the Middle Pleistocene. 'Ubeidiya fauna clearly show Early Pleistocene developments, which can be characterized by an increase in Palearctic species at the expense of tropical species. Middle Pleistocene cold phases could have favored better-adapted northern species, eliminating some Ethiopian-originating species that were shifted to lesser adaptive ecozones. Several species that survived the northern emigration persist in the Middle East today, and account for 15–20% of contemporary fauna. The great diversity of Palearctic species in 'Ubeidiya demonstrates their entrenchment in the Jordan Valley before 1.4 Myr. Interestingly, despite this faunal collision, the ancient Villafranchian species survived the entire period.

The quasi-isolation of the southern Levant, from the Taurus-Zagros Mountains in the north, and from the Red Sea, Nile delta and Saharo-Arabian desert in the south, permitted better biogeographic and biotic relations with the east (Mesopotamia and central Asia). During periods when no north–south connections were established, the similarity between southwest Asian and Asian biota increased, as during the late Middle Pleistocene (Stages 7 and 6). Gesher Benot Ya'akov was probably the last large-scale Afro-Eurasian biotic and hominid exchange until late Stage 5.

Dissemination of African species into the Levant continued during the Pleistocene at a decreasing rate. Most of the fauna were restricted to the Levant, south of the Zagros-Taurus Mountains. Southward-northward shifts of the Palearctic regime fluctuated throughout the Pleistocene, with widening intensification of the arid belt (Tchernov 1975). During these cold and warm phases, some Palearctic populations were cut off from their main distribution area, and gene exchanges with ancestral populations ceased. Intense Pleniglacial desiccation and swift temperature rise probably caused a general retreat of Palearctic species from the Levantine deserts. The populations that remained survived in refugium enclaves, mostly on higher mountains (Tchernov 1981a).

The Zagros, Taurus, Lebanon and Anti-Lebanon Mountains acted as a barrier for southern Levantine biota. Surrounded by desert, mountains and desiccation, the area encouraged autochthonous speciation, and only major environmental change would enable the introduction of different biota in such a state of quasi-isolation. However, dynamic change did occur in some micromammals, upon which biochronologic and paleoecologic studies have been based.

Efforts to establish a reliable chronology for the southern Levant during the late Middle and Upper Pleistocene, which includes the evolution of modern humans, have been hampered by lack of agreement in interpreting geomorphologic and faunal data. The scarcity of radiometric dates has caused us to rely on relative dating methods. Even recent uranium/thorium (U/Th) (Schwarcz *et al.* 1980), thermoluminescence (TL) (Valladas *et al.* 1987, 1988) and electron-spin resonance (ESR) (Schwarcz *et al.* 1988, 1989; Stringer *et al.* 1989; Grün *et al.* 1991) dating techniques leave critical issues unresolved. For example, the chronology of Tabun D (Mt. Carmel), for which micromammals have been used to build a sequence of Late Acheulean, Acheulo-Yabroudian, Mousterian and Upper Paleolithic sites, remains in dispute.

A long cultural Mousterian sequence has been revealed in the Mediterranean zone of the southern Levant; yet, none of the sites contained a continuous, undisturbed depositional and/or cultural sequence. Thus, stratigraphic, cultural and biotic correlations among the sites are difficult. At Kebara, on Mt. Carmel, and Hayonim, in western Galilee, the base of the Middle Paleolithic has not yet been excavated. Although the formation and depositional history of the eastern Mediterranean caves may be complex, Mousterian sites have evolved through the same general stages. The microvertebrate component (*e.g.*, micromammals, passeriform birds, small species of reptiles, amphibians and most terrestrial gastropods) of all the caves was non-anthropogenically deposited. However, osseous debris of larger vertebrates were deposited mainly by humans. The distribution of microfaunas may be correlated with the roosting place of birds of prey, for example, the barn owl (*Tyto alba*). Thus, *Tyto alba* pellets can provide clues to the nature and abundance of small vertebrates in and around cave sites.

A more complete knowledge of Pleistocene paleocommunities and the biochronology and evolution of human-animal interactions will be possible only when the data from previously excavated sites, such as Tabun, are revised, Middle Paleolithic sequences are recovered from Levantine sites, such as Hayonim and Kebara, and analyses of the faunas of more recently excavated sites, such as Qafzeh, are completed.

MICROMAMMALIAN COMMUNITIES AND THEIR BIOSTRATIGRAPHIC SEQUENCES

Oumm-Qatafa Cave

Oumm Qatafa is in the Judean desert, southeast of Jerusalem and east of Bethlehem. The site was excavated by Neuville (1951), who described a long sequence of prehistoric cultures. However, the faunal assemblage indicates a relatively short period of deposition, at least of the bone-bearing beds (Haas 1951; Tchernov 1968b). Rust (1950) believed that at least some of the cultural stages of Oumm Qatafa are older than the Yabroudian industry, and hence, are pre-Würmian. The cave's micromammalian assemblage is comparable (Table 1) with the fauna of Tabun G, which is "Tayacian" (Bate 1937a,b, 1942, 1943). Howell (1959) stated that Layer E of Oumm Qatafa represents a pluvial stage prior to the "Last Interpluvial", thus corresponding to part of the Riss. Woldstedt (1962) suggested the Eem Interglacial (excluding Layers C and B, which are sterile) (120,000 yr) as a maximum age.

TABLE 1. Comparison of micromammalian assemblages from late Acheulian, Acheulo-Yabrudian and Mousterian deposits from Israel. When available, date and references have been added to each site. The assemblages of the late Middle Paleolithic sites, Amud (Galilee), Sefunim and Geula (Mt. Carmel) have been identical with the Mousterian complex of Kebara.

SITE	OUMM QATAFA (Judean Desert)	ZUTTIYEH (Galilee)	TABUN (Mt. Carmel)	TABUN (Mt. Carmel)	QAFZEH (Galilee)	TABUN (Mt. Carmel)	HAYONIM (Galilee)	HAYONIM (Galilee)	TABUN	KEBARA (Mt. Carmel)	TABUN
Layer	B-C-D-E-F-G		Tabun E	Tabun D (Unit IX)**	(XV-XXV)	Tabun D (Unit I)*	(Lower E)	(Upper E)	Tabun C	(Units VI-XII)	Tabun B
Periods	Late Acheulian	Acheulo-Yabrudian	Acheulo-Yabrudian	Lower Mousterian	Lower Mousterian	Lower Mousterian	Upper Mousterian	Upper Mousterian	Upper Mousterian	Upper Mousterian	Upper Mousterian
Date		1. U-TH = 164 ±21 kyr.* 2. U-TH = 148 ±6 kyr.** 3. No microfauna described		ESR (LU) = 145-245 kyr** ESR (EU) = 95-155 kyr** Faunal descriptions include a mixture of all (I-IX) lithostratigraphic units	TL = 92(x) kyr* ESR (LU) = 92±5 kyr**	ESR (LU) = 145-245 kyr** ESR (EU) = 95-155 kyr** Faunal descriptions include a mixture of all (I-IX) lithostratigraphic units			ESR (LU) = 100-130 kyr* ESR (EU) = 85-120 kyr*	TL(VI-VII)=47-52 kyr* TL(VIII-IX)=57-58 kyr* TL(X-XII)=60-61 kyr*	ESR (LU) = 90-120 kyr* ESR (EU) = 85-105 kyr*
SPECIES											
RODENTIA											
Hystrix indica	++		+++		+++		+++	+++	+++	+++	+++
Sciurus anomalus	...		+++		+++		+++	+++	+++	+++	+++
Mesocricetus auratus	...		+++		...		+++	+++	+++	+++	+++
Allocricetus jesreelicus	+++		+++		...		+++	...	...	...	...
Allocricetus magnus	+++		+++		...		+++	...	...	...	...
Cricetulus migratorius	...		...		...		+++	+++	+++	+++	+++
Rattus haasi	+++		...		...		...	...	...	...	...
Mastomys batei	+++		+++		+++		...	...	...	...	...
Arvicanthis ectos	+++		+++		+++		...	...	...	...	...
Apodemus mystacinus	+++		+++		+++		+++	+++	+++	+++	+++
Apodemus sylvaticus	++		+++		+++		+++	+++	+++	+++	+++
Apodemus flavicollis	...		...		...		...	...	...	...	...
Mus macedonicus	++		+++		+++		+++	+++	+++	+++	+++
Gerbillus dasyurus	+++		...		+++		...	...	...	...	...
Meriones tristrami	+++		+++		+++		+++	+++	+++	+++	+++
Psammomys obesus	+++		...		...		+++	...	...	...	...
Ellobius fuscocapillus	+++		+++		...		+++	+++	...	...	...
Microtus guentheri	+++		+++		+++		+++	+++	+++	+++	+++
Spalax ehrenbergi	+++		+++		+++		+++	+++	+++	+++	+++
Myomimus judaicus	++		...		...		...	...	...	...	...
Myomimus qafzensis	...		+++		+++		...	...	...	...	...
Myomimus roachi	...		...		...		+++	+++	+++	+++	+++
LAGOMORPHA											
Lepus capensis	+++		+++		+++		+++	+++	+++	+++	+++
Ochotona sp.	+++		...		...		...	...	...	...	...
INSECTIVORA											
Crocidura leucodon	+++		+++		+++		+++	+++	+++	+++	+++
Crocidura russula	+++		+++		+++		+++	+++	+++	+++	+++
Suncus etruscus	...		...		+++		+++	+++	+++	+++	+++
Suncus cf. murinus	...		...		+++		...	...	...	...	...
Talpa chthonia	...		...		...		+++	...	+++	...	...
References	*Gisis and Bar-Yosef 1974. **For pre-Yabrudian layer: Schwarcz et al. 1980			**Jelinek 1981,1982a,b. **Grün et al. 1991	*Valladas et al. 1988. **Schwarcz et al. 1988.	*Jelinek 1981,1982a,b. **Grün et al. 1991			*Grün et al. 1991	*Valladas et al. 1988.	*Grün et al. 1991

The spatial and chronologic distribution of lagomorphs in the southern Levant indicates a short interval during the Late Acheulean when the genus, *Ochotona*, appeared in the region, at Oumm-Qatafa, and a post-Acheulean replacement of *Ochotona* by *Lepus*, at Tabun F and E (Tchernov 1981b, 1988a,b). The disappearance of *Ochotona*, together with other ancient animals, such as *Myomimus judaicus* and *Rattus haasi* and the first appearance of *Lepus capensis*, *Sciurus anomalus* and *Myomimus qafzensis* (Daams 1981; Haas 1972, 1973) place the complex of Tabun F and E well after the faunal beds of Oumm Qatafa, and within the Acheulo-Yabroudian range of Zuttiyeh. This agrees with Bar-Yosef's (1989) statement that Tabun F and E are best placed in late Stages 7 and 6.

The relative antiquity of the micromammalian assemblage of Oumm Qatafa (*Rattus haasi*, *Arvicanthis ectos*, *Mastomys batei* (Muridae), *Myomimus judaicus* (Gliridae)), and the unique appearance of *Ochotona* sp., Ochotonidae, Lagomorpha, some of which were never recovered from younger lithic deposits (Tchernov 1981b, 1984b), suggest that the cave's osseous beds antedate all Acheulo-Yabroudian lithic assemblages in the Levant. Further, several Palearctic genera are not yet represented in the southern Levant during this period, *e.g.*, *Lepus* (Leporidae, Lagomorpha), *Talpa* (Talpidae, Insectivora) and *Sciurus* (Sciuridae, Rodentia). This assemblage may best be correlated with Tabun G (Farrand 1979; Jelinek 1981, 1982a,b), Yabroud I rock-shelter (Copeland and Hours 1981; Bar-Yosef 1989), or Birket Ram (Goren-Inbar 1985), all of which may be assigned to Stage 7. Thus, Oumm Qatafa may delineate a biostratigraphic baseline for all later Acheulo-Yabroudian and Mousterian faunal sequences.

Zuttiyeh Cave

The Acheulo-Yabroudian macrofauna of Zuttiyeh cave (Bate 1932) may be correlated with part of Tabun F and E, yet the paucity of faunal remains prevents finer correlation. The industry resembles that of Tabun E (Gisis and Bar-Yosef 1974). The levels above the Acheulo-Yabroudian provided dates of 95,000 ± 10,000 and 97,000 ± 13,000 yr, whereas dates from below these layers are 148,000 ± 6000 and 164,000 ± 21,000 yr (Schwarcz *et al.* 1980), which place it well within Stage 6.

Qafzeh Cave

The Mousterian sequence of Qafzeh has been divided into two complexes: 1) the upper part (V–XIII), rich in lithics and large mammal remains, but poor in human remains; 2) the lower part (XIV–XXIV), poor in lithics but rich in microvertebrates and human burials (Vander-meersch 1981). The entire Mousterian sequence is dominated by lithics manufactured using the Levallois technique, with clear preference for radial preparation (Boutié 1989).

During the past ten years, dates of the Mousterian levels of Qafzeh have been heavily debated (Tchernov 1981b, 1984b, 1988b, 1989; Bar-Yosef and Vandermeersch 1981; Jelinek 1982a,b; Trinkaus 1984; Bar-Yosef 1988, 1989). The paleontologic age estimate, based on the micro-mammalian assemblage, placed them at *ca.* 100,000 yr, or Stage 5. This would mean that anatomically modern humans occupied the cave before Neanderthals made their first appearance here. Such unexpected antiquity was rejected by several scholars. To explain more clearly Qaf-zeh Cave's unique biostratigraphic position, I will describe the micromammalian community.

The micromammals of Qafzeh are similar to the Acheulo-Yabroudian faunas of Tabun F and E (Bate 1942, 1943). It is significant that the two archaic forms of Muridae (*Mastomys* and *Arvicanthis*) remain to this day. The subgenus, *Mastomys*, as well as the genus, *Praomys*, to which it belongs, is endemic to sub-Saharan Africa. It was first recorded from Tabun E and D (Bate

1942), and then from Oumm Qatafa (Haas 1951) (Table 1). Tchernov (1968a,b) described it as a new species, *Mastomys batei*, endemic to the southern Levant. Haas (1972) referred to the *Mastomys* population from Qafzeh as a new species, *Mastomys nazerensis*, but it was later found to be very similar to other Levantine communities of *Mastomys batei* (Tchernov 1981b, 1986a). Bate (1942) also described another African rat, *Arvicanthis ectos*, from Tabun F and E; this was the first reported occurrence of this genus outside Africa (apart from *Arvicanthis niloticus naso* from southern Arabia). These two genera have been confined to the Middle East since the Early Pleistocene (Tchernov 1986a). Qafzeh is the only known site outside Africa where both of these genera were found in a Middle Paleolithic level. Jelinek (1982b) believes that these archaic African species remained in Qafzeh because of its proximity to the Jordan Rift Valley "refugium". Yet, no other Mousterian sites in the Jordan Valley, *e.g.*, Shovakh (Binford 1966) and Amud (Suzuki and Takai 1970) yielded *Mastomys* or *Arvicanthis* fossils. Thus, these archaic murids probably existed in Qafzeh not because of ecologic preference, but because of the great antiquity of the deposits. Although *Mastomys batei* is also found in Tabun D (possibly Unit IX; see below), the genus, *Arvicanthis*, is absent from this layer, and neither species has been found in later Mousterian deposits or elsewhere in Asia.

Gerbillus dasyurus (Gerbillidae) is known from the 'Ubeidiya Formation (Tchernov 1986) and the Give'at Shaul Fissure Filling (Tchernov 1968a). This species was also retrieved from the Late Acheulean deposits of Oumm-Qatafa (Tchernov 1968a,b, 1981a,b) (Table 1). The only Mousterian deposits in which this species was found, in small quantities, are Qafzeh and lower Layer E of Hayonim. Neither has it been recovered from any Upper Paleolithic deposits in the eastern Mediterranean. It is only during the Late Epipaleolithic that *Gerbillus dasyurus* reappears in the Mediterranean Levant (Kebara and Hayonim Layer B). The total lack of Gerbillidae fossils during the Middle and Late Würm is not well understood. Episodic evidence of Gerbillidae along the Mediterranean Levant is probably negatively correlated with the amount of plant cover, and hence, connected with the north-south shifting of biogeographic belts. A large-scale reduction of Mediterranean growth could have encouraged this species to re-occupy desiccating landscapes during relatively dry periods.

A unique species of glirid, *Myomimus qafzensis*, was identified both by Haas (1972, 1973) and by Daams (1981) as endemic to Oumm Qatafa, Tabun E and Qafzeh. Once again, Qafzeh is the only Mousterian site in which a unique form is known. In all later sites, including Tabun D, from the Mousterian to the Bronze Age, this dormouse was replaced by a modern Euro-Siberian species, *Myomimus roachi* (Tchernov 1986a).

Cricetines are completely absent from the Mousterian deposits of Qafzeh, which cannot be due to local ecology, as cricetines, *Mesocricetus* and *Cricetulus* (Table 1), occur in Upper Paleolithic deposits of this site (Tchernov 1981b). Sample size cannot be a factor, as thousands of rodent remains were sifted from the Mousterian levels. See below, for more discussion.

The genus, *Suncus*, is unknown from the Acheulean and Acheulo-Yabroudian deposits of the eastern Mediterranean. It first appeared as *Suncus etruscus* in the Middle Paleolithic (Tabun C, Qafzeh, Hayonim E). Another species of *Suncus*, which is closely related to the Arabian species, *Suncus murimus* (Haas 1972; Tchernov 1989), occurs in the Mousterian deposits of Qafzeh. This is the only period during the Pleistocene in which a typical Arabian species is found at such a northern latitude, which suggests a large-scale northward shift of the desert belt. There is neither evidence of cricetines, nor other Palearctic species, such as *Talpa* (Insectivora), *Ellobius* (Microtinae) and *Apodemus flavicollis* (Muridae) in the Mousterian deposits of Qafzeh. The Qafzeh assemblage is dominated by open-country, steppe or savanna species: Arabian *Gerbillus dasyurus*; giant Arabian shrew, *Suncus murimus*; typical savanna rodents, *Mastomys* and *Arvicanthis*, associated with abundant African antelope, *Alcelaphus buselaphus*, *Gazella gazella*, *Rhinoceros hemitoechus*, as well as *Camelus dromedarius* (Payne and Garrard 1983). If one considers that arboreal *Apodemus flavicollis* and all cricetines are absent from the rodent assemblage of Qafzeh, one can conclude that the Early Mousterian of this site was deposited during a relatively dry climate corresponding to late Stage 5, or to the end phase of the Last Interglacial (Tables 1, 2).

In all other Mousterian deposits in the southern Levant, excluding Tabun D (Unit II) (see below), several archaic micromammals became extinct or disappeared from the Levant: *Myomimus qafzensis*, *Mastomys batei*, *Arvicanthis ectos*, *Suncus murimus*, temporarily, *Gerbillus dasyurus*, and probably *Camelus dromedarius*. However, other species associated with more mesic environments or arboreal habitats appeared: *Myomimus roachi*, *Apodemus flavicollis* and all the cricetines (Tables 1, 2).

It is difficult to accept a later Mousterian date for the hominid and bone-bearing layers of Qafzeh, as stated by Jelinek (1982a,b), when *ca.* 40% of the micromammals are different from any other Mousterian assemblage in the Levant. If there were an intra-Mousterian faunal break in the southern Levant, it would have occurred during the transition from the Mousterian complex of Qafzeh to later Mousterian phases (Tabun D, Unit IX, see below; Tabun C and B), or from Stages 5 to 4.

If the Mousterian assemblage of Qafzeh antedates all other Mousterian phases (excluding Tabun D, Unit IX), it may fill the stratigraphic hiatus between Tabun C, D, Unit II, and E, as claimed by Farrand (1979), Jelinek *et al.* (1973) and Jelinek (1982a,b). It might also explain Qafzeh's unique archaic microfaunal assemblage. The faunal and dating evidence indicate that the stratigraphic position of Tabun D, in the general sequence of the Mousterian, is far from clear (see below), but it is crucial for understanding the southern Levantine Middle Paleolithic.

Biochronologically, the Qafzeh micromammalian community fits only within an old Mousterian phase in the southern Levant. Recent TL dates (Valladas *et al.* 1988) give an average age of 92,000 yr, and clearly support the relative antiquity of microfauna associated with the burials. ESR dates (Schwarcz *et al.* 1988) reinforced this estimate by showing an average of 92,000 ± 5000 yr (early uptake (EU)) and 115,000 ± 15,000 (linear uptake (LU)) for these layers.

Tabun Cave

According to Bar-Yosef and Goldberg (1988), Tabun D industry generally comprises blades and points removed from Levallois unipolar cores. Elongate points, racloirs and some Upper Paleolithic types are the most frequent forms. These authors believe that if the Hummalian industry from El-Kowm, which dates between the Late Acheulean and Mousterian, belongs in this horizon, then Tabun D may be contemporaneous with this non-Levallois technique (Copeland 1985). Hence, Tabun D best fits into a stage between the Acheulo-Yabroudian and the Early Mousterian of Qafzeh, or within Stage 5e (127,000–117,000 yr). This stage correlates with the Enfean II Formation (Gvirtzman *et al.* 1983–1984) and contains *Strombus bubonius*. During this period, the westernmost sandstone (*kurkar*) ridge along the Mediterranean coast was consolidated. Thus, the sand layers of Tabun F and E belong to an accumulation of sand that occurred during Stage 6; the consolidation of their sandy sources along the coast took place during Stage 5e, or Tabun D, or within the Last Interglacial prior to the Mousterian complex of Qafzeh (Bar-Yosef and Goren 1981).

TABLE 2. First Appearance and Last Occurrence of Micromammals (and Relevant Large Mammals) During the Late Middle and Upper Pleistocene in the Southern Levant

Age (kyr)	Oxygen Isotope Stage	Principal Cultural Sequence	Reference Locality	Taxa Restricted to the Reference Level	Taxa Occurring in the Reference Fauna			
					First Appearance	Last Occurrence	Last Intermittent Occurrence*	First Intermittent Appearance*
10		Neolithic	Various sites		** Meriones sacramenti, ** Gerbillus allenbyi, ** Gerbillus pyramidum, (Gazella dorcas)			
10.5 12.5	Early 1	Epipaleolithic Naufian	Hayonim B, Hayonim Terrace (Galilee), Eynan (Huleh Valley)			Apodemus flavicollis, Sciurus anomalus, (Capra aegagrus), (Equus caballus)		
12.5 22	Late 2	Epipaleolithic Kebaran	Hayonim C		Acomys cahirinus	(Dicerorhinus hemitoechus)		Gerbillus dasyurus
22 37	Early 2 Late 3	Upper Paleolithic	Hayonim D, Kebara D		Eliomys melanurus, Rattus rattus	(Crocuta crocuta)		
40 60	Early 3	Late Mousterian	Hayonim (Upper E), Kebara E (XI-XII), Tabun C+B; Sefunim (Mt. Carmel)	‡Cricetulus migratorius				Apodemus flavicollis
60 75	4	Mousterian	Hayonim (Lower E), #Tabun D (Unit I)		†Myomimus roachi, Suncus etruscus, Suncus murimus	Ellobius fuscocapillus, Allocricetus magnus, Talpa chthonia		
90 110	5a-c	Early Mousterian	Qafzeh (Galilee)	Suncus murimus	†Myomimus qafzensis, Suncus etruscus, Suncus murimus	Arvicanthis ectos, Suncus murimus, Mastomys batei	Apodemus flavicollis, Gerbillus dasyurus	
120 130	5d-e	Early Mousterian	#Tabun D (Units IX)					
140 160	6	Acheulo-Yabrudian	Tabun E		Lepus capensis, †Myomimus (?)qafzensis, Sciurus anomalus, Mesocricetus auratus	Allocricetus jesreelicus	Apodemus flavicollis, Allocricetus magnus, Mesocricetus auratus	
~200	7	Late Acheulian	Oumm-Qatafa (Judean Desert)	Ochotona sp., Rattus haasi	Ochotona sp., Rattus haasi, Ellobius fuscocapillus, ≠Allocricetus jesreelicus, ≠Allocricetus magnus, §Mesocricetus auratus	Ochotona sp., Rattus haasi, †Myomimus judaicus		

* A few species of rodents intermittently appeared and disappeared from the Mediterranean region of the southern Levant in correlation with climate fluctuations. During cold phases, *Apodemus flavicollis* dispersed southward from the Palearctic region; during arid periods, *Gerbillus dasyurus* dispersed northward (Tchernov 1989).

** First appearance of Saharan elements during the Early Holocene, a dispersal event restricted to the southern Levantine coastal plains (Tchernov 1989)

‡ Probably replacing the extinct genus, *Allocricetus*, in the Levant (an event that occurred much earlier in the Palearctic region outside the Levant (Tchernov 1986a))

\# The fauna of the complex layers of Tabun D were treated as a single assemblage; earlier and later Mousterian communities were mixed. Tabun D is considered here as two entities as suggested by Jelinek (1982a,b). Fauna from Tabun D (units I+II) would have shown close relation to the assemblage of Qafzeh, while Tabun D, unit IX, is closer to the assemblage of Qafzeh, while Units I and II in Tabun are essentially Tabun C.

† Described by Bate (1937b) as a new genus (*Philistomys*), it was later re-identified as a member of the genus, *Myomimus*, probably *M. qafzenzis*.

≠ Probably replacing *Allocricetus bursae* (Tchernov 1986a)

§ Probably replacing the Lower Pleistocene extinct species, *Mesocricetus primitivus* (Tchernov 1986a)

The conflict between the geochronologic and cultural interpretations and the biochronologic sequence focuses on this point, as our minimal knowledge about the micromammals of Tabun D
(from Bate 1937a,b, 1942, 1943) shows that: 1) Tabun D includes only Palearctic species, thus
implying a new wave of immigration from higher latitudes; and 2) some species are known for
the first time in the area, and at least one is a new modern species. To clarify this contradiction, I will discuss the evolution of some rodent groups in this region (Tables 1, 2).

The extinct genus, *Allocricetus*, is important for correlating biostratigraphies. The Early Pleistocene *Allocricetus bursae* survived in the eastern Mediterranean until the Middle Pleistocene
(Tchernov 1968a, 1986a,b) long after it became extinct elsewhere. During the Middle Pleistocene, it probably underwent a swift *in-situ* speciation into *Allocricetus magnus* (Tchernov
1986a) and *Allocricetus jesreelicus* (Bate 1943). The latter became extinct at the start of the
Last Interglacial, whereas *Allocricetus magnus* continued to survive until the "middle" Mousterian, coinciding with the introduction of *Cricetulus migratorius* into the region. The post-Qafzeh
appearance of *Cricetulus* in the southern Levant is an important biochronologic event. It is the
only surviving cricetine in Israel today. *Ellobius fuscocapillus* (Microtinae) is known from Tabun Layers E, D and C (*Ellobius pedorychus*) (Bate 1937a,b) and from Oumm Qatafa (Haas
1951). This species was also found in the lower part of Layer E in Hayonim Cave (Tchernov
1988b, 1989).

Middle Pleistocene *Myomimus qafzensis* (Gliridae) is known from Oumm Qatafa, Tabun F and
E, and Qafzeh, and was replaced by the modern species, *Myomimus roachi*. *Talpa chthonia* was
first described by Bate (1932, 1937b) from Tabun F and E, and reappears only in Hayonim
Lower E and Tabun C. This species became extinct during the Upper Mousterian (Table 1). Its
absence from Tabun D, as well as from Qafzeh, could have been the result of a temporary
northward retreat from the region.

The broken chronologic sequence of the cricetines, *Ellobius* and *Talpa* (Tables 1, 2), which
never adapted to eremian conditions in the Old World, and were always confined to mesic habitats, is important biochronologically, as the occasional appearance of these species in the
southern Levant indicates a southward dispersal event. Although missing from the Qafzeh
Mousterian complex, individuals of this group were found in Tabun D. The appearance of
cricetines in Tabun D cannot be explained logically, as this should place it earlier than Stage 5.
If the entire sequence of Tabun D is older than Qafzeh, a very cold phase should have been
recorded during Stage 5, or during the Last Interglacial. There is no evidence for such a phase.
However, Bar-Yosef and Goldberg (1988) believed that a very early Mousterian lithic
assemblage from Tabun D should be placed before the Qafzeh assemblage. I will now attempt
to deal with the problem of Tabun D.

On the basis of the stratified deposits of Tabun Cave, the Levantine Mousterian is subdivided
into three phases, named by Copeland (1975) "Tabun D"-type, "Tabun C"-type and "Tabun B"-
type. Ronen (1979) and Jelinek (1981, 1982a,b) grouped them into nine lithostratigraphic units:
I for Tabun B and C, and II–IX for Tabun D, where Units III–VIII were designated disturbed
layers. It is also important to note that Jelinek (1982b) included Unit II within Tabun C,
whereas, in 1981, Unit II was still included in the latest stratum of Tabun D. The two faunal
assemblages, Tabun D and Qafzeh, cannot belong, by any ecologic or evolutionary criteria, to
the same general period, *i.e.*, the Last Interglacial. All the Units between II and IX are disturbed and mixed; thus, a long hiatus should exist between the two units. This unusually long
interval for a seemingly unique "cultural phase" is illogical, which was well demonstrated in
Grün, Stringer and Schwarcz's (1991) dates for Tabun D. Their results show a total duration

for Tabun D (LU or EU) of 100,000 yr. Because of the lack of detailed provenience for the Tabun sequence, Bate (1937a,b, 1942, 1943) assigned the faunal remains of Tabun D to a single unit.

Grün, Stringer and Schwarcz (1991) agree that these dates are far from conclusive. Sampling material from this old excavation might have yielded ambiguous results, as some of Garrod's stratigraphic units cross time boundaries, and might also have crossed significant breaks in sedimentation (Jelinek 1982a). Further, some of the teeth used for ESR dating, which were considered stratigraphically homologous, could have derived from both sides of a break or an erosional hiatus. This may well explain the wide range of dates obtained by Grün et al. (1991). Accepting the consistent TL results of Valladas et al. (1988), Schwarcz et al. (1988) and Tchernov's faunal sequence (1981b, 1988b, 1989), the Qafzeh Mousterian deposits date at ca. 100,000 yr. Grün et al.'s (1991) ESR dates for Tabun B and C give an average age of either ca. 90,000 (EU) or 110,000 (LU) yr, and hence, should be contemporaneous with Qafzeh. However, the two faunal assemblages are basically different, and we need to know how, within a distance of 30 km, the Qafzeh assemblage is dominated by East African and Arabian eremian species, some of which are extinct, while Tabun C and B contain only modern Palearctic species. It is now generally accepted that the age of the Kebaran Mousterian complex (Layers X–XII with the Neanderthal burial) is ca. 60,000 yr (Valladas et al. 1988). If Tabun B and C date to ca. 100,000 yr, it is difficult to explain the similarity between the two faunal assemblages located 12 km apart, but temporally separated by 40,000 yr. The ESR age estimate of Grün, Stringer and Schwarcz (1991) should be viewed as an important attempt to produce a more realistic absolute chronology for the Tabun sequence.

The stratigraphic complexity of Tabun D (Jelinek 1981, 1982a,b) is the main cause for uncertainties in the faunal composition, as well as the lithic industries) of Tabun D. If the bovid teeth for the ESR analysis (Grün et al. 1991) were collected at random, the uncertainties might be explained. Following Jelinek (1981, 1982a,b), it seems that we must separate Unit IX, at the base of Tabun D, from Unit II, at the top, or consider it, as Jelinek (1982b) suggested, as related to early Tabun C. This approach may also clarify the correlation between the Qafzeh and Tabun sequences. It will also explain the illogical co-existence of Acheulo-Yabroudian species and modern immigrants similar to those found in Tabun C and Lower E of Hayonim Cave. I believe that Unit IX antedates the Early Mousterian complex of Qafzeh (Layers XXV–VI), and Tabun D Unit II postdates Qafzeh, which explains the arrival of a swarm of Palearctic species at the dawn of Stage 4. The 40,000–50,000 yr of Units VIII–III, which may be partly contemporaneous with Qafzeh, should be ignored for the meantime. Radiometric dates should be measured separately from the different units of the complex and mixed layers of Tabun D, and should not rely on "Garrod's collection".

I suggest that Tabun D (Unit IX) antedates the Qafzeh complex, and contains all the Afro-Arabian species known from that sequence; hence, Unit IX is older than Qafzeh, but still within Stage 5. However, Unit II postdates the Qafzeh complex, and includes all the newly arrived Palearctic elements, which may designate the onset of the Last Glacial, or early Stage 4 (Tables 1, 2).

Skhul Cave

The small rockshelter of Skhul (Garrod and Bate 1937) contains a lower Unit C, unconformably overlain by Unit B, which contains hominid burials. The erosional phase between B and C was correlated by Bar-Yosef (1989) to the erosional phase that truncated the top of Tabun D;

i.e., 60,000–80,000 yr. Recent ESR data (Stringer *et al.* 1989) gave an average date of 81,000 ± 15,000 yr (EU), and 101,000 ± 12,000 yr (LU). This wide range and paucity of microfaunal remains prevent a final date for Skhul. Alternately, Unit B may represent a long period of depositional or erosional phases, and the human burials may have been sparsely spaced over a long period (Bar-Yosef, personal communication), but no stratigraphic evidence for this hypothesis is preserved.

Hayonim Cave

The Mousterian complex so far excavated at Hayonim Cave was divided into Units Lower E and Upper E (Tchernov 1981b, 1984a), based on their different faunal assemblages. Lower E retains some of the old taxa (*Ellobius fuscocapillus*, particularly *Allocricetus magnus*), but none of the Afro-Arabian elements (*Arvicanthis, Mastomys, Gerbillus dasyurus*). This assemblage contains only typical Palearctic taxa, as well as *Talpa chthonia*. None of these species appears in Tabun C and B (Haas 1973), Hayonim Upper E, Kebara (Units VI–XII), Sefunim (Tchernov 1981b, 1984a,b) Amud B (Suzuki and Takai 1970), Geula B (Heller 1970), or Shovakh (Binford 1966). Thus, it is apparent that Lower E of Hayonim antedates all Mousterian units that seem to belong to a unique climatic stage, but is biochronologically younger than both Qafzeh and Tabun D (Unit IX). Biostratigraphically and ecologically, Lower E of Hayonim Cave may best be placed within early Stage 4 (Tabun D Unit II). In terms of faunal composition, Bar-Yosef's (1989) estimate for Tabun C, from 60,000 to 90,000 yr, agrees with the faunal sequences, but disagrees with the ESR dates (Grün *et al.* 1991), which placed both Tabun C and B within Stage 5, or contemporaneous with Qafzeh.

Kebara Cave

The latest excavations at Kebara (Bar-Yosef *et al.* 1992) exposed a successive and intensive human occupation, with an increased sedimentation rate and a lithic industry that resembles "Tabun B-type" (Meignen and Bar-Yosef 1988, 1989). A series of TL dates indicates that Units XII–VI spans the range of 60,000 to 48,000 yr (Valladas *et al.* 1988). ESR dates (Schwarcz *et al.* 1988) suggest a range of 60,000 to 64,000 yr for Units X–XI. If the estimated age of the first Neanderthal occupation is *ca.* 65,000 yr, then this occupation started at the end of Stage 4, when Neanderthals already dominated the region. Layers V–XII manifest no faunal changes, and are very similar to the other "Upper" Mousterian phases (Tabun B and C, Sefunim, Hayonim Upper E, Geula, Amud and Shovakh), all of which may be largely placed within Stage 3 (Table 1); this represents a unique and stabilized climatic phase.

It seems that, during the latter part of the Mousterian, the faunal communities in the southern Levant stabilized; almost no changes were recorded in the transition from the Middle to the Upper Paleolithic. Generally, no strict correlation exists between the rate of mammalian turnover (extinction *versus* immigration) and Pleistocene environmental changes in the eastern Mediterranean. Greater correlation is shown (Tchernov 1981b) between relative frequencies of species and on body sizes rather than on differential extinction; species responded to climate changes by moving to another ecologic regime or changing their ecologic amplitudes. A population may either follow its optimal valence (amplitude) (Endler 1977) through spatial changes or remain in one location by adjusting its phenotypic characters to the changing environment. The magnitude of environmental changes in the Levant was usually great enough to affect the genetic construction of the population and, unlike the more catastrophic situation in northern latitudes, was not always strong enough to cause an overall faunal turnover.

BIOCHRONOLOGY AND CHRONOSTRATIGRAPHY

The updated information on mammalian assemblages presented here is not complete, but it is sufficient to draw an outline of the sequences of mammalian lineages during the Last Inter-glacial and Late Pleistocene periods. Correlation of cave deposits is based on the better-known mammalofaunal assemblages. Several points are worthy of note:

1. The fossiliferous beds of Oumm Qatafa have a limited time range within the Late Acheul-ean (Fig. 1), and their fauna, particularly the micromammals, may be used as a base line for all later mammalian lineages in this region. *Ochotona* sp., *Rattus haasi* and *Myomimus judaicus*, as well as the Late Acheulean lithics from Levels F–B, place these important faunal beds before any Acheulo-Yabroudian assemblage in the Levant. Layer G, at the base of the sandy infilling of Tabun (Goldberg 1973), is the only coastal site stratum that can be related to the assemblage of Oumm Qatafa.

2. The Acheulo-Yabroudian separates the Late Acheulean from the Mousterian (Jelinek 1981), as it does in the El-Kowm basin (northeast Syria), Jerf 'Ajla Cave, (Palmyra region), Yabroud Rockshelter I (Anti-Lebanon Mountains) and Tabun Cave. In the Bezez (Lebanon) and Zuttiyeh Caves, the Acheulo-Yabroudian is overlain by Mousterian deposits, but no Late Acheulean has been found beneath this level. Jelinek (1982a,b) claimed that Unit X in Tabun shows the only known transition from the Acheulo-Yabroudian (Mugharan tradition *sensu* Jelinek) to the Mousterian of Levallois facies. Garrod (1962) noted that the human skull (a late endemic form of *Homo erectus*) from Zuttiyeh Cave was found under an Acheulo-Yabroudian industry complex that can be related to Tabun E. This was later con-firmed by Gisis and Bar-Yosef (1974). The fauna from Tabun E (and F) show that some ancient Middle Pleistocene or Acheulean species continued, such as *Allocricetus jesreeli-cus, Ellobius fuscocapillus* (old Palearctic elements), *Arvicanthis ectos, Mastomys batei* (ancient African elements). In addition, two species were introduced to the southern Le-vant: *Talpa chthonia* and *Lepus europaeus*, which probably excluded the genus, *Ochotona* or *Lagomys*. Stalagmitic layers above and below the Acheulo-Yabroudian were dated by U/Th. The overlying layers yielded dates of 95,000 ± 10,000 and 97,000 ± 13,000 yr, and below, 148,000 ± 21,000 yr (Schwarcz *et al.* 1980), and hence, are related to Stage 6 (Tables 1, 2, Fig. 1).

3. Biochronologically, the lower layers in Qafzeh (XIV–XXIV) should correlate to a very early Mousterian phase, which may fit in the E–D hiatus (Farrand 1979; Jelinek 1982a, b) in the Tabun sequence. During the beginning of Stage 4, several archaic species of micro-mammals became extinct, or disappeared from the Levant: *Myomimus qafzensis, Mastomys batei, Arvicanthis ectos, Suncus murinus* and, temporarily, *Gerbillus dasyurus* and *Camelus dromedarius*. All the cricetines, *Ellobius fuscocapillus, Apodemus flavicollis* and *Capreolus capreolus*, reappeared in the southern Levant, along with a new Euro-Siberian species, *Myomimus roachi*. Bate (1937a,b, 1942, 1943) lists these species from Tabun D and C. I suggest that these species specifically belong to Unit II within the sequence of Tabun D and C. This hypothesis is reinforced by a similar list from Lower E of Hayonim Cave, all of which can be attributed to early Stage 4 (Fig. 1). This significant faunal break between Stages 5 and 4, or between Qafzeh and Unit II of Tabun, and Lower E of Hayonim, is associated with a large-scale southward dispersal of Palearctic elements and the introduc-tion of Neanderthals in this region, pushing many of the Afro-Arabian species southward. Early Stage 4 and its faunal turnover was associated in the Levant by a lowering sea level, particularly evident from Mt. Carmel southward to Sinai, and dune activity resulted in the

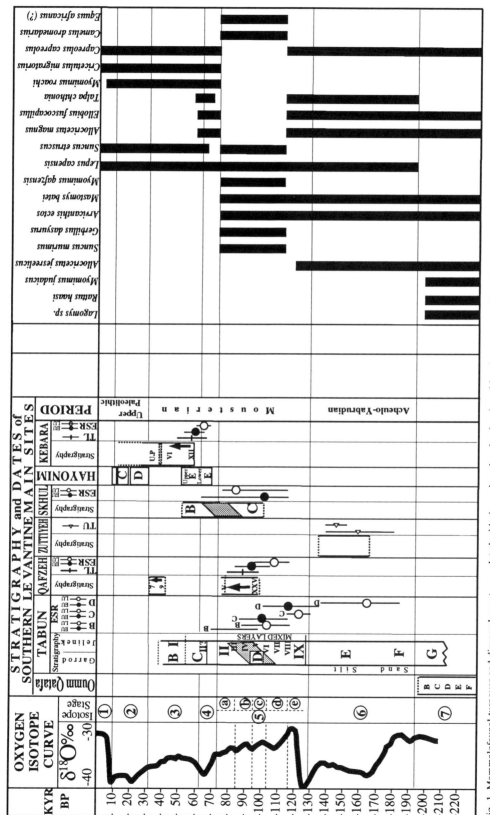

Fig. 1. Mammalofaunal turnover and dispersal events correlated with the main cultural units, depositional sequence and hominid replacements in the principal historic sites of the southern Levant. The sequence covers the late Acheulian, Middle Paleolithic and early Upper Paleolithic cultural periods. Oxygen isotope curve is a composite of several published curves (Modified from Tchernov (1991))

development of *kurkar* ridges along the coast. Typical African elements, such as *Arvicanthis ectos* and *Mastomys batei*, still exist. The endemic Acheulo-Yabroudian *Myomimus qafzensis* is still common. The appearance of Arabian elements, such as *Suncus murimus* and *Gerbillus dasyurus*, as well as *Camelus dromedarius* and probably *Equus africanus* and the predominance of ostrich (*Struthio camelus*) eggshells point to a significant northward shift of the Saharo-Arabian desert belt. This is further manifested by the absence of all the cricetines, as well as *Ellobius fuscocapillus*. A strong Afro-Arabian influence marks the fauna of Qafzeh, indicating savanna conditions during this period. I suggested (Tchernov 1981b, 1988b, 1989) late Stage 5 for the animal community of Qafzeh. The most recent TL dates (Valladas *et al.* 1988) confirm the biochronologic status of Qafzeh.

4. If the Mousterian complex of Qafzeh were placed with the "Upper Mousterian" (Jelinek 1982a,b), the transition from the Mousterian of Qafzeh to the Upper Paleolithic would show a faunal break. No extinction is known in the transition to the Upper Paleolithic. Five fossil species indicate that the Qafzeh Mousterian assemblage is closely related to Oumm-Qatafa and Tabun E and F. The idea that fossil species, such as *Mastomys batei* and *Arvicanthis ectos*, continue to survive in the vicinity of the Jordan Rift Valley (Jelinek 1982a,b) is improbable; they did occur along the coast during the early sedimentary cycle at Tabun, but were not recorded from the inland Shovakh Cave adjacent to the central Jordan Valley (Fig. 1). The position of Tabun D within the Mousterian sequence remains unclear. However, the lithic material (Bar-Yosef 1989) indicates a pre-Qafzeh Mousterian phase. This contradiction may be resolved by direct TL or ESR dating of this layer. I thought that the lithics should be sampled from Tabun D (Unit IX); Bate's faunal analyses, and, consequently, Grün *et al.*'s (1991) ESR dates treated the whole sequence of Tabun D (II–IX, including mixed Units III–VIII), as a single entity, which caused much confusion.

5. One observes gradual elimination or exclusion of faunal species from the region, rather than faunal breaks. The Levantine communities seem to be temporarily stabilized during the Late Mousterian and the Aurignacian. The transition to Stage 3 can be represented by the assemblage of Hayonim Upper E, the latter part of Tabun C and Tabun B, the whole complex of the Mousterian deposits in Kebara Cave (Layers XII–VI), Amud, Shovakh, Sefunim and Geula. All these late Mousterian complexes are characterized by the disappearance of *Talpa chthonia* and *Ellobius fuscocapillus* from the Levant (Fig. 1).

6. It seems that, during the latter part of the Mousterian, the faunal communities of the southern Levant were completely stabilized (Saxon 1974; Davis 1977; Tchernov 1981b, 1984a,b). The few ossiferous beds from the early Late Paleolithic, such as Qafzeh 7–9 and Kebara, indicate that no faunal change occurred during the Mousterian to Upper Paleolithic transition or throughout the Upper Paleolithic. What did occur was a significant change in the relative frequencies of the rodent communities (Tchernov 1984b), and most probably in the ungulates as well. During late Stage 3, modern humans reappeared in the region, but this time, no faunal exchange with Africa was related to this event.

Several research tools were used to build this suggested sequence of mammalian-hominid cultural chronostratigraphy of the southern Levant. Apart from the known faunal assemblages, the geochronologies of relevant cave sites and their industrial sequences, and sea-level data for the Mediterranean coast, radiometric dates are proving useful in addressing anthropological problems. By combining our knowledge of stratigraphic contexts with radiometric dates, we can begin to reconstruct a complete Levantine Middle Paleolithic sequence, and establish a clearer model for the association between biotic and hominid dispersal events.

REFERENCES CITED

Bar-Yosef, O.
1988   The data for the southwest Neanderthals. In *L'Homme de Néandertal*, Vol. 3, edited by M. Otte, pp. 31–38. Université de Liège, Liège.
1989   Geochronology of the Levantine Middle Paleolithic. In *The Human Revolution*, edited by P. Mellars and C. Stringer, pp. 589–610. Edinburgh University Press, Edinburgh.

Bar-Yosef, O., A. Belfer-Cohen, A. Goren, I. Hershkovitz, O. Ilan, H. K. Mienis and B. Sass
1986   Nawamis and habitation sites near Gebel Gunna, southern Sinai. *Israel Exploration Journal* 36:121–167.

Bar-Yosef, O. and P. Goldberg
1988   An outline of the chronology of the Middle Palaeolithic in the Levant. In *L'Homme de Néandertal*, Vol. 3, edited by M. Otte, pp. 13–20. Université de Liège, Liège.

Bar-Yosef, O. and N. Goren
1981   Notes on the chronology of the Lower Palaeolithic in the Southern Levant. In *Las Industrias Más Antiguas Pre-Achelense y Achelense*, edited by J. D. Clark and G. L. Isaak, pp. 28–42. UISPP Congress, Mexico City.

Bar-Yosef, O. and E. Tchernov
1972   *On the Palaeo-Ecological History of the Site of 'Ubeidiya*. Israel Academy of Sciences and Humanities, Jerusalem.

Bar-Yosef, O. and B. Vandermeersch
1981   Notes concerning the possible age of the Mousterian layers in Qafzeh cave. In *Préhistoire du Levant*, edited by J. Cauvin and P. Sanlaville, pp. 281–125. Maison de l'Orient, CNRS, Lyon.

Bar-Yosef, B. Vandermeersch, B. Arensburg, A. Belfer-Cohen, P. Goldberg, H. Laville, L. Meignen, Y. Rak, J. D. Speth, E. Tchernov, A. M. Tillier and S. Weiner
1992   The excavations in Kebara Cave, Mt. Carmel. *Current Anthropology* 33:497–550.

Bate, D. M. A.
1932   On the animal remains obtained from the Mugharet-el-Zuttiyeh in 1925. In *Prehistoric Galilee*, edited by F. Turville-Petre, pp. 27–52. British School of Archaeology, London.
1937a   Palaeontology: The fossil fauna of the Wady-el-Mughara caves. In *The Stone Age of Mount Carmel*, edited by D. A. E. Garrod and D. M. A. Bate, pp. 137–240. Clarendon Press, Oxford.
1937b   New Pleistocene mammals from Palestine. *Annals and Magazine of Natural History*, Series 10 (20): 397–400.
1942   Pleistocene Murinae from Palestine. *Annals and Magazine of Natural History* 9:465–486.
1943   Pleistocene Cricetinae from Palestine. *Annals and Magazine of Natural History* 11:823–838.

Binford, S. R
1966   Me'arat Shovakh (Mugharet as Shubbabiq). *Israel Exploration Journal* 16:96–103.

Bouchud, J.
1974   Etude préliminaire de la faune provenant de la grotte du Djebel Qafzeh, près de Nazareth, Israël. *Paléorient* 2:87–102.

Boutié, P.
1989   Etude technologique de l'industrie Moustérienne de la grotte de Qafzeh (près de Nazareth, Israël). In *Prehistoric Investigations of the Southern Levant*, edited by O. Bar-Yosef and B. Vandermeersch, pp. 213–230. BAR International Series 497, British Archaeological Reports, Oxford.

Copeland, L.
1975   The Middle and Upper Palaeolithic in Lebanon and Syria in light of recent research. In *Problems in Prehistory: North Africa and the Levant*, edited by F. Wendorf and A. E. Marks, pp. 317–360. Southern Methodist University Press, Dallas.

Copeland, L. and F. Hours
1983   Le Yabrudien d'El Kowm (Syrie) et sa place dans le Paléolithique du Levant. *Paléorient* 9:21–38.

Daams, R.
1981   The dental pattern of dormice *Dryomys, Myomimus, Microdyromys* and *Peridyromys*. Utrecht Micropaleontological Bulletin (Special Publications) 3:1–115.

Davis, S.
1974   Animal remains from the Kebaran site of Ein-Gev I: Jordan Valley, Israel. *Paléorient* 2:453–462.
1977   The ungulate remains from Kebara cave. *Eretz-Israel* 13:150–163.

Davis, S. J. M.
1982   Climatic change and the advent of domestication: The succession of ruminant artiodactyles in the late Pleistocene-Holocene in the Israeli region. *Paléorient* 8:5–15.

Endler, J. A.
    1977   *Geographic Variation, Speciation and Clines.* Monographs on Population Biology 10. Princeton University Press, Princeton.

Farrand, W. R.
    1979   Chronology and palaeoenvironment of Levantine prehistoric sites as seen from sediment studies. *Journal of Archaeological Science* 6:369–392.

Garrard, A. N.
    1982   The environmental implications of the re-analysis of the large mammal fauna from the Wadi-el-Mughara caves, Palestine. In *Palaeoclimates, Palaeoenvironments and Human Communities in the Eastern Mediterranean Region in Later Prehistory*, edited by J. L. Bintliff and W. van Zeist, pp. 165–198. BAR International Series 133, British Archaeological Reports, Oxford.

Garrod, D. A.
    1962   The Middle Paleolithic of the Near East and the problem of the Mount Carmel man. *Journal of the Royal Anthropological Institute* 92:232–259.

Garrod, D. A. E. and D. M. A. Bate
    1937   *The Stone Age of Mount Carmel.* Clarendon Press, Oxford, 240 pp.

Geraads, D. and E. Tchernov
    1983   Fémur humain du Pléistocène moyen de Gesher-Benot-Ya'akov (Israël). *L'Anthropologie* 67:131–141.

Gisis, I. and O. Bar-Yosef
    1974   New excavations in Zuttiyeh cave, Wadi Amud, Israel. *Paléorient* 2:175–180.

Goldberg, P.
    1973   Sedimentology, Stratigraphy, and Paleoclimatology of et-Tabun Cave, Mount Carmel, Israel. Ph.D. Dissertation, University of Michigan, Ann Arbor.

Goren-Inbar, N.
    1985   The lithic assemblage of Berekhat Ram Acheulean site, Golan Heights. *Paléorient* 11:7–28.

Goren-Inbar, N. and S. Belitzky
    1989   Structural position of the Pleistocene Gesher Benot Ya'akov site in the Dead Sea zone. *Quaternary Research* 31:371–376.

Grün, R., C. B. Stringer and H. P. Schwarcz
    1991   ESR dating of teeth from Garrod's Tabun collection. *Journal of Human Evolution* 20:231–248.

Gvirtzman, G., E. Schachnai, N. Bakler and S. Ilani
    1983–   The stratigraphy of the Kurkar group (Quaternary) of the coastal plain of Israel. *Geological Survey of*
    1984   *Israel, Current Report* 70:70–82.

Haas, G.
    1951   Remarques sur le microfaune de mammifères de la grotte d'Oumm Qatafa. In *Le Paléolithique et le Mésolithique du Désert de Judée*, edited by R. Neuville, pp. 218–239. Archives de l'Institute Paléontologique Humaine, Mémoire 24, Paris.
    1972   The microfauna of Djebel Qafzeh cave. *Paleovertebrata* 5:261–270.
    1973   The Pleistocene glirids of Israel. *Verhandlungen der Naturforschenden Gesellschaft in Basel* 83:76–110.

Heller, J.
    1970   Small mammals of Geula cave. *Israel Journal of Zoology* 18:1–49.

Hooijer, D. A.
    1959   Fossil mammals from Jisr Banat Yaqub, south of Lake Huleh, Israel. *Bulletin of the Research Council of Israel* G8:177–179.
    1960   A stegodon from Israel. *Bulletin of the Research Council of Israel* G9:104–107.
    1961   The fossil vertebrates of Ksar 'Akil, a Palaeolithic rock shelter in the Lebanon. *Zoologische Verhandlanger* 49:1–67.

Howell, F. C.
    1959   Upper Pleistocene stratigraphy and early man in the Levant. *Proceedings of the American Philosophical Society* 103:1–65.

Jelinek, A. J.
    1981   The Middle Paleolithic in the southern Levant from the perspective of the Tabun cave. In *Préhistoire du Levant*, edited by J. Cauvin and P. Sanlaville, pp. 265–280. Maison de l'Orient, CNRS, Lyon.
    1982a   The Tabun cave and Paleolithic man in the Levant. *Science* 216:1369–1375.
    1982b   The Middle Paleolithic in the southern Levant with comments on the appearance of modern Homo sapiens. In *The Transition from Lower to Middle Palaeolithic and the Origin of Modern Man*, edited by A. Ronen, pp. 57–104. BAR International Series 151, British Archaeological Reports, Oxford.

Jelinek, A. J., W. R. Farrand, G. Haas, A. Horowitz and P. Goldberg
   1973   New excavations at the Tabun cave, Mount Carmel, Israel, 1967–1972. A preliminary report. *Paléorient* 2:151–183.
Kurtén, B.
   1965   The Carnivora of the Palestine caves. *Acta Zoologica Fennica* 107:1–74.
Meignen, L. and O. Bar-Yosef
   1988   Variabilité technologique au Proche Orient: L'example de Keabara. In *L'Homme de Néandertal*, Vol. 4, edited by M. Otte, pp. 81–95. Université de Liège, Liège.
Neuville, R. (editor)
   1951   *Le Paléolithique et le Mésolithique du Désert de Judée*. Archives de l'Institute Paléontologique Humaine. Mémoire 24, Paris.
Payne, S. and A. Garrard
   1983   *Camelus* from the Upper Pleistocene of Mount Carmel. *Journal of Archaeological Sciences* 10:243–247.
Ronen, A.
   1979   Palaeolithic industries. In *The Quaternary of Israel*, edited by A. Horowitz, pp. 300–305. Academic Press, New York.
Rust, A.
   1950   *Die Hohenfunde von Yabrud (Syrien)*. Karl Vacholtz Verlag, Neumünster.
Said, R.
   1975   The geological evolution of the river Nile. In *Problems in Prehistory: North Africa and the Levant*, edited by F. Wendorf and A. E. Marks, pp. 7–44. Southern Methodist University Press, Dallas.
Saxon, E. C.
   1974   The mobile herding economy of Kebarah cave: An economic analysis of the faunal remains. *Journal of Archaeological Science* 1:27–45.
Schwarcz, H. P., W. M. Buhay, R. Grün, H. Valladas, O. Bar-Yosef and B. Vandermeersch
   1989   ESR dating of the Neanderthal site, Kebara Cave, Israel. *Journal of Archaeological Science* 16:653–659.
Schwarcz, H. P., P. Goldberg and B. Blackwell
   1980   U-series dating of archaeological sites in Israel. *Israel Journal of Earth Sciences* 29:157–165.
Schwarcz, H. P., R. Grün, B. Vandermeersch, O. Bar-Yosef, H. Valladas and E. Tchernov
   1988   ESR dates for the hominid burial site of Qafzeh in Israel. *Journal of Human Evolution* 17:733–737.
Stringer, C. B. and P. Andrews
   1988   Genetic and fossil evidence for origins of modern humans. *Science* 239:1263–1268.
Stringer, C. B., R. Grün, H. P. Schwarcz and P. Goldberg
   1989   ESR dates for the hominid burial site of Es Skhul in Israel. *Nature* 338:756–758.
Suzuki, H. and F. Takai
   1970   *The Amud Man and His Cave Site*. Tokyo University Press, Tokyo.
Tchernov, E.
   1968a   *Succession of Rodent Faunas During the Upper Pleistocene of Israel*. Mammalia Depicta, Paul Parey, Hamburg and Berlin.
   1968b   A Pleistocene faunule from a karst fissure filling near Jerusalem, Israel. *Verhandlungen der Naturforschenden Gesellschaft in Basel* 79(2):161–185.
   1973   *On the Pleistocene Molluscs of the Jordan Valley*. The Israel Academy of Sciences and Humanities, Jerusalem.
   1975   Rodent faunas and environmental changes in the Pleistocene of Israel. In *Rodents in Desert Environments*, edited by I. Prakash and D. K. Ghosh, pp. 331–362. W. Junk, The Hague.
   1981a   The impact of the postglacial on the fauna of Southwest Asia. In *Contribution to the Environmental History of Southwest Asia*, A (8), edited by W. Frey and H.-P. Uerpmann, pp. 197–216. Dr. Ludwig Reichert Verlag, Weisbaden.
   1981b   The biostratigraphy of the Middle East. In *Préhistoire du Levant*, edited by J. Cauvin and P. Sanlaville, pp. 67–97. Maison de l'Orient, CNRS, Lyon.
   1984a   Faunal turnover and extinction rate in the Levant. In *Quaternary Extinctions: A Prehistoric Revolution*, edited by P. S. Martin and R. G. Klein, pp. 528–552. The University of Arizona Press, Tucson.
   1984b   The fauna of Sefunim cave, Mt. Carmel. In *Sefunim Prehistoric Site, Mount Carmel, Israel*, edited by A. Ronen, pp. 501–519. BAR International Series 230, British Archaeological Reports, Oxford.
   1986a   The rodents and lagomorphs from 'Ubeidiya Formation. In *The Lower Pleistocene Mammals of 'Ubeidiya (Jordan Valley)*, edited by E. Tchernov, pp. 235–350. Mémoires et Travaux du Centre de Recherche Français de Jerusalem 5, Association Paléorient, Paris.

Tchernov, E.

1987   The age of 'Ubeidiya Formation, an early Pleistocene hominid site in the Jordan Valley, Israel. *Israel Journal of Earth-Sciences* 36:3–30.

1988a   The paleobiogeographical history of the Southern Levant. In *The Zoogeography of Israel*, edited by Y. Yom-Tov and E. Tchernov, pp. 159–250. W. Junk, The Hague.

1988b   Biochronology of the Middle Palaeolithic and dispersal events of hominids in the Levant. In *L'Homme de Néanderthal*, Vol. 2, edited by M. Otte, pp. 153–168. Université de Liège, Liège.

1989   The Middle Palaeolithic mammalian sequence and its bearing on the origin of *Homo sapiens*. In *Prehistoric Investigations of the Southern Levant*, edited by O. Bar-Yosef and B. Vandermeersch, pp. 25–42. BAR International Series 497, British Archaeological Reports, Oxford.

1991   Biological evidences for human sedentism in Southwest Asia during the Natufian. In *The Natufian Culture in the Levant*, edited by O. Bar-Yosef and F. R. Valla, pp. 315–340. International Monographs in Prehistory, Ann Arbor.

Tchernov, E. (editor)

1986b   *The Lower Pleistocene Mammals of 'Ubeidiya (Jordan Valley)*. Mémoires et Travaux du Centre de Recherche Français de Jerusalem 5, Association Paléorient, Paris.

Tchernov, E. and Guerin, C.

1986   Conclusion sur la faune du gisement Pléistocène ancien d'Oubeidiyeh (Israël): Implication paléoecologique, biogéographique et stratigraphique. In *The Lower Pleistocene Mammals of 'Ubeidiya (Jordan Valley)*, edited by E. Tchernov, pp. 351–405. Mémoires et Travaux du Centre de Recherche Français de Jerusalem 5, Association Paléorient, Paris.

Tchernov, E. and M. Volokita

1986   Insectivores and primates from the early Pleistocene of 'Ubeidiya Formation. In *The Lower Pleistocene Mammals of 'Ubeidiya (Jordan Valley)*, edited by E. Tchernov, pp. 45–62. Mémoires et Travaux du Centre de Recherche Français de Jerusalem 5, Association Paléorient, Paris.

Trinkaus, E.

1984   Western Asia. In *The Origins of Modern Humans: A World Survey of the Fossil Evidence of Modern Humans*, edited by F. H. Smith and F. Spencer, pp. 251–293. Alan R. Liss, Inc., New York.

Valladas, H., J. L. Joron, J. Valladas, B. Arensburg, O. Bar-Yosef, A. Belfer-Cohen, P. Goldberg, H. Laville, E. Tchernov, A.-M. Tillier and B. Vandermeersch

1987   Thermoluminescence dates for the Neanderthal burial site at Kebara in Israel. *Nature* 330:159–160.

Valladas, H., L. Reyss, J. L. Joron, J. Valladas, O. Bar-Yosef and B. Vandermeersch

1988   Thermoluminescence dating of Mousterian Proto-Cro-Magnon from Israel and the origin of modern man. *Nature* 331:614–616.

Vandermeersch, B.

1981   *Les Hommes Fossiles de Qafzeh (Israël)*. Centre National de la Recherche Scientifique, Paris.

Vaufrey, R.

1951   Etude paléontologique, I: Mammifères. In *Le Paléolithique et le Mésolithique du Désert de Judée*, edited by R. Neuville, pp. 198–217. Archives de l'Institute Paléontologique Humaine, Mémoire 24, Paris.

Williams, M. A. J and F. M Williams

1976   Evolution of the Nile basin. In *The Nile*, edited by J. Rzoska. W. Junk, The Hague.

Woldstaedt, P.

1962   Ueber die Gliederung des Quartärs und Pleistozäns. *Eiszeitalter und Gegenwart* 13:115–124.

RADIOCARBON DATING LEVANTINE PREHISTORY

H. T. WATERBOLK

Biologisch-Archaeologisch Instituut, Poststraat 6, 9712 ER Groningen, The Netherlands

INTRODUCTION

At the request of the editors of this volume, I have attempted a critical summary of the results of radiocarbon dating in eastern Mediterranean archaeology. I base my considerations mainly on date lists and archaeological labels of the authors. I also add some dates that apparently escaped their attention, or that were published only recently. The total number of dates is about 1000. My focus is on the best estimates of the chronological boundaries between the stratigraphic units within the individual sites, and between regional archaeological stages, as far as such estimates are possible with existing ^{14}C evidence. Apart from a considerable number of new ^{14}C determinations, we now also have a significant number of accelerator mass spectrometric (AMS) dates (*e.g.*, Housley 1994). This chapter is a sequel to the paper I presented at the 1986 CNRS symposium (Waterbolk 1987).

^{14}C dates are quantitative assays subject to statistical laws, yet samples from which they originate are archaeological materials that require individual assessments of particular characteristics, such as depositional and post-depositional history, and provenience (Mook and Waterbolk 1985). Calculations of mean values of groups of dates or graphic representations *à la* Gasco (1991) mask specific differences in samples and should be avoided or treated with caution. Singularity of dates derives not only from the nature of the sample (*e.g.*, wood, grain, textile, bone, eggshell, shell) and from contextual uncertainties (*e.g.*, age before use, reworking, admixture, contamination, unrecognized intrusions), but, unfortunately, also from the quality of the laboratories that processed the samples and the date the sample was analyzed. For example, the 1950s solid carbon dates of the Chicago laboratory (Jarmo and Jericho) are now only of historical interest due to large standard deviations incurred by the earlier technology. Other early gas-counting results must also be discarded (*e.g.*, Geochronological Laboratory (GL) and early British Museum (BM) dates from Jericho) (see Waterbolk 1987).

Obvious are differences in precision that show in the magnitude of the statistical uncertainty (sigma or σ) and that always should be considered when comparing series of dates. Differences also derive from pretreatment of difficult samples, such as bone, the results of which can be more variable than statistics alone can explain. Single bone dates are always suspect. For a complete explanation of the hazards of bone dating, see Hedges and van Klinken (1992). Other quality differences are less easy to detect. As demonstrated by the International Collaborative Study (Scott, Long and Kra 1990), some laboratories produce dates on wood that vary more than statistics explain; others show a systematic offset of a few hundred years. High-precision laboratories are less subject to these unexplained errors than other labs. Of course, we expect that improvements will continue, but if we are dealing with large series of dates produced during the past 30 yr by *ca.* 40 laboratories, we are faced with a substantial problem (Waterbolk 1990).

As for the problem of admixture, AMS dates have a definite advantage over most radiometric dates in that they may be based on a single seed, bone or piece of wood charcoal. Unfortunately, date lists are not always explicit about whether, for example, a charcoal sample comes from a single piece of wood or from an assemblage of heterogeneous elements. Some dates differ considerably from the expected age. Although a laboratory error can never be excluded, it has been my exper-

Late Quaternary Chronology and Paleoclimates of the Eastern Mediterranean
Edited by O. Bar-Yosef and R. S. Kra. RADIOCARBON 1994, pp. 351–371

351

ience that most aberrant dates that cannot be easily explained document a human activity, albeit at a moment other than that expected by the submitter. Some dates included here represent this problem; however, they should not be rejected. An aberrant date can provide valuable information on the reliability of other dates from the same site.

For young dates (<10,000 BP), the contamination problem is relatively unimportant, but such considerations as age before use, old wood and re-use of wood make the youngest dates of a group most useful for defining boundaries. For old dates (>30,000 BP), the opposite is true; a minute quantity of remanent contamination can lead to a date that is too young. Thus, the oldest dates of a series should define the boundaries of interest. However, outliers are always suspect. I do not address the issue of calibrating ^{14}C dates in this chapter. I prefer to use uncalibrated dates for analyzing data, and calibration curves only for placing ^{14}C ages of abstracted chronological boundaries on the historical time scale. Calibration curves are not yet available for the greater part of the Near Eastern ^{14}C time scale. The reader is encouraged to calibrate dates for the younger periods.

In the following, I discuss separate periods: 50,000–20,000 BP; 20,000–15,000 BP; 15,000–10,000 BP; and 10,000–5000 BP. I also focus on the following subareas: the Levantine coast; the Jordan Valley; southeast Anatolia; northern Syria; Deir ez-Zor/Palmyra; Damascus Basin; eastern Jordan; Azraq; Araba; Negev/Jebel Maghara; southern Sinai; and Egypt. As for Mesopotamia and Cyprus, I discuss only the chapters by Kozłowski, and Simmons and Wigand, and dates between 5000 and 3000 BP for the Negev, following Avner, Carmi and Segal's chapter.

50,000–20,000 BP (Figures 1A–1F)

I assisted John C. Vogel in preparing for publication some early Groningen (GrN) ^{14}C date lists (Vogel and Waterbolk 1963, 1964), which included dates in the 50,000 to 30,000 BP range from the Levantine sites, Tabun, Ksar 'Akil, Kebara and Ras el-Kelb. Later GrN lists included dates from Geulah and Yabroud (Vogel and Waterbolk 1967). We also had unpublished dates from Ras Beyrouth, Lebanon and Douara, Syria. The dates still play a role in the present discussion.

Thermoluminescence (TL) and electron-spin resonance (ESR) dates from Tabun discussed in this volume (Schwarcz, Mercier and Valladas, Farrand) make clear that the first GrN dates on charred bone from Tabun C (GrN-2729: 40,900 ± 1000 BP) and Tabun D (GrN-2170: 35,400 ± 900 BP) cannot be correct. Later, for Tabun C, three more dates were produced (GrN-7408: >47,900 BP; GrN-7409: 51,000 ± 4800 BP; and GrN-7410: 45,000 +2100/−1600 BP. A determination of >52,000 BP (GrN-2556) was measured for a Mousterian level at Ras el-Kelb, thought by Garrod to be contemporary with Tabun C. Apparently, complete removal of all contaminants was impossible at Tabun. This difficulty is further illustrated by a series of ten La Jolla (LJ) dates for Tabun C and D, which all fall between 38,000 and 23,500 BP, and are much too young (not included in Figure 1A). In this context, the single date for overlying Level B at Tabun (GrN-2534: 39,000 ± 800 BP) should be regarded with equal caution.

That sample pretreatment has not been fully effective in the Tabun samples does not imply that all finite GrN dates between 50,000 and 40,000 BP are wrong. GrN-2561 (41,000 ± 1000 BP) from Kebara is from the uppermost Mousterian level at a depth of 2.5 m. The youngest TL date for Kebara, from a depth of 4 m, is 48,000 ± 3500 BP (Mercier and Valladas 1994). Statistically, these determinations are very close. In addition, the date of 43,750 ± 1500 BP (GrN-2579) for a sample from 1 m below the top of the Mousterian levels at Ksar 'Akil may well be correct. At Kebara and Ksar 'Akil, we now have a series of mainly Oxford Accelerator (OxA) dates from Upper Paleolithic layers that postdate the Mousterian measurements and follow the stratigraphic sequence.

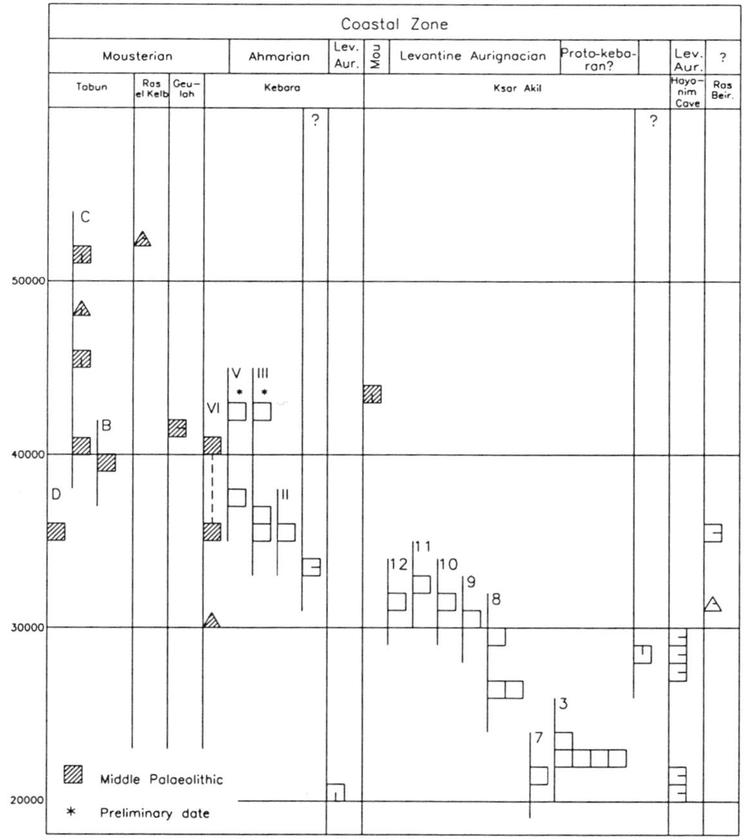

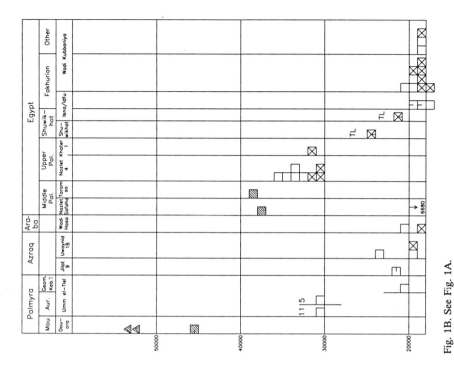

Fig. 1B. See Fig. 1A.

Fig. 1A–C.(A). (50,000–20,000 BP) Middle Paleolithic GrN dates specified in the text. Other Middle Paleolithic dates—Kebara, Rosh ein-Mor, Boker Tachit (after Weinstein 1984). Main source of Upper Paleolithic dates (Phillips, this volume). Additional dates from Kebara, Nazlet Safaha and Taramsa (Housley, this volume); Umm el-Tlel (Cauvin and Stordeur, this volume). Key to symbols follows Fig. 6.

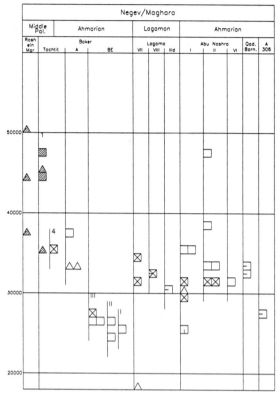

Fig. 1C. See Fig. 1A.

For Kebara, Housley (1994) mentions two more unpublished dates for the Upper Paleolithic: 42,100 ± 2100 BP and 42,500 ± 1800 BP. Again, these are not statistically different from GrN-2561 for the overlying Mousterian.

In the Palmyra area (Fig. 1B) we have three unpublished dates from Middle Paleolithic layers in the Douara cave (GrN-7599: >52,000 BP on charcoal; GrN-8058: >53,000 BP on eggshell; GrN-8638: 46,700 +2200/−1700 on eggshell). In the Negev (Fig. 1C) is a succession of Middle Paleolithic and early Upper Paleolithic (Ahmarian) layers at Boker Tachtit. Four dates exist for charcoal from a fire pit in Level 1: >35,000 BP (GX-3642); >45,490 BP (SMU-184); 44,930 ± 2420 BP (SMU-259); and 47,280 ± 9050 BP (SMU-580); the average age is *ca.* 47,000–46,000 BP. From Level 4 (Ahmarian) is a date of 35,055 ± 4100 BP (SMU-579). This date falls within the range of dates for the Ahmarian in another Boker site and in various sites in the northern Sinai. These dates form a dense cluster between 38,000 and 25,000 BP. SMU-2372, dated at 48,250 ± 2810 BP from charcoal from Abu Noshra II, is a single outlier that must be regarded with caution. Two other Zürich (ETH) dates and 4 other SMU dates exist for this site; they range between 38,924 ± 1529 and 31,023 ± 8537 BP. However, 48,250 ± 2810 BP is not too far from 38,924 ± 1529 BP (at 2 σ, they overlap statistically); from this, one cannot derive any good ^{14}C evidence for an earlier start of the Ahmarian in the Levant than *ca.* 40,000 BP. By implication, the finite Mousterian dates from Ksar 'Akil, Kebara, Douara, Boker Tachtit and perhaps Tabun B may well be acceptable.

For Egypt (Fig. 1B), we have 2 OxA dates from "Late Middle Paleolithic" extraction pits at Nazlet-Safaha (OxA-2601: 37,200 ± 1300) and Taramsa (OxA-2601: 38,100 ± 1400) and a cluster of 9 GrN dates for the Upper Paleolithic flint mines of Nazlet Khater (36,000–30,000 BP). This is another indication that the introduction of Upper Paleolithic flintknapping might have occurred *ca.* 40,000 BP throughout the Levant. On the basis of existing ^{14}C evidence, no subarea can claim priority, as Phillips (1994) seems to suggest for the Negev in relation to the Carmel area, or Schwarcz (1994) for the Negev in relation to Europe.

The age of anatomically modern man is a discussion that must be kept separate from that of Upper Paleolithic flint industries. To date, TL and ESR measurements in the Levant have concentrated mainly on the dating of levels containing human fossils and not flint industries. In the Carmel area, the Ahmarian is replaced by the Levantine Aurignacian at *ca.* 32,000 BP. From Ksar 'Akil, a good series of dates follow the stratigraphic sequence. At this site, the Aurignacian is followed by the Proto-Kebaran at *ca.* 23,000 BP. In the Negev, the Ahmarian continues up to *ca.* 24,000 BP.

"Lagaman" dates are equivalent to early Ahmarian dates. Determinations between 25,000 and 20,000 BP were obtained for the Azraq area (Jilat, Uwaynid and Wadi Hasa) (Fig. 1B) and Egypt (two TL dates from Shuwikhat and Isna/Idfu and conventional ^{14}C dates from Wadi Kubbaniya).

20,000–15,000 BP (Figures 2A–2F)

In the Carmel caves (Fig. 2A), Kebaran dates range from 19,000 to 15,600 BP. The principal site in the Jordan Valley (Fig. 2B) is Ohalo II, for which we have 16 dates, ranging from 20,100 to 15,000 BP; such a wide range is highly unlikely in view of the nature of the site (an unstratified lake-edge settlement). The samples were dated by three laboratories: Pretoria (Pta) measured 3 dates between 20,100 and 19,400 BP on unknown material; Oxford measured 3 dates on wild barley seeds between 19,310 and 18,680 BP; Rehovot (RT) dated 10 samples of unknown material from 19,800 to 15,500 BP. The Pta and OxA dates form clusters, OxA being clearly younger. This could be expected if the Pta samples were of charcoal of old wood. The range of the RT dates is too wide. From these data, it seems that the actual Ohalo occupation occurred for a few centuries *ca.* 19,000 BP.

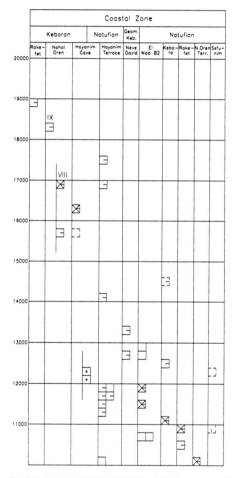

Four other sites in the Jordan Valley have yielded dates in the 20,000 to 15,000 BP range: Wadi Hammeh 26 (contemporaneous with Ohalo II); Fazaël (two dates that the excavator considers "both provocative and problematic" since he expected them to be of Upper Paleolithic age (Housley 1994)); Salibiya 9 (labeled Natufian) and a burial at Ein Gev. The ^{14}C evidence is meager here.

In the Azraq area (Fig. 2D), dates from Uwaynid 18 and 14 and Jilat 6 fall early, respectively late in the period. From the Wadi Arabah (Fig. 2D) area is a good series of dates between 17,000 and 15,400 BP for Wadi Hasa. In both areas, sites are assigned to the non-Natufian Microlithic (Byrd 1994). The Negev/Maghara region (Fig. 2E) well documents the period, 20,000–15,000 BP, with a stratigraphically dated series from Ein Aqev and a cluster of dates from Shunera 16 and isolated dates from Nahal Zin, Hamifgash and Azariq.

Fig. 2A–F. (A). (20,000–10,000 BP) Main sources of dates (Byrd, this volume). Additional dates from Hayonim Cave, Kebara, Azariq 13 (Housley, this volume); Salibiya 9, 'Iraq ed-Dubb, Gesher, Netiv Hagdud, Hallan Çemi Tepesi (Kuijt and Bar-Yosef, this volume); Qualkhan (Henry 1988); Mureybet (Aurenche and Evin 1987). Key follows Fig. 6.

In Egypt (Fig. 2F), this period is represented by many dates from the Isna/Idfu and Wadi Kubbaniya areas, primarily attributed to the Fakhurian and the Kubbaniyan. Fakhurian dates range widely, which may be because some dates are on shells (Isna/Idfu), and others are on small quantities of charcoal, which resulted in a large statistical error. Most Kubbaniyan samples are from three stratified sites in Wadi Kubbaniya (E78-3, E78-4, E81-1) with

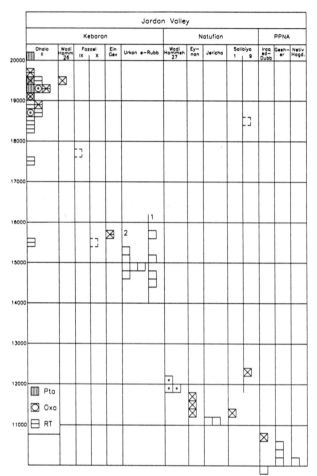

Fig. 2B. See Fig. 2A.

slightly different ages. Because the dates do not follow the stratigraphy, the sites must have existed only briefly, and at different times. Judging from the dates on annual plant material (*Cyperus* and *Scirpus*), these three sites must have existed only from *ca.* 18,000–17,500 BP. Many outliers among these dates show a large statistical error. Because most Fakhurian dates precede 18,000 BP, this might well be the best estimate for the boundary between both cultural stages. *Ca.* 20,000 BP might be a reasonable estimate for the beginning of the Fakhurian. All AMS dates on cereals from these sites were recent or subrecent (Housley 1994). Apparently, the intrusion of younger materials is a common phenomenon at Kubbaniyan sites. Thus, the few dates younger than 17,500 BP are not reliable.

15,000–10,000 BP
(Figures 2A–2F and 4)

For the Carmel area (Fig. 2A), we have no good ^{14}C evidence for the period between 15,600 and 13,400 BP. The Geometric Kebaran is represented only by two dates on charred bone (*ca.* 13,000 BP). For the Natufian are dates from Kebara, Hayonim (Cave and Terrace), El Wad (including some recently published dates, *cf.* Weinstein-Evron 1991), Rakefet, Nahal Oren Terrace and perhaps Sefunim (labeled Upper Paleolithic). These dates suggest that the transition from the Geometric Kebaran to the Natufian occurred here *ca.* 12,800 BP.

During this period, occupation in the Jordan Valley (Fig. 2B) started with the well-dated Kebaran site, Urkan e-Rubb (*ca.* 15,000–14,500 BP). The Geometric Kebaran is not represented in the dated sites. The Natufian is found in Wadi Hammeh 27, Eynan, Salibiya 1, perhaps Salibiya 9 and 'Iraq ed-Dubb, and most assuredly, Jericho. The earliest well-dated site (with a cluster of three dates *ca.* 12,000 BP) is Wadi Hammeh 27. Only two dates can be used for Jericho (*ca.* 11,000 BP).

In SE Anatolia (Fig. 2C) the site of Hallan Çemi Tepesi, has given dates between 11,900 and 9700 BP. For the upper level, two dates cluster at *ca.* 10,700 BP. The Kebaran and the Geometric Kebaran are not observed in dated sites in the Euphrates Valley (Fig. 2C). The Natufian is well dated at Abu Hureyra and Mureybet; at the former, the dates broadly follow the stratigraphy (Moore 1992) and form a cluster between *ca.* 11,200 and 10,400 BP, with one older outlier (a date on grain with a high σ) and a series of suspect younger bone dates (Fig. 4D). Other outliers include an unexplained charcoal date, BM-1719: 9100 ± 100 BP, and a seed date, OxA-882: 6100 ± 120 BP, which must be an intrusion. On the basis of the seed dates, the site existed from *ca.* 10,900–10,400 BP. At Mureybet (Phase Ia), the six dates fall between 10,400 and 10,000 BP. The six dates for Phases Ib and II (labeled Pre-Pottery Neolithic A (PPNA)) fall between 10,600 and 10,000 BP, and thus, are not younger. The ^{14}C evidence indicates that Natufian occupation at both these sites lasted no longer than 500 yr.

In the Azraq and Arabah areas (Fig. 2D), only the period, 13,600–12,000 BP, is well dated at more than one site, including a stratified series from Jilat 22. Most dates outside this range are from bone. These widely spread dates from Kharaneh and Madamagh illustrate the difficulties of dating bone (see Hedges and van Klinken 1992). Jilat 10 and 22 contain non-microlithic stone industries; Beidha and Wadi Judayid 2 are assigned to the Natufian. Kharaneh 4, Jilat 9 and Madamagh are classified as non-Natufian microlithic. Existing ^{14}C evidence shows no chronological distinction among these three groups. The Natufian sites fall within 12,800 and 12,000 BP, with two younger outliers at Beidha.

The Geometric Kebaran, Mushabian, Natufian and Harifian are a well-documented sequence in the Negev (Fig. 2E). The dates for the Geo-

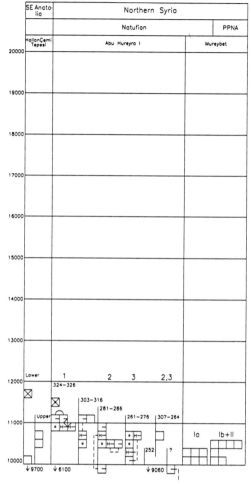

Fig. 2C. See Fig. 2A.

metric Kebaran start at *ca.* 14,500 BP, which are the same as the youngest Kebaran dates from the Jordan Valley (Urkan e-Rubb). I have already discussed the boundary between the Geometric Kebaran and the Mushabian at 13,700 BP (Waterbolk 1987). The overlaps between these complexes are due to systematic differences between laboratories. For the Mushabian, the youngest dates are from Shunera Site 4. Shunera dates overlap sightly with Natufian dates from Rosh Horesha and Saflulin. A good estimate for the boundary between Mushabian and Natufian is *ca.* 11,200 BP. The three Harifian sites, Maaleh Ramon, Ramat Harif and Abu Salem, produced clusters of dates that follow the stratigraphic sequence and lie between 10,500 and 10,000 BP. Thus, the Mushabian of the Negev overlaps both late Geometric Kebaran and early Natufian in other areas. Egyptian dates younger than 16,000 BP are not discussed here.

At first glance, the Akrotiri dates (Fig. 3) present a problem. I do not think that the explanations of Simmons and Wigand (1994) bring us any closer to the true age of the site than a careful evaluation of the nature of the samples and the magnitude of the statistical error. The bone dates especially are scattered too widely and should be discarded. In contrast, the charcoal dates form a cluster between 10,900 and 10,200 BP, with one outlier with high σ at 11,700 BP. The shell dates with low statistical errors are slightly older than the charcoal dates. This may well be due to a

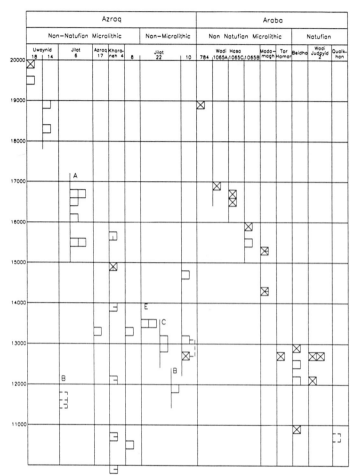

Fig. 2D. See Fig. 2A.

reservoir effect. The dates for the lower layer (4) do not differ significantly from those of the upper layer (2). The charcoal dates from the lower part of Layer 2 are somewhat older than those for the upper part. The true range of the whole occupation may have been shorter than that indicated by ^{14}C dates (*e.g.*, 10,500–10,300 BP). There is little doubt that the site was contemporaneous with the later Natufian in the Levant.

10,000–5000 (3000) BP
(Figures 4A–H and 5, 6)

The earliest dates for this period along the Levantine coast (Fig. 4A) are two OxA dates on seeds and bone from Late Natufian contexts at Hayonim Terrace. Both differ significantly from the six dates between 12,000 and 11,000 BP from the same site (Fig. 2A). As they are fairly close together, they may well represent a true occupation, whether Natufian or not. The date, 6970 ± 80, on seeds from the same Natufian provenience demonstrates clearly that the late Neolithic occupation capped the Natufian levels (Housley 1994).

PPNA is found only at the inland site of Nachcharini; however, PPNB has been dated at Horvat Galil, Sefunim, Nahal Bezet, Atlit Yam and Ras Shamra. At Nachcharini, Sefunim and Ras Shamra (Vc), the dates vary widely; some are problematic and cannot be used. Only at Ras Shamra do we have reasonably good data, with 2 outliers in Phase Vc and 1 in Va. The dates suggest a PPNB habitation from *ca.* 8300–7100 BP and a PNA occupation at *ca.* 6000 BP. The PNA dates of Labwe, Tell Judaidah, Tel Hariz and Byblos are contemporaneous with Ras Shamra; those of Ard Tlaili, Kefar Samir, Nizzanim and Neve Yam are younger. Several sites have generated dates from Chalcolithic contexts, suggesting continuity of habitation in the general area. The Shiqmim dates suggest that the Chalcolithic started here at *ca.* 5700 BP.

Traditionally, the Jordan Valley (Fig. 4B) is associated with PPNA. Data sets are available from Gilgal I, Gesher, Netiv Hagdud and Jericho. However, since there are no Final Natufian dates in the area, the beginning of the PPNA cannot be dated accurately. The best estimate is *ca.* 9800 BP. The youngest PPNA dates come from Jericho at *ca.* 9200 BP.

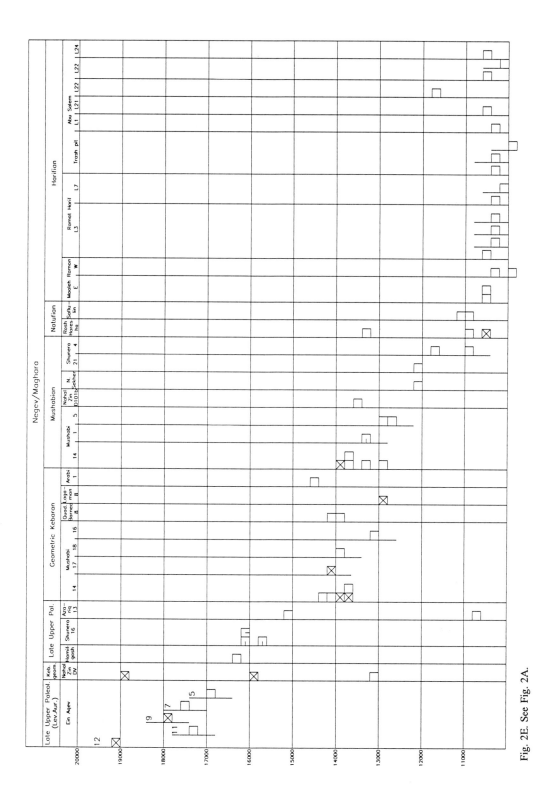

Fig. 2E. See Fig. 2A.

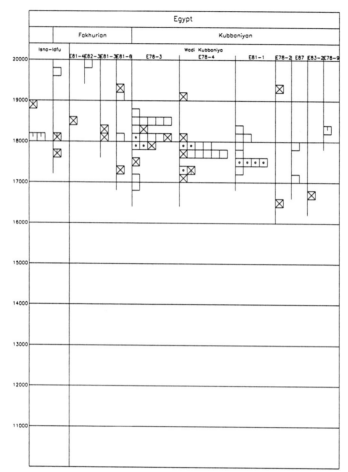

Fig. 2F. See Fig. 2A.

At Netiv Hagdud, one observes a difference between the dense cluster of 4 Pta dates (9660 ± 70 to 9780 ± 90 BP) and the wider scatter of 7 less reliable RT dates (9400 ± 180 to 10,180 ± 300 BP). The single OxA date falls into the narrow Pta range. As at Ohalo II, I must conclude that the RT dates suffer from greater variability than statistics alone can explain. The Gesher dates illustrate the same problems.

In the Jordan Valley, the PPNB has been dated between 9200 and 8500 BP at Jericho, 'Ain Ghazel, Yiftahel and Munhata. The stratified upland site of 'Ain Ghazel has provided 23 charcoal dates, analyzed by four laboratories. Apparently, there were difficulties with sample preparation; dates with errors of >150 yr were nearly all young. If they are disregarded, we have an acceptable series of dates from the Arizona AMS Facility (AA), OxA and GrN, which does not exactly follow the stratigraphic sequence (not indicated in the graph), with only one unexplained outlier. There is no systematic difference between the 4 AA and the 14 GrN dates. The 2 OxA dates are relatively young. Of the 5 imprecise results from the University of California, Riverside (UCR) laboratory, 2 are much too old and 2 are young. I feel comfortable only with the main cluster of dates between 9100 and 8700 BP. The site of Yiftahel has provided dates between 8900 and 8600 BP.

The next dates from the Jordan Valley are about a millennium later—isolated dates from Munhata (Fig. 4B) and Tsaf and a cluster of dates from Teleilat el-Ghassul. The Chalcolithic is represented by a few dates from 5500 BP onward.

In southeast Anatolia (Fig. 4C), the earliest Neolithic site is Çayönü, with many ¹⁴C dates. After a few old dates on doubtful material (mudbrick, charcoal + organic material), a dense cluster starts at 9300 BP, which must be a *terminus post quem* for the beginning of the occupation. After 8700 BP, dates are widespread, which may be due to the presence of a much later occupation of the site (probably at *ca.* 6000 BP), reworking older materials, or (also) a more localized, continued occupation up to *ca.* 7600 BP. Four other PPNB sites in southeast Anatolia have yielded dates between

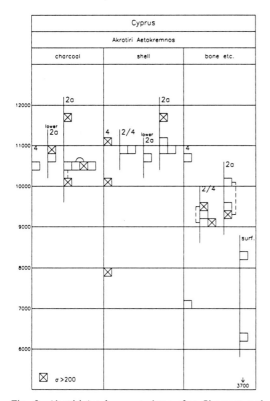

Fig. 3. Akrotiri-*Aetokremnos;* dates after Simmons and Wigand (this volume). Key follows Fig. 6.

9000 and 7600 BP—Çafer, Gritille, Hayaz and Kumar. Pottery-bearing sites, Girik-i-Hacyan and Fatmali, were dated to after 7000 BP. "Bronze Age" dates begin, with one exception, at 5600 BP, and are from Hayaz and Icme.

In northern Syria (Fig. 4D), the transition from Natufian to PPNA is documented at Mureybet, where the youngest Natufian dates (Layer Ia) are *ca.* 10,000 BP (Fig. 2C). Dates for the PPNA Layers Ib and II are the same, and dates for PPNA Layers IIIa and IIIb are 10,000–9500 BP. I can only conclude that the PPNA started at *ca.* 10,000 BP, and that the first Neolithic people used the same old wood as the Natufians. The PPNB continues, in Layers IVa and IVb up to *ca.* 9000 BP.

PPNA is absent from neighboring Abu Hureyra, where PPNB dates cluster between 8700 and 7800 BP, with 1 outlying younger bone date and 4 outlying older dates. In Figure 4D, the dates are grouped according to phases A and B distinguished by Moore (1992) on the basis of a shift in the animal economy from gazelle hunting to sheep and goat herding. The change took place *ca.* 8400 BP. The high dates are probably due to the use of bitumen at the site. Contrary to Housley (1994), I doubt that the occupation extended much beyond 8700–7800 BP. The Assouad occupation falls within the same period, with one old outlier. Slightly younger is the PNA site of Damashlia. Combining evidence from Abu Hureyra and Damashlia, pottery may have been introduced in the area *ca.* 7900 BP.

For an accurate estimate of the beginning of the Halaf culture, the site of Sabi Abyad is very important (Akkermans 1991; Akkermans and Verhoeven, in press). A series of stratified dates suggests that the transition from pre-Halaf PNA to the true Halaf culture occurred *ca.* 7000 BP. If GrN-2660 from the site of Halaf really represents Halaf occupation, it seems too old. Slightly younger Halaf dates (up to 6400 BP) are from Arjoune in northwest Syria. Later occupation in northern Syria is evidenced by ^{14}C dates from Hamman et-Turkman, Aqab, Sukas, Arjoune and Qala'al Mudiq.

Natufian and PPNA are absent from the Deir ez-Zor/Palmyra steppe area (Fig. 4E). PPNB is present at es-Sinn, Bouqras, El-Kowm I and II and Qdeir. The introduction of pottery is well documented at Bouqras, where it appears as early as 8200 BP (see Waterbolk 1987). One outlying date at Bouqras and 3 at El-Kowm must be due to the presence of bitumen at these sites. A hiatus in the Bouqras series may be due to a steep part in the calibration curve and need not mean an interruption of occupation. All the wood used at the site is of short-lived poplar tree. Es-Sinn yielded the oldest date, GrN-9833: 8650 ± 50 BP, which may be due to slight bituminous contamination, but because the sample was collected from the basal tell layers, it may also be accurate.

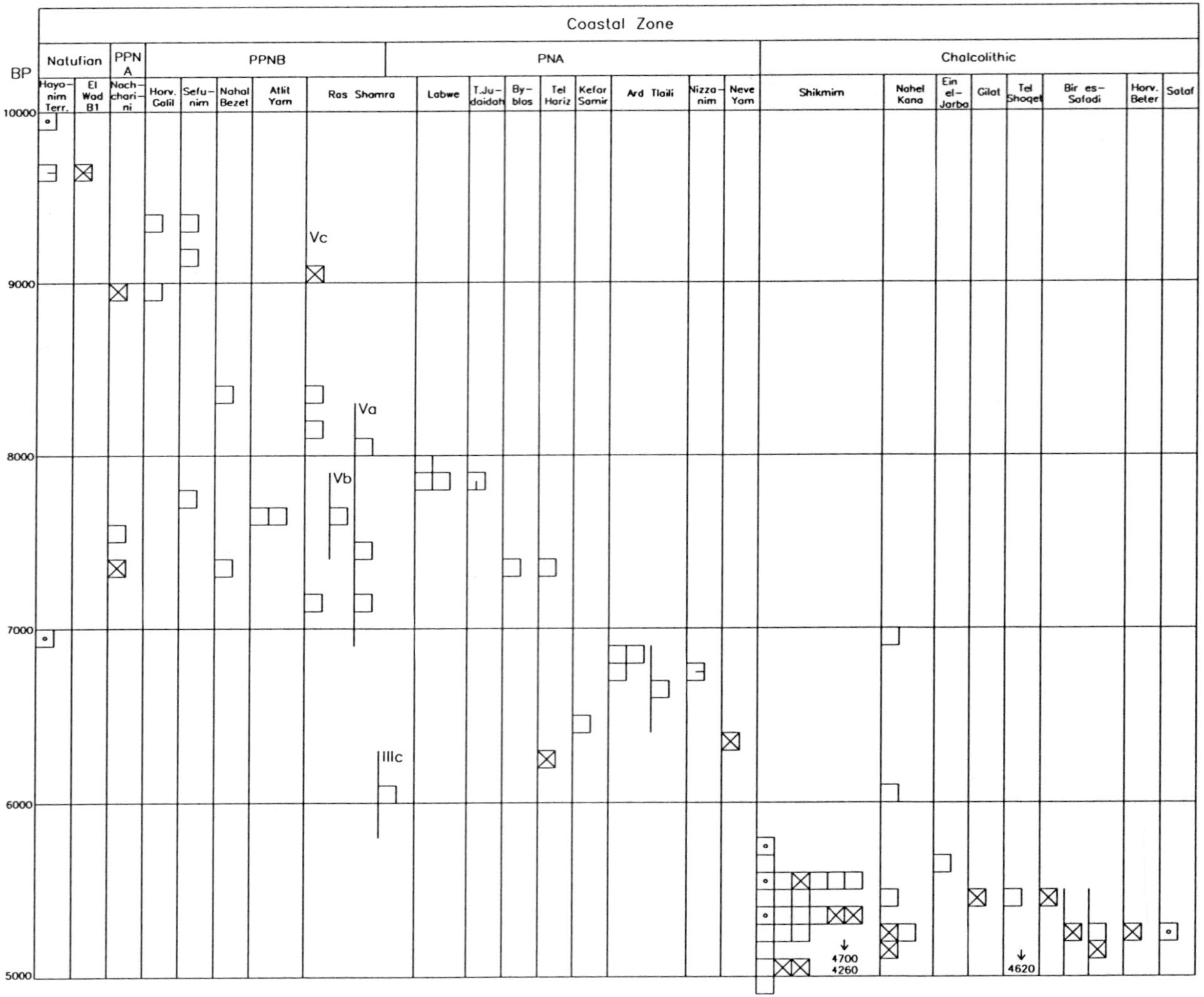

Fig. 4A–H. (A). (10,000–5000 BP) Main sources of dates—Kuijt and Bar-Yosef (this volume); Avner, Carmi and Segal (this volume). Additional dates from Hayonim Terrace, Shikmim, Sataf, Wadi Makhuk, Arjoune, Shulat Qeren (Housley, this volume); Shikmim, Neve Yam, Ein el-Jarba, Bir es-Safadi, Horvat Beter, Munhata, Tsaf, Teleilat el-Ghassul, Nahal Hever, Rosm Harbush (Weinstein 1984); 'Ain Ghazel, 'Iraq el-Barud, Çayönü, Mureybet, Abu Hureyra, Tell Aqab, Halaf, Bouqras, El-Kowm (Aurenche and Evin 1987); Çafer, Kumar (Cauvin 1987); Hammam et-Turkman (Mook and van Loon 1988); El-Kowm, Qdeir (Cauvin and Stordeur, this volume); Damashlia, Sabi Abyad (Akkermans 1991; Akkermans and Verhoeven, in press); Azraq area (Garrard, this volume); Kharaneh 4, Shunera 2, Shunera 3 (Byrd, this volume); Horvat Galil, Nahal Bezet, Atlit Yam, Tel Hariz, Kefer Samir, Shikmim, Nahal Kana, Tel Shoqet, Gilat, Bir es-Safadi, Gilgal, Gesher, Netiv Hagdud, Qumran, Nahal Mishmar (Carmi and Segal 1992). Key follows Fig. 6.

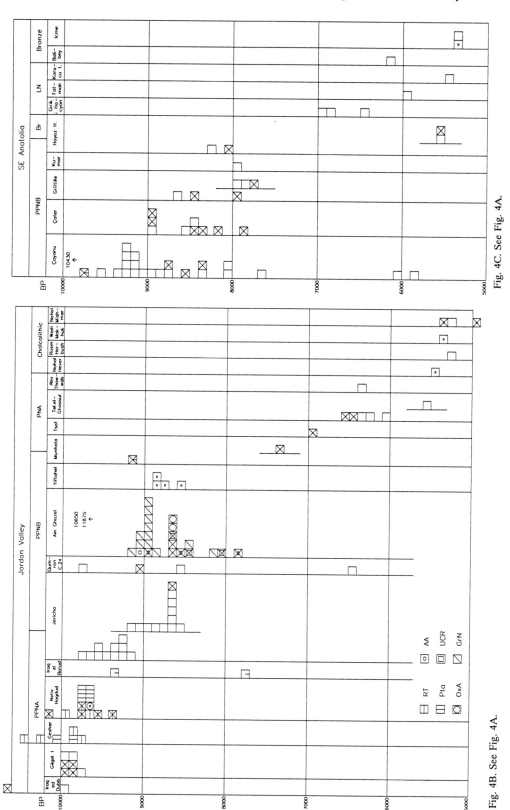

Fig. 4C. See Fig. 4A.

Fig. 4B. See Fig. 4A.

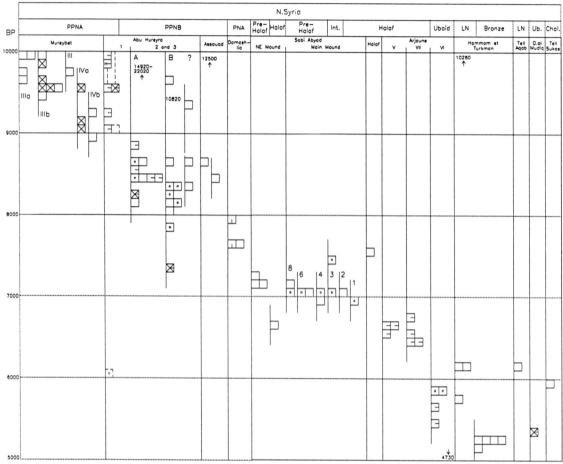

Fig. 4D. See Fig. 4A.

Older layers than those excavated might also exist, at Bouqras, under the core of the tell. The youngest dates in the area are from El-Kowm I at *ca.* 7300 BP (see Cauvin and Stordeur 1994).

From the Damascus basins (Fig. 4E) is a good series of stratified dates from Aswad, Ghoraife and Ramad between 9800 and 7800 BP, with one suspect outlier, from Ghoraife, at *ca.* 7000 BP. Aswad Ia, with dates *ca.* 9700 BP, is assigned to the PPNA. The oldest PPNB dates, at Aswad Ib, are *ca.* 9300 BP. An accurate determination of the transition between PPNA and PPNB is not yet available, nor are reliable younger dates for the area.

Evidence for PPNB at 8300–7000 BP is found at various Burqu' sites, Dhuweila and Jebel Naja, in the dry inland areas of eastern Jordan (Fig. 4F). Dates cluster between 8300 BP and 6900 BP and between 7400 BP and 6900 BP. In the Azraq area (Fig. 4F), habitation is documented at 8800–7800 BP. At Jilat 7 is an unexplained date of *ca.* 5800 BP, close to the Chalcolithic date of 5200 BP from Jilat 27.

In the Wadi Arabah region (Fig. 4G), the PPNB site of Beidha (Waterbolk 1987) is accompanied in time by the Basta site, which is slightly younger (Becker 1991). Together, the sites document

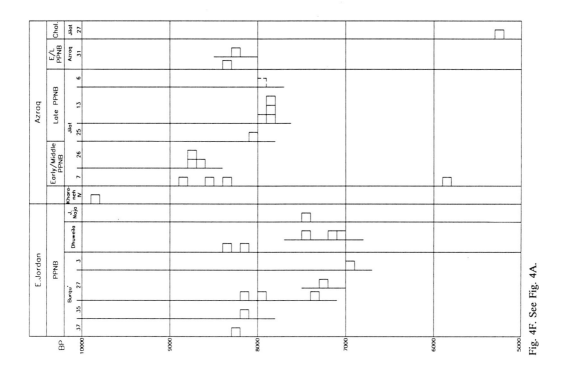

Fig. 4F. See Fig. 4A.

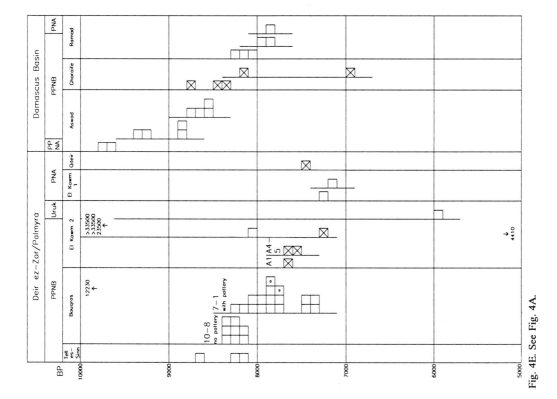

Fig. 4E. See Fig. 4A.

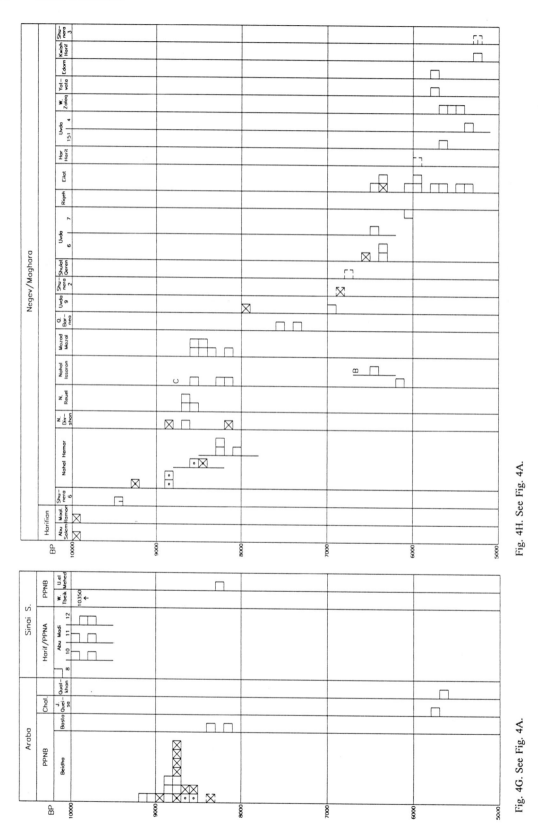

Fig. 4H. See Fig. 4A.

Fig. 4G. See Fig. 4A.

a PPNB occupation from *ca.* 8900–8100 BP. The Chalcolithic is represented by two dates from J. Queisa and Qualkhan (Henry 1988).

The Neolithic habitation in the Negev (Fig. 4H) starts shortly after 8900 BP, with five sites yielding dates up to 8000 BP. The period between the Harifian and the Neolithic is represented only by a date on carbonaceous material from Shunera 6 and an outlier date with high σ on linen from Nahal Hemar. The latter site has produced a well-stratified series of dates. Qadesh Barnea is the only site that yielded two dates from 8000 to 7000 BP. Dates cluster again at *ca.* 6500 BP, and the area seems to have been inhabited continuously until *ca.* 5300 BP. Seventh-millennium dates from two Mushabian sites (Shunera 2 and Shlulat Qeren) may represent intrusions in this period.

A gap still exists between 5300 and 4700 BP in the Negev (Fig. 5), and evidence becomes meager after 3600 BP. As discussed above, other gaps or probable gaps in Negev habitation exist between 9700 and 8900 BP, and between 8000 and 7000 BP. Thus, it is premature to attribute continuous human activity in the Negev from the Neolithic to Early Bronze Age IV (EB IV), as Avner, Carmi and Segal do in this volume. I would also like to note that, although most sites were short-lived, they often yield widely scattered dates (Uvda 9, 16 and 166, Dimona, Timna). Most of these dates were measured by the Rehovot laboratory.

One stratified PPNA site (Abu Madi) has been found in the southern Sinai (Fig. 4G), yielding dates between 10,100 and 9800 BP. Of 2 PPNB sites, 1 (Wadi Tbeik) produced a date before 10,000 BP. A date of *ca.* 8200 BP was obtained for Ujrat el-Mehed.

NEMRIK, M'LEFAAT AND JARMO (Figure 6)

A large series of dates from the PPN site of Nemrik (Fig. 6), measured by the Gdansk/Gliwice (Gd) laboratory, range from >40,000 to 5200 BP. Laboratory error is evident if we compare 20

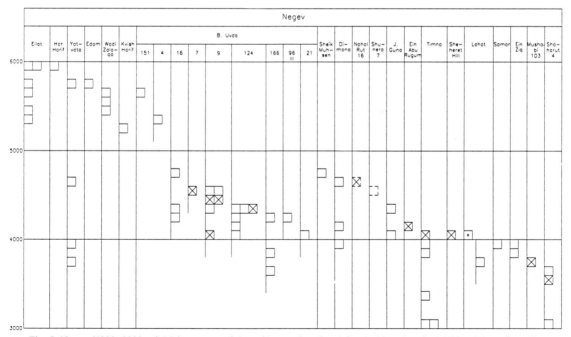

Fig. 5. Negev (6000–3000 BP) Main sources of dates (Avner, Carmi and Segal, this volume). Additional dates from Har Harif, Timna (Weinstein 1984); Shunera 7, Nahal Rut 17 (Byrd, this volume); Lahat, Shaharut 4 (Carmi and Segal 1992). Key follows Fig. 6.

dates with serial numbers, Gd-6000 and up, with 64 earlier dates with serial numbers, Gd-2000–5000. The former range only from 10,200 to 8200 BP, and mostly follow the stratigraphy. Considering this, I estimate *ca.* 10,000–8150 BP as the maximum duration of the site, which overlaps both the PPNA and PPNB of the area. The eight dates from M'lefaat are equally poor. If we use only Gd-6000 + dates, the site may have been contemporaneous with the earlier phases of Nemrik. The Jarmo dates discussed in Kozłowski (1994) are largely unreliable (Geochronological Laboratory (GL) and Chicago (C) dates should be rejected). However, the U.S. Geological Survey (W) and Heidelberg (H) charcoal dates, and perhaps the GrN potsherd date, can still be used. These range from 8830 ± 200 to 7600 ± 75 BP, which means that Jarmo could be contemporaneous with PPNB sites on the Syrian Euphrates. Interestingly, the IGAN date from the site of Magzalya 10 (Kozłowski 1994) falls within the same period. The site is in northern Mesopotamia, halfway between Jarmo and the Syrian sites.

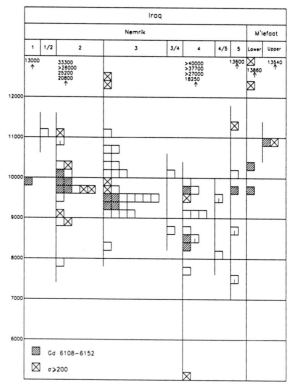

Fig. 6. Nemrik and M'lefaat—dates after Kozlowski (this volume)

CYPRUS

As for Cyprus, my analysis of the Neolithic dates (LeBrun 1987) concludes with an aceramic occupation of 7700–7100 BP (sites of Khirokitia, Dhali Agridhi, Kalevasos-Tenta and Andreas-Kastros) and a ceramic Neolithic occupation from 5800 BP onwards (sites of Khirokitia, Dhali Agridhi and Ayios Epiktikos Vrysi).

CONCLUSION

For the period, 50,000–20,000 BP, dates in quantity are available only for the Carmel area, the Negev and Egypt. In all three subareas, more dates are needed for the transition of the Mousterian to the Upper Paleolithic. For now, *ca.* 40,000 BP is the best estimate for the area as a whole.

The summary graph covering the period, 20,000–5000 BP, illustrates the habitation

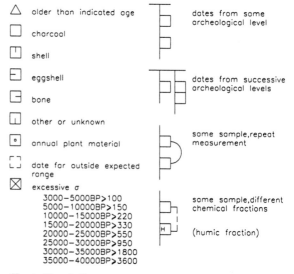

Key to Figs. 1–6

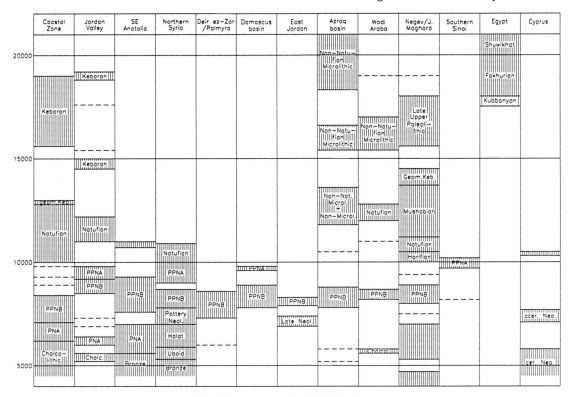

Fig. 7. Summary graph—20,000–5000 BP

periods documented by ¹⁴C dates (Fig. 7), as well as the many hiatuses in our knowledge. It also gives an overview of possible general trends for future research. One notes, for example, the early appearance of the Natufian in the coastal zone and Wadi Araba, compared to northern Syria and the Negev, or the generally synchronous appearance of PPNA at *ca.* 10,000 BP in all four subareas where it is well documented. Much less synchronous are the spread of the PPNB over practically all areas between 9300 and 8300 BP, and its disappearance between 8500 and 7000 BP. The aceramic Neolithic occupation of Cyprus is contemporaneous with the later part of the PPNB in the coastal area. Continuity of habitation after the PPNB is well documented only in the coastal area and northern Syria.

ACKNOWLEDGMENTS

The AutoCAD graphs for this chapter were prepared by Huib J. Waterbolk.

REFERENCES CITED

Akkermans, P. M. M. G.
    1991   New radiocarbon dates for the later Neolithic of northern Syria. *Paléorient* 17(1):121–126.
Akkermans, P. and M. Verhoeven
            An image of complexity: The burnt village at Late Neolithic Sabi Abyad. *American Journal of Archaeology*, in press.
Aurenche, O. and J. Evin
    1987   List of the ¹⁴C dates from the archaeological sites of the Near East from 14,000 to 5700 BP. In *Chronologies du Proche Orient*, edited by O. Aurenche, J. Evin and F. Hours, pp. 687–744. BAR International Series 379, British Archaeological Reports, Oxford.

Avner, U., Carmi, I. and Segal, D.
   1994   Neolithic to Bronze Age settlement of the Negev and Sinai in light of radiocarbon dating: A view from the southern Negev. This volume.
Becker, C.
   1991   The analysis of mammalian bones from Basta, a pre-pottery Neolithic site in Jordan: Problems and potential. *Paléorient* 17(1):59–76.
Byrd, B.
   1994   Late Quaternary hunter-gatherer complexes in the Levant between 20,000 and 10,000 BP. This volume.
Carmi, M. and D. Segal
   1992   Rehovot radiocarbon measurements IV. *Radiocarbon* 34(1):115–132.
Cauvin, J.
   1987   Chronologie relative et absolue dans le Néolithique du Levant Nord et d'Anatolie entre 10,000 et 8,000 BP. In *Chronologies du Proche Orient*, edited by O. Aurenche, J. Evin and F. Hours, pp. 325–342. BAR International Series 379, British Archaeological Reports, Oxford.
Cauvin, J. and Stordeur, D.
   1994   Radiocarbon dating El-Kowm: Upper Paleolithic through Chalcolithic. This volume.
Farrand, W. R.
   1994   Confrontation of geological stratigraphy and radiometric dates from Upper Pleistocene sites in the Levant. This volume.
Garrard, A., Baird, D. and Byrd, B.
   1994   The chronological basis and significance of the Late Paleolithic and Neolithic sequence in the Azraq Basin, Jordan. This volume.
Gasco, J.
   1991   Traitements graphiques des dates radiocarbone: Application au Proche Orient. In *Chronologies du Proche Orient*, edited by O. Aurenche, J. Evin and F. Hours, pp. 151–176. BAR International Series 379, British Archaeological Reports, Oxford.
Hedges, R. E. M. and G. J. van Klinken
   1992   A review of current approaches in the pretreatment of bone for radiocarbon dating by AMS. *Radiocarbon* 34(3):279–291.
Henry, D. O.
   1988   The Epipalaeolithic sequence within the Ras En Naqb–El Quweira area, southern Jordan. *Paléorient* 14(2): 245–256.
Housley, R.
   1994   Eastern Mediterranean chronologies: The Oxford AMS contribution. This volume.
Kozłowski, S. K.
   1994   Radiocarbon dates from Aceramic Iraq. This volume.
Kuijt, I. and O. Bar-Yosef
   1994   Radiocarbon chronology for the Levantine Neolithic: Observations and data. This volume.
Le Brun, A.
   1987   Chronologie relative et chronologie absolue dans le néolithique Chypriote. In *Chronologies du Proche Orient*, edited by O. Aurenche, J. Evin and F. Hours. pp. 528–548. BAR International Series 379, British Archaeological Reports, Oxford.
Mercier, N. and Valladas, H.
   1994   Thermoluminescence dates for the Paleolithic Levant. This volume.
Molist, M. and M. C. Cauvin
   1990   Une nouvelle séquence stratifiée pour la préhistoire en Syrie semidésertique. *Paléorient* 16(2):55–64.
Mook, W. G. and M. N. van Loon
   1988   Radiocarbon dates. In *Hammam et Turkman II. Report of the University of Amsterdam's 1981–1984 Excavations in Syria*, edited by M. N. van Loon, pp. 717–718. University of Amsterdam.
Mook, W. G. and H. T. Waterbolk
   1985   *Radiocarbon Dating*. Handbooks for Archaeologists 3. European Science Foundation, Strasbourg.
Moore, A. M. T.
   1992   The impact of accelerator dating at the early village of Abu Hureyra on the Euphrates. *Radiocarbon* 34(3): 850–866.
Phillips, J.
   1994   The Upper Paleolithic chronology of the Levant and the Nile Valley. This volume.
Schwarcz, H.
   1994   Chronology of modern humans in the Levant. This volume.

Scott, E. M., A. Long and R. S. Kra (editors)
    1990   Proceedings of the International Workshop on Intercomparison of Radiocarbon Laboratories. *Radiocarbon* 32(3):253–397.

Simmons, A. and Wigand, P.
    1994   Assessing the radiocarbon determinations from Akrotiri *Aetokremnos*, Cyprus. This volume.

Vogel, J. C. and H. T. Waterbolk
    1963   Groningen radiocarbon dates IV. *Radiocarbon* 5:63–202.
    1964   Groningen radiocarbon dates V. *Radiocarbon* 6:349–369.
    1967   Groningen radiocarbon dates VII. *Radiocarbon* 9:107–155.

Waterbolk, H. T.
    1987   Working with radiocarbon dates in Southwestern Asia. In *Chronologies du Proche Orient*, edited by O. Aurenche, J. Evin and F. Hours, pp. 39–59. BAR International Series 379, British Archaeological Reports, Oxford.
    1990   Quality differences between radiocarbon laboratories illustrated on material from SW Asia and Egypt. In *Proceedings of the Second International Symposium, 14C and Archaeology, Groningen 1987*, edited by W. G. Mook and H. T. Waterbolk, pp. 141–158. PACT 29, Strasbourg.

Weinstein, J. M.
    1984   Radiocarbon dating in the southern Levant. *Radiocarbon* 26(3):297–366.

Weinstein-Evron, M.
    1991   New radiocarbon dates of the early Natufian of el-Wad cave, Mt. Carmel, Israel. *Paléorient* 17(1):95–98.